NEW RESEARCH ON KNOWLEDGE MANAGEMENT MODELS AND METHODS

Edited by **Huei-Tse Hou**

New Research on Knowledge Management Models and Methods
Edited by Huei-Tse Hou

Published by InTech

Janeza Trdine 9, 51000 Rijeka, Croatia

Publishing Process Manager Anja Filipovic

Technical Editor Teodora Smiljanic

Cover Designer InTech Design Team

Additional hard copies can be obtained from orders@intechopen.com

New Research on Knowledge Management Models and Methods,
Edited by Huei-Tse Hou
p. cm.
ISBN 978-953-51-0190-1

For EU product safety concerns:
IN TECH d.o.o., Prolaz Marije Krucifikse Kozulić 3, 51000 Rijeka, Croatia,
info@intechopen.com or visit our website at intechopen.com.

Meet the editor

Dr. Huei-Tse Hou is an Assistant Professor of Graduate Institute of Applied Science and Technology, National Taiwan University of Science and Technology, Taiwan. He has received the Ta-You Wu Memorial Award (Young Outstanding Researcher Award) (Year 2010) by the National Science Council, Taiwan. His research interest focuses on knowledge management/sharing, e-Learning behavioral pattern analysis, e-Learning system development, and game-based learning systems. Prof. Hou has published many academic papers in famous SSCI indexed journals such as Computers in Human Behavior, Computers & Education, Educational Technology & Society, British Journal of Educational Technology, and Interactive Learning Environments.

Contents

Preface

In a highly interactive Internet environment, the research issues in knowledge management vary based on the development of new technology and modes of interaction in the knowledge community. Due to the development of mobile and Web 2.0 technology, knowledge transfer, storage and retrieval have become much more rapid. The technologies and methods continue to get more and more diverse. At the same time, the types of online communities with high levels of interaction become more and more multi-dimensional. To optimize organizational performance and further promote knowledge innovation and knowledge management in organizations, new and expanded strategies for sharing knowledge within and between knowledge communities are required.

In recent years, there have been more and more new and interesting findings regarding theories, methods, and models in the research field of knowledge management. There are also innovative technologies and tools in knowledge management technology. It is worth noting that the technologies, tools, and models in technology have been applied to more fields (e.g., education and digital learning) as technology and management concepts have continued to develop. These trends speak to the importance of studies of knowledge management, and the studies expand their influence on more multidisciplinary applications. New research issues in knowledge management await researchers. A comprehensive understanding of these novel research issues will assist with the academic development and practical applications in the field of knowledge management.

Therefore, this book aims to introduce readers to the recent research topics in knowledge management, it is titled "New Research on Knowledge Management Models and Methods" and includes 19 chapters. The focus is on the exploration and coverage of the innovations of all knowledge management models and methods as well as deeper discussion.

I expect this book to provide relevant information about new research trends in comprehensive and novel knowledge management studies. This information will serve as an important resource for researchers, teachers and students, and will further scholarly work and the development of practices in the knowledge management field.

Prof. Huei-Tse Hou
Graduate Institute of Applied Science and Technology
National Taiwan University of Science and Technology
Taiwan

1

Three Postulates that Change Knowledge Management Paradigm

Michel Grundstein
MG Conseil, Nogent sur Marne, LAMSADE Paris Dauphine University, Paris France

1. Introduction

In the foreword of the book untitled "The New Age in Knowledge" (O'Dell and Hubert 2011) Larry Prusak describes some of the main principles focused on knowledge management at the beginning days (p. xi): i) Knowledge is a fixed pool, a collection of resources that can be measured and used by standard management techniques; ii) Technology is the key tool to unlock the value of this resource - more technology, the better; and iii) Individuals are the critical unit of analysis in working with knowledge - the more productive the individual is the more knowledge is being used. He concludes: "It is now clear in hindsight that these principles were developed with information in mind, not knowledge, and that they were not at all suitable to working with such elusive intangible. It is because of these ideas that many knowledge management efforts ran into problems and that the whole subject began to fade in the minds of busy executives."

However, although it does not always get the expected outcomes when put at work in organizations, the positivist paradigm of KM, influenced by computer science and information technology, is the most implicitly recognized paradigm by researchers and practitioners in KM. From our viewpoint, this paradigm needs to be enlarged to a general view resting on a constructivist paradigm.

In this chapter we put down background theory and assumptions; notably, we introduce the concept of "commensurability of interpretative frameworks," and we propose an empirical model (DITEK) that attempts to describe the transformation process from data to information and from information to tacit and explicit knowledge. Then, we suggest a constructivist paradigm of KM within organizations based on three fundamental postulates. This leads to envisage new KM perspectives that induce specific KM Governance, and leads towards a technological, managerial, and socio-technical well-balanced KM approach within organizations referring to general model for knowledge management within organization so called MGKME. Finally, we sketch out the architecture of an enterprise's information and knowledge system (EIKS), and we propose a well-balanced KM initiative strategy within organizations.

2. Background theory and assumptions

2.1 Research motivations, method, and objectives

Our research follows a constructivist paradigm that is deeply rooted in our pragmatic experience in the real field. As a practitioner having to manage deployment of innovative technologies (such as computer aided design, knowledge based systems, and others) in large companies just when these technologies were conceived into universities and laboratories, we observed that we always needed to elaborate a model with socio-technical perspectives, which could be used as a pattern of reference for all stakeholders in order to engender the essential learning process that leads people to appropriate and use these technologies. Later on, when becoming Associate Researcher in the domain of KM, we perceived the lack of general model of KM that integrates socio-technical perspectives. This point of view is often disregarded when considering the technical approach of KM, although hundred of frameworks can be found in the literature (CEN-CWA 14924-1, 2004). As a practitioner we always had to consider the constructivist paradigm that underlies the creation of knowledge, and consequently KM approach. As a researcher we always had to be confronted with the positivist paradigm that most often considers knowledge independently of its links with action, and the context of organizations. Thus, our researches, notably in the domain of KM, are continuously oriented towards a well-balanced use of positivist and constructivist paradigms within organizations.

2.2 The dominant positivist paradigm of KM

Numerous authors analyzed the notions of data, information and knowledge. Let us quote notably Davenport and Prusak (1998, pp.1-6), Sena and Shani (1999), Takeuchi and Nonaka, (2000), Amin and Cohendet, (2004, pp. 17-30), Laudon and Laudon, (2006, p. 416). Besides, Snowden (2000,) makes the following synthesis: "The developing practice of knowledge management has seen two different approaches to definition; one arises from information management and sees knowledge as some higher-level order of information, often expressed as a triangle progressing from data, through information and knowledge, to the apex of wisdom. Knowledge here is seen as a thing or entity that can be managed and distributed through advanced use of technology…The second approach sees the problem from a sociological basis. These definitions see knowledge as a human capability to act (pp. 241-242)."

The dominant positivism paradigm of KM is implicit in the DIKW (Data-Information-Knowledge-Wisdom) hierarchy model. This model induced numerous computers and information researches. For example, (Rowley, 2007) revisiting the DIKW hierarchy by examining the articulation of the hierarchy in a number of widely read textbooks in information systems and knowledge management preferably published in 2003 and later, noted that "there is a consensus that data, information and knowledge are to be defined in terms of one another, although data and information can both act as inputs to knowledge; the tangle of concepts can be explored at two levels - the relationship between data and information, and the relationship between information and knowledge p.174);" and she raised the question: "Is there a sharp divide between data, information and knowledge, or do they lie on a continuum with different levels of meaning, structure and actionability occurring at different levels (p. 175)."

More recently, (Muller and Maasdorp 2011) point out the dominance of the DIK model in information science. They have three conjectures as to why knowledge management practitioners and authors prefer the DIK model. The first one concerns information theory background, the second one is about simplicity, and the third one rests on accumulative worldview. Their ideas are closely akin to ours. Let's quote some of their conjunctures: "the first possible explanation for the dominance of the DIK model in KM is that it is an effect of background in information theory or communication theory of the practitioner or the author; the second conjecture is that simplicity counts in management and that this has the effect of privileging a theoretical position that is clearly linked to a working and productive legacy in information system but more importantly, clears up the messy situation of exactly understanding the notion of knowledge in organizations; the third conjecture is painted on an even broader canvas. If one has a worldview that is cumulative and sees the world as consisting of innumerable little bits (now not in the technical sense) of matter that all add up to the while by the process of accumulation and simple organization and categorization, then a data information knowledge model would make sense…That means that a mechanistic and positivist worldview is to be found at the base of the easy acceptance of the DIK model."

In fact, we think that, beyond all these studies, we have to position our thoughts in the contextual field where the notion of data, information, and knowledge are used: in our case, the field of enterprises and more generally organizations. That leads to conceive how the transformation process should be envisaged using the concept of commensurability of interpretative frameworks highlighted by (Tsuchiya 1993).

2.3 The concept of commensurability of interpretative frameworks

2.3.1 Creation of Individual's tacit knowledge

Our approach is built upon the assumption emphasized by Tsuchiya concerning knowledge creation ability. He states, "Although terms 'datum', 'information', and 'knowledge' are often used interchangeably, there exists a clear distinction among them. When datum is sense-given through interpretative framework, it becomes information, and when information is sense-read through interpretative framework, it becomes knowledge (p.88)".

In other words, we can say that tacit knowledge that resides in our brain results from the sense given, through our interpretative frameworks, to data that we perceive among the information transmitted to us. Or rather, Knowledge exists in the interaction between an Interpretative Framework (incorporated within the head of an individual, or embedded into an artifact), and data.

In a different way, Wiig (2004) who highlights a discontinuity between information and knowledge describes this process clearly. He states, "The process, by which we develop new knowledge, uses prior knowledge to make sense of the new information and, once accepted for inclusion, internalizes the new insights by linking with prior knowledge. Hence, the new knowledge is as much a function of prior knowledge as it is of received inputs. A discontinuity is thus created between the received information inputs and the resulting new knowledge (p. 73)."

Consequently, we postulate that knowledge is not an object processed independently of the person who has to act. So, we can say that formalized and codified knowledge that are independent from individual, are not more than information. Furthermore, as emphasized by Haeckel (2000) we must discern "the knowledge of knower and the codification of that knowledge (p. 295)."

2.3.2 Conditions for considering information as knowledge

Tsuchiya emphases how organizational knowledge is created through dialogue, and highlighted how "commensurability" of the interpretative frameworks of the organization's members is indispensable for an organization to create organizational knowledge for decision and action (ref. Fig. 1). Here, commensurability is the common space of the set of interpretative frameworks of each member (e.g. cognitive models or mental models directly forged by education, experience, beliefs, and value systems). Tsuchiya states "It is important to clearly distinguish between sharing information and sharing knowledge. Information becomes knowledge only when it is sense-read through the interpretative framework of the receiver. Any information inconsistent with his interpretative framework is not perceived in most cases. Therefore, commensurability of interpretative frameworks of members is indispensable for individual knowledge to be shared (p. 89)."

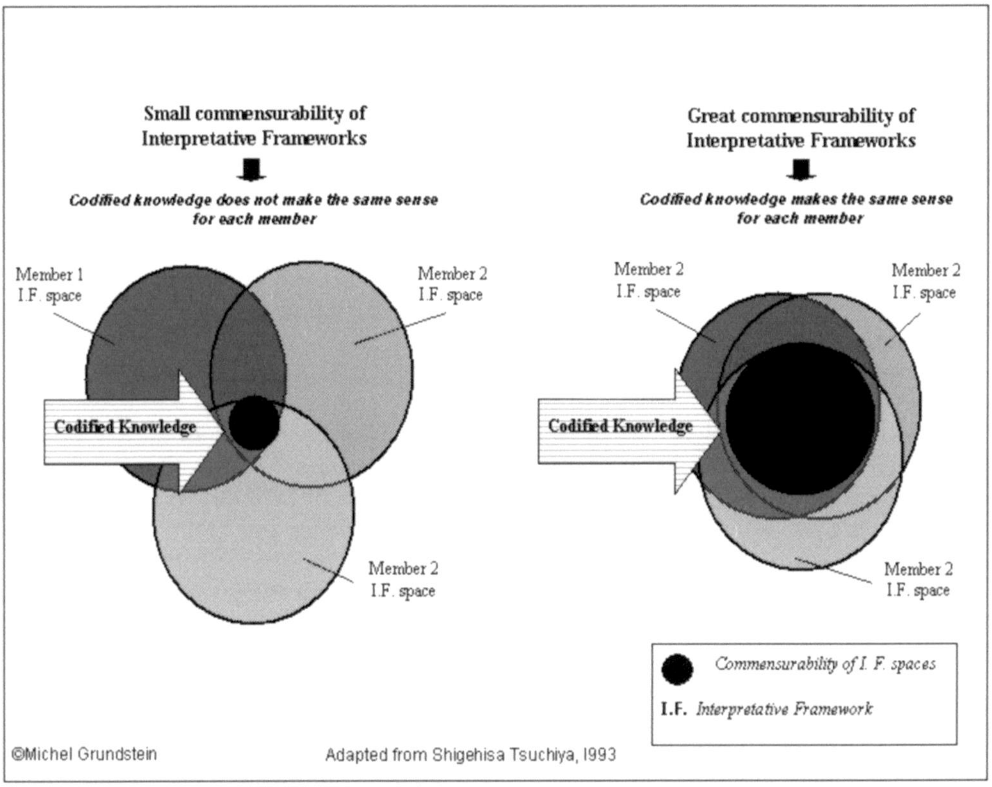

Fig. 1. Commensurability of Interpretative Frameworks (I.F.) and Individual Sense-Making

Consequently, information can only be assimilated to knowledge when members having a large commensurability of their set of interpretative frameworks commonly understand it in the same way. In that case, we call it "*information source of knowledge for someone*." Such is the case for members having the same technical or scientific education, or members having the same business culture. In these cases, formalized and codified knowledge make the same sense for each member; that enables to speak of knowledge bases, and flows of knowledge. However, one must take into account that interpretative frameworks evolve in a dynamic way: they are not rigid mindsets. Especially, when considering that, as time is going on, contexts and situations evolve. Thus, the contribution of scientific results, techniques and new methods, the influence of young generations being born with Web (Y generation or Digital Native), the impact of identity crisis and multiple cultures, modify the interpretative frameworks, and create a gap between individuals' commensurability of interpretative frameworks.

3. From data to information, and tacit and explicit knowledge: The DITEK process model

Relying to the theories and assumptions set out above, we elaborated a model that attempt to describe the transformation process from data to information, and from information to tacit and explicit knowledge. This model, called DITEK process model, describes at a first level the relationship between data and information, and at a second level the relationship between information, and tacit and explicit knowledge (ref. Fig. 2 and Fig. 3). Contrary to the idea of continuum between the concepts of data, information, and knowledge induced by the DIKW hierarchical model, DITEK process model shows a discontinuity between these concepts.
At a first level, we have to consider the relationship between data and information. This level must be thought as a basic process where data are discrete raw elements perceived, gathered, and filtered by a person before to be aggregated, supplemented, and organized into information (ref. Fig. 2).

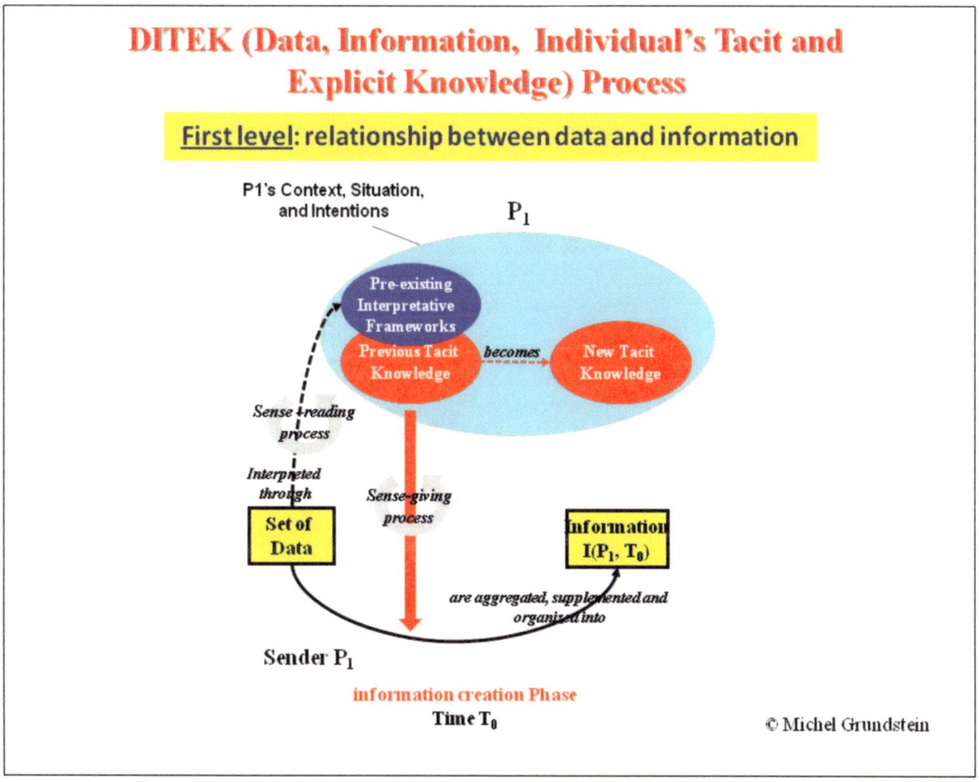

Fig. 2. DITEK process model level 1: From data…to information

At a second level, we have to consider the relationship between information, and tacit and explicit knowledge. This level is in rupture with the first one, it presupposes that information already exists whatever are time and context in which it was created. Let's describe the transformation process.
A sender P_1 is acting in specific context and situation at time T_0. P_1 has pre-existing interpretative frameworks, previous tacit knowledge, and intentions. In an information

creation phase, P_1, has direct access to a set of data outside himself. Then, P_1 according to a sense-reading process - that depends of his pre-existing interpretative frameworks activated depending of his context, his situation, and his intentions, filters some of these data that take sense for him. At the same time, a sense-giving process using P_1's previous tacit knowledge enables P_1 to aggregate, supplement and organize selected data into information $I(P_1, T_0)$. Once created this information becomes a static object independent from P_1, and time. It is this information that is passed-on by the individuals or by means of the digital information system (DIS) where it is stored, treated and transmitted as a stream of digital data. During this process, P_1's pre-existing interpretative frameworks are not changing; previous tacit knowledge can be reorganized and modified into new tacit knowledge.

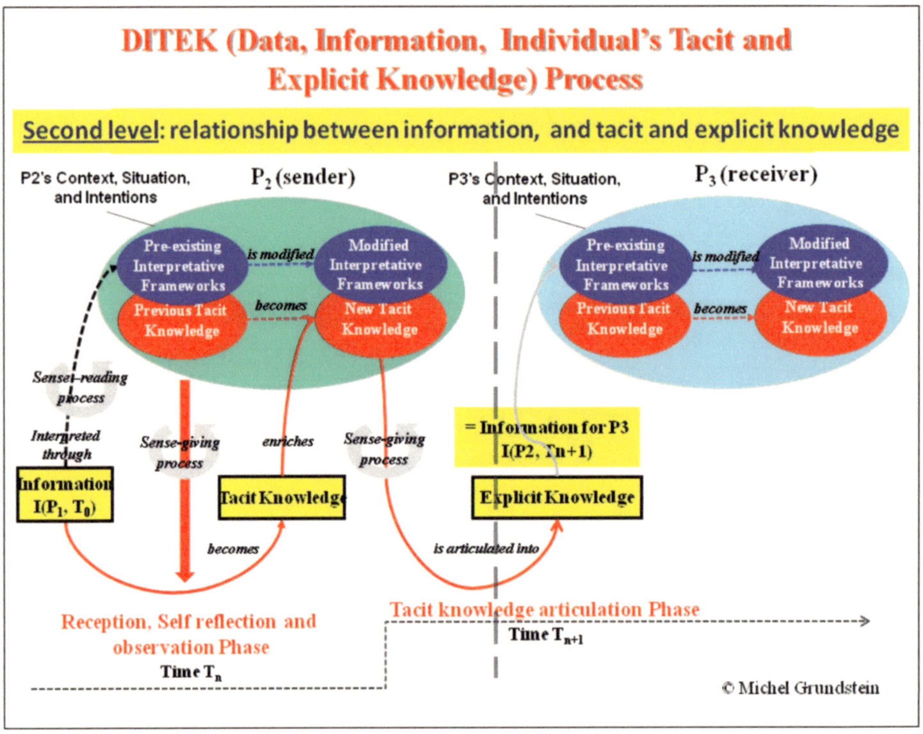

Fig. 3. DITEK process model level 2: From information…to tacit and explicit knowledge

At a later stage of the first level process, at time T_n, when P_2 perceives the information $I(P^1, T_0)$ during a reception, self-reflection and observation phase, this information (P_1,T_0) is captured by P_2, who is in different context and situation than P_1 who elaborates it. P_2 has his own intentions. Then, P_2 according to a sense-reading process, interprets this information (P_1, T_0), filtering data through his pre-existing interpretative frameworks activated depending of his context, his situation, and his intentions. At the same time, a sense-giving process that uses P_2's previous knowledge operates, and engenders new tacit knowledge. That's the way that changes P_2's pre-existing interpretative frameworks, and enriches P_2's previous tacit knowledge enabling P_2 to understand his situation, identify a problem, find a solution, decide, and act. The results of this process are modified interpretative frameworks, and new tacit knowledge.

The process of transformation of information into tacit knowledge is a process of construction of knowledge. Created knowledge, can be very different from one individual to another when the commensurability of their interpretative frameworks is small, whatever are the causes of it. There are large risks that the same information takes different senses for each of them, and consequently generates a construction of different tacit knowledge in the head of the decision process stakeholders. Unlike the information, knowledge is dynamic. Once constructed it cannot be considered as an object independent from the individual who built it, or the individual who appropriates it to make a decision and to act.

Later on, at time T_{n+1}, when P_2 as a sender communicates with a receiver P_3, during *a* tacit knowledge articulation phase, a sense-giving process enables P_2 to articulate a part of his new tacit knowledge into explicit knowledge that is no more than information $I(P_2,T_{n+1})$ for P_3.

As a result one can understand the importance to clearly distinguish static factual information, which allows describing the context and the situation that raise a problem, from the tacit knowledge of the individual who processes this information to learn and get knowledge he needs to carry out his tasks.

Consequently, paraphrasing (Kautz and Kjaergaard 2008) if technology provides the possibility of making information available across time and space (p. 49), we always have to keep in mind the role of individual in the knowledge sharing process, but we do also pay attention to how individual uses technology to share knowledge (p. 43).

Our approach is inspired by a KM constructivist paradigm. It induces to consider tacit and explicit knowledge as the outcome of a sense-giving process that involves people engaged in actions, and mainly depend of the organizational context. It implies three fundamental postulates and leads to a definition a KM focused on activities and processes opening on Technological, Managerial, and Socio-technical Well-balanced KM Initiative Strategies within Organizations

4. A constructivist paradigm of KM

4.1 Three fundamental postulates

Our observations and experiments within the industry, led us to set forth three postulates: (i) Knowledge is not an object; (ii) Knowledge is linked to the action, and (iii) Company's knowledge includes two main categories of knowledge. We define these postulates below.

4.1.1 Postulate 1: Knowledge is not an object

Knowledge exists in the interaction between an interpretative Framework (incorporated within the head of an individual, or embedded into an artifact), and data. This postulate comes from the assumption emphasized by Tsuchiya (1993) concerning tacit knowledge creation ability.

4.1.2 Postulate 2: Knowledge is linked to the action

From an organization perspective, knowledge is created through action. Knowledge is essential for the functioning of support, and value-adding processes (Porter, 1985). Activities contributing to these processes utilize and create knowledge. Thus, the actions finalize the organization's knowledge. This viewpoint takes into account the context and the situation, which allow utilizing and creating knowledge. In particular, we must analyze the role and intentions of the actors - decision-makers - involved with these activities in order to achieve the organization's missions. Therefore, knowledge is linked to their decisions, their actions, and their relations with the surrounding systems (people and artifacts).

4.1.3 Postulate 3: Company's knowledge includes two main categories of knowledge

Within organizations, knowledge consists of two main categories (ref.Table.1).

EXPLICITED KNOWLEDGE (KNOW-HOW)	TACIT KNOWLEDGE EMBODIED BY INDIVIDUALS (SKILLS)	
Collective knowledge (*Knowledge that can be though as objects)*	**Collective knowledge** (*Routines)*	**Personal knowledge** *(Private knowledge)*
- Knowledge formalized within documents and/or codified in knowledge-based systems and databases. - Knowledge embedded in automated management systems, conception systems, production systems, and products.	- Knowledge incorporated within models, and regular and predictable behaviors.	- People's abilities, - Professional knack, - Knowledge of company history, and decisional contexts, - Knowledge of the environment (customers, competitors, technologies), and socio-economic factors
Information source of knowledge for someone	**Defensive Routines** - Knowledge that is an obstacle to change **Constructive Routines** - Knowledge that favors innovation and change	**Specific knowledge belonging to each individual** - Knowledge that is a volatile intangible resource, which depends on the continuity of the presence of employees in the company

Table 1. The two main Categories of Company's knowledge

On the one hand, explicited knowledge includes all tangible elements (we call it "know-how"); and on the other hand, tacit knowledge (Polanyi, 1966), includes intangible elements (we call it "skills"). Tacit knowledge can or cannot be articulated into explicit knowledge. The tangible elements are collective knowledge. They take the shape of formalized and codified knowledge in a physical format (databases, procedures, plans, models, algorithms, and analysis and synthesis documents), or are embedded into automated management systems, in conception and production systems, and in products. The intangible elements are inherent to the individuals who bear them, either as collective knowledge - the "routines" that are non-written individual or collective action procedures (Nelson and Winter, 1982) or personal knowledge (skills, crafts, "job secrets", historical and contextual knowledge of environment, clients, competitors, technologies, and socio-economic factors).

4.2 Knowledge management perspectives

Relying to the postulates mentioned above, it appears that, KM addresses activities, which utilize and create knowledge more than knowledge by itself. With regard to this question,

since 2001, our group of research has adopted the following definition of KM (Grundstein and Rosenthal-Sabroux, 2003):
"KM is the management of the activities and the processes that enhance the utilization and the creation of knowledge within an organization, according to two strongly interlinked goals, and their underlying economic and strategic dimensions, organizational dimensions, socio-cultural dimensions, and technological dimensions: (i) a patrimony goal, and (ii) a sustainable innovation goal" (p.980).
The patrimony goal has to do with the preservation of knowledge, their reuse and their actualization; it is a static goal. The sustainable innovation goal is more dynamic. It is concerned with organizational learning that is creation and integration of knowledge at the organizational level.
This definition of KM induces a specific KM governance, and leads towards a technological, managerial, and socio-technical well-balanced KM initiatives within organizations referring to general model for knowledge management within organization so called MGKME (Grundstein, 2005a, 2007, 2008), which integrates managerial guiding principles, *ad hoc* infrastructures, socio-technical environment, support and value adding processes, organizational learning processes, generic KM processes, and relevant methods and supporting tools. MGKME is described section 6. Furthermore, distinguishing information from knowledge leads to conceive what we call Enterprise's Information and Knowledge Systems (EIKS).

5. Knowledge management governance

After having considered the Corporate Governance and the Information Technology Governance concepts, we attempt to tackle with a Knowledge Management Governance perspective drawing a link with the Corporate and IT Governance principles.

5.1 The OECD corporate governance

OECD (Organization for Economic Co-operation and Development) corporate governance principles were originally issued in 1999. They have since become the international benchmark for corporate governance. OECD governments in April 2004 agreed the new Principles, and define Corporate Governance as shown on figure 4 (OECD, 2004, p.11).

5.2 The COBIT® IT Governance

Control Objectives for Information and related Technology (COBIT®, 2000, 2002, 2005) was initially published by the Information Systems Audit and Control Foundation, Inc. in 1996. Guldentops (2004) states that "COBIT® presents an international and generally accepted IT control framework enabling organizations to implement an IT Governance structure throughout the enterprise" (p. 277). A fourth edition has been edited in 2005. In the Executive Summary IT Governance is defined as shown on figure 4 (COBIT®, 2005, p.6).
IT governance provides the structure that links IT process, IT resources and information to enterprise strategies and objectives. To achieve success, corporate governance and IT governance can no longer be considered separate and distinct disciplines. The COBIT® Management Guidelines helps to support these needs. They have identified specific Critical Success Factors, Key Goal Indicators, Key Performance Indicators and an associated Maturity Model for IT Governance.

5.3 KM Governance Perspectives

Corporate Governance and IT Governance do not explicitly mention to consider Intellectual Capital as a resource in the enterprise strategies. Even so, as pointed out by Edvinsson and Malone (1997), "The core of the so-called *knowledge economy* is huge investment flows into human capital as well as information technology" (p. 12). However, we think that the knowledge economy will oblige to take into account Intellectual Capital. Consequently, we need to study the link between KM, and Corporate Governance and IT Governance. To enable such a study, we must refer to a KM pattern of reference to elaborate KM Governance principles.

5.3.1 Towards a unified KM pattern of reference

Despite the fact that numerous Knowledge Management Frameworks have been suggested all over the world, it does not exist a unify pattern of reference supporting our definition of KM as described in the paragraph 4.2. For example, let us consider *The European Guide to Good Practice in Knowledge Management* (CEN-CWA 14924-1, 2004). The project team has collected, categorized and analyzed more than 140 KM Frameworks. We can notice that this work has produced a high-quality practical outcome that is a reference point to achieve a good understanding of KM. Nevertheless, as contributors to this project, we underline the predominant positivist paradigm, and the information management approach of KM that have inspired the project team. Moreover, we have observed that few of them were "*people-focused*" as Wiig (2004) states: "our emphasis is on people and their behaviors and roles in enterprise operations (p. XXV)." Furthermore, we have distinguished two main approaches underlying KM: (i) a technological approach that answers a demand of solutions based on the technologies of information and communication (ICT); (ii) a managerial approach that integrates knowledge as resources contributing to the implementation of the strategic vision of the company.

Therefore, we suggest two KM Governance Perspectives depending on the first or the second approach (ref. Fig. 4).

On the one hand, the technological approach leads to reduce knowledge to codified knowledge that is no more than information. In that case, we can manage KM projects in the same way than IS projects. Specific criteria inherent to KMS must connect KM Governance and IT Governance principles. On the other hand, the managerial approach that integrates knowledge as a resource focuses on the core business processes and the people. Corporate Governance principles must integrate the risks linked to the utilization and creation of knowledge

These aspects involve elaborating Management Governance Guidelines for KM as COBIT® is for IT. The aim of the Model for General Knowledge Management within the Enterprise (MGKME), described hereafter, is to contribute to elaborating a guiding framework that serves as a pattern for KM Governance Guidelines.

6. MGKME, A Model for General Knowledge Management within the Enterprise

6.1 KM Empirical Model versus KM System

KM becomes a reality in the implementation of a system. The purpose of this system is to amplify the utilization and the creation of knowledge to improve the enterprise's effectiveness. This system is often called Knowledge Management System (KMS). Therefore,

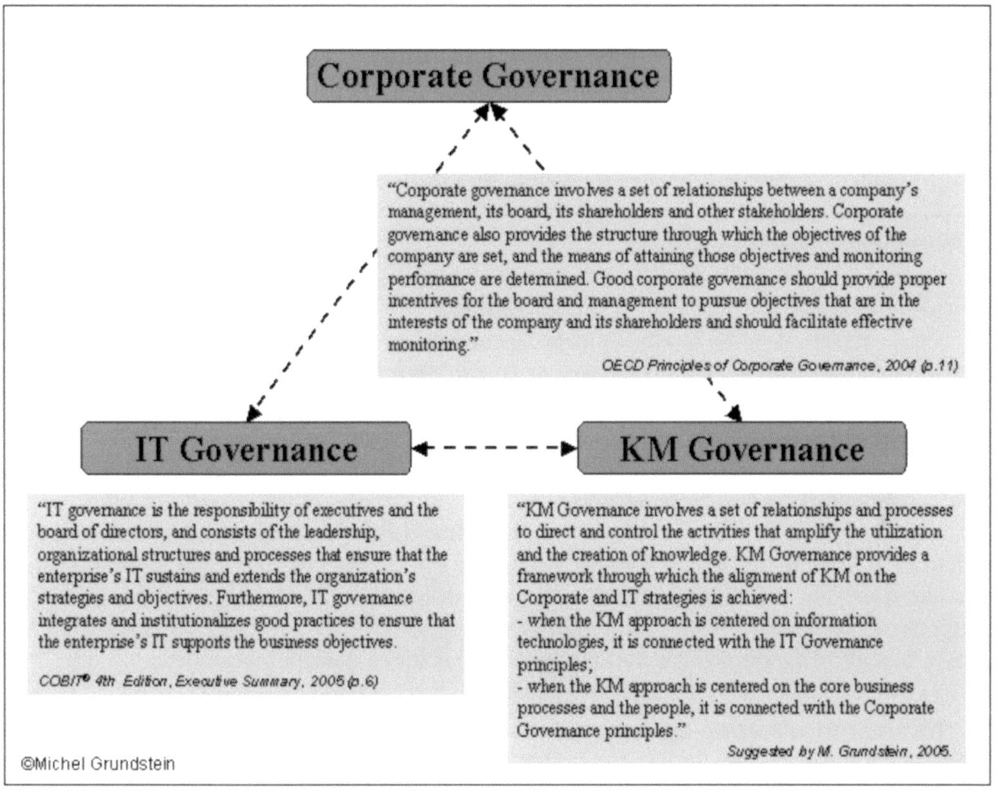

Fig. 4. KM Governance Perspective

we have to distinguish between the notion of KM Empirical Model that is a template, and the notion of KM System - a context dependant system, which is the implementation of this template in the real world (ref. Fig. 5).

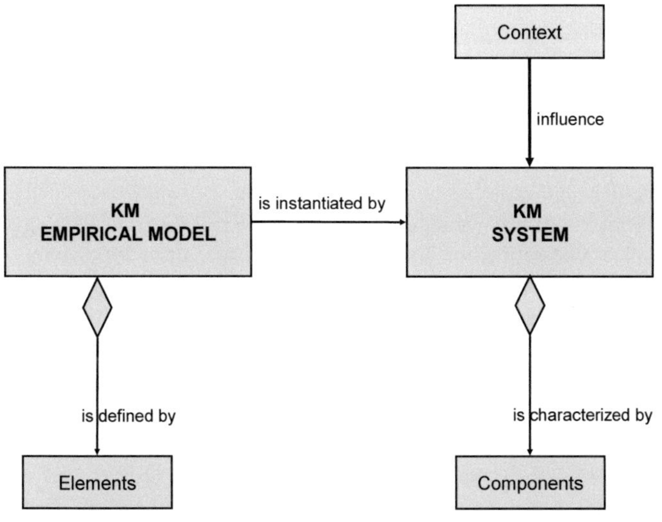

Fig. 5. KM Empirical Model and KM System

To implement KMS components, Enterprises need a general model that is a pattern of reference (a template) in order to integrate KM Governance principles in their strategic vision, and to use KM as a factor that enable improving their efficiency and competitiveness. In this chapter, we refer to MGKME, our Model of General Knowledge Management within the Enterprise (Grundstein, 2005a, 2007, 2008) that articulates the enterprise's sociotechnical environment, the enterprise's value-adding processes, the managerial guiding principles specific to KM and the *Ad-hoc* infrastructures, the generic KM processes, and the organizational learning processes.

6.2 The enterprise's sociotechnical environment

E. Coakes (2002) defines sociotechnical approach as "*the study of the relationships and interrelationships between the social and technical parts of any system*" (p. 5). From KM viewpoint, the Socio-technical Environment constitutes the social fabric where autonomous individuals, supported by Information and Communication Technologies (ICT) and tangible resources, interact and are conversing through physical or virtual places (coffee machines, collaborative workspaces, weblogs, wikis, CoPs).

The socio-technical approach leads to emphasizing the link between knowing and action, with due regard to the basic constraints of the social system that is to give a sense to working time. Thus, KM initiative should result in Knowledge Management System (KMS) components that take into account the individuals, both as components and users of a system that allows them to be autonomous and to achieve their potentialities.

6.3 The enterprise's value adding processes

Value adding processes derive from the value chain described by Porter (1985) who identifies nine value-adding activities that he classifies into two main categories. The "primary activities" are: 1) in-bound logistics, 2) operations, 3) out-bound logistics, 4) marketing & sales, and 5) Services. The "support activities" are: 1) business infrastructure, 2) human resource management, 3) technological development, and 4) supplies. In this way, Value-adding processes represent the organizational context for which knowledge is essential factors of performance. It is in this context that is implanted a KM initiative.

6.4 The managerial guiding principles specific to KM and the *Ad-hoc* infrastructures

The Managerial Guiding Principles should bring a vision aligned with the enterprise's strategic orientations, and should suggest a KM Governance principles by analogy with COBIT®. In particular, we established KM indicators. Numerous publications and books relates to that subject. From our viewpoint, we constructed two main categories of indicators in order to monitor a KM initiative: (i) a category of indicators that focus on the impacts of the initiative that favor enhancement of intellectual capital, (ii) a category of indicators that insure monitoring and coordination of KM activities, measuring the results, and insuring the relevance of the initiative.

In addition (ref. Fig. 6), we suggest a way to get a good articulation between the Deming's cycle PDCA (Deming,1982), and Argyris and Schön's Organizational learning (Argyris and Schön, 1996).

Firstly, we refer to the PDCA cycle of activities - plan, do, check, and act; this cycle well known as the *Deming's Cycle* by Quality Management practitioners, has inspired the ISO 9004 (2000) Quality Standards in order to get a continuous process improvement of the

Quality Management System. Secondly, we refer to the *Single-Loop Learning* and *Double-Loop Learning* defined in the Argyris & Schön's organizational learning theory
Furthermore, we should think about the *Ad-hoc* infrastructures, which are adapted sets of devices and means for action. Beyond a network that favors cooperative work, it is important to implement the conditions that will allow sharing and creating knowledge. An *ad hoc* infrastructure must be set up according to the specific situation of each company, and the context of the envisaged KM initiative. The SECI spiral of conversion Model proposed by Nonaka and Takeuchi (1995) and the Japanese concept of *Ba* inspire this infrastructure (Nonaka and Konno, 1998; Nonaka, Toyama, and Konno, 2000; Grundstein, 2011).

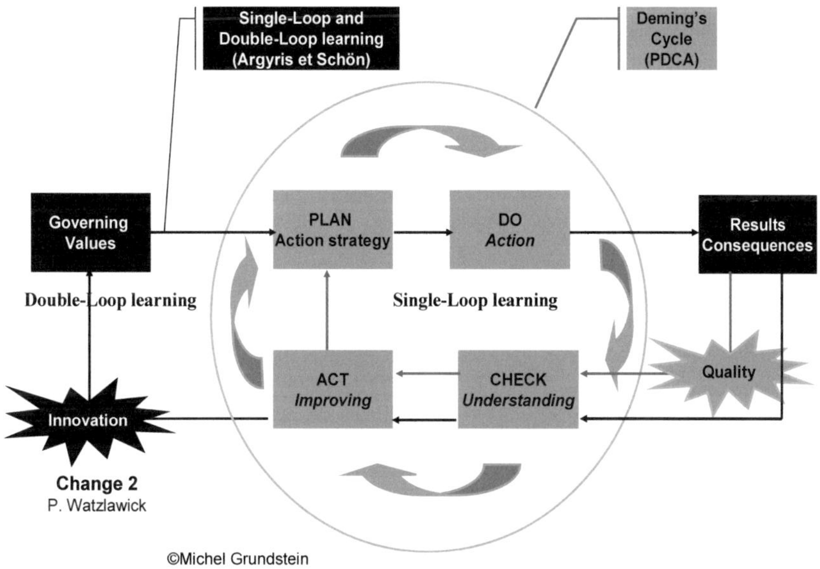

Fig. 6. Deming's cycle and Argyris & Schön's Organizational learning

6.5 The generic KM processes

The generic KM processes answer the problem of capitalizing on company's knowledge defined in the following way (Grundstein, 1996) "*Capitalizing on company's knowledge means considering certain knowledge used and produced by the company as a storehouse of riches and drawing from these riches interest that contributes to increasing the company's capital*" (p. 141).
Several problems co-exist. They are recurring problems for a company. These problems constitute a general problematic that has been organized in five categories. Each of these categories contains sub-processes aimed to contribute a solution to the set of overall problems (ref. Fig. 7).
The **Locating KM Process** deals with the location of Crucial Knowledge, that is, Knowledge (explicit or tacit) that is essential for decision-making processes and for the progress of the support and value-adding processes. One can mention GAMETH® (Grundstein, 2000; Grundstein & Rosenthal-Sabroux, 2004), an approach that provides the elements that lead to identifying the problems, clarifying the needs for knowledge, identifying and locating potential crucial knowledge, specifying the value-based assessment of this knowledge, and finally, determining "crucial knowledge".

The **Preserving Process** deals with the retention of knowledge and skills. When knowledge can be articulated into words, it is necessary to acquire it with the bearers of knowledge, to represent it, to formalize it, and to conserve it. This leads to Knowledge Engineering activities notably described in (Schreiber et al, 2000). When knowledge cannot be articulated, then interactions through communities of practice or other types of networks must be encouraged.

The **Enhancing Process** deals with the benefit of knowledge and skills. It is necessary to make them accessible according to certain rules of confidentiality and safety, to disseminate them, to share them, to use them more effectively, to combine them, and to create new knowledge. Here is the link with innovation processes.

The **Actualizing process** deals with the actualization of knowledge and skills. It is necessary to appraise them, to update them, to standardize them and to enrich them according to the returns of experiments, the creation of new knowledge, and the contribution of external knowledge. Here is the link with business intelligence processes.

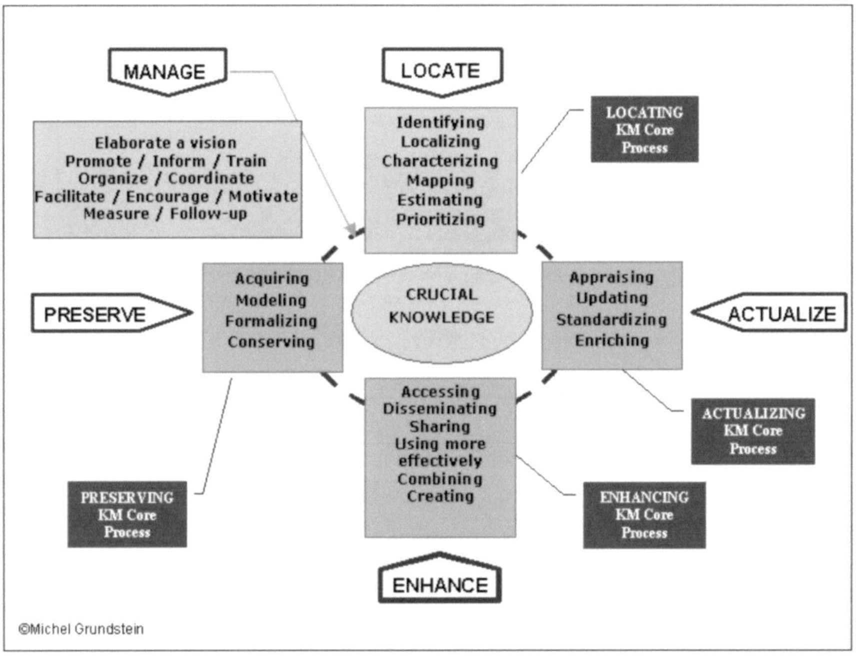

Fig. 7. The Generic KM Processes

6.6 The organizational learning processes

The Organizational learning processes underlay the whole generic KM processes. The aim of the organizational learning process is to increase individual knowledge, to reinforce competencies, and to convert them into a collective knowledge through interactions, dialogue, discussions, exchange of experience, and observation. The main objective consists in fighting against the defensive routines that make barriers to training and change. Therefore, it is a question of helping the members of the organization to change their way of thinking by facilitating an apprenticeship of a constructive way of reasoning instead of a defensive one.

6.7 MGKME description

The MGKME, described hereafter (ref. Fig. 8), supports our full meaning of KM as defined in paragraph 4.2. It is an empirical model based both on our experience within the industry, and on our research works. MGKME rests on a Sociotechnical approach. It focuses on people and value adding processes. Moreover, the MGKME presents an attempt to articulate the Deming's Cycle PDCA and the Single-Loop Learning and Double-Loop Learning defined in the Argyris & Schön's organizational learning theory. It suggests "*ad hoc* infrastructures" derived from the Nonaka and Takeuchi's SECI model and the Japanese concept of "*BA*". It highlights four generic KM processes (Grundstein, 2007): Locating crucial knowledge process; Preserving crucial knowledge process; Enhancing crucial knowledge process; and Actualizing crucial knowledge process.

MGKME is composed of two main categories of elements: (I) the underlying elements consist of (1) socio-technical environment and (2) value adding processes; (II) the operating elements focus on the underlying elements. They consist of (3) managerial guiding principles, (4) *ad hoc* infrastructures, (5) generic KM processes, (6) organizational learning processes, and (7) methods and supporting tools.

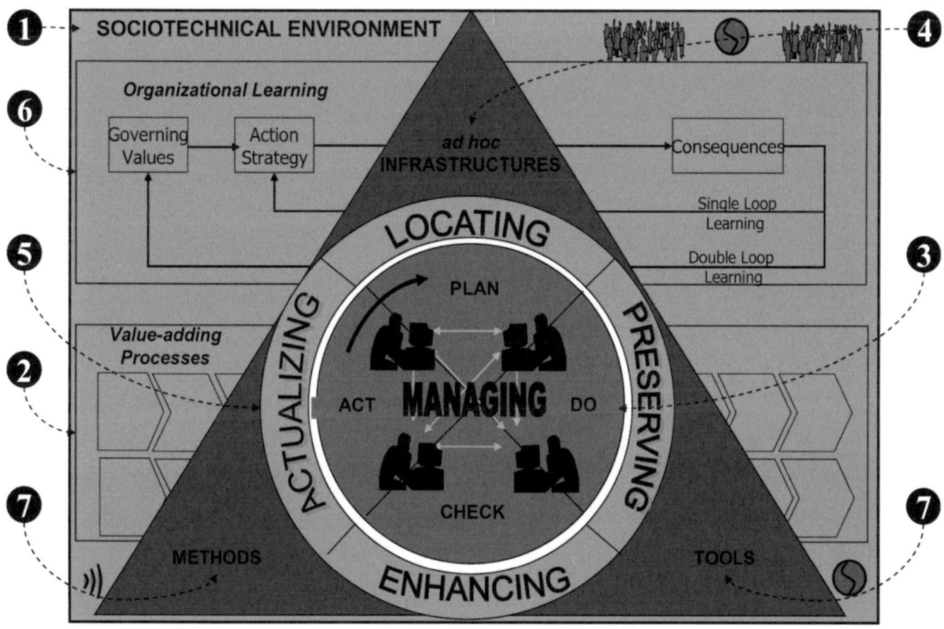

©Michel Grundstein

Fig. 8. Model for Global Knowledge Management within the Enterprise

Key Issues to address for every elements of each level are synthesized in Table 2 and 3.

Table 2 represents the underlying level of MGKME. The Underlying level of the MGKME contains the elements of MGKME that underlie the operating components of the Knowledge Management System. The core knowledge is embodied in people heads, and their abilities to utilize them and to generate new knowledge at the same time. The information technologies and the tangible technical resources enhance their competence, while value-adding processes and organizational infrastructures are structuring their activities. Nevertheless, their social interactions are essential factors, which leverage their potentialities, and that actually enable them to achieve effective results. Therefore, from our perspective, socio-technical environment❶, and value-adding processes❷ are fundamental components of the Knowledge Management System.

	Elements	Key Issues
UNDERLYING LEVEL	❶ Sociotechnical Environment	Enterprise 's Activities (sector, key value-chain elements, geographical distribution, size, market, mass or batch manufacturing processes, product lifecycle, oral or written culture) Relations and Interactions between ICT, Structure, and People: their roles, their tasks Capability to learn and Innovate Social and Intellectual Capital Management Involvement
	❷ Value-adding Processes	Porter's Primary and Support Activities : Running Processes Business Processes Design and Development Processes Innovative Product and Services Processes

Table 2. MGKME's underlying Level

Table 3 represents the operating level of MGKME. The operating level of MGKME contains the elements of MGKME that focus on the underlying components of the Knowledge Management System, and consist of managerial guiding principles❸, ad hoc infrastructures❹, generic KM processes❺, organizational learning processes❻, and methods and supporting tools for KM❼.

7. The enterprise's information and knowledge system (EIKS)

The enterprise's information and knowledge system (EIKS) consists mainly in a set of individuals and digital information systems (ref. Fig. 9).

EIKS rests on a socio-technical context, which consists of individuals in interaction among them, with machines, and with the very EIKS. It includes:

- Digital Information Systems (DIS), which are artificial systems, the artefacts designed from information and communication technologies (ICT)
- An Information System (IS), constituted by individuals who, in a given context, are processors of data to which they give a sense under the shape of information. This information, depending of the case, is passed on, remembered, treated, and diffused by them or by the DIS.

Model Level	Elements	Key Issues
II OPERATING LEVEL	❸ Managerial Guiding Principles	Vision KM Governance Principles (strategic alignment, articulation between quality and organizational learning management) Main Development Axes Indicators
	❹ *ad hoc* Infrastructures	Content and Document Management Systems Collaborative Information Systems Organizational conditions encouraging interaction, communication, and knowledge sharing
	❺ Generic KM Processes	Locating Process Preserving Process Enhancing Process Actualizing Process
	❻ Organizational Learning Process	Team Learning Processes New Organizational Structures Experiments General Vision, and Systemic Approach Routines (defensive or constructive) Knowledge Dissemination Constant Evolution versus Change (Alter, 2000)
	❼ Methods and Supporting Tools	General Methods and Tools Knowledge Engineering, Artificial Intelligence (Semantic WEB and Ontology) CSCW -Computer Supported Cooperative Work (Multi-agents Systems) Social Networks (Identification, Visualization, and Informal Social Network Analysis Systems) Impact of Web 2.0

Table 3. MGKME's operating Level

- A Knowledge System (KS), consisting of tacit knowledge embodied by the individuals, and of explicit knowledge formalized and codified on any shape of supports (documents, video, photo, digitized or not). Under certain conditions, digitized knowledge is susceptible to be stored, processed and spread with the DIS. In that case, knowledge is no more than information.

We insist on the importance to integrate the individual as a component of the system. In fact, relying to our assumptions, we argue that knowledge resides primarily in the heads of individuals, and in the social interactions of these individuals. Knowledge is dependent of the individual's interpretative frameworks, and the context of his action. Consequently, as mental models and interpretative frameworks are directly forged by cultural factors, it induces to stress the role of cultural factors when social interactions, information sharing and knowledge transfer are essential to enable efficiency in the global economy. Here, knowledge transfer must be understood as transmission, plus absorption and use of knowledge (Davenport and Prusack 1998 p.101). Therefore, the project manager should consider the individual (knowledge worker and decision-maker) both at once as a user, and a component of the EIKS. In EIKS, the information and knowledge portals have become essential for the knowledge workers who have to share with colleagues disseminated all around the world.

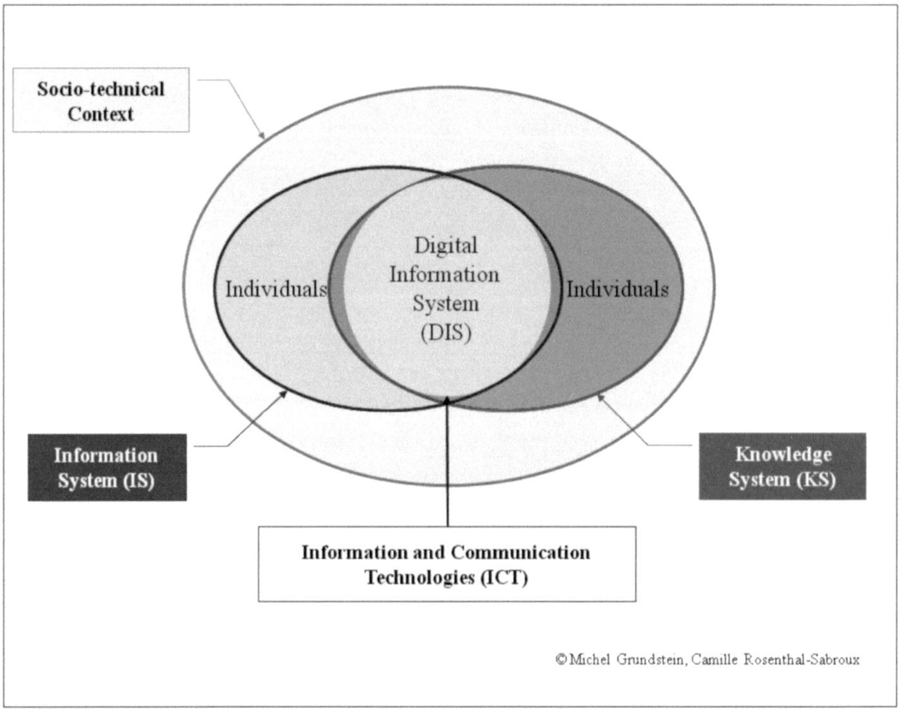

Fig. 9. The enterprise' information and knowledge system (EIKS)

8. A well-balanced KM initiative strategy within organizations

A general KM initiative shows willingness, at the highest level of the enterprise, to encourage all the steps, and to implement all the means leading to capitalize on knowledge to pull strategic advantages of it. Afterwards, we refer to our own studies about general KM initiative (Grundstein, 2005b).

There exist three main development phases: (i) The Strategic Orientation Phase which aim is to establish KM Initiative outline and agenda; (ii) Operational Management Phase which aim is to design and specify specific projects linked to capitalizing on knowledge problems; and (iii) Projects Deployment Phase which aim is to monitor and implement EIKS. For the purpose of this chapter, we will focus on the first phase, the strategic orientation phase.

8.1 Strategic orientation phase

The strategic orientation phase of general KM initiative leads to establish KM initiative outline and agenda, taking into account priorities and available resources. It includes four steps (ref. Fig. 10): (i) Elaborating the Enterprise's KM Vision; (ii) Aligning KM Strategy on

Enterprise's Strategies; (iii) Monitoring KM Maturity Study; and (iv) Establishing KM Initiative Program. Questions which must be considered focus notably on achieving alignment of the KM strategy on the organization's strategy:

- How to articulate the general KM initiative with the Enterprise's strategic orientations?
- How to make the Enterprise's members, whatever are their hierarchical level, aware of KM interest for them, and the Enterprise?
- How to assess the Enterprise's KM maturity and its capacity to implement KM projects?
- How to identify IS needs, KS needs, and EIKS needs?
- How to define the KM initiative outline, and the agenda?
- What are predictable impacts?
- How to gather constructive conditions?
- What are the activities to develop and promote?
- What are the indicators to set up?
- How to establish *Ad-hoc* organizational structures, and to attribute roles to stakeholders?
- How to create and support organizational learning processes leading towards more information sharing, and knowledge transfer?

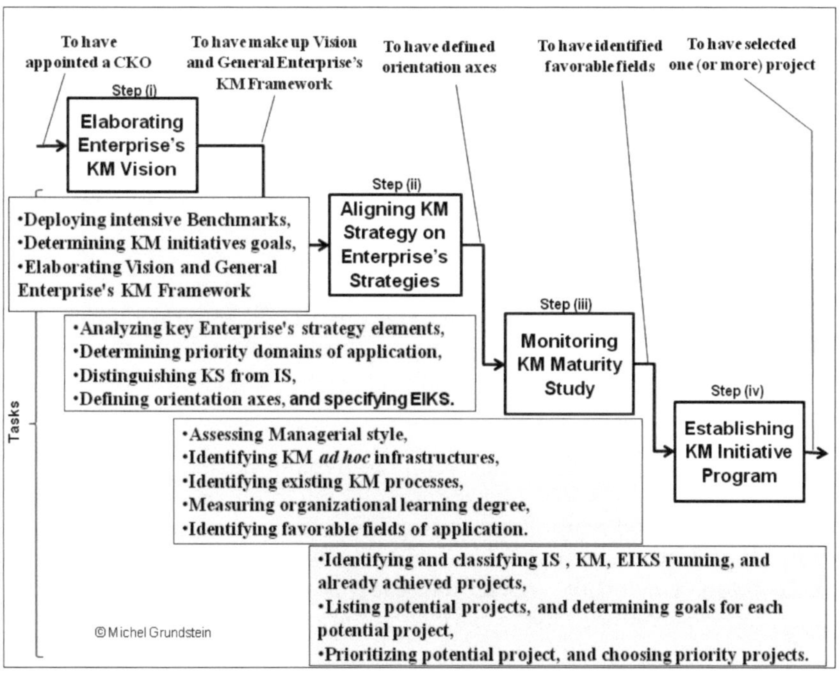

Fig. 10. The Strategic Orientation Phase

The strategic orientation phase is crucial and can avoid getting KM resources outcomes unused. We argue that, most of time, IT approach leads confusing notions of information and knowledge, and misunderstanding the goals: do we have to develop an Information System or do we have to implement an EIKS that integrate people as users and components of the system? Therefore, the strategic orientation phase must help to build a general KM vision that makes a clear distinction between technology as a support to share individual's tacit knowledge, and technology as a means to collect, store, and distribute explicit and codified knowledge that is no more than information. Beyond benchmarking studies, to deal with the strategic orientation phase, Enterprises need a Meta model that is a pattern of reference (a template) in order: (i) to integrate KM Governance principles; (ii) to adapt it to their own situation; (iii) to monitor KM Maturity study (Grundstein, 2008, p. 424); and (iv) to envision integrating Information systems and KM systems in the same both digital and human system that we call EIKS.

9. Conclusions and perspectives

Most of time, the positivist paradigm of KM thought as a means to acquire, codify, store and disseminate knowledge, considers knowledge as an object, and so disregards the importance of individual's tacit knowledge used in action. Although this paradigm of KM is greatly shared, without awareness when elaborating KM initiative's strategy, we can confuse the notions of information and knowledge. The constructivist paradigm of KM proposed in this paper is founded on the DITEK process model, and three postulates. It brings an open definition of KM focused on the activities and processes that enhance the utilization and the creation of knowledge within organizations; in doing so, it induces a well-balanced technological, managerial and socio-technical KM initiative strategy. Therefore, to avoid misunderstanding during the strategic orientation phase of a KM initiative, we pointed out that it was fundamental to clearly distinguish the notion of information from the notion of knowledge.

The three postulates that change the paradigm of KM induce an open definition of KM that leads to integrate the whole dimensions that should be involved in a KM initiative. They induce a specific KM governance, and lead towards a technological, managerial, and socio-technical well-balanced KM initiatives within organizations referring to general model for knowledge management within organization so called MGKME. Furthermore, distinguishing Information from Knowledge opens our mind on a different view of information systems: these systems based on Digital Information System (DIS) integrate people, both at the same time, as users and components of the system. This pragmatic vision needs thinking about the architecture of an Enterprise's Information and Knowledge System (EIKS), which must be a basis of discussion during the strategic orientation phase of a general KM initiative.

10. Acknowledgement

This work is dedicated to Dany my wife. With her dynamism, joie de vivre, love and trust towards me, she always supported and encouraged me to go ahead in my works and my researches, making the conditions allowing us to live with a complete peace of mind.

I am grateful to Camille Rosenthal Sabroux who gave me the opportunity to collaborate with Paris Dauphine University, and all the students whose continuous contribution and relevant questioning encouraged me to clarify and improve the models.

11. References

Alter, N. (2000) *L'innovation ordinaire*. Paris:France Presses Universitaires de France.

Amin, A., Cohendet P. (2004) *Architectures of Knowledge, firms, capabilities, and communities*. New York US: Oxford University Press Inc.

Argyris, C., Schön, D.A. (1996) Organizational Learning II. Theory, Method, and Practice. Readings, MA: Addison-Wesley Publishing Company.

CEN-CWA 14924-1 (2004). Knowledge Management Framework. In European Guide to Good Practice in Knowledge Management (Part 1). Brussels: CEN, CWA 14924-1:2004 (E). Retrieved June 19, 2004, from ftp://cenftp1.cenorm.be/PUBLIC/CWAs/e-Europe/KM/CWA14924-01-2004-Mar.pdf

Coakes, E. (2002) Knowledge Management: A Sociotechnical Perspective. In E. Cokes, D. Willis & S. Clarke (Eds), Knowledge Management in the Sociotechnical World (Chapter 2, pp.4-14). London, Springer-Verlag.

COBIT® (2005) Control Objectives for Information and Related Technology. Control Objectives, Management Guidelines, Maturity Models, (4th Edition). Rolling Meadows Illinois: IT Governance Institute.

Davenport T. H., Prusak L. (1998) Working Knowledge. Harvard Business School Press, Boston.

Deming, W.E. (1982): *Out of the Crisis*. MIT Press International

Edvinsson, L. & Malone, M. S. (1997). Intellectual Capital. Realizing your Company's True Value by Finding its Hidden Brainpower. New York, NY: HarperCollins Publisher, Inc.

Grundstein, M. (1996). "CORPUS", an Approach to Capitalizing Company Knowledge. P. Ein-Dor (Ed.) Artificial Intelligence in Economics and Management (pp.139-152). Tel-Aviv, Boston, MA: Kluwer Academic Publisher.

Grundstein, M. (2000). From capitalizing on Company's Knowledge to Knowledge Management. In D. Morey, M. Maybury, & B. Thuraisingham (Eds), Knowledge Management, Classic and Contemporary Works (chapter 12, pp. 261-287). Cambridge, Massachusetts: The MIT Press.

Grundstein, M. (2005a). MGKME: A Model for General Knowledge Management within the Enterprise. 2nd International Conference on Intellectual Capital, Knowledge Management and Organizational Learning, Proceedings. American University in Dubai, UAE, (ICICKM05 Proceedings pp.201-211). Reading, UK: ACL.

Grundstein M. (2005b) Pilotage d'un projet Global de Knowledge Management (PGKM). Research Report #12. Paris, France: MG Conseil (www.mgconseil.fr).

Grundstein M. (2007) Knowledge Workers as an Integral Component in Global Information System Design. In Wai K. Law (Ed.), Information Resources Management: Global Challenges (Chapitre XI, pp. 236-261). Hershey PA: Idea Group Publishing, 2007.

Grundstein, M. (2011) Establishing an Ad Hoc Infrastructure for Innovative Technologies Deployment: The Case of Knowledge-Based Systems. In E.N. Murthy (Ed.) , The IUP Journal of Infrastructure, Vol. IX No. 2, Andhra Pradesh: India: The Icfai University Press.

Grundstein, M. (2008) Assessing the Enterprise's Knowledge Management Maturity Level. Int.J. Knowledge and Learning, Vol.4, No. 5, pp. 415-426.

Grundstein M., Rosenthal-Sabroux C. (2003) Three Types of Data For Extended Company's Employees: A Knowledge Management Viewpoint. In M. Khosrow-Pour (Ed.), Information Technology and Organizations: Trends, Issues, Challenges and Solutions, 2003 IRMA Proceedings (pp. 979-983). Hershey, PA: Idea Group Publishing.

Grundstein, M., & Rosenthal-Sabroux, C. (2004). GAMETH®, A Decision Support Approach to Identify and Locate Potential Crucial Knowledge. In D. Remenyi (Ed.), Proceedings 5th European Conference on Knowledge Management (pp. 391 - 402). Reading, UK: Academic Conferences Limited.

Guldentops, E. (2004). Governing Information Technology through COBIT®. In W. V. Grembergen (Ed.), Strategies for Information Technology Governance (chap. XI, pp. 269-309). Hershey, PA: Idea Group Inc.

Haeckel, S., H. (2000) Managing Knowledge in Adaptive Enterprises. In C. Despres and D. Chauvel (Eds), Knowledge Horizons (chap. 14, pp. 287-305). Woburn, MA: Butterworth-Heinemann.

Kautz, K., Kjaergaard, A. (2008) Knowledge Sharing in Software Development. In P. A. Nielsen and K., Kautz (Eds), Software Processes & Knowledge. Beyond Conventional Software Process Improvement (Chapter 4, pp.43-68). Aalborg, Denmark: Software Innovation Publisher, Aalborg University.

Laudon K C, Laudon J P. (2006) Management Information Systems; Managing the Digital Firm. Upper Saddle River, New Jersey: Pearson Education, Inc, (Ninth edition).

Muller, H. & Maasdorp, C. (2011) The data, information, and knowledge hierarchy and its ability to convince. Fith International Conference on Research Challenges in Information Science, Gosier, Guadeloupe, France, RCIS proceeding

Nelson, R.R., & Winter, S.,G. (1982) An Evolutionary Theory of Economic Change. Cambridge, MA: Harvard University Press.

Nonaka, I., Konno, N. (1998) The Concept of "Ba": Building a Foundation for Knowledge Creation. California Management Review, spring 1998, Vol. 40 No. 3, 40-54.

Nonaka, I., Takeuchi, H. (1995) The Knowledge Creating Company. New York: Oxford University Press

Nonaka, I., Toyama, R., Konno, N. (2000) SECI, Ba and Leadership: a Unified Model of Dynamic Knowledge Creation.Long Range Planning 33, 5-34. Elsevier Science Ltd

O'Dell, C. and Hubert, C. (2011) The New Edge in Knowledge, How Knowledge Management is Changing the Way we Do Business. APQC, Hoboken, New Jersey: John Wiley & Sons.

OECD (2004). OECD *Principles of Corporate Governance*. Retrieved September, 2005, from http://www.oecd.org/document/49/0,2340,en_2649_34813_31530865_1_1_1_1,00. htmlPolanyi, M. (1966) The Tacit Dimension. London: Routledge & Kegan Paul.

Polanyi, M. (1966). The Tacit Dimension. London: Routledge & Kegan Paul.

Porter, M. E. (1985) Competitive Advantage: Creating and Substaining Superior Performance. New York: The Free Press.

Rowley, J. (2007) The Wisdom hierarchy: representations of the DIKW hierarchy. Journal of Information Science, 33 (2), pp. 163-180. Retrieved from http://jis.sagepub.com/cgi/content/abstract/33/2/163

Schreiber, A.Th., Akkermans, J.M., Anjewierden, A.A., de Hoog, R., Shadbolt, N.R., Van de Velde, W., & Wielinga, B.J. (2000). Knowledge Engineering and Management. The CommonKADS Methodology. Cambridge, Massachusetts: The MIT Press.

Sena J.A., Shani A.B. (1999) Intellectual Capital and Knowledge Creation: Towards an Alternative Framework. In J. Liebowitz (Ed.), Knowledge Management Handbook (chapter 6, pp. 6.1-6.29). Boca Raton, Florida: CRC Press LLC.

Snowden, D. (2000) The Social Ecology of Knowledge Management. In C. Despres & D. Chauvel (Eds) Knowledge Horizons (chap. 12, pp. 237-365). Woburn, MA: Butterworth-Heinemann.

Takeuchi H., Nonaka, I. (2000) Theory of Organizational Knowledge Creation. In D. Morey, M. Maybury, B. Thuraisingham (Eds), Knowledge management, Classic and Contemporary Works (Chapter 6, pp. 139-182). Cambridge, MA: The MIT Press.

Tsuchiya S. (1993) Improving Knowledge Creation Ability through Organizational Learning. ISMICK'93 Proceedings, International Symposium on the Management of Industrial and Corporate Knowledge, UTC, Compiègne.

Wiig, K., 2004. People-Focused Knowledge Management: How Effective Decision Making Leads to Corporate Success. Burlington, MA: Elsevier Butterworth-Heinemann.

2

Analytical Models for Tertiary Education by Propaedeutic Cycles Applying Knowledge Engineering and Knowledge Management

Alfonso Perez Gama

Fundacion de Educacion Superior San Jose FESSANJOSE – Bogota Colombia*

1. Introduction

A Knowledge based system model to face the new methodological strategy on Higher Education in Colombia by propaedeutic cycles. A great challenge is presented to Superior Education Institutions: to establish the link between traditional cycles: professional-technical, technology and university ones with the secondary, basic and media levels. Our solution is presented linking each phase with a propedaeutic component discussed in a model. The model is dialogically integrated by cognitive an informational components.

Leontief III Millenium: we present the problem resituation from the Inter-industry Economy Model, to the new Knowledge and Information Economy, by recontextualizing the W. LEONTIEF Model from the Industrial Society to the Knowledge Society, and by innovating it with the Process and Knowledge Engineering, Artificial and Computational Intelligence, Fuzzy Logic and General Systems Theory in order to face the most critical problems in Superior Education in Colombia. A structural system to determine and analyze the cohesion and coherence of the propedaeutic cycles between competences and the curriculum knowledge. This construct enables curricular knowledge management inside the media and higher education. Several types of matrices are developed; firstly regarding columns: the longitudinal one in time (semesters); secondly the cross one grouped by curriculum subjects, (additionally each cell of them can be expressed by fuzzy values); thirdly regarding the structure: the input/output for optimization purposes.

Also an individualized model of student productivity to be integrated to counteract the stereotypes which considers the technical and technological cycles as relegated careers in higher education. This model is an intelligent knowledge based one which was validated with a software prototype just implemented in the FESSAJOSE. This construct has as its mission the guarantee of quality assurance of student's propaedeutic cycles.

These initiatives are focused on Research, Development, Innovation and Experimentation with application of knowledge and ICT architectures. They are synthesized with a model designed and implemented to confront the four main problems frequently found in third world countries:

---

* FESSANJOSE is a Technology Institution of Superior Education redefined by Propaedeutic cycles as a social project with student coming from lower economic strata at Bogota: www.fessanjose.edu.co.

- Student desertion in tertiary education which represent USD$300 million looses yearly in Colombia, by 2009
- The propaedeutic cycle's methodology for Higher Education in this country
- The academic governability for universities and the sustainability
- The low productivity in students and teachers with serious consequences in the competitiveness national wide.

Our response rests on 3 dimensional worlds with the mathematical and computational model: the Real world, the Virtual world and the Student and Lecturers world

- Firstly with a set of analytical-mathematical tools that enables the curricular knowledge management: FESSJ-PROP Model, which is a structural system to analyze and structure and cohesion and coherence between the propaedeutic cycles, supported in knowledge engineering, knowledge management, Artificial intelligence, Process Engineering and Fuzzy Systems.
- Secondly with a intelligent coaching systems called iCOACH to improve Student and lecturers productivity. It contains an individualized Student Model to address the dropout, and improve productivity in the process of articulation from the Secondary Education to the Professional one with additional propaedeutic complements.
- Thirdly with several Leontief Model extensibilities by Linear Programming, LP and Input-Output I/O, which analyses the dropout complexity and the other problems mentioned above. The LP Objective Function has 3 student levels
- They are integrated with a multidimensional flexibility system, which enables management of the complex and heterogeneous environment.

Several parts of the model we present in this chapter have been submitted in several international conferences showing the progress in our research. Also it was included by the Colombia Education Ministry as one of the BEST PRACTICES in Superior Education in Colombia†.

In Section 1 we introduced the higher education sector analysis presenting several problems currently affects this sector. In following section we present the FESSJ-PROP Model for curricular analysis through the Coherence Matrix. The third section we present to initiative leading to develop the education software architecture facing student desertion. Next section the integration Linear Programming an Leontief model for the study of education sector problems like student desertion costs, academic governability, sustainability and the intellectual capital and the knowledge activities. Finally we present the methodology issues we developed to undertake these projects.

2. Preliminary

2.1 Research development rationale

The higher education system model by propaedeutic cycles that has been named FESSJ-PROP is a complex curricular architecture for implementation and analysis in all Higher Education Institutions in Colombia. A great challenge is presented to Superior Education Institutions: to establish the link between traditional cycles: technical, technology and professional ones with the secondary, basic and media levels. This Architecture is integrated to the Plan of Studies coherent of the three Propaedeutic Cycles; Professional Technical, Technology, and Professional. The model is supported on several dialogical components;

† National Bank of Significant Higher Education Experiences: www.colombiaaprende.edu.co

structural components or matrix model for curriculum coherence verification and knowledge management, the management system of flexibility, and the student's productivity formation. The tests and validation of the model were initially supported on the rational on the use of the mathematical and computational instruments and, then, on the approach of the system measurement, the same rationale of the study theoretical frames, contrasting then, with the real application of the curriculum coherence matrix during the inspection on quality conditions of the Academic Peers for testing in Bogotá (March and April 2009) in all verified programs; additional a computer simulation model was designed and implemented for complementary validation. The consistence and the prediction power of the model was demonstrated along with the development of other information construct called iCOACH as a learning prototype , which is working to an experiential learning ; iCOACH is an intelligent system based on knowledge used as a student's individual productivity tool.

2.2 Student desertion and repetition issues

Student dropout is a phenomenon cultural and Socioeconomics. Several studies in Colombia have found statistics and figures in excess of 50% that significantly affect the efforts made for increasing the coverage and quality education. Similarly close to one of every two students entering the Systems do not completes successfully or do in times higher than expected. Some determinants of the phenomenon have been analyzed using Statistical and Sociological techniques. Important factors that are the following:

- Economic impact of more than 1/4 part of them.
- Academic with almost half of the students highlighting that most of the student population of the institution FESSANJOSE belongs to lower income strata: 1, 2 and 3 of Bogota. Also it is shown that the 1/3 of the deserters is first semester students who entered in 2007 at the Institution.
- Academic and psychological aspects represent a marked influence on desertion inside institutions, within the academic aspects we can emphasize: low academic performance, non-compliance with the expectations of students and poor vocational preparation from high school, which is demotivation and causes deviation of the students admitted their personal goals and objectives, forcing the student voluntarily to remain in academic conditionality and / or outside the program or even outside the university.
- The psychological aspects as the lack of screenning personnel and professional, the failure to adapt to the college environment and learning environment are significant and are presented in the students since the start of their studies and can be identified from their income the institution; It is directly linked to academics, because they affect the student's academic performance.

It requires among other: Virtual systems for verification of concepts and deepening of meaningful learning, monitoring progress of individual students and motivation Programs, counseling, vocational guidance reinforced through academic tutoring, life project. In the Section 5 we deal with methodology aspects related to these problems. However it is important to point out that the problem is worsened by increasing educational coverage and the global crisis: every time we have more students, larger classes, less contact with them, increasing the teaching load and higher costs that many students spend more time on making any income economy.

2.3 Tertiary education quality and competitiviness

The educational work has been understood as reconstructive science of the knowledge. That we want to motivate student from which the challenge for educators in the emerging Knowledge Society motivation lies in the appropriation of knowledge that encourages students to generate new knowledge as a way to confront the serious problems of backwardness and dependency of our own countries.
To understand the new role of lecturers is necessary to clarify what is the model that will go to rationalize and legitimize the claim to educational practices and especially the role of the teacher in the order produced by modernity and post-modernity in the informatics context; what is clear is that the traditional pedagogy of the lecturer seems to have fulfilled their life cycle. Education with information and knowledge technology based (EDUMATICS, COGNIMATICS) is an option of the lecturer from the standpoint of pedagogy which is due to its characteristic modifier for the training of future generations of engineers.
The theoretical framework of our project is also supported on models and systems including: Model of software engineering and architecture education, computational model of pedagogy, instructional model, System focused on Innovation and Learning System of thinking processes. This theoretical and conceptual framework is documented in a number of publications.

2.4 Governability & sustainability problems

It is a concept that goes beyond what administration is and is associated with the conditions of the institutional capacity to deliver the educational goods and services, the ease for decision making, the management of the new intellectual capital and related, to meet the needs of government, business and society in general. It is affected by the overload of demands and social requirements and also by factors such as the trust, the participation and the consensus building.
University Governance and Sustainability are closely associated. And as it is not a matter exclusively of educators, the sustainability is not a purely financial issue, but financially it is a strategic component of the strength of educational institutions. A model of corporate governance is the composition consistent, coherent, concerted, committed, participatory and assumed by the set of systems and actors, about ways of thinking, decision taking, acting and learning that shows an institution in the different dimensions of its strategy. In Section 4 we present the I/O model to quantitatively analyze these problems involved.

2.5 A hybrid system to face superior education sector problems: A computational and mathematical model

FESSJ-PROP and iCOACH integrate the model. Firstly, the structural system to determine and analyze cohesion and coherence of the propaedeutic cycles, between competences and the curriculum knowledge. This construct enables curricular knowledge management inside the media and higher education. Several types of matrices are developed; firstly regarding columns: the longitudinal one in time (semesters); secondly the cross one grouped by curriculum subjects, (additionally each cell of them can be expressed by fuzzy values); thirdly regarding the structure: the input/output for optimization purposes. Secondly an individualized model of student productivity to be integrated to counteract the stereotypes which considers the technical and technological cycles as relegated careers in higher education. This hybrid model is an intelligent knowledge based one which was validated with a software prototype just implemented. This construct has as its mission, the guarantee of quality assurance of student's propaedeutic cycles.

2.6 The propaedeutic cycles in higher education for the knowledge society

Formation through the propaedeutic cycles is a strategy responding to new dynamics of knowledge society, and the pace of the labor market. It is characterized by developing and organizing in a flexible, sequential and complementary curriculum programs of the university. There are three levels of postsecondary education: first, the professional technician, and second, technology, and third, the university, where each level is preceded by a previous preparatory cycle. Perez Gama Alfonso et al.(2010)

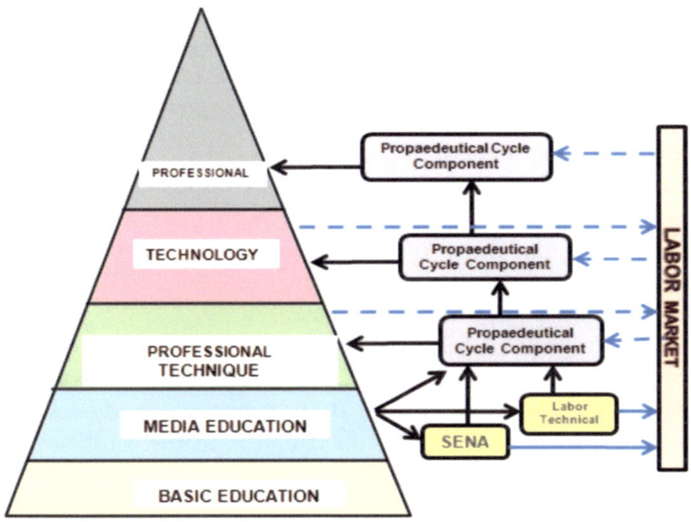

Fig. 1. Education System Pyramid with articulation: flexible, sequential and complementary

This means that a person must be able, in parallel with secondary education, starting in the tenth grade their technical training. Upon completion of this first level with the skills acquired will have access to employment. But also, if he or she has successfully completed high school and professional technical program, will be able to carry out technology studies: the second formation cycle.

According to the regulations mentioned in cycles propaedeutic formation becomes a model for access to higher and more complex levels of professional competitiveness, and a response to the need to adapt the educational supply of the continually changing and expanding labor market coverage as a manifestation of the right to knowledge. Education turns its gaze towards the productive sector to inquire about their new occupational demand and to offer from a scientific and technological training, responses and solutions to their problems and needs, using new skills.

A propaedeutic cycle is an intermediate step in a sequence that allows the student to progress in their education based on their interests and capabilities; each level carries a preparatory component which enables continuity of skills throughout their training. Propaedeutic cycles form a system that follows the principles of lifelong education is related to labor market trends (local and global) in terms of adaptability to new and diverse occupational and professional opportunities, and also mobility-mediated joint and possibilities of completing a cycle that provides the foundation for subsequent cycles continue, taking account among others:

- It is characterized by the relationship between theory and practice in matters directly related to the world of production, technological innovation and job performance ratings, allowing alternating study and work;
- It is projected as a strategy for expanding coverage, and provides answers to a country where professional training by levels and shorter periods, helping to reduce high dropout rates.
- Academic rigidity promoted by the Colombia Act 30, and forcing the student to a route inflexible, monolithic and binding, represents high economic and social costs to him or her for the institution and the educational system in general. It becomes more obvious in cases of desertion, death or change of career. In general the curriculum so far is a reflection of the academic organization of subject areas in schools and often distantly related to each other, in order to study phenomena or concepts from single disciplinary approach.

2.7 Required flexibility per propaedeutic cycles

A flexible curriculum could be defined as an alternative response to the linear and inflexible studies in higher education, which breaks with the system of serial and mandatory courses. To deal with rigidities it is required a comprehensive system of flexibility as the antithesis to the same. The high repetition and dropout rates are economic and cultural phenomena that have affected the higher education system in general.

As mentioned before the actual Education System is rigid, hard and forces the student to reentry as contrasting with propaedeutic cycles in which the flexibility is mandatory. The curriculum is defined as the set of criteria, study programs, methodology and processes contributing to the integral formation and to the national identify construction, including aids the scholar human resources to put into practice the policy to carry out the PEI (Institutional Educational Project acronym). The flexibility refers to the curricular, academic, pedagogical and administrative ones, that is, the use of the university autonomy to manage knowledge as well as the study plan for whom do not accomplish with the requirements to come up to higher cycles, and besides to relocate learning contexts supported by ICT. We describe them bellow

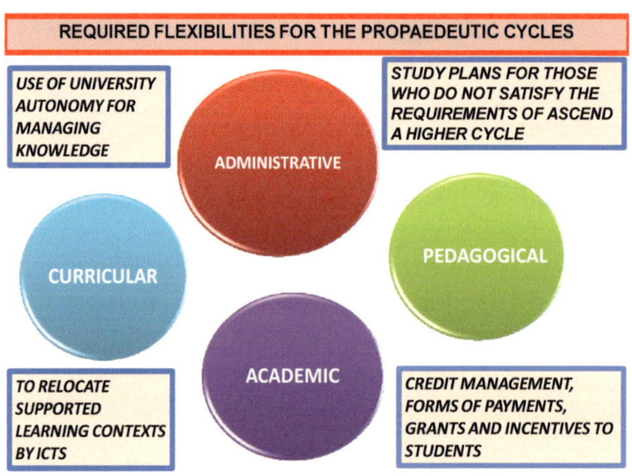

Fig. 2. Flexibility Required

Curricular flexibility is the structure defined as the content organization, methodologies, and selected vocational training to develop study plans of school programs in which the contents are selected according to their importance, pertinence, appropriateness, technological, scientific, social and economic impact on account of the competences wanted to be cultivated and developed in the technician-professional, technologist, and engineer. The structure has been provided with a solid common nucleus in each cycle and elective subjects which will consult the stage of this art. The broad experience of in the first cycle consolidates the possibilities of this flexibility.

Academic flexibility is an open and dynamical organized system which intends to transform the rigid structures which are uncoupled as it corresponds, wherein prevails the integrated work in the application and search of knowledge, defining the professional area. An open system promotes self management and self regulation. The strategic alignment of an institution is an imperative: PEI (Institution Educative Project).

Pedagogical flexibility that applies the educational strategy as a coherent unified, and integrated framework of school decisions promoted by the educational model, underlies the mentioned self-regulation and self-control by a student in his learning enabled by the ICTs, which allows him to enter to diverse learning spaces and environments tending to new educational communicative and interaction forms and also knowledge access In the same way the controls on the student about how to reach knowledge are implemented via electronic, information, and cognitive micro-worlds cultivating the competences which were already explicated as well as the involved strategies in the educational model that:

- Considers the integration of Academic Credit units of each engineering aspect.
- Creates educational mastery linking education, research, and social projection as pointed by, and
- Entails to new virtual spaces and contexts of personal autonomy in the students' learning, besides admitting that they perform an integrated project of each propaedeutic cycle.

Administratively, the flexibility supposes a range of possibilities to the educational offer within the culture of educational service to the research, the academic units which compose a outstanding institution as from the policies which assigns it for relevant, important, and appropriate making-decisions according to the FESSANJOSE Development Plan 2008-2015. This flexibility entails to the necessary reengineering of the administrative processes for its ISO certification.

To change, if required, the policies and flexible strategies, that is, it is necessary to state the actions in different university forms for the adjustment to the organizational change that implies to manage the Technician- Professional cycle to a broader level the Technology and the Engineering level. The earlier requires thinking over the sense, purpose of the Management Model, the curricular and scholar systems, which are coherent, appropriate, and suitable to the as a Higher Education Institution. It is required: flexible policies and strategies for change, i.e. the actions must be posed in different instances, in this case the University, to adapt to organizational change that involves the passage of Cycle Professional Technician to a much wider: the cycle of technology and the University cycle. This call requires reflection on the meaning and purpose of models of management and academic systems and curriculum, seeking to be consistent, relevant and proper for the Institution of Higher Education.

The formation by propaedeutical cycles in all the areas of competence of the systems engineering, will facilitate the relevance of professionals of the knowledge that will work in the global society and on behalf of a growing country where the intellectual capital should be distinguished for its formation in architectures and engineering of software, the capacity of investigation, development of intelligent systems, under the paradigms of government of the ICT and of the management information systems, taking care of the environment and in defense of the values and life.

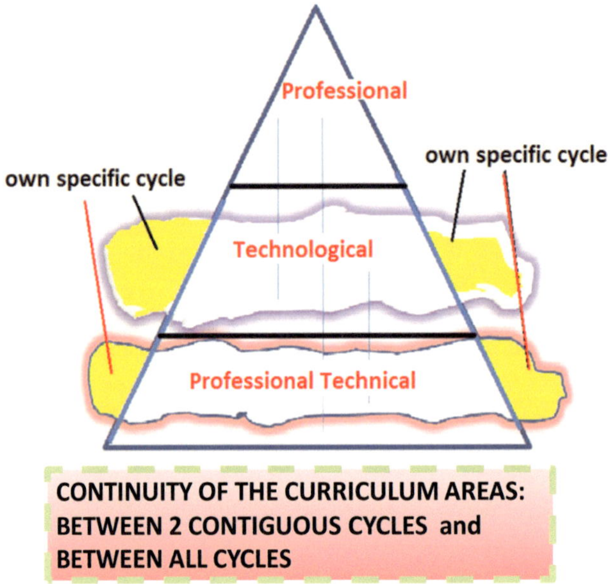

Fig. 3. Continuity cycle: flexible, sequential and complementary

This Figure 3, emphasizes that propaedeutic cycle education is more robust than the traditional model: an *all terrain professional*.

2.8 Section I syntehsis

We have presented a scope of the superior education sector mentioning some critical problems we have faced in our research which is presented in the following section.

3. Curricular and coherence matrix

One of the most important work we have developed and have been submitted to different international scenarios of high technical and scientific, is discussed in this section

3.1 Leontief input output model innovation

Leontief III Millenium: we present the problem resituation from the Interindustry Economy Model, to the new Knowledge and Information Economy, by recontextualizing the W. LEONTIEF Model from the Industrial Society to the Knowledge Society, and by innovating it with the Process and Knowledge Engineering, Artificial and Computational Intelligence, Fuzzy Logic and General Systems Theory in order to face the most critical problems in Superior Education in Colombia mentioned in the previous Section I. A structural system to determine and analyze the cohesion and coherence of the propedaeutic cycles between competences and the curriculum knowledge. This construct enables curricular knowledge management inside the media and higher education. One example of several types of matrices is presented bellow.

3.1.1 Objetives of FESSJ-PROP model

The Leontief innovation started by changing the monetary unit by the academic credit as usual in education. The concept of industry at macro-economic level we changed at university micro-economic level and changing by education process: knowledge (of the study plan) and competences as it is illustrated in Figure 4 bellow. It is searches:

- To reduce the high complexity of the propaedeutic cycle harmonization which are facing the Colombian Universities undertaking these projects
- To offer major clarity to the educational community
- To contribute to the democratization of the involved knowledge within this methodological strategic.
- To articulate efforts within the policy of the Government of Colombia that seeks to increase the educational supply to a major access of the marginalized social population and of those of lower income in order to fulfill the right to information and to the democratization of knowledge executed by the National Constitution.
- To improve the prospective scope as a tool for constructing future in institutions.

3.1.2 Specific objectives

- To enable the curriculum analysis in time power, by periods, and in the knowledge power by areas and assignments. This analysis includes all propaedeutic cycles in higher education.
- To quantify the university production in knowledge development for the student by propaedeutic cycle.
- To apply the new tendencies of engineering which are approached by models: model driven engineering, showing the good applicability of the model by propaedeutic cycles
- To enable the comprehension and management of the methodological strategic by propaedeutic cycles.
- To face accurately, the complexity involved in multiple dimensions leading to the optimization of a study plan in terms of balancing efforts, definitions, scope and projections of subjects and competences/expertise.
- To demonstrate that the student productivity and higher education quality run hand in hand in each propaedeutic cycle.

3.2 Relationships description and architecture

It refers the logical-cognitive relationships among the architecture parts of an educational system. It is as much an analysis instrument as a linear mathematical structure that communicates (all communication action is a pedagogical one), enabling the justification of a study plan and giving it as an organized and complex totality interlinking the interior and external coherency and consistency. Among the objectives are:

- To manage knowledge enabling a morphologic analysis to a study plan on higher education.
- To eliminate inconsistencies and make viable the curriculum optimization of the PEI.

- To improve the prospective scope of the PEI.
- To quantify the production of the universities in the development of knowledge in students (competence culture) by propaedeutic cycles to redesign the expertise areas in each cycle as well as the know-how.
- To give priority to and classify the competence areas.
- To contribute to develop a curriculum without errors and ambiguities.
- To construct the input/out matrix or as a foundation of the optimization and structural analyses.

The curriculum coherence is the strategic alignment between a study plans with its objectives, justification, given the purpose and view, duly articulated with the PEI:

- Non-complex comprehension of the methodology strategy by propaedeutic cycles.
- Optimization of university resources.
- The curricular coherence model is expressed as a matrix which is as much an instrument analysis as a lineal mathematical structure, enabling the justification of a study plan, which gives a sense as an organized and complex totality.

The external coherence refers to the alignment of the educational style of FESSANJOSE to the professional profiles and intellectual capital which demand the industry, the government, science, and technology in a global society. The model based on educational processes according to the curriculum study plan, where an assignment (including classes, workshops, tutorials, laboratories etc.) is associated to an expertise unit. The matrix method is of morphological type to obtain a system contradictions free without the unwanted entropy. The coherence also implies harmony, and articulation between teaching and apprenticeship, alignment, and synchronization.

The system diagram of the matrix model is expressed as follows: rows representing expertise of each level against columns in which the corresponding curricula subjects is arranged (See the whole Matrix Figure 4).

The link is expressed as a propaedeutic component formed by the intelligent iCOACH in order to increase the student productivity in each cycle and also some assignments of connecting in order to meet the prerequisites of each cycle. It is suggested to have both a terminal cycle with their corresponding competences with and the cycle for following higher levels. We did the design for Systems Engineering and it was presented to obtain the Qualified Register of the program.

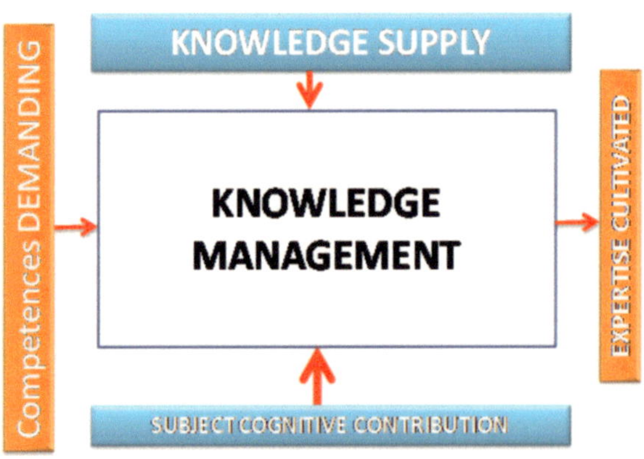

Fig. 4. Matrix model system schema

The *COHERENCE* additionally implies: It has the characteristic of holistic and integral view i.e. the entire complexity of the curricular system transcends knowledge in all its conceptual administrative, methodological, educational, normative dimensions. The academy management is coherent with the PEI when the difference between the achieved in face to the wanted is null, curricular coherence. The PEI is the expression of the proper philosophical comprehension of the educational task and it acts as definition of identity, exercising the university autonomy, recognized by the Constitution and Law.

3.3 Matrix and sub-matrix applications in curriculum analysis

In this subsection we discuss the Curricular Coherence Matrix which is an arrangement between Competences of the study plan and the knowledge involved in the courses and subjects involved.

3.3.1 Background: Mathematical Leontief model for systems analysis

The linear model focused on curricular coherence matrix is both an instrument of analysis as a linear mathematical structure, enabling the justification of curriculum and making sense as an organized and complex. The re-contextualization and re-situation Leontief Model Analysis enables Governance and Sustainability with the extension of the matrix A of technical coefficients, larger.

3.3.2 Generation of a hyperspace matrix for analysis

The Curricular coherence matrix in a linear arrangement between the knowledge represented in a curriculum and competencies that are expected to develop in students during their student life.

$$\mathrm{Y} = \mathrm{AX} \qquad t= T_0 \tag{1}$$

$$\mathrm{X} = \mathrm{A}^{-1}\mathrm{Y} \qquad t= T_1 \tag{2}$$

Where Y is the vector of endogenous (1) and vice versa in (2)
Vector X is the independent or exogenous (1) educational processes related to each subject and vice versa (2).
The matrix A is M x N where:
The M rows represent levels of competence / expertise of the curricular organization of an academic program.
The N columns represent the unit and functional areas (educational processes involving classes, workshops, tutorials, laboratories, workshops, etc.) knowledge of the Plan.
This cell may contain other qualitative values (fuzzy logic or ambiguity). Each value represents the incidence between the subject and competition.

$$[a_{i,j}] = \{\text{yes, not}\} \text{ (black, white), or}$$

$$[a_{i,j}] = \{\text{null, medium, high}\} \text{ (white, red, and blue for a dashboard chart).}$$

See Figure 5.
Next figure we show the whole curricular coherence matrix for Systems Engineering career at the FESSANJOSE with the strategy of the propaedeutical cycles, namely: The Professional Technician in Software Development as the 1st level, the Technology in Software

Architectures as the 2nd cycle and the University cycle in Systems Engineering. All of them rightly articulated by the corresponding Propaedeutical component.

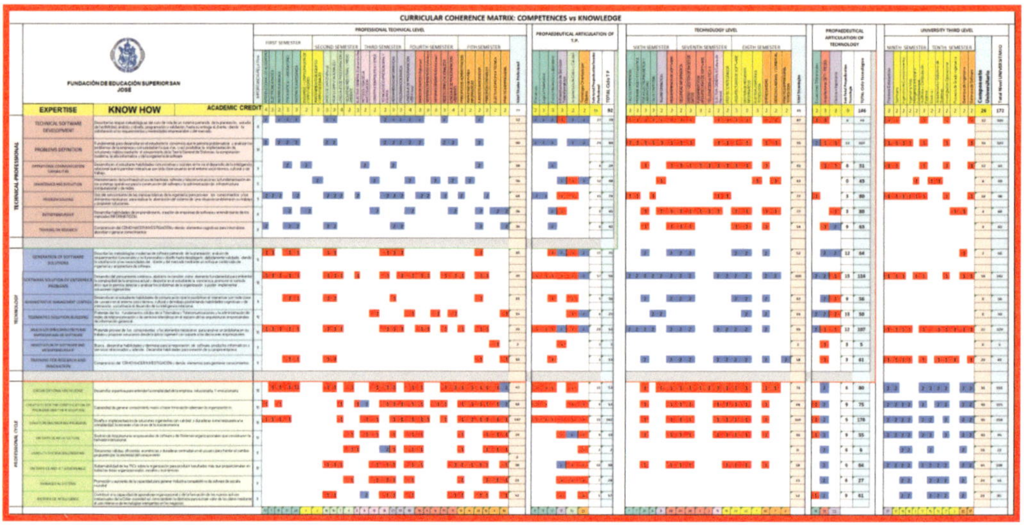

Fig. 5. Systems Engineering Curriculum Coherence Matrix

3.4 Quantitation of curricular knowledge curriculum

Another chart shows the metric for how well the systmens courses and subjects within each propaedeutic cycle features are integrated to provide specific expertise of the skills deployed in the cross-coherence curricular matrix consistency: from the quantified matrix can be obtain for each cycle the productions in systems, namely in terms of compuational expertise cultivated by the engineering educational process. This type of Matrix can be of several classes, i.e. grouped by areas of knowledge (basics, professional specific, professional, etc), organized in time (by academic semesters of the study plan) and also presented by each propaedeutic cycle with/without articulation. Bellow is presented a way (metaphor) to express a space for the several matrices with fuzzy values just specified earlier.

Fig. 6. Curricular Coherence Matrix hyperspace

In this work we present the re-contextualized linear model as did Buckley (1992) of the open model of input-output technical coefficients which are expressed by fuzzy numbers. There are some basic assumptions: A process or unit of knowledge can feed one or more competencies. On the other hand provides the linearity between the skills and knowledge. Furthermore the constancy of the technical coefficients of the matrix A is supposed in the medium term. Unlike the Leontief model in which the unit of measure is of monetary type in our unit of measurement is the Academic Credit is properly normalized.

Our proposed model makes better use of academic information available. The Leontief model associates industries with academic units in cluster. The corresponding architecture is represented in the Sub-Section 4.5.1, the Table 1. The analysis is based on academic governance system flexibilities of FESSANJOSE as discussed in the sub-section 1.7 and quantified by the equation (1), to observe endogenous or exogenous changes in either the skills or the same knowledge, equation (2)

$$\Delta Y = \Delta A X \tag{3}$$

3.4.1 Curricular quantification from the matrix: Cognitive contribution

The cognitive contribution of the j^a subject is obtained by the following relation:

$$\sum_{i} a_{i,j} n_j = d_j \tag{4}$$

Where n_j is the corresponding subject credits d_j is the cognitive contribution of the j^a subject for each propaedeutic cycle (columns). Bellow contribution in the last row present the cognitive for the first level, Professional Technician on Software Development corresponding to the Systems engineering matrix depicted in Figure 5.

	FIRST SEMESTER					
IMPORTANCIA RELATIVA	INTRODUCCION A LOS ALGORITMOS	ELECTRONICA BASICA	MATEMATICA BASICA	FISICA BASICA Y LABORATORIO	MATEMATICA INTEGRADA	ENSAMBLE Y CONFIGURACION DE COMPUTADORES
	4	3	2	3	3	2
	13	7	11	17	24	4

	SECOND SEMESTER					
IMPORTANCIA RELATIVA	MANTENIMIENTO DE EQUIPOS COMPUTACIONALES	BASES DE DATOS I(Mysql)	REDES COMPUTACIONALES I	LENGUAJES DE PROGRAMACION VIS	SEGURIDAD INDUSTRIAL Y MEDIO AMBIENTE	ELECTIVA GENERAL (Cultura y/o Dep
	3	3	3	4	2	1
	2	16	16	7	4	5

	THIRD SEMESTER				
IMPORTANCIA RELATIVA	METODOLOGIA DE LA INVESTIGACION	CONSTITUCION POLITICA Y ETICA	TECNICAS DE EXPRESION ORAL Y ESCRITA	HERRAMIENTAS INFORMATICAS	PROGRAMACION BASICA
	2	2	2	3	3
	8	10	16	21	13

	FOURTH SEMESTER					
IMPORTANCIA RELATIVA	LENGUAJE DE PROGRAMACION WEB I (Java)	BASES DE DATOS II (Sqlserver)	SISTEMAS OPERATIVOS I (Windows)	SISTEMAS OPERATIVOS II (Linux)	REDES COMPUTACIONALES II	LENGUAJE DE PROGRAMACION WEB II(PHP)
	4	3	3	3	3	4
	18	14	5	4	11	11

	FITH SEMESTER						
IMPORTANCIA RELATIVA	PRINCIPIOS DE ADMINISTRACION	MARKETING DE PYMES INFORMATICAS	EJERCICIO INTEGRADOR	PRINCIPIOS CONTABLES	ELECTIVA ESPECIFICA TECNICA	PRACTICA EMPRESARIAL	PROFESSIONAL TECHNICIAN LEVEL
	2	2	2	2	2	2	77
	12	6	20	12	9	16	

Fig. 7. Software Development Professional Technician Subjects Contribution

Similarly for the Technology level of Software Architecture, the cognitive contribution is presented jointly with the propaedeutical component of the 1st level, Professional Technician, as shown in Figure 7.

For the 3rd Cycle, Professional on Systems Engineering similarly is shown in Figure 9 with the propaedeutical component correspondent of the previous Technology level.

Level	Group	Subject	Value	Contribution
PROFESSIONAL TECHNICIAN	PROPAEDEUTIC ARTICULATION	Precalculo	2	11
		Logica Matematica	3	11
		Fisica Mecanica y Laboratorio	3	17
		Infraestructura de Servicios Teleinformaticos	3	17
		Arquitectura de Datos y Calidad	2	18
		Tecnologia Orientada por Objetos	2	21
		PROPAEDEUTIC OF PROFESSIONAL TECHNICIAN	15	
		TOTAL OF PROFESSIONAL TECHNICIAN CYCLE	92	
TECHNOLOGY	SIXTH SEMESTER	CALCULO DIFERENCIAL	3	7
		PROBABILIDAD Y ESTADISTICA	3	7
		FISICA ELECTROMAGNETICA Y LABORATORIO	3	20
		CALULO INTEGRAL	3	9
		TELEINFORMATICA I	2	9
		REQUERIMIENOS DE SOFTWARE	2	20
	SEVENTH SEMESTER	SEGURIDAD INFORMATICA	2	20
		DISEÑO Y GESTION DE BASES DE DATOS	3	20
		FUNDAMENTOS DE ARQUITECURAS DE SOFTWARE	3	3
		TELEINFORMATICA II	2	3
		ELECTIVA GENERAL II (Cultura y/o Deporte)	2	15
		PROYECTO INTEGRADOR	2	15
	EIGTH SEMESTER	ARQUITECTURAS DE SOFTWARE	3	20
		GESTION DE RECURSOS INFORMATICOS	3	22
		ELECTIVA ESPECIFICA TECNOLOGIA	3	1
		EMPRESARISMO	2	22
		DERECHO LABORAL Y COMERCIAL	2	7
		PRACTICA EMPRESARIAL TECNOLOGIA	2	2
		Techology Level	45	
	PROPAEDEUTIC ARTICULATION	Ecuaciones Diferenciales	3	14
		Arquitecturas SI/TI - PESIG	3	31
		Ciencia e Ingeniería	3	11
		Sub-total of Technology Propedeutic	9	
		TOTAL OF TECHNOLGY CYCLE	146	

Fig. 8. SoftwareArchitecture Technology Subjects Contribution: TP articulated

Level	Group	Subject	Value	Contribution
Technology PROPAEDEUTICAL ARTICULATION		Ecuaciones Diferenciales	3	14
		Arquitecturas SI/TI - PESIG	3	31
		Ciencia e Ingeniería	3	11
		Sub-Total Propedeutico Tecnologia	9	
		TOTAL Ciclo Tecnológico	146	
UNIVERSITY THIRD CYCLE	NINTH SEMESTER	Procesos Estocasticos	3	17
		Seminario	2	17
		Ingenieía de Connocimientos	2	19
		Ingeniería Web	2	18
		Inteligencia Artificial y Computacional	2	3
		Auditoria y Computación Forence	3	17
	TENTH SEMESTER	Electiva I	2	15
		Arquitectura y Gobierno de Sistemas	2	13
		Investigación Operacional	2	21
		Proyecto de Grado Ingeniería	2	3
		Gerencia de Ingeniería	2	20
		Gerencia de Software	2	17
		Componente Universitario	26	
		Total Nivel UNIVERSITARIO	172	

Fig. 9. 3rd cycle Professional on Systems Engineering Subjects Contribution technology articulated

These values (added by subjects) for each subject to compare the cognitive contribution per semester and also allows:
To identify orphan subjects which have not been established or are too weak implications.
To identify any overestimation
The above would require a review by the Curriculum Expert Group.

3.5 Other metrics obtained from the matrix: Production

The cultivated expertise is given by the production i as follows:

$$\sum_{j} a_{i,j} n_j = b_i \tag{5}$$

Where b_i is the i^a production, expressed as cultivated expertise for each competence unit (rows). For each cycle see bellow the corresponding values obtained.

The Figure 10 bellow shows the values of Expertise cultivated in the student for each cycle, by the competences of the 1st cycle of Technician-Professional.
The Figure 11 expresses the same by the competences of the Technology cycle. The Figure 13 the same for the University cycle.

TECHNICAL-PROFESSIONAL COMPETENCES	TECHNICAL-PROFESSIONAL Level	Propedeutical of TP	TOTAL TP Cycle	Technology Level	Propedeutical of Technology	TOTAL Ciclo Tecnológico	University Component	Total of University Component
ACADEMIC CREDITS	77	15	92	45	9	##	26	172
TECHNICAL SOFTWARE DEVELOPMENT	52	27	79	87	6	93	12	105
PROBLEMS DEFINITION	60	24	84	95	12	107	16	123
OPERATIONAL COMMUNICATION	18	6	24	45	6	51	12	63
MAINTENACE AND EVOLUTION	36	12	48	43	0	43	6	49
PROBLEM SOLVING	64	15	79	77	3	80	18	98
ENTREPRENEURSHIP	36	9	45	77	3	80	4	84
TRAINING ON RESEARCH	36	6	42	54	9	63	0	63

Fig. 10. Expertise cultivated in the student for each cycle, by the competences of the 1st cycle

3.5.1 Systems engineering skills by cycles, expertise and know-how

In the diagram of the Figure 5 it can be seen how they develop skills throughout student academic life. It is noted that development of basic skills is permanent or continuous Salthouse (1991) backed by numerous studies in which skill or expertise has a behavior of someone who continually learns, throughout his life: a Normal Distribution. This may be associated with the occupational skills of the three cycles preliminary in Systems Engineering.

The Systems Professional expertise requires the definition of specialized skills or outstanding tasks i. e. SUPERIOR PERFORMANCE or represented in a domain that are described as KNOW HOW. The cognitive processes associated with learning mechanisms are of more complex.

EXPERTISE approach involves the development of skills as a dynamic continuum and is associated with learning processes throughout life that are affected by change and social practices, industry behavior, science and technology. As a result, the structure of competence is variable in itself, change usually associated with a requirement of living space in which it is used. In concluding synthesis:

FUNDACIÓN DE EDUCACIÓN SUPERIOR SAN JOSÉ

		IMPORTANCIA RELATIVA	PROFESSIONAL TECHNICIAN LEVEL	PROPAEDEUTICAL OF PROFESSIONAL TECHNICIAN	TOTAL OF PROFESSIONAL TECHNICIAN CYCLE	Techology Level	Sub-total of Technology Propedeutical	TOTAL OF TECHNOLGY CYCLE	Third Level	Total UNIVERSITY CYCLE
	EXPERTISE		77	15	92	45	9	146	22	168
TECHNOLOGY	GENERATION OF SOFTWARE SOLUTIONS	8	16	15	31	52	12	64	0	64
	SOFTWARE SOLUTION OF ENTERPRICE PROBLEMS	10	39	17	56	109	15	124	14	138
	ADMINISTRATIVE MANAGEMENT CONTROL	9	11	5	16	47	9	56	0	56
	TELEMATICS SOLUTION BUILDING	10	15	6	21	35	15	50	0	50
	ANALYSIS & DESIGN OF SOFTWARE ENTERPRICE ARCHITECTURES	10	33	20	53	95	12	107	18	125
	NEGOTIATION OF SOFTWARE AND ENTERPRENEURSHIP	8	2	3	5	2	3	5	0	5
	TRAINING FOR RESEARCH AND INNOVATION	8	10	3	13	58	3	61	18	79

Fig. 11. Competences cultivated in the student for each cycle, by the competences of the 2nd cycle

PROFESSIONAL CYCLE COMPETENCES	TECHNICAL-PROFESSIONAL Level	Propedeutical of TP	TOTAL TP Cycle	Technology Level	Propedeutical of Technology	TOTAL Ciclo Tecnológico	University Component	Total of University Component
ACADEMIC CREDITS	77	15	92	45	9	146	26	172
ORGANIZATIONAL KNOWLEDGE	43	10	53	74	6	80	36	116
CREATIVITY FOR THE IDENTIFICATION OF PROBLEMS AND THEIR SOLUTION	44	9	53	66	9	75	40	115
SOLUTION ENGINEERING PROBLEMS	147	15	162	169	9	178	40	218
ENTERPRISE ARCHITECTURE	24	9	33	46	9	55	40	95
USABILITY SYSTEMS ENGINEERING	0	2	2	0	6	6	16	22
ENTERPRICE AND ICT GOVERNANCE	38	10	48	58	6	64	44	108
MANAGERIAL SYSTEMS	21	7	28	21	6	27	24	51
ENTERPRICE INTELLIGENCE	52	5	57	52	9	61	24	85

Fig. 12. Expertise cultivated in the student for each cycle, by the competences of the 3rd cycle

- The ability of generalization, abstraction, conception, analysis (decomposition), integration, design and composition (synthesis).
- Ability to apply high-level knowledge in exercise and professional practices.
- Ability to organize and plan the implementation time and wise use of resources entrusted him/her to social responsibility and civic commitment.
- Ability to communicate orally and in writing and to develop methods and techniques geared to the user, i.e. usability or user oriented, because the systems demand, apart from the machine communication, working with people is required.

- Ability to define problems: the creativity needed to identify problems and also the creativity needed to solve complex technical problems in order to face the turbulence of the global Millennium III: this is the imperative of our research.

The imperative demands of ICT and its domain expertise in different environments as enshrined in the Colombia National Plan of ICT, but the recent ICT Law passed by the local Government.

3.5.2 Inputs skills / expertise in systems engineering

For each of the cycles shows the quantification of the lecturing services, extension, research, mentoring, support, laboratories, experiment, practice and other which is acquired by every competence in the cognitive process of each student.

In these plots, the row number refers to the number of credits each course feeding the competence offered in this cycle: Professional Technician on Software Development.

Each value allows us to visualize the relative importance of a subject. If zero or very low one, tells us that is isolated or de-contextualized and deserves a critical review.

The model of the first cycle of the FESSANJOSE provides five semesters, has been successful in the national context, obtaining several years in the top ECAES (professional examinations of official national wide). The technology cycle visualize the design possibilities and advantages of this cycle. Applying the formulas (1) and (2) we obtain the corresponding values for competences cultivated for each propaedeutic cycle and the valued added of the courses. See Figures 10, 11 and 12.

3.6 Input / otput matrix

In this matrix each cell is expressed as follows:

$$\widetilde{\boldsymbol{a}}_{i.j} = \frac{d_j}{b_i} \tag{6}$$

Technical Coeficient: input fraction by production unit: Where each $\boldsymbol{a}_{i,j}$ coefficient is the ratio of cognitive inputs by unit of cultivated competence production.

With this matrix (called of the technical coefficients), it can be performed the OPTIMIZATION analysis, adding quality objectives, capacity restrictions as costs, academic objectives, scholars population, lecturers, university resources and many others related. Also this matrix can be extended to complete the Leontief I/O matrix with the remaining sectors as shown in the Table 1 of the sub-section 4.1.4.

The Systems Engineering curriculum design based in propedeutical cycles and also in EXPERTISE have cognitive and structural features distinctive, the first of which is an academic structure articulated, sequential, complementary and flexible, whose cornerstone is the development of professional and occupational engineering skills. This assumption allows defining: Firstly the **Feedback sub-matrix** corresponding to the cycle objective, which can be quantified knowledge articulation, processes subsequent courses to strengthen the competencies implied. See Figure 13 bellow.

The **Feedforward sub-matrix,** to quantify the knowledge articulation of the processes of the current cycle and feeding skills training for senior cycle (upper).

There are many possibilities for analysis, to meet the socio-economics demands in terms of such competences.

Are they balanced?

Is there bias?

What if a new competence is included due to the Systems, Software and related industries demand?
What is the effect of restructuring a subject or a course or a subset of them in missionary terms?
Can you explain the lower/higher values?
Is it necessary to revise a subject content regarding the competence impact?
Is it necessary to redefine the scope and the limitation of a competence?
Is it a group of subjects of the study plan, biased or underestimated?
Is it necessary to recalculate the number of credits assigned to each subject initially proposed, after changes?

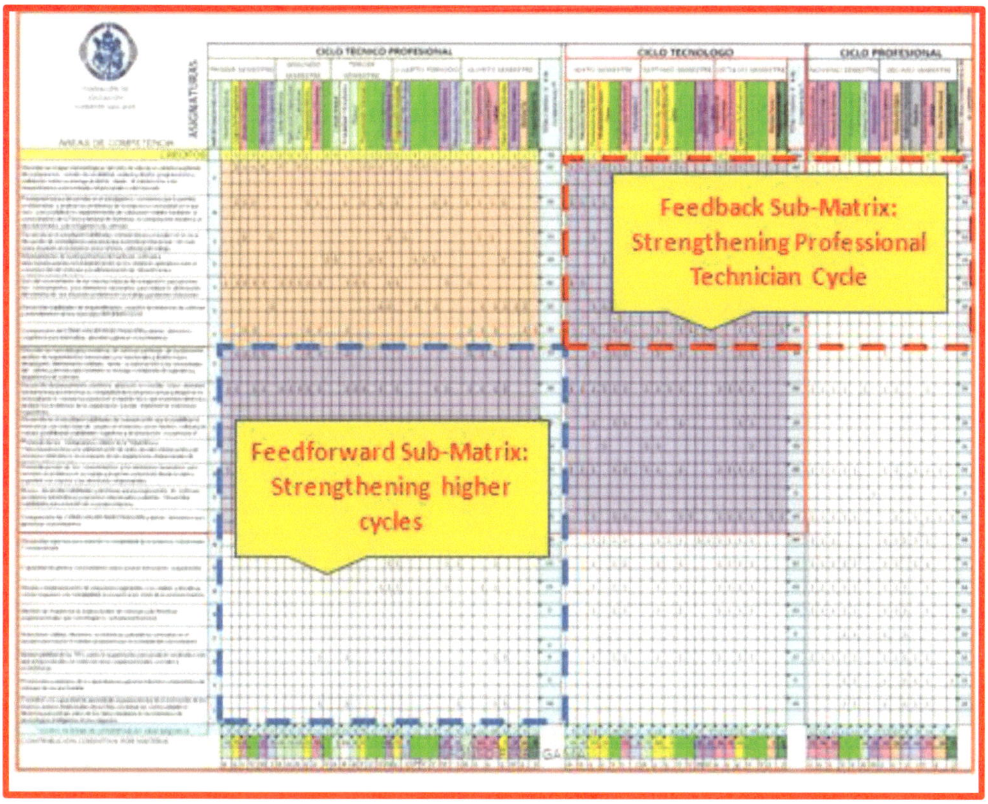

Fig. 13. Feedback and Feedforward Matrices

4. Education software architecture: Facing student desertion in Colombia higher education

The Student Desertion National wide problem is very critical by its cultural, economics and family impact. Several IES (Superior Education Institutions) have performed studies leading to point out this problem as a recurrent and prevalent one. The design and implementation of iCOACH which is an intelligent tool knowledge based is presented here as a instrument of high computing to follow up each student in the academic first terms of the engineering faculty at the FESSANJOSE, The software architecture have 3 main parts: Edumatic builder (as a tool for Professor), the Student Model, and the third one is the Knowledge Base for concept verification and security. Several previous works have preceded this project so our methodology and related are very experienced. A prototype was built to demonstrate the iCOACH validity and applicability and also as an instrument of academic productivity. This effort is part of a greater system called FESSJ-PROP which is an analytical model for Propedeutical Cycles Higher Education Strategy in Colombia. Perez Gama Alfonso et al.(2010).

4.1 Diagnosis and justification

Student dropout is a phenomenon cultural and Socioeconomics. Several studies in Colombia have found statistics and figures in excess of 50% that significantly affect the efforts made for increasing the coverage and quality education. Similarly close to one of every two students entering the Systems do not completes successfully or do in times higher than expected. Some determinants of the phenomenon have been analyzed using Statistical and Sociological techniques. Important factors that are the following:

- Economic impact of more than 1/4 part of them.
- Academic with almost half of the students highlighting that most of the student population of the institution FES belongs to strata 1, 2 and 3 of Bogota. Also it is shown that the 1/3 of the deserters is first semester students who entered in 2007 at the Institution.
- Academic and psychological aspects represent a marked influence on desertion inside institutions, within the academic aspects we can emphasize: low academic performance, non-compliance with the expectations of students and poor vocational preparation from high school, which is demotivation and causes deviation of the students admitted their personal goals and objectives, forcing the student voluntarily to remain in academic conditionality and / or outside the program or even outside the university.
- The psychological aspects as the lack of screening personnel and professional, the failure to adapt to the college environment and learning environment are significant and are presented in the students since the start of their studies and can be identified from their income the institution; It is directly linked to academics, because they affect the student's academic performance.

It requires among other: Virtual systems for verification of concepts and deepening of meaningful learning, monitoring progress of individual students and motivation programs, counseling, vocational guidance reinforced through academic tutoring, life project.

The problem is worsened by increasing educational coverage and the global crisis: every time we have more students, larger classes, less contact with them, increasing the teaching load and higher costs that many students spend more time on making any income Economy.

4.2 Anti-drop methodology

A program within the university by intelligent monitoring provide assistance ranging from the process of adaptation to university life to the completion of their studies, aiming to drop the risk is minimal, plus academics critical cases in the work is more specialized towards the student remained in college, monitoring for first semester students will be using our system: Intelligent Coach, we used to call iCOACH, to identify and strengthen weaknesses of students in those subjects where students show academic deficiencies, in this institution that the problems start from the basic courses. Individual causes are: Age, gender and civil status, home calamities, college change, life project and disease. Academic causes: High school deficiencies, Poor performance, No flexibilities (pedagogical and administrative). External causes: social Stratum, personal and parent's employment, household costs, city residence change. We conducted inside FESSJ, a survey and choose the following factors: Economic Difficulties, Life Project, Semester deferral, Academic performance, Career Change, City residence Change, family problems, disease, or working.

4.3 General objective problem for solving with iCOACH

Reduce the student's academic mortality index in first terms of each university program and also improve quality performance. The first goal is to develop an intelligent and computational system for monitoring student progress and also for be able for academic reinforcement to the student, way virtual tutoring and intensive courses in his college life. This intelligent tool is able student training and concepts verification with wide knowledge base of questions and testing previous to the taking examinations with the final purpose of entrenchment theirs mental and cognitive abilities for significant learning in his/her career. The second one is to evaluate academic and socioeconomic factors related to the student drop out using statistical metrics which are generated by the own intelligent tool, for quantification purposes. So with this to design emergent strategies more suited. The last one is to formulate complementary actions or programs leading to reduce. The most final goal of the Project is to improve academic student's quality.

4.4 Computational project description

Recent advances in ICT and hypermedia are offering opportunities with no precedent to comply with new student need or unsolved ones for all level. Actually the education sector in Colombia which is one of the most of the 4 axis in the ICT National Planning supported by web wide networks face several problems, as:

- Poor pedagogical services in which are attempted manage the student free time within the concept of ACADEMIC CREDIT. Regarding 18 articles of the 2566 Decree and the 1188 Education ACT an academic credit is "the estimated time of student academic activities as a function of academic expertise's which an academic program is expected to develop ". Its more essential , definition the term allows: to incorporate within the concept, not only the presence hours with/or without the lecture direct accompanying but also is being taking account the independent student work for preparation and practice. The later implies the managerial of the student free time way personnel autonomy in his learning under student control.
- The inadequacy of evaluative models for cognitive progress student as a countermeasure the desertion in Higher education.
- Failing protuberant in the feedback quality information and monitoring of the student progress.
- Few educational answers with based ICT technology to the increasing educational requirements, for all level.
- Few support to the Scientific and Technology sector, given the few opportunities for financial resources of continued researches which are involved in the relevant knowledge generation.
- Also huge considerations regarding Intelligent Computer Education and all digital technology are marginal options in process and darkness that the same education has to be re-contextualized (adequacy of a curriculum), redefined and resituated.

4.4.1 Antidesertion computational problem formulation

It was precede an intensive work in several research projects, something like EIDOS at the National University of Colombia and FESSANJOSE, in such areas as artificial Intelligence and cognimatics computing education and related, undergraduate and M Sc thesis as well as subjects as virtual and distance education. In several universities as The National of Colombia, District City University, and many others and also studying several international edumatics experiences in presence and virtual learning methodologies giving that an unusual interest in continuing these concerns exploring the electronics book production leading to a virtual library exploring related areas. It is required:
Firstly, of having good student models with feedback and forward monitoring leading to the user cognitive evaluation and individualized following up to each subject. Secondly to have lecturer tools (edumatics builders) in order to design tests intelligent wise, sure, and consistent, based in random and structured selection form knowledge bases. Thirdly, the new lecturer with the characteristics and new player roll of having the possibility for concreting the pedagogy as knowledge rebuilder for recontextualisation of all education materials for one user who will be alone doing his/her learning under his control and autonomy. To build a system for verification of student's concepts , it was undertaken the project within the edumatics and software engineering to establish the planning, analysis, identification of pedagogical training requirements and software to specify the design of a edumatics intelligent system, systemic and cognitive with assessment with the students to virtual mode. The system specified included the following: An edumatics builder, wich is the test and examination generator for students, which is a lecturer tool and cognitive evaluator of students for verification of concepts, controlled by an intelligent tutoring agent and a virtual knowledge base of questions and tests with a fully re-organized structure. It also identified the need for a comprehensive systems or basic models: Model of the System, functional model, data model and the student model, which included general information on knowledge bases to be used. On the other hand the market is demanding educational products, packages and systems to which the person learns what they want, anytime and anywhere, it also costs have to be attractive, as is being displayed in the electronic marketplace.

4.4.2 Theoretical context

The educational work has been understood as reconstructive science knowledge. That we want to motivate student from which the challenge for educators in the emerging Knowledge Society motivation lies in the appropriation of knowledge that encourages students to generate new knowledge as a way to confront the serious problems of backwardness and dependency of our own countries. To understand the new role of lecturers is necessary to clarify what is the model that will go to rationalize and legitimize the claim to educational practices and especially the role of the teacher in the order produced by modernity and postmodernity in the informatics context; what is clear is that the traditional pedagogy of the lecturer seems to have fulfilled their life cycle. Education with information and knowledge technology based (EDUMATICs, COGNIMATICS) is an option of the lecturer from the standpoint of pedagogy which is due to its characteristic modifier for the training of future generations of engineers. The theoretical framework of our project is also supported on models and systems including: Model of software engineering and architecture education, computational model of pedagogy, instructional model, System focused on Innovation and Learning System of thinking processes. This theoretical and conceptual framework is documented in a number of publications. The following is a brief description. The theoretical framework of our project is also supported on models and systems including: Model of software educational engineering, computational model of pedagogy, instructional model, System Focused on Innovation and Learning System of thinking processes. This theoretical and conceptual framework is documented in a number of publications.

4.4.3 Developing model of educational architecture

The model was developed, presented and discussed in many venues nationally and internationally. Taxonomically includes several models for students seeking a formal specification for use in modern software engineering practice and also in the architecture of educational software. The above mentioned is complemented by other models: the cognitive, conceptual or syllabus, and the Instructional Tutorial Planning. This software engineering education has been used to enable the stimulation of intelligence and the extension of the knowledge based on personal autonomy in learning supported by technology. The theme is very suggestive.
The rationale of the educational activities is focused on motivating higher mental abilities: this is a major challenge in research. ¿Why is the reason to have a computer model approach? Without going into a taxonomic discussion, we emphasize the approach of computational models to establish a differentiation primarily with mathematical models, which can closed express structures and behaviors, among others in addition to explicitly recognize the complexity of "model" as regards cognition. ¿How support the student personal autonomy in his/her learning? It considers learning as an essential part of the educational problem is even more true in regard to a new build of Educational Computing education - with the support of a knowledge-enabling staff carrying autonomous student learning in the field of robotics have shown significant progress in artificial learning.
One aspect of innovation in education is to understand that intelligence is a skill that can be educated: Learned (act of the individual) and education (opportunity for the teacher). We point out numerous scientific researches and the teaching practice and show intelligence as a result of thought. The correctly thinking is not a function of the innate intelligence nor education. Phenomenologically associated power of some subjects in the curriculum, to develop thinking (eg mathematics of all the ways to teach thinking is basically another way of addressing the educational problems throughout the area: kindergarten to higher education. If we start from the assumption of the modifiability of cognition, how much can be done more intelligently to people with or without the support of information technology in a meaningful and lasting? Regarding the educability of the intelligence is so intelligent behavior must be considered as a goal of educational activities, pari passu with other aspects such as emotional and psychomotor; also that the construction of data objects, so tecnofactum or mentefactum/ cerebrofactum (mental/brain artifacts) to extend their cognitive potential of the student. In summary, we propose an electronic and computer environment for learning, as dual use: machine or artificial learning (machine learning) to evolve the knowledge base and development of higher mental abilities by the student.

4.4.4 Software architecture and engineering methodology

Our methodology involves the use of multiple paradigms, ranging from engineering information, to modern software engineering/architecture with artificial intelligence and obviously web engineering. It includes evolutionary prototyping method.

4.4.5 Outcome

The products to obtain:

- Construction of an intelligent agent for monitoring student progress towards the verification of concept learned.
- Construction of an intelligent for the generation of tests and examinations and the presentation of individualized assessments, via the Internet. Includes a knowledge base manager of problems, a response handler for results and a statistical system. The intelligent evaluation using international standards. Repository or knowledge bases tested educational content on specific subjects, including a system of meta-cognition, e. g. conceptual or cognitive maps (digital maps).
- Generation of statistics for monitoring student progress in real time
- A management system safe and secure on the Internet for communication with the student to allow access 24 hours a day, 7 days a week, both the systems evaluated to establish electronic communication.
- With a website to see e. g. frequently asked questions and answers, news and more.
- Simulation Model for iCOACH and the full implementation.

4.5 Computer constructor of tests & exmination for knowledge verification

The software platform is designed as a tool for educational to be used by managers, tutors and learners, to facilitate the construction of tests for testing concepts and the generation of an intellectually demanding action space, allowing interaction of the various actor involved in the process. The constructor in with the general functional model of the project, through the following agents: Professor: individual or object that provides the system of disciplinary knowledge, ponders the complexity of knowledge, design tests with which to assess learning, provides the answers and lead the process of cognitive apprenticeship. Student: Is the person on which rests the teaching institution and who is responsible for the quantity and quality of knowledge acquired. The system serve as coach potentiates cognitive skills, accredited skills and explore their results critically. Manager: individual or object that performs the monitoring and feedback of student progress, uses statistical information on academic performance, monitors the implementation of curriculum plans and ensures compliance with the institutional offer.

4.5.1 Operationality

The system must control access to the authorized players through verification of the validity of a login and a password and only allows access to certain information service in accordance with the privileges of that user as a certain level it. In the same vein should give special attention to the process designed to protect from an unauthorized access over the network and safeguarding the integrity and confidentially of information.

4.5.2 Security

The system must control access to the players authorized through verification of the validity of a login and password and only allows access to certain information services in accordance with the privileges of that user as a certain level it. In the same vein should give special attention to the processes designed to protect from unauthorized access over the network and safeguarding the integrity and confidentiality of information.

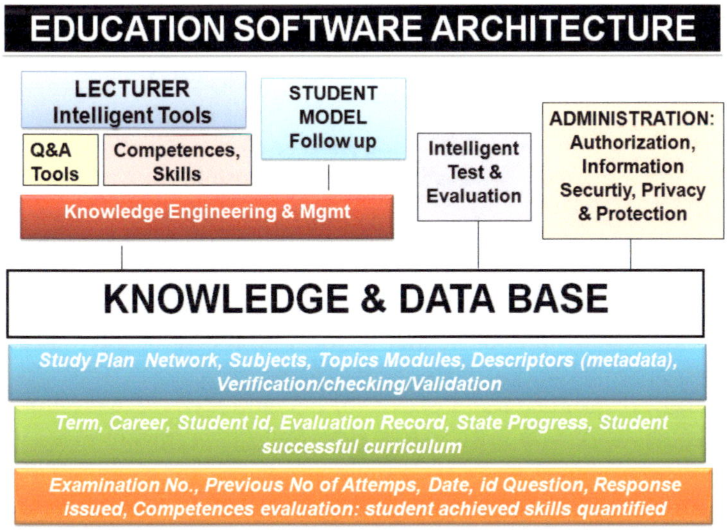

Fig. 14. iCOACH Architecture

4.5.3 Architecture

Functional components interact independently of the builder, so in most cases the transfer of parameters is absent or reduced to a minimum. Each function corresponds to a visual interface for easy operation, flexibility and self significantly.

4.5.4 Conclusions and future work

iCOACH allows to design strategies by monitoring individual student progress, to identify deserters and perform follow up of them with the additional support of the FESSANJOSE Welfare Department. The system implementation of flexibilisation: the administrative (i.e. payment by quotes, the pedagogical (i.e. transfers. ICT strategies) and related. iCOACH is also a management tool to the student surplus time for their learning controlled by him/herself. Other major conclusion of this effort is to have obtained the design specifications and the requirements for the professional software development for iCOACH: the maturity model.

The future work: is to extend iCOACH to all academic programs inside FESSANJOSE and to offer coaching services to all academic community in Colombia using SOA (Services Oriented Architecture). The iCOACH Professor-side is to extend the Knowledge base developing parameterized and intelligent queries/questions for knowledge verification with natural language processing in order to have a knowledge base fully re-organizing and intelligent one.

5. Integration of input-output model and linear programming: Linear programming with leontief input output model

5.1 Background: Mathematical Leontief model for systems analysis

The linear model focused on curricular coherence matrix is both an instrument of analysis as a linear mathematical structure, enabling the justification of curriculum and making sense as an organized and complex. The re-contextualization and re-situation Leontief Model

Analysis enables Governance and Sustainability with the extension of the matrix A of technical coefficients, extended. The first part of this modelwas presented in Section and we illustrated with several matrices. Perez Gama Alfonso et al. (2011).

5.1.1 Mathematical Leontief model for economic analysis

The model defines the main characteristics of sectored performance of a country's economic system interacting industries.

$\mathbf{X}_j$: It is considered in the model increases or decreases linearly to changes in the gross value of production.

Although the model usually assumed that cutting the input current flows in each sector are proportional to the level of output in that sector, in the case of inter-industry flows this assumption is not appropriate.

Economic activities are grouped into n sectors or industries, where X (vector of production), Y (vector of final demand. X, Y ∈ Rn values represent the vectors of gross production and final demand, respectively. The matrix technical coefficients is denoted by A = $[a_{i,j}]$, are transactions between industries i and j per unit industrial output j.

With the above matrix can perform optimization analysis of institutional, with the addition of objective functions, capacity constraints, unit costs for credit, the target student population, limited resources and many other related university items as mentioned above.

Production is assumed that X is distributed to some intermediate consumption and the rest to the final consumer. Whereas the vector of exogenous final demand, the solution vector is obtained by clearing the gross value of production:

$$X = (I - A)^{-1}Y, \tag{7}$$

Where **I** is the identity matrix

Leontief matrix, which describes the total needs of direct and indirect inputs, such that its diagonal elements must be greater than or equal to 1, which means that to produce one additional unit to meet the net final demand of social production, is necessary to increase the production of each academic unit at least one unit. Among other questions asked in this analysis, would include:

¿ How much should increase the production of the P_i process to meet the increase of one unit of competence demanded further of that process and how much to increase the production of other processes?

$$\Delta X = (I - A)^{-1}\Delta Y \tag{8}$$

This equation allows us to quantify and predict the output **X** and other institutional variables: cost, value added etc. of university academics in different periods.

This model generates a lot of information in such a way that enables us to analyze the financial sustainability and enriches the PEI (Institutional Educational Project) planning process and specially favors the strategy formation process.

5.1.2 Other considerations on the Leontief matrix

The main underlying causes of the alteration of the coefficients over time are:

- Technological change in academic production e.g. by introducing ICT and Virtualization.

- The knowledge change in the state of the art
- The increase in the benefits arising from economies of scale e.g. content generation for personal independent learning.
- Substantial increases in student cognitive productivity through the use of intelligent virtual tutors as our prototype iCOACH.
- The changes in relative prices (as Leontief coefficients arising from a monetary valuation.)
- Changes in patterns of exchange (purchase of books and knowledge contents generated by lecturer-authors, etc.).

Final Demand at the institutional level is represented by all the activities of Social Projection, University Extension Services and Consulting, Research Projects. The changes in the final demand composition may result from the:

- Requirements of the Higher Education legislation
- Need to meet national and international standards of the Curriculum.
- Changes in the scientific production and new knowledge.
- Demand for Consulting by the company and the government in this country.
- Generation of new knowledge as a result of research and innovation processes

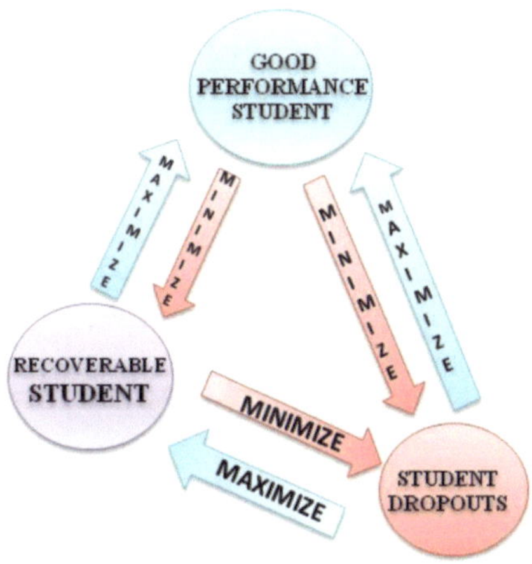

Fig. 15. Student Levels Flows for Optimization

5.1.3 Linear programming with Leontief input output Model

One application of process engineering is the application of the Leontief model combined with linear programming, as many authors assert, and we have shown by applying these models in the Health Sector in Colombia (National Department of Planning) Ortegón Edgar et al.(1973). The following Table 1 shows the model architecture. Construction of these matrices requires a significant budget to develop the study field for several months within FESSANJOSE.

The Linear Programming with Leontief Input Output Model involves 3 Student levels: Good Performance, Recoverable and the Dropout. See Figure 15.

5.1.4 Mathematical knowledge architecture

The architecture presented in Table No. 1 comprises the matrix of Leontief Input-Output in a system either at the micro level (i.e. a program of study) or a higher level of an institution or country. This architecture has 3 components: the inter-sector subset, the restriction and threshold values and the multiple objective functions.

The model was integrated with linear programming to analyze together the services of Education in the Tertiary Sector of the economy (trade and services), with the primary sector and the manufacturer sector.

The optimization criteria are shown schematically in Figure No. 15, which shows the levels of students in higher education mentioned above.

FUNDACIÓN DE EDUCACIÓN SUPERIOR SAN JOSÉ	*Multisectorial Model: Linear Programming & Leontief Input-Output for Higher Education*			Higher Education											Rest of Final Demand				
		Primary	Manufacture Industry	Basic Sciences	Professional Basics	Socio-Humanistic	Communications	Found. Scientific Technical	Social Projectn & Research	Rest of Commerce & Services	Households	Government	Exports	Imports	Physical Capital	Intelectual Capital	Others		RHS
Industry & Knowledge ECONOMY	Primary Sector																	=	0
	Manufacture Industry																	=	0
Higher Education	Basic Sciences															k1		=	0
	Professional Basics															k2		=	0
	Socio-Humanistic						(I - A)				-H	-G	-1X	-1M	-df1	k3		=	0
	Communications															k4		=	0
	Found. Scientific Technical															k5		=	0
	Social Projection & Research															k6		=	0
	Rest of Commerce, Services & TICs															k7		=	0
	Remunerations	f1	f2	f3	f4	f5	f6	f7	f8	f9	-1							=	0
	Government	t1	t2	t3	t4	t5	t6	t7	t8	t9		-1						=	0
	Exports	ex1	ex2	ex3	ex4	ex5	ex6	ex7	ex8	ex9			-1					=	0
	Imports	m1	m2	m3	m4	m5	m6	m7	m8	m9				-1				=	0
	Rest Added Value	r1	r2	r3	r4	r5	r6	r7	r8	r8							-1	=	0
	Restrictions and Thresholds																		
FIT	Seats			q1	q2	q3	q4	q5	q6									≤	b1
	Human Resource			l1	l2	l3	l4	l5	l6									≤	b2
	Capacity			v1	v2	v3	v4	v5	v6									≤	b3
	Minimun Coverage			i1	i2	i3	i4	i5	i6									≥	b4
	Multiple Objective Functions																		Z
CRITERIA	STUDENT LEVEL			q1	q2	q3	q4	q5	q6									=	Opt
	Student repetition Avoided			l1	l2	l3	l4	l5	l6									=	Max
	Desertion Avoided			v1	v2	v3	v4	v5	v6									=	Max
	Gross benefits			i1	i2	i3	i4	i5	i6									=	Max

Table 1. Linear Programming with Leontief & Input-Output Model: Knowledge Architecture

The flows within these levels of students are outlined and quantified in the multiple objective functions.

$$f(X, D_{f}) = 0 \tag{8}$$

D_fIs the final demand: Households, Inversion, Government, Δ Inventories, Rest of the world…
Political function issues:
Max

$$Z= f(\Delta Students\ Level) \tag{9}$$

$$(I - A)X \ - \ D_f = 0 \tag{10}$$

$$\text{F (resources)} \leq b_i \text{ availability} \tag{11}$$

5.1.5 Strategies analysis

- *Among the questions that can be analyzed and quantified would be:*
- *What would the cost of changing a student from one level to another?*
- *What would be the opportunity cost of losing a student from a higher to a lower level?*
- *What management strategies of type economic, academic or pedagogic, respond better in order to maximize the number of students who leave school?*
- *Which strategy is more responsive to the maximization of repetition avoided?*
- *How an institution responds to the demands facing in improving the quality and competitiveness economic and curricular without breaking?*
- *How much does it cost for an institution to improve its quality?*
- *How much does it cost for an institution to improve competitiveness?*
- *What additional financial and technological resources an institution needs to maintain good government?*
- *What is the value of intellectual capital accumulated in a university?*
- *What is the new cost of an academic credit, after optimization?*
- *How many credits are assigned to a subject?*

Many other questions can be done to this model giving possibilities for simulations running. As can be seen this mathematical tool, allow analyzing and quantifying a variety of strategies ranging from economic to academic and pedagogical, to reach optimum levels in terms of dropout, repetition and improvement in student performance and in general better IES governability.

5.2 Some conclusions and future work

This study has indicated the Leontief Model re-situation towards social sector: academic world of knowledge, and from the inter-industry economy to the new knowledge industry. At the same time the model allowed us to analyze the problems of Academic Governance and Financial Sustainability of Higher Education Institutions.

- The Model architecture shows a model suitable for the knowledge society as displayed in Table 1
- International Peers in evaluating our work have acknowledged that the literature is very scarce in this educational purpose. Also our mathematical system for analyzing the

desertion, curricular coherence consistency for the propaedeutic cycles and many other educational issues has been emphasized as a social innovation and pioneer in the international arena.

- The integrated model for the knowledge society promises to be a tool for analyzing and quantifying the Competitiveness of Higher Education in this country.
- Substantial rescue of the propaedeutic cycles, in particular: major industrial and social credibility of the TP-T education is expected.
- Major preference of young people, for education by propaedeutic cycles, due to the possibility of achieving better long-term career, prospected as a project life.
- Best potential for high quality accreditation by the TP-T institutions.
- Finally once we have our completed model it is verified, tested, validated and accepted, we make it serve the all country's academic community in Colombia.

6. Methodology issues

The problems presented was faced with multiple paradigm methods which are required to implement several complementary actions.

We have of a complex information system, called SIFES which involves the education software architecture with which we have historical information of the student cohorts, period to period. We have implemented the mentioned architecture shown in (See Figure 14) order to obtain information in real-time student and the student record the information including all incidents and risk factors. It is included:

- Student Communication System In Real-Time: is an additional module of the student web portal that allows each student to write their concerns, problems and suggestions so that the Welfare Department of the FESSANJOSE may consult such information once the student has registered, to be analyzed in order to determine the trouble spots by career or journey and also make direct intervention with students and thus further mitigating the chances of dropping out.
- Individualized Follow Up in Real-Time of the student of the FESSANJOSE, allowing the generation of new information from the SIFES database.
- SIFES As mentioned above, is a system of academic information FESSANJOSE is a system developed with high standards of engineering and advanced security controls, which have the academic record and financial participants such as teacher education project and students. Regarding students can consult their resume, medical exams, schedules, materials recorded, self-assessment results and institutional and historical grades of the semester, approvals, assistance, educational aid, and payments recorded. Front SIFES teachers have information on their resume, studies, time availability, results of teacher evaluation, contracts, schedules, attendance records, typed notes. SIFES generates reports for various agencies, report early warning dropout prevention such as low results in more than one material, appropriate controls on payments and attendances.
- BOARD OF CONTROL: This system allows monitoring the possible state of desertion based on variables such as attendance, grades and financial commitments and compliance with these indicators can be set for each student, using a mathematical model to determine the probability of dropping further with each student so they can make appropriate interventions as may be evidenced in the variables that make up the information and decrease the probability of a given student. Virtual and includes tutoring

with an emphasis for students with deficiencies and low performance, the implementation of training workshops to promote student retention, teachers, managers and administrative (use of technological support and also includes Parent Involvement).

6.1 Fieldwork survey methodology

The variables of the model are enriched with the national SPADIES (Prevention and Analysis System of the Attrition in Higher Education Institutions) that offers the National Education Ministry which allows us to compare the figures of dropout, repetition, retention, and others. One problem is reconciling the concepts in determining how to understand the dropout, how many academic periods without registering, if it is included students graduating from each program who have not received and others.

Institutionally implemented a system of engineering of organizational processes with dual-use ISO certifying institution and feed the model discussed in this chapter for quantified architecture model that includes obviously the intellectual assets.

6.2 Knowledge engineering methodology: Towards a knowledge engineering methodology: An attempt to its formalization

Our research effort represents ongoing work with several University projects and unpublished graduate works and also consulting works for institutions in Colombia. In the FESSANJOSE the model has evolved to our proposal of social innovation Leontief Model that incorporate the knowledge sector.

The Knowledge Engineering Methodology presented in this paper is an attempt for reducing the complexity involved: is part of that effort and has not obeyed to a large-scale project with good funding. They have been serene developments that we want to share with the academic community. We describe an attempt to formalize a KE methodology in 8 steps which are presented in detail, the mix of ideas coming from both Engineering and Management we tried to integrate in this construct. Also we discuss briefly our understanding between knowledge engineering and knowledge management.

6.2.1 Background of the method

For several years we have been involved in building expert systems, intelligent systems and courseware development in areas such Strategic Planning, Information Systems Architectures based on knowledge and building intelligent tools for Superior Education Sector, which has resulted in an empirical study we have gradually put on several congresses.

In particular we have faced the problem of Higher Education in Colombia for Propaedeutical Cycles, which faces many serious problems of student dropout and mainly the lack of competitiveness of the sector. The foregoing led us to rethink the matrix of input/ output in terms of curricular knowledge and competences to be cultivated in students to submit papers in several international conferences. In recent years we have redefined the architecture of the Leontief model by introducing the sector of knowledge and applied to our university, FESSANJOSE. The Knowledge Engineering Methodology presented in this paper is an attempt for reducing the complexity involved: is part of that effort and has not obeyed to a large-scale project with good funding. They have been serene developments that we want to share with the academic community. Our work has been developed with academic rigor, disciplined and continued: the documentation of the project is a key part of the methodology we use to formalize and enrich our research ideas and innovation. They are subjected to the contrasting, in international meetings, world class, and obviously by systematizing the feedback provided by international pairs of very high scientific level.

6.2.2 Proposals towards a knowledge engineering methodology

Knowledge engineering (KE) is considered as the systemization of intelligence and relies on the work of organization, representation and knowledge management as a substitute for human reasoning and reasonable basis to encapsulate solutions to hard problems and difficult tasks, also serves to identify the layers of knowledge of an information system. In itself, the KE, is the technology for building expert systems and intelligent agents. Clearly the maturity of the KE requires a disciplined work and treatment of problems, analysis and solutions, supported by knowledge.

6.2.3 Some implications of intelligent engineering solution

We found that extensive knowledge in the subject or study target, informal or explicit is one of the consequences. Also, the use of knowledge representation with a model of expertise and the application of search techniques in the appropriate information structure. It is required the support for heuristics analysis or for the same creativity. Finally the main competences required are: the ability to infer knowledge, the ability to reason or symbolic processing and the ability to apply an appropriate logic of the problem. In e-Commerce, the increase in business intelligence (BI) is impressive, supported by ES (expert systems) and intelligent systems. An ES is seeking a satisfactory solution, good enough for the job, although not optimal. The output of an ES depends on the amount of knowledge and depth of analysis is made on the knowledge of experts.

6.3 Engineering of the knowledge

This construct refers to the techniques of obtaining knowledge, representing, building and using it appropriately to assemble and explain reasoning of the knowledge based system, creating a product which tries to solve the involved problem. The following defined steps were indentified: The following describes graphically the proposed methodology of Knowledge Engineering.

The two phases is related to the problem Definition and Determination, namely:

- Cognitive Planning: defining the system (structure and components), model (behavior), detailed specification of the problem, selecting methods and techniques, user requirements and interface, identifying the data types and objects and solution quality.
- Learning: Acquisition of knowledge or machine learning process: acquisition of knowledge required by the system, in a systematic or automatic or with help from the experts. This knowledge can be specific when the problem domain and solution procedures are the same, or may be general knowledge, i.e. knowledge across an enterprise.

The subsequent 3 phases are related to the development of the intelligent system:

- Ontology, representation and organization of knowledge: how it is distributed, classified, organized, developed the map of knowledge and is represented by some formalism or structured information or objects in the KB, to enable computer use.
- Knowledge Acquisition Methods
- Problem Solving Design alternatives and selection of the solution.

The final 3 phase are related to the system construction.

- Prototype Construction.
- Verification, validation, contrasting and legitimacy: the methodology used successfully for the problem? Verify sources of knowledge. Legitimate and check that the knowledge is represented in the KB, is correct. To demonstrate that the solution and conclusions are expected. The inference is based on the design of software, which allows the computer to infer on the knowledge represented in the BC. This includes: Explanation and justification.
- Obtaining the Final System and Evolution.

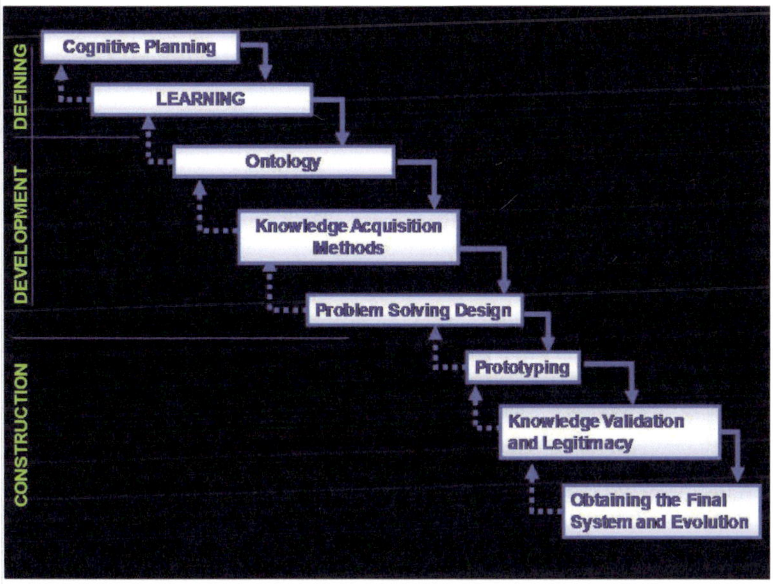

Fig. 16. Knowledge Engineering Life cycle

In the following sections we develop each of the mentioned phases.

6.3.1 KE cognitive planning

We begin by establishing the commitment of senior management and stakeholders and also the involvement of the group of domain experts. Preliminary meetings are held with this group, which reviews the key issues to consider in connection with the layers of knowledge to add. Planning is also made as to form and means to acquire such skills.

6.3.1.1 System determination

It refers to the identification of its *structure, the architecture, the model i.e. behavior and components (knowledge objects)*. Also includes the specification of the problem with its domain, computational requirements, scenarios, construction of an example of a user session, decision on the methods and techniques, user requirements and interface, identifying objects and data types and quality of the solution. It is very important to assess cost / benefit and identification and definition of dictionaries and concepts represented in the KB with the knowledge to select the really relevant.

6.3.1.2 Determination of the subsystem to incorporate knowledge

The analysis of the results of the application of the requirements engineering is included. Also, for purposes of choosing the corresponding subsystem, in order to recompose the architecture of the involved knowledge.

6.3.1.3 Determination of the specific module

Once chosen the subsystem, is analyzed functionally and, according to the priority of the modules and the requirements of users choose one of them for adding layers of knowledge.

6.3.1.4 Phase outcomes

Classes of knowledge.
The identification of the layers of the knowledge of the company (knowledge architecture).
Determination of intellectual assets.
The specification of the methodology, tools and techniques.
A portfolio of the intelligent subsystems.
The Intellectual capital resources.
Scheduling and Time table.
Quality Assurance Plan.

6.3.2 Knowledge acquisition phase: Learning

Taking the problem and its modular decomposition, followed by the conceptualization of relevant knowledge, must define its scope. When knowledge has been collected, must be analyzed, coded and documented so that these activities take place according to the chosen acquisition technique. It also should be prioritized to represent in the KB. Later must be formalized to determine the method of acquisition. The acquisition stage can be difficult to the extent that knowledge is extracted directly from human experts. Once the execution is carried out, it should be the implementation, which includes programming and coding of knowledge in the computer, designing a prototype that allows refining and contrasting the results. Finally, the knowledge engineer test at the KB by means of examples (cases) and compares the results with experts to examine the validity of knowledge.

6.3.2.1 Phase outcomes

Knowledge Recovery
Knowledge Bases
Repositories
Conceptual Map of the Knowledge or Syllabus
Knowledge Structures.

6.3.3 Knowledge representation phase: Ontology

The representation of knowledge involves the consistent use of mathematical logic and information structures. The KE theories fall into two categories: mechanisms and content. Ontologies are content theories about classes of objects, their properties and their interrelationships, which allow the specification in the domain of knowledge. The representation has several roles:

- As a substitute for human reasoning for knowledge automation
- As an ontological agreement to reason about the world
- As a component or part of intelligent reasoning

- As a means to achieve high computational efficiency
- As a means of the human expression to express things, about the world.

6.3.3.1 Phase outcomes

Knowledge Bases with fully reorganization
Internal and External Networks
Portfolio Capabilities: Assimilation, Strategic Technology and Innovation

6.3.4 Knowledge acquisition methods

Working with KE involves a trans-disciplinary team, in which the engineer is the intermediary between the KB and the Experts, refining and representing the KB. There are at least three types of methods for the acquisition of knowledge such as: manual, semi-computer based and automatic: artificial or machine learning.

SELECTING THE APPROPRIATE METHOD

- Applicability to a wide margin in the domain of problems, adequate both to the company and the system in question.
- Tutorial Capabilities, online help or learning environment, to reduce the need for a exhausting training expert and have less dependence on software manufacturer or distributor. It is a condition to motivate the user.
- Ability to work in parallel to analysis with the detection of flaws and inconsistencies in the reasoning process.
- Ability to incorporate multiple sources of knowledge.
- Analysis of the available tools

6.3.4.1 Phase outcomes

Assessed and appropriate method
Determination of appropriate computational resources
Tutorial Online Help
Determination of alternative sources of knowledge

6.3.5 Problem solving solutions design

The design of responses to problems or needs raised to be knowledge based is presented in several steps which are described as follows.

6.3.5.1 Defining of potential solutions

The first step, the knowledge domain organization related to the selected module, is to list all possible solutions, inputs, outputs, responses, alternatives and recommendations. It should identify the precise outputs to be presented to the user on the computer screen. The aim of this step is that the KB provides advice at the time required and not suddenly, a conclusion based on momentary must know every possible answer across time.

6.3.5.2 Determining the knowledge related to the relevant parts of the module

Knowledge Layers to be introduced should be raised at different levels of the organization. At this point is to be determined the operational knowledge, i.e. what is related to the application or specific system´s functionalities.

Domain knowledge module: determines the knowledge that the user needs to perform properly in the company.
Inferred knowledge: knowledge which is needed that can be inferred through the use of AI which supports the user.
Knowledge of processes and tasks of the module: identify the knowledge required for the development of system tasks, and relates to the basis of plans. These layers also serve as support for strategic planning and tactical levels, and are used in the plan generation and plan recognition.

6.3.5.3 Determining of knowledge related for problem solving

Layers of knowledge that are introduced should also support the management at the tactical and operational level, so should determine the knowledge that supports the resolution of problems.
Knowledge of **management skills**: includes the reasoning and decision-making DSS (Decision Support System), taking into account the user's management style in order to identify the subspace and data-information required by the executive for making their decisions in each application that contains the specific module. These layers of knowledge must be determined according to the administrative level support, i.e., differentiating strategic as tactical. Knowledge of **user interface**: where should the user's knowledge representation and should be considered cognitive style and managerial. In this respect it pursues a natural language interface to work with the system databases

6.3.5.4 Tasks decomposition

Tasks are evaluated regardless of the user model. At this point should answer:
¿What tasks can be decomposed?
¿Is there any difference between the user's perspective and that of the expert?
The second question is useful for determining if it is necessary to analyze and develop a comprehensive plan to draw conclusions. The tasks that are discussed are related to the tasks performed by the experts to solve their problems and do their job. These tasks should be decomposed into subtasks or sub-functions according to the natural order in which they develop.
To analyze the order of tasks: It should be a state diagram of the tasks previously listed, considering their order. With this diagram, it should do an analysis to determine if the order is correct, any extra work, or can be rearranged for performance optimizing.
Construction of the model: The model of a KB is useful to the extent as it constitutes a pattern of knowledge, easily interpretable, which determines how it will solve the problem in the KB. This model must be designed by determining the knowledge islands and regions.
Designing the architecture of the KB: Should design the hardware architecture of the KB, in which represents the different components and their relationships to have a "map" (e.g. semantic network or cognitive map) of the KB and facilitate construction. The conceptual design of the map gives the main idea or structure of meta-knowledge on the KB and the way they are going to solve problems. Should exhibit the capabilities and the interfaces with other MIS.

6.3.5.5 Identifying of production rules

To determine the rules of the tasks and subtasks is important to consider the solutions, inputs, outputs, responses, alternatives and recommendations that were identified previously, considering the following aspects:

- Need to identify questions to collect the necessary data from the IF portion to trigger rules lead to the conclusion.
- Should list all required data system called "facts" (or symptoms) the user will enter the system.
- Each conclusion should be in the THEN portion of the rule.
- A decision tree is a good help if the elements of knowledge can be arranged quickly in a tree format. If so, proceed directly to the construction of a tree from them. Some of them are so large that KB may require a decision tree for the entire domain; however, to simplify the work, you can build decision trees for subsets of the domain.
- Define rules for each output.

6.3.5.6 Identifying of meta-rules and frameworks

Once have determined the rules concerning the problem domain defined those who exercise control over the other and the process of inference.
By identifying, the frames: Select the objects on which the knowledge requires modeling.
By determining meta-knowledge: Control over knowledge, or "knowledge of knowledge" must be determined to have domain information and the inference process.

6.3.5.7 Phase outcome

Selected Method for solving the problems identified.
Problem solution domain.
Meta-cognition.
Specifications accomplished.

6.3.6 Prototipyng

The first objective is to build a small prototype, for which selects a subset of the KB and carries to the KE tool, which must be done quickly. The result is a prototype which can quickly verify the implementation and testing and verifying ideas. In this sub-step is the representation of knowledge with the tool by means of a prototype, since this technique to identify weaknesses and strengths of the model developed, by which you can refine the results to get quality. A prototype is also a good way to test the concepts before investing in a larger program. With the use of a shell can quickly assemble a small prototype to determine if you are on the right track. It allows for demonstrations, as its assessment will also be important in determining the quality of the result.

6.3.6.1 Graphical representation of knowledge layers

When rules and frameworks have led to the KB by using the tool must be plotted to assess the concatenation rules, relationships and inheritance between frames, i.e. to determine if the model is represented which really needs.
Elaboration of the rules diagram. There is a network diagram of the rules and actions for each of the layers of knowledge, which will have a broad overview of the KB and make the adjustments necessary to refine the model.
Elaboration of the diagram of the frames. There are graphically represented all the objects, taking into account the inheritance and relationships between them.

6.3.6.2 Inference proof

From the KB, the inference process is made to assess the results based on the reasoning process was implemented.

6.3.6.3 Phase outcome

Verified operational prototype and with quality assurance
Documentation of software testing and prototype
Effective and proven outcomes
Prototype of Dual-Use: as a Professional Tool and for Powered Training Tutorial

6.3.7 Knowledge validation and legitimacy

A used specific case to test the quality of the KB is acceptable, verifying that the source of knowledge is accurate.

6.3.7.1 Validation and contrasting of results with the experts

A workshop is held with experts in order to present the results obtained with the KB, for analysis and give their opinions. The main criterion should be used for the tests, is the opinion of domain experts, as they can tell if the results are satisfactory or not. Potential users can also serve as judges, with criteria regarding the usability, the interface and the clarity of the explanations.

6.3.7.2 Refinement

Based on the different opinions of experts, an analysis of BC and, as if the knowledge engineer finds it necessary, the redesign or restatement is realized.

6.3.7.3 Assessment

There is a close relationship between evaluation and refinements of the ES as the evaluation may reveal cases handled by the rules of the system and as a result, we add new rules or modify old ones, such changes can have unexpected negative effects on some parts of the system.

6.3.7.3.1 Verifying

The purpose of this evaluation is to check if the system implements its specifications and there are good logical consistency (i.e. the problem of verifying that the method is correct) for this purpose is the assessment obtained, taking into account actual performance levels. The prototype and system upgrades should be tested for performance in the laboratory and in the field. The initial evaluation is conducted in a simulated environment, the system is exposed to test problems (e.g., case histories or suggested by users.).

It also examines whether the system can be used efficiently and if it is cost-effective. The assessment should consider the quality of the messages presented, i.e., design and programming of the explanatory power of the BC to determine to what extent they meet the proposed objectives.

6.3.7.3.2 Validation

Should test the system and application performance, which makes comparison with expert, to establish that the system built to solve the problem is correct and will perform at an acceptable level of accuracy. The decrease in response time and quality of the conclusions may be a good initial approach to evaluate an ES.

For this purpose we used the modified Turing test, with which they are presented to potential users or administrators are two solutions to one problem: the first is the result of expert opinion and the other the result of IMIS (Intelligent Management Information

Systems). Without knowing the source, are asked to compare the solutions. With the results of the comparison determines how valid the results of IMIS are. To use this approach should consider potential disagreement between the criteria of the evaluators, since the problems can be so complex that occur disagreements over its interpretation and solution.
Other requirements to be considered in validating the final system are:

- Should meet a recognized and important business needs or assistance, counseling, tutoring.
- The processing speed of the system must be very high.
- The system must be able to increase the skills of the user: dual learning, man-machine.
- Error correction should be easy to perform.
- The system must be able to answer simple questions.
- The system should ask questions for additional information.
- Knowledge should be easily modified (allow add, delete and modify rules.)
- Make the user feel the control system to encourage its use.
- It must be reasonable degree of physical and mental effort of a novice user.
- Must be clear requirements in terms of data entry and should be simple to obtain.

6.3.7.4 Phase outcome

Correct source of knowledge.
Methodology used properly
The solutions checked and conclusions as expected.
Refined knowledge System.

6.3.8 Obtaining the final system and evolution

One advantage of rule-based systems is that they are modular, so can build subdivisions of large systems and then test them step by step, which is made possible with prototypes.
One approach is using the evolutionary prototyping, where a prototype is enhanced until obtaining the final system, which can be built gradually by adding pieces, parts or modular components. This is a cyclical process, which is an advantage that can improve the result and get the best approach to user requirements and needs of knowledge of IMIS.
If each subsection is evaluated and approved separately, the final system will most likely work the first time.
In this sub-step is performed integration of subsystems that is, if KB is created different or heterogeneous in terms of sources, we must take into account the need to create interfaces between them, allowing optimal operation and communication between the system and users.

6.3.8.1 Phase outcome

Integrated, Robust intelligent System
Populated Knowledge Bases
Institutional Learning System
Intellectual Assets
Institutional Memory
Tutorial Intelligent Engineering Knowledge

6.3.9 Section summary and work ahead

This proposal is an attempt in the way to formalize a methodology that allows the intelligence of information systems within the business, adding layers of knowledge. It provides methods that reduce the complexity of knowledge management which are required to enterprises of the Third Millennium. We have relied on experiential learning working primarily with our students for several years and also with external projects. We are aware that more empirical work is required complementary and many theoretical efforts.

The research has resulted in a tool that has allowed us to quantify our goals, to make viable and to face the serious problems of the Colombia Higher Education Sector for which we have innovated the Inter-industry model I/O W. Leontief incorporating the knowledge as a sub-sector of the economy, by the identification of a model architecture.

In Colombia there is an unusual demand for seminars and postgraduate courses in KM but little or no mention of the KE; it is imperative to migrate in this direction, especially when the economy demands more knowledge-based systems that require more rigorous engineering to improve competitiveness. This requires people, processes and methods and not only technology.

The world has become more complex, enterprise application development requires new engineering approaches and architectural approaches. Similarly, more specialized cognitive abilities around the working groups.

It takes audacity KE alternatives, systems architecture and design, taking into account the systemic qualities and cost-benefit to the organization.

6.3.9.1 Synthesis: Knowledge engineering vs. knowledge management

KE	KM
Tend to use technology low level	Work at high level
Application design & development	Govern of ICT/IMIS
Low Level Programming	User´s View
Workshop with experts	Logistic management
Knowledge Base Design and Implementation	Strategy alignment of the Corporate Plan
Resources Optimization	Best Practices
Requirements Engineering	User´s Requirements

6.3.9.2 Prospect work

Our models are implemented at institutional at FESSANJOSE but we want to undertake to the design and implementation national wide as a national purpose to face several higher education problems mentioned above as student desertion and the academic governability in which knowledge based systems are the key support.

In other hand we want to develop a knowledge a more complex architecture to support the knowledge engineering efforts which includes the knowledge model.

6.4 Chapter conclusions

It is very import to point out that literature related to the propaedeutic cycles in Superior Education is very scarce. Most of our works discussed in this chapter has been considered as a pioneering effort in order to face most of problems in Tertiary Education. In the first section we introduced the higher education sector analysis with theirs several problems currently affects this sector. In following section we present the FESSJ-PROP Model for curricular analysis through the Coherence Matrix. The third section we have presented our initiative iCOACH, leading to develop the education software architecture facing student desertion. Next section as a complementary of the previous Section we presented the integration linear programming an Leontief model for the study of education sector problems like student desertion costs, academic governability, sustainability and the intellectual capital and the knowledge activities. Finally we present the methodology issues we developed to undertake these projects.

As future work we have undertaken the development of intelligent authoring tools for digital 3D interactive contents leading to the promotion of a knowledge industry in this country but mainly to increase the teachers productivity regarding his/her own cognitive style, the student style and the knowledge characteristics.

7. Acknowledgment

To "Fundacion de Educacion Superior FESSANJOSE", to Lecturers and Officers, especially to SAN JOSE EIDOS INTERNATIONAL RESEARCH TEAM including Dr Carlos F. Pareja, Dr Rocio Paramo, Dr Guillermo Hoyos, Byron Alfonso Pérez G., Leyini Parra. Special mention of our Graduate Students: Hada Jessica Perez G, Raúl A. Alonso Marroquín, Javier H, García-Torres, Alcira Fernandez F, Dr. Oscar Vanegas and to our Secretary Diana Paola Cano to all of them a debt of gratitude.

8. References

Abelardo Pardo et al. (2010) Current Issues with Assessment Formats and Interoperability; IEEE EDUCON 2010 Global Conference in Engineering Education; Madrid Spain Apbril 2010. Conference Book ISBN 978-84-96737-70-9. CD ROM IEEE CATALOG CFP10 EDU-CDR ISBN 978-1-4244-6569.

Buckley J.J. (1992). Solving fuzzy equations in economics and finance Fuzzy Sets and Systems 48. North-Holland , pp. 289-296 15th International Conference on Input Output Techniques. Renmin University of China Beijing 2005.

Ortegón Edgar et al. (1973) "Aplicaciones de la Programación Lineal en la Planeación del Sector Salud" Revista de Planeación y Desarrollo Volumen V No. 3 ISSN 0034-8686 (Depto Nacional de Planeación) Septiembre 1973; Also published by the AID Sector Analysis Series: "Linear Programming Uses for Health Planning"; Bureau for LatinAmerica Agency for International Development # 17 USAID WASHINGTON January 1974 USA.

Perez Gama Alfonso et al. (2010) A Knowledge Based Analytical Model of Propaedeutic Cycles: Linking Media Education To Higher Education In Colombia; Ieee EDUCON 2010 Annual Global Engineering Education ConferencE; Madrid España Abril 2010. Conference Book ISBN 978-84-96737-70-9.

Perez Gama Alfonso et al. (2010-2) Education Software Architecture: Facing Student Desertion in Colombia Higher Education with an Intelligent Knowledge Based Coaching System; IEEE ANDESCON 2010 Bogotá Colombia. ISBN 978-1-4244-7172-0 Sept 2010.

Perez Gama Alfonso et al. (2011) Knowledge for the Society: Social Inclusion to the Superior Education High Competetivity: A Knowledge-Based Governability Model for the Higher Education in Colombia by Propaedeutic Cycles; IEEE EDUCON 2011 Annual Global Conference Engineering Education - Amman Jordan APRIL 4-6 2011. ISBN: 978-1-61284-641-5.

Salthouse Timothy A.(1991) : EXPERTISE AS THE CIRCUMVENTION OF HUMAN PROCESSING LIMITATIONS; in Toward a General Theory of Expertise Prospects and Limits. Edited by K. Anders Ericsson and Jacqui Smith - Published 1991

3

Knowledge Recycling and Transformation in Design

Buthayna Hasan Eilouti
Prince Sultan University
Saudi Arabia

1. Introduction

In most design fields, many design processing activities are directly or indirectly information-driven and knowledge-based. However, major storage, retrieval and processing tasks that are usually associated with design knowledge management are redundantly repeated for each design assignment. In addition to management problems, there is a deficiency in knowledge networking where information in different areas are not sufficiently linked. In other words, in many cases, knowledge existing in one discipline can inform and inspire problem solving methods in others if represented properly.

This chapter introduces proposals of knowledge recycling and modeling where precedent-based prototypes can be reused to generate new designs. It also introduces an approach to knowledge transformation, where knowledge extracted in one discipline can inform innovative solutions in another. Both, knowledge recycling and transformation are argued to help eliminate redundant search for knowledge and aide in making knowledge base in one field more accessible and usable in another.

2. Knowledge in design

Knowledge is essential for design derivation in all processing phases: pre-design reasoning, design development and post-design evaluation, as well as in the linkage of all of these in recursive refinement cycles. Major tasks, especially in the pre-design phase, consist of basic prototypical ingredients such as component analysis, relational matrices, topological studies, zoning diagrams and sequential flow charts. Despite the common structure underlying their applications, many design-related knowledge-based activities are redundantly repeated in various design assignments. As such, recycling and transforming knowledge within and between disciplines become increasingly necessary to eliminate redundant repetitions and to facilitate accessing and applying previous knowledge to new designs. In this chapter, examples of knowledge recycling and transformation are demonstrated and discussed.

Within the scope of this chapter, knowledge management is studied in the context of engineering design. It includes methods for recycling, transformation, networking and modeling of the data underlying design processing tasks.

Research in design knowledge management is significant for design theory, practice and education. On the theoretical level, the study introduced in this chapter aims to reveal new models that form sources of inspiration for concept derivation and to help in the transformation of abstract knowledge constructs into applied design models.

On the practical level, when clear transformation and recycling methods and models are described, the applied knowledge developed from the abstract knowledge constructs can be implemented to derive more optimum processes and perhaps more innovative designs.

On the pedagogical level, this research may contribute to mapping complex problems to potential solutions through grouping combinations of sub-models to generate various alternative solutions; or through using existing models in other fields of study as points of departure for problem-solving in design. Each of the developed transformation and mapping methods may provide guidance with which designers and students can avoid the problem of repeating previous solutions and reach satisfactory design solutions with relative ease and speed. In addition, the generated hybrid and cross-disciplinary models are expected to contribute to the education of design through explicit and externalized templates. Knowledge recycling and transforming models aim to contribute to new systematic design derivation methods and to explore new sources of inspiration and innovation in design.

As an extension of this research, the applicable models and processes can be developed into computer aids that may assist designers generate their products more efficiently. These automated aids may be built as blocks and hyper-linked documents. They can also form a basis for a knowledge base for design problem solving and derivation.

3. Knowledge recycling in design

The scope of this research is limited to architectural design. Within this scope, building design generation can be considered the core and ultimate goal of knowledge cycle management. For the purpose of this study, the source of information in this cycle will be building precedents. As such, the knowledge cycle starts from data as embedded in precedent documented representations (see Figure 1). Upon interpretations of raw data and assignment of semantic attributes to them, data mutate into information. The latter, upon organizing and classifying its contents, can be transformed into abstract knowledge prototypes. These, in turn, subject to proper representation methods can be translated into applied knowledge models. Combined with informed design methodologies, the applied knowledge models can be implemented to produce new designs that may be documented to represent new precedents that, if communicated properly, may represent a new point of departure for future designs. The intention of design knowledge recycling models is to translate their contents into applied knowledge that can be transformed into new design products. They can be arranged in the pre-design phase of designing to embody chunks of knowledge as needed in order to interpolate their information to derive new alternatives. The proposed models are introduced and discussed in the knowledge modeling section that follows.

4. Design knowledge processing

In the context of engineering design in general, and in architectural design in specific, the most significant activities associated with knowledge management are:

1. Knowledge analysis
2. Knowledge organization
3. Knowledge modeling

4. Knowledge derivation
5. Knowledge implementation
6. Knowledge communication
7. Knowledge documentation , and
8. Knowledge evaluation

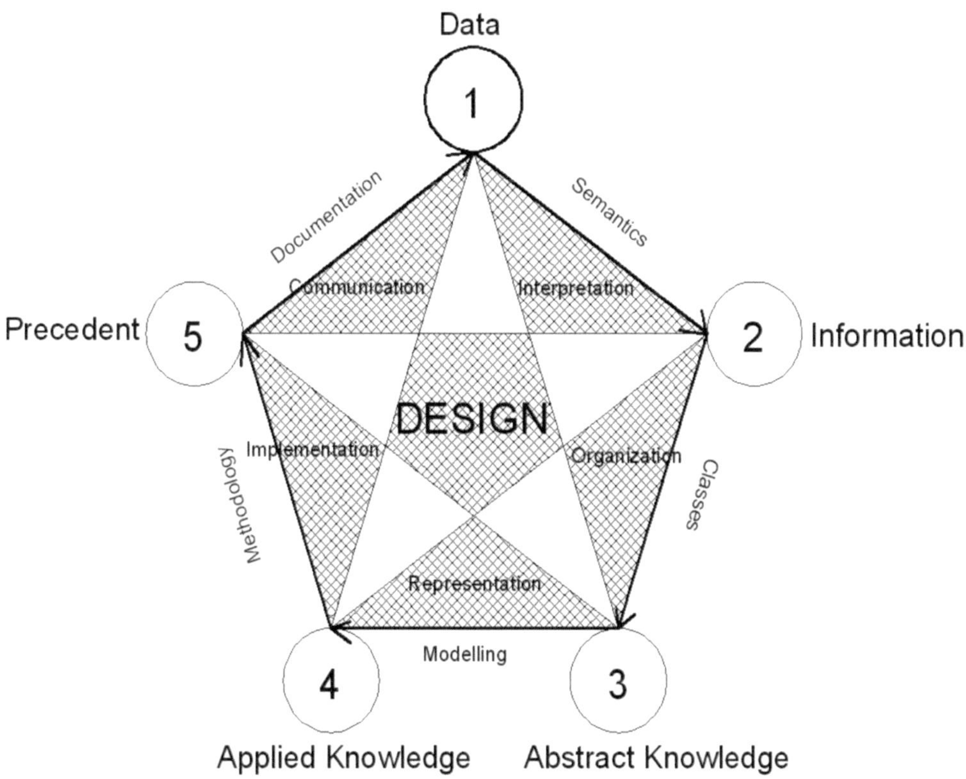

Fig. 1. Knowledge recycling pentagon

These eight design-related knowledge management areas are illustrated in Figure 2. They are represented as a knowledge management octagon where the transition from one station into the next requires additional layers of interpretation to clarify its premises and present its processing phases and resultant products. Some of these areas were emphasized in previous researches (Eilouti, 2007, 2009, 2011). However, the recycling octagon introduced in Eilouti, 2009 is revised here to fit the context of this chapter. In this revised octagon, the design knowledge processing sequence starts with design analysis, where knowledge from documented designs in previous case studies can be extracted, analyzed and assessed to prepare reusable parts for the generation of new knowledge. Upon its extraction, the analyzed design knowledge needs organization to categorize its contents based on pre-defined criteria and goals. Based on knowledge organization, it becomes possible to model knowledge either in easier to understand abstract models, or in easier to implement applied models. Knowledge is then represented in applicable models which, in turn, can be applied to produce new designs. This cycle from knowledge analysis to modeling uses layers and components of knowledge in an inductive reasoning approach to conclude wholes from parts. The next cycle departs from the knowledge-based implemented models. These need to be synthesized in the form of multiple alternatives of design proposals and filtered to develop design derivation. This sub-cycle represents the main core of the designing process; which is design development. The generated designs are then evaluated to test their weaknesses and strengths in order to revise any of the previous sub-cycles if necessary. The communicated representations need then to be documented for future reference. This sub-cycle from knowledge communication to knowledge evaluation encompasses post-design activities and mainly is concerned with re-presentation of produced designs in different formats, and with the study of the derivation and analysis processes. The design activities included in this cycle are mostly deductive and represent the pre-design phase of future designs. In this phase, design compositions are analyzed to be later assembled from the basic elements that are embedded in precedent-based generated knowledge. The two main areas of concern of this knowledge processing octagon in this research are the knowledge modeling, and knowledge recycling. This latter recursively loops between documented precedent-based design knowledge and generated product. These two knowledge areas- modeling and recycling- will be discussed in more detail in this section and the following sections.

The transition from each knowledge-related activity to the next in the management octagon requires a major task that is possibly associated with multiple minor ones. For example, the deductive cycle of the design recycling loop starts from studying previously documented designs, it requires *reasoning* to analyze existing knowledge. Upon analyzing its contents, precedent-based knowledge as embedded in case studies can be subject to *critical assessment* to evaluate what parts can be reused and how they function. Next, new knowledge can be inferred from evaluated previous experiences to generate new guidelines that may inform future designs. The main task needed for the transition from knowledge derivation to knowledge implementation is the organization of its associative data and information. This task requires *classification* and *categorization* of the relevant information. Similarly, a prototyping of organized data is required to prepare managed knowledge to be modelled in more usable formats in the next stage. This task uses typology and classification to help prototype given knowledge body in recognizable and reusable models. Then, these models need to be synthesized in many forms as a point of departure for the generation process. Upon modeling in more usable formats, knowledge-based prototypes require adopting a clear methodology to explain how they will be implemented to generate new products. When implemented, the product designs need to be presented in different formats including text, graphics, and mock ups to make them executable and comprehensible by other design parties. This requires *visualization* and *representation* methods. After proper communication of the design product, its associative knowledge requires archiving for future reference. The documented representations of designs take typically the form of archiving them as precedents or design cases.

5. Knowledge modeling

One of the major stations in the knowledge recycling pentagon (Figure 1) and in knowledge management octagon (Figure 2) represents knowledge modeling. In the first, it is represented as the transitional stage from abstract knowledge to applied one. In the second, it is represented directly as the design knowledge modeling station.

Within the framework of model structuring as illustrated in Figures 1 and 2, the main concern of this research is the development of applied models which can serve as both

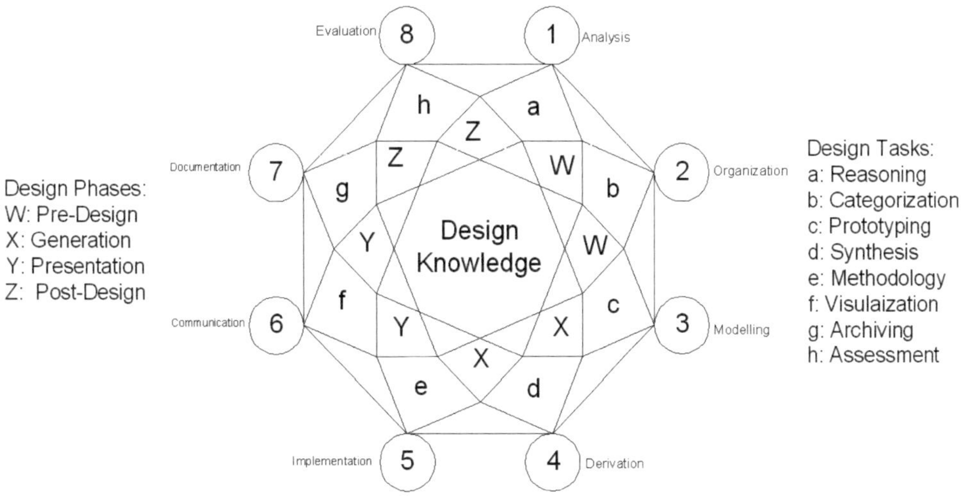

Fig. 2. Knowledge management octagon

analogical and metaphorical references, as well as inductive and deductive inference resources for design generation. The models are developed based on a study of related precedents and therefore called Precedent-Based Design (PBD) models. The PBD models are classified into seven classes. These are:

1. Scenario-Based Models (SCBM)
2. Prototype-Based Models (PTBM)
3. System-Based Models (SYBM)
4. Concept-Based Models (CNBM)
5. Component-Based Models (CMBM)
6. Principle-Based Models (PRBM)
7. Rule-Based Models (RLBM)

All of these models are based on studying examples of existing precedents and analyzing them according to either retrospective or prospective approaches. In the retrospective approach, a designer starts with a given design problem and analyzes precedents that are relevant to it. In the prospective approach, a designer synthesizes existing PBD models into multiple alternatives and develops one of them based on continuous evaluation and generation cycles. Reasoning with one of the PBD models depends on the features of emphasis it details. Classification of the models is based on the type of data extracted from precedents, and on the way the extracted data is expected to be implemented and manipulated. The seven models are illustrated in Figure 3.

Precedents in each model are analyzed to conclude a group of interrelated properties that can be assembled in a layer of coherent data. As such, similar functions are assembled in separate layers as a mechanism for the classification of data in terms of predefined criteria and goals. Such a classification enables users to hide or exclude data temporarily from the design as needed. In addition, this classification facilitates searching of entities of more interest to users and isolating them as the design processing phase requires. The seven models and their associated layers of information include:

1. The first type is the Component-Based Model (CMBM). In this type, a layer may represent a set of homogeneous components that belong to one category, such as the vocabulary elements that correspond to the functional components of a building program such as classrooms,

meeting halls and exhibition spaces. A layer may also consist of a designer's toolkit that may summarize design key goals, constraints, methods, strategies or techniques; reasoning or synthesis methods of a design; and tools of representation and media employment. A layer may emphasize and isolate building blocks such as the sets of roofs, windows, walls and masses used in design. Furthermore, a layer may highlight the patterns of functional clustering such as those described by Alexander's patterns (Alexander, 1977), which are based on resolving conflicts that may result from behavioral tendencies of grouping different building spaces.

2. The second type is the Principle-Based Model (PRBM). In this model, principles of form composition are deduced from a morphological analysis of the structures of studied precedents. They include visual and aesthetic principles such as rhythm, symmetry, proportion, scale, balance, integration, unity, character, and part-to-whole or void-to-solid ratios. The principles also include those that highlight the codes and regulations such as the ones used to control barrier-free or emergency exit regulation compliance that are concluded from precedents and formulated to define and restrict new designs. In addition, they include pre-defined standards that are typically used to guide the generation of an aesthetic design, such as the golden section proportional system, the ergonomic quality assurance requirements and the optimum sizes of functional spaces that can be found in architectural and engineering standardization references.

3. The third type represents Rule-Based Model (RLBM), in which the syntactic rules underlying the derivation of precedent designs are inferred. These are then represented either in the form of relational rules or process-related rules. In the first, rules emphasize the morphological structure of a composition and how components are topologically and mathematically related in space. In the second, rules are concluded to guide the incremental evolution sequence that emphasizes the procedural aspects of form making and the steps and phases of producing the final product. Both types of rules (relational and procedural) are represented in shape grammars. So, a shape grammar of precedents can propose guidelines about the morphological structure and designing process for future similar designs. As examples of shape grammar studies see Eilouti et. al.(2007, 2009).

4. The fourth type is Scenario-Based Model (SCBM). A precedent in this type is portrayed in its entirety for performance evaluation purposes. The functionality of a case may be investigated in different situations and for different purposes. A what-if game can be played to test different aspects of a case performance. As such, a particular behavioral aspect can be simulated in a precedent. For example, a precedent may be tested to check how it may function from the viewpoint of potential users; that is a user-based analysis. User-based simulation of space utilization aims to study pedestrian movement patterns and space flow and accessibility. Consequently, the user-based scenario simulation findings can be used as input for future design decisions. A precedent can also be evaluated against a hypothetical event that may occur daily, weekly, monthly or yearly; that is an event-based analysis. In event-based performance simulation, the building at hand is investigated for its performance satisfaction of a pre-defined criterion such as escape routing, emergency exits, or its comfort assurance and compliance in response to directed tests such as those related to lighting, airflow, acoustics, and visual and thermal comfort.

5. As in the previous type, each case in a Prototype-Based Model (PTBM) is portrayed in its entirety. A set of attributes in precedent designs is captured in its holistic character to be transformed into future designs. Its transformation entails its adaptation to generate another solution. In this model, a design template or a prototype can be inferred from a precedent to serve as a point of departure for relevant new designs. A prototypical model may be developed based on the functional components of precedents, or their formal aspects. For example, spaces

of a hospital could be clustered according to a given functional template as concluded from previous successful hospital designs. Similarly, a specific shape in plan may work well for many existing hospitals, which proposes a formal template for future hospital plans.

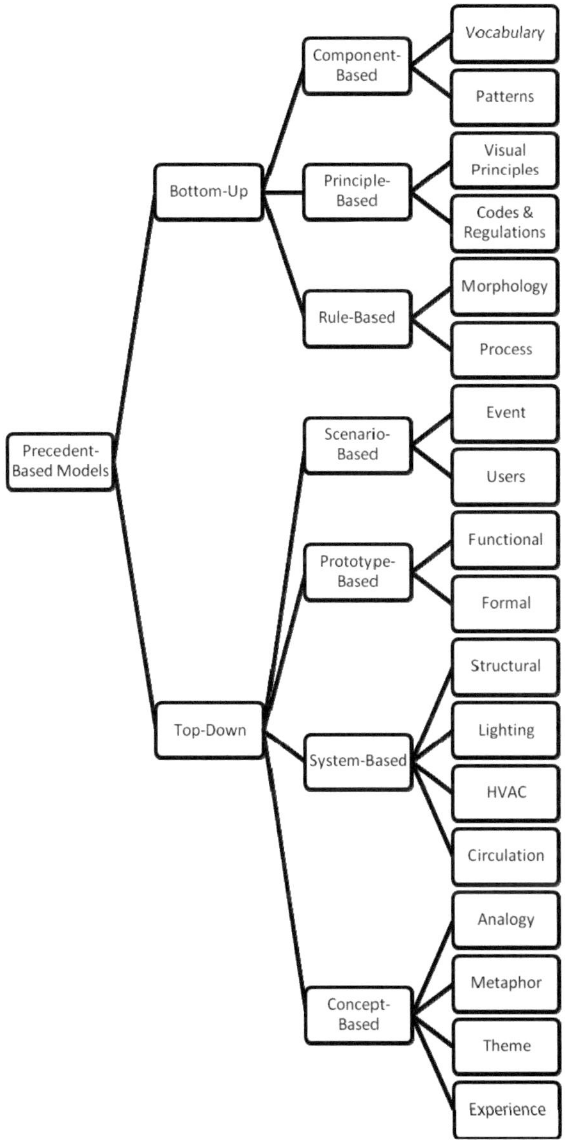

Fig. 3. The seven precedent-based models

6. Similar to the fourth and fifth types, a System-Based Model (SYBM) highlights a precedent as a whole. SYBM is based on the inference of systems in each of which a class of similar functional or formal elements is grouped. Possible systems that can be emphasized in a set of precedents include: structural, circulation, signage, HVAC and lighting systems.
7. In the previous models, most of the layers discussed so far are tangible. However, other intangible layers can be identified in them. The intangible layers are intensively represented in

the conceptual model defined as Concept-Based Model (CNBM). This model encompasses the philosophical, semantic and symbolic aspects underlying a precedent design. Within this model, the design philosophy of the precedent case at hand can be concluded, or a possible analogy, metaphor, scheme or theme can be drawn from it. In CNBM, the significant factors that may enhance creativity and imagination in a precedent are explored. For example, a theme or a story can be tailored from its composition. Similarly, an aspectual analogy can be drawn from comparing physical elements of a precedent with other known products or creatures. Or, some semantic layers can be borrowed in a metaphorical reference. In CNBM, an attempt can be made to capture the spirit of a designer's style of designing. A future design based on CNBM may cast the internal stylistic spirit on a new design that the same designer could hypothetically produce in different temporal or contextual settings.

6. Knowledge transformation

This section demonstrates an example of knowledge transformation. Such a transformation is represented by Biomimetics, where solutions offered by natural organisms are studied to inform innovative design problem solving in engineering applications. In this context, Biomimetics represents a transformation of environmental knowledge into engineering design. As such, it links knowledge learned from nature to concepts of man-made product generation. The epistemological and methodological assumptions underlying knowledge transformation in Biomimetics are based on a cross-disciplinary understanding and approach to knowledge building. In this approach, knowledge is transformed from biology to other design-oriented disciplines such as engineering. As a result of knowledge networking, natural organisms and man-made products are mapped to draw some solutions from the former to inform the latter. Upon mapping, nature can be imitated directly as a template or indirectly as a metaphor to solve design problems. Such mapping is referred to as Biomimicry. The "Biomimicry" term represents a concatenation of "bio" which means life and "mimesis" meaning imitation. In its study of nature, biomimicry analyzes living organisms for their shapes, models, behaviors, systems, morphologies, anatomies, components, topologies and processes as well as their fitting in their communities and natural environments. The study then uses analogical or metaphorical reasoning to imitate or take creative inspiration from them to derive sustainable and optimal solutions for human design problems.

Based on biomimicry, Biomimetics -or biologically-inspired technological application- is most frequently used in scientific and engineering literature to indicate the process of applying biological principles that underlie the morphology, structures and functionality of biological entities to manmade designs (Benyus, 1997). In this process, natural organisms are investigated to extract solutions from their adaptation techniques to their environments. Consequently, new concepts may be derived through partial or holistic extrapolation from natural solutions to artificial ones.

Scholarly works and research projects in the areas of Biomimicry and Biomimetics and their applications in engineering design are relatively new and increasingly growing (Reap et. al., 2005; Rosemond and Anderson, 2003; Todd, 2004; Wainwright et. al., 1976). Examples of Biomimetics applications include spidersilk that is used as building material, and fuel cells that power automobiles and release water instead of carbon dioxide.

While engineering applications of Biomimetics are increasingly growing, a much slower rate of knowledge networking between Biomimetics and architectural design is witnessed.

Although some examples exist in architecture (Berkebile and McLennan, 2004; Hansell, 2005; Knowles, 2006; Feuerstein, 2002) and mostly on the urban/environmental level (Hastrich, 2006; Kibert, 2006; Pedersen and Storey, 2007); using Biomimetics as a point of departure to approach architectural design in ways other than formal analogy is still under researched. In the following section, a biomimetics-based design approach is proposed. The approach is discussed, developed and implemented as a project in a real design studio to test its applicability. The approach that is summarized in the following sections is further detailed in a separate research (Eilouti, 2010).

7. Biomimetic approach to design

A proposal for a new biomimetics-based design approach is represented as an exercise on inter-disciplinary knowledge networking. The exercise aims to develop new formal and functional treatments that evolve from contextual fit considerations and users' changing needs as well as product lifecycle factors. In this exercise, the inter-disciplinary knowledge transfer and deployment is preceded by a cross-disciplinary development of a new approach to architectural designing that shifts conventional paradigms of design thinking, which are mostly centered about formal attributes, into behavior-centered and function-oriented design formations. As such, the approach proposed in this study is concerned with the development of design solutions from the context and environment of a designated design not only to generate organic forms but also to develop environment-friendly functions, systems and solutions.
The approach uses new resources of inspiration that are simulated by digital studio tools. It is described, implemented, reflected on and discussed in digital design studio settings for third year architectural engineering students in Jordan University of Science and Technology (JUST). The approach is presented to introduce a new style in architecture, which we called "BioTecture". It is represented as a Biomimetic-Inspired Design (BID) project and is based on the application of principles of biomimetics on architectural design using various points of departure. All departure paths map buildings to living creatures, but vary in order of station points. The approach includes three methods (Figure 4). These are:

1. Building-Based Design (BBD),
2. Organism-Based Design (OBD) and
3. Application-Based Design (ABD).

7.1 Building-based design method

In this method, a designer starts from the building that needs designing. For its design, s/he:

1. Defines a specific design problem
2. Finds an organism in a specific biome that exhibits a partial or total solution to the problem defined in the first step. This search may include more than one organism that shares various aspects with the subject of designated design problem and a biome that shares some aspects with the design context or environment
3. Extracts information from the selected organisms and biomes as needed
4. Maps the extracted information to the design problem
5. Develops a design solution or proposes potential alternatives from the match between the information and building aspects
6. Evaluates the design product using criteria from the original organisms and biomes that are used for inspiration or imitation

7.2 Organism-based design method

In the organism-based method, a designer studies an organism and its relationships to its biome, and then draws partial solutions from the analysis. In this method, a designer:

1. Identifies an organism the features of which seem inspiring for a design solution
2. Extracts detailed information about the organism
3. Defines a design problem that seems relevant to the features defined in the first step and the information extracted in the second
4. Maps the extracted information to the design problem
5. Develops a design solution or proposes potential alternatives from the match between the information and building aspects
6. Evaluates the design product using criteria from the original organisms and biomes that are used for inspiration or imitation

7.3 Application-based design method

In the application-based method, a designer starts from an application that is inspired by organisms or natural systems and draws parallels between that application and buildings or design problems that share some aspects with it. In this method, a designer:

1. Finds an application that offers promising solutions to architectural design problems
2. Defines a design problem that seems relevant to the application identified in the first step
3. Extracts detailed information about the application and the solutions embedded in its design including the original organisms/biomes that inspired the application
4. Extrapolates the extracted information to the design problem
5. Develops a design solution from the match between the application aspects and the building desired attributes
6. Evaluates the design product using criteria from the application's successful accomplishments and from the original organisms that are used for inspiration or imitation

8. BioTecture project

Based on the above described approach, a biomimetics-inspired design (BID) project was assigned to the JUST students. It is mainly concerned with the design of a self-sufficient adaptive house that changes its structures and configurations according to inhabitants' needs. The house is also supposed to respond to climatic changes, and to mutate in form and spatial organization during its lifecycle. Since the project views a building as a living creature that continuously changes in response to internal and external factors, and since it is inspired by living creatures, the project's style is called "Biotecture".

Reflections and feedback about the approach and the project implementation are measured by structured questionnaire. The questionnaire was given to the students who worked on the project after they finished the term in which they were assigned the project (Eilouti, 2010) to guarantee neutral feedback.

The results of the project implementation seem to encourage adopting its associative environmental problem-solving techniques and inter-disciplinary approaches as complementary for conventional functional- or formal-oriented problem-solving approaches as points of departure for design generation. However, the new design approach has some limitations as its participants pointed out. One of these is that it limits expressing the designer's personality in the generated design.

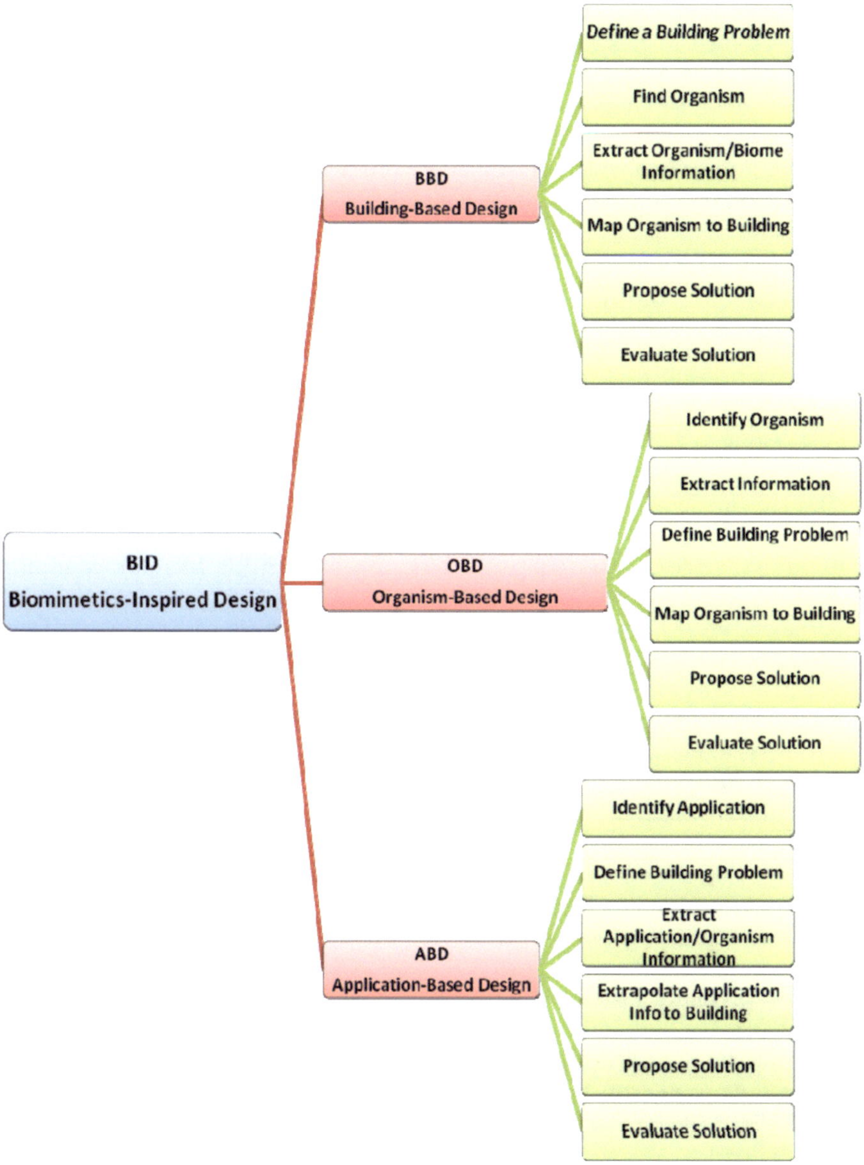

Fig. 4. The biomimetics-inspired design methods

Future extensions of this line of research include the automation of databases that are relevant to biosystems and that may be matched to artificial artifacts through computer-aided software. Such software may help in the external and internal referencing between entities and in the knowledge linkage and networking between databases in different disciplines.

9. Conclusion

Given that knowledge is essential for most design tasks, it can be made more accessible, applicable and useful if approached and represented in new forms. It can be recycled by analyzing relevant design precedents and re-synthesized to derive new emergent solutions. These are represented in this chapter as seven precedent-based design recycling models. Knowledge can also be made more useful if transformed from one discipline into another. This is shown in this chapter as biomimetics-inspired design (BID) approach to architectural design. In all of these knowledge management methods including recycling, modeling and transformation; problem-solving can be made more externalized, informed and systematic. Furthermore, applying these methods may provide new sources not only for learning but also for innovation.

10. References

Alexander, C. (1977). *A Pattern Language: Towns, Buildings, Construction.* Oxford University Press

Benyus, J. (1997), *Biomimicry: Innovation inspired by Nature*. New York: William Morrow.

Berkebile, B. and McLennan, J. (2004), The living building: biomimicry in architecture, integrating technology with nature. *BioInspire* 18.

Eilouti, B (2007) Models for the Management of Precedent-Based Information in Engineering Design, pp. 326-331, the *11th World Multi-Conference on Systemics, Cybernetics and Informatics*, USA

Eilouti, B. and A. Al-Jokhadar. 2007. A Generative System for Mamluk Madrasa Form-Making, *Nexus Network Journal* Vol 9, No.1, pp. 7-30, Birkhäuser, Basel, Switzerland

Eilouti, Buthayna H., Al-Sha'ar, Jamil, 2012, Shape Grammars of Traditional Damascene Houses, *International Journal of Architectural Heritage,* Vol 6 (4), Taylor & Francis, pp. 1-21, UK

Eilouti, B.H. (2009), Design knowledge recycling using precedent-based analysis and synthesis models, *Design Studies,* Elsevier Vol 30, No.4, pp. 340-368

Eilouti, B. H. (2010), Biomimetically Correct, International Journal of Architectural Research , *Archnet,* MIT Press, Vol 4, 2/3 USA, pp 429-442

Eilouti, B. H. (2011), Environmental Knowledge in Engineering Design Processing, *The 5th International Conference on Knowledge Generation, Communication and Management: KGCM 2011*, Orlando, Florida, USA, pp 370-375

Feuerstein, G. (2002), *Biomorphic Architecture - Human and Animal Forms in Architecture,* Stuttgart, Edition Axel Menges.

Hansell, M. (2005), *Animal Architecture,* New York, Oxford University Press.

Hastrich, C. (2006), The Biomimicry design spiral, *Biomimicry Newsletter*, 4.1, p. 5-6.

Kibert, C. J. (2006), Revisiting and reorienting ecological design. *Construction Ecology Symposium*. Massachusetts Institute of Technology, Cambridge, MA.

Knowles, R. (2006), *Ritual House: Drawing on nature's rhythms for architecture and urban design.* Island Press.

Pedersen Zari, M. and Storey, J. B. (2007), An ecosystem based biomimetic theory for a regenerative built environment. *Lisbon Sustainable Building Conference* 07. Lisbon, Portugal.

Reap, J., Baumeister, D. and Bras, B. Holism (2005), biomimicry and sustainable engineering. *ASME International Mechanical Engineering Conference and Exposition.* Orlando, FL, USA.

Rosemond, A. D. and Anderson, C. B. (2003), Engineering Role Models: Do Non-Human Species have the Answers? *Ecological Engineering,* 20, p. 379-387.

Todd, J. (2004), Restorer eco-machines for the culture of aquatic animals and the restoration of polluted aquatic environments. *BioInspire* 19.

Wainwright, S. A. (1976), Biggs,W. D., Currey, J. D., Gosline,J. M., *Mechanical Design in Organisms,* New York, Wiley.

4

A Stakeholder Model for Managing Knowledge Assets in Organizations

Constantine Imafidon Tongo
Department of Human Resource Management and Organizational Behaviour, Lagos Business School, Pan African University, Ajah, Victoria Island, Lagos Nigeria

1. Introduction

The valuable and visible things that were made centuries ago to make life meaningful for men in the earth never fell from the skies; they were first of all produced in human minds, and those that will be created in future shall also spring from the same source. The above adage suggests that the specific knowledge required to produce these things in olden days preceded their physical existence. Nevertheless, from time immemorial, knowledge has played the second fiddle to other factors of production like land, capital and labour within organizations. This is a bit absurd, especially when we consider the fact that there is no single product or service that organizations can offer to markets without being first of all produced in the minds of people in the form of a specified knowledge needed for it to see the light of day.

Therefore one wonders that it is only a few years ago that knowledge as an asset was brought into the mainstream of organizational theory. It is now very clear that the primary business of organizations is to sell knowledge based products and that competitiveness hinges on the effective management of all organizational knowledge assets (Grover and Davenport, 2001; Hillman and Keim, 2001; Alavi and Leidner, 2001; Anand, et. al., 2002; Quinn, 2005).

Given the above truism, how can knowledge assets be effectively managed in organizations? This question is very pertinent since the knowledge management literature is rife with the idea that these assets can exist in various forms (Falconer, 2011; Lytras and Ordonez de Pablos, 2009; Schiuma, 2009; Alavi and Leider; 2001; Becerra-Fernandez and Sabherwal, 2001; Akbar, 2003). Hence they all need to synergistically interact and depend on each other for the promotion of organizational effectiveness. However, in order to achieve synergy in the management of knowledge assets, it is important to know the specific roles that each knowledge asset will be playing within organizations. This can only be achieved by extensively differentiating them according to the purpose that they are meant to serve in organizations.

Previously, the process of differentiating knowledge assets has been mainly based on the forms by which they exist (i.e. tacit and explicit knowledge), their sources (i.e. knowledge generated within organizations and externally generated knowledge) and where they are stored (e.g. knowledge in human mind, organizational structure, culture and process, etc.). However, differentiation of knowledge assets in terms of what forms they exist, their sources and where they are stored in organizations would not appreciably promote their effective management; as these do not inform us about the usefulness of these assets. Rather, knowing the purpose for accumulating each of them should be the pre-requisite for managing them successfully in organizations. Like any other organizational asset or resource, the purpose of all knowledge assets must be well articulated by managers before they can be properly coordinated to promote organizational effectiveness.

Nevertheless, contemporary knowledge management theorists have not yet unanimously defined the purpose of the different forms of organizational knowledge assets. According to Grover and Davenport (2001), knowledge managers often take a highly inconclusive approach to the management of knowledge assets. In practice, what they actually manage under the banner of knowledge management is a mix of knowledge information, and unrefined data- in short, whatever any knowledge manager finds useful and easy to store in an electronic repository (Grover and Davenport, 2001). Indeed, this uncoordinated approach to the management of knowledge assets would not yield any meaningful results. Nonetheless, it suggests that modern knowledge managers do not really know the purpose of all the different organizational knowledge assets at their disposal.

Presently, there are three main types of organizational knowledge assets (i.e. structural knowledge, human knowledge and relational knowledge) that the current knowledge management literature recognizes; and only the purpose of one of them has been well defined by the literature (De Long and Fahey, 2000). That asset is termed relational knowledge or relational capital. Its purpose is to build better relations with primary stakeholders like employees, customers, suppliers, shareholders and communities (Hillman and keim, 2001). The purpose of the other knowledge assets (i.e. structural knowledge and human knowledge) has not yet been articulated in relation to the goals of any modern organization.

Since most modern organizations thrive to satisfice the interests of their stakeholders in order to survive (March and Simon, 1958; Cyert and March, 1963; Simon, 1982; Freeman, 1984; Hillman and Keim, 2001; Schneider, 2002) and only relational knowledge or capital has been known to pursue this objective; it therefore means that if other knowledge assets are tailored towards other disparate objectives, they would lack the capacity of being synchronized with relational knowledge or capital for the benefit of stakeholders.

In other words, the objective of relational knowledge and those of other knowledge assets (i.e. structural knowledge and human knowledge) could be diametrically opposed to each other. Thus, while relational knowledge seeks to satisfice stakeholders' interests; the objectives of other knowledge assets may counteract the mission of relational knowledge. Consequently, the long term wealth generating capacity of the different organizational knowledge assets would not be effectively synchronized to meet stakeholders' interests. This will be very counter productive for any organization.

Therefore I assert in this article that despite the variability of these assets, their ultimate purpose is to satisfice stakeholders' interests. As a matter of fact, the accumulation of any knowledge asset by organizations is worthless unless it is meant to meet the needs of some stakeholders.

Based on this view of organizational knowledge assets, the objective of this article is to differentiate them according to their ultimate purpose, which is satisficing stakeholders' interests; as well as provide mechanisms for their integration so that they could be effectively managed.

This is particularly important because recent studies have been placing more emphasis on the analysis of the interactions and interdependencies of the various types of organizational knowledge assets (Bontis, 1996; Ordonez de Pablos, 2001; Tsan and Chang, 2005; Falconer, 2011). However, much more detailed research involving the purpose of the different types of knowledge assets is needed to understand their nexus with each other as they create value for organizations.

Further more, while many past studies have attempted to provide key indicators that can track down the performance of knowledge assets; aspersions are now been cast on these studies because they have woefully failed to accurately discern the purpose of all the knowledge assets. Without defining the purpose of each of them, it will be impossible to derive the key indicators that can assess their performance. Since this article is geared towards differentiating them according to their purpose, we can be more certain that this purpose driven differentiation would significantly help to derive the key indicators required for their performance. This shall be treated in the latter part of this article.

In order to achieve the objective of this article, it shall be divided into six sections. The first section will present the previous taxonomy for knowledge assets. Since knowledge assets are strategic resources (Lytras and Ordonez de Pablos, 2009; Tongo, 2010; Schiuma, 2009); the second section shall attempt to link the management of knowledge assets to business strategy. This shall be followed by a discussion on the rationale for proposing the stakeholder model for managing organizational knowledge assets in the third section. A detailed analysis of the model shall ensue in section four. The fifth section would cover the theoretical and practical managerial implications of the model and then the sixth section concludes the article.

2. Previous taxonomy for organizational knowledge assets

Organizational knowledge assets, otherwise known as intellectual capital in the knowledge management literature have been construed as any information, belief or skill that the organization can apply to its various activities (Anand, et. al., 2002). According to this view, it can exist in multiple forms. It may refer to the specific scientific knowledge possessed by an organization's research department, or information about an oversee market, or skills that enable managers to make effective decisions in rapidly changing environments (Anand, et. al., 2002). However, irrespective of the various forms in which organizational knowledge exists, it has been broadly differentiated into two types. These are tacit knowledge and explicit knowledge (Polanyi, 1962, Nonaka, 1994; De Long and Fahey, 2000; Markus, 2001; Anand et. al., 2002).

The tacit dimension of knowledge comprises both cognitive and technical elements (Nonaka, 1994). The cognitive element refers to an individual's mental models consisting of mental maps, beliefs, paradigms, and viewpoints. The technical component consists of concrete know how, crafts and skills that apply to a specific organizational context (Alavi and Leidner, 2001). According to De Long and Fahey (2000), tacit knowledge is what we know but cannot explain. Consider, for example, a quality control engineer who through years of experience can identify the quality of a newly manufactured engine by its sound and vibrations on testing the engine. Such tacit knowledge cannot be transferred through a written document, and yet it is very important in the organization (Anand, et. al., 2002).

Explicit knowledge, on the other hand, is articulated, codified, and communicated in symbolic form and/or natural language (Alavi and Leidner, 2001). Explicit knowledge can easily be communicated and shared among individuals. For instance, information about market size and regulations in an overseas market can be precisely transferred to a report that can be shared within the organization (Anand, et. al., 2002).

It is important to note that both tacit and explicit knowledge are stored within individuals, organizational systems and processes. Tacit knowledge that exists within individuals is referred to as human knowledge or human capital. Human knowledge is the combined knowledge, skill, innovativeness and ability of individuals to realize organizational tasks and goals (Tongo, 2010; Skandia, 1996; Alas, 2009; Joia and Sanz, 2009; De Long and Fahey, 2000). It also includes wisdom, experience, intuition, and even spirituality of organizational members (Lytras and Ordonez de Pablos, 2009). Human knowledge is the property of individual employees which does not belong to the corporate entity (Tongo, 2010; Lytras and Ordonez de Pablos, 2009). Even though employees may possess some explicit knowledge alongside their unique tacit knowledge, such explicit knowledge is not part of human knowledge because it is common to some or the entire members of the organization.

Knowledge that is explicit and common to organizational members is called structural knowledge or capital. Structural knowledge signifies knowledge assets that remain in the organization when it does not take into consideration human knowledge (Ordonez de Pablos, 2009). Structural knowledge connotes organizational knowledge that has moved from individuals or from the relationships between individuals embedded in organizational systems and processes, such as organizational routines, policies, culture, or structure (Lytras and Ordonez de Pablos, 2009).

According to Lytras and Ordenez de Pablos, structural knowledge can be further broken down into technological knowledge and organizational knowledge. Technological knowledge represents industrial and technical knowledge, such as results from research and development and process engineering. Organizational knowledge includes all aspects that are related to the organization of the company and its decision making capabilities and processes. For instance, organizational knowledge comprises organizational culture, organizational structure design, coordination mechanisms, organizational routines, planning and control systems, among others (Bontis, Chong, and Richardson, 2000; Skandia, 1996).

Apart from human and structural knowledge, the literature on knowledge management also recognizes another class of knowledge assets. It is termed relational knowledge or capital. It is also called social capital or social knowledge by some knowledge management theorists (Anand, et. al; 2002; De Long and Fahey; 2000). Unlike human and structural knowledge, relational knowledge can exist in both explicit and tacit forms (Anand, et. al; 2002). Explicit relational knowledge can be obtained from external sources through the use of impersonal communication media such as electronic data interchanges, as well as faxes and letters. On the other hand, tacit relational knowledge requires personal communication that allows for direct and intense interaction among individuals (Anand, et. al., 2002).

Both the explicit and tacit forms of relational knowledge constitute the value of organizational relationships. In general it has been accepted that these relationships are mainly focused on parties that are external to the organization. This includes customers, suppliers, shareholders, etc. (Ordonez de Pablos, 2005). Nevertheless, it must be appreciated that the relationship of an organization with its employees creates value. So for this strategic reason it is necessary to put them in mind. Therefore, to advance in the study of relational knowledge, it is convenient to differentiate between internal relational knowledge and external relational knowledge (Ho, 2007; and Ordonez de Pablos, 2009).

Internal relational knowledge includes the value of the strategic relationships created between the organization and its employees (Menon and Pfeffer, 2003; Lytras and Ordonez, de Pablos, 2009). External relational knowledge represents the external perspective of relational knowledge and includes social relations of the organization with principal agents: customers, suppliers, shareholders, local government and communities, etc. (Lytras and Ordonez, de Pablos, 2009; Ho, 2007; Menon and Pfeffer, 2003).

Based on the stakeholder theory (Freeman, 1984); a firm can only exist through the interaction, transactions and exchanges carried on with those who have vested stakes in it. In the long run the firm must operate in such a way that each stakeholder is satisfied. The primary goal of the firm is survival, the more dissatisfied its stakeholders are, the more certain it is that the company's activities will cease (Freeman, 1984; Carroll, 1989; Nasi, 1982; 1995). Therefore, the long term wealth generating capacity of organizational knowledge assets can only be guaranteed when potential and existing stakeholders are satisfied (Stewart, 1997; Nielsen, et. al., 2009; Joia and Sanz, 2009; Schiuma, 2009; Lytras and Ordonez de Pablos, 2009; Hillman and Kiem, 2001).

Given the importance of satisficing the needs of stakeholders, only relational knowledge cannot achieve this goal; however, the contemporary knowledge management literature has inadvertently restricted both human knowledge and structural knowledge from undertaking the task of meeting stakeholders' interests. A growing number of researchers and consultants have argued that relational knowledge is the only valid notion of knowledge that managers should be concerned with (De long and Fahey, 2000). Hence the literature has failed to incorporate the purpose of human and structural knowledge into the overall organizational goal of putting stakeholders' interests at the centre of business activities. This shortfall shall be arrested by the latter sections of this article. But before this issue is treated I shall first of all link knowledge management to business strategy. This is important because organizational knowledge assets are strategic resources (Lytras and Ordonez de Pablos, 2009; Tongo, 2010; Schiuma, 2009) and the consideration of all stakeholders of organizations borders on the pursuance of a particular business strategy.

3. Linking knowledge management to business strategy: Past, present and future

Every approach to strategy conceives sources of wealth creation and the essence of the strategic problem faced by organizations differently (Teece, et.al., 1997). The competitive forces' approach pioneered by Porter (1980), views the strategic problem in terms of industry structure, entry deterrence, and positioning; game theoretic models see the strategic problem as one of interaction between rivals with certain behavioural expectations about each other; resource based perspective asserts that long run superior performance is associated with the possession of scarce, valuable and inimitable firm-specific resources-human, material and physical resources (Barney, 1991; Teece, et. al., 1997; Penrose, 1959; Wernerfelt, 1984; Studdard and Darby, 2011). However, the knowledge based perspective to strategy, which is the crux of this study, postulates that the services rendered by these firm specific resources is basically a function of the knowledge assets possessed by the firm (Alavi and Leidner, 2001; Grant, 1996).

This position stems from the notion that knowledge as a focal asset creates unique advantages for governing economic activities through a logic that is very different from traditional resources' management. Unlike other resources that are governed by the law of diminishing returns; every additional unit of knowledge that is effectively utilized results in a marginal increase in performance (Malhotra, 2000). Consequently, the success of modern corporations is often attributed to the fact that every additional unit of knowledge based product or service would result in an increase in marginal returns (Malhotra, 2000).

This therefore implies that knowledge must be seen as the most important factor of production. However, just as not all forms of labour and material are required by every organization, the type of knowledge required by each business entity must be tailored towards its own unique peculiarities. Consequently, in order to effectively harness knowledge as a factor of production, each business organization must be able to accumulate certain "knowledge assets" that are relevant and specific to its diverse operations (Tongo, 2008; Tongo, 2010).

From a practitioner's perspective, much of the work undertaken on knowledge management has been accomplished without immense change on how organizations do business (Grover and Davenport, 2001). Nevertheless, organizations that have reached the initial plateau of knowledge management now realize that the long run complete success at using knowledge for business advantage requires change in many core aspects of business (Grover and Davenport, 2001). In the first phase, the emphasis was on the knowledge management project. According to Grover and Davenport, projects are a good way to get started with knowledge management, but they are by definition peripheral to the rest of the business. Projects "bottle up" knowledge and treat it as something separate. What firms must do in the second phase of knowledge management is to integrate it with business strategy (Grover and Davenport, 2001).

In this regard, the definition and formulation of a business strategy aimed to support and drive organization's value creation in global business have to consider the nature of knowledge assets and its relationship with business strategy (Schiuma, 2009). This means that the identification of the strategic knowledge assets at the basis of organizational effectiveness needs to be taken into account; both as intrinsic objects of business strategy and as instrumental lever to achieve strategic outcomes (Schiuma, 2009). With respect to the Schiuma's assertion, organizations can adopt two main approaches in designing strategy: (i) managers can explicitly and directly focus their attention on knowledge assets and include their development in the objectives of the business strategy or (ii) managers can focus the strategy definition around business and performance objectives and afterwards identify the strategic organizational knowledge resources grounding the achievement of targeted strategic objectives (Schiuma, 2009).

It suffices to state that while in the first approach, the knowledge assets available to the organization are the main drivers of its strategic direction; the second approach peripherally integrates knowledge assets into the mainstream of business strategy. In other words, implied in this latter approach is the second fiddle which knowledge assets play in relation to other organizational resources; as they are only tangentially considered after other resources must have been tailored towards the achievement of strategic goals. Conversely, the first approach implies that organizational strategic design stems from its knowledge assets. However, very little attempts have been made to link up business strategy to knowledge assets management (Grover and Davenport, 2001). Hence the first approach to strategy design as outlined above by Schiuma has been largely ignored.

Presently, the knowledge management literature has only paid an over arching emphasis on the second approach of strategy design which has precisely relegated knowledge assets to the background. The balance scorecard which is the most renowned contemporary business model that attempts to link knowledge management to business strategy is a product of this second approach.

The balance scorecard is a strategic planning and management model that aligns business activities to the vision and strategy of the organization. It was developed by Kaplan and Norton (1996), as a performance measurement framework that added strategic non-financial performance measures to traditional financial metrics to give managers and executives a more "balanced" view of organizational performance.

According to Kaplan and Norton (1996), the balance score card retains traditional financial measures, but financial measures only tell the story for industrial age organizations for which investments in long term capabilities and customer relationships were not critical for success. These financial measures are inadequate, however, for driving knowledge based organizations towards the creation of future value through investment in customers, suppliers, employees, processes, technology and innovation (Kaplan and Norton, 1996).

The balance scorecard suggests that business strategy must be viewed from four perspectives, and that organizations should develop metrics, collect data and analyze them relative to each of these perspectives.

The four perspectives are (i) learning and growth perspective- which focuses on employee training (ii) business process perspective- focusing on internal business processes (iii) customer perspective- dealing with the need to satisfy customers (iv) financial perspective- pertains to timely and accurate provision of financial data to investors (Kaplan and Norton, 1996).

While the balance score card acknowledges the importance of building the capacities of some intangible or knowledge assets, especially those derived from the three non- financial perspectives in order to promote the future growth of organizations; it fails to see the accumulation of these knowledge assets as the basis for strategy design.

From its point of view, strategy design is about integrating the four perspectives in a way that leads to the satisfaction of three business stakeholders. These are investors, customers and employees (Kaplan and Norton, 1992, 1993, 1996). Apart from the fact that other important stakeholders like government and host community are not covered by the analysis of the balance score card; it accords little or no significance to the role that organizational knowledge assets could play in promoting stakeholders' welfare.

Hence the balance score card actually hinges on the resource based view, rather than the knowledge based view of the firm. It proposes that through the efficient management of financial and non- financial resources of the firm; investors, customers and employees could be satisfied through a business strategy that seeks their diverse interests. However, this business strategy is not fundamentally derived from the knowledge assets available to the organization; it is more or less designed around financial and non-financial resources of the firm. It is for this reason that the balance score card centers around Schiuma's (2009) second approach to strategy design as described above.

More recent business models have been proposed for the strategic management of knowledge assets. The Skandia Navigator (Edvinsson and Malone, 1997); Intangible Assets Monitor (Sveiby, 1997); Danish guideline for Intellectual Capital Accounting developed by the Danish Ministry of Science, Technology and Innovation and the Intellectual Capital Report (Ordonez de Pablos, 2004) are examples of these models. Unlike the balance score card, these other models were mainly designed for measuring the performance of organizational knowledge assets, but they had little or nothing to do with the mapping out of the strategic direction of organizations. Organizational strategy design was never the preoccupation of these more recent business models. They only provided many disparate indicators that could be used in tracking down the performance of knowledge assets in organizations. Besides the very tenuous relationship that these business models have with business strategy; they were not unanimous in defining the purpose or role of each of the different knowledge assets in relation to all stakeholders' interests. Given this scenario, what then do these business models portend for the effective management of knowledge assets?

First of all, these business models are grossly inadequate in providing the key indicators required for measuring the performance of knowledge assets since they have largely ignored the interests of some organizational stakeholders.

Secondly, ignoring the interests of some stakeholders may threaten the long term survival of organizations and this is precisely what managers of organizational knowledge assets should seek to avoid (Hillman and Kiem, 2001).

Thirdly, without integrating the long term wealth generating capacity of knowledge assets into business strategy it will be impossible to ascertain how they create value for organizations (Andriessen, 2004). In support of this notion, strategy researchers have found out that organizational value creation derives in large part from intangible assets such as organizational learning, grand equity, and reputation (Penrose, 1959; Rumelt, 1984, 1987; Barney, 1986; Spender, 1994; Grant, 1996); and knowledge is arguably the most important intangible asset that firms possess (Penrose, 1959; Winter, 1988).

Therefore because the three points highlighted above would not promote the effective management of knowledge assets towards long term organizational competitiveness; I therefore developed a model that recursively links the different knowledge assets to a business strategy that seeks to satisfice stakeholders' interests. This model is referred to as the "stakeholder model of organizational knowledge assets" in this article. The subsequent section provides the basis for the necessity of the model.

4. Stakeholder model of organizational knowledge assets

The recent emphasis on knowledge assets as the main driver of organizational value creation has its own historical antecedents. It is imperative that these antecedents be briefly reviewed in order for us to understand why knowledge assets should drive the process of creating organizational value.

Prior to the post industrial period i.e. before the end of World War II, managers thought they operated within a "closed system" that was made up of two main parties- management and employees. Competitors ought to be a third party, but the business environment that preceded the post industrial period was not quite competitive, and so businesses were somewhat insensitive to the activities of competitors. Therefore the only two parties existing within the so called "closed system" of businesses were assumed to be primarily motivated by the need to satisfy their own selfish interests.

The above point was made very clear by Adam's Smith rational economic man concept and his theory of the firm. According to him, while the managers on one hand would seek the maximization of profits for their owners; employees on the other hand sought maximization of their economic gains. However, the selfish tendencies of both parties were only implicitly implied by Elton Mayo's perspective of the human nature and organizational functioning. But it suffices to state that Mayo's social man could only attain psychological uplifting if his social needs at work are satisfied as long as this does not undermine the maximization of profits that the organization pursues. In other words, while the social man is basically concerned with his own selfish social needs, the firm that employs him can only accommodate the satisfaction of these social needs provided its own profits are not tampered with.

Hence the "closed system" that both classical management and human relations theorists espoused before the post industrial period was chiefly concerned with satisfying the selfish interests of just the two parties- management and employees. However, the changing business environment that ushered in the post industrial economy and the subsequent need to view organizations as "open systems" made it expedient for organizations to consider other stakeholders (competitors, suppliers, consumers, government, society e.t.c) of their businesses, apart from management and employees that were hitherto relegated to the background. These stakeholders became increasingly important for business survival. It therefore became imperative for businesses to be socially responsible to these stakeholders.

Consequently, the theoretical landscape of management was altered during the post industrial period by those who thought that businesses could only survive through paying substantial attention to their entire stakeholders. This implies that organizations must be viewed as "open systems" which can affect and be affected by many stakeholders outside its boundaries. Renowned management scholars like Robert Katz, Daniel Kahn, William Scott, James Thompson, Fremont Kast, James Rosenzweig Michael Hannan, John Freeman e.t.c belonged to this management school of thought (Shafritz and Ott, 1996). Due to constraints posed by paper space it will be impossible to discuss some of the unique contributions of these management scholars to the above discussion.

Nevertheless, one debate that typifies the post industrial period and still lingers in mainstream economics and management pertains to the overall motive of businesses that now have to function as "open systems". Are they required to maximize profits given the fact that they need to satisfy a number of stakeholders with diverse interests?

Friedman (2002) posits that profit maximization is the principal responsibility of businesses. According to him, those who proclaim that business must have a "social conscience" are preaching pure and adulterated socialism. For Friedman (2002), profit maximization should take care of all the social needs of business' stake holders.

Freeman (2002), disagrees with the above position. Rather he asserts that managerial capitalism is better served by extending the fiduciary relationship from shareholders to include other stakeholders. Business organizations have stakeholders, that is, groups and individuals who benefit from or are harmed by business activities and whose rights are violated or respected by corporate actions (Freeman, 2002).

Albeit, in spite of the heated debates for or against the profit maximization motive of businesses which this article is less concerned about, it is important to note that for the very first time in management history the moral basis or ethical dimension of managing businesses was brought to the fore. And this occurred during the post industrial period.

During the post industrial period, organizations were seen as "open systems" that made use of only tangible resources- land, machines, labour, material, money, e.t.c.- to satisfy the diverse interests of their stakeholders. However, the dawning of the 21st century ushered the global business community into an era of the knowledge economy in which knowledge -an intangible resource- has replaced the traditional factors of production to become the most strategic resources needed for satisfying the pluralized interests of business stakeholders (Chang and Lee, 2007; Houghton and Sheetan, 2000; Hsu, 2009).

Nations are currently being forced to compete in a global knowledge economy where ideas, information and knowledge have no boundaries, but are instead multiplying at a fast pace

(Petty and Guthrie, 2000). In this knowledge economy, information and knowledge are seen as the principal drivers of value creation and competitive advantage, generating the increasingly critical intangible assets of contemporary organizations. Therefore making the management of knowledge assets very imperative (Cuganesan, 2005).

It is now commonly believed that building better relations with primary stakeholders like employees, customers, suppliers, and communities (Freeman, 1984), could lead to increased shareholders' wealth through the accumulation of knowledge assets that can be sources of competitive advantage (Hillman and Kiem, 2001; Saenz and Gomez, 2008). These knowledge assets in turn lead to a positive relationship between stakeholder management and shareholder value, wherein effective stakeholder management leads to improved financial performance (Hillman and Kiem, 2001; Saenz and Gomez, 2008).

Going by these findings, how can synchronization of the different knowledge assets (i.e. structural knowledge, human knowledge and relational knowledge) towards the satisficing of stakeholders' interests for organizational value creation be achieved? In this article, it is believed that this could be achieved by the development of a business strategy that links the long term wealth generating capacity of highly differentiated and integrated forms of these knowledge assets to the ultimate goal of meeting the diverse interests of stakeholders. This is depicted in the next section. This section shall differentiate and integrate the various facets of the stakeholder model. There after some light will be shed on the theoretical and practical managerial implications of the model.

5. Differentiating and integrating knowledge assets by stakeholder model

The rationale for the differentiation of organizational knowledge assets stems from Simon's (1991) principle of bounded rationality. This principle recognizes that the human brain has limited capacity to acquire, store and process knowledge. The result is that efficiency in knowledge production requires that individuals specialize in particular areas of knowledge (Grant, 1996). This therefore implies that experts are almost invariably specialists, while jacks-of-all trades are masters of none (Grant, 1996).

Implied in the principle of bounded rationality is the fundamental assumption that there are gains from specialization in knowledge acquisition and storage, and that production requires the input of a wide range of differentiated knowledge. Without benefits from specialization in knowledge there is no need for organizations comprising multiple individuals (Grant, 1996).

Therefore based on the principle of bounded rationality, it is assumed that individuals that make up organizations can be differentiated in terms of some specific, unique and bounded knowledge that they possess for meeting the needs of the relevant stakeholders of their organizations. However, because this knowledge may be tacit and not easily transferred to other organizational members, it therefore falls within the realm of *human knowledge*, as previously conceptualized in section two of this article. Albeit, this *human knowledge* that is resident within the individual is potentially useful for satisficing the needs of a particular stakeholder. Since stake holders are many, it becomes expedient to differentiate *human knowledge* according to the number of primary stakeholders often associated with organizations.

X-raying the vast literature on corporate social responsibility provides the identification of eight primary stakeholders. These are employees, shareholders, creditors, customers, competitors, suppliers, communities and government. What this implies is that a specific tacit *human knowledge* is always targeted towards meeting the needs one of these stakeholders at a given period of time. Therefore it will be useful to develop new concepts about *human knowledge* that effectively capture all organizational stakeholders. Towards this end, five new concepts pertaining to the different facets of *human knowledge* are presented. These are: (i) Human Knowledge about Product Market **(HKPM)** (ii) Human knowledge about Labour Market **(HKLM)** (iii) Human Knowledge about Financial Market **(HKFM)** (iv) Human knowledge about Technological Process **(HKTP)** (v) Human knowledge about External Environment **(HKEE).**

HKPM is tacit knowledge located within the minds of employees about the behaviour of customers in relation to products or services that the organization offers both its actual and potential markets. It also entails employees possessing some form of tacit knowledge about the behavioural orientation of customers towards competing products or services. Consequently, HKPM is basically directed to two organizational stakeholders. These are customers and competitors. However, its ultimate goal is to utilize the entire HKPM to satisfice the interests of customers.

HKLM corresponds to tacit knowledge domiciled within employees' minds about the nature of both internal and external labour markets in terms of the various skills, values, and competences required for organizational performance. HKLM directs attention to the sources of rare talents required to drive organizational value; as well as the utilization and development of such talents.

HKFM pertains to tacit knowledge resident within human minds about the most viable sources and applications of the firm's financial resources for increasing shareholders' wealth. It also has to do with knowledge about the impact of exigencies occurring within the financial markets on shareholders' wealth and credit worthiness of the organization. Hence HKFM focuses on satisficing the needs of shareholders and creditors.

HKTP addresses tacit knowledge about the various inputs, machines, equipment, etc., that is associated with the firm's process of production; as well as other alternatives to this production process. Suppliers of raw materials, valuable inventions and machines are the main stakeholders that HKTP is concerned with.

HKEE borders on tacit knowledge about the host communities, business laws, as well as the political climate and social values of the country in which business is conducted. HKEE focuses on two primary stakeholders. These are government and host communities.

In terms of quantity of human knowledge available to organizations, two key indicators can easily be identified. These are: organizational tenure of employees and number of employees focusing on all the differentiated forms of human knowledge. It is believed that the longer the employees remain in their organizations, the deeper would be the level of their organizational learning; which ultimately impacts positively on the ability of employees to generate new human knowledge. Also, the greater the numerical strength of employees that specialize in an area of human knowledge, the more likelihood of generating higher levels of human knowledge in this specialized area.

With regards to the quality of human knowledge available to the organization per time, two key indicators were identified. These are: number of trainings employees have undergone and the number of times employees in the five differentiated areas of human knowledge have been rewarded for generating a novel idea within a specific period of time.

The performance of the five types of human knowledge depends on both the quality and quantity of tacit knowledge that is resident in human minds about all organizational stakeholders at a specified period in time within organizations. Therefore, in order to identify the key indicators required for the measurement of their performance, these two parameters must be taken into account.

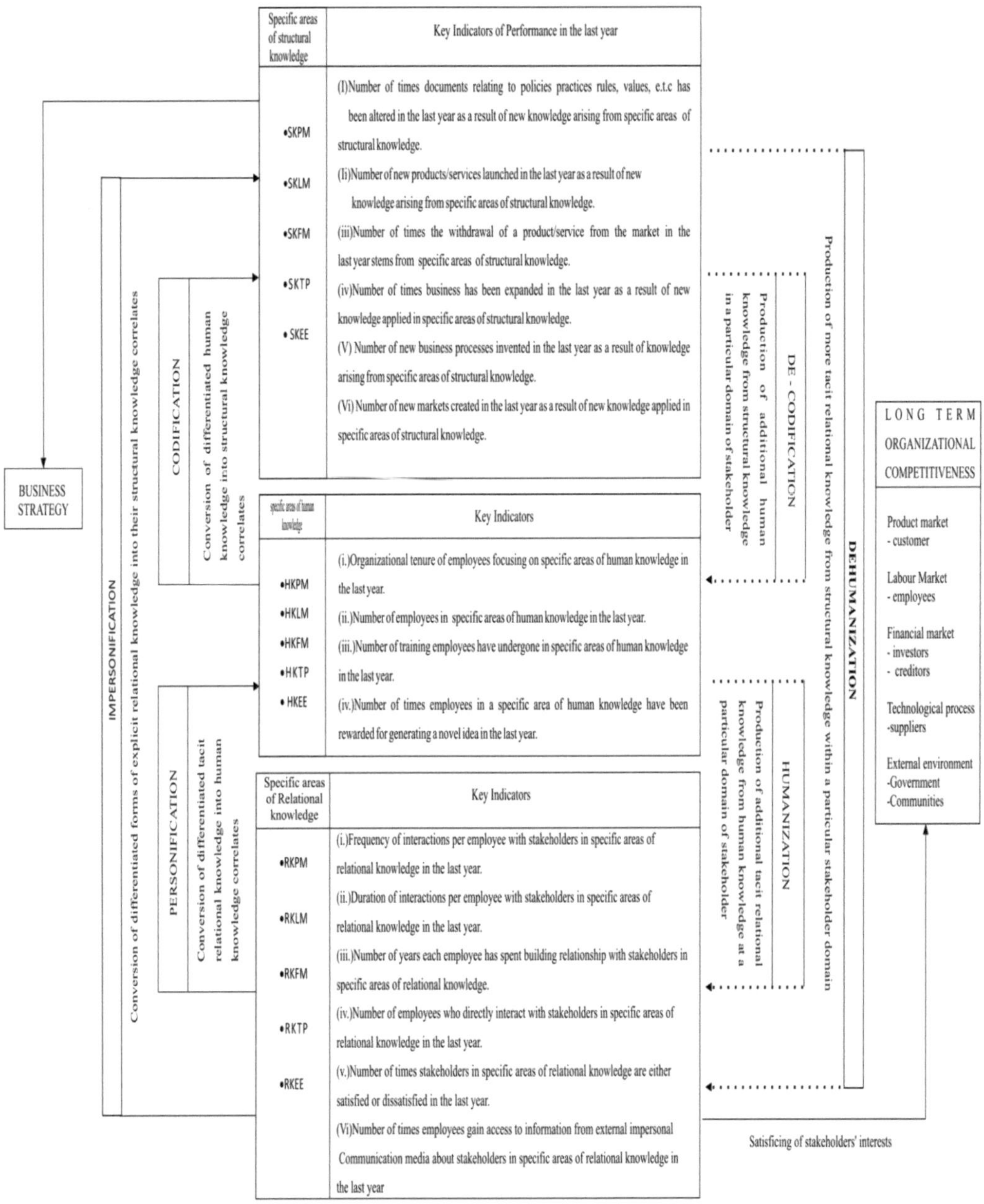

STAKEHOLDER MODEL OF ORGANISATIONAL KNOWLEDGE ASSETS

Fig. 1.

Hence four key indicators (organizational tenure, number of employees per time, number of employees' training per time, and number of times employees have been rewarded for generating a novel idea per time), would measure the performance of all the differentiated forms of human knowledge.

But recall that the differentiated forms of human knowledge all exist in their tacit states. However, it is possible that over time, the different brands of human knowledge will be transformed into explicit knowledge. Through *codification* of human knowledge explicit knowledge is produced (Nonaka, 1994; Hansen, et. al., 1999; Lytras and Ordonez; 2009; Grover and Davenport, 2001; Becerra-Fernandez and Sabherwal, 2001). Once this is achieved, they cease to be called human knowledge. Rather they have been metamorphosed into their *structural knowledge* correlates.

Such metamorphosis yields the following conversions: HKPM is converted to Structural Knowledge about Product Market **(SKPM)**. HKLM is converted to Structural Knowledge about Labour Market **(SKLM)**. HKFM is converted to Structural Knowledge about Financial Market **(SKFM)**. HKTP is converted to Structural Knowledge about Technological Process **(SKTP)**. HKEE is converted to Structural Knowledge about External Environment **(SKEE)**.

The codification process harnesses the differentiated forms of human knowledge to produce structural knowledge that is visible or shared amongst organizational members and aims at meeting the needs of stakeholders within the five areas of specialized knowledge. The codification process entails converting invisible human knowledge into visible structured knowledge that creates value for one or more stakeholders of organizations. Six of such visible end results that ensue the codification process are as follows: alteration of documents relating to policies, practices, rules, values, etc; the launching of new products and services; withdrawal of a product or service from the market; expansion of business activities through the establishment of new subsidiaries; invention of new business processes and the creation of new markets.

All of these visible end results which constitute the structural knowledge of organizations are propelled by specialized human knowledge in one or more of the five areas that encapsulate the interests of organizational stakeholders. These visible end results are the key indicators required for measuring the performance of structural knowledge.; and they periodically influence the direction of business strategy. It is for this reason that it would be impossible to extricate business strategy from structural knowledge; as changes in the formation of structural knowledge may often result to alterations in business strategy (De long and Fahey, 2000).

Nonetheless, both the formation and sharing of structural knowledge by organizational members leads to the production of more human knowledge. Unlike the direct conversion of the differentiated forms of human knowledge into their structural knowledge derivatives, already shared structural knowledge may not just produce its exact replica in the form of human knowledge. Instead through the process of *de-codification,* additional human knowledge could be produced from structural knowledge within the domain of a particular stakeholder.

For example, an organization may have an employment policy that forbids the employment of contract staff. This policy was informed by the experiences of those who have some HKLM. These persons have found out that past employees who have left the organization expropriate valued knowledge to competing firms. However, a new organizational specialist in HKTP, who has become conversant with the antecedents of this employment policy, may also become sensitive to the fact that inventors who are presently in the pay roll of the organization divulge valued ideas to outsiders for some personal gains.

From the above example, we can see that while HKLM led to generation of SKLM that forbids the employment of contract staff. However, this SKLM produced a new HKLM, which will need to be converted into its specific SKLM in order for the organization to guide against its inventors divulging important information to third parties. This observation leads to the first two propositions of this study which attempt to integrate human knowledge with structural knowledge, as shown below.

H_1: The process of codification directly converts all differentiated forms of human knowledge into their structural knowledge derivatives.

H_2: De-codification of all sorts of structural knowledge would only increase human knowledge within the domain of a particular stakeholder.

The formation and sharing of structural knowledge that is explicit amongst employees should presupposedly guide and regulate the way they relate with their organizational stakeholders. Especially those employees that are directly interacting with stakeholders that have been affected by the structural knowledge that has been newly formed and shared. These employees would need to fully understand the impact of the newly formed structural knowledge on their stakeholders, and periodically adapt behaviours that would enable them maintain their relationships with the affected stakeholders. It is at this point that relational or social knowledge is reconstructed.

Relational knowledge is actually the knowledge asset that directly comes in contact with the stakeholders. It is that knowledge that organizations can directly access using their employees and also through formal and informal ties with their various stakeholders (Anand, et. al., 2002). It is important to note that just as we have the five differentiated forms of human and structural knowledge; relational knowledge can also be differentiated in terms of the stakeholder interests that it seeks to address. Hence the differiented forms of relational knowledge are as follows: (i) Relational Knowledge about Product Market **(RKPM)** (ii) Relational Knowledge about Labour Market **(RKLM)** (iii) Relational Knowledge about Financial Market **(RKFM)** (iv) Relational Knowledge about Technological Process **(RKTP)** and (v) Relational Knowledge about External Environment **(RKEE)**.

However, because these differentiated forms of relational knowledge can either be in their tacit and explicit states (Anand, et. al; 2002), the processes by which they are integrated with human and structural knowledge are quite different. Tacit relational knowledge requires personal communication that allows for direct and intense interaction with a particular stakeholder. For instance, the tacit form of RKLM could only be acquired through intense personal interaction with members of both internal and external labour markets. When this effectively takes place, RKLM will be converted to HKLM, which in turn may be converted to SKLM via the codification process.

Nevertheless, the diffentiated forms of tacit relational knowledge are converted to their human knowledge correlates via the *personification* process (e.g. RKLM is converted to HKLM through the process of personification). This process involves the personification of tacit relational knowledge. Therefore, it can be assumed that as a specific form of tacit relational knowledge increases, its human knowledge correlate would also increase. This leads to the third proposition of this study, which is as follows:

H_3: The process of personification directly converts all differentiated forms of tacit relational knowledge into their human knowledge correlates; and so as relational knowledge of a particular stakeholder increases, its human knowledge correlate also increases.

Human knowledge obtained from relational knowledge can influence future interactions with a specific stakeholder to produce additional relational knowledge needed for dealing with the concerned stakeholder. For instance, through RKPM, it is possible for an organization to perceive that its customers are dissatisfied with its products or services. Through the personification process this RKPM is converted to HKPM, which subsequently could change future direct interactions with the customers to produce another RKPM that views its customers as being satisfied. Hence there is a process by which human knowledge generates additional form of relational knowledge within the domain of a specific stakeholder. This process is called *humanization* and so it can be posited that this process can produce more tacit relational knowledge that is quite different from the one that initially produced it. This leads to the fourth proposition of the study, which is as follows:

H_4: The process of humanization would lead to the production of additional tacit relational knowledge that derives from human knowledge within the domain of a particular stakeholder.

The process of humanization does not only produce more tacit relational knowledge. For it is possible to produce more tacit relational knowledge without the agency of the human mind. Since apart from personal interactions with stakeholders, relational knowledge can also be obtained explicitly from external sources through the use of impersonal communication media such as electronic data interchanges, internet, news papers, information from radio and TV stations (Anand, et. al; 2002); it could be possible to produce more tacit relational knowledge from these impersonal external sources. However, via a different process that is termed *de-humanization*. For the purpose of this article, the word "dehumanization" does not hold any English literary meaning. Rather, it serves to differentiate between accumulation of more tacit relational knowledge as a result of the functioning of the human mind (i.e. via humanization process) and the direct derivation of this knowledge via impersonal external sources that has been codified into structural knowledge required to satisfice the interests of a particular stakeholder. As a result of the import of the dehumanization process to the production of more tacit relational knowledge, the fifth proposition of this study is posed below.

H_5: The process of de- humanization would produce additional tacit relational knowledge that derives from structural knowledge within the domain of a particular stakeholder.

However, explicit relational knowledge within the domain of a particular stakeholder is directly converted into its structural knowledge correlate without the direct input of the human mind. The process of codifying explicit relational knowledge gained from impersonal external sources is termed *impersonification*. Thus, leading to the formulation of the sixth proposition, as shown below:

H_6: The process of impersonification directly converts explicit relational knowledge into structural knowledge within the domain of a particular stakeholder.

Like human and structural knowledge, the performance of relational knowledge can also be measured. Six key indicators can help us assess the performance of all differentiated forms of relational knowledge per time. These are: frequency of interactions per employee with stakeholders; duration of interactions per employee with stakeholders; number of years each employee has spent building relationship with stakeholders; number of employees who directly interact with stakeholders; number of times stakeholders in specific areas of relational knowledge are either satisfied or dissatisfied; number of times employees can gain access to information from external impersonal communication media about stakeholders in the specific areas of relational knowledge.

The six key indicators highlighted above for performance measurement of relational knowledge would enable organizations understand how they fare in terms of satisficing the interests of their stakeholders in a bid to gain long term organizational competitiveness.

It is worth noting that the above propositions about the interdependencies and interrelationships between the three types of knowledge assets (i.e. human knowledge, structural knowledge and relational knowledge) that are geared towards meeting the diverse interests of stakeholders have both theoretical and practical implications for managing organizations. This is treated in the next section of the article.

6. Theoretical and practical managerial implications of the stake holder's model

The knowledge based processes (i.e. codification, de-codification, personification, impersonification, humanization, and de-humanization) that integrate all the differentiated forms of human knowledge, structural knowledge and relational knowledge should occur discontinuously in organizations for them to sustain long term organizational competitiveness. In other words, organizations should strive to experience concurrent cycles of these processes. However, cycles of these processes would not just happen by abracadabra. Organizations must proactively ensure that the necessary conditions required for the effective management of these processes are created in order for them to successfully and continuously experience cycles of these processes.

First of all, modern organizations must embrace a stakeholder´s perspective of conducting business. This suggests that they need to identify all their primary stakeholders and incorporate them into their business strategy. This is very imperative given the position held in this article that pinpoints the basis for the accumulation of all knowledge assets, which is, the satisficing of all stakeholders´ interests. After organizations have been able to identify all their stakeholders, it would then be necessary to differentiate their employees based on areas of specialized knowledge that they possess in relation to these stakeholders. The stakeholder model of organizational knowledge assets depicted above recognizes five areas of such specialized knowledge. These are: human knowledge about product market(HKPM); human knowledge about labour market (HKLM); human knowledge about financial market (HKFM); human knowledge about technological process (HKTP), and human knowledge about external environment (HKEE).

The stakeholder model implies that all organizational employees would be located within the five broad areas of specialized knowledge needed for meeting the needs of business stakeholders. However, the main challenge lies in utilizing the tacit (*human*) knowledge that is domiciled within them in the five broad areas of specialized knowledge for the production of both structural and relational knowledge needed for the improvement of stakeholders´ welfare. Recall that apart from the processes of de-humanization and impersonification, the other four processes (i.e. codification, de-codification, personification and humanization) cannot take place without the input of the human mind; and these four processes are needed for the formation of structural and relational knowledge. Human knowledge is precisely the conduit through which these four processes can be experienced in organizations. Consequently, there is need for us to place a lot of emphasis on managing this facet of organizational knowledge assets.

In his article on the Knowledge based theory of the firm, Grant (1996), dealt with two organizational variables that can influence the full expression of human knowledge. These are: the role of hierarchy and the distribution of decision making authority in organizations. According to Grant, the recent emphases for team based structures where team membership is fluid, depending upon the knowledge requirements of the task at hand, is one response to the deficiencies of hierarchy. The importance of a team based organization is the recognition that coordination is best achieved through the direct involvement of individual knowledge specialists, and that knowledge managers cannot effectively coordinate knowledge assets if they cannot harness the requisite specialist knowledge (Grant, 1996).

The spread of the team based approach to conducting business is occasioned by the notion that the critical knowhow is located among knowledge specialists. Hence the displacement of scientific management by various forms of participative, employee-empowering management approaches partly reflects the motivational benefits of these systems, but is also the result of the greater efficiency of these systems in harnessing and integrating the relevant human knowledge (Grant, 1996).

Also, in order to effectively harness human knowledge, the locus of decision making in organizations must be considered (Grant, 1996). According to Grant, the quality of organizational decisions depends on their being based upon the relevant human knowledge. If the human knowledge relevant to a particular decision can be concentrated at a single point in the organization, then centralized decision making is feasible. However, must of the time the human knowledge required to make decisions may be widely dispersed in organizations, and so it would be needful to deploy decentralized decision making to fully access and harness such knowledge(Grant, 1996).

The arguments brought forward by Grant lead to the submission that team based organizations that decentralize decision making to those who have relevant human knowledge would be favourably disposed to catalyzing the processes of codification, de-codification, personification, and humanization required for the formation of structural and relational knowledge that could improve stakeholders´ welfare.

However, while variables that pertain to organizational structure and decision making as delineated above by Grant(1996), may be very important for the harnessing and accessing of human knowledge; contemporary research in knowledge management has ignored the import of personal factors in the expression of human knowledge. Organizations can design their structures in ways that facilitate the production of structural and relational knowledge from human knowledge; however, if individuals lack motivation, job satisfaction and commitment towards their organizations, they may resist the utilization of their tacit human knowledge. This challenge leads the discussion to the concept of knowledge markets.

Grover and Davenport (2001), aver that organizations should be seen as knowledge markets in which knowledge is exchanged for other things of value- money, respect, promotions, or other knowledge. The concept recognizes the interest that individuals have in holding onto the knowledge they possess (Grover and Davenport, 2001). Yet there is paucity of research on the behavior of various knowledge markets. For instance, the capacity of organizations to unleash tacit human knowledge about product market, labour market, financial market, technological process and external environment, may vary depending on the behavior of specialists in the five different knowledge markets.

Therefore for organizations to constantly experience the dynamics of the knowledge based processes (i.e. codification, de-codification, personification, and humanization) that must depend on the functioning of the human mind, both organizational and personal variables that could influence the production of structural and relational knowledge from human knowledge must be given considerable attention by knowledge assets´ managers. But in addition to these, the four key indicators (i.e. organizational tenure of employees, number of employees focusing on all differentiated areas of human knowledge, number of trainings employees have undergone per time, number of employees in all differentiated areas of human knowledge that have been rewarded for generating a novel idea within a specific period of time), required for tracking down the performance of all brands of human knowledge must be regularly monitored to ensure the flourishing of these four processes in organizations.

The other two processes (i.e. de-humanization and impersonification) which enable the addition of stocks of explicit knowledge to differentiated forms of relational knowledge and structural knowledge without the rigorous functioning of the human mind can be kept alive in organizations by exploring and exploiting various impersonal sources of information that expose organizational members to the interests of their stakeholders.

Finally, the discontinuous functioning of all the six knowledge based processes also depends on the nexus between structural knowledge that has been shared amongst all organizational employees and the sustenance of the network of relationship that the organization has with its stakeholders. As already stated in an earlier section of this article, organizational structural knowledge would always influence business strategy and this should not adversely affect the network of relationship between organizations and their stakeholders. Consequently, structural knowledge and relational knowledge must mutually reinforce each other in order for these integrative processes to concurrently and discontinuously produce the different forms of knowledge assets needed for long term organizational competitiveness.

7. Conclusion

With the emergence of the knowledge driven economy, knowledge assets have become the most important factor of production in 21st century organizations. This therefore suggests that knowledge assets should drive the long term competitiveness of these organizations. However, without satisficing the pluralized interests of stakeholders, it would be impossible for knowledge assets to achieve this objective.

This present article has identified six different processes (i.e. codification, de-codification, personification, impersonification, humanization, and de-humanization) by which different knowledge assets (i.e. structural knowledge, human knowledge and relational knowledge) can be synchronized or integrated with a business strategy that seeks the satisficing of organizational stakeholders´ interests.

It is worth noting that for the very first time in the history of knowledge management, the interrelationships and interdependencies between the different knowledge assets; and the ways by which they create value for organizations was well delineated by the stakeholder model that was developed in this study.

Further more, with the use of extant material in the field of knowledge management, it was impossible to define the functionality of all the different knowledge assets. However, this problem has been largely ameliorated through the purpose driven differentiation typology adopted for the naming of these knowledge assets. Based on this typology, any facet of these assets could be specifically targeted by knowledge assets´ managers for performance improvement.

Most importantly, this purpose driven differentiation of knowledge assets is superior to extant categorization of knowledge assets because it affords us the opportunity of properly discerning the key indicators required for tracking down the performance of these knowledge assets; as well as providing the leeway for their effective management to the betterment of organizational stakeholders for long term organizational competitiveness.

It is suggested here that empirical studies should be undertaken to test the various propositions posed in this study; as this would help validate the veracity of the six aforementioned processes that integrate the different types of knowledge assets. Finally, one philosophical stance of this article hinges on employees´ knowledge specialization; but it may be possible for an employee to possess some tacit knowledge in two or more areas of specialized knowledge. Such situations in which some employees may be jack of all trades will be the subject of another article.

8. References

Akbar, H. (2003). "Knowledge Levels and their Transformation: Towards the Integration of Knowledge Creation and Individual Learning", *Journal of Management Studies,* Vol. 40: 1998-2019.

Alas, R. (2009). "Organizational Learning During Changes in Estonian Organizations" in Lytras, M. and Ordonez de Pablos, P. (eds.) (2009). *Knowledge Ecology in Global Business: Managing Intellectual Capital,* New York: Information Science Reference.

Alavi, M. and Leidner, D. (2001). "Knowledge Management and Knowledge Management Systems: Conceptual Foundations and Research Issues", *Management Information Systems,* Vol. 25, No. 1: 107-136.

Anand, V.; Glick, W.; and Manz, C. (2002). "Thriving on the Knowledge of Outsiders: Tapping organizational Social Capital", *Academy of Management Executive,* Vol. 16. No. 1: 87-101.

Andriessen, D. (2004). *Making Sense of Intellectual Capital,* Elsevier Butterworth Heinemann: Burlington.

Barney, J. (1986). "Strategic Factor Markets: Expectations, Luck, and Business Strategy", *Management Science,* Vol. 32: 1231-1241.

Barney, J. (1991). "Firm Resources and Sustained Competitive Advantage", *Journal of Management,* Vol 17: 99-120.

Becerra- Fernandez, I. and Sabherwal, R. (2001). "Organizational Knowledge management: A Contingency Perspective", *Journal of Management Information Systems,* Vol 18. No. 1: 23-55.

Bontis, N. (1996). "There's a Price on your Head: Managing Intellectual Capital Strategically", *Business Quarterly,* Summer, 41-47.

Bontis, N., Chong, W., and Richardson, S. (2000). "Intellectual Capital and Business Performance in Malaysian Industries," *Journal of Intellectual Capital,* Vol 1, No 1: 85-100.

Carroll, A. (1989). *Business and Society,* Cincinnati: South Western, 2nd Edition.

Chang, S. and Lee, M. (2007). "The Effects of Organizational Culture and Knowledge Management Mechanisms on Organizational Innovation: An Empirical Study in Taiwan", *The Business Review, Cambridge,* Vol 7. No 1: 295- 301.

Cuganesan, S. (2005). "Intellectual Capital in Action and Value Creation", *Journal of Intellectual Capital,* Vol. 6, No. 3: 357-373.

Cyert, R. and March, J. (1963). *A Behavioural Theory of the Firm,* Englewood Cliffs, N.J.: Prentice Hall.

De Long, D. and Fahey, L. (2000). "Diagnosing Cultural Barriers to Knowledge Management", *Academy of Management Executive,* Vol. 14, No. 4: 113-127.

Edvinsson, L. and Malone, M.(1997). *Intellectual Capital: Realizing your Company's True Value of Finding its Hidden Brain power,* New York: HarperCollins.

Falconer, J.(2011). "Rewinding History: Paradoxes, Evanescence, and Hubris in Learning/Knowledge Exploration, *International Journal of Learning and Intellectual Capital,* Vol. 8, No. 1: 18-29.

Freeman, R. (1984). *Strategic Management: A Stakeholder Approach,* Marshfield (MA): Pitman.

Freeman, R. (2002). "A Shareholder Theory of the Modern Corporation" in P. Hartman (ed), *Perspectives in Business ethics,* London: Mc Graw Hill, 171-181pp.

Friedman, M. (2002). *Capitalism and Freedom,* Chicago: University of Chicago Press.

Grant, R. (1996). "Toward a Knowledge Based Theory of the Firm", *Strategic Management Journal,* Vol. 17: 109-122.

Grover, V. and Davenport, T. (2001). "General Perspectives on Knowledge Management: Fostering a Research Agenda", *Journal of Management Information Systems,* Vol. 18. No. 1: 5-21.

Grover, V. and Davenport, T. (2001). "General Perspectives on Knowledge Management: Fostering a Research Agenda", *Journal of Management Information Systems,* Vol. 18, No. 1: 5-21.

Hansen, M.; Nohria, N.; and Tierney, T. (1999). "What's your Strategy for Managing Knowledge?", *Harvard Business Review,* March-April Issue: 106-116.

Hillman, A. and Keim, G. (2001). "Shareholder Value, Stakeholder Management, and Social Issues: What's the Bottom Line?", *Strategic Management Journal,* Vol. 22, No. 2: 125-139.

Ho, C. (2007). "Identifying Stakeholders' Position through Value Creation System", *The Business Review, Cambridge,* Vol 7. No 1: 254-262.

Houghton, J. and Sheetan, P. (2000). "A Primer on the Knowledge Economy", *Centre for Strategic Economic Studies,* Victoria University, Australia.

Hsu, H. (2009). "Managing the Information Technology: Knowledge Transfer in Virtual Teams", in Lytras, M. and Ordonez de Pablos, P. (eds.) (2009). *Knowledge Ecology in Global Business: Managing Intellectual Capital,* New York: Information Science Reference.

Joia, L. and Sanz, P. (2009). "The Conundrum of Valuing a Company's Intellectual Capital: The Role of Taken for Granted Indicators", in Lytras, M. and Ordonez de Pablos, P. (eds.) (2009). *Knowledge Ecology in Global Business: Managing Intellectual Capital,* New York: Information Science Reference.

Kaplan, R. and Norton, D. (1992). "The Balanced Scorecard- measures that drive performance" *Harvard Business Review,* January- February: 72-79.

Kaplan, R. and Norton, D. (1993). "Putting the Balanced Scorecard to Work", *Harvard Business Review,* September-October: 134-147.

Kaplan, R. and Norton, D. (1996). "Using the Balanced Scorecard as a Strategic Management System", *Harvard Business Review,* January-February, 76.

Lytras, M. and Ordonez de Pablos, P. (2009). "The Building of the Intellectual Capital Statement in Multinationals: Challenges for the Future" in Lytras, M. and Ordonez de Pablos, P. (eds.) (2009). *Knowledge Ecology in Global Business: Managing Intellectual Capital,* New York: Information Science Reference.

Malhotra, Y. (2000). "Knowledge Assets in the Global Economy: Assessment of National Intellectual Capital", *Journal of Global Information Management,* Vol 8, No. 3: 5-15.

March, J. and Simon, H. (1958). *Organizations,* New York: Wiley.

Markus, M. (2001). "Toward a Theory of Knowledge Reuse: Types of Knowledge Reuse Situations and Factors in Reuse Success", *Journal of Management Information Systems,* Vol. 18, No 1: 57-93.

Menon, T. and Pfeffer, J. (2003). "Valuing Internal vs External Knowledge: Explaining the Preference for Outsiders", *Management Science,* Vol. 49, No. 4: 497-513.

Nasi, J. (1982). "Towards a Deeper Comprehension of the Social Responsibility of Firms: Some Philosophical, Conceptual and Methodological Frameworks for Scientific Research", *Turku School of Economics and Business Administration, Series A.*

Nasi, J. (1995). (ed.) *Understanding Stakeholder Thinking,* Helsinki: LSR-Publications.

Neilsen, C., Roslender, R., and Bukh, P. (2009). " Intellectual Capital Reporting: Can a Strategy Perspective Solve Accounting Problems?" in Lytras, M. and Ordonez de Pablos, P. (eds.) (2009). *Knowledge Ecology in Global Business: Managing Intellectual Capital,* New York: Information Science Reference.

Nonaka, I. (1994). "A Dynamic Theory of Organizational Knowledge Creation", *Organization Science,* Vol. 5, No 1: 14-37.

Ordonez de Pablos, P. (2001). "Relevant Experiences on Measuring and Reporting Intellectual Capital in European Pioneering Firms", in N. Bontis and C. Chong (eds.), *Organizational Intelligence: The Cutting Edge of Intellectual Capital and Knowledge Management,* London: Butterworth-Heinemann

Ordonez de Pablos, P. (2004). "Knowledge Flow Transfers in Multinational Corporations: Knowledge Properties and Implications for Management" *Journal of Knowledge Management,* Vol 8, No 4: 105-116.

Ordonez de Pablos, P. (2005). "Intellectual Capital Accounts: What Pioneering Firms from Asia and Europe are doing Now." *International Journal of Knowledge and Learning,* Vol 1. No 3: 249-268.

Penrose, E. (1959). *The Theory of the Growth of the Firm,* Wiley: New York.

Petty, R. and Guthrie, J. (2000). "Intellectual Capital Literature Review", *Journal of Intellectual Capital,* Vol. 1: 155-176.

Polanyi, M. (1962). "Personal Knowledge", in *Meaning,* M. Polanyi and H. Prosch (eds.) (1975), Chicago: University of Chicago Press, pp22-45.

Quinn, B. (2005). "The Intelligent Enterprise of a New Paradigm", *Academy of Management executive,* Vol. 19, No. 4: 109-120.

Rumelt, R. (1984). "Towards a Strategic Theory of the Firm", In R.B. Lamb (ed.), *Competitive Strategic Management,* Prentice-Hall: Englewood Cliffs, N.J.

Rumelt, R. (1987). "Theory, Strategy, and Entrepreneurship", in D. Teece (ed.), *The Competitive Challenge,* Ballinger: Cambridge, MA. pp.556-570.

Saenz, J. and Gomez, J. (2008). "Intangible Disclosure, Market Performance and Business Reputation- the case of Spain", *International Journal of Learning and Intellectual Capital,* Vol. 5, No. 1: 83-99.

Schneider, M. (2002). "A Stakeholder Model of Organizational Leadership", *Organization Science,* Vol. 13, No. 2: 209-220.

Schuima, G. (2009). "Strategies for Assessing Organizational Knowledge Assets" in Lytras, M. and Ordonez de Pablos, P. (eds.) (2009). *Knowledge Ecology in Global Business: Managing Intellectual Capital,* New York: Information Science Reference.

Shafritz, J. and Ott, S. (1996). *Classics of Organization Theory,* New York: Harcourt Brace College Publishers.

Simon, H. (1982). *Models of Bounded Rationality,* Vols. 1 and 2, MIT Press.

Simon, H. (1991). "Bounded Rationality and Organizational Learning", *Organization Science,* Vol. 2: 125-134.

Skandia. (1996). *Customer Value.* Supplement to Skandia's 1996 Annual Report.

Spender, J. (1994). "Organizational Knowledge, Collective Practice and Penrosian rents", *International Business Review,* Vol. 3: 353-367.

Stewart, T.(1997). *Intellectual Capital: The New Wealth of Organizations,* New York: Doubleday/Currency.

Studdard, N. and Darby, R. (2011). "Social Entrepreneurship: Managing Strategic Decisions in Social Entrepreneurial Organizations", *International Journal of Social Entrepreneurship and Innovation,* Vol 1. No. 1: 66-78.

Sveiby, K. (1997). *The New Organization Wealth: Managing and Measuring Knowledge Based Assets,* San Francisco: Berett-Koehler.

Teece, D.; Pisano, G. and Shuen, A. (1997). "Dynamic Capabilities and Strategic Management", *Strategic Management Journal,* Vol. 18: 509-533.

Tongo, C. (2008). "Building the Intellectual Capital of African Enterprises in a Knowledge Economy: Impediments and Requirements", *International Journal of Learning and Intellectual Capital,* Vol 5. No 1: 33-47.

Tongo, C. (2010). Accounting for Intellectual Capital: A 21st Century Responsibility for Strategic Managers, *Journal of Management Systems,* Vol. 22, No. 1: 39-51.

Tsang, W. and Chang, C. (2005). "Intellectual Capital System Interaction in Taiwan", *Journal of Intellectual Capital,* Vol. 6, No. 2: 285-298.

Wernerfelt, B. (1984). "The Resource Based View of the Firm", *Strategic Management Journal,* Vol. 5: 171-174.

Winter, S. (1988). "Knowledge and Competence as Strategic Assets", In D. Teece (ed.), *The Competitive Challenge: Strategies for Industrial Innovation and Renewal,* Ballinger, Cambridge, MA.

5

Performance Innovation Through Applied Knowledge Management: Thought Leadership in Organizations

Michel Soto Chalhoub
Chairman, ISIS Group
Engineering and Management Consulting
Lebanon

1. Introduction

Organizations experience the competitive advantage of innovation as they face a globalizing knowledge economy. In that regard, knowledge management has evolved as one of the most important sources of competitive advantage (Drucker 1988; Senge 1990; Davenport and Prusak, 1998; Srikantajah and Koening, 2000; Tang, 2011). Many of the older companies remain on the forefront of their markets, and sustain their superiority over supposedly aggressive and nimble start-ups through their ability to manage knowledge and innovation in a steady and paced manner (Brand, 1998; McAdam, 2000; Swanborg, 2010). As concepts of the learning organization evolved over the last decades, knowledge management became synonymous to competitive advantage. Since knowledge is the catalyst to the development of core competences, it is a main driver of innovation in the organization. This is particularly important in the current globalization wave that is pressuring companies to go beyond traditional self-renewal techniques such as the acquisition of external technologies or the purchase of modern assets. Organizations are pushed to create an internal, self-propelling process for product innovation that would keep it steps ahead of competition (Ahuja, 2011; Yang 2007).

2. A typology of knowledge: Management choices

As the idea of knowledge management made it into corporate practice, processes were put in place to make the idea operational. The field then grew to include a typology of knowledge; namely two major types - codified knowledge and tacit knowledge (Handy, 1989; Millar, 1998; Chalhoub 1997; Senge, 1990). While codified knowledge lends itself to being embedded in repetitive processes within daily operations, tacit knowledge requires various types of direct interaction in between parties for knowledge to be exchanged and ideas to evolve (Wetlaufer, 1999; Adva 2011). Codified knowledge requires what is called extraction processes and mechanisms so that companies could use it in the form of intranets, electronic or traditional media, and signs and symbols that could be interpreted by anyone acting independently or with minimal interaction (Chalhoub, 2010; Hansen et al. 1999). Although codification techniques have proven to be helpful especially in cases of turnover, tacit knowledge is favored by various schools of thought including Japanese corporate practice. Deeply rooted in Japan's cultural environment, the exchange of knowledge between workers is based on a dynamic interaction that results in idea generation, experience sharing, and applied advice (Nonaka and Takeuchi, 1995). Tacit knowledge requires ways to be created, evaluated, monitored, and most importantly utilized by its human resources for company performance. Interestingly, this soft asset turns out to be the hardest to duplicate by competitors (Zhang and Kim, 2011).

Knowledge mobility poses a challenge in linking it to performance measurement. As one of the managers that we interviewed in Pasadena, California, put it when describing his company "95% of our company assets and financial worth leave the company everyday ..." he said "only to get them back in-house the following morning" describing the thousand and some engineers working in the premises. While mobility contributes to competitive advantage, it puts the organization in a vulnerable position if the latter does not have the requisite culture that appreciates and retains knowledge workers (Theriou and Chatzoglou, 2008; Nonaka and Takeuchi, 1995). This is the type of culture that keeps senior managers fully aware of, and concerned about, the well-being of knowledge workers to manage a paradoxical relationship: mobility yet stability (Zheng et al., 2010). Tacit knowledge is also attributed to corporate entrepreneurship whereby a network of knowledge workers collaborate and launch entrepreneurial activity embedded in an established corporation (Floyd and Wooldridge, 1999).

3M is known for its philosophy of competition through continuous innovation. The company instilled policies that encourage managers to look for new ideas and launch new products. But the company goes well beyond policies and processes in its philosophy; 3M relies on tacit knowledge. For tacit knowledge to be effective in driving performance, the company culture must foster sharing and collaboration. Despite the common perception that start-ups are usually more aggressive than older industry counterparts in terms of innovation, older companies such as 3M, which was founded in the 1890s, can be a role model for self-renewal through knowledge management.

3. Analysis framework in knowledge management

The use of analysis frameworks provides a roadmap for the academician and the practitioner in pursuing an idea from concept to application. Analysis frameworks became an integral part of organizational strategies in order to provide fact-based and consistent policies (Yanga et al., 2010; Norton and Kaplan, 2001).

We propose an operation's level framework of analysis in knowledge management. One of the advantages of the proposed framework is that it assists the analyst in using an organized and structured approach in dissecting and solving a problem. Before proceeding, we define performance in the context of work environment. Performance at work requires the ability to understand the process that you are driving, the content needed within that process to make decisions, the ability to distinguish between results that meet requirements from those that do not, and the ability to change the process under certain conditions (Liao and Wu, 2010). We identified four components of knowledge management that are operational performance drivers and we linked them through an analytical framework. Figure 1 shows the framework schematically and illustrates how the process steps, decision points, and knowledge inputs and results (as outputs) are laid out. This is not to be confused with process reengineering or workflow design. It rather helps the analyst set the stage for building a learning organization. The main question becomes: how does the organization create, disseminate, and channel those knowledge elements in the third layer of figure 1 to drive faster and better decision-making, while performing daily processes and without disrupting operations?

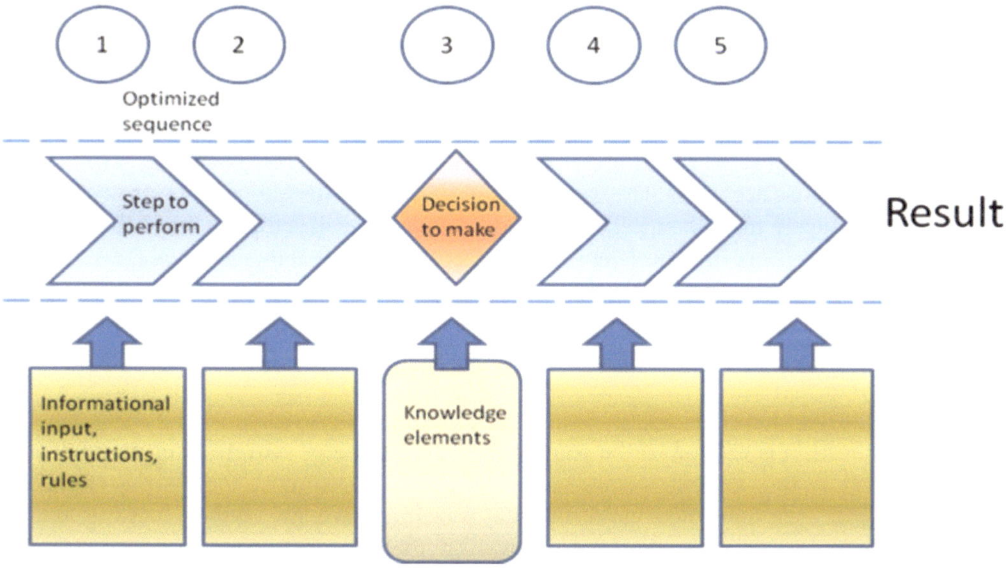

Fig. 1. Schematic representation of knowledge elements in decision-making

Consider the framework in figure 1. The practitioner can now focus her workshop or focus interviews on key research questions. The first question is related to decision-making. No matter how detailed or long-drawn is the process laid out for a certain department or in a certain company function, the main challenging points are those key decisions that the knowledge worker is expected to make to run the business or perform within that process. For example, if a person is ultimately responsible for the purchasing and procurement processes, he will always face decisions related to supplier selection, quantities ordered, or the set of quality or technical specifications to be met. A CEO, who is ultimately responsible for company strategy, will always face decisions about the choice of the next country of physical expansion, decisions about market entry, market exit, choice of alliances or strategic partnerships. Therefore the first question that the knowledge worker needs to ask is:

Q1: what are the key decisions that I need to make better and faster than in my existing performance level?

Note that the question is phrased in a way that the point of reference is the existing or current performance and the aim is to exceed it into a superior or desired performance level. It is therefore understood that comparative business analyses, benchmarking, competitor analysis, environmental scan and the like should be implicitly practiced by the organization a priori, and that the manager should already be aware of where the organization stands with respect to its competitors. Therefore, knowledge management practices should embed comparative analyses to track changes in performance. The analyst at this point needs to

identify and list those decisions in collaboration with the most relevant human resources to that particular decision process.
The second question is related to the support that the decision-maker needs in order to make decisions. This is where knowledge availability becomes an important determinant in the success of the decision-making process. Within this question, the analyst is advised to go through what is called knowledge extraction. The question is then:
Q2: what do I need to know to make faster and better decisions in relation to the particular business process at hand?
The third question is related to decision rules or a logical set of criteria that help the decision-maker reach a yes or no type of decision, or a certain choice among a set of choices. The yes or no types of decisions are encountered when a clear cut action is required after the decision is made. Consider for example the case of a defective component in a car that is causing or may cause accidents. The company would need to decide whether or not to recall the model completely from the market. To recall or not to recall is the nature of the decision. To make such decision, the decision-maker needs to know data about accidents, their nature, their gravity (a defect in the stereo system is of a different gravity from a defect in a gas pedal that gets stuck while driving), the credibility of the reports, the source of the reports, the impact of not recalling the model on the market and customer base, etc … The third question is:
Q3: What is the decision rule?
The fourth question is related to the sequence of process steps required before a decision can be reached. In this context, we are not looking for any sequence that works, especially that process design does not yield unique solutions. We are rather looking for an optimized sequence of steps that are minimized in terms of number and complexity, while maximized in terms of impact on the end result. For example, most screening activities that we normally do in a natural manner fall in this category. When looking for a home to buy, reading the police report about three neighborhoods where you may potentially buy should logically precede touring every house on the market in each of these neighborhoods. Narrowing the touring activity further by using a price bracket as decision rule, and looking at the proximity from a bus or metro station (especially if you do not like driving or owning a car in the city) would certainly precede physical visits to each property. Now these examples were chosen as somewhat trivial for illustrative purposes, but the same concept of optimization in sequencing and minimizing process steps applies to the most complex situations. In fact, the more complex the situation, the more the decision-maker would need to simplify the process schematics and keep things manageable. The fourth question is:
Q4: What is the optimal number and sequence for the process steps?
In the following section, we provide an empirical application of the framework above.

4. Empirical applications

Once the theoretical framework is explained and practiced in workshop sessions, in executive seminars, or in the classroom (case of university instruction), we turn to empirical applications. Empirical applications typically bring into the discussion field observations that support (or not) the theory. Many empirical research projects published in literature confirmed the relationship between various aspects of knowledge management and organizational performance. The way tasks and roles are distributed in a knowledge-sharing environment have a significant and positive effect on performance (DeGiovanni, 2010). Another research project examined a production management model applied to shop-floor automotive operations. The variables included production organization and work organization (type of groups) in the context of knowledge management. Floor personnel were interviewed to collect empirical data and it was found that these variables are positively related to performance (Muniz et al., 2010). Other researchers found empirical evidence about the importance of the process used to manage knowledge in driving innovation (Lin et al., 2010).

In our current project, primary data was collected from 323 business entities and was analyzed using linear regression models to test the following hypotheses:

H1: Managers who identify and manage key decisions in their processes reach higher performance levels than those who do not.

H2: Processes where knowledge requirements are identified and made readily available lead to higher performance than the ones that are not.

H3: Managers who clearly disseminate decision rules facilitate decision-making better than the ones who do not.

H4: Processes where number and sequence of steps are optimized perform better than the ones where they are not.

Primary data analysis and numerical calculations, which were left outside the scope of this chapter, showed that the four hypotheses above were accepted and that the independent variables representing each of the components were significantly and positively correlated with overall organizational performance. Performance is measured in interim process steps as well as the end result, or put differently, the extent to which the end result meets the initial requirements. Meeting initial, or agreed upon requirements, is a commonly used definition of the term quality. Analysis showed that quality is correlated with the way knowledge is created, disseminated, and managed.

Consider the case of the automotive industry, whereby companies compete on specific dimensions of competition. Kia Motors, for example, used external and internal knowledge to make decisions in the process of developing, manufacturing, and launching the Picanto model. Rise in gasoline prices, increased environmental awareness across all automotive buyer segments, change in attitudes towards driving, increased concern about safety in city streets, and other trends in consumer behavior were successfully translated by Kia Motors into clear operational and specific technical requirements. As a result, a small 1,200 cm3 engine was put together that has enough horse power to lift four or five passengers in steep slopes, or circulate in busy city streets. Kia Motors went eagerly after consumer feedback in 2009 and 2010 about weakness in the gear box, and about the mildly unattractive body shape. Shortly within 2011, the company launched its 2012 edition with an improved gear box, a more attractive body shape, dashboard, and optimal cabin room. In addition, internal knowledge components within the manufacturing process led to a fluid and efficient process that minimizes defects. Result: a successful product.

There are many cases where manufacturers and engineering entities create bonds that bridge across various organizations in search for external knowledge. This experience is enriching as it brings new input into the internal knowledge loop.

There is ample literature on the identification and use of components of innovation as drivers of performance. Many frameworks focus on implementation because they consider that knowledge management theory has been overly addressed and that real effects start when those ideas are put to practice (Anantatmula and Kanungo, 2010).

5. Role of culture in managerial decision-making

Clarity in managerial decision-making mechanisms is often credited to hierarchy. This concept started with Max Weber's administrative management theory (Weber, 1947). But clarity in lines of authority should serve another purpose; gravitating towards those who have the most relevant knowledge about the managerial or technical problem at hand. We coin this concept as knowledge-based role distribution. Although seemingly simple, it is not easy to apply. In most organizations, and in most national cultures, personal or prior social relationships, informal networks of friends and family, are a few examples of how appointments are made in many high level positions (McDermott and O'Dell, 2001). These appointments are often followed by exchange of favors. It is believed that such factors exist in many regional or national cultures and several models have been developed to account for power distance and its effect on behaviors in society and in business dealings (Hofstede, 1985). Hofstede (1985) uses five dimensions to describe the extent to which power differentials within society and organizations are accepted. More recent studies established some level of relationship between power distance, societal traditions, and personal value systems and beliefs (Basabe and Ros, 2005). Nevertheless, many studies have shown that the positive role of knowledge-sharing in employee growth and organizational performance transcends national boundaries and societal norms, is driven by globalization trends, and is influenced by a global convergence in the use of quality and business standards (Chalhoub, 2009). We propose that, for multinational organizations, knowledge creation and sharing be the prerequisite for business performance, while we maintain that these other relational factors - local societal traditions and national cultures - would certainly be important checkpoints.

The role of culture becomes even more important in fostering the use of objective and factual decision-making processes. It becomes a matter of culture and conviction to let problem-solving gravitate toward those best equipped with relevant knowledge (Hatch and Schultz, 1997). It is culture that presents knowledgeable people as an opportunity to the business owner or senior manager, and not as a threat. This approach provides access to different realms of ideas, different groups of people, and offers different opportunities for utilizing resources for the competitiveness of the firm. It was argued that culture makes a great difference as to how knowledge management initiatives evolve within the organization ranging on a spectrum of a simple repository of information all the way to a highly collaborative system among employees and across organizational boundaries including e-communities of practice (Leidner et al., 2006).

6. Organizational thought leadership – A path of transformation

The learning organization has moved from a concept, written and talked about in the 1980s, to a practical application based mostly on behavioral management theories (Drucker, 1995). Behavioral theories pioneered by Follett (1918) and developed further by other researchers and practitioners are mainly concerned with leadership behaviors, contingencies, and transformation. In order to develop sustainable competitive advantage, one needs to look at knowledge management as a long term transformation rather than just a simple daily

process. Designing and driving the knowledge management process in daily operations becomes part of a larger, strategic transformational program that can be amended and improved. Compare and contrast this concept to the Ford model mostly based on scientific management theory, on efficiency, and on applying process rules with little departure from the status quo (Taylor, 1911 ; Ford and Crowther, 1922). Scientific management surely has its advantages in terms of cost avoidance, risk minimization, reaching business targets quantitatively, and predictability of the final product. But it may be misused within the organization to a point where it stifles creativity. Further, processes and company policies could be used sometimes by those who do not encourage change, or who have reached a comfort zone, or those who have managerial power and do not wish to relinquish it.
This leads us to the second framework related to transformational leadership in the organization. The basic hypothesis that we test is that companies that approach knowledge management from a transformational leadership perspective are better positioned to innovate and launch new products successfully than the ones that do not.

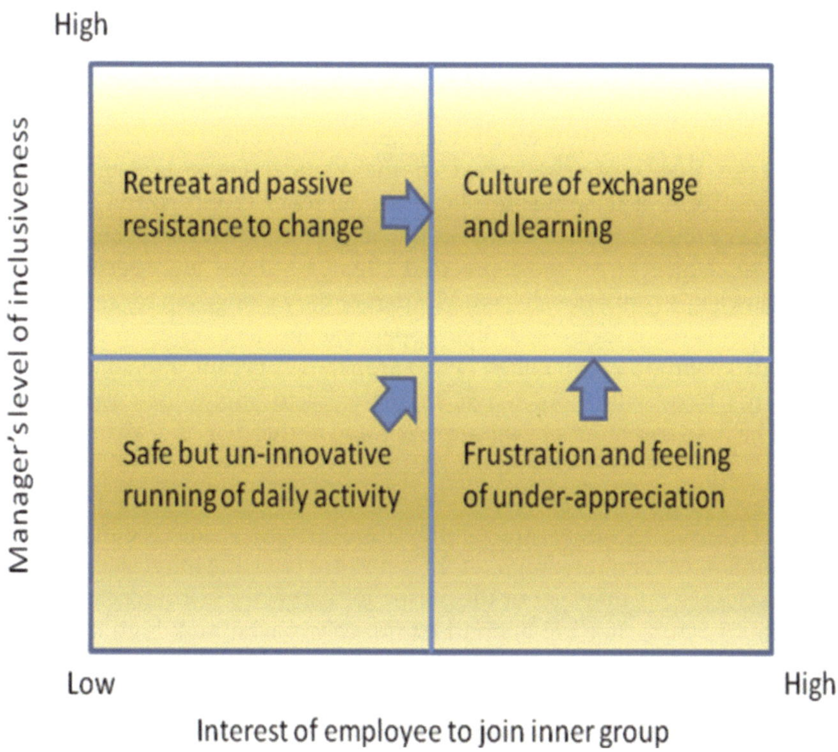

Fig. 2. The manager as a leader: fostering a culture of exchange and learning.

Leadership behaviors result in very specific capabilities that are not easy to translate into a physical or codified form. The first reason is that such leadership capabilities require tacit knowledge. Tacit knowledge is demonstrated only in its direct use and application as opposed to representing it through media such as company intranet, e-mail, or technical reports. The second reason is that knowledge management is based on people (Drucker, 1999). Practically, you will always find a gap between what people actually do on the job to excel in fulfilling their roles, and what is documented in company manuals - if at all.

Further, this gap is often difficult to close. There are other reasons related to real life situations at work; employees with superior knowledge often get subjected to office politics. As a result, those who occupy positions of authority are not always those with the highest levels of knowledge. Literature makes a clear distinction among sources of power, namely the difference between position or legitimate power on one hand, and expert power on the other hand (Yukl, 2002). Simply put by one of the managers whom we interviewed in our sample, "those who are too busy with internal politics hardly have time to evolve intellectually … but those who are good at acquiring knowledge and excelling on the job, have too little time to engage in office politics." As a result, those who are good at politics survive over those who are busy at work, unless there is transformational leadership that reestablishes the balance and sets direction. Yukl (2002) interprets Schein's work on how a transformational leader influences organizational culture (Schein, 1992). Attention, reaction to crises, role modeling, rewards, and clarity of criteria for evaluation, are all measures that Schein (1992) presents as factors that influence culture. Whether instilling culture in a newly created organization, or changing culture in an existing organization, leaders would need a mechanism to embed knowledge transfer in daily operations and be able to dismantle dysfunctional and counterproductive styles of management (Kets De Vries and Miller, 1984).

One of the theories that shed light on click formation within the organization is the leader-member exchange (LMX) theory, rooted in the Vertical Dyad Linkage (VDL) theory (Dansereau et al., 1975). It describes the inner versus outer group within the organization whereby the inner group is formed based on the quality of the exchange between the leader and the follower. However, in most practical situations those high performers who, by nature, seek knowledge continuously could be part of the outer group for reasons other than performance. This is the critical point that upper management needs to carefully identify and handle (Truckenbrodt, 2000). Follett (1924) argued that organizational authority should gravitate towards those with knowledge. If this were to apply, then the organizational culture would be the integrator between expertise and authority rather than encourage click formation.

Figure 2 shows an expanded model that uses dimensions similar to the ones used in the LMX theory. The x-axis represents the employee's eagerness to join the inner group, from low to high. Employees who rank high on the x-axis are typically interested in being part of an inner group close to the manager or the person in charge, try to influence outcomes, or be aware of decisions before they are announced. Managers who rank high on the y-axis are the ones interested in including an employee or a group of employees in that inner circle. One of the strengths of the LMX approach is that if the manager plays a leadership role, he or she becomes a facilitator and a coach who knows how to create a dynamic group exchange while moving employees to the upper right part of the model. In this case, individual knowledge creation becomes an integrated part of organizational knowledge management (Gao et al., 2008). One of the weaknesses of the LMX approach is that it may create uneven distances between the leader and the followers; the leader would not be at equal distance from his or her employees. Nevertheless, leadership has been often described as an organizational quality recognizing that leadership has to flow through networks of people, and would be carried through knowledge sharing (Ogawa and Bossert, 1995). In that regard, knowledge management is considered as a prerequisite for transformational leadership.

7. Conclusion and recommendations

For knowledge management to become a competitive edge, it requires a balance between creativity and systems-orientation at the same time. This paradoxical relationship, challenging as it may be, can be managed successfully in the presence of an organizational culture that is conducive to knowledge sharing.

A theoretical model is presented to describe the relationship between business performance and four innovation drivers. The model is then discussed in light of empirical evidence about the correlation between decision-making, intellectual capital, and leadership.

It is also shown that managing internal knowledge systematically is critical to individual and organizational performance provided there is a company culture that encourages and drives participation. Therefore, it is important to reach a culture where employees pro-actively engage in knowledge sharing, and particularly exchange tacit knowledge, in a self-sustained manner. Processes that are designed for systematic intelligence gathering make it possible to create a balance between innovation and speed in moving in new directions, on one hand, and stable slower-paced movements on the other hand.

In organizations that are not culturally prepared, innovators may be perceived as causing disturbances or discontinuities. In such environments, managers that are often selected on the basis of hierarchy may engage in thwarting the innovators or causing them to flee the organization. If company culture is not ready for knowledge management, the more innovators contribute to radical departures from the status quo, the more they may be subjected to resistance and internal politics. This is where the role of transformational leaders comes in to protect and nurture innovation.

Establishing the culture of a learning organization is driven by transformational leadership behaviors to make deliberate decisions and take actions. An organizational leadership diagnosis could, in this case, be performed with a modified LMX model which would account for group dynamics rather than just inner and outer groups.

8. References

Adva, D. (2011), "Tacit Knowledge Taxonomy and Transfer: Case-Based Research," Journal of Behavioral and Applied Management, May 2011.

Ahuja, I. P. S., (2011) "Managing Research and Development for Core Competence Building in an Organization," Journal of Technology Management & Innovation, March 2011, Vol. 6, No. 1, pp. 58-65.

Anantatmula, V. S. & Kanungo, S. (2010), "Modeling Enablers for Successful KM Implementation," Journal of Knowledge Management, 14(1), pp. 100-113.

Basabe, N., Ros, M., (2005), "Cultural Dimensions and Social Behavior Correlates: Individualism-Collectivism and Power Distance," Revue Internationale de Psychologie Sociale, Vol. 18, No. 1, pp. 189-225.

Brand, A. (1998) "Knowledge Management and Innovation at 3M", Journal of Knowledge Management, Vol. 2, Issue 1, pp.17 - 22.

Chalhoub, M.S., (1997) "Knowledge: The Timeless Asset that Drives Individual Decision-Making and Organizational Performance," Journal of Knowledge Management, Cap Gemini, Cambridge.

Chalhoub, M.S., (2010), "Tacit Knowledge and Sources of Power: Beyond Organizational Boundaries," Working Paper in Leadership Development Program MEDA-EU Program, ISIS Group, Cambridge.

Chalhoub, M.S., (2009), "Employee Growth and Development through Knowledge Management in the Global Environment: Effects on the Competitiveness of Firms in a Multinational Context," Journal of Knowledge Globalization, Vol. 2, No. 2.

Dansereau, F., Graen, G., and Haga, W.J., (1975) "A Vertical Dyad Linkage Approach to Leadership within Formal Organizations: A Longitudinal Investigation of the Role Making Process," Organizational Behavior and Human Performance," Vol. 13, No. 1, pp. 46-78.

Davenport, T. H., & Prusak, L. (1998). *Working Knowledge: How Organizations Manage what they Know.* Boston, MA: Harvard business School Press.

DeGiovanni, P. (2010), "The Impact of Knowledge Tasks and Roles on Firm Success and Performance: A Structural Model," International Journal of Knowledge Management Studies, Vol. 4, No. 3, pp. 265-280.

Drucker, P.F. (1988), "The Coming of the New Organization," Harvard Business Review, pp. 45-53.

Drucker, P.F. (1995). *Managing in a Time of Great Change.* Butterworth-Heinemann, Oxford.

Drucker, P.F. (1999). *Management Challenges for the 21st Century.* Butterworth-Heinemann, Oxford.

Floyd, S.W., and Wooldridge, B., (1999) "Knowledge Creation and Social networks in Corporate Entrepreneurship: The Renewal of Corporate Entrepreneurship," Entrepreneurship: Theory and Practice, Vol. 23, No. 3, pp. 123-143.

Follett, M. P., (1918). *The New State: Group Organization the Solution to Popular Government.* Pennsylvania State University Press.

Follett, M.P., (1924). *Creative Experience.* Bristol, UK, Thoemmes.

Ford, H., and Crowther, S., (1922). *My Life and Work.* Doubleday, Page & Company.

Gao, F., Li, M., and Clarke, S., (2008) "Knowledge, Management, and Knowledge Management in Business Operations," Journal of Knowledge Management, Vol. 12, No. 2, pp. 3-17.

Handy, C. (1989). *The Age of Unreason.* HBR Press: Boston, MA, USA.

Hansen, M. T., Nohria, N., and Tierney, T. (1999) "What's your Strategy for Managing Knowledge?" *Harvard Business Review,* 77(2), pp. 101-116.

Hatch, M.J., and Schultz, M. (1997) "Relations between Organizational Culture, Identity, and Image," European Journal of Marketing, Vol. 31, No. 5/6, pp. 356-365.

Hofstede, G., (1985) "The Interaction between National and Organizational Value Systems," Journal of Management Studies, Vol. 22, No. 4, pp. 347-357.

Kaplan, R. S., and Norton, D. P. (2001). *The Strategy-Focused Organization.* Boston, MA: Harvard Business School Press.

Kets De Vries, M.F.R., and Miller, D., (1985). *The Neurotic Organization: Diagnosing and Changing Counterproductive Styles of Management.* Jossey-Bass: San Francisco.

Leidner, D., Alavi, M., and Kayworth, T. (2006), "The Role of Culture in Knowledge Management: A Case Study of Two Global Firms," International Journal of e-Collaboration, Vol. 2, No. 1, pp. 17-40.

Liao, S. H. and Wu C., (2010) "System Perspective of Knowledge Management, Organizational Learning, and Organizational Innovation," Expert Systems with Applications, Vol. 37, No. 2, pp. 1096-1103.

Lin, R .J., Chen, R. H. & Chiu, K. K. S. (2010), "Customer Relationship Management and Innovation Capability: An Empirical Study," Industrial Management & Data Systems, Vol. 110, No. 1, pp. 111-133.

McAdam, R. (2000), "Knowledge Management as a Catalyst for Innovation within Organizations: A Qualitative Study," Knowledge and Process Management, Vol. 7, No. 4, pp. 233-241.

McDermott, R. and O'Dell, C. (2001), "Overcoming Cultural Barriers to Sharing Knowledge," Journal of Knowledge Management, Vol. 5, No. 1, pp. 76-85.

Millar, W. (1998), "Fostering Intellectual Capital," HR Focus, Vol. 75, pp. 9-11.

Muniz, J. Jr., Dias Batista, E. Jr., Loureiro, G. (2010), "Knowledge-Based Integrated Production Management Model Applied to Automotive Companies," International Journal of Knowledge Management Studies, Vol. 4, No. 3, pp. 301-318.

Nonaka, I. and Takeuchi, H. (1995). The Knowledge Creating Company: How Japanese Companies Create the Dynamics of Innovation. Oxford University Press: New York.

Ogawa, R.T., and Bossert, S.T., (1995) "Leadership as an Organizational Quality," Educational Administration Quarterly, Vol. 31, No. 2, pp. 224-243.

Schein, E.H. (1992). Organizational Culture and Leadership. Jossey-Bass. San Francisco.

Senge, P. M. (1990). *The Fifth Discipline: The Art and Practice of the Learning Organization.* Currency Doubleday, New York.

Srikantajah, T. K., & Koening, M. E. D. (2000): Eds. *Knowledge Management for the Information Professional.* Medford, New Jersey: ASIS Monograph Series.

Swanborg, E. (2010), "Social Networks in the Enterprise: 3M's Innovation Process," CIO, April 29, 2010.

Tang, F., (2011), "Knowledge Transfer in Intra-Organization Networks," Systems Research and Behavioral Science, Vol. 28, Issue 3, pp. 270-282.

Taylor, F.W., (1911). Scientific Management. Harper & Row: New York.

Theriou, G. N. and Chatzoglou P. D. (2008), "Enhancing Performance through Best HRM Practices, Organizational Learning and Knowledge Management: A Conceptual Framework," European Business Review, Vol. 20, No. 3, pp. 185-207.

Truckenbrodt, Y. (2000) "The Relationship between Leader-Member Exchange and Commitment and Organizational Citizenship Behavior," Acquisition Review Quarterly, Summer 2000.

Weber, M., (1947). The Theory of Social and Economic Organization. Translated by Henderson, A.M., and Parsons, T., Edited by Parsons, T. Oxford University Press: New York.

Wetlaufer, S. (1999), "Driving Change: An interview with Ford Motor's Jacques Nassir," Harvard Business Review, Vol. 77, No. 2, pp. 76-88.

Yang, J. (2007) "The Contingency Value of Knowledge in New Product Creativity," International Journal of Technology Management, 40(1/2/3), pp. 101-113.

Yanga, C., Fang, S. and Linc, J. L. (2010), "Organizational Knowledge Creation Strategies: A Conceptual Framework," International Journal of Information Management, Vol. 30, No. 3, pp. 231–238.

Yukl, G. (2002). *Leadership in Organizations.* Fifth Edition. Upper Saddle River. NJ: Prentice Hall.

Zhang, W. and Kim, M. (2011), "Harnessing Explicit Knowledge," Journal of Economics and Behavioral Studies, Vol. 2, No. 3, Mar 2011, pp. 97-107.

Zheng, W., Yang, B. and McLean, G. N. (2010), "Linking Organizational Culture, Structure, Strategy, Knowledge Management in Higher Education and Organizational Effectiveness: Mediating Role of Knowledge Management," Journal of Business Research, Vol. 63, No. 7, pp. 763-771.

6

Managing Tacit Knowledge in Strategic Outsourcing

Karin Širec, Miroslav Rebernik and Barbara Bradač Hojnik
University of Maribor, Faculty of Economics and Business
Slovenia

1. Introduction

The globalization of modern economies and transition to integral knowledge society brings along complex issues of mastering outsourced activities, especially in managing tacit dimensions of knowledge transfer that takes place in outsourcing relationships. Relationships can be divided into several groups, among which the traditional and strategic ones are the most distinguished (Reuvid & Hinks, 2001; Espino-Rodriguez & Padron-Robaina, 2004; Linder, 2004). Traditional outsourcing is interpreted as a relationship in which the outsourcing provider can perform only well-controlled activities. This mindset has changed over the time due to fact that outsourcing providers usually have significant capabilities and a higher level of knowledge than outsourcers. Consequently, traditional outsourcing has evolved and transformed into problem solving (strategic) outsourcing (Linder et al., 2002), which seeks to achieve major changes in the company's performance (e.g., changes in business processes, access to new technology, innovation, productivity improvements) and is mostly based on long-term cooperation between companies that often develops into a business partnerships. Such outsourcing also enables companies to fully exploit investments of external providers, their innovations, and specialized skills and knowledge that would otherwise be very costly and almost impossible to replicate within company. In strategic outsourcing objectives and relationships between participants become very important; consequently, tacit knowledge dimensions (Polanyi, 1958, 1966; Howels, 1996; Rebernik & Širec, 2007) should be appropriately managed.

This chapter discusses some fundamental issues related to the importance of knowledge management in the outsourcing relationship. Managing the outsourcing relationship is incorporated primarily in the outsourcing process itself, and no special attention is paid to it, although it is crucial for the effectiveness of the outsourcing relationship. Such an approach neglects the importance of governing, supervising, and developing the relationship with the outsourcing provider, particularly because the outsourcing literature relates mainly to large companies (Rebernik & Bradač, 2009). A considerable number of organizations have had negative experiences with outsourcing because no relationship management had been established; this is an area in which a great deal of effort should be applied during the outsourcing process (Embelton & Wright, 1998). Rather, organizations have tended to establish teams of employees who govern the outsourcing process. In this process, participants involved in outsourcing activities share various information and exchange different types of knowledge and skills. Not only do they learn from each other, but they also need to unlearn some previously used procedures, routines, and ways of doing business that have become obsolete in newly established outsourcing relations.

In particular, in a knowledge society aimed at sustainable development, the exchange of knowledge among different agents is becoming increasingly important. To embrace the knowledge and use it productively, a critical mass of knowledge and skills has to be present already in the company. Without an appropriate knowledge base, new knowledge cannot be absorbed (Cohen & Levinthal, 1990; Zahra & George, 2002; Schmidt, 2005). In this knowledge exchange, learning and unlearning are continually taking place in all knowledge areas and with all types of knowledge. It makes the phenomena of strategic outsourcing very complex and hard to comprehend. The processes are not only mutually dependent on social, cultural, economic, and political contexts, which differ from country to country, but are also concealed by tacit knowledge (Tominc & Rebernik, 2007).

We will investigate problems of managing tacit knowledge together with the importance of unlearning it. We will also examine possible opportunistic behavior in strategic outsourcing relationships and indicate possibilities for avoiding it. Based on surveys in the literature, we will discuss several types of knowledge and issues related to sharing, learning, and—most importantly—unlearning obsolete tacit knowledge dimensions as well as several important aspects of managing successful outsourcing relationships. When we take into account the needed collaboration, the holistic perception of business processes demonstrates that participants must be interdependent, be aware of their interdependence, and have a long-termed strategic interest in cooperative relationships. As the main problem of managing tacit knowledge lies in the fact that it escapes observation and measurement, an adequate framework that would make some dimensions of tacit knowledge visible and manageable has to be developed. To overcome the perpetual elusiveness of tacit knowledge, we present a framework that could help highlight dimensions of tacit knowledge that can be mobilized and observed through the manifestation of different behaviors. It is to a certain degree possible to make explicit some dimensions of tacit knowledge that not only contribute to successful sharing and mutual learning, but also enable the identification of those parts of knowledge that hinder the ability to accept novelties and should be unlearned. The better we understand the process of creating and using new knowledge and discarding obsolete knowledge, the more likely it is that companies will foster innovative behavior in companies and that the outsourcing processes will be sustainable in the long run.

This chapter contributes to a better understanding of the importance of knowledge management related to managing tacit dimensions on the level of cooperation between companies. The aim is to develop a model for managing different types of knowledge in strategic outsourcing relationship in such a way that it will develop into a sustainable outsourcing partnership. First, we introduce the strategic outsourcing relationship and its major management areas among which knowledge management is in the focal point. Furthermore, we explore the complexity of different types of knowledge and the learning/unlearning process of tacit knowledge dimensions in the management of the outsourcing relationship. In the turbulent and ever-changing business environment, tacit knowledge dimensions grow obsolete very rapidly and hinder change processes, so ways of unlearning this obsolete knowledge have to be found. To develop a sustainable outsourcing partnership in the long term, it is necessary to recognize possible opportunistic behavior that might occur at both parties in the outsourcing relationship and find ways to avoid such behavior.

2. Strategic outsourcing relationship

Outsourcing is a widely accepted business tool for transferring part of the business activities to another company to achieve different business goals. Commons (1931), Coase (1937), and Williamson (1983) explained that companies outsource when costs of in-house activities are higher than buying products and services on the market. According to Sharpe (1997), outsourcing is a management tool that affects the competitiveness of a company in such a way that its business strategies are based on core activities while non-core or supportive activities are outsourced. The concept is to have the management and/or day-to-day execution of one or more activities performed by a third outsourcing provider who is internally providing those same activities. We suggest classifying the outsourcing concept into three main parts regardless of its type, each with its own specifics and characteristics (Rebernik & Bradač, 2009): (1) the decision to outsource or not, (2) the outsourcing process, and (3) management of the outsourcing relationship. We focus primarily on the third part, in which problems of managing tacit knowledge are especially important.

Widely spread knowledge about outsourcing and its permanent growth has led to the extension of its use in all business areas. Based on the review of the literature, authors have classified outsourcing according to its effects; the commonly used classifications are traditional, which some authors call tactical (e.g., Espino-Rodriguez & Padron-Robaina, 2004), as well as strategic and transformational. The conventional concept of outsourcing indicates that the outsourcing provider can perform only well-controlled activities. Activities that could cause problems must be carried out in the outsourcer's company (Reuvid & Hinks, 2001). This mindset has changed over time as outsourcing providers may have significant capabilities and even higher levels of expertise. Consequently, the traditional outsourcing has evolved into more sophisticated problem-solving outsourcing. Other authors have similarly defined the traditional form (e.g., Greaver, 1999; Linder, 2004; Linder et al., 2002) and believe that this type of outsourcing focuses on cost reductions in order to achieve control in those areas in which the company does not achieve sufficient quality. Its foundation is to improve capacity at the operational level through the implementation of the same activities but better, faster, and cheaper. In such cases, the impact on the fundamental changes in the company is small.

Strategic outsourcing differs from the traditional outsourcing, which is based on the concept of performing the same activities at a lower cost while cooperation is static and unchangeable. Strategic outsourcing is based on changes in the management's perceptions and on continuous adaptations to needs and changes on the market (Reuvid & Hinks, 2001). The fundamental differences between traditional and strategic outsourcing lie in their objectives and in the relationship between the participants (Capgemini, 2004). The traditional form is typically used for outsourcing support and simple activities in order to lower costs due to economies of scale. Meanwhile, the strategic outsourcing focuses on core and supportive activities; it seeks to achieve further major changes in the company's performance (e.g., changes in business processes, access to new technology, innovation, productivity improvements). Its aim is predominantly to make a company more competitive by enabling it to stay focused on its core competencies. Strategic outsourcing—the core of our discussion—is focused on innovation and business improvements. Its main characteristic is a long-term relationship in which both parties stimulate and facilitate continuous and mutual business change in order to create value, develop capabilities, and manage uncertainty (Capgemini, 2004). As the strategic outsourcing relationship develops over time, it relates to a deepening partnership and an increasing range of skills and has a more fundamental and significant business impact. Companies increasingly outsource activities that are crucial to the competitive advantage of the firm. In itself, this type of outsourcing can be beneficial if rents can be obtained from the relation (Mol, 2007).

Two main criteria for defining outsourcing as strategic are (1) strategic policy at the company level concerning outsourcing and (2) preparation to consider the outsourcing of core activities (Alexander & Young, 1996). Strategic outsourcing offers the possibility to manage step-by-step changes in the organization. It focuses on three main areas: technology, business, and finance. The essence of strategic outsourcing is the strength of an outsourcing provider that can take on existing services, implement new technology and business processes, and bundle these initiatives in an appropriate management of the relationship with the outsourcer to develop common knowledge and innovation.

In the management of outsourcing relationships, several issues need special attention. Power et al. (2006) classify these into six major areas: work administration, communication management, knowledge management, personnel management, training and education, and financial management (see Figure 1).

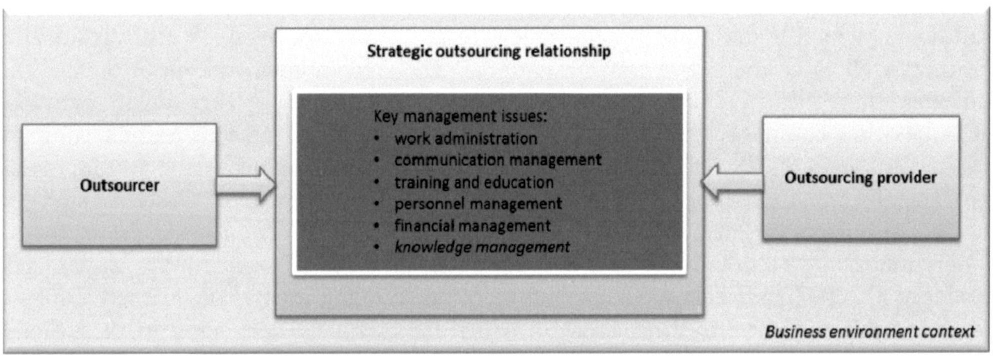

Fig. 1. Strategic outsourcing relationship management framework

Work administration ensures that the work undertaken is done and involves tracking work assignments, deliverables, and resource consumption as well as ensuring that the timeline is reached (Power et al., 2006). Communication management is especially crucial in the early stages of the relationship, when partners do not know each other. However, managers and entrepreneurs often believe that, when the contract is signed, their work is done. Over time, communication is simplified as the partners get to know each other. Training and education (Power et al., 2006) of the leader and involved employees is an inevitable part of process of building successful outsourcing relationships because cooperation with the other company brings about different ways of doing things, as cultures, forms of communication, and other issues are very often different. During outsourcing, the entrepreneur is constrained to gain new knowledge and experiences. Personnel management involves managing the employees involved in the outsourcing process and, when appropriate, establishing different teams (e.g., a governance team, a financial team). Financial management is the area in which monitoring and controlling are crucial, particularly in the early stages of cooperation and particularly if performance standards have not been implemented as agreed. Knowledge management involves sharing best practices, ideas, and innovations and improving processes with the outsourcing provider, which involves establishing new routines (Power et al., 2006); as such, old routines have to be unlearned, and efforts have to be made to manage different dimensions of tacit knowledge that could hamper the introduction of new routines. As knowledge management is one of the most important areas in strategic outsourcing relationship, we will focus on this dimension of managing relationships.

3. Types of knowledge important in strategic outsourcing

Knowledge is a living asset; dynamic and volatile, it is often difficult to observe and understand. Unlike information, it is not final and stored, but emerging and being constantly recreated and socially reconstructed in particular work contexts. Knowledge may be tangible or intangible by its nature. Know-how, when articulated into the organization's database and operating technologies, is tangible. Similarly, explicit knowledge is tangible because it has been encoded into documents, databases, or some other permanent medium (Meso & Smith, 2000, p. 232).

All kinds of knowledge together, as an emerging synergy, make knowledge a system that, in combination with values, needs, and possibilities, is the starting point of any human action (Mulej et al., 2000). Thus, knowledge is an important part of a more complex system. On the other hand, organizations' knowledge resources have pertinently been described as an iceberg (Svelby, 1997; Haldin-Herrgard, 2000). Structured, explicit knowledge is the visible top of the iceberg; this part of the knowledge resource is easy to find and recognize, and therefore also rather easy to share. Beneath the surface of conscious thought lies a vast sea of tacit knowledge, derived from a lifetime of experience, practice, perception, and learning. This concept is captured in Polanyi's (1958, 1966) often-quoted statement, "We know a lot more than we can express"; therefore, this part of the intangible knowledge resource can be more difficult to share (Haldin-Herrgard, 2000, p. 358).

Tacit knowledge often enables us to perform at a higher level than our explicit knowledge does. For example, novices cannot become experts simply by being exposed to explicit information; they need to experience the activity itself and the cooperation relating to it. For these reasons, the success of a manager is heavily dependent on tacit knowledge. Therefore, supporting the sharing of tacit knowledge throughout the company will be possible with methods like apprenticeship, direct interaction, networking, and action learning that includes face-to-face social interaction and practical experiences. Four categories of tacit knowledge exist (Lubit, 2001, p. 166):

1. Hard-to-pin-down skills. "Know-how"; the word *skill* implies tacit knowledge. People need to repeatedly practice skills, receive feedback, and get a feel for them.
2. Mental models. We draw on mental models or schemas when trying to make sense of a situation; they determine how we understand and analyze situations—that is, how we understand cause-and-effect connections and what meaning we attribute to events. The schemas we use are often subconscious abstractions rather than explicit models we consciously employ; therefore, they belong to tacit knowledge. They affect whether or not we see people as trustworthy, whether we see opportunity in a situation, and how we judge risk.
3. Ways of approaching problems. Tacit knowledge underlies the decision trees people use.
4. Organizational routines. Much of a company's tacit knowledge is stored in its routines. This tacit knowledge embedded in routines includes an intuitive grasp of what data to focus on and of the relative priority of competing demands. In time, managers leave, but the routines remain as a legacy of their knowledge.

The difficulty of expressing, codifying, and transmitting tacit knowledge makes it easier for a company to protect it than explicit knowledge. Moreover, tacit knowledge may only be effective when embedded in a particular organizational culture, structure, and set of processes and routines. The difficulty of copying tacit knowledge enables tacit knowledge to be the basis of an inimitable competitive advantage (Rebernik & Širec, 2007).

In many industries, success in today's markets depends on the ability to learn about emerging market opportunities and rapidly develop and spread the knowledge necessary to exploit them, rather than the ability to engage in careful long-term planning. The key driver of superior performance today is the ability to change when the business environment calls for it and to find the shifting sources of advantage. As a result of these changes, the ability to acquire, develop, and spread new knowledge has become an indispensable core competence. When considering strategic outsourcing, such abilities are of special importance.

The ability to create new and valuable breakthroughs offers companies an unambiguous competitive advantage. Therefore, it is vital for a company to enable an organizational environment that will encourage unique, original, and unexpected innovations that are far more valuable from a competitive standpoint than innovations that are predictable, incremental, or mundane (Lynn et al., 1996).

Such an imperative requires a shift in the role of management in the strategic outsourcing relationship. Managers have to manage the organizational environment or context in which the relationship is performed rather than control the workers themselves (Stewart, 1997; Svelby, 1997). The management of the outsourcing relationship has to serve as a coach and facilitator, a boundary-buster, and head cheerleader. His or her role will be to eliminate the barriers that prevent individuals from performing at their optimum levels. Success in the strategic outsourcing relationship requires a new form of vision-based leadership (Davenport, 1993, pp. 117-37). This problem is multidimensional in its nature. Outsourcer and outsourcing provider have to consider a number of factors simultaneously. These factors, which exist at different levels, are presented in Figure 2.

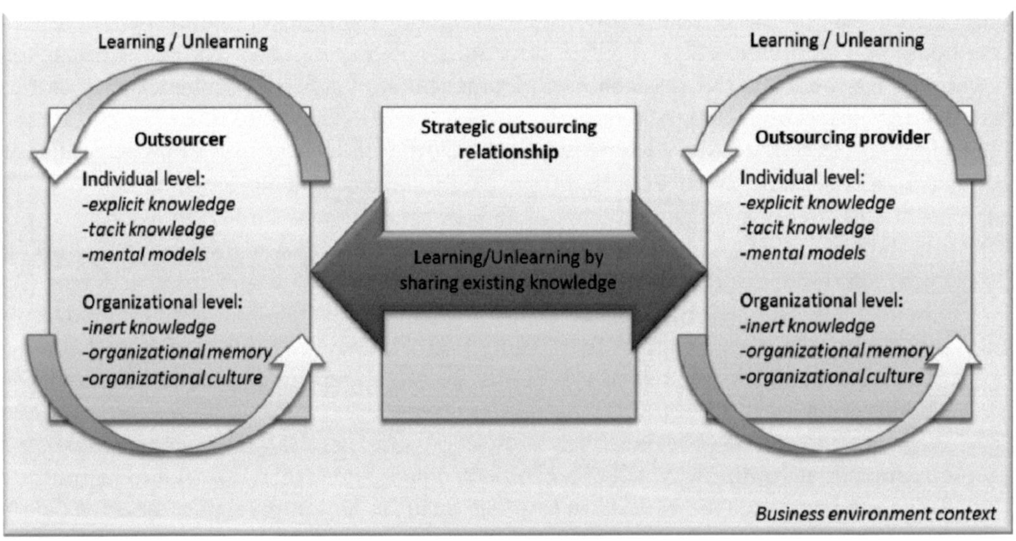

Fig. 2. Knowledge management attributes in the strategic outsourcing relationship

In the strategic outsourcing relationship, the outsourcer and outsourcing provider should get closer and closer in terms of common knowledge base, which requires sharing existing knowledge on individual, organizational, and environmental levels together with learning and unlearning obsolete knowledge. However, a particular problem always occurs when the knowledge must become visible to the other company.

At the individual level, researchers and writers have identified the difference between explicit and tacit knowledge. Explicit knowledge is widely accepted as knowledge that is recognized by the individual and therefore easily expressed or articulated (Nonaka & Takeuchi, 1995; Durrance, 1998; Newell et al., 2002; Roy & Roy, 2002). Explicit knowledge is sometimes referred to as codified knowledge. Tacit (or implicit) knowledge entails information that is difficult to express, formalize, and share. It stands in contrast to explicit knowledge, which is conscious and can be put into words. People experience tacit knowledge mostly as intuition rather than as a body of facts or instruction sets they are conscious of having and can explain to others. Tacit knowledge is obtained by internal individual processes, such as experience, reflection, internalization, or individual talent. Therefore, it cannot be given in lectures and found in databases, textbooks, manuals, or internal newsletters for diffusion. It has to be internalized in the human body and soul (Haldin-Herrgard, 2000, p. 358).

The third level considered within the model focuses on the individual level's mental models (Kim, 1993) and the organizational level's culture. In addition to mental models, many other terms can be found in the literature, such as frames of reference (Mezirow, 2000, as cited in Becker, 2006), cognitive maps (Huber, 1991), schemas (Barrett et al., 1995), theories of action (Hedberg, 1981), and paradigms (Markoczy, 1994 as cited in Becker, 2006). We follow the definition of Mezirow, who describes mental models as those deep-seated underlying values and belief systems that guide, shape, and dictate the individual's everyday attitudes and behaviors. Culture has long been seen as the shared or commonly held beliefs, assumptions, values, and taken-for-granted norms and behavior that govern organizations (Becker, 2006).

At the organizational level, explicit knowledge is generally captured in a static form. This knowledge, which is easily articulated and documented, can be found in organizational policies, procedures, and processes as well as in documentation such as performance management systems and position descriptions (Becker, 2006). At the organizational level organizational memory in many ways reflects tacit knowledge, although more has been written about organizational memory in the field of information technology than in the general management literature. Many authors propose different definitions and explanations for organizational memory (Argyris & Schon, 1978; Levit & March, 1988; Stein, 1995; Paoli & Principe, 2003), and they all recognize that organizational memory is not just explicit knowledge that is captured, but more importantly also has a tacit dimension.

At the business environment level, companies face the challenge of exchanging knowledge among different agents. Social, cultural, economic, and political contexts in which companies operate and undertake outsourcing activities differ from country to country. The knowledge gained in one business environment context is therefore not easily transferred (Rebernik, 1997; Tominc & Rebernik, 2007) and is very often of limited usefulness.

4. Learning and unlearning explicit and tacit knowledge

An abundance of literature has examined organizational learning (see, e.g., Hedberg, 1981; Cummings, 2003; Argyris, 2004; Esterby-Smith & Lyles, 2005), and many concepts and theories of learning exist. By definition, an organization learns in only two ways: (a) through the learning of its members or (b) by incorporating new members who have knowledge the organization did not previously have (Simon, 1991, p. 125). We should also pay attention to the individual level, as learning and unlearning take place at both levels. When a company outsources, it has to adapt on two levels: the company and the individual. This adaptation takes place with the help of learning—namely, the acquisition of new knowledge from persons able and prepared to use acquired knowledge in decision making and influencing other organizations (Miller, 1996). Adaptation also takes place at the organizational level because new organizational routines have to be created and performed so that newly established outsourcing ties and deployment of activities can take place. Successful learning results in modified behavior (MacDonald, 1995); in other words, the result of learning is adaptation. Furthermore, in the process of adaptation, the entrepreneur and organization have to unlearn many previously set rules and ways of doing business.

Looking at organizational learning from this perspective and understanding outsourcing as a learning process, one can expect a company to outsource if the entrepreneur is willing and able to learn and is capable of delegating some business tasks to the outsourcing partner. When current knowledge and required new knowledge are closely related, learning is not difficult; however, when a wide gap exists between current knowledge and new knowledge, individuals and organizations have to invest in the learning process. An important part of investment is unlearning obsolete knowledge and values that impede our ability to absorb new information and exploit it.

Any understanding involves both learning new knowledge and discarding obsolete and/or misleading knowledge. Sometimes the unlearning may be as important as the acquisition of new knowledge (Hedberg, 1981). Organizations' conceptual understanding as information-processing systems draws our attention to experiential knowledge that is stored in organizational memory (Andersen et al., 2003). Although experiential knowledge is often equated with tacit knowledge, in reality not all of it is tacit; indeed, some of it can be articulated and shared. The real problem is that much of the experiential knowledge collected in the "pre-outsourcing period" may have become obsolete and should be disposed of because it has become useless and impedes the accumulation of new knowledge as well as the creation of sustainable relationships. The presence of certain knowledge may constrain learning or even encourage ineffective learning (Cummings, 2003). It has been suggested that the proponents of experiential knowledge may be the worst at unlearning, as the accumulation of such experiential knowledge requires considerable investment of time and resources. Knowles and Saxberg (1988) also suggest that those who have invested heavily in their current knowledge may not be willing to unlearn. It would stand to reason that long-held views and knowledge acquired and reinforced over time may be considered more difficult to unlearn than recently acquired knowledge, to which the individual has less of an emotional attachment. This viewpoint contrasts with that which relates to absorptive capacity, which claims that—without an appropriate knowledge base—new knowledge cannot be absorbed. Nonetheless, regardless of whether previously acquired knowledge helps unlearning or hinders it, previously acquired knowledge is recognized as having some influence on unlearning. Tacit knowledge, in particular, raises issues in relation to unlearning due to the fact that it is less easily identified or articulated, meaning it may be less easily challenged as part of the unlearning process (Becker, 2006).

Similarly, as a company must "disorganize" some part of its knowledge store (Holan et al., 2004), disorganization must take place at the individual level as well. For unlearning to take place, intentional unlearning of some parts of existing individual and organizational knowledge is needed. Cohen and Levinthal (1990) coined the term "absorptive capacity" to describe the observation that prior related knowledge enables the recognition of the value of new information, its assimilation, and its application to commercial needs. They emphasized that "the ability to assimilate information is a function of the richness of the pre-existing knowledge structure: learning is cumulative, and learning performance is greatest when the object of learning is related to what is already known" (Cohen & Levinthal, 1990, p. 131). Thus, learning is more difficult when individuals and organizations are faced with an unfamiliar situation.

If sharing tacit knowledge is a demanding task, its unlearning is even more difficult. To study non-expressed knowledge, an adequate methodology has to be developed. To summarize our understanding on managing tacit knowledge, we propose a theoretical framework on how the process that will enable long-term viability of business systems should occur (Rebernik & Širec, 2007):

1. recognition of the tacit dimension on an individual as well as organizational level;
2. observation of the behavior deriving from individuals as well as organizational teams according to possessed tacit knowledge;
3. the making of the behavior explicit by sharing it;
4. learning of the new knowledge and simultaneous unlearning of obsolete and inadequate knowledge.

Although tacit knowledge constitutes a major part of what we know, it is difficult for organizations to fully benefit from this valuable asset because tacit knowledge is inherently elusive; in order to capture, store, and disseminate it, it first has to be made explicit. However, such a process is difficult and often fails for three reasons (Stenmark, 2001, p. 9):

1. we are not necessarily aware of our tacit knowledge;
2. on a personal level, we do not need to make it explicit in order to use it; and
3. we may not want to give up a valuable competitive advantage.

Our understanding of the phenomena derives from the fact that tacit knowledge in its entirety is very difficult to recognize and benefit from. Thus, we propose bringing forward tacit knowledge that can potentially be mobilized and observable through different manifestations of behavior in order to make it explicit as only its explicitness would enable us to share it as well as learn what needs to be learned and unlearn those things that are outdated and obsolete. At this point, it should be stressed that not all dimensions of tacit knowledge foster processes of introducing novelties. Thus, an important knowledge management task would be to separate the tacit knowledge dimension, which both supports and contradicts the introduction of novelties—in our case, newly established outsourcing routines. Having done this, it should be less difficult to incorporate different management efforts into the learning processes of those who support the learning processes and those who are against the unlearning processes for novelties to be introduced (Rebernik & Širec, 2007).

5. Problems with opportunistic behavior

In the outsourcing partnership, both parties have to work together, but they can either cooperate or participate. The distinction between cooperation and participation is described by Webster's Dictionary (1999), where *cooperate* is described as "to act, work or associate with others especially for mutual benefit" and *participate* is described as "to engage or have a share in something in common with others". Indeed, a difference exists between participative and cooperative relationships; a relationship could be participative but non-cooperative or both participative and cooperative at the same time. Cooperative participation occurs if all participants have a common benefit. In non-cooperative participation, individuals do not cooperate to achieve a mutual benefit, but rather an individual one—even at the loss of other participants (Rebernik & Mulej, 1999).

A successful strategic outsourcing relationship requires both parties (client and the service provider) "to be on the same page" (Karen & Black, 2004). The most significant obstacles that could prevent an efficient (principal-agent) outsourcing arrangement are:

1. misunderstanding of client's objectives, policy and culture;
2. client disagrees with the provider's objectives and policy;
3. communication and monitoring problems; and
4. both sides controlling.

Cooperative participation presumes information exchange. Cooperation is impossible if participants do not share their internal information (Rebernik & Mulej, 1999). According to this process, bounded rationality, information asymmetry, and opportunistic behavior (Williamson, 1983; Barney & Ouchi, 1986) become influential. The concept of bounded rationality indicates that the human mental capabilities are limited and humans cannot rationally define and solve complex problems. For this reason, we have to cooperate because individually we are not capable of solving complex problems on our own. Information asymmetry means that two parties involved in a transaction do not have equal information about things that are important for the transaction. Between the two contracting parties, information asymmetry means that one party has private information, which brings about the so-called information rent.

Information asymmetry can cause pre- and post-contractual opportunistic behavior. Pre-contractual or ex-ante opportunistic behavior is also known as adverse selection (Akerlof, 1970). It shows up when one party in a potential transaction owns private information about something that can cause damage to the other party in the course of contract implementation. Post-contractual or ex-post opportunistic behavior is known as the moral hazard. It shows up when one of the contractual parties, because of its own benefit, does not undertake the agreed activities and the other party in the transaction cannot control the contract implementation in its entirety. If we observe participation in strategic outsourcing as an information sharing or exchange, it can imply the chance of both the moral hazard and adverse selection.

Cooperation needs to include sufficiently shared, common (public) information, making the platform for cooperation able to be initiated in the first place. In the case of cooperative participation, every participant will make available all required private information. Some participants may behave in an opportunistic way and disclose less private information than the others do; they may not own the information, or they may be only fictitious team members. They may also tend to hide their private information because they expect to attain some information rent.

An important learning objective is to prevent the outsourcing partner from possible opportunistic behavior. In business relationships, it is impossible to foresee every relevant possibility or incident that could happen during a relationship. It is reasonable to be prepared for possible opportunistic behavior. This does not mean that participants in outsourcing have completely different goals, but rather that their interests in some circumstances may be contradictory. Because of information asymmetry and the possible worst-case scenario of the outsourcing contract being a failure, one must admit not only the possible opportunistic behavior of participants, but also any unintentional harmful actions arising from bounded rationality. Therefore, some safeguards to prevent the outsourcing partner from acting opportunistically have to be established in advance (Rebernik & Bradač, 2006).

6. Managing tacit knowledge in strategic outsourcing relationships

The sub-consciousness of tacit knowledge and the difficulty of expressing it are commonly found as the main problems in tacit knowledge diffusion. It is not only that we have difficulty expressing and articulating what we know; we may not even be conscious of what we know or how tacit knowledge connects to our explicit knowledge. In this section we present some of the most influential elements that effective management of tacit knowledge in strategic outsourcing relationship has to overcome.

The most important elements of managing tacit knowledge in strategic outsourcing relationship are:

1. time for internalization of tacit knowledge;
2. powerlessness;
3. emotional commitment and deep personal involvement;
4. procedural justice in decision making;
5. effective communication and common culture development;
6. distance vs. personal contacts; and
7. an appropriate rewards system.

By successfully managing these elements, partners in a strategic outsourcing relationship create the platform for the disclosure of tacit knowledge and can jointly create a common knowledge thesaurus that can be shared. A conceptual framework of managing tacit knowledge in strategic outsourcing relationships to create and share the thesaurus and achieve sustainable outsourcing partnership is provided in Figure 3.

The consumption of time that the internalization of tacit knowledge requires is the first element to be considered in the sharing process. In today's business world, time is a scarce resource, and the internalization of new experiences or knowledge is a process over time (Halding-Herrgard, 2000, p. 361). The dimension of time is attributed to personal tacit knowledge as well as to more organizational forms. In the strategic outsourcing relationship parties face time-consuming constraints regarding the reflection of gained experiences. For both parties, the time allotted for the introduction of such experiences is often insufficient. The rapid rate of change in today's business environment calls for continual learning as well as unlearning. However, few organizations reserve sufficient time for these processes to jointly create a common knowledge.

We should also point out the problem of powerlessness. Knowledge is a basis for power and respect, and people are often hesitant to share knowledge lest their power decreases. Moreover, sharing knowledge requires that time be taken away from other responsibilities that have a higher priority. People are hesitant not only to share what they have, but also to use the knowledge of others. This has been referred to as the "not invented here" syndrome.

Perhaps, the most important step toward harnessing the tacit knowledge of individuals and teams is to allow it to flow from the pull of emotional commitment and deep personal involvement (Glynn, 1996, as cited in Mascitelli, 2000, p. 185). Therefore, the challenge for managers is to inspire, guide, excite, encourage, and shape without overwhelmingly imposing arbitrary structures that might destroy the fragile essence that has to be built and nurtured in strategic outsourcing relationship.

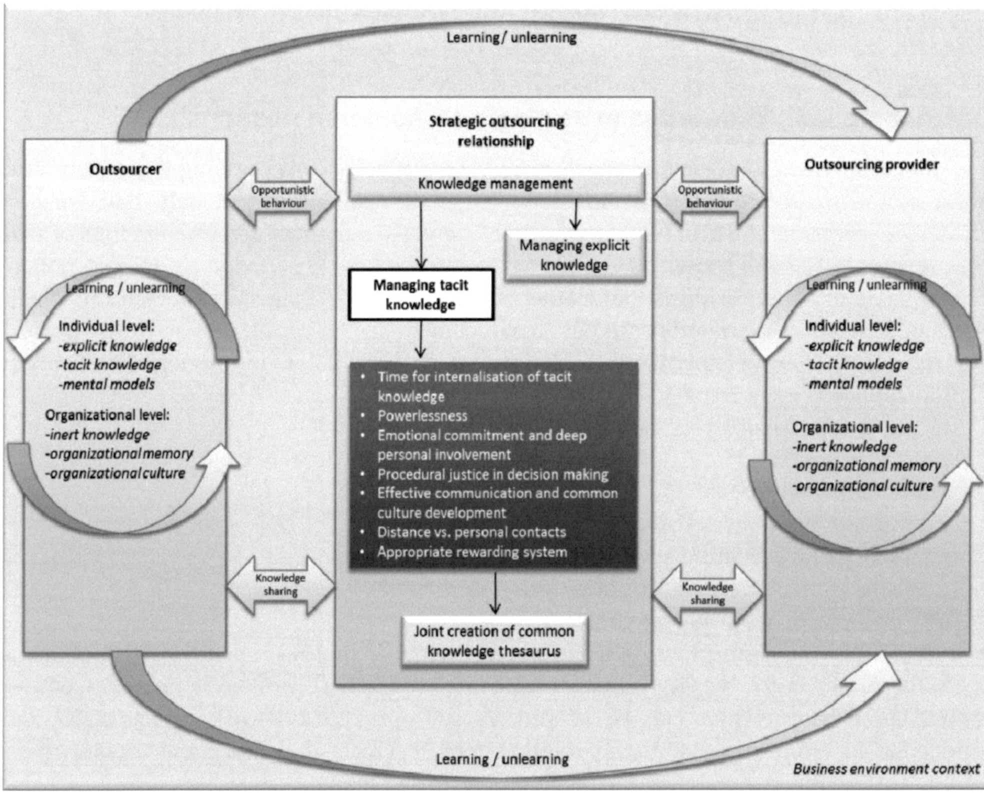

Fig. 3. Conceptual model to manage tacit knowledge in strategic outsourcing relationship

For example, managers can foster the genuine commitment of design team members on three different levels (Mascitelli, 2000, p. 187) by:

1. crafting a "culture of innovation" for the company as a whole;
2. establishing a strong sense of group identity, importance, and purpose among project team members; and
3. creating a generative environment for knowledge sharing, in which learning—as well as unlearning—occurs.

Another element for encouraging knowledge sharing is procedural justice in decision making. Research (Lubit, 2001, p. 175) has shown that, when managers feel strategic decision-making processes are fair, they tend to cooperate voluntarily. Procedural justice has three aspects: engagement, explanation, and clarity. When these three aspects of procedural justice are fulfilled, company employees are most likely to both share their ideas and carry out decisions that are made.

Effective knowledge management includes dealing with the defensive mechanisms that impede communication. Common defensive mechanisms include avoiding the discussion of important issues, ambiguous messages, and distorted information. Avoiding these phenomena is critical for developing a culture that values openness, tolerates failures, encourages questioning of the way in which things are conducted, and permits workers to challenge their superiors (Lubit, 2001, p. 175). The limited efficacy of most knowledge management efforts has come about because they have overwhelmingly focused on creating electronic means to capture and store information and improve communication. Far more attention needs to be given to the task of convincing people to effectively use the information system (Lubit, 2001, p. 173).

Further constraints in managing tacit knowledge in the strategic outsourcing relationship stem from the distance. Social interaction is often seen as a necessity for the diffusion of tacit knowledge. As such, the globalization, diversification, and virtualization of business that obstruct face-to-face interaction are a threat to tacit knowledge diffusion. Tacit-to-tacit exchanges are greatly enhanced through close personal contact, which is why physical co-location and face-to-face interaction can be important catalysts for innovation (Nonaka & Takeuchi, 1995; Holtshouse, 1998; Mascitelli, 2000, p. 193). Modern ways of doing business that have become completely intertwined with global and outsourcing networks do not improve the conditions for the exchange of tacit knowledge. In the "flat world" (Friedman, 2007) with overnight global deliveries, there is no time for sharing tacit knowledge. This is contrary to the popular notion that information technology can eliminate barriers to knowledge exchanges across oceans and time zones. However, if we accept the concept that tacit knowledge is fundamentally based on bodily experiences and emotional involvement, it is hard to imagine that something so personal can be digitized and downloaded. This is not to say that groupware and intranets are not essential tools for strategic outsourcing; their effectiveness in the sharing of explicit knowledge is undeniable. Rather, we are suggesting that simple steps can be taken to achieve important results in this regard. The frequent use of brief "stand-up meetings" for example, can help ensure continuous interaction among team members and encourage socialization and collaboration in outsourcing relationship.

The authors of the book *Enabling Knowledge Creation* (Von Krogh et al., 2000) go even further in their discussion about effective knowledge creation within an organization. They argue that groups of people working together are more than just teams; they are micro-communities of knowledge. This is an important distinction because "larger communities of knowledge can share certain practices, routines and languages, but for new tacit knowledge to emerge through socialization, the group must be small" (Von Krogh et al., 2000, p. 162). These teams are in a better position not only to create competitive position-enhancing knowledge, but also to communicate and integrate this knowledge back into their own areas and across the organization. One major challenge is that these micro-communities are typically not stable or perpetual. Unfortunately, through the dissolution of such micro-communities, most tacit knowledge gained and developed by them is lost. This knowledge can be retained only through the interactions that exist within the micro-community itself, not through documents or manuals (Allred, 2001, p. 162).

Finally, the implementation of new knowledge and best practices must be measured and rewarded, supported by the culture and recognized by promotion decisions. Without attention to the implementation of knowledge, people are likely to learn information, but then fail to change their behavior in beneficial ways.

In the strategic outsourcing relationship, the nature of the relationship is based on knowledge sharing; participants take a more active role and assume more responsibility and risks in developing the relationship. The successful strategic outsourcing relationship depends on forging strong links among the management, system, and process functions that lead the organization to cooperate. The collaborative relationship is closer and broader with more teams working together on a wide range of functions; as a result, the contract is typically longer. Managing an effective strategic outsourcing relationship requires commitment from all included parties. The success of the relationship depends on cooperation among participants, who must share their business information and knowledge; otherwise, cooperation is not possible. In this process bounded rationality, information asymmetry and opportunistic behavior manifest. Viewing cooperation as information sharing implies the possibility of both the moral hazard and adverse selection. As we have already underscored, cooperation needs private information and a requisite minimum of shared, common, public information, making the platform establish cooperation. In the case of cooperative participation, every participant will also make his or her private information available. There is always a possibility that some participants may behave in an opportunistic way and put less private information on the table than others, they may not own it, pretend to be team members, or tend to hide their private information because they expect to benefit from it later in the process.

As in strategic outsourcing, the ownership of intangible assets of cooperating companies can be challenging to define; thus, it is important that cooperating parties "contractually specify who will have control over each dimension of each asset in each particular future contingency" (Grossman & Hart, 1986, p. 716). A theory of the firm provides a conceptual background for understanding the strategic outsourcing relationship. A successful relationship requires that the outsourcer and the provider disclose all information to ensure mutual benefits. To make the relationship efficacious, all parties need to exchange all relevant information. A provider is not only a performer of services, but also a partner who is included in the joint development of processes and products in both companies.

7. Conclusions

Over the years traditional outsourcing has evolved into long-term problem-solving strategic outsourcing focused on changes in business processes, productivity improvements, technology, and innovation. Instead of delegating simple routine tasks aimed at cost-effectiveness, today's outsourcing is concentrated on long-term cooperation between companies, developing it into business partnerships. The specialized skills and knowledge of outsourcing partners that would otherwise be very costly and almost impossible to obtain within a single company can be shared and exploited. Two main problems appear in such partnerships: the tacit dimension of knowledge in each company and the possibility that outsourcing partners will behave opportunistically. For a sustainable outsourcing relationship, these issues must be managed effectively.

The most important element of the strategic outsourcing relationship is knowledge management as both parties must share their knowledge to jointly create and exploit a common knowledge thesaurus. As any knowledge base consists of tacit and explicit knowledge and the explicit knowledge is relatively easy to share, special attention must be paid to tacit knowledge. The main prerequisite for sharing tacit knowledge is to make it clear to the partner what can be done by investing enough time for the internalization of tacit knowledge, taking care of powerlessness, appreciating emotional commitment and deepening personal involvement, ensuring procedural justice in decision making, establishing effective communication and common culture development, cultivating personal contacts despite the distances, and establishing an appropriate rewards system.

Participants involved in outsourcing activities not only learn from each other, but they also need to unlearn obsolete knowledge and skills contained in procedures, routines, and ways of doing business from the pre-outsourcing period. Sharing tacit knowledge is a demanding task, but its unlearning is far more difficult. In the era of ever-increasing globalization and transcontinental outsourcing, the management of knowledge—especially its tacit dimension—is becoming one of the key drivers of competitiveness. To overcome the perpetual elusiveness of tacit knowledge, we presented a conceptual model that could help manage the outsourcing relationships and contribute to the creation of a common knowledge thesaurus for outsourcing partners. In any relationship where information asymmetry exists, opportunistic behavior can arise. Policy makers and strategy developers should pay attention to such a possibility; otherwise, no sustainable relationship can be established among outsourcing partners.

Investigating strategic outsourcing in light of managing tacit knowledge raises many issues that future research should examine, especially in the area of opportunistic behavior in the outsourcing relationship and the creation of appropriate policy measures and strategic moves to prevent such behavior. The unlearning is another field in which appropriate models for immediate use in business practice still have to be developed. There is also a lack of empirical research on tacit knowledge, which could prove a number of findings and theoretical constructions that many authors have already developed.

8. References

Akerlof, G. A. (1970). The Market for 'Lemons': Quality Uncertainty and the Market Mechanism. *The Quarterly Journal of Economics*, Vol.84, No.3, pp. 488-500, ISSN 0033-5533

Alexander, M. & Young, D. (1996). Strategic Outsourcing. *Long Range Planning*, Vol.29, No.1, pp. 116-119, ISSN 0024-6301

Allred, B. (2001). Enabling Knowledge Creation: How to Unlock the Mystery of Tacit Knowledge and Release the Power of Innovation. *The Academy of Management Executive*, Vol.15, No.1, (February), pp. 161–162, ISSN 1079-5545

Andersen, P. H.; Christensen, P. R.; Damgaard, T. & Munksgaard, K. B. (2003). Internationalization of Sourcing and Knowledge Development: An Organizational Routine Perspective. Paper presented at *LOK Research Conference*, (December 1-2, 2003), 13.8.2011, Available from http://www.lok.cbs.dk/images/publ/PHA%20og%20PRC%20og%20TD%20KBM.pdf

Argyris, C. & Schon, D. A. (1978). *Organizational Learning: A Theory of Action Perspective*. Addison-Wesley Publishing Company, ISBN: 0-201-00174-8, Massachusetts

Argyris, C. (2004). *On Organizational Learning* (2nd ed. reprinted), Blackwell, ISBN 0-631-21308-2, Malden, US

Barney, J. B. & Ouchi, W. G. (1986). Learning from Organizational Economics, In: *Organizational Economics*, J. B. Barney & W. G. Ouchi (Eds.), pp. 423-445, Jossey-Bass, ISBN 978-1555420154, San Francisco

Barrett, F. J.; Thoman, G. F. & Hocevar, S. P. (1995). The Central Role of Discourse in Large-Scale Change: A Social Construction Perspective. *Journal of Applied Behavioral Science*, Vol.31, No.3, pp. 352-373, ISSN 0021-8863

Becker, K. (2006). Individual and Organisational Unlearning: Directions for Future Research. *International Journal of Organisational Behaviour*, Vol.10, No.4, pp. 659-670, ISSN 1440-5377

Capgemini. (2004). *Adapting to Change: Strategic Change Enabled through Transformational Outsourcing*, 3.10.2006, Available from http://www.capgemini.com

Coase, R. H. (1937). The Nature of the Firm. *Economica*, Vol.4, pp. 386-405, ISSN 0013-0427

Cohen, W. M. & Levinthal, D. A. (1990). Absorptive Capacity: A New Perspective on Learning and Innovation. *Administrative Science Quarterly*, Vol.35, No.1, ISSN 0001-8392

Commons, J. R. (1931). Institutional Economics. *American Economic Review*, No.21, pp. 648-657, ISSN 0002-8282

Cummings, J. (2003). *Knowledge Sharing: A Review of the Literature*, The World Bank, Washington, US, 15.08.2011, Available from http://lnweb90.worldbank.org/oed/oeddoclib.nsf/docunidviewforjavasearch/d9e389e7414be9de85256dc600572ca0/$file/knowledge_eval_literature_review.pdf

Davenport, T. H. (1993). *Process Innovation: Reengineering Work through Information Technology*, Harvard Business School Press, ISBN 0875843662, Boston, MA

Durrance, B. (1998). Some Explicit Thoughts on Tacit Learning. *Training and Development*, Vol.52, No.12, pp. 24-29, ISSN 1055-9760

Easterby-Smith, M. & Lyles M. A. (Eds.) (2005). *The Blackwell Handbook of Organizational Learning and Knowledge Management* (1st paperback), Blackwell, ISBN 978-1405133043, Malden, US

Embleton P. R. & Wright, P. C. (1998). A Practical Guide to Successful Outsourcing. *Empowerment in Organisations*, Vol.6, No.3, pp. 94–106, ISSN 0968-4891

Espino-Rodrıguez, T. F. & Padron-Robaina, V. (2004). Outsourcing and its Impact on Operational Objectives and Performance: A Study of Hotels in the Canary Islands. *International Journal of Hospitality Management*, Vol.23, pp. 287-306, ISSN 0278-4319

Friedman, T. (2007). *The World is Flat: A Brief History of the Twenty-First Century*. Picador, ISBN-978-0374292881, New York

Glynn, M. A. (1996). Innovative Genius: A Framework for Relating Individual and Organizational Intelligences to Innovation. *Academy of Management Review*, Vol.21, pp. 1081–1111, ISSN 0363-7425

Greaver, M. (1999). *Strategic Outsourcing: A Structured Approach to Outsourcing Decisions and Initiatives*, American Management Association, ISBN 0-8144-0434-0, US

Grossman, S. & Hart, O. (1986). The Costs and Benefits of Ownership: A Theory of Vertical and Lateral Integration. *Journal of Political Economy*, Vol.94, No.4, pp. 691-719, ISSN 0022-3808

Haldin-Herrgard, T. (2000). Difficulties in Diffusion of Tacit Knowledge in Organizations. *Journal of Intellectual Capital*, Vol.1, No.4, pp. 357-365, ISSN 1469-1930

Hedberg, B. (1981). How Organizations Learn and Unlearn, In: *Handbook of Organizational Design* (Volume 1), P. Nystrom & W. Starbuck (Eds.), pp. 3-27, Oxford University Press, ISBN 978-0-19-827241-0, London, UK

Holan de, P.; Phillips N. & Lawrence T. (2004). Managing Organizational Forgetting. *MIT Sloan Management Review*, Vol.45, pp. 45-51, ISSN 1532-9194

Holtshouse, D. (1998). Knowledge Research Issues. *California Management Review*, Vol.40, No.3, pp. 277-280, ISSN 0008-1256

Howells, J. (1996). Tacit Knowledge, Innovation and Technology Transfer. *Technology Analysis & Strategic Management*, Vol.8, No.2, pp. 91-106, ISSN 0953-7325

Huber, G. P. (1991). Organizational Learning: The Contributing Processes and the Literatures. *Organization Science*, (February), pp. 88-115, ISSN 1047-7039

Karen M. G. & Black R. T. (2004). Agency Risks in Outsourcing Corporate Real Estate Functions. *Journal of Real Estate Research*, Vol.26, No.2, pp. 137-160, ISSN 0896-5803

Kim, D. H. (1993). The Link between Individual and Organizational Learning. *Sloan Management Review*, Vol.35, No.1, pp. 37-50, ISSN 0019-848X

Knowles, H. P. & Saxberg, B. O. (1988). Organizational Leadership of Planned and Unplanned Change: A Systems Approach to Organizational Viability. *Futures*, Vol.20, pp. 252-265, ISSN 0748-1578

Levitt, B. & March, J. G. (1988). Organizational Learning. *Annual Review of Sociology*, Vol.14, pp. 319-340, ISSN 0360-0572

Linder, J. (2004). Outsourcing as a Strategy for Driving Transformation. *Strategy & Leadership*, Vol.32, No.6, pp. 26-31, ISSN 1087-8572

Linder, J.; Cole, I. M. & Jacobson, L. A. (2002). Business Transformation through Outsourcing. *Strategy & Leadership*, Vol.30, No.4, pp. 23-28, ISSN 1087-8572

Lubit, R. (2001). The Keys to Sustainable Competitive Advantage: Tacit Knowledge and Knowledge Management. *Organizational Dynamics*, Vol.29, No.3, pp. 164-178, ISSN 0090- 2616

Lynn, G. S.; Morone, J. G. & Paulsen, A. S. (1996). Marketing and Discontinuous Innovation: The Probe and Learn Process, *California Management Review*, Vol.38, pp. 8-37, ISSN 0008-1256

MacDonald, S. (1995). (1995). Learning to Change: An Information Perspective on Learning in the Organization. *Organization Science*, Vol.6, pp. 557-568, ISSN 1047-7039

Markoczy, L. (1994). Modes of Organizational Learning: Institutional Change and Hungarian Joint Ventures. *International Studies of Management & Organization*, Vol.24, No.4, pp. 5-31, ISSN 0020-8825

Mascitelli, R. (2000). From Experience: Harnessing Tacit Knowledge to Achieve Breakthrough Innovation. *Journal of Product Innovation Management*, Vol.17, No.3, pp. 179-193, ISSN 0737-6782

Meso, P. & Smith, R. (2000). A Resource-Based View of Organizational Knowledge Management System. *Journal of Knowledge Management*, Vol.4, No.3, pp. 224-234, ISSN 1367-3270

Mezirow, J. (2000). Learning to Think Like an Adult: Core Concepts of Adult Learning Theory, In: *Learning as Transformation: Critical Perspectives on a Theory in Progress*, J. Mezirow (Ed.), pp. 3-33, Jossey-Bass, ISBN: 978-0-7879-4845-0, San Francisco

Miller, D. (1996). Configurations Revisited. *Strategic Management Journal*, Vol.17, pp. 505-512, ISSN 0143-2095

Mol, M. J. (2007). *Outsourcing: Design, Process and Performance*, Cambridge University Press, ISBN 978-0521682787, Cambridge

Mulej, M., et al. (2000). *Dialektična in druge mehkosistemske teorije (podlaga za celovitost in uspeh managementa)*, University of Maribor, Faculty of Economics and Business, ISBN 961-6354-01-9, Maribor

Newell, S.; Robertson, M. J.; Scarbrough, H. & Swan, J. A. (2002). *Managing Knowledge Work*, Palgrave MacMillan, ISBN 978-0333962992, London

Nonaka, I. & Takeuchi, H. (1995). *The Knowledge Creating Company: How Japanese Companies Create the Dynamics of Innovation*, Oxford University Press, ISBN 10-0195092694, New York

Paoli, M. & Principe, A. (2003). Memory of the Organization and Memories within the Organization. *Journal of Management & Governance*, Vol.7, No.2, pp. 145, ISSN 1385-3457

Polanyi, M. (1958). *Personal Knowledge: Towards a Post-Critical Philosophy*, Routledge & Kegan Paul, ISBN 0-203-044215-6, London

Polanyi, M. (1966). *The Tacit Dimension*, Doubleday & Co., 1966, Reprinted Peter Smith, 1983, ISBN 0844659991, Gloucester, Massachusetts

Power, M. J.; Desouza, K. & Bonifazi, C. (2006). *The Outsourcing Handbook*, Kogan Page, ISBN 978-0749444303, London

Rebernik, M. & Bradač, B. (2006). Cooperation and Opportunistic Behaviour in Transformational Outsourcing. *Kybernetes*, Vol.35, Issue7/8, pp. 1005-1013, ISSN 0368-492X

Rebernik, M. & Bradač, B. (2009). The Role of Adaptation and Learning of Entrepreneurs in Managing Outsourcing Relationships, In: *The Management of Small and Medium Enterprises*, M. Fink & S. Kraus (Eds.), pp. 282-298, Routledge, ISBN 978-0-415-46724-7, New York

Rebernik, M. & Mulej, M. (1999). On Cooperative and Effective Participation, *Problems of Participation and Connection: Book of Abstracts Edited by Gerard de Zeuuw*, pp. 44-46, Center for Innovation and Cooperative Technology, Amsterdam, April 1999

Rebernik, M. & Širec, K. (2007). Fostering Innovation by Unlearning Tacit Knowledge. *Kybernetes*, Vol.36, No.3/4, pp. 406-419, ISSN 0368-492X

Rebernik, M. (1997). Beyond Markets, Hierarchies and Ownership Mania in Transitional Countries. *Systems Research and Behavioural Science,* Vol.14, No.3, pp. 83-194, ISSN 1099-1743

Reuvid, J. & Hinks, J. (2001). *Managing Business Support Services: Strategies for Outsourcing and Facilities Management* (2nd edition), Kogan Page, ISBN 978-0749439002, United Kingdom

Roy, P. & Roy, P. (2002). Tacit Knowledge Management in Organizations: A Move towards Strategic Internal Communications Systems. *Journal of American Academy of Business*, Vol.2, No.1, pp. 28-32, ISSN 1540-1200

Schmidt, T. (2005). What Determines Absorptive Capacity?, In: *CEA 39th Annual Meetings*, 14.8.2011, Available from http://economics.ca/2005/papers/0149.pdf

Sharpe, M. (1997). Outsourcing, Organizational Competitiveness, and Work. *Journal of Labor Research*, Vol.18, pp. 535-549, ISSN 0195-3613

Simon, H. (1991). Bounded Rationality and Organizational Learning. *Organization Science*, Vol.2, No.1, pp. 125-134, ISSN 1047-7039

Stein, E. (1995). Organizational Memory: Review of Concepts and Recommendations for Management. *International Journal of Information Management*, Vol.15, No.2, pp. 17-32, ISSN 0268-4012

Stenmark, D. (2001). Leveraging Tacit Organizational Knowledge. *Journal of Management Information Systems*, Vol.17, No.3, pp. 9-24, ISSN 0742-1222

Stewart, T. A. (1997). *Intellectual Capital: The New Wealth of Organizations*, Doubleday, ISBN 0-38-548228-0, London

Svelby, K. E. (1997). *The New Organizational Wealth: Managing & Measuring Knowledge-Based Assets*, Berrett-Koehler Publisher, ISBN 1-57675-014-0, San Francisco, CA

Tominc, P. & Rebernik, M. (2007). Growth Aspirations and Cultural Support for Entrepreneurship: A Comparison of Three Post-Socialist Countries. *Small Business Economics*, Vol.28, No.2/3, pp. 239-255, ISSN 0921-898X

Von Krogh, E.; Ichijo, K. & Nonaka, I. (2000), *Enabling Knowledge Creation: How to Unlock the Mystery of Tacit Knowledge and release the Power of Innovation*, Oxford University Press, ISBN 0-19-512616-5, New York

Webster's Dictionary. (1999). *Webster's II New College Dictionary*, Houghton Mifflin, ISBN 0395962145, Boston and New York

Williamson, O. E. (1983). *Markets and Hierarchies, Analyses and Antitrust Implications*, The Free Press, ISBN 978-0029347805, New York

Zahra, S. & George, G. (2002). Absorptive Capacity: A Review, Reconceptualization and Extension. *Academy of Management Review*, Vol.27, No.2, pp. 185-203, ISSN 0363-7425

7

Assessment of Operational Experience as Strategy for Knowledge Acquisition and Learning in Organizations

Pedro Solana González and Daniel Pérez González
University of Cantabria
Spain

1. Introduction

In the current economic environment characterized by increasing competition and the pursuit of excellence, companies need to increase the efficiency of their production processes and management. In this sense, the policy of continuous improvement in organizations must be based on knowledge acquisition according to the experience of the company in the development of their activities and learning through the analysis of the operational experience. In recent literature several authors have found evidence of how the communications about observations, experiences and incidents are an important requisite for learning (Edmondson 1996; Van Dyck et al., 2005; Solana and Pérez, 2011). Even incidents without severe consequences also have considerable learning potential (Homsma et al., 2009).

Researchers have recognized the significance of organizational learning and its related concepts like the process of improving actions through better knowledge and understanding (Fiol and Lyles, 1985); the collective ability of a group to continuously expand its capacity to create the future in terms of personal mastery, shared vision, systems thinking, and team learning (Senge, 1990), identifying four necessary components: knowledge acquisition, information distribution, information interpretation and organizational memory (Huber, 1991); a structured and systematic method applied by an organization to motivate employees to learn (Dodgson, 1993). A gradual learning process by which staff learns through experiences and cooperate with other colleagues (Marchand et al., 2000).

The analysis of operating experience in organizations, whether it is a requirement that comes from external bodies, as if it is a policy promoted internally to the organization, is a relevant strategy of acquiring knowledge and learning for companies (Pérez and Solana, 2011). This strategy has proven effective in industries such as nuclear, to maintain a high level of efficiency and contribute to the improvement of processes and activities in such organizations, being able to apply this methodology in other companies and activity sectors.

The implementation of organizational learning programs requires that the managerial attention should create opportunities for the work staff to engage in communication about incidents in order to allow for the development of shared knowledge about error incidents. Opportunities for employees to interact and discuss incidents openly may promote organizational learning (Homsma et al., 2009).

In this chapter we will explain how companies can develop organizational learning programs based on an adequate strategy of acquiring knowledge through the analysis of the experiences of its activity, a strategy which at the same time is based on the communication processes, sharing of knowledge, workflow management and collaboration. This work presents a model of knowledge acquisition and organizational learning that can serve as reference and be applied in different companies to improve their operational and management processes. The model is based on processes developed by the nuclear industry and is the result of the strict regulation and controls of its activity.
Following the chapter deepens first on the acquisition of knowledge in organizations and their relationship to organizational learning, for which a review of literature on the subject is realized by taking as a focus the experience based learning. Secondly, it discusses the need to establish formal procedures in organizations of knowledge acquisition in order to develop organizational learning, procedures that can be implemented with the help of techniques to design and specify complex workflow based on collaboration and sharing of knowledge. In this regard, it is presented workflow and Petri nets as a suitable technique for the specification of workflow processes with these characteristics. Then it is developed a methodology that enables organizations to implement a program of acquiring knowledge based on the phases of communication of experiences, event analysis, evaluation and implementation of improvement actions. This methodology of work it is formally specified as a learning model based on operating experience of the organization, a model that has been successfully implemented in the nuclear industry and can be applied to other companies. Finally, we present the conclusions and future lines of work.

2. Review of literature

In the next paragraph we present a review of the literature for the two disciplines that are studied in this chapter, knowledge management and organizational learning, and discuss the various theories and approaches on how organizations acquire knowledge and its relationship with organizational learning.

2.1 Knowledge management

The information is the result of the interpretation of data resulting from the observation (Buckland, 1991), however the next cognitive level, knowledge, represents a contribution of value-added to information: theoretical and practical understanding of a subject, synthesis process in which the information is compared to another and combined to establish meaningful relationships, applied information or the result of adding the experience to information. In addition, the various representations of knowledge (observations, rules, procedures, guidelines) have to be interpreted by the people, putting knowledge in context to apply it when necessary to act in a certain situation (Lueg, 2002). However, the acquisition and interpretation of knowledge in organizations is a complex matter, in so far as it is not presented as a monolithic image, but as an heterogeneous and dynamic system of different knowledge (Bonifacio et al., 2000) that are dynamically created in time (Newell, 1982).
Although there is no unique definition of Knowledge Management (KM) universally accepted, it should be noted some especially interesting. Lueg (2002) refers to KM as the discipline that deals with the collection and dissemination of knowledge for the benefit of an organization and the people who make and Swan et al. (1999) defines it as any process or

practice of creating, acquiring, sharing and use of knowledge to improve learning and performance of organizations.

Some authors relate the knowledge management with learning in organizations (Nonaka and Johansson, 1985; Huber, 1991; Quinn, 1992), in this sense Dodgson, (1993) links the Organizational Learning (OL) with the ways in which companies build, increase and organize the knowledge and, Sánchez and Heene, (1997) associate it with the processes of creating new knowledge in the bosom of individuals and groups within a company, and processes to effectively enhance the knowledge within the organization. Organizational learning is linked to the processes through which the organization creates knowledge or expands the knowledge base that has, line in which are also located the contributions of Nonaka, who considers knowledge creation as the central core of organizational learning (Nonaka and Takeuchi, 1995; Nonaka and Ichijo, 1997; Nonaka, et al., 1998).

Other authors that relate KM in the organization with the concept of organizational learning make it from different points of view: Amponsem (1991) associates organizational learning to the process through which individual knowledge becomes in knowledge of the entire organization; Marengo (1991) considers organizational learning as the process of generating new organizational competencies that involve knowledge creation in turn; Andreu and Ciborra (1994), Revilla (1995) and Andreu and Sieber (1998) associate organizational learning with the process of problem solving that enables to expand the knowledge base of the organization through the incorporation of the generated knowledge.

From the management point of view, the inclusion of the organizations into the knowledge economy requires the reorganization that allows them to integrate the knowledge in their conventional operation in order to convert it in a true strategic active (González et al., 2009). The recent literature shows the explanatory power of knowledge management on the organizational performance (Pedraja et al., 2009) what makes knowledge management a fundamental discipline for business competitiveness. Organizational effectiveness requires achieve an effective integration of specialized knowledge (Grant, 1996) that together with the management of intangible assets are key factors for obtaining competitive advantages by organizations (Teece, 1998).

Finally, within the literature review, a series of recent works of special interest are included below, analysing various issues relating to knowledge management.

2.2 Organizational learning

The concept of OL is taking a significant rise in both the academic and business context, by contributing to the improvement of the understanding of organizations and their activities. However, organizational learning is faced with a relative lack of empirical works, and in particular of case studies, to try to induce theory from practice.

The organizational learning literature has taken mainly two perspectives (Durand et al. 1996; Von Krogh, 1998; Easterby-Smith et al. 1998; Gherardi, 1999): the cognitive (or perceptual) and the social (or constructive). Spender (1996 a), Backler (1995), Cook and Brown (1999) also identify two approaches about the nature of knowledge; which emphasized that the knowledge is or has and the one who believes that knowledge is created, i.e. it is a process. These perspectives and approaches are related, so two fundamental approaches can be considered: the cognitive-possession and the social process.

The cognitive perspective takes two orientations (Cook and Yanow, 1996); the first that focuses the learning of the organizations in the processes of learning of individuals and assumes that organizations can learn as they have the same or similar skills that the

Author	Objective of the study	Main result
Bueno et al. (2004)	Design a model for the analysis of the conceptual relationships between business processes and knowledge processes.	Knowledge processes explain the critical intangible resources and the essential capabilities for organisational achievement. Learning processes contribute to the improvement of business processes.
Kuan (2005)	Studies the KM in small and medium enterprises (SMEs)	Identify the critical success factors that can act as a list of items for SMEs to address when adopting KM.
Teresa et al. (2006)	Develop a strategic contingency model to identify the interrelationships among KM capability and innovation	KM capability could enhance organizational learning and knowledge integration; levels of organizational learning, knowledge integration, and KM capability have significant impact on a firm's innovation.
Moreno and Pelayo (2007)	Integrate in a model of internal knowledge management the human, technological and organizational focus.	The KM promotes organizational learning. The technological, human and organizational factors are enablers of organizational learning (model Thalec).
Chin and Siong (2009)	Explore KM performance measurement from the angle of KM process effectiveness	Significant interactions were found between KM success factors (business strategy, K audit, K map, KM team) and KM elements of strategies (technology, culture, leadership, measurement) with KM process effectiveness.
Krogh, Nonaka and Rechsteiner (2011)	Investigate the leadership in organizational knowledge creation	Develop a framework for leadership in organizational knowledge creation based on three layers: a core layer of local knowledge creation; a layer that provides the resources and context; and a structural layer that forms the overall frame and direction for knowledge creation.

Table 1. Review of recent literature on KM

individuals (Cyert and March, 1963; Daft and Weick, 1984; Levitt and March, 1988; Weick, 1991), while the second considers the organizational learning as the learning from individuals in organizational contexts (Simon, 1991; March and Olsen, 1976; Shrivastava, 1983). The organizational learning is perceived as something more than the sum of individual learning of its members, while emphasizing the key role of individuals and their learning (Huysman, 1999).

In the social perspective, learning has a relational character that takes on special importance the context and the dynamics of organizational change (Lave and Wenger, 1991; Brown and

Duguid, 1991; Blackler, 1993; Weick and Roberts, 1993; Weick and Westley, 1996; Cook and Yanow, 1996; Spender, 1996 b; Sánchez and Heene, 1997; Dixon, 1994; Gherardi and Nicolini, 2000), is not based on the individual but arises from social interactions and is acquired through participation in the daily practice of the organization. Focuses on the way in which people interpret or give meaning to their work experiences. The social perspective understands the knowledge as a process of construction or creation. In this sense, the activity theory of Vygotsky (1962) maintains that the knowledge is continuously evolving and considers that it is not something that people and organizations have but something they do, which is constantly built and developed.

On the other hand, Hendlund (1994) and Nonaka (1994) studied the interaction between individual and collective knowledge and how the individual knowledge contributes to the collective. In this sense, it is not necessary that the members of the organization learn what others know, but join and integrate their knowledge (Grant, 1996).

The literature of the organizational learning is also referred to the concept "learning organization" (Senge, 1990; Goh and Richards, 1997; Leonard, 1992; Ulrich et al., 1993) in reference to the organizations that have institutionalized processes of reflection and evaluation that allows them to acquire a new competence, learning to learn, and create shared knowledge. A learning organization is one that builds intentionally structures and strategies to maximize organizational learning (Dogson, 1993) and formalizes learning methods (Moreno and Pelayo, 2007).

The knowledge of an organization is continuously created through activities that are developed (Tsoukas, 1996) and the people for their participation in the same accumulate knowledge through experience (Nonaka, 1994). Learning is the process whereby knowledge is created through the transformation of experience (Kolb, 1984). However, these aspects while necessary, are not sufficient, since the organizational knowledge should be shared, it is conditioned by people can establish formal and informal relations and the need of an evaluation from the observation of the organization of itself (Von Krogh et al., 1994).

In this sense, the organizations which are willing to implement the management of knowledge, must be able to collect in a formal way the experience of the organization, which is ultimately determined by the interaction between people and their organizational structures, and between the organization and its environment (companies of the same sector of activity, customers and suppliers). The experiences that in an organization contribute to a greater extent to the acquisition of knowledge and organizational learning originate in the activity itself that this develops, materialized across their business processes, but also on the experiences and knowledge shared with other organizations (enterprises in the same sector), or that are acquired through the surveillance activities of competition.

3. Processes specification: Workflow and Petri nets

A business process can be defined as the set of activities and performances to be carried out in an integrated manner to achieve a more general organizational goal. These processes are usually performed within an organizational structure in which there are various functional roles and hierarchical relationships. A process can be developed entirely in a single business unit or can be applied to various and even to different organizations (inter-organizational processes) as the processes with customers and suppliers, or collaborative processes in which knowledge is shared between different organizations.

Business processes can involve formal or relatively informal interactions among participants. Some of the activities of the process can be automated, in which case it is the system the responsible for carry them out. Manual activities however, are outside the control of the system being made directly by people (WFMC-TC00-1011 Issue 3.0, 1999). The business processes of organizations, generally involve the development of complex workflows that are part of their daily activity.

A workflow refers to a process or work procedure (susceptible to be automated using informatics methods and systems) in which involves different knowledge (relational data, documents, experience) and the tasks performed by the participants according to a defined set of rules, to contribute to the achievement of a business objective (Hollingsworth, 1995).

The design of workflows requires develop specifications that describe an abstraction of the processes of the company. The workflow specification languages are used for this purpose to create workflow models that support the structure of the process activities (control flow) and the exchange of information (data flow) between such activities (Mentzas et al. 2001).

The classic model of representation allows to specify the workflow based on a set of activities (with a total or partial order) and its dependencies, and enables reference the objects are handled (resources, knowledge) and the actors involved in the process (people, according to their role, and the system that can automate some activities).

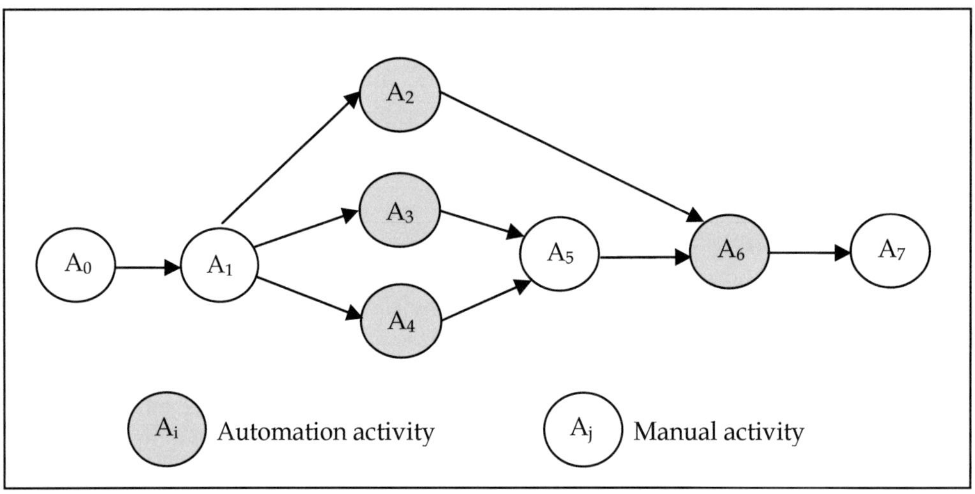

Fig. 1. Workflow model based on activities

This technique is suitable to model processes from a logical point of view, but is insufficient when you need to have a detailed specification when you want to automate such processes. The use of formal techniques that offer a greater capacity for analysis and verification of the process that is being designed help to overcome this limitation (Solana, 2006).

In general, systems are increasingly oriented towards the idea of process, which is leading to the development of collaborative environments that have ever greater capabilities to manage the knowledge of organizations.

3.1 Petri nets

In the literature on information systems have been proposed various techniques to model the process perspective. Some of these techniques are not formal in the sense that the diagrams used have not a defined formal semantics. This kind of techniques (Data Flow Diagram or Structured Analysis and Design Technique) but allow to design and discuss about processes, are not the most appropriate when it is trying to design complex workflow processes, because they are incomplete and subjective (Aalst, 2002).

However, Petri nets for its formal semantics are an effective tool for modeling and analyzing business processes of organizations, and its main features include: 1) provide a natural form of representation and a high expressiveness, 2) its graphical language allows to specify complex workflows according to the workflow primitives of Workflow Management Coalition[1] (WfMC), 3) the theory of Petri nets provides a powerful analysis tool to verify the correctness of the definition of workflow processes and 4) Petri nets can represent the states of a process as elements of "first class", in contrast to other modeling techniques that focus exclusively on the active parts of the process, on the activities.

In this chapter the Petri nets are used to formally specify the model of knowledge acquisition and organizational learning that is presented, which has interest as case of study, because it allows to contrast some of the theories and ideas developed by the different authors to which we have referred above.

3.2 Formalization of Petri nets

A Petri net is a directed graph that uses two different types of nodes, called places and transitions. The places are represented by circles (○) and the transitions as rectangles (□). The nodes are connected to each other through directed arcs (○ → □) and are not allowed connections between two nodes of the same type.

The formal definitions that constitute the basic theoretical framework of this technique and that we have considered convenient to collect are the following (Aalst, 1998):

Definition 1. (Petri net). A Petri net is a triple (P, T, F), where:

- P is a finite set of places.
- T is a finite set of transitions, such that ($P \cap T = \Phi$).
- $F \subseteq (P \times T) \cup (T \times P)$ is a set of arcs (flow relation).

The arcs are considered of weight one because in the context of workflow processes the places are achieved when certain conditions are fulfilled.

Definition 2. (Input place). A place p is called an input place of a transition t iff there exists a directed arc from p to t.

Definition 3. (Output place). The place p is called an output place of transition t iff there exists a directed arc from t to p.

Be the place p and the transition t, then:

- $\bullet t$ denote the set of input places for a transition t.
- $t\bullet$ is the set of output places for a transition t.
- $\bullet p$ denote the set of transitions sharing p as output place.

---

[1] Founded in May 1993 is a global organization of adopters, developers, consultants, analysts, as well as university and research groups engaged in workflow and Business Process Management (BPM). The WfMC creates and contributes to process related standards and interoperability of workflow management systems. http://www.wfmc.org.

- p• is the set of transitions sharing p as an input place.

Definition 4. (State of a Petri net). The state M of a Petri net is a distribution of tokens (●) over places. We will denote $n_1p_1 + n_2p_2 + n_3p_3 + \ldots + n_kp_k$, the state of a Petri net such that there are n_1 tokens in the place p_1, n_2 tokens in p_2, n_3 tokens in p_3 and so on n_k tokens in the place p_k. The number of tokens can change during the execution.

Transitions are the active components in a Petri net, change the state of the net according to the following firing rules:

1. A transition t is said to be enabled iff each input place p of t contains at least one token.
2. An enabled transition may fire. If a transition t fires, then t consumes one token from each input place p of t and produces one token in each output place p of t.

Given a Petri net (P, T, F) and a state M_1, we establish the following notations:

- $M_1 \rightarrow^{t} M_2$: transition t is enabled in state M_1 and firing t in M_1 results in state M_2.
- $M_1 \rightarrow M_2$: there is a transition t such that $M_1 \rightarrow^{t} M_2$.
- $M_1 \rightarrow^{\sigma} M_n$: the firing sequence σ = t1, t2…, tn-1 leads from state M_1 to state M_n, i.e., $M_1 \rightarrow^{t1} M_2 \rightarrow^{t2} \ldots \rightarrow^{tn-1} M_n$.

3.3 Workflow nets

The Petri nets that are applied to modeling of workflow processes are called workflow nets (WF-net), are based in network theory proposed by Carl Adam Petri at the beginning of sixties (Petri, 1962) and whose basic theoretical principles have just presented.

The workflow nets allow to define the workflow processes, modeling using graphical elements the process activities (transitions), the states (places) that can be found as a result of the development of such activities and the dynamics of the process. In a workflow net the transitions are the active parts of process, the places are the passive parts and the arcs between transitions and places represent relations of causality (Aalst, 2002).

The workflow nets let model different cases or instances of the process, as layers in the WF-net which are represented by tokens (●) on the network places. The overlapping of the different cases allow to view the execution status of the process and perform an analysis of its situation in a certain moment (eg. when a place has a large number of tokens, indicates that there is a bottleneck in that place).

The workflow nets can represent the routing or dynamic of transitions between the process places, for which are used routing constructors. The constructors AND-split, AND-join, OR-split and OR-join, allow to represent sequential models, conditional, parallel and iterative. It is also possible to represent under what conditions are triggered the execution of the activities, for which are used attributes or control variables.

The AND-split constructor allows to model that multiple activities are executed simultaneously. The AND-join constructor models the synchronization of two or more activities whose execution can be developed in parallel, so that the next activity does not start until they are completed. The OR-split constructor (it is a exclusive OR) models the case that for a given activity, as a result of compliance with certain conditions, begins a single subsequent activity. The OR-join constructor models the case in which a certain activity begins after the completion of one of the alternatives precedents activities, not being required the synchronization of these (WfMC-TC00-1011 Issue 3.0, 1999).

The difference between explicit OR and implicit OR is that in the latter case, the time of the election, which is normally done in terms of fulfillment of some condition, is made as late as possible.

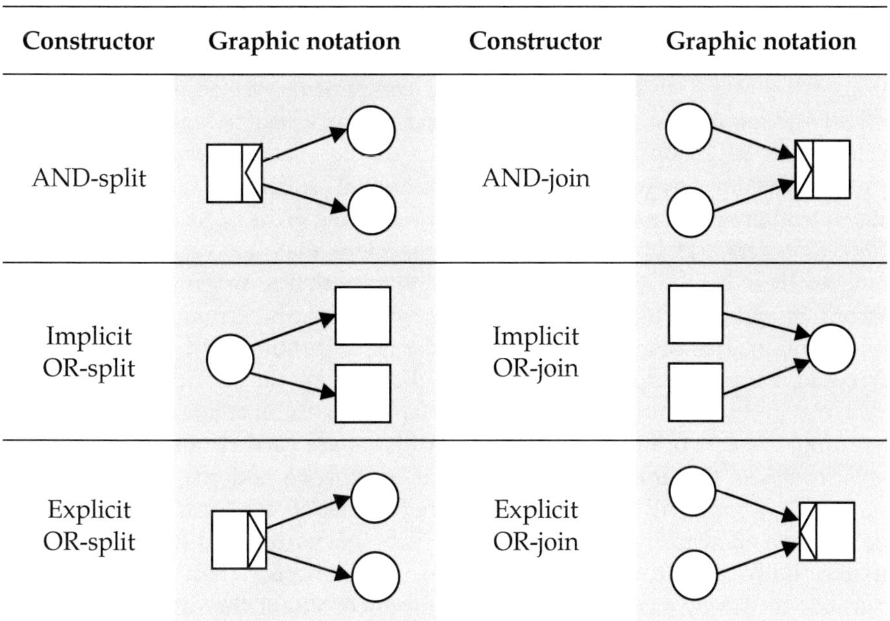

Source: Elaborated by the authors from Aalst (1998)

Fig. 2. Symbolic notation of constructors for workflow nets

4. Organizational knowledge and learning model

The next paragraph contains the empirical development of research, which has designed a model of knowledge acquisition based on analysis and evaluation of operational experience and has developed an organizational learning system that has been brought to practice successfully in Nuclenor, company that manages the operation of the nuclear power plant of Santa María de Garoña in Spain. Following are commented the background and organizational context in which the work has been developed, are characterized the organizational roles involved in the model and are described the activities of the process of analysis of operational experience and acquisition of knowledge, to finalize presenting learning model developed using workflow nets as a technique of specification.

4.1 Background and organizational context

Currently the development of policies of continuous improvement in the organizations can be achieved through the implementation of organizational learning processes and the evaluation of operational experience, according to the phases of detection, communication, evaluation and, correction and improvement of findings, events or incidents reported.

Following is presented a methodology for the acquisition of knowledge and learning based on experience, this methodology is been used to improve the efficiency in Nuclear Power Plants, which for the strict and rigorous control that they are subjected, can provide the basis for other industries.

The Nuclear Security Council in Spain carried out periodically a review of the security of Nuclear Power Plants, through the evaluation of the operational experience required to the holders of energy production plants. It must demonstrate that the power plants maintain a high level of efficiency and operational safety, through an adequate system of acquiring knowledge from the experience, so that the existence or the development of potentially dangerous states of the structures, systems and components will be detected and analyzed exhaustively taking measures and corrective and improvement actions which will be more suitable (GS-1.10/08, 2008).

An event is defined as any unwanted and unintentional sequence of occurrences that results or could potentially give rise to consequences in different areas of the organization as plant operation or safety, (PCN-A-039, 2010). While there may be various types of events according to their degree of importance and characteristics, much of the events can be categorized as minor incidents, that is, unexpected results, errors or incidences in the activity, conditions that detects any service of the organization, which is considered to have had or could have an impact on security, reliability of the installation, organizational efficiency, risk and the health of people, industrial plant equipment or environment.

The detection, correction and prevention of incidents are carried out mainly through two different processes: the analysis of operational experience and the probabilistic security analysis which works with historical data. In this paper we focus on the first process because it works on abnormal or unexpected events that correspond to situations that occur during the daily activity in the industrial installations. These events are unique opportunities to detect, analyze and correct imperfections of the organizational practices and human error.

The implementation of an organizational learning process of these characteristics, based on the analysis of the operational experience, requires to define the set of activities to follow in a methodological form, to carry out the evaluation of the events occurred in the organization, since these are detected until the actions to correct them are executed: record of the event, communication, evaluation and definition of actions to take, execution of these and close of the event. The aim of this process is to ensure that the appropriate actions are taken to increase the security and reliability of the industrial plant, and the efficiency in the management of the organization, taking into account for the future the recommendations and lessons learned issued from this analysis.

This learning process includes all the activities guided to compare the functioning of processes and activities of an organization with the established expectations. The activities and issues that must be corrected or improved are derived from the comparison between the results and expectations.

The working method employed, allow tracking of each situation and know the status of the events in its different phases; propose actions to take, and get reports for both the enterprise and other organizations. The aim pursued is to identify, document, analyze and evaluate inadequate trends, and adopt the actions to resolve the nonconformities detected.

The first phase in the evaluation of an event is to describe and record the circumstances that have surrounded the incident, which may occur as a result of inappropriate actions in the design, maintenance, non-fulfillment of procedures and practices, inappropriate communications or lack training (PG-017, 2007).

Once registered and documented the event, first the direct cause is analyzed, that is, the failure, action, omission or condition which immediately produces or leads to the occurrence of the event.

It then proceeds to perform the process of evaluation properly speaking, which starts by analyzing the root causes, that is, the fundamental causes that if are corrected will prevent the repetition of the event or adverse condition, and continues determining the corrective actions that prevent the future recurrence of the condition or adverse trend that carries again to the event occurs. In this sense, it will record the set of actions to be performed, indicating if they involve the correction or improvement of some aspect, their priority and the training to give when appropriate, establishing the business unit that will implement (execute) them and within what time.

The actions to be executed by each business unit are communicated to the unit responsible, starting then the implementation phase of the actions; process that ends when the last action is executed, giving the incident by closed.

Likewise, the general coordinator of the process will carry out in parallel form the tasks of control and monitoring of the process on those events that are in evaluation or open (in phase of implementation of actions). The monitoring of the actions being executed will be recorded, indicating the date on which it is tracking, the evolution in the implementation of the action (difficulties, delays incurred, etc.), which may give rise to coordination actions when was necessary.

4.2 Organizational roles of the process

The process of knowledge acquisition and learning based on operating experience of the organization requires the coordination of the various business units and the participation of their staff. To implement this process in a satisfactory way in the organization it is necessary consider the following roles:

General Coordinator of the Process (GeCoorPr): is responsible for managing the program of operational experience, including the following tasks (PG-017, 2007):

- Tracing coordinators of the various units for the process be carried out satisfactorily.
- Maintain the database that supports the process updated, which involves record the events, determine the direct cause and appoint the coordinator responsible for its evaluation (BuUnCoor. Resp. Eval.).
- Perform the activities to control and monitor the implementation of actions to correct the events and incidents detected.

Business Unit Coordinators (BuUnCoor): the coordinators of each business unit are responsible for the performance of the following tasks (PCN-A-039, 2010):

- Verify the fulfillment of criteria for the event be analyzed and document the events generated by their unit, completing the report of the event.

Coordinators of business units responsible for evaluation (BuUnCoor Resp. Eval.): in this case the business unit coordinator has the following functions:

- Evaluate the events affecting their unit, for which they will generate an evaluation report, identify the root causes of the event and propose actions to perform by different units of the organization to correct the incident.
- Maintain the database of operational experience updated recording the information referred to above, including the evaluation report.
- Inform to the general coordinator when finalize the evaluation of the events.

Coordinators of business units responsible for execution (BuUnCoor Resp. Exec.): will be the responsible for the following functions:

- Lead the implementation of actions within the competence of their business unit.
- Inform to the general coordinator when the personnel of their business unit will go executing and closing the corrective actions assigned.

Personnel of the organization and external (PerOr-Ex): any person who while performing their job detects an incident, must inform the coordinator of the unit providing the necessary data to determine if applies record and evaluate the event.

4.3 Activities of knowledge acquisition and learning

The entire process by which the organization acquires knowledge from its experience and learn, begins with the detection and analysis of each event, and ends one the actions oriented to its correction or improvement are executed. The various activities that are part of this process of organizational learning are the following:

Activity code	Name	Description
Act. A	Detection and communication of the event.	Event detection and communication of it, usually by email, to BuUnCoor of the person who detects.
Act. B	Initial analysis and verification of criteria.	The BuUnCoor makes a preliminary analysis of the event and determines if it satisfies the criteria for reporting and analyzing.
Act. C	Fulfillment event report.	The incident is described fulfillment for it an event report, which is done by BuUnCoor following an established electronic format.
Act. D	Sending the event report to GeCoorPr	The BuUnCoor send by email the event to the GeCoorPr.
Act. E	Event record and sending to BuUnCoor Resp. Eval.	The GeCoorPr records the event, identifies the direct cause and assigns the unit responsible for the evaluation, sending the recorded event to BuUnCoor responsible for the evaluation.
Act. F	Identification of root causes and proposed actions	The BuUnCoor responsible for the evaluation determines and assigns the root causes and propose corrective and improvement actions to make, indicating: action number, description, priority, if require give training, the limit date of execution and the unit responsible for do it.
Act. G	End of the evaluation: record evaluation date and pass on to the open state.	The end of the evaluation implies that the event becomes opened setting the valuation date, from this point it will proceed to execute the actions set out to correct it.
Act. H	End of the evaluation: sending actions to BuUnCoor Resp. Exec.	When the BuUnCoor responsible for the evaluation indicates that it has finished (when all the actions must be implemented have been registered), the event and the whole of its information associated is sent to BuUnCoor of the units responsible for execution of the actions.
Act. I	Control and monitoring activities.	The GeCoorPr performs control activities and monitoring the execution of actions to avoid unwarranted delays and coordinating the process.
Act. J	Execution and closing actions by units.	The responsible for performing actions, execute them in time, indicating the date and documentation of closing, and inform to the GeCoorPr.
Act. K	Closing event when closing the last action.	Once has closed the last action assigned to the event, it is considered closed (set status to closed) and terminates the process.

Table 2. Activities of the knowledge acquisition and learning process

Part of the activities outlined can be automated at least partially by the system itself triggering (from the database manager) processes that are associated with certain events:

Activity code	Automation process
Act. E	The event is sent to BuUnCoor Resp. Eval. when the incident is recorded in the database.
Act. G	The state of the event is changed as opened and the valuation date is set, when the BuUnCoor Resp. Eval. indicates that has completed its evaluation.
Act. H	It is automatically sent the record of the event and the actions that are determined to take to the BuUnCoor Rep. Exec. (may be several), once the BuUnCoor Resp. Eval. indicates that it has finished it.
Act. J	Are reported (by sending a message) to GeCoorPr when is registered the closing date of each action.
Act. K	It changes the state of the event to the closed state when the closing date is assigned to the last action.

Table 3. Activities which trigger automation processes

Figure 3 shows the flowchart of the process which has been described, indicating in grey colour the activities that are partially automated.

4.4 Model specification of organizational learning

The process of knowledge acquisition and organizational learning from the analysis of operational experience can be modeled formally applying the theory of Petri nets. This technical of specification is used with the purpose of any organization can develop and implement the process through an information system that helps to realize an efficient management of workflow and the issues analyzed.

The Petri net model presented allows to specify a complex organizational process, of structured type, with a high level of detail, both with respect to the activities that should be considered as the flow of information and communication that occur.

The organizational learning model presented has been implemented successfully in Nuclenor, company with 400 employees that manages the nuclear power plant of St. Mª de Garoña in Spain. The results achieved reveal a high degree of involvement of company staff in the communication of events and their active participation in all phases. For reasons of confidentiality does not provide specific data of the company in this regard, although it is an intensive program in knowledge management, both for the number of events analyzed (knowledge creation) as the quantity of actions implemented (organizational improvement) and knowledge sharing.

The experiences analyzed are a shared knowledge base that is available to all departments and personnel of the company, so that in the resolution of any problem or incident go first to the existing knowledge base and take into consideration the results derived from the analysis of similar operational experiences. By the importance of enhancing the security and efficiency of the installation, being an industrial company which is part of an strategic sector, this knowledge base also includes experiences reported by other Spanish and international nuclear plants, so that the incidents could be applied to the nuclear plant are analyzed with the purpose of learn from the experience of other companies in the sector and avoid similar situations in the future.

The system now constitutes a program of organizational learning and continuous improvement for the company, which provides periodic evaluation of a set of performance indicators in the various departments and areas of the company (installation security, risk and health of people, internal management and environment).

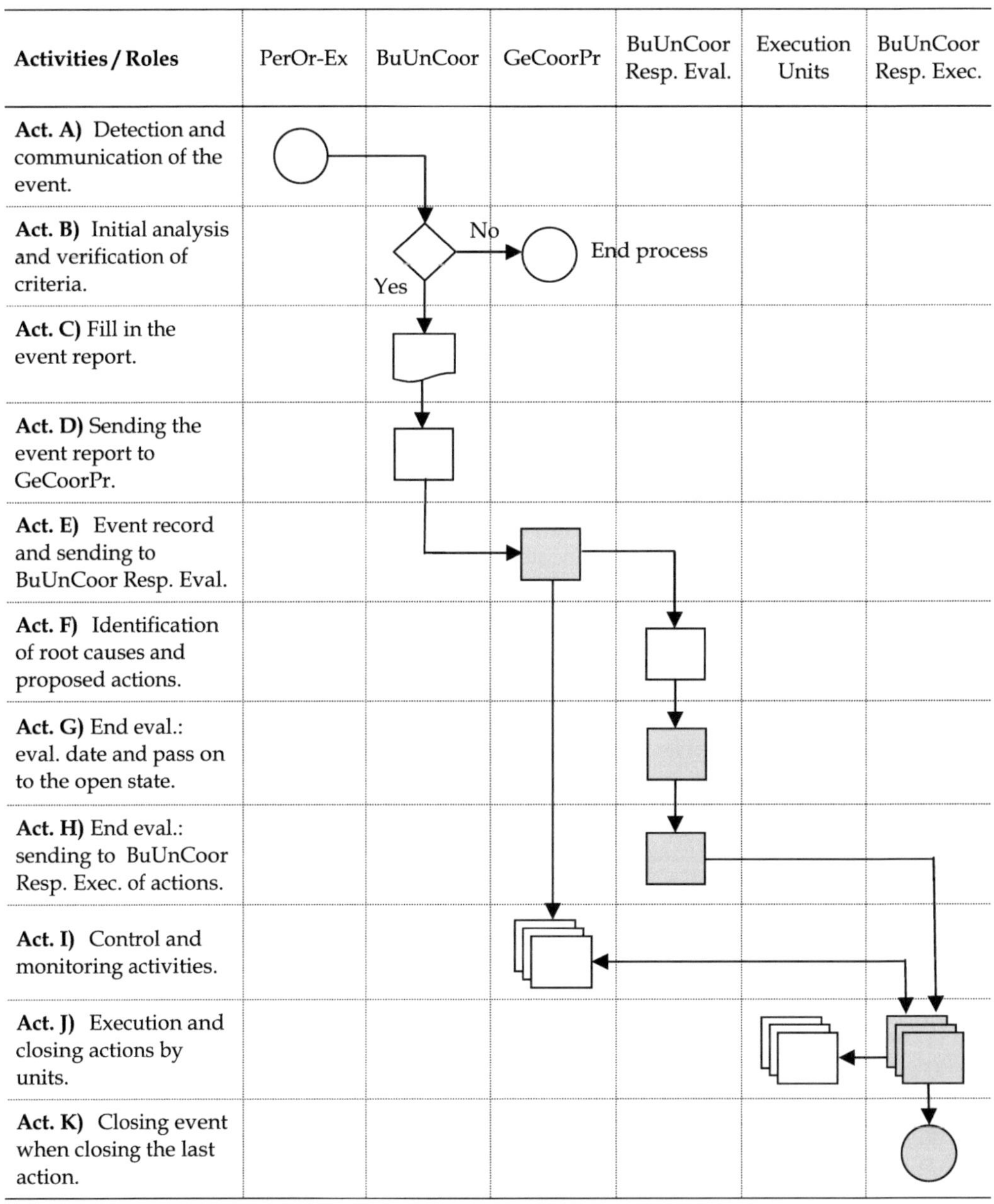

Fig. 3. Process diagram of knowledge acquisition and organizational learning

Based on the analysis performed in the preceding paragraphs, is presented below the workflow model that specifies the organizational learning process described in this chapter.

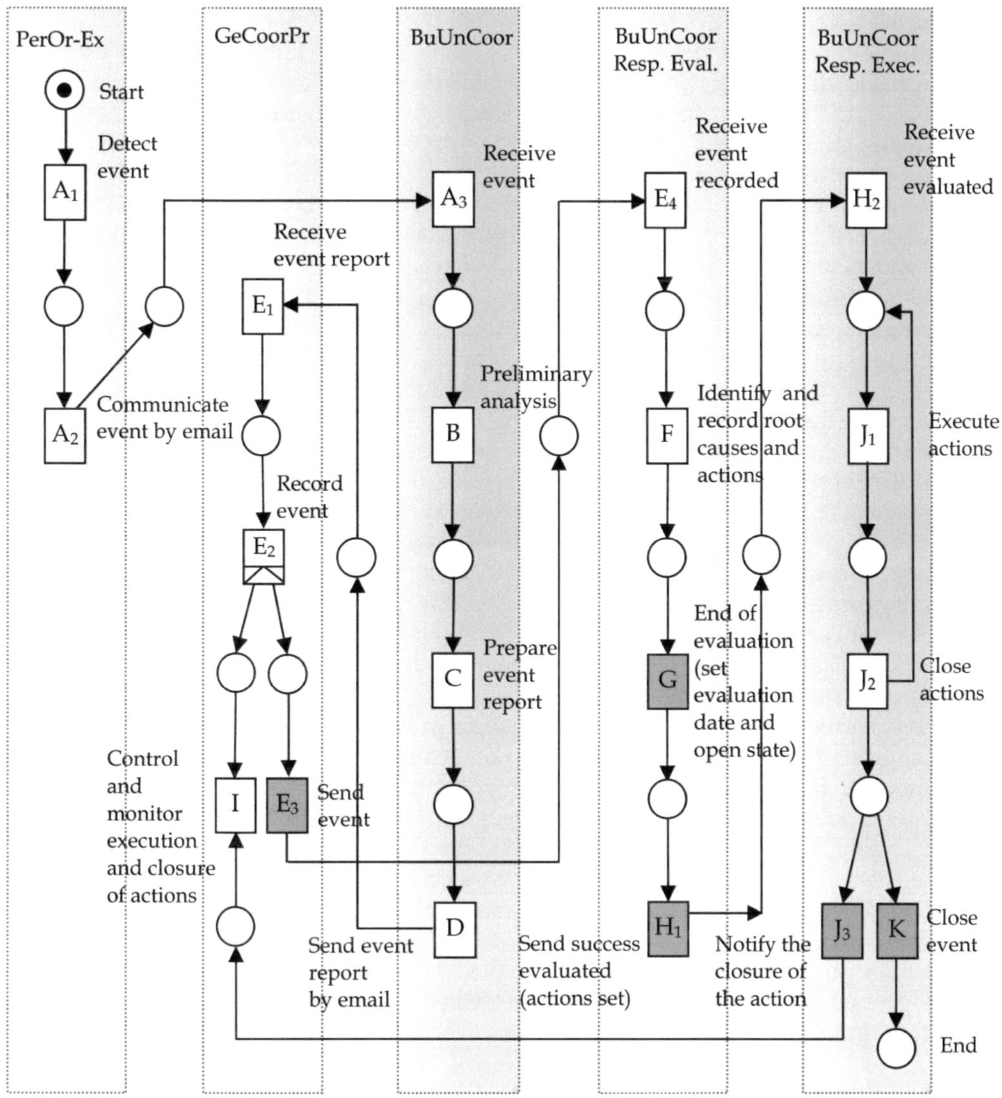

Fig. 4. Model for knowledge acquisition and organizational learning

5. Conclusion

This chapter has been addressed the organizational learning as one of the key approaches of knowledge management. Knowledge and learning are closely related, the organizational learning is the ability of the organization, from existing knowledge, create new knowledge or extend the knowledge base of the organization.

The organizations are complex systems in which the concept of learning can be applied to persons (individual learning) working teams (group learning) and organizations themselves (organizational learning). Individuals learn from their experiences and errors, teams learn from shared experiences and work in groups and organizations learn from the activities and business processes that take place as part of their daily dynamic, in all these cases the experience is a key element of learning.

For learning to occur in the organization is necessary to establish the structures and mechanisms to convert knowledge of individuals and teams into collective knowledge. It is not sufficient to know that the organization learns from its experience, letting the learning and knowledge acquisition are developed in natural and spontaneous form, but to maximize learning the organization needs to develop relational contexts, workflows and formal learning processes, which help to institutionalize the knowledge so that it can be shared and used by the entire organization. In this sense, the organization should develop a core competency, learn to learn.

For the organization learn it is necessary to consider the perspectives: strategic, organizational, technological and human resources. In the strategic perspective will be necessary to align the organizational learning strategy with business strategy and objectives, in the organizational perspective will have been to create the structures and formal processes that support the learning strategy, in terms of technology will be require put into serve of the organization the technological advances to manage and share knowledge (collaborative systems and knowledge bases) and in the perspective of human resources will be necessary to coordinate human capital in a context of learning and knowledge sharing.

Along the chapter has addressed all these issues and how organizations can acquire knowledge through the analysis of experience in their activities. It has presented a methodology based on the procedures of the nuclear industry that allows other companies to implement programs of knowledge acquisition and organizational learning. The organizational learning model has been presented allows to obtain a valuable information from the analysis and evaluation of daily experience, processes that together with taking preventive, corrective and training actions, can improve greatly the efficiency of operative and management processes, avoiding future non-compliance, human errors and potentially dangerous state for people, structures and components of the organization.

The model of knowledge acquisition and organizational learning proposed has interest as empirical study, because it has been implemented successfully in the nuclear industry. This work has relevance to the business community because the model has been presented can be applied to other companies and activity sectors with the adaptations required for each particular business context. From an academic perspective, the case study makes contributions that allow contrast some of the theories of organizational learning and knowledge management have been shown in the review of literature, and may help to infer theory from practice in future works.

6. Acknowledgment

This work has been possible thanks to the financing provided by Nuclenor, that has allowed the development of knowledge that has been presented and apply it in the own company through various research projects, and also thanks the support for the research provided by the Leonardo Torres Quevedo Foundation.

7. References

Aalst, W. M. P. (2002). Making Work Flow: on the Application of Petri Nets to Business Process Management. En: J. Esparza, C. Lakos (Eds.): Lecture Notes in Computer

Science, Vol.2360, pp. 1-22: *23rd International Conference on Applications and Theory of Petri Nets*, Adelaide, Australia, Junio 2002. Springer Verlag.

Aalst, W. M. P. (1998). The Application of Petri Nets to Workflow Management. *The Journal of Circuits, Systems and Computers*, Vol. 8, No. 1, pp. 21-66.

Amponsem, H. (1991). *Organizational Learning through Internal Systems, Strategic Alliances and Networks*. Doctoral Tesis. Queen's University at Kingston. Canadá.

Andreu, R. & Ciborra, C. (1994). Information Systems for the Learning Organization. Conference on Information Technology and Organisational Change. Nijenrode University.

Andreu, R. & Ciborra, C. (1996). *Core Capabilities and Information Technology: An Organizational Learning Approach*. In: Moingeon, B. and Edmondson, A., Organizational Learning and Competitive Advantage. Sage.

Andreu, R. & Sieber, S. (1998). Knowledge and Problem Solving: a Proposal for a Model of Individual and Collective Learning. Working Paper, n° 99/1. IESE.

Blackler, F. (1995). Knowledge, Knowledge Work and Organisations: and Overview and Interpretation. *Journal of Management Studies*, Vol. 30, No. 6, pp. 863-884.

Blackler, F. (1993). Knowledge and the Theory of Organisations: Organisations as Activity Systems and the Reframing of Management. *Organisation Studies*, Vol. 16, No. 6, pp. 1021-1046.

Bonifacio, M.; Bouquet, P. & Manzardo, A. (2000). A Distributed Intelligence Paradigm for Knowledge Management. In: Staab, S. and O' Leary, D. (eds.) Bringing Knowledge to Business Processes. *Papers from the 2000 AAAI Spring Symposium*. Technical Report SS-00-03. ISBN 1-57735-109-6. The AAAI Press. CA, USA.

Brown, J. S. & Duguid, P. (1991). Organizational Learning and Communities of Practice: Toward a Unified View of Working, Learning and Innovation. *Organization Science*, Vol. 2, No. 1, pp. 40-57.

Buckland, M. K. (1991). *Information and Information Systems*. Praeger, New York.

Bueno, E.; Ordonez de Pablos, P. & Salmador M. P. (2004). Towards an integrative model of business, knowledge and organisational learning processes. *International Journal of Technology Management*, Vol. 27, No 6-7, pp. 562-574.

Chin, C. & Siong, C. (2009). Knowledge Management Process Effectiveness: Measurement of Preliminary Knowledge Management Implementation. *Knowledge Management Research & Practice*, Vol. 7, No. 2, pp. 142-151.

Cook, S. & Brown, J. S. (1999). Bridging Epistemologies: the Generative Dance between Organizational Knowing. Organization Science, Vol. 10, No. 4, pp. 381-400.

Cook S. & Yanow D. (1996). *Culture and organizational learning*. In: Cohen M., Sproull L., eds. Organizational learning. Califórnia: Sage. pp. 455-430.

Cyert, R. M. & March, J. G. (1963). *A Behavioural Theory of the Firm*. Prentice Hall, Englewood Cliffs, NJ.

Daft, R. L. & Weick, K. E. (1984). Toward a Model of Organisations as Interpretation Systems. *Academy of Management Review*, Vol. 9, No. 2, pp. 284-295.

Dixon, N. (1994). *The Organizational Learning Cycle*. McGraw-Hill.

Dodgson, M. (1993). Organizational Learning: a Review of Some Literatures. *Organization Studies*, Vol.14, No.3, pp. 375-394.

Durand, T.; Mounoud, E. & Ramanantsoa, B. (1996). Uncovering Strategic Assumptions: Understanding Managers Ability to Built Representations. *European Management Journal*, Vol. 14, No. 4, pp. 389-397.

Edmondson, A. (1996). Learning from Mistakes is Easier Said than Done: Group and Organizational Influences on the Detection and Correction of Human Error. *J Appl Behav Sci,* Vol. 32, No. 1, pp. 5-32.

Easterby-Smith, M., Snell, R.; Gherardi, S. (1998). Organizational learning: Diverging Communities of Practice?. *Management Learning,* Vol. 29, No. 3, pp. 259-272.

Fiol, C. M. & Lyles, M. A. (1985). Organizational Learning. *Academy of Management Review,* Vol. 10, No. 4, pp. 803-813.

Gherardi, S. (1999). Learning as Problem-driven or Learning in Face of Mystery? *Organization Studies,* Vol. 20, No. 1, pp. 101-24.

Gherardi, S. & Nicolini, D. (2000). To Transfer is to Transform: the Circulation of Safety Knowledge. *Organisation,* Vol. 7, No. 2, pp. 329-348.

Goh, S. & Richards, G. (1997). Benchmarking the Learning Capability of Organisations. *European Management Journal.* Vol. 15, No. 5, pp. 575-583.

González, A. J.; Joaquí, C. Z. & Collazos, C. A. (2009). Karagabi KMmodel: Modelo de Referencia para la Introducción de Iniciativas de Gestión del Conocimiento en Organizaciones basadas en Conocimiento. *Ingeniare,* Vol. 17, No. 2, pp. 223-235.

Grant, R. M. (1996). Toward a Knowledge-Based Theory of the Firm. *Strategic Management Journal,* Vol. 17, Winter Special Issue, pp. 109-122.

GS-1.10/08 (2008). *Guía de Seguridad nº 1.10. Revisiones Periódicas de la Seguridad de las Centrales Nucleares.* Colección Guías de Seguridad del CSN. Consejo de Seguridad Nuclear.

Hedlund, G. (1994). A Model of Knowledge Management and the N-Form Corporation. *Strategic Management Journal,* Vol. 15, pp. 73-90.

Hollingsworth, D. (1995). *The Workflow Reference Model.* Document number WFMC-TC00-1003 Issue 1.1. Workflow Management Coalition (WfMC).

Homsma, G. J.; Van Dyck, C.; De Gilder, D.; Koopman, P.L. & Elfring, T. (2009). Learning from Error: the Influence of Error Incident Characteristics. *Journal of Business Research,* Vol. 62, No. 1, pp. 115-122.

Huber, G. P. (1991). Organizational Learning: the Contributing Process and Literatures. *Organization Science,* Vol. 2, No. 1, pp. 88-115.

Huysman, M. (1999). Balancing Biases: a Critical Review of the Literature on Organisational Learning. In Easterby-Smith M., Burgoyne J. and Araujo L. *Organisational Learning and the Learning Organisation,* pp. 59-74. Sage, London.

Kolb, D. (1984). *Experiential Learning.* Englewood Cliffs, Prentice Hall.

Krogh, G.; Nonaka, I., and Rechsteiner, L. (2011). Leadership in Organizational Knowledge Creation: A Review and Framework. *Journal of Management Studies.* DOI: 10.1111/j.1467-6486.2010.00978.x

Kuan W. (2005). Critical Success Factors for Implementing Knowledge Management in Small and Medium Enterprises. *Industrial Management & Data Systems,* Vol. 105, No. 3, pp.261-279.

Lai, M.; Lin, Y.; Lin, L.; Wang, W. & Huang, H. (2009). Information Behavior and Value Creation Potential of Information Capital: Mediating Role of Organizational Learning. *Expert Systems with Applications,* Vol. 36, No. 1, pp. 542-550.

Lave, J. & Wenger, E. (1991). *Situated learning: Legitimate peripheral participation.* Cambridge University Press. New York.

Leonard, D. (1992). The Factory as a Learning Laboratory. *Sloan Management Review,* Vol. 4, No. 1, pp. 23-38.

Levitt, B. & March, J. G. (1988). Organisational Learning. *Annual Review of Sociology*, Vol. 14, pp. 319-340.

Lueg, C. (2002). Presentación. Gestión del Conocimiento y Tecnologías de la Información: Relaciones y Perspectivas. Monografía: Gestión del Conocimiento y TIC. *Novática*, enero - febrero, No. 155, pp. 4-7.

March, J. G. & Olsen, J. P. (1976). *Organizational Learning and the Ambiguity of the Past.* In: March, J.G. and Olsen, J.P. (eds.), Ambiguity and Choice in Organizations, pp. 54-68. Universitetsforlaget. Bergen. Noruega.

Marchand, D. A.; Kettinger, W. J. & Rollins, J. D. (2000). Information Orientation: People, Technology and the Bottom Line. *MIT Sloan Management Review*, Vol. 41, No. 4, pp. 69-80.

Marengo, L. (1991). *Knowledge, Coordination and Learning in an Adaptive Model of the Firm.* Doctoral Tesis. Sussex University. U.K.

Mentzas, G.; Halaris, C. & Kavadias, S. (2001). Modelling Business Processes with Workflow Systems: an Evaluation of Alternative Approaches. *International Journal of Information Management*, Vol. 21, pp. 123-135.

Moreno, M. J. & Pelayo, Y. (2007). Thalec: Modelo para la Gestión Interna del Conocimiento. *Capital Humano*, No. 208, pp. 68-82.

Newell, A. (1982). The Knowledge Level. *Artificial Intelligence*, No. 18, pp. 87-127.

Nonaka, I. (1994). A Dynamic Theory of Organisational Knowledge Creation. *Organisation Science*, No. 5, pp. 14-37.

Nonaka, I. & Ichijo, K. (1997). *Creating Knowledge in the Process Organization.* In: Shrivastava, P., Huff, A. S. and Dutton, J. E. (eds.), Advances in Strategic Management, Vol. 14, pp. 45-52. JAI Press, Inc.

Nonaka, I. & Johansson, J. K. (1985). Japanese Management: What about the "Hard" Skills?. *Academy of Management Review*, Vol. 10, No. 2, pp. 181-191.

Nonaka, I.; Reinmoeller, P. & Senoo, D. (1998). The "Art" of Knowledge: Systems to Capitalize on Market Knowledge. *European Management Journal*, Vol. 16, No. 6., pp. 673-684.

Nonaka, I. & Takeuchi, H. (1995). *The Knowledge-Creating Company*. Oxford University Press.

PCN-A-039 (2010). *Tratamiento de la Experiencia Operativa*. Nuclenor.

Pedraja, L.; Rodríguez, E. & Rodríguez, J. (2009). La Influencia de la Gestión del Conocimiento sobre la Eficacia Organizacional: un Estudio en Instituciones Públicas y Empresas Privadas. *Revista Facultad de Ingeniería*. No. 47, pp. 218-227.

Pérez, D. & Solana, P. (2011). *CRM 2.0 and E-government: Challenges for Public Administration and Social Effects*. Chapter six, in: Colomo-Palacios, R.; Varajão, J. & Soto-Acosta, P. (2012). *Customer Relationship Management and the Social and Semantic Web: Enabling Cliens Conexus*. DOI:10.4018/978-1-61350-044-6

Petri, C. A. (1962): Kommunikation mit Automaten. PhD thesis, Institut für Instrumentelle Mathematik, Bonn.

PG-017 (2007). *Seguimiento de Normativa y Tratamiento de la Experiencia Operativa Interna y Externa*. Nuclenor.

Quinn, J. B. (1992). *Intelligent Entreprise*. Free Press.

Redding, J. C. & Catalanello, R. F. (1994). *Strategic Readiness*. Jossey-Bass. San Francisco.

Revilla, E. (1995). *Factores Determinantes del Aprendizaje Organizativo: un Modelo de Desarrollo de Productos*. Doctoral Tesis. Valladolid University. Spain.

Sadiq, S. W. & Orlowska, M. E. (2000). On Capturing Exceptions in Workflow Process Models. *Business Information Systems, 4th International Conference on Business Information Systems*, pp. 3-19.

Sánchez, R. & Heene, A. (1997). *Strategic Learning and Knowledge Management.* John Wiley and Sons. Nueva York.

Senge, P. M. (1990). *The Fifth Discipline: the Art and Practice of the Learning Organization,* New York: Doubleday.

Shrivastava, P. (1983). A Typology of Organizational Learning Systems. *Journal of Management Science,* Vol. 20, pp. 2-24.

Simon, H. A. (1991). Bounded Rationality and Organizational Learning. *Organization Science,* Vol. 2, No. 1, pp. 125-134.

Solana, P. (2006). *Modelización de Sistemas de Información para la Automatización de Procesos de Negocio y el Control de la Documentación en las Organizaciones.* Doctoral Tesis. Cantabria University. Spain.

Solana, P. and Pérez, D. (2011). Security Model Applied to Electronic Records Management: Experiences and Results in the Nuclear Sector. *International Journal of Technology Management,* Vol. 54, No. 2/3, pp. 204–228.

Spender, J. C. (1996 a). Organizational Knowledge, Learning and Memory: Three Concepts in Search of a Theory. *Journal of Organizational Change Management,* Vol. 9, No. 1, pp. 63-78.

Spender, J. C. (1996 b). Making Knowledge the Basis of a Dynamic Theory of the Firm. *Strategic Management Journal,* Vol. 17, No. 1, pp. 45-62.

Swan, J.; Scarbrough, H. & Preston, J. (1999). Knowledge Management - the Next Fad to Forget People ?. *Proceedings of the 7th European Conference on Information Systems (ECIS' 99),* Copenhagen, Denmark, pp. 668-678.

Teece, D. T. (1998). Capturing Value from Knowledge Assets: the New Economy, Markets for Know-How, and Intangible Assets. *California Management Review,* Vol. 40, No. 3, pp. 55-79.

Teresa L. J.; Chia-Ying L. & Tien-Shiang L. (2006). A Contingency Model for Knowledge Management Capability and Innovation. *Industrial Management & Data Systems,* Vol. 106, No. 6, pp. 855-877.

Tsoukas, H. (1996). The Firm as a Distributed Knowledge System: a Constructionist Approach. *Strategic Management Journal,* No. 17, pp. 11-25.

Ulrich, D.; Jick, T. & Von Glinow, M. A. (1993). High-impact Learning: Building and Diffusing Learning Capability. *Organizational Dynamics,* 22, 2, 52-79.

Van Dyck, C.; Frese, M.; Baer M. & Sonnentag, S. (2005). Organizational Error Management Culture and its Impact on Performance: a Two-Study Replication. *J Appl Psychol,* Vol. 90, No. 6, pp. 1228-1240.

Von Krogh, G. (1998). Care in Knowledge Creation. *California Management Review,* Vol. 40, No. 3, pp. 133-153.

Von Krogh, G.; Roos, J. & Slocum, K. (1994). An Essay on Corporate Epistemology. *Strategic Management Journal,* No. 15, pp. 53-71.

Vytgotsky, L. S. (1962). *Thought and Language.* MIT Press, Mass.

Weick, K. E. (1991). The Nontraditional Quality of Organisational Learning. *Organisation Science,* Vol. 2, No. 1, pp. 116-123.

Weick K. E. & Roberts, K. H. (1993). Collective Mind in Organizations: Heeding Interrelating on Flight Decks. *Administrative Science Quaterly,* Vol. 38, pp. 330-358.

Weick, K. E. & Westley, F. (1996). *Organizational Learning: Affirming an Oxymoron.* In Clegg, S.R., Hardy, C. and Nord, W.R. (Eds.). Handbook of organizational studies, Sage, pp. 440-458. London.

WFMC-TC00-1011 Issue 3.0 (1999). *Terminology & Glossary,* Workflow Management Coalition (WfMC).

8

What's Wrong with Knowledge Management? And the Emergence of Ontology

Mark Burgess
CTO CFEngine
Norway

1. Introduction

Knowledge Management (KM) is undoubtedly the challenge of this decade, and it is destined to shape the way we go about a wide range of fields of human activity for decades to come. Yet, while technologies claiming to enable KM abound, there is little sign that any wide reaching principles have been clearly understood or articulated, or that current research approaches have any positive benefit beyond brute force searching for answers, see Hicks et al. (2006). Nor is there any realistic alternative to the two major approaches to information organization: random search and retrieval (indexing), versus catalogue classification (the directory or table of contents).

In this essay, I should like to discuss some of the principles of knowledge organization, as I see them, from a perspective that has yielded some success in the related area of configuration or pattern management, see Bergstra & Burgess (1994-now); Burgess (2005). In order to keep things concise and focused, I will concentrate on spelling out a few specific criticisms of current approaches to KM, and then go on to propose adjustments to these approaches that could lead to large improvements in the current state of the art. Finally I'll set some challenges for future investigation.

2. Background

Knowledge management, or knowledge engineering (KE) today conjours up associations like: database, catalogue, ontology, semantic reasoning, etc. Yet, before information technology (IT) arrived on the scene, thousands of years of human development came up with quite different answers to the problem of passing on knowledge:

- Exploring and Discovering.
- Storytelling.
- Teaching and apprenticeship.

Only with the arrival written word, see Wolf (2007), did libraries begin to consider ways of managing large amounts of information, to accumulate knowledge and set about the task of organizing it. Today, however, those who work with knowledge (knowledge engineers, if we may call them that) feel that there is no mileage in these simple matters and are now only concerned with stockpiling and organizing information, then retrieving it, assuming that its simple existence as some form of documentation is enough to guarantee its usefulness.

Concepts like 'taxonomy' and 'ontology' abound, both of which we must return to in this essay, and methods are borrowed from computer logic to try to reason about categories of information, see et al. (2003); Strassner (2007).
The state of the art in knowledge management today, may be summarized by these things, in my view:

- Databases.
- The Web, and its search engines.
- Wikis for collaborative writing.
- Ontology or semantic modelling as a dream of something better.

The bulk of information today is available on 'the Web'. Although the web is only a publishing mechanism, it has played a genuine role in encouraging the documentation and dissemination of knowledge, by making it easy (cheap) for people to participate in a shared process. Wikis have helped to make this happen (with flagship examples like Wikepedia), but the ways in which Wikis are used, in a wider context, suggests that they have a less than effective track-record as long-term repositories of knowledge (see below for some speculations on this).
Today, we aspire to greater sophistication. Semantic technologies attempt to go beyond the pure text-search approach to using the web, by attaching actual intended meaning to words. Tools like RDF, see W3C (n.d.), Topic Maps, see Moore (2001); Pepper (2009), OIL, OWL, Protegé, see Strassner (2007), etc., attempt to use intended meaning to provide better hints and suggestions to knowledge-seekers by wrapping information in 'meta-data' – or information for computers to use in cataloguing and reasoning to capture domain expertise.
Semantic webs or networks (often called ontologies today) begin with the desire to classify topics 'meaningfully'. One reason is to be able to disambiguate different patterns of usage as we talk about things. An ontology is a model of someone's particular 'world view'. Technically, an ontology is defined as 'a set of specialized concepts within a domain' (from the Greek logos (talk about) and ontos (that which exists)). It is the term used for describing domain knowledge.
Judging both from my own personal experience and from existing research, ontologies are notoriously hard to create for a number of reasons, see Dicheva & Dichev (2005); Moench et al. (2003). They typically represent domain expertise, they need to be populated with knowledge by domain experts; however, the technologies for doing so are not user-friendly and so these trained experts need other experts (trained knowledge engineers) to make the models on their behalf – experts, requiring more experts. All this places a high cost on creating useful systems, and it has essentially killed most efforts to use semantic technologies, by trying to be too clever. This is one of the issues I would like to address here. The other main problem with technologies today is that they have little capacity to teach users about new things they didn't already know of. So we would like to find a way to offer new insights to users, as they interact with a knowledge base.

3. The shortcomings of databases and search

Stockpiling information does not increase knowledge in any real sense, but this is what we do in libraries and databases. According to the IT Infrastructure Library's knowledge management guide, see of Government Commerce (2000), the knowledge ladder goes through four phases: DIKW, or from mere Data (numbers, texts, assertions, etc), to Information that has some context around it, which in turn becomes knowledge when we are able to apply it and use it as a tool. Then finally there is Wisdom, down the line as something we aspire to.

The ability to search within such a repository can throw up all kinds of possibilities, but usually either too few or too many to make real sense of. With the advent of Google's PageRank, we have come to trust statistical 'mass-voting' as a guide to relevance. Popular voting a normative process in which common habits converge and encourage the spread of the habit to others. What is interesting about the enormous success of Google is that is does not try to be too sophisticated. It basically offers up some sorted data to users, who must then use their brains and exploring skills to rummage through he results. I believe we should learn something from this.

Databases store data row upon row, like a warehouse. They form the bread and butter technologies for storing data in a retrievable way, by associating names and addresses with information, so that a catalogue of entries can be made and searched by users. The limitation of most databases is that they have fixed tabular structures or schemas into which all information must fit. They are just 'data' - void of interpretation, and inaccessible to non-specialists. This makes sense from the viewpoint of machine retrieval, but it puts a burden of creativity on the user to standardize something that it perhaps only loosely understood. As a result, tidy database models tend to bloat into garbage dumps for all kinds of semi-intended annotation.

I shall argue that this is part of a common flaw in approaches to Knowledge Management: the first flaw of KM is that the user is expected to subsidize the technology in order to make it work. The tools of knowledge management, far from helping, often put up barriers and costs for the user. It is interesting to see the great leaps and bounds that have been made in user interface design, and compare this to the poverty of progress in knowledge management.

A second problem with database search is the attempt to use formal logic to whittle away at a large number of possible matches, see Strassner (2007). Even today's experimental derivative technologies for semantic search try to use assumed facts to reason in first order logic, hoping to find enlightenment. The problem with logic is that is needs strictly defined, inflexible categories to work with – and this is the second flaw of knowledge modelling. As one whittles away results, the result tends to be either utterly obvious, or empty due to over constraint.

4. Knowledge representations

Knowledge is what you get when you combine context and experience with information so that its consumers can form their own mental model, believe it and apply it for themselves.

The way we represent this mixture can vary enormously. Examples range from the obvious to the subtle, and as scientists we should also have the humility to recognize art as a form of semantic commentary with a definite role to play in communicating things with cultural context.

Definition 1 (Knowledge Representation). *A piece of work that attempts to communicate observations about something, e.g. experiences, opinions, or some other form of human understanding.*

Examples of Knowledge Representation include the obvious books, articles, stories. We also have keywords, titles, tables of contents, index entries, pointers, references and relationships to other works. Paintings, songs, music, and all other forms of communicable works may be thought of as different representations for knowledge.

How do we know when something is knowledge? This brings us to the third flaw with Knowledge Management. It is generally assumed in the field of Knowledge Management that facts and knowledge are authoritative, i.e. that which is knowledge is defined for the masses by schools and universities or experts, or other figure-heads. This however is patently false. Accepting something as knowledge is an entirely voluntary choice that every one of us makes at our discretion. No one can force us to believe or accept what is represented. We must therefore adopt a model of knowledge based on voluntary adoption if we hope to understand something significant.

Definition 2 (The three flaws of knowledge engineering). *Current approaches to knowledge make three errors:*

1. *Users are expected to work too hard to interact with knowledge.*
2. *Knowledge is treated as a logical framework.*
3. *Knowledge categories are defined authoritatively, but users only accept them voluntarily, if the context of their own experience.*

4.1 Topic maps and RDF

One of the representations of knowledge index that has been developed over the years is the Topic Map, see Pepper (2009). Topic Maps are a form of subject index with detailed annotations that explain the relevance of associations. Topic maps have been made into a standard for the representation and interchange of knowledge. The ISO standard is formally known as ISO/IEC 13250:2003.

Topic Maps have several competitors in this space, the Resource Description Framework (RDF) being the best known, see W3C (n.d.). What makes Topic Maps interesting is that they were designed for human consumption, where the emphasis for RDF is on artificial machine reasoning.

A topic map represents information using an index model called TAO:

- Topics, or subject fragments (atoms).
- Associations that explain relevance and meaning.
- Occurrences of independent information about topics.

Every knowledge item we want to talk about is a topic which has a name and a type-category. Relationships to related issues are made by association (e.g. see also ...). Finally, occurrences are pointers to specific documents or other representations of knowledge that are asserted to be relevant to the named topic.

As I studied Knowledge Management in the beginning, I was drawn to topic maps over RDF and OWL, as it seemed to avoid wallowing in syntax and logic. Even Topic Maps have sought validation through this kind of formal computer science approach however, and I believe that the biggest flaw in Topic Maps was in choosing to model in the classic database approach. This led to unnecessary constraints, such as non-overlapping type categories, see Dietz (2006); Kipp (2003); W3C (n.d.).

The reason this approach has failed is a basic limitation on human willingness to get involved in highly technical reasoning. Modelling knowledge with logic is very hard, and not very convincing as knowledge is based on human faculties which are seldom fully rational and are never uniquely structured. On a scale of posting a note on the refrigerator to publishing a scientific paper in Nature, Topic Maps and RDF are much closer to the latter. That is simply too hard for most users, and hence these technologies curse Knowledge Management to be the domain of wizards and kings, unable to capture the knowledge of everyman.

5. Promises as a model for knowledge

To motivate a solution to the three problems above, I want to take a simple point of view based on a modelling framework known as *promise theory*[1], which has yielded some success in understanding issues related to knowledge management: organization and cooperation. Promise theory is a way of describing how individual 'agents' advertise their behaviour so that they can form expectations of one another. They do this by communicating promises. An agent can be a human, group of humans, or some other entity being steered by humans.
Like all models, it is intentionally simplistic, but I shall claim (in the interests of knowledge) that this approximation can be a good anchor point from which to begin a more sophisticated understanding.

5.1 The promise model

Promises are about trying to understand and govern expectations, given that we (i.e. people or agents) have at best incomplete information about the world. If we knew everything, there would be no use for promises. Promises made by agents to each other act as a kind of signalling mechanism to raise or lower expectations. Promise theory is uniquely suited to studying knowledge management because it captures something about the human condition: subjective individuals working together in a partially cooperative environment.

Definition 3 (Promise). *The public expression of something that is, has been, or might be intended, made by an individual agent (the promiser), to a limited audience called the scope of the promise, which generally includes the promisee(s), i.e. the intended recipient(s) of the promise.*

A *promise*, in this technical meaning, is a statement of intent, by an agent, that is meant to reinforce another's expectation that the intention will turn out to be true. For instance:

1. I promise to feed your cat – expectations about what might happen in the future and cannot yet be confirmed.
2. I promise I have fed your cat – expectations about what might have happened in the past but has not yet been verified.
3. Feed cats seems a promising strategy – we speak of the expectation that feeding cats will bring positive outcomes in the future.

Clearly each of these statements can be considered a matter of knowledge. In each case, promises are about expectations[2]. Consider next the following promises about someone's understanding of certain terms:

- I promise that a 'chapter' means a part of a book, in the context of literature.
- I promise that a 'chapter' means a sub-division of a religious order, in the context of churches.
- I promise that chapters consist of words, in the context of literature.

[1] Actually this phrase was coined rather loosely, and its authors have tried to find a more specific name for it such as 'micro-promises' that is less omnipotent in its claims, but simplicity often reigns above reason, as we shall see in this essay.

[2] In philosophy, promises are usually thought of as a moral issue, but here we shall discard any moral connotations and deal exclusively with expectations. The promise of good weather, for instance, means that there is some expectation on the part of listeners that the weather will turn out well. This is not a promise made by morally good or evil clouds, but rather an imagined intention (embodying a harmless anthropomorphism) made by holiday-makers and wedding planners, etc.

- I promise that chapters consist of persons, in the context of religious orders.

These are promises about what an agent thinks he/she/it knows. Does anyone actually know these things for certain, i.e. are they facts? I think not. When, as individuals, we say 'a chapter is a part of a book' this is a confident statement, steeped in self-assurance. Anyone haunted by a modest amount of scientific humility would be less unilateral in making this kind of assertion and would probably try to qualify it with all kinds of uncertainty. Of course, what we mean is: to the best of my knowledge and belief, this knowledge is correct – please trust me, see Bergstra & Burgess (2006). We must not call these statements facts, but rather subjective expressions that might or might not be confirmed by others' viewpoints, thus essentially a promise.

Promises themselves constitute what we think we know, but they also discuss another level of knowledge. By thinking of knowledge as something that agents (i.e. you and I) have to promise to know, we will be able to reverse the simple design error in modern information systems that assumes authoritativeness, and turn logical ontology databases (designed by committees) back into simple language and hearsay that ordinary people own.

5.2 Basic principles of promises

There are two ways in which we are going to apply promises in this discussion: as a model of the people interacting with knowledge, and as a model of the knowledge itself. I will use the term 'topic' as a shorthand for knowledge item. Moreover, there are two kinds of promises that we should mention:

- Promises to offer or give something, e.g. I claim to be an expert in Foo.
- Promises to use or accept something, e.g. I believe your claim.

Both underline the individuality or autonomy of an agent, and we can use the term voluntary cooperation to express this freedom to disbelieve or not accept.

In the promise theory view, a promisee is not obliged to accept something promised by another agent. He or she must promise to accept a given promise in order for communication to be complete.

The basic principles of promises may be applied as follows, see Bergstra & Burgess (1994-now):

1. Anything that can be independently expressed or can change in some way can be an agent (promiser), entitled to its own viewpoint, and can make promises about its condition. We use this to say that any topic we can think of is assumed to exist and can promise to be related to any other, in the mind of an agent.
2. An agent (promiser) can only make promises about itself, not about other agents. Thus, in our case, a topic is only responsible for what it claims to know about itself and how it claims to relate to other topics.

Each topic is therefore self-contained, independent and can be unique in an individual's context, while still allowing for multiple interpretations. This allows multiple, private viewpoints.

5.3 Applying promises to knowledge indexing

The modern approach to category design is grounded in the goal of making sophisticated indices to make information accessible and to codify experience. To discuss how humans interact with knowledge, we shall make people (i.e. the users of knowledge) into the role of promise-agents, in the first case. They will make certain promises to one another, which will involve agreeing about meanings, responsibility to learn and use concepts, etc. This is fairly unambiguous.

To apply promises to the representation of knowledge itself, we have to think more abstractly. Each topic, or item of knowledge, will be an agent that can make promises. The promises a topic can make are like the following:

- A topic promises a brief explanation of itself, in a given context.
- A topic promises to be *associated* with another topic in a particular way.
- A topic promises references *occurrences* of information that are about itself.

According to the rules above, no one else can make these promises. An example of the latter might be written like this:

```
topics:
 literature::
    "Odyssey"    # The topic/promiser
        comment => "A book from classic Greek literature",
    association => a("was written by","Homer");
 authors::
    "Homer" comment => "A Greek writer from around 850 BC",
        association => a("wrote","Odyssey");
television::
    "Homer" comment => "Usually refers to Homer Simpson";
```

Promises therefore have two relationships to knowledge:

- Every time we propose to know something, the inevitable uncertainty on the part of the involved parties (promiser and the promisee), means that the assertion at best has the status of a promise, not a fact.
- Such a promise, once made, becomes a form of meta-information that describes the structure of knowledge, and is thus useful for analysis and reasoning.

We might write the above in a formal promise language, just to drive the point home:

```
topics:
 knowledge::
   "uncertainty"
        comment => "Incomplete information about something",
    association => a("is a basic assumption of","promises");

   "promises"
      association => a("may be viewed as","meta-information");

    "meta-information"
          comment => "Information about some other information";
```

Promises themselves constitute information and hence may be perceived as a kind of knowledge; moreover promises may be about knowledge itself. Conversely, knowledge about a promise can influence the behaviour of agents who are not the intended promisee, so knowledge about knowledge can be discussed with promises. From an engineering viewpoint, the scope can have an important influence on behaviour.

Why introduce these notions? The most compelling answer is that this model has several useful properties: it defines atomic 'topics' with a minimum of assumed structure, but embodies some principles that preserve things we know to be true about knowledge: that knowledge is subjective in both content and structure, and is defined by a collaborative process by individuals.

5.4 Graphical representations - knowledge maps

Whenever things are interrelated, they form networks. In mathematics, the technical term for networks is *graphs*. The World Wide Web is one such network. There is a science of networks and their properties that has been studied at length in the literature, see Albert & Barabási (2002); Newman (2003). Since networks play such a large role in knowledge transfer, any theory of knowledge management must take their properties into account.

The agent making the promise (called the promiser) often directs it at a particular agent (one or more promisees), but others may also know about the promise. We call the set of agents who know about a promise the *scope* of the promise. There is thus communication from

$$promiser \rightarrow (promisee + scope) \tag{1}$$

We define a knowledge map as follows:

Definition 4 (Knowledge Map). *A directed graph $\Gamma(T, A)$, where T is a set of nodes representing topics, and A is a set of edges or links representing associations between topics.*

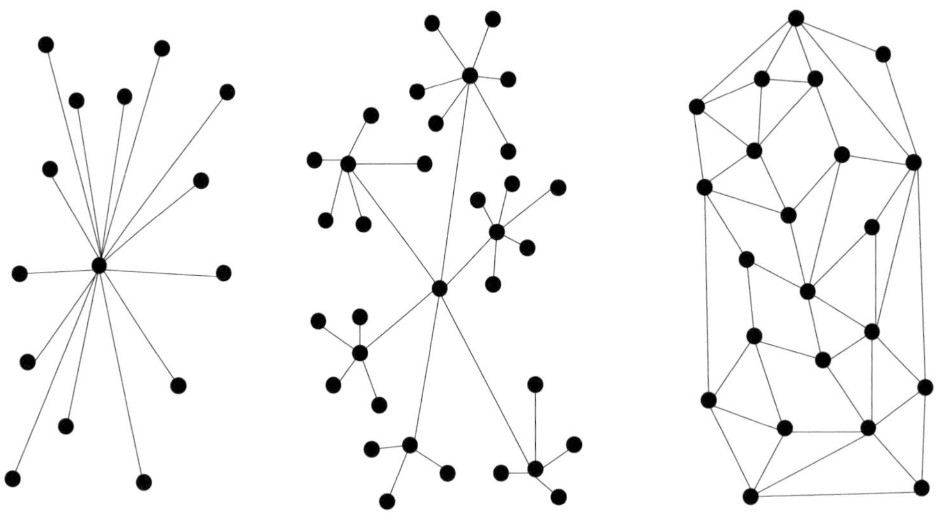

(a) (b) (c)

Fig. 1. Networks with different shapes: (a) A star network, (b) a tree, (c) a mesh.

Graphs or networks have many different shapes. If we begin to associate ideas freely, we end up with a 'mesh' (see fig 1 (c)). On the other hand, if we try to subdivide topics into categories in a 'branching process', we get a tree or hierarchy (see fig. 2 (b)). A tree is also called an acyclic graph (or DAG for Directed Acyclic Graph) because it contains no loops. A single category looks like the figure (a).

When we subdivide subject categories in the manner of a hierarchy, we are laying an artificial tree on top of the mesh network and pretending that the new shape is a good representation of the old shape (see fig. 2). It is clear to see that we can lay many different trees across

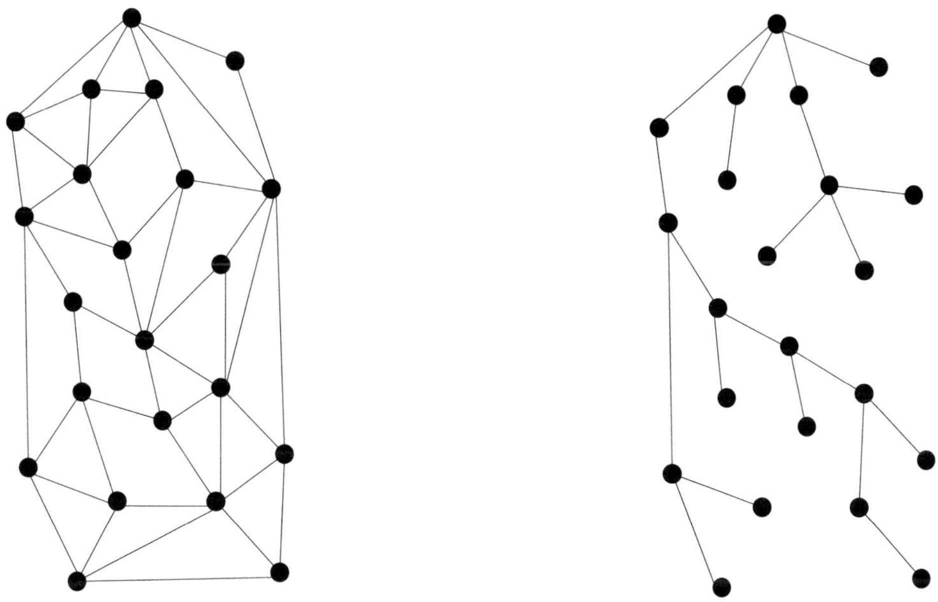

(a) (b)

Fig. 2. Illustration of a spanning tree (b) for a general network (a).

a generalized set of topics, and so there is is no unique tree that represents a given set of knowledge items.

Definition 5 (Spanning tree). *Any DAG (tree) that starts from an arbitrary root node in a graph and covers all the nodes once only.*

Taxonomies have the property of a spanning tree (see sections below and fig. 3).

Definition 6 (Singleton). *An isolated node in a graph, unconnected to any other. In our case, this is a topic with no associations.*

For the evaluation of graphs, let us define one more thing.

Definition 7 (The degree of a node). *Denoted k. The number of associations a node has.*

If we plot a frequency diagram of $n(k)$, the number of nodes if degree k, this degree-distribution can be used to characterize the processes behind the structure.

5.5 Agreement and consensus

In discussing what individuals know as a group, we will have use for the notion of agreement. The term agreement is often confused with 'contract' in economics and social sciences, but that is a derived meaning. We are only concerned with what agents claim to agree about. This is also a matter of promises, it turns out, because agents cannot know if they actually have the

same understanding as any other. At best they can promise to agree to something given their best understanding.
Agreement is what happens when two or more agents seem to arrive at a common understanding. For example, two parties can agree that $2 + 2 = 4$. Two agents may or may not know about their common state of agreement. By promising to agree, they can make this public.

Definition 8 (Proposal). *A proposal P is a prototype promise, i.e. the statement of an intention that has not yet been been made public, or acted upon.*

Definition 9 (Agreeing). *Agents are said to agree about a proposal P, if they independently promise to adopt P i.e. if they formally promise to use the proposal and make the promise themselves.*

Agreement is the basis of most of cooperation, and it is the way in which agents arrive at a common understanding. It is therefore central to knowledge management.
Agreement, about some body of information, can thus be viewed as a number of promises. In a contract, for example, one writes down a number of proposals for each side to follow (which are themselves prototype promises), and then the parties promise to subscribe to these by signing. If all parties promise that a set of proposals will be honoured, then an agreement may be expressed as a promise to keep some specification or promise proposals. This may be called the *body* of the agreement. The term contract is also used here.

Definition 10 (Agreement). *A promise agreement is a pair of use-promises between two parties to acknowledge and adopt the body of a proposal.*

Now, armed with this briefest introduction to the promise model, we can get back to the main story: knowledge.

6. Knowledge maps

6.1 Some definitions

To speak of a technology for knowledge maps, we need to formulate a more precise and technical definition of categories, using a promise model. Let's begin with some core concepts.

Definition 11 (Taxonomy). *A hierarchy of topics organized into categories in the manner of a tree with parent (container) concepts and children belonging to parent-categories.*

Taxonomy has been one of the main tools for classifying 'things' in the world, especially in biology. It is a way of putting things, concepts and ideas into one and only one box. Because every concept can only belong to a unique part of the tree hierarchy, the structure of knowledge is fragile to mistakes in choosing the wrong categories for something. Because everything that follows depends on the decisions made, making a change to a tree can be an expensive operation that requires unpicking and redesigning. Moreover, trees are branching processes, they tend to lead to too many different locations for information to reside, and trade complexity of information for complexity of categorization[3].

[3] I often refer to this as the depth versus breadth problem. If we try to hide complexity inside category containers, and sub-containers we simply turn a one dimensional list into a two-dimensional structure, but the total number of things one has to deal with can still be the same, depending on the effectiveness of the categories.

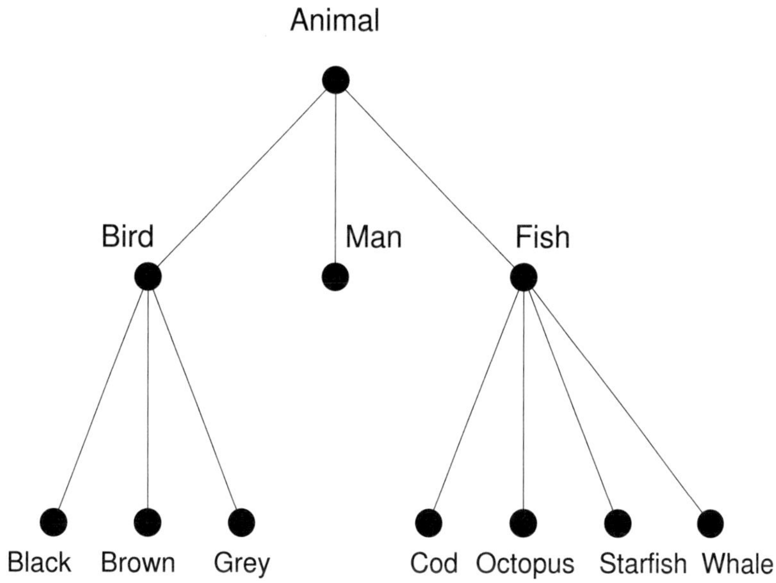

Fig. 3. A taxonomy usually has the structure of a tree - which has the technical name of Directed Acyclic Graph (DAG).

Since taxonomies are non-unique (they are merely arbitrary spanning trees, viewed from a particular starting point), they cannot be considered fundamental. They are design structures, often decided by committees or standardizing bodies, in order to achieve a consensus.
Taxonomies are about putting things in one special box with a special name. A less contrived structure approach to classification is to use a network representation where names are less important than qualities. Semantic webs, or the ontologies they represent, are designed to allow this by letting anything associate itself with anything else, without due regard for boundaries, by using flexible associations.

Definition 12 (Ontology). *A mesh of topics and categories, supplemented by promises of associations to other topics.*

The state of IT ontologies today borrows a lot from taxonomy, in that it is usual for concepts or topics still to be arranged into hierarchical boxes. In this respect, ontology has been unable to divorce itself from hierarchical taxonomy. This seems to be more a case of habit than actual judgement – a hangover from computer science's database modelling and object orientation doctrines. However, and I would like to propose that this causes more problems than it solves.

6.2 Survivability of an ontology

If taxonomy and ontology pretend authority from arbitrariness, what might then be fundamental? Promise theory emphasizes that 'fundamental' is a subjective issue: it belongs to a specific agent's point of view, which in turn is limited by what information is available to it. If we are to build something fundamental, we must therefore base it on subjective viewpoints. Indeed, it suggests that everyone has to build their own viewpoint. This is what ontologies try to achieve and fail at because they retain a notion of authority.
A set of associations can just as effectively capture worthwhile aspects of hierarchy, by documenting which concepts are generalizations of others. For example 'animal' is sometimes

the right generalization for 'bird' or 'fish', but not always. It is also true that information classified as applying in any context generalizes information true only in a special context. These are set relationships, not hierarchical ones. With a 'generalization promise', any topic can bear allegiance to a number of possible generalizations in different contexts, without pre-designed limitations.
The survival of an ontology depends on its being used, which in turn depends on the agreement of all agents: i.e., keeping the promises to use the terms correctly, by all those who participate in it.
How does one know if a taxonomy (or technical ontology) has been a success? In our promise approach, we can simple measure this as the extent to which users keep the promises to support the ontology.

7. The economics of knowledge

The giving and receiving of promises quickly turns into a question of economics. There are motivations, incentives to act and costs involved in acting to keep promises. The economics of knowledge will be central to understanding both the weaknesses of current approaches to knowledge management, and the way towards a more 'natural' or less contrived approach. By taking an economic approach to the subject we join the ranks of scientific models in which rational modelling (or bounded rationality) is the explanation for motivations.
Knowledge management involves activities like the following:

- Acquiring knowledge, with associated gain and cost of effort.
- Retaining knowledge, a maintenance cost.
- Disseminating knowledge, with cost of effort. This might be written off against the maintenance above, but it is normally a cost. Disseminating knowledge can also be considered a long term investment however – investing in others' educations, means that we might save on work down the line.

The extent to which knowledge continues and grows in the minds of agents is therefore a question of the individual economic considerations of those agents. It costs little and brings rewards, knowledge will flourish. If the cost is too high, knowledge will not be maintained or spread.
The expected payoffs can be short term or long-term, and any human interpreting the value of a knowledge promise will form their own value-judgement based on how long they are willing to wait for a payoff. Through the promise model, there is a natural connection with economic game theory here, see Burgess & Fagernes (n.d.).
To model what we may expect of knowledge and its usefulness, we start by writing down the promises that are relevant, and what the benefits and costs of having these promises kept might be. Due to the subjective nature of promises, we can only suggest these things in broad terms, and it will remain for specific contexts to determine values for these things.
Agents (humans, machines or service centres, etc) can promise

- To reveal information.
- To use information revealed to them.
- To document or write down information.
- To train or teach others to interpret information.
- To search for answers.

7.1 The value of promised knowledge

It is not easy to come up with a universal measure of value for knowledge, of course, but in the spirit of modelling that is what we are going to pretend. Since there is no standard for this, we are free to invent one based on the promise model.

Definition 13 (The value of a promise). *Let $V(\pi)$ denote a function, which when applied to a promise π returns a real number with the interpretation of a payoff/return. A negative value represents a net cost associated with keeping the promise.*

Let us suppress, for now, the issue of when the payoff occurs, and assume that keeping the promise leads to rewards that we are accounting for far off in the future, at some final reckoning. We may add up values over the time each time the status of a promise is assessed, with values for:

1. A promise found to be kept, positive if good or negative if bad.
2. Costs associated with keeping the promise (always negative).
3. The promise was not kept leads to a possible loss for the promisee.

However we choose to account for these values, they are perceived very clearly in our minds when we interact with knowledge.
The hypothesis I propose is then that it must be possible to increase the net value of knowledge by adopting some simple strategies.

Hypothesis 1 (Increase value and reduce cost). *Some principles:*

- *Knowledge is made more accessible by reducing the cost of lookup.*
- *The value of information rises when accompanied by bonus associations to related topics.*
- *The cost of knowledge assimilation can be reduced by avoiding knowledge management overheads.*

The cost of knowledge includes the work done acquiring, using, transmitting it, etc. If we use accounting terminology, it is a simple matter of time and materials. The cost of information retrieval or lookup by either a person or a computer is related to the algorithmic complexity of the search required to find it. This translates most likely into the time a user has to invest in accessing information.
The costs are probably quite different depending on the representation of the knowledge items one uncovers while searching. For instance a book is likely easier to interpret than a painting, As a general question we would like to know how such costs that inhibit the learning and dissemination of knowledge can be reduced.

7.2 The cost of categories

Classification into categories plays a central role in this essay because it has been such an important activity in knowledge engineering for centuries. Why is it so popular? It was introduced in order to cluster together books about similar subjects. The contention is that this reduces tangibly the cost of finding relevant information, assuming that you understand the classification in the first place[4]. Let us test this idea.
Suppose there are T topics divided into C categories. In a linear search (starting at the beginning and running through until we find the right one). If there is only one category, then the cost of finding a topic on average is about half the length of the search list:

$$\chi_1 = \frac{1}{2}T \tag{2}$$

[4] Librarians are trained knowledge engineers who learn classifications and became smart assistants.

If there are multiple categories, this generalizes to:

$$\chi_C = \frac{1}{2}T/C + \frac{1}{2}(C-1) \quad (3)$$

So, if categories are to have any economic value,

$$\frac{1}{2}T/C + \frac{1}{2}(C-1) < \frac{1}{2}T. \quad (4)$$

This gives us a quadratic constraint for χ, which is easily solved to give $T > C$. In other words, introducing categories is always likely to reduce search times a little for any number of categories, assuming that one knows which category the topic belongs to. The saving $\Delta\chi = \chi_C - \chi_1$ actually shrinks with the number of categories however, since, if we write the total number of topics $T = t + C$, as there cannot be more categories than topics, then the saving is

$$\Delta\chi = \frac{1}{2}(t - t/C), \quad (5)$$

where t is the number of 'pure topics', i.e. those that are not themselves subject categories. $\Delta\chi$ gives a constant saving for large C at around half the number of non-categories. Thus the saving is not large if we go berserk with sub-categories. The cost does not depend on whether the topics are arranged in a flat partitioning or in a tree either[5], so hierarchy does not help here either.

7.3 Cost of adding a category: missing freedoms

Categories form lists that we call directories, that we are still familiar with today (e.g. yellow pages, and Yahoo). These stem from a time when libraries were the most important search engine. Classification was conceived of as a cost saving mechanism, and for a few privileged scholars with more expert knowledge, it also worked to identify larger patterns that enhanced the meaning of the information. This worked because scholarly subjects were handled by a few well-trained people, and subjects were placed into relatively few categories or fields of study. There was little focus on overlap, more on the 'nobility' of knowledge.

For most users, however, the cost of categorization gets counted twice: both when using knowledge and contributing knowledge. The cost χ_C, above, is the cost of lookup, but also the minimum cost of adding something to the category structure, since placement requires us to parse the model to look up the right place to add something. There can be additional overheads:

- A search for the correct category is required.
- If a new category is needed, it must be localized and agreed upon by the authorized designer of the taxonomy.
- If no category can be added, topics become orphaned.

The cost of agreeing on a change to the taxonomy depends on its governance, for instance:

- All agents must agree.

[5] The approach of introducing categories is similar to the use of hashing algorithms to locate values by replacing a linear search with a cheap constant-cost function that finds the approximate location of a value, but the difference is that there is no semantic hashing function to reduce the cost of finding subject categories in a list.

- An elected body must agree.
- Anyone can decide to change the categories.

A significant cost of working with knowledge thus comes from the need to anchor the topic in a particular place. If we could simply dump knowledge in a known location (e.g. treat every instance of the word as simply a word) then this can be done with essentially zero cost[6].
What this shows is that, from the perspective of someone wanting to contribute to knowledge, the presence of categorization adds a large cost deterrent to the activity. This is a plausible reason for the failure of ontology and semantic modelling so far today.
This need to choose a unique category is major hindrance to creating the model, and getting data into the model. What if I make a mistake? Every programmer knows that putting data into the wrong class or structure causes huge problems down the line, so you'd better get it right! But wouldn't it be nice if you didn't have to be so careful? Isn't the computer supposed to help us, not the other way around?

7.4 The cost of knowledge maintenance: memory and repetition

Repetition is a key tactic in learning and training. Repetition serves two goals: to gather experience about the consistency of information, as well as confirming and reinforcing a fixed message, thus increasing its value. The scientific method, for example, is based on the idea that verification of knowledge increases its value.
It will come as no surprise to anyone that merely documenting something cannot be viewed as an automatic strategy for increasing anyone's knowledge about it. Promising to write something does not imply an obligation on the part of a reader to read it. There must be a corresponding promise to read what has been written in order for it to be effective. Once read, knowledge must be remembered in order to be used. This suggests that there must be an approach for memory.
There are three kinds of memory:

- Rehearsed memory (e.g. muscle reflex memory).
- Short term memory (brute force, short-lived cramming).
- Long term cognitive memory (associative pathways).

In economics one uses dilemma games, to estimate the trade off between short and long term strategies, see Burgess & Fagernes (n.d.). I have no comments to make on that here. What this suggests is the following: if we are to improve the actual utility of knowledge over time, then we have

Hypothesis 2 (Knowledge requires practice)**.** *Any knowledge management scheme must encourage user to interact with it regularly.*

Positive reinforcement is needed to turn information into knowledge, and this repetition incurs a cost.

7.5 The Dunbar numbers

It is worth mentioning, as an addendum to the economic question, some limitations we should expect to bump into in knowledge engineering. Science always throws up certain scales that need to be attended to in understanding organized phenomena. The Dunbar numbers could be such scales for Knowledge Management.

[6] This is the logic behind hash tables in computing.

Studies by anthropologists, interested in the origin of human intelligence, have demonstrated statistical evidence for the idea that our capacity to perceive and know things and people well is limited by our brain size, see Dunbar (1996); Zhou et al. (2004). The evidence for this assertion comes from studies of inter-human relationships, but from there it is not a huge stretch to imagine that similar limitations apply to any kind of learned acquaintance, such as acquaintance with knowledge in its various forms.
The so-called Dunbar hierarchy identifies some key numbers that suggest economics limits on level of intimacy we can have to knowledge, because more intimate knowledge has a greater cognitive cost. The precise implications for knowledge management are, as far as I know, not fully understood, but the following numbers can be expected to appear if the hypothesis is correct (parentheses describe the original inference).

5	Detailed intimate interactions (close friends).
15	Team-level or frequent interaction (teams).
30	Daily working group size (tribe, workgroup, extended family, etc).
100	Things we recognize and understand (acquaintances).

Table 1. Key numbers from the Dunbar hierarchy, relating cognitive cost.

These numbers might appear anywhere cognitive cost plays a role. When presenting knowledge, for instance, we can expect people to have difficulty in relating to large numbers of choices and interrelationships, e.g. returned search results, number ingredients in an idea, number of steps in a recipe, etc. It would not be right to speculate unduly on how the Dunbar numbers might apply to knowledge management, but it is worth flagging this subject as worthy of further study.

8. From type hierarchy to overlapping contexts - a cheaper solution to encourage participation

Experience seems to show that users rarely contribute their own expertise back to projects that attempt to build taxonomies or strongly typed ontologies. It costs them too much. The same applies to Wikis that are organized hierarchically, because users either cannot find the right place to put something or they put it in the 'wrong' place, creating little value. The problem lies in quickly knowing how things should be organized in relation to one another.
Why is it so hard to know what topics should be related and how, to see what information is going to be needed and in which context? The answer is simply that this decision involves creative design. It is not a matter of pre-determined fact, but an arbitrary choice – but we don't like arbitrariness, so we look for agreement within a group or permission from an authority, etc. What started out as a simply desire to share, becomes an exercise in multi-party logistics. There is thus a significant 'mental computation' involved in this.
Suppose we could add a topic wherever we pleased, with some context to explain our usage. Then the cost of adding would be reduced by the entire cost of searching for the right place. Instead of an $O(N)$ search, we have an $O(1)$ insertion, costing the user little effort. Let's examine this idea further.

8.1 The meaning of domain and context

Users embellish facts with contextual information and want to emphasize certain aspects of knowledge. This freedom must be allowed in any account of KM. Terminology might begin as a set of unique terms, but quickly becomes distorted by ordinary linguistic creativity into slang and jargon in special contexts. Context is therefore both highly important, and somewhat neglected in knowledge research, see Deutsche (2006).

Users further seek generalizations of things, because we all look for common patterns as a way of compressing a large number of special instances to a single representative category[7]. The danger is that we become obsessed with dividing and subdividing knowledge into precise categories, perhaps spurred on by a feeling that information will get lost if we don't put everything into exactly the right box. The problem with packing things into boxes, as many will have experienced, is how to find the right box again later as the number of boxes grows large. Moreover, we often change our minds about how to classify information so what was classified last year is not findable tomorrow unless we refresh our understanding of context.

The first step in traditional classification schemes is to break things into a taxonomy. But a majority perhaps of concepts do not merely fall into just one category and so this artificial notion works against us once things go beyond the trivial. One has to either be an expert on a particular model of categorization or perform a brute-force search through the model to find the appropriate category.

If we look more critically at the way humans think outside of what we've been taught in school, this is not what we do. Our minds tend to do the opposite: we generalize from little evidence into much broader categories, implying that we are not that consumed with an obsessive compulsion for semantic correctness.

8.2 Topic type, a redundant concept

Topics play a dual role in the topic map standard, as:

- Subject identifiers that point to explanatory documents and semantic relationships (t).
- Context 'containers' or categories for other subjects (C).

In my own testing of knowledge modelling, attempts to use typing of topics have proven excessively difficult, and have thrown up many conflicts and singletons from unnecessary repetition during modelling. The fixation on 'type', apparently shoehorned into ontology languages from the historical origins of database modelling, seems to have been both a red herring and an expensive hindrance to locating useful information. To see what we can replace type with, we need to define some terms.

If knowledge is to be used and interacted with regularly, it will become the domain of a particular social group. Let's assume that such a group converges on a basic set of ideas. A knowledge domain is then any set of topics claimed by a group of individuals.

Definition 14 (Knowledge domain). *An arbitrary set of topics used commonly by a group of users, forming a cultural body of knowledge.*

Unlike the case of type annotation, there is no limitation on overlapping between different knowledge domains. The contention in topic map modelling is essentially that data-types model different cases. Again, this seems to flow more from a classic computer science dogma, based on some kind of entity relation model, rather than on a clear philosophy of the problem. In addition to a domain of knowledge, there is also the idea of usage in circumstances that are governed by factors far outside of the domain itself, such as time and environment.

Definition 15 (Context). *Any set of topics, either associated with one another or not, that describe the current situation of an agent when using or searching for information.*

---

[7] This is the basic approach behind all data compression.

Contexts are words and phrases we attach to a topic to disambiguate its usage. A context need not be either semantically or categorically related to the topic it describes. For example, the knowledge about 'tea' can be in the context of 'flavours', 'botany', 'drinking', 'suppliers', or even 'afternoon' none of which has any particular affinity to tea other than by association.
As mentioned above, it seems that, more by habit than reason, one has used a hierarchy of non-overlapping category types to disambiguate usage in different contexts. This seems to be a simple error of modelling. The problem is that it mixes up two different models unnecessarily: a description of generalizations or 'type' (which is forced unnaturally to be unique) and a model of brainstorming relationships to related things. We do not need a type to disambiguate usage, just another existing topic within the model, with no special status.

8.3 Contextualization is not strongly ordered

To illustrate why context is not at all hierarchical, consider this example of a geographically distributed organization, with finance, engineering and legal departments in three countries. Let us suppose that the organization has headquarters in 'usa', 'uk' and 'norway', and each branch has departments for 'finance', 'engineering' and 'legal' matters.
We have now two choices when making a hierarchy for the organization, depending on what we happen to think is of primary importance. In the first version, we treat geography as the primary distinction, and can express the full hierarchy like this:

```
usa.finance
usa.engineering
usa.legal
uk.finance
uk.engineering
uk.legal
norway.finance
norway.engineering
norway.legal
```

In this notation, the dot has the apparent interpretation of 'member' because the departments are smaller than the countries and are contained within them.
A different agent might feel that this model is upside down and that one should consider the finance department to be a unified global entity, with branches in three different countries. In that case, you would write

```
finance.uk
finance.usa
finance.norway
```

and so on. This example highlights the fact that we often want to slice and dice complex concepts in different ways, and attending too closely to a single hierarchical model prevents that.
If we think technically for a moment, the key observation is to notice that the '.' (dot) operator is really an intersection of sets (AND)[8], and that this is a much more flexible notion than hierarchy.

[8] It is a commutative operator, which is why it makes sense to write both `usa.finance` and `finance.usa`.

Underlying hierarchies and networks is the concept of *sets*. A set or *collection* of something is just a number of instances that satisfy some property. For example, the *set of all vending machines*, or the *set of times between 2 and 3 o'clock*. Sets can be thought of as networks in which the elements are all joined to each other by a common relationship 'in the same set as'.
We often write subset membership using a membership '.' character, e.g. if `linux` is the set of hosts with property 'linux', then a subset (or sub-class) of these hosts is 'debian' (see figure). The class *64 bit hosts* is not a subset of linux, as part of it lies outside. It is a subset of *hosts*.

usa.finance
usa AND finance
usa $\cap$ finance

Context sets have the property that

```
usa.finance = finance.usa
```

i.e. the commutativity of membership ordering. Hierarchies do not have this property.
Sets can be made hierarchical when every subset is contained entirely by one and only one parent set, and in turn contains zero or more whole subsets which it does not share with any other. The problem with hierarchical sets is that they are too restrictive. If you design them incorrectly in the first place, you shut parts of the organization inside a box that prevents other parts from accessing them.
With sets, we can perform filtering based on logical reasoning, just as with search languages – but in a very efficient way. We can promise to association meanings by set-computation:

```
classes:

 "english_speaking"
     expression => "(usa|uk).!legal";
```

Thus the English speakers promise to identify themselves as those entities belonging to the USA 'OR' to the UK, excepting the legal department (`!` means NOT).
Henceforth, I will use the notation 'context::topic', e.g. 'X::Y' to mean a mention of a topic Y in context X.

8.4 Topics in multiple contexts

Consider a slightly different case of 'homonyms', i.e. words that have multiple meanings in different contexts. As an example, I shall borrow from the Topic Map literature a fascination with opera as a knowledge domain, see Pepper (2009), by examining the topic "Peter Grimes" which is a character from a poem made famous through Benjamin Britten's acclaimed opera. What type or types should this topic have? We might interpret a mention of the name in multiple ways:

- As a name, e.g. 'names::Peter Grimes'.
- One or more persons with the same name, e.g. 'names.friends::Peter Grimes', 'names.tv_show::Peter Grimes'.
- An opera, e.g. 'opera::Peter Grimes'.
- A libretto from an opera, e.g. 'opera.libretto::Peter Grimes'.
- A character from an opera, e.g. 'names.opera::Peter Grimes'.

- A character in a poem (The Borough) on which the opera was based, e.g. 'names.poem::Peter Grimes'.

And so on. The list is potentially infinite.

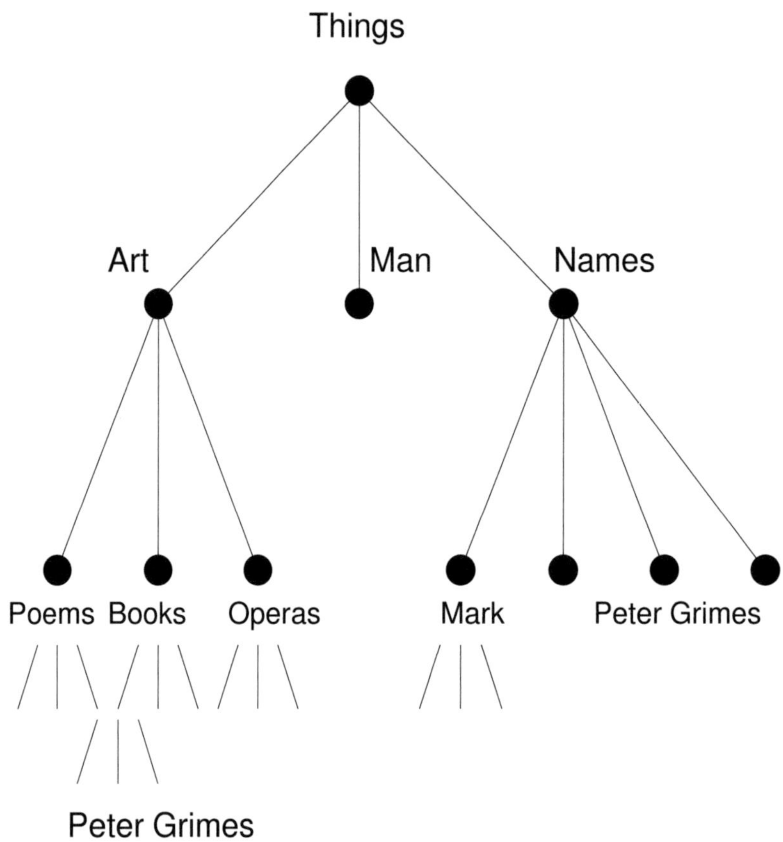

Fig. 4. A single topic, like 'Peter Grimes' is really a linguistic element, that has usage in many different contexts. Arranging topics in a tree confuses context with parent-node, which is wrong.

The desire for simplicity and parsimony encourages people to think about topics as falling into neat, mutually exclusive categories, but what we see is really something with a much more linguistic freedom: a single phrase 'Peter Grimes' used in a wide variety of overlapping contexts, with slightly different meanings.

At this point, most people feel an uncomfortable need to anchor the righteous place of each usage in their model by making an exclusive choice. Suppose this is to place this name within the category of opera, along with Aida and The Ring cycle, etc, but what criterion does one have for deciding on types? In fact, a type is just a topic itself, and the entire type notion could be eliminated in favour of an association: Aida "is an" opera, as one does in an object oriented model approach.

8.5 Reasoning about categories in searches

Consider occurrence of text for different interpretations of Peter Grimes. There is a book of the libretto

```
occurrences:

  peter_grimes.opera::

     ''http://onlinebooks.com''
        represents => { ''Book about the opera''};

     ''http://onlinescores.com''
        represents => { ''The complete score of the opera''};

  peter_grimes.name::

     ''http://names.com''
        represents => { ''The origin of the name''};
```

In our new set interpretation, the sub-set operation '.' is commutative and reflexive. So it doesn't matter if we consider `peter_grimes` to the the superset or opera to be the super-set. Suppose however that the first book contains the complete text of the libretto and the etymology of the name, an explanation of the poem, etc. Then it is relevant to all these contexts, or indeed in a generic context 'any' and should appear in the results of any search.
If we interpreted `opera,libretto,poem,name` as type categories that do not overlap (e.g. as a conventional topic map) then it would be necessary to register this book as an occurrence in every single category – i.e. with multiple registrations; that is because the combination type+topic is a unique entity, and thus multiple types significantly increases the cost of documenting this information for users. The overlapping set model collapses all these registrations into one, but is not broken by multiple references, so we achieve two things: a reduction in cost of inserting data, and robustness to inserting multiple times.
Using context sets, we have many more possible ways to give useful information. Suppose we search for `peter_grimes.opera`, returning results for peter grimes in any category is generally more helpful than unhelpful to a human being. The issue then becomes for whom are the results intended? If we admit that humans play a role in the process (because they are far superior reasoning agents than software) then a freer interpretation is the correct one. This requires less expertise to set up and leads to better results.
Conversely if machines are to do all the work, users must have access to a complete and mathematically correct technical ontology, with type-correct documentation to yield precise search results. The only way to address this is the Topic Maps standard is the introduction of a search language, which pushes the complexity back onto the user, violating the first principle. The user is forced to fight the logic of the system rather than using it for inspiration. In practice it is rare that we want to restrict information so stringently as through a logic of types – and when we do so, we often end up finding nothing because the data are so over-constrained that the intersection of all constraints is the empty set. We need to simplify all this structure drastically.

9. Emergent norms and common knowledge – the recipient's view

An interesting and highly relevant question is thus the following: given a free approach to ontology, based on context rather than a pre-arranged taxonomy of types, would a free user process of adding topics and associations converge to a graph that auto-selects a set of attractors we might call popular 'well known concepts'?

It is tempting to answer: yes, this must be so, since our natural language evolves in basically this way, and seems to have achieved just that. However, we also know from natural language that, when a sufficient number of individuals is involved, languages fragment and sub-cultures emerge. All of these things are natural from a network point of view however. Let's sketch out how one might go about discovering whether this is possible.

9.1 Norms, swarms and attractors

We would like to know if a group of agents, making no promises to obey a predetermined ontology, would effectively promise to follow an emergent ontology after a sufficient amount of time. Understanding this hypothesis fully goes beyond the scope of this essay, but we can sketch out some of the issues.

The concept of emergent behaviour is tied to so-called swarm intelligence, see Bonabeau et al. (1999) and has enjoyed a fashionable period over the past 20 years. It has brought both insight and a lot of hype to modelling. Let us focus on a simple promise model of swarming that attempts to bring a simple but clear meaning to how swarming and emergent norm-formation (normation) takes place, see Burgess & Fagernes (2007a;b).

A swarm is simply a flock of agents (birds, insects, etc) that seem to exhibit collectively organized behaviour, even though each of the agents is a free entity with only weak links to its nearest neighbours. Swarms often come together to minimize costs of some kind, e.g. the cost of protecting each agent against predators. We call such behaviour 'emergent' because it is not explicitly designed, but is perceived as a side effect of something else, by a particular user's perspective.

In promise theory, emergent behaviour is explained by noting the indistinguishability of certain collections promises from others. Without getting into details, we say that a system has emergent properties if it seems to promise something, from the viewpoint of an external observer who in scope, that in fact it does not explicitly promise, see Burgess & Fagernes (2007a) In the same way, it is possible for a knowledge model to make no explicit design promises about category and yet still form a structure that appears to cluster around certain 'attractor topics' in the manner of a hierarchy.

The spontaneous formation of hierarchies is a relatively well-known phenomenon in network science, see Newman et al. (2001); Watts (1999) and is related to the 'small worlds' phenomenon. This could provide an explanation for the preponderance of attention given to hierarchical organization. Put simply, what happens is that certain early-defined topics acquire an economic advantage to being used. Topics that have the most associations and usage tend to attract even more attention, and therefore acquire the status of an anchor point or emergent category for knowledge. This phenomenon is called 'preferential attachment'. For a simple review, see , see Barabási (2002).

What is exciting about this model is that it can be tested by looking at the statistics of the graphs that result from such a free collaboration. Preferential attachment leads to long-tailed or power-law distributions in the node degree k of the association graph, of the form $N(k) \sim 1/k^n$, for some n, whereas a designed hierarchy would likely show a much sharper distribution of node degrees, see Barabási (2002); Newman et al. (2001).

Hypothesis 3 (Convergence of knowledge graph). *A knowledge map will converge to a graph with a power-law degree distribution if a type-free context model is used.*

We are not able to say what result a graph will converge to as users add associations and topics.

- An arbitrary choice by policy of a desired outcome for the meaning of a norm.
- An attractor or potential surface with a unique minimum, e.g. based on popularity.

We identify semantic 'votes' for discrete subjects, although many of the concepts might view things less precisely, living only in the suburbs of these concept's centra. Any suitable model must account for this uncertainty, and multiplicity of viewpoints (a town can have many districts).

10. Emergence friendly rules for ontology

Let's summarize what minor changes to, say Topic Maps, are needed to encourage spontaneous ontology, and lower the cost of knowledge development. The data model for topic maps contains no major errors or omissions, but it contains one unnecessary constraint that makes topic maps hard to build models with. That is the constraint that topic types should be non-overlapping categories, see Kipp (2003).

Hypothesis 4 (Correction of Topic Maps). *We replace non-overlapping types with overlapping contexts so that a topic can belong to more than one contexts. Topic types become contexts, and topic names are registered only once, with associations and occurrences belonging to contexts, and topics existing universally as pure syntax.*

The beauty of this reinterpretation is that it does very little violence to existing technology, but extends the possible interpretation of the data in potentially valuable ways.
Under this new regime, we can assume that:

- All topics exist, whether defined or not.
- Only topic associations need be explicitly promised, including in which context they are relevant, i.e. in which context a topic promises certain properties.
- The context of a topic (i.e. the usage of the term or phrase) explains its semantics, not a classification of its type within a separate ontological spanning tree.

The 'current context' in a topic search, for instance, can be assumed from the path taken by the user through the history of topics, etc. This also motivates the idea of stories below.
The transition from selection by taxonomic classification to selecting topics by usage is subtle but wide ranging. It's not what the topic is, but how the term is used that is important. In other words, topics themselves are reinterpreted from labelled semantic concepts to being simple syntactic fragments.

11. Roles and collective promises – user-perceived black boxes

The Dunbar numbers, mentioned previously, suggest that cognitive complexity is related to the number of things we need to (promise to) know at different levels of intimacy. So a relevant economic question is: how can we reduce this number of items, and thereby reduce the cognitive cost for end users of information?
Categories are clearly an attempt to do reduce the numbers by providing umbrella concepts, but their introduction is often overwhelmed by hiearchical design issues. I believe that too great an emphasis is placed on the hierarchical aspect of the taxonomic category trees. Promise theory's basic tenets lead to a suggestion for this reduction that is simpler: spanning sets – or

what I shall call *roles*, see Bergstra & Burgess (1994-now). A role is simply a group of things that identifies some pattern amongst knowledge items (agents). If these agents or topics make similar kinds of knowledge promises, then they must play a similar role in the scheme of things too. Put simply, a role is a bundle of topics that make similar knowledge promises.

Some examples help to make this clear. For instance, at a low level, different categories of words play certain roles in the construction of knowledge; e.g. some words promise to be verbs, some promise to be nouns or 'things', and so on. These roles are functional and therefore have a practical value. Next, one might have other roles, like 'colour' or 'animal', which are less clearly functional, but more an attempt to put a name on a perceived phenomenon.

We can define such roles simply in terms of the promises they make:

Definition 16 (Promise role). *A collection of agents or things that is assessed by a user as making the same kind of promise (or collection of promises).*

Patterns like this tie in with the use of repetition to emphasize learning, as mentioned before, and thus patterns are related to our notion of learning by rote.

Now, consider a different type of knowledge promise that is not about describing an intrinsic property of a single item, but is rather about interpreting the result of a collaboration between different promises that individuals might classify in very different ways. Take, for example, the concept of a radio. Someone might call a particular group of functional elements (e.g. electronic components) a radio. Each of the components promises certain properties like 'will act as a switch' or 'which store electric charge', if this collective set of components keeps the promise to play music from various radio stations, we might indeed call it a radio.

The attachment of a concept like 'radio' to a set of collaborating relationships is nothing like the naming that happens in a standard taxonomy: it is an interpretation, based on probably an incomplete understanding of the structure of the internal properties, based on a superficial evaluation of its behaviour. In a hierarchical decomposition one would separate the components into rigid categories like 'resistor', 'capacitor', 'transistor', or 'plastic' and 'metal', none of which say anything about what these parts contribute to.

A radio is thus an emergent property of a collaborative network of properties that has no place in a taxonomic categorization related to its parts. A radio is not more than the sum of its parts, as we sometimes like to say, but rather it forms a collaboration which comes alive and takes on a new interpretation at a different level. Typical taxonomic decompositions are reductionistic, leaving no room for the understanding of this as a collective phenomenon. This defect can really only be repaired if we understand that it is the *observer* or recipient, not the designer, that ultimately makes the decision whether to accept the assessment of a set of component promises is a radio or not.

Definition 17 (Collective role). *A collection of agents that is assessed to form a collaborative role, if the agents work together to keep a promise that requires the participation of all the agents collectively.*

The concept of a radio is clearly much cheaper to maintain as a new and separate entity than a detailed understanding of how the components collaborate to produce the effect. We frequently use this kind of information hiding to reduce the cost of knowledge, but clearly knowledge gets lost in this process.

Definition 18 (Black box). *The purposeful forgetting or discarding of knowledge in order to reduce the cost of accepting a collective role.*

The ability to replace a lot of complexity with a simple label brings great economic efficiency for end-users of knowledge, which one could measure in concepts per role. However, I believe that it is not the size of a group or role that is the best indicator for providing a reduction in perceived complexity, but rather the affinity that a receiver who promises to *use* this role's defining pattern feels for the concept. In other words, how well does a user identify with the pattern?

When things combine to play a collaborative role, a single recipient can use the promise as an entity, i.e. a 'black box'– and experience a cognitive simplification. The cost of understanding this functional collaboration is greatly reduced.

The important point here, as we see repeatedly in this essay, is that it is the way that these terms are perceived by the user, i.e. the *usage* (not the definition) of these terms that is the crucial element here. If I talk about 'Mr Green' and understand this usage as a decription of the man's colour, and you interpret it to be a name, the intended implication will not be passed on. We therefore require a binding of terms or ontologies between different agents who engage in knowledge interactions.

Definition 19 (Knowledge bindings). *A binding occurs between the author of knowledge and the recipient when there is something in common between their promised interpretations. If the recipient's promised understanding of concepts about the original intention does not overlap at all with the meaning promised by the author, then nothing will be communicated.*

The interpretation of knowledge made by a recipient clearly depends formally on both the original promised usage of terms by the author/promiser of the knowledge and whatever terms the recipient has promised to accept.

It follows straightforwardly from promise theory that what is offered is only a pre-requisite. It is what is *accepted* or used by agents that is important. Clearly, it is true that knowledge that no one accepts or uses is valueless.

12. Making usage the knowledge enabler

How might we use this cost reduction approach by grouping things effectively for users? One approach might be to simply write down items, as suggested before, and wait for natural social processes to normalize usage into common knowledge, but this can take significant time and can lead to an explosion of new items. One would likely need to go back and re-organize the stored information later to eliminate redundancy. All this accomplishes, however, is to delay the inevitable cost of organizing the information in the first place.

While there might be optimum ways of approaching categorizations that reduce the cost of knowing everything, this suggests that there is an intrinsic cost to knowing something that is associated with the what the receiver of the knowledge has decided is an acceptable set of category bundles. This is such an important observation, it is worth turning it into a hypothesis

Hypothesis 5 (Knowledge has a minimum cost). *There is an intrinsic minimum cost to comprehending information that depends on the complexity of the model used to interpret information by the recipient, i.e. the complexity of the recipient's use-promise.*

This hypothesis harks of Shannon's entropy theorem for intrinsic information, and is almost certainly related through the definition of modelling 'alphabets', see Burgess (2004); Shannon & Weaver (1949). As Einstein remarked: everything should be made as simple as possible but

no simpler. The subjectivity of this intrinsic cost might also explain why some people find it harder than others to learn or accept knowledge from certain sources than others.
The economic perspective we are pursuing here suggests a simple strategy for reducing personal cost by an end user that has to do with short-circuiting others' predefined or authoritative categories by recategorizing everything in his or her own set.

Hypothesis 6 (Personal simplification strategy). *Each individual student or recipient of knowledge begins by remapping apparent categories of information used by the source into a personal reduced set of trusted categories, according to their own world view and experience. In this way the cost of lookup, mistrust and unfamiliarity is reduced.*

In modelling terms, we can imagine forming usage-categories called, say, 'virtual bundles of knowledge promises', i.e. virtual roles for the things a user promises to accept, which any knowledge agent is free to edit and manipulate as it sees fit.
More work will be needed to identify what the optimum approach might be in certain circumstances, and this could depend on a number of factors, so I shall leave the subject dangling on this point, as an opportunity for future work.

13. How can we be certain about meaning?

If an ontology is not determined by a standardizing authority, how can we be certain that anyone will end up understanding each other? The story of the Tower of Babel comes to mind, as one advocates tearing down the standard ontologies. In fact, I believe that the underpinning of knowledge by these spanning trees is entirely unnecessary. It is rather up to each and every user to apply such a tree as a filter if they so desire.
What the promise model underlines is that every agent individually promises only its own intended meaning, and in fact no two agents can truly know if they mean the same thing. Rather than seeing this as a problem to be forced into submission, it is better to accept this as the nature of reality and deal with the uncertainty. Only an independent third party can determine whether or not they *seem* to agree for all intents and purposes. The frequency of use will determine how stable word usage is. Note that the irregular verbs are those that are most frequently used. Less well used words tend to be normalized into common patterns quickly to reduce the cost of recall.
The main difference in the emergent approach is the distribution of cost. For the authoritative ontology, the up-front cost of contribution and usage is high, and it assumes expert knowledge. For the emergent context approach, there is no initial cost, but rather one must promise to practice over time to retain meaning. The advantage of a purely linguistic classification is that it is not a separate rehearsal from daily usage. We have little choice but to practice language, so in some ways the overhead is gratis, or at least can be 'charged to a different account'.

14. Curiosity, inspiration, learning and understanding – narratives

Turning to the future now, the promise model has some other nice features. Often, we claim to have understood something when we are happy to stop looking for further explanation. This usually happens when we are able to construct a satisfactory story or explanation about it. These stories or explanations stop in often arbitrary places – they are more about sating our curiosity to some level of satisfaction than total revelation. Humans evolved language through story telling. It is entirely possible that our brains are wired to support this form of narrative.

Consider what might happen if we looked up Einstein's famous equation $E = mc^2$ in a knowledge base. This simple looking equation is associated with a huge amount of popular culture about Einstein, and most people would immediately think of him, but there is nothing unique or 'copyrighted' about it. A nutrition expert who had never read any physics might use this formula for something quite different, such as "Eating is munching and chewing twice".

Still, one context dominates above all others and that is physics. Under this context, there are many associated ideas. When we think of $E = mc^2$, we might associate it with the atomic bomb, or nuclear power, or mass-energy conversion, or with a funny photograph of Einstein pulling tongues at the camera.

In a book one could integrate all of these apparently unrelated meanings from cover to cover, weaving them into a story, with a progressing storyline that explains, organizes and blazes a repeatable trail for all these ideas, or one could go directly to look up keywords in an index. The table of contents in a book spans the highlights of the story, whereas the index is a quite different covering of the subjects that pays little attention to the ordering or developments in narrative, or the totality of the theme in the book.

The concept of a story is large in human culture, but as far as I can tell very little attention has been given to them in Knowledge Management research. In work with Alva Couch, I have tried to remedy this by exploring a simple notion of stories, including the notion of automated storytelling, by identifying causal associations between topics, see Burgess (2009); Couch & Burgess (2009; 2010). A table of contents, in a book, is a rough outline of the story told by the book at a very high level. It gives a different perspective on a book's content than the index does (yet the index is what current KM technology is almost exclusively focused on). Knowledge technology needs to support the idea of storylines, in which ideas and information build upon the context of earlier information, because this is how humans communicate, see Wolf (2007).

Definition 20 (Story). *A collection of topics connected together by associations in a causative thread.*

Causality (i.e. cause and effect) can be embodied in associative relationships such as 'affects' or 'always happens before', 'is a part of' etc. These relationships have a transitivity that most promised associations do not have, and this property allows a kind of automated reasoning that is not possible with arbitrary associations.

Automated story generation has been discussed by myself and Alva Couch in , see Couch & Burgess (2009; 2010), so I will not repeat the detailed arguments here. Today, there are no semantic knowledge models that are able to model creative narratives by association, or even ordered tables of contents in books for that matter! This is an extraordinary omission and a key capability in integrating random access knowledge with documents.

It is worth studying this possibility to derive new and 'unknown' stories from emergent repositories of knowledge promises. In this way, one could imagine discovering a new story about $E = mc^2$ that has never been told before, derived perhaps from the contributions of a swarm of twenty different individuals who were not even thinking about this matter.

Understanding more about the principles of story detection could also have more far-reaching consequences for knowledge than just automated reasoning. In school, not all students find it easy to make their own stories from bare facts, and this could be why some students do better than others in their understanding. We tend to feel we understand something when we can tell a convincing story about it. With more formal principles behind an effort to understand stories, technology could help struggling students to grasp connections better, and one could imagine a training program to help basic literacy skills.

We don't have time to explore all these details in this essay, except to point to this as a promising (pun intended) area of research for the future. I think that storylines combined with a linguistic approach to ontology can go a long way to addressing the deficiencies of today's web ontology methods.

15. Conclusions and challenges

There are many questions pending after this short essay, too many to provide many plausible answers to even a few; this is both regrettable and very exciting. The potential for future work is large, and the aim here has rather been to highlight the challenges ahead. I believe that current research has to some extent lost its way in trying to impose the intricacies of formal ontologies, and that instead of designing new standards of representation for descriptive logics, we need to re-examine some basic ideas about the aims of Knowledge Management and its relationship to pedagogy.

With a few modifications, we abandon the idea of searching for the 'right place' to put topic information, and put it anywhere with some context labels. The promises will then self-organize into an emergent pattern. Users could also use the idea of storytelling to organize their knowledge:

- Write down topic atoms and try to combine them into a network of associations.
- Write down complete stories and break them down into simplified narratives that can be represented as milestone topics linked by association.
- Start by defining a hierarchy of categories and sub-categories. This is still possible, but not recommended.

For the future we still have to demonstrate the validity of this approach:

1. Prove the independent compatibility of multiple ontologies, using promise theory.
2. Show how different ontological viewpoints can emerge from groups and norms/swarming.
3. What is the process for refactoring and establishing norms?

Teaching skills are bound to become a more valuable resource as society enters a truly knowledge oriented era. Without these, we might have massive data storage, but all of it will be largely wasted. An important aspect of learning is selective forgetting, and one can question the wisdom of stockpiling information forever. But as humans we tend to hold on the the past somewhat irrationally.

In this essay, I have proposed using a model for knowledge engineering based on autonomous cooperation, as a way of working around the modelling errors of hierarchical categorization most commonly used today. By stripping away unnecessary structure, a promise approach to knowledge grants knowledge the freedom for it to evolve in a direction dictated by common collaborative culture, see Ostrom (1990). I believe that organized ontology has a limited usefulness, in much too specialized circumstances to be generally useful, and that we must return to a simpler linguistic approach to documenting ontologies.

Three important focus areas come to mind to explore further:

- The neglected role of narratives and storylines in knowledge representation.

- The role of repeated interaction in cementing normative language.
- The economics in the dynamics of agreement.

The tension between the desire to hierarchically divide and conquer subjects and the freedom to develop storylines unconstrained is likely to haunt knowledge management for many years to come. In the writing of this essay, for instance, I have striven to seek a balance between serving two masters: to organize things into a simple hierarchy of sections (for later 'dipping into the story' i.e. for reference), while at the same time recognizing that the whole narrative much be readable from start to finish. It is through the storyline that the illusion of understanding is most likely to emerge, because there we control the context of information from moment to moment. A novel never has to satisfy the former constraint, and is therefore a purer form of writing.

The likelihood that we will ever unify meaning into a single, standard, crystalline tree of concepts is about the same as the likelihood of unifying all the world's cultures into one. The evidence from social networking, see Newman (2003); Watts (1999), suggests that the human desire for social interaction evens out and normalizes: like swarming behaviour, we follow involuntarily the influences of others, and this leads to a condensation that has manageable proportions.

The final answers about knowledge management lie probably with social anthropology. It will be a challenge for more empirical studies to come up with evidence for the success or failure of the suggestions contained here. In the mean time, there seems to be little to lose by trying a promise approach, so I leave it to readers to explore these simple guidelines in practice.

16. References

Albert, R. & Barabási, A. (2002). Statistical mechanics of complex networks, *Reviews of Modern Physics* 74: 47.

Barabási, A. (2002). *Linked*, (Perseus, Cambridge, Massachusetts).

Bergstra, J. & Burgess, M. (1994-now). *An engineering approach to promises*, work in progress.

Bergstra, J. & Burgess, M. (2006). Local and global trust based on the concept of promises, *http://arxiv.org/abs/0912.4637* .

Bonabeau, E., Dorigo, M. & Theraulaz, G. (1999). *Swarm Intelligence: From Natural to Artificial Systems*, Oxford University Press, Oxford.

Burgess, M. (2004). *Analytical Network and System Administration — Managing Human-Computer Systems*, J. Wiley & Sons, Chichester.

Burgess, M. (2005). An approach to understanding policy based on autonomy and voluntary cooperation, *IFIP/IEEE 16th international workshop on distributed systems operations and management (DSOM), in LNCS 3775*, pp. 97–108.

Burgess, M. (2009). Knowledge management and promises, *Lecture Notes on Computer Science* 5637: 95–107.

Burgess, M. & Fagernes, S. (2007a). Laws of systemic organization and collective behaviour in ensembles, *Proceedings of MACE 2007*, Vol. 6 of *Multicon Lecture Notes*, Multicon Verlag.

Burgess, M. & Fagernes, S. (2007b). Norms and swarms, *Lecture Notes on Computer Science* 4543 (Proceedings of the first International Conference on Autonomous Infrastructure and Security (AIMS)): 107–118.

Burgess, M. & Fagernes, S. (n.d.). Voluntary economic cooperation in policy based management, *IEEE Transactions on Network and Service Management* p. (submitted).

Couch, A. & Burgess, M. (2009). Compass and direction in topic maps, *(Oslo University College preprint)*.

Couch, A. & Burgess, M. (2010). Troubleshooting with human-readable automated reasoning, *Proceedings of the Twenty-Fourth Systems Administration Conference (LISA XXIV) (USENIX Association: Berkeley, CA)*, p. (unnumbered pages).

Deutsche, G. (2006). *The unfolding of language*, Arrow.

Dicheva, D. & Dichev, C. (2005). Authoring educational topic maps: Can we make it easier?, *Proceedings of Fifth IEEE International Conference on Advanced Learning Technologies (ICALT'05), ISBN: 0-7695-2338-2*.

Dietz, J. (2006). *Enterprise ontology*, Springer.

Dunbar, R. (1996). *Grooming, Gossip and the Evolution of Language*, Faber and Faber, London.

et al., F. B. (ed.) (2003). *The Description Logic Handbook*, Cambridge.

Hicks, R., Dattero, R. & Galup, S. D. (2006). The five-tier knowledge management hierarchy, *Journal of Knowledge Management* 10: 19–31.

Kipp, N. (2003). A mathematical formalism for the topic maps reference model, *Technical report*.

Moench, E., Ullrich, M., Schnurr, H. & Angelc, J. (2003). Semanticminer – ontology-based knowledge retrieval, *Journal of Universal Computer Science* 9(7): 682–696.

Moore, G. (2001). Rdf and topicmaps: An exercise in convergence, *Technical report*, XML Europe.

Newman, M. (2003). The structure and function of complex networks, *SIAM Review* 45: 167–256.

Newman, M. E. J., Strogatz, S. & Watts, D. (2001). Random graphs with arbitrary degree distributions and their applications, *Physical Review E* 64: 026118.

of Government Commerce, O. (ed.) (2000). *Best Practice for Service Support*, ITIL: The Key to Managing IT Services, The Stationary Office, London.

Ostrom, E. (1990). *Governing the Commons*, Cambridge.

Pepper, S. (2009). *Encyclopedia of Library and Information Sciences*, CRC Press, ISBN 9780849397127, chapter Topic Maps.

Shannon, C. & Weaver, W. (1949). *The mathematical theory of communication*, University of Illinois Press, Urbana.

Strassner, J. (2007). *Handbook of Network and System Administration*, Elsevier Handbook, chapter Knowledge Engineering Using Ontologies.

W3C (n.d.). Defining n-ary relations on the semantic web: use with individuals. http://www.w3.org/TR/2004/WD-swbp-n-aryRelations-20040721/.

Watts, D. (1999). *Small Worlds*, (Princeton University Press, Princeton).

Wolf, M. (2007). *Proust and the Squid*, Harper Collins.

Zhou, W., Sornette, S., Hill, R. & Dunbar, R. (2004). Discrete hierarchical organization of social group sizes, *Proc. Royal Soc.* 272: 439–444.

9

Knowledge-Based Enterprise Framework: A Management Control View

Saulius Gudas
Vilnius University
Kaunas Faculty of Humanities, Kaunas
Lithuania

1. Introduction

Contemporary organizations need to manage not only data, but the whole data-information-knowledge continuum; this is why the role and structure of the enterprise repository or enterprise knowledge base have to change adequately too. The concept of computerised knowledge base becomes important with the emergence of such intensively computer-based organizational forms as supply chains, virtual organizations etc. Organizations require having not only data in virtual environment (i.e. shared data bases), but also digital knowledge about those data, as well as about the data structure and semantics; knowledge about enteprise infrastructure and processes; process management up to strategic intentions (Gudas, 2009a).

Knowledge management is the business activity intended to solve critical enterprise adaptability and competitiveness issues in a rapidly changing environment. The main goal of the knowledge management in enterprises is to create an organizational context for effective creation, storage, dissemination and use of enterprise knowledge, which are essential for securing enterprise competitiveness against the changing business environment and for setting the environment towards a desirable direction (Maier, 2004).

The main goal of the knowledge management in enterprises is to create organizational context for effective creation, store, dissemination and use of enterprise knowledge, which are essential for enterprise competitiveness in changing business environment.

There are some well-known knowledge management models (Holsapple, Joshi 1999), which highlight some important knowledge management aspects and knowledge management components aimed at implementing knowledge management in organizations.

In spite of the variety of knowledge management models and tools, there is a gap between these theoretical models and the practical implementation of knowledge management systems in organizations. This problem of adjustment of business requirements and IT capabilities is known under the name "Business and IT alignment" (Henderson, Venkatraman 1990).The investigations in knowledge management area are closely related to developments in the field of enterprise architecture (EA) frameworks (J.Schekkerman, 2003), enterprise modelling (EM) frameworks (Zachman, Sowa, 1992; Maes, et al., 2000; Ulrich, 2002) and languages (Vernadat, 2002). Enterprise domains and aspects of the enterprise knowledge identified in the various EM and EA methodologies and frameworks reflect the semantics of the concept "enterprise knowledge component".

The most IT-based enterprises today are data–driven: enterprise management activities are supported by management (functional) IS based on the Data Base Management Systems services. The integrated enterprise knowledge base is concerned as a tool for solving a range of business problems: business transformation into the knowledge-based business, business and IT alignment, and the IT-based support of business management activities.

There are three concepts related to the knowledge processes in enterprise: "knowledge-intensive", "knowledge-centric" and "knowledge-based". Appropriate name for any enterprise, based on knowledge intensive work, or knowledge intensive products is a "knowledge-intensive" organization or firm (Zack, 2003).

Even if the definition of the knowledge-centric enterprise does not emphasize the use of the information technologies (IT) in the enterprise, it should be noted, that research presented here is concerned with the contemporary enterprise, which uses IT extensively for the support of the management of its business processes. On the basis of the literature analysis "knowledge-based" enterprise is defined as an enterprise, which integrates enterprise knowledge base into the overall framework of business management and development.

The newest vision of the Real Time Enterprise (RTE) as the most adaptive and responsive enterprise is expressed by Gartner Group (Gartner Group, 1999). Y. Malhotra (Malhotra, 2005) has analysed the knowledge gaps which arise when implementing knowledge management in Real Time Enterprises and has pointed out the two main KM models: strategy-pull and technology-push models, thus indicating two interrelated RTE domains: business (strategy) domain and technology domain. Henderson and Venkatraman (Henderson, Venkatraman, 1990) have also analysed business-IT alignment problem and proposed a seminal Strategic Alignment Model (SAM) for business–IT alignment; the model was aimed to support the integration of information technology (IT) into business strategy by advocating alignment between and within four domains. In the SAM two interrelated aspects of computerised enterprise are defined: 1) business domain and 2) IT domain, decomposed into two levels of detail: 1) infrastructure and processes level, 2) strategic level.

Two types of knowledge inherent to the Knowledge-Based Enterprise should be pointed out. The first type of knowledge comprises all the organizational memory, which consists of various types of human knowledge, handled by managers daily to perform and manage organizational activities. This type of knowledge is referred to as *organizational knowledge.*

Another type of knowledge is a subset of knowledge stored in the Enterprise KB, and is named *enterprise knowledge.* It comprises virtual (digital) knowledge about the problem domain, i.e. digital knowledge about activities of Knowledge-Based Enterprise.

The Knowledge–Based Enterprise (KBE) framework is based on the internal modeling paradigm applied for enterprise management modeling (Gudas, 2009), (Gudas, 2008), (Gudas, Brundzaite, 2006a). The dependency map of the major concepts involved in the development of KBE framework (i.e. external modeling, internal modeling, knowledge, control, management system, management function, elementary management cycle, knowledge management framework, etc.) is presented and major concepts are described.

The control view-based perspective is applied for analysis of enterprise modeling methods (Gudas, 1991), (Gudas, et al., 2005) aimed for refinement of knowledge modeling aspects and management layers.

The M. Porter's Value Chain model (Porter, 1985), as well as Strategic Alignment Framework (Henderson, Venkatraman, 1990), is modified and used for the analysis and structuring of enterprise domains, management information transactions and content of information, developing the control view-based definition of enterprise management

function, identification of enterprise components, related to knowledge management. The internal structure of enterprise knowledge component is motivated and defined.
The Enterprise Knowledge Space is defined, delineating the boundaries and granularity of enterprise knowledge layers and components.

2. Concepts of enterprise knowledge management modeling

A rough overview of the concepts and their dependencies involved for development of the control view-based approach to Enterprise Knowledge Management modeling is given in Fig. 1.

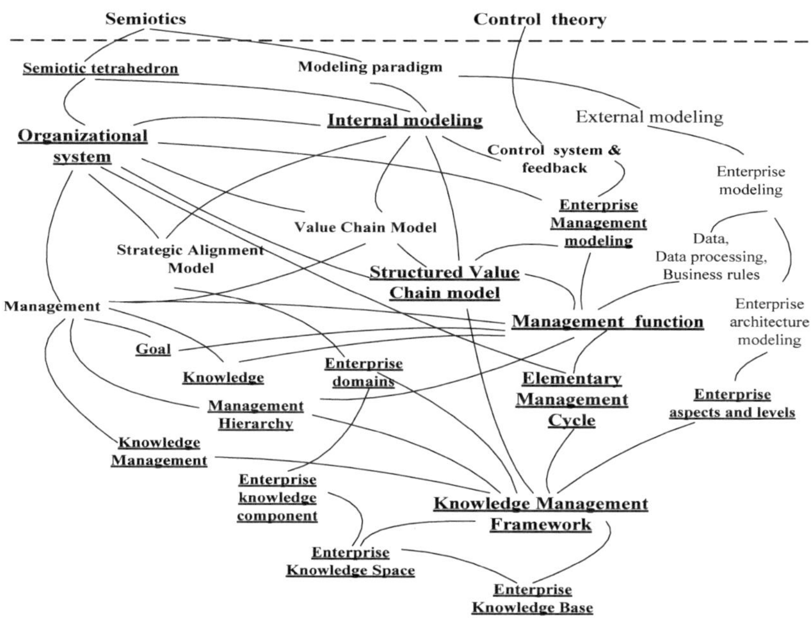

Fig. 1. Dependency map of major concepts involved for development of Enterprise Knowledge Management framework

Semiotics and *Control theory*. The top two concepts in Fig. 1 are on the level of theories, namely, *„Semiotics"* and *„Control theory"*. Semiotics gives for Enterprise Knowledge Management modeling the concept of *Semiotic tetrahedron* of FRISCO [Falkenberg et al., 1998], which affords a predefined methodological structure for *Organizational System* modeling using *Internal modeling* paradigm.
The Control theory gives the concept *"Control System"* for developing the *control view* approach to *Organizational System management* modeling. The concept *"Control System"* is a background for developing the feed back loop of the *Management Control System*, formally defining the Enterprise *Management* as a hierarchy of *Management Functions* comprised of *Data, Knowledge* and *Goal* components and interactions in the information feedback loop. The internal structure of *Management Function* is information processing framework defined as *Elementary Management Cycle* (Gudas, et al., 2005).
The *External modeling* paradigm. The *External modeling* paradigm denotes the branch of empirical Enterprise modeling methodologies and methods, relevant and formally

described by "Black Box" approach (Gudas, 2009]. Enterprise modeling is a well developed field of business process modeling, closely related with Business Process Re-engineering (BPR) and Information System Engineering (ISE), development of CASE methods and tools. Enterprise modeling affords a set of methodologies, enterprise architecture modeling frameworks, methods, standards and languages for manifestation (representation) of empirical information acquired by system analyst in the business domain. Enterprise models developed for BPR and ISE needs correctly empirically represents the identified data (information flows), processes, events, organizational units, workflows or few other component types (constraints, business rules, etc.) of business domain.

The development of Knowledge -Based Modeling methods is related with understanding differences of two modeling paradigms: *an external modeling* paradigm and *internal modeling* paradigm.

An external modeling paradigm is based on the Black Box model of W. Ross Ashby (Fig. 2). A Black Box model highlights the origin of empirical models: components and (functional) behaviour of a system are acquired by external (empirical) analysis and represented by analyst using definite modeling language (notation).

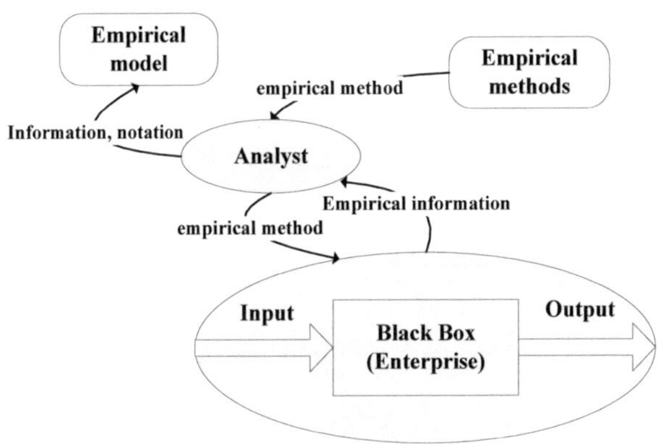

Fig. 2. The External modeling paradigm is relevant to Black Box model

The *Internal modeling* paradigm. The *Internal modeling* paradigm denotes the branch of *Knowledge-based approaches* to modeling, relevant and formally described by "White Box" approach (Gudas, 2009). The *Internal modeling* paradigm gives background to extend Enterprise modeling views and aspects, a set of Enterprise components' types and interactions.

An Internal modeling paradigm is based on the White Box principle (Fig. 3). *A White Box* principle highlights the origin of knowledge-based approaches - the representation (model components, structure and the operation of a system) are validated by analyst against some predefined knowledge (theory) related to the internal transformations of *Domain*. For instance, the high level *business model* - Value Chain Model (VCM) (Porter, 1985), as well as the Strategic Business&IT Alignment Model (SAM) (Henderson, Venkatraman, 1990), is classified as internal models of Enterprise. *A Control view-based* approach to Enterprise management and knowledge modeling (Gudas, et al., 2005) fits to *Internal modeling* paradigm based on the White Box principle. The Internal modeling paradigm (Fig. 3) highlights the formal model of *Domain* as the essential component of knowledge-based modeling.

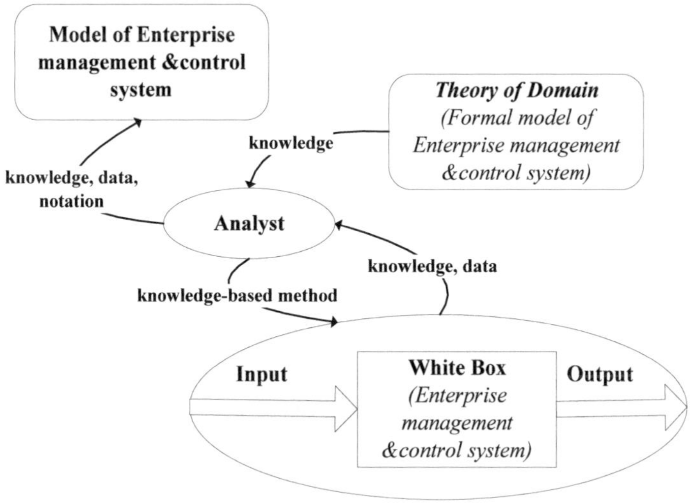

Fig. 3. The Internal modeling paradigm is relevant to White Box principle

The Semiotic tetrahedron of FRISCO. The concept of *semiotic tetrahedron* is a methodological structure for understanding the relation between "model"and "business domain" (*„the relation of symbols to reality")* (Falkenberg, et al., 1998).
The *semiotic tetrahedron* in the Fig.4 (*Domain, Conception, Actor (Interpreter&Representer), Representation*) is key predefined structure for understanding the *internal modeling* paradigm and its application for *Organizational System* management modeling as well as for understanding the concepts *Interpretation* and *Elementary Management Cycle* (Gudas et al, 2005).
The Semiotic tetrahedron reflects the view of FRISCO to the relation of reality (*Domain*) and model (*Representation*): there is a *domain* (the Real World) observed by analyst called the *Actor*. As a result of these activities (namely, *perception* and *interpretation*), the *Actor* forms *A Conception* (an internal semantic model of Real World) and *A Representation* (an external semantic model of Real World).
The semiotic triangle is a helpful tool for explaining the enterprise management as a semiotic process - a sequence of steps and transformations of information (data, knowledge and goals).

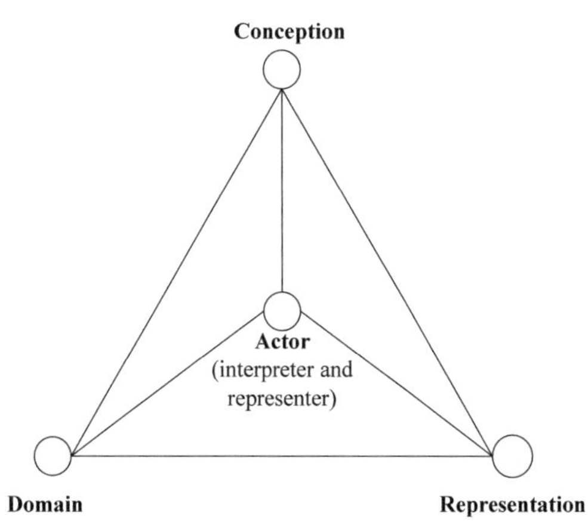

Fig. 4. The semiotic tetrahedron of FRISCO (Falkenberg et al., 1998)

Enterprise management&control as White Box. *A control* is an activity of managing or making control over some another activity. *A control system* is a system for controlling the operation of another system. A feedback control concept is applied to technical, social, economic systems modeling as well as to enterprise management and knowledge management modeling (Gudas, et al., 2005).

Definitions of management mostly include activities as follows: *planning, organizing, directing, and controlling* of the enterprise's operation so that objectives can be economically and efficiently achieved through others. So, the definition of the *management* includes the *control* concept.

Enterprise (Organizational System) is managed by management and control system, which performs a definite set of *Management Functions* {Fj} aimed to control enterprise *Processes* {Pi} (Fig. 5). Any *Management Function* is comprised of two components, namely, *Information Processing* (goal driven data processing and decision making) activity and *Information Feedback loop.*

Enterprise (management and control) modeling is based on the assumption as follows: any Enterprise is under control if each Enterprise *Management Function* includes the closed loop cycle of information transitions: a) takes (makes measurements of) *a Process state attributes,* b) calculates and decides a *Process control attributes* and in that way c) influences the *state of a Process.*

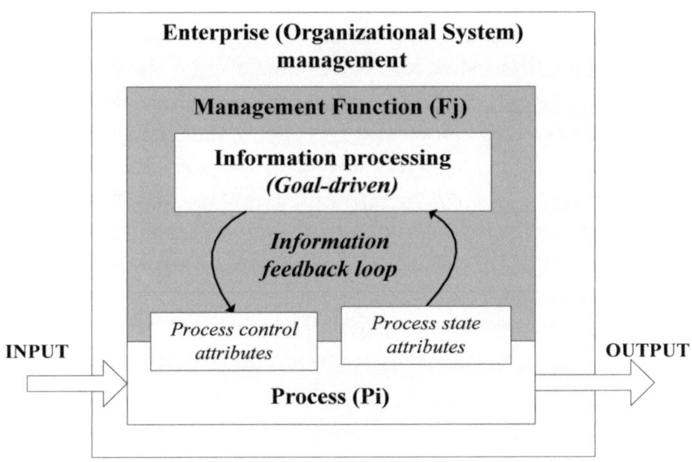

Fig. 5. The White Box model of Enterprise *Management Function*

According to Firestone (Firestone, 1999), organizational knowledge management activity "is aimed at integrating the various organizational agents, components, and activities of the organizational knowledge management system into a planned, directed process producing, maintaining and enhancing an organization's knowledge base". The enterprise knowledge base along with its organizational and technological components constitutes enterprise knowledge management system (KMS). Knowledge management activity, as any other enterprise activity, is arranged in a hierarchy, which can have some reasonable number of interrelated levels.

Data, information, and knowledge. The analysis of *knowledge management* area requires well defined conceptual basis - relevant definitions at least for *management, data, information, knowledge, goal/objective* concepts. "The lack of consistent definitions for data, information, and knowledge make rigorous discussions of Knowledge Management difficult" (Hicks, et al., 2006).

One major problem related with enterprise management and knowledge management is a problem of understanding *data, information, knowledge, goals* and their inter-relationships (Muller, Schappert, 1999), (Liew, 2007), (Hicks, et al., 2006). In the classical interpretation (based on the semiotic triangle) the concept "data"is associated with syntax (has no meaning), information corresponds to semantic (*information* is context interpreted *data*) and *knowledge* takes the pragmatic part (*knowledge* is action interpreted information) (Muller, Schappert, 1999).

The definitions of data, information, and knowledge could be concerned as problem, because data and information, as well as information and knowledge are perceived as interchangeable, it depends on activities and situations (Muller, Schappert, 1999).

And what about one more type of information - a *goal (an objective)*, representing the key feature of Organizational Systems and management activities - a goal-driven behaviour? The semiotic tetrahedron of FRISCO extends the content of semiotic triangle including *an Actor* (interpreter and representer of percepted (acquired) *Data*) related with *Knowledge* and *Information* components. *An Actor* must be considered as an active component of *Organizational System* (as goal driven component), i.e. an Actor is considered as a goal seeking component of semiotic triangle. Consequently, the modified semiotic triangle that includes a *Goal* component interrelated with *Data, Information* and *Knowledge* components is presented in Fig. 6.

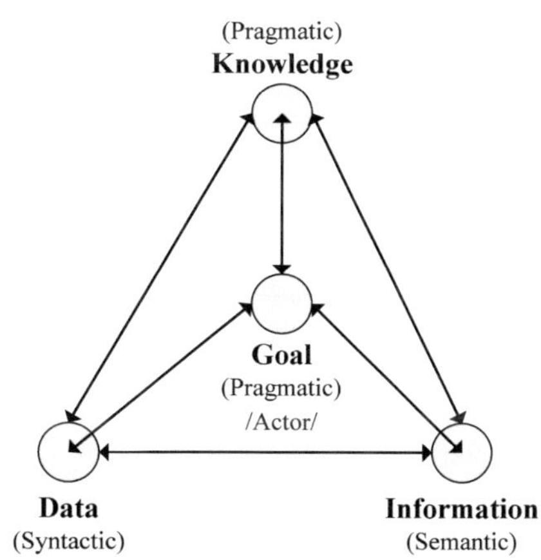

Fig. 6. The modified semiotic triangle

The inter-relationships of *Data, Knowledge, Goal, Information* and *Real World (RW)* are presented in the Fig. 7. A Goal is considered as domain interpreted information (pragmatic aspect - RW related). Knowledge is considered as action interpreted information (pragmatic aspect - management related, predefined (constrained) by *Goal*)).

Enterprise modelling. Enterprise modelling usually involves the definite set of aspects: function, behaviour, information, resource and organization (Vernadat, 2002) (GERAM, 1999). In addition, it is possible to distinguish one more aspect of an Enterprise modelling, defined as *the management point of view*. From this point of view, the new major Enterprise modelling constructs are identified. In the management control systems' literature, similar aspect is called *the management control perspective* (Anthony, Govindarajan, 2003), (Merchant, 1999). The management control perspective focuses on the organisation management and control issues; meanwhile the particularity of *the management-control point of view* is the refinement of information processing constructs and their interactions in the Enterprise. Some business systems are able to choose their own behaviour. Business processes in such systems are guided by the *decision-making mechanism*. That is why the modelling of *management process* and *management information flows* must be taken into account as mandatory aspects of Enterprise modelling. The scope of management process modelling is the internal structure of management information (Enterprise knowledge, data, objectives) and the management information processing as well.

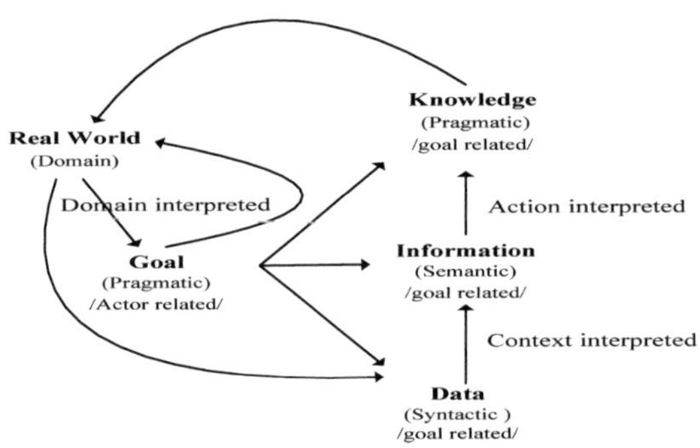

Fig. 7. Inter-relationships of data, information, knowledge, goal, and reality (domain)

It is claimed in Systems and Control Theory that a system can be controlled effectively only if some *feedback loops* (also called *control loops*) are implemented. Consequently, the components of the control loop should be included into Enterprise model.

It should be pointed out that the term *Control flow* (in the sense of *workflow*) is associated with the concept *Activity* in the UEML 1.0 (Vernadat, 2001). However, the earlier version of UEML core (UEML, 1999) includes separate modelling constructs *Function* and *Process,* and that makes this UEML core closer to the Enterprise modelling from the management point of view.

Further, the Control Theory defines the typical structure of a *System* - a real world System with internal "mechanism" of control. *A System* involves the following mandatory (complex) constructs: a real world *Process,* a *Control System* and a *Feedback Loop* which creates *an Information flow* (*Control flow*) between a *Process* and a *Control System* (Gupta and Sinha, 1996). *A Control System* performs a definite set of activities (*Functions,* related to a definite *criterion)* aimed to control *a Process.* Any *Function* takes (makes measurements of) *a Process state attributes,* calculates a *Process control attributes,* in this way making influence on the state of a *Process.*

Before we go further, let us define that any item (structural unit) of *a System* is named *an object. An object* could be conceptualised as *an entity* or *a class* (of the UML), or in some other way in accordance with particular modelling methodology.

3. Four domains of enterprise strategic alignment

Henderson and Venkatraman have analysed business-IT alignment issue and proposed a Strategic Alignment Model (SAM) (Henderson, J., Venkatraman, N., 1990).

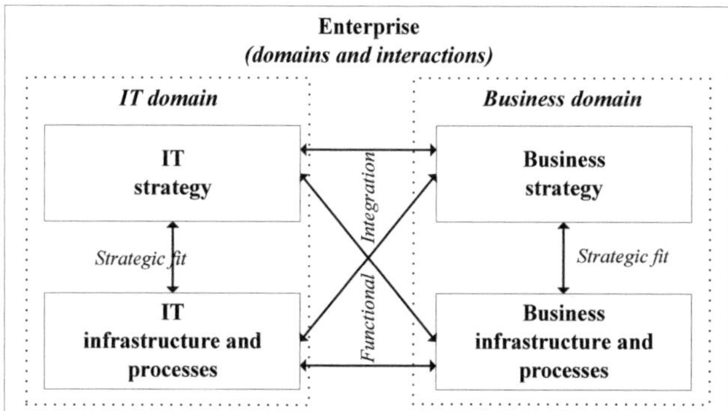

Fig. 8. Domains of Enterprise in the Strategic Alignment Model (SAM) (Henderson, Venkatraman, 1990)

The model is aimed to support the integration of information technology (IT) into business strategy by advocating alignment between and within four enterprise domains and is classified as internal model of Organizational System (Fig. 8).

The major constructs of SAM - enterprise domains (namely, *Business domain* and *IT domain*) and views (*Business strategy, Business infrastructure, IT strategy, IT infrastructure)* are selected as criterions for the analysis of the major concepts of various Enterprise Modeling and Enterprise Architecture methodologies and frameworks (see Table 1).

The interactions of Business and IT domains and views, namely *functional integration* and *strategic fit* are considered as knowledge manipulation processes, supported or not supported by enterprise information systems (data bases and knowledge bases). Alignment of business strategy and IT strategy is an intensive knowledge process, it requires particular knowledge about at least four views: *Business strategy, Business infrastructure, IT strategy, IT infrastructure* of enterprise.

Knowledge -Centric Enterprise Structure. The knowledge-centric organization, regardless of whether its products are tangible or not, here is defined according to the concept of knowledge-based organization, presented by M.H.Zack (Zack, 2003) and is based on the resource-based view of the firm; namely, knowledge-centric organization: a) recognizes knowledge as a key strategic resource, b) rethinks their business processes in the knowledge-oriented sense (i.e. "it takes knowledge into account in every aspect of its operation and treats every activity as a potentially knowledge-enhancing act." (Zack, 2003), c) aligns its knowledge management activity with its strategy.

Even if the definition of the knowledge-centric enterprise do not emphasizes the use of the information technologies (IT) in the enterprise, it should be noted, that research presented here is concerned with the contemporary enterprise, which extensively uses IT for the support of the management of its business processes.

Contemporary organizations use the integrated data repositories which have to be identified within the enterprise model (the *Data Base* and *Data Warehouse* components in Fig. 9).

In order to illustrate the conception of the contemporary enterprise, which is knowledge-centric enterprise, the SAM model has to be complemented by additional components. According to the definition of the knowledge-centric organization, it rethinks its processes in the knowledge-oriented sense and aligns its *knowledge management activity* with its strategy. Consequently, in the knowledge-centric enterprise there exist some infrastructure for the knowledge management - the knowledge management (KM) layer; thus SAM model is complemented with additional structural elements - business *knowledge and IT knowledge management components* (see Fig. 9).

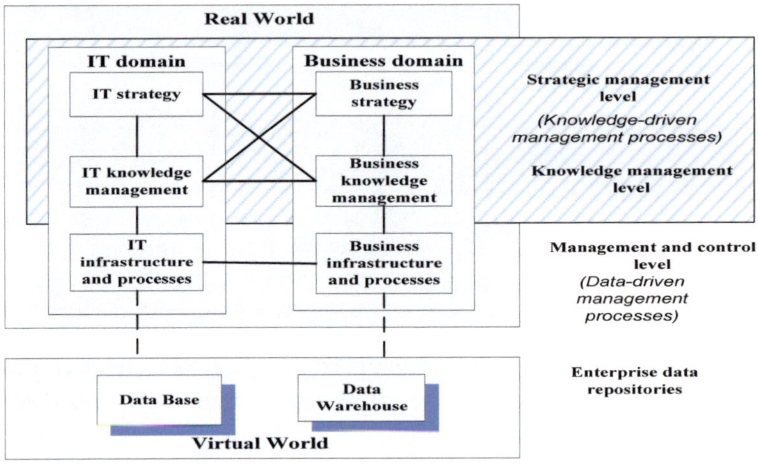

Fig. 9. The Knowledge-Centric Enterprise structure

To sum up, business and IT domains of SAM can be decomposed into three levels of management hierarchy: strategic management level, knowledge management level, and business management&control level.

The management processes on the strategic level and knowledge management level are *knowledge -driven* because these top level management activities require particular knowledge about strategies and management methods, and etc. The management processes on the business and IT management and control level require definite (time related) data about the state of business and IT processes, thus this level of management essentially is *data-driven.*

Knowledge-centric enterprise, as any other contemporary organization, possibly uses the integrated data repositories which are presented in the SAM as the Enterprise *Data repositories* component (Fig.9).

Even if knowledge management activities of Knowledge-Centric Enterprise are under control, there is a possibility for the knowledge flow bottlenecks left, because the valuable knowledge two interrelated enterprise domains required for the management solutions about *(i.e. Business domain, IT domain)* typically resides in the heads of the managers and employees, in the unstructured documents etc. As the business-IT alignment is continuous decision making process, it should be supported with reliable information (*Real World d*ata and *digital* data) and knowledge (*Real World* knowledge only) accessible across the enterprise.

4. Two worlds of the knowledge-based enterprise

In Strategic Alignment Model (Henderson, Venkatraman, 1990) two interrelated components of the enterprise are defined: 1) Business domain and 2) IT domain. According to the definition of the Knowledge-Based Enterprise, another two important components of the enterprise management are identified: Knowledge domain and Data domain. All these four components are interrelated domains (see Fig. 16), which have to be taken into account when transforming business enterprise into Knowledge-Based Business Enterprise (Gudas, Brundzaite, 2006a).

The scheme presented in Fig. 10 sums up findings made in the chapter. The peculiarity of this abstraction is that it clearly separates the Knowledge domain from Data domain, in contrast to other conceptual enterprise models (e.g. presented in (Hettinger, 2003) or (Iyer, Gottlieb, 2004). For instance, the well-known ISA framework (Zachman, Sowa, 1992) does not concern knowledge domain at all. Though comparing ISA model with the presented abstraction of the Knowledge-Based Enterprise domains, different purposes and tasks of the ISA and Enterprise Knowledge Modelling framework should be noted.

The concept of the *knowledge base* is also used in the sense of computerized meta-data repository when implementing large-scale data management and business intelligence systems in the contemporary organizations. Meta-data repository helps to provide business data as well as data about data for business and for IT departments and to make adequate decisions regarding data management in organizations. Contemporary organizations need to manage not only data, but the whole data-information-knowledge continuum; this is why the role and structure of the enterprise repository or enterprise knowledge base have to change adequately too (Gudas, Brundzaite, 2006a).

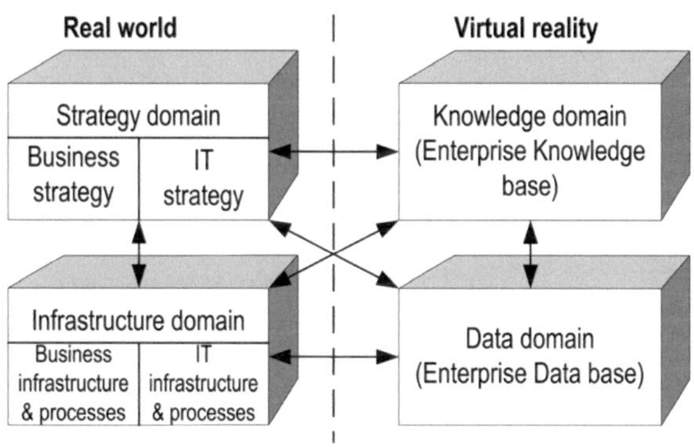

Fig. 10. Two worlds of the knowledge-based enterprise

The concept of computerized knowledge base become important with the emergence of such intensively computer-based organizational forms as supply chains, virtual organizations etc. Organizations require for having not only shared data bases in virtual environment, but also knowledge about those data, as well as about the data structure and semantics; knowledge about its infrastructure and processes; process management up to strategic intentions.

The solid lines in Fig. 10 represent the knowledge management activities which are used to assure integration of the enterprise knowledge base into overall enterprise management and development framework, as well as support of inter-domain alignment tasks. Knowledge management activity has to be managed and explicitly modelled either (Gudas, Brundzaite, 2006a).

5. Knowledge-based enterprise structure

The scope and structure of the organizational knowledge in the knowledge management literature is investigated. This structure has the name of *organizational memory* or *corporate*

memory. The organizational memory is concerned with the organizational learning processes. Organizational memory comprises all the possible forms of organizational knowledge: tacit, explicit, computerized, not-computerized, etc (Zack, 2003).
There are a lot of possible facets for characterising knowledge (Zack, 2003), although it is important in this situation to analyse knowledge in the sense of its "objective" and "subjective" characteristics. According to J.M. Firestone (Firestone, 1999), there are two kinds of knowledge:

1. "Knowledge viewed as belief… Such knowledge is "subjective" in the sense that it is agent-specific, whether the agent is an individual, group, team, or organization".
2. "Knowledge viewed as validated models, theories, arguments, descriptions, problem statements etc. This kind of knowledge, further, is "objective." It is objective in the sense that it is not agent specific and is shared among agents. Finally, it is objective because, since it is sharable, we can sensibly talk about community validation of this kind of knowledge."

Business-IT alignment is a continuous decision making process and it should be supported with reliable information and knowledge. As it was noted in the beginning of the article, enterprise knowledge basd is intended to be used as the source of knowledge about the problem domain (i.e.) also for IS engineering tasks in the IS requirements' development stage. Resuming it should be stated that enterprise knowledge base is shared and it stores the enterprise knowledge (*digital knowledge*) in the form of validated Enterprise Knowledge Models. According to the Knowledge-Based Modeling (internal modeling) paradigm enterprise knowledge models have to be validated according to the formal model of enterprise management&control thus ensuring reliability of the acquired knowledge about problem domain.
Besides, it is suggested, that Knowledge-Based Enterprise uses Enterprise Knowledge Base (KB) together with explicitly modelled knowledge management activity as obligatory enterprise management component.
The concept of the Knowledge-Based Enterprise is illustrated further by using **Strategic Alignment Model (SAM)** (Henderson, Venkatraman, 1990). Therefore, Strategic Alignment Model is complemented by one more additional structural element - Enterprise *Knowledge Base* (see Fig. 11), which supports enterprise knowledge management activities and allows continuous cross-domain alignment process and also helps to eliminate knowledge flow bottleneck across enterprise.
Consequently, *Knowledge-Based Enterprise* here is defined by enhancing the Knowledge-Centric Enterprise (as defined above) with Enterprise knowledge repository. The *Knowledge-Based Enterprise* uses *Enterprise Knowledge Base* as obligatory enterprise management, as well as information system development component.
In Fig. 11 the structural element *Enterprise Goal's Base* is abstracted, which could be as the part of the Enterprise knowledge base too.
Contemporary enterprise modelling methods are conceptual methods in the sense how the models are created and what knowledge they represent; they allow to acquire empirical knowledge about the problem domain (i.e. enterprise), which can be hardly validated. *Enterprise Knowledge Base* (EKB) here is considered as the computerised Enterprise Knowledge Model, which consist of integrated set of enterprise knowledge sub-models and is validated against the formalized enterprise knowledge model. Thus, EKB is the reliable knowledge source for a support of business management decision making, business and IT alignment, as well as for support of knowledge management and information systems development processes.

The peculiarity of the abstraction, presented in Fig. 11 is that it clearly separates the Knowledge domain and Data domain, in contrast to other conceptual enterprise models (e.g. presented in (Iyer, Gottlieb, 2004)).

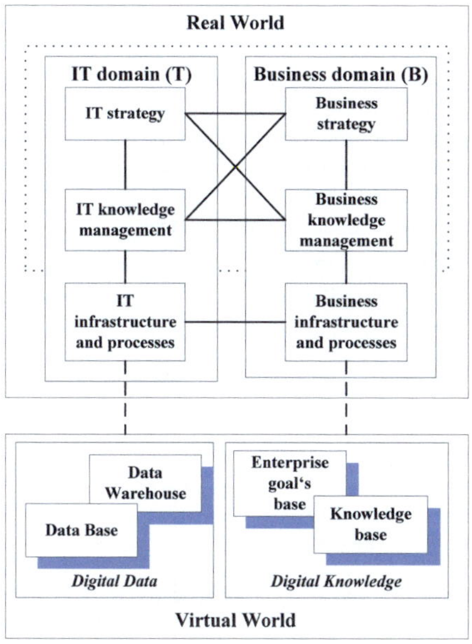

Fig. 11. Knowledge-Based Enterprise structure

Knowledge-Based Enterprise uses knowledge as a key strategic resource, as it was said before (see also Fig. 11). It became evident that the *organizational knowledge (non-digital knowledge)* is human knowledge used (and hidden in the Fig. 11) in the *business* and *IT domains* as integral components of any enterprise.
Meanwhile, *enterprise knowledge* (virtual, digital knowledge stored in the Enterprise KB) is an obligatory component of Knowledge-Based Enterprise, integrated with all enterprise domains. Accordingly, three tiers Knowledge-Based Enterprise Architecture (in the Fig.12), it includes Enterprise KB as key component, integrated with knowledge management systems (Gudas, Brundzaite, 2007a).

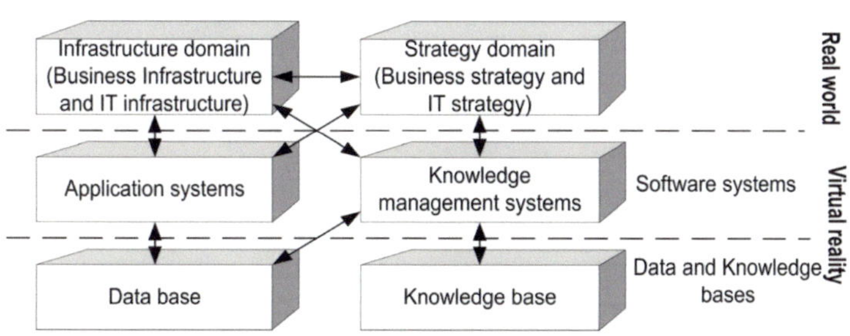

Fig. 12. Knowledge-based Enterprise Architecture

The Knowledge-Based Enterprise Architecture co-relates with the A Multi-Layer Architecture for Knowledge Management Systems (*Strategy; Organization; Information System)* presented by Ulrich Frank (Ulrich, 2002).

6. Enterprise domains and aspects of the knowledge

Having defined Knowledge-Based Enterprise architecture independently from the products the enterprise produces, the following knowledge management modeling approach is concerned with the identification of the types and actual content of the enterprise knowledge.

Modelling Framework	Enterprise domains and aspects of the Enterprise knowledge			
Henderson, Venkatraman, 1990	*Business domain, Business strategy*	*Business domain, Businessinfrastructure*	*IT domain,IT strategy*	*IT domain,IT infrastructure*
J.Zachman, ISA Framework (Zachman, Sowa, 1992)	Business domain; Motivation, Time	Business domain; Processes/Functions, Data,People, Network	IT domain; Goals/Objectives, Time, Peoples	IT domain; Functions,Data structure,Network,
B. Iyer, R. Gottlieb, 2004	Business process domain	Organization domain	Information/ knowledge domain	IT infrastructure domain
M.Porter's value chain model (Porter, 1985)	Business domain, Support activities	Business domain, Primary activities		
GERAM (GERAM, 1999), (Williams, Li, 1995)	Business domain; Management & control,Customer service	Business domain; Resource,Organization, Information, Function	IT domain; Human, Machine	IT domain; Software, Hardware
Multi-Perspective Enterprise Modeling (MEMO) (Ulrich, 2002a)	Business domain; Goal(competitiveness), Resource (Human resource technology), Structure(Strategic Business units), Process (Value Chain)	Business domain; Operational goals Employees,machinery, Organization structure, Task process,	Information System (domain); Requirements metrics, Architecture, Object model,	Information System (domain); Application, transaction workflow
Maes, R., Rijsenbrij, D., Truijens, O., Goedvolk, H. (2000).	Business domain; Strategy, Structure	Business domain; Information and communications; Operations	Technology domain; Strategy, systems, structure	Technology domain; Infrastructure, Operations
ARIS (EPC) (Scheer, 1999)	Business domain; Event, Function, Work, Control flow	Business domain; Information flow, Resources, Organization unit, Role,		
UEML (Vernadat, 2002)	Business domain; Event, Process, Activity, Role	Business domain; Organization unit, Enterprise object (Product, Order, Resource (Human, Machine));	IT domain; Resource (Human)	IT domain; Enterprise object Resource (Application, Machine)

Table 1. Enterprise domains and aspects of the Enterprise knowledge

The investigations in knowledge management area are closely related with developments in the area of enterprise architecture (EA) frameworks (J.Schekkerman, 2003), enterprise modelling (EM) frameworks (Zachman, Sowa, 1992); (Maes et al., 2000); (Ulrich, 2002) and languages (Vernadat, 2002).
B. Iyer, R. Gottlieb decomposition of enterprise architecture (Iyer, Gottlieb, 2004) identifies four domains: business process domain, information/knowledge domain, infrastructure domain and organization domain.
Enterprise modelling (EM) and Enterprise architecture (EA) frameworks underlies our theoretical findings. In the contemporary EM and EA methods the three basic aspects of the enterprise knowledge *business strategy; business; information systems and technologies)* are separated, and used to construct layered architecture. The analysis of the EM methods is presented in (Gudas, Brundzaite, 2006).

7. Structured value chain model

The Value Chain model comes from M. Porter's book (Porter, 1985). A Value Chain is a high level business model, a model that breaks down an organization into a series of value-generating activities. Two major interacting parts of VCM are *Support Activities* and *Primary Activities* (Porter, 1985).

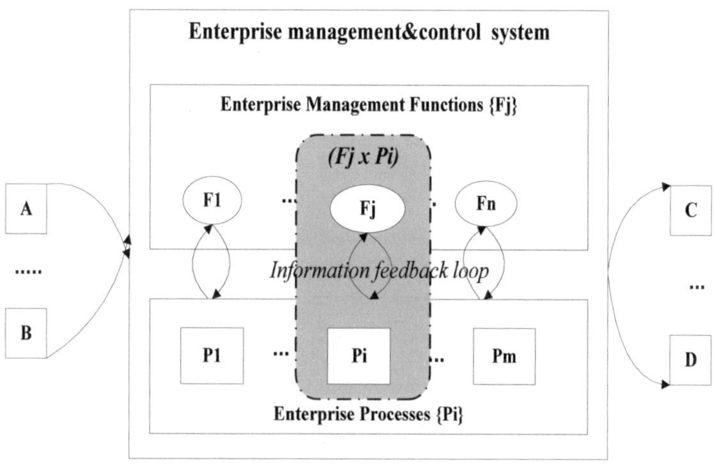

Fig. 13. The structured Value Chain Model (SVCM)

The analysis of the Enterprise modelling from *the management (control) point of view* gives some new aspects for the Enterprise modelling itself (Gudas et al., 2005):

- The matter under investigation is a content of information, information processing and decision-making activities in the Organizational System (Enterprise).
- It is aimed at the enhancement of the Enterprise model that can be used as a source of domain knowledge for business management analysis and development of advanced IS engineering methods;
- A set of EM constructs and their types of relation should be revised *from the management point of view*. These constructs should include a definite set of structural elements and relations for the modelling of Enterprise management functions and information interactions.

From *the management (control) perspective* the major parts of M.Porter's Value Chain Model are renamed as follows (Fig. 13):

- *Support Activities* are information processing activities (for instance data processing, decision making), consequently they are renamed as *Management Functions* {Fj};
- *Primary Activities* are material flow processing activities (for instance, manufacturing), consequently they are renamed as *Enterprise Processes* {Pi};
- *The interaction of Management Functions* {Fj} and *Enterprise Processes* {Pi} is considered as information feedback, it is the obligatory component of enterprise management (control) system.

The Structured Value Chain model is used to identify the information transactions between *Management Functions* and *Enterprise Processes. The Structured VCM* refines the enterprise management & control as a system of closed loop interactions of Management Functions {Fj} and Enterprise Processes {Pi}:

$$\mathbf{SVCM = \{Function\ (Fj)\ x\ Process\ (Pi)\}.\quad i = 1,m;\ j = 1,n;}$$

The interaction of *Function* and *Process.* The interaction of Enterprise model core elements *Process* and *Function* is formally assumed as a *Control Process*. It is defined as a *Feedback Loop* between *Process P*(i) and *Function F*(j). The analysis of the *Function- Process* interaction is a background of the formalized model of the organizational system (an Enterprise model) described in (Gudas, 1991).

Fig. 4 presents the structured model of the *Function-Process* interaction. The concept *Process* is assumed as "a Black Box". The internal structure of *Process* is unstudied, the concept *Process* is characterized by a set of *Process state attributes* (this set comprises subsets of *Input flow attributes, Output flow attributes* and *Process attributes*) and it is influenced by the output of a management *Function* – a set of *Process control attributes* (Gudas et al., 2005).

From the management point of view, *Process P(i)* is defined by two sets of attributes: a set of *Process state attributes* and a set of *Process control attributes.* A set of *Process state attributes* includes the *Process input* (material flow) *attributes, Process output* (material flow) *attributes* and the *attributes* of the particular *Process P(i).*

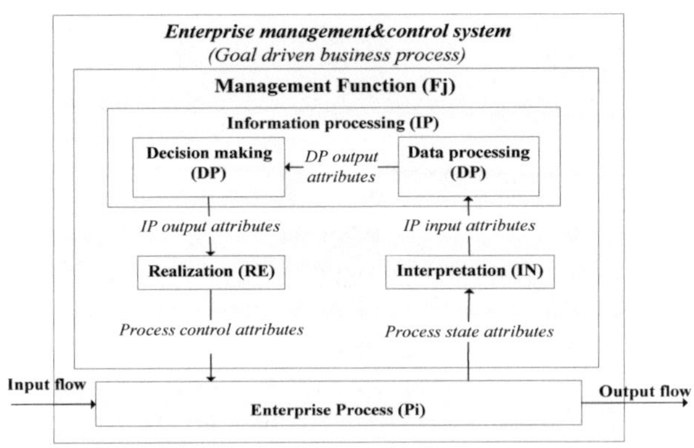

Fig. 14. The structured model of the *Function-Process* interaction

A management *Function* consists of the predefined sequence of mandatory steps of information transformation (*Interpretation, Information Processing, Realization*); these steps compose a management cycle (a feedback loop). A definite set of attributes (a set of

information items) is formed and transmitted during each management step. A management *Function F(j)* is initiated by some *Event* – a fact or a message associated with some internal or external (environmental) object. This definition of *Function* is close to the definition of function presented in (ENV 40003, 1990). This paper presents more detailed content of *Function F(j)* since it defines a sequence of definite types of interacting information activities (*Interpretation, Information Processing, Realization*) directed to control *Process P(i)* (Fig. 13).
All other constructs of *Function-Process* interaction (except constructs *Process, Input flow* and *Output flow*) in the structured model are assumed to be the components of the construct Enterprise *Management Function* (Fig. 15).

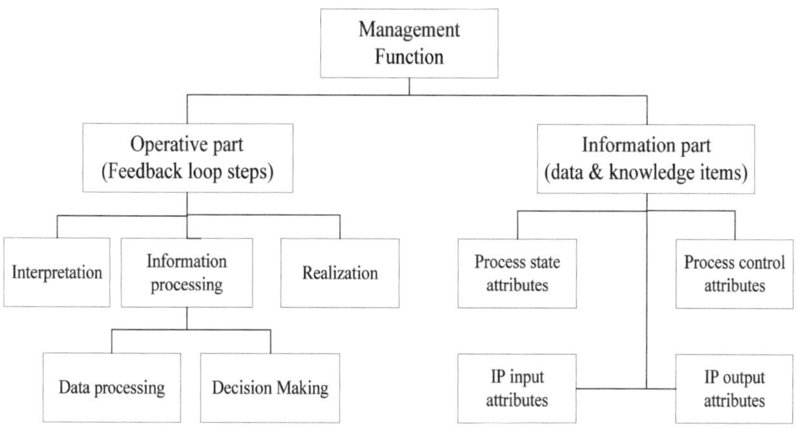

Fig. 15. The control view based structure of Management Function (Gudas et al., 2005).

It is assumed, that *Process* and *Management Function* are activated by some *Event*. A definite set of *state attributes* of an activated *Process* is the information flow defined as an input of (one or more) specific management *Function* that is activated by some particular *Event*.
It should be pointed out, that the set of attributes of management *Function* is closely related to the description of function presented by CIMOSA (ENV 40003, 1990). The CIMOSA specification of function includes the structural part (the list of sub-functions is used), the functional part (goals, limitations, functional description, necessary equipment, input, output) and the part of an attitude (goals, limitations, procedural rules, events, end state).
The Elementary Management Cycle (EMC). The structured model of the *Function-Process* interaction (Fig. 14) is formally specified as **Elementary Management Cycle (EMC)** at Fig. 16. The Elementary Management Cycle (EMC) is the basic construct of Enterprise management modelling, refines the components of management (control) cycle as well as content of management information transformations (Gudas, 1991), (Gudas et al., 2005).
The semantics of *Elementary Management Cycle (EMC)* transactions at Fig. 16 are co-related with the description of modified semiotic tetrahedron of FRISCO (Fig. 4, Fig. 6).
A new perspective - control view perspective of Enterprise management modeling is beneficial and constructive for advancing of Business Process modeling and IS engineering methods. An Enterprise Management Model provides the theoretical background for system analysis of management information processes, identification and more detailed decomposition of enterprise data and knowledge components *Function, Process, Activity, Information flow, Control flow, etc.*

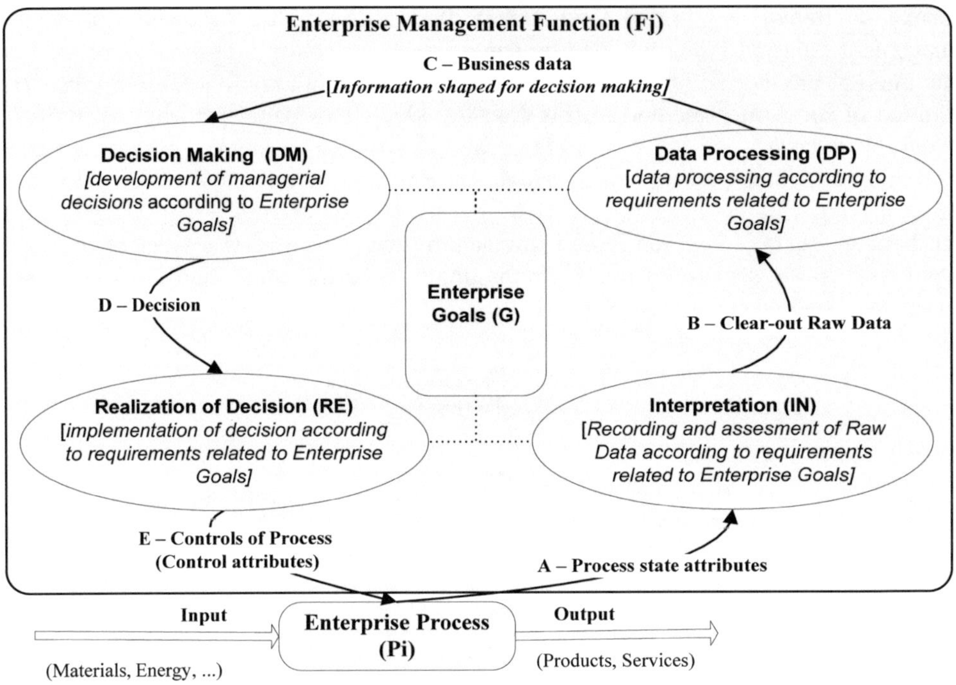

Fig. 16. The Elementary Management Cycle (EMC) - specification of *Function-Process* interaction

8. Enterprise knowledge component

Enterprise domains and aspects of the enterprise knowledge identified in the various Enterprise Modeling (EM) and Enterprise Architecture (EA) methodologies and frameworks (Table 1) reflect the semantics of the concept "enterprise knowledge component" (Gudas, Brundzaite, 2006).

Summarizing the above given overview of enterprise modelling domains and aspects (Table 1), we make a premise, that there are three integrated aspects of the Enterprise management activities modeling (Henderson, Venkatraman, 1990):

- Modeling of business strategy, infrastructure and processes;
- Modeling of IT strategy, infrastructure and processes;
- Modeling of Enterprise Business and IT integration (Business and IT alignment activities).

Performance of all these Enterprise management activities require adequate diverse knowledge, namely, first type of knowledge is knowledge about business processes (*B*), second type - knowledge about information technologies (*T*) and, finally, knowledge about enterprise management (*K*) (Gudas, Brundzaite, 2006).

So, the key enterprise management activities are supported by the differing types of interrelated knowledge, depicted as *enterprise knowledge component* in Fig. 17. Enterprise management activities required to be supplied as well by actual data stored in the enterprise data repositories (data base). Hence, the enterprise knowledge component e(b, t, k) is associated with *data* items as well (see Fig. 18).

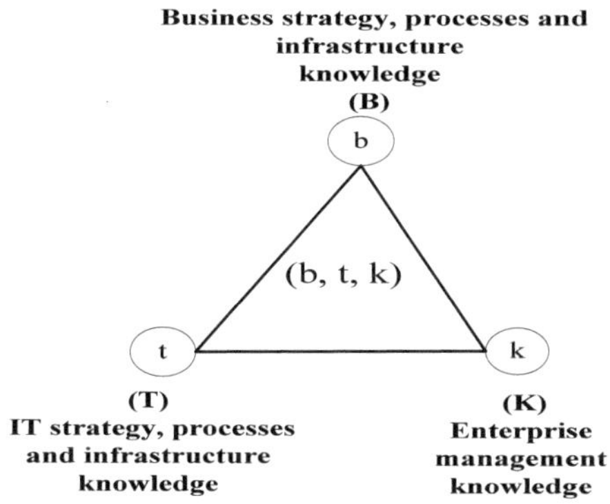

Fig. 17. Knowledge component e (b, t, k) for enterprise management activities

The internal structure of the enterprise knowledge component (b, t, k) (see Fig. 17) represents a new viewpoint to enterprise knowledge modelling: the enterprise management facilities (decision making units of organizational structure) should be supplied and operate with *complex integrated knowledge* about different Enterprise domains as follows: business knowledge (B), IT knowledge (T) and knowledge about enterprise management modeling (K) (Gudas, Brundzaite, 2006).

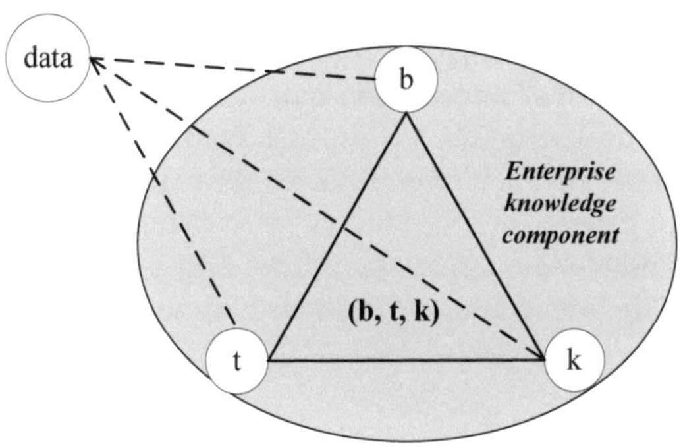

Fig. 18. Enterprise knowledge component e (b, t, k) is integrated with enterprise data items

The depicted enterprise knowledge component (Fig. 18) represents a structural viewpoint to enterprise knowledge modeling: the Knowledge Base should include *integrated enterprise knowledge* (validated models, theories, arguments, descriptions, problem statements) about business strategy and infrastructure (*B*), IT strategy and infrastructure (*T*), enterprise management modelling knowledge and knowledge management methods (*K*).
On the basis of the internal structure of enterprise knowledge component (b, t, k) the abstract space (the Universe of Discourse) for Enterprise knowledge modeling is defined as follows (Fig. 19): Enterprise Knowledge Space (B, T, K), in which B – axis of business process knowledge hierarchy; T – axis for IT management knowledge hierarchy, K – axis of enterprise management knowledge hierarchy (Gudas, Brundzaite, 2006).
The Enterprise Knowledge Space axes (B, T, K) reflect the different management knowledge types, each axis having its own hierarchical structure. Semantics of the enterprise knowledge hierarchy levels (partition of the axes B, T, and K) is discussed in the following chapter.

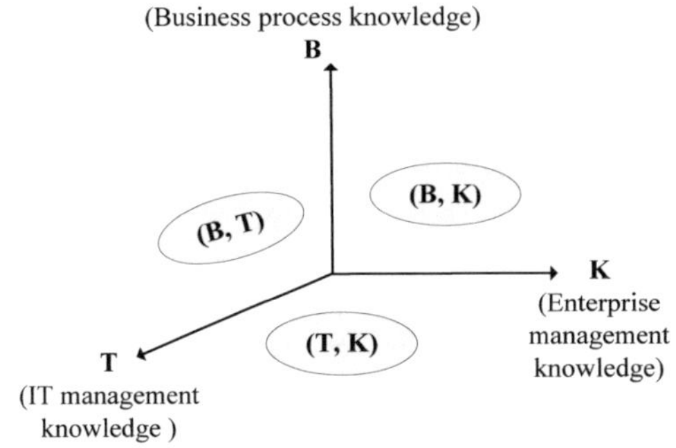

Fig. 19. Enterprise Knowledge Space (B, T, K) axes

9. The enterprise knowledge space

In this chapter we explore the granularity of the enterprise knowledge with the purpose to develop enterprise knowledge base which will be applicable for transformation of enterprise into the knowledge-based enterprise, for the enterprise IT management and alignment with business goals and the range of other business management functions.

The contemporary organizational theories distinguish between four hierarchical levels in organizations: strategic level, tactical level, knowledge level and operational level (Laudon, Laudon, 2004). On the basis of such hierarchical system, it is possible to define four adequate levels in organizational information management processes. We have modified a slightly ordinary hierarchical structure by placing knowledge management in the second level of the business management hierarchy (axes B), because of the overall nature of the knowledge management processes. The Enterprise Knowledge Space (Fig. 20) was derived by fitting integrated knowledge model component (see Fig. 18) with the hierarchical information structure of the organizational systems (Gudas, Brundzaite, 2006).

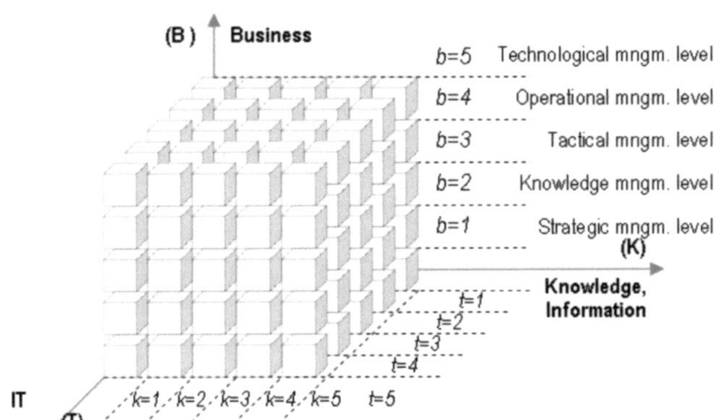

Fig. 20. Enterprise knowledge space *E(B,T,K)*

The enterprise knowledge space *E (B, T, K)* is developed for the systematization of the enterprise knowledge modelling area; it is aimed to be employed for the development of practical enterprise knowledge modelling and management methods.

Each item *e* in the Enterprise Knowledge Space *E (B, T, K)* is identified along 3 axes:

$$e(b;t;k) \in E, \quad \forall b,t,k \in \{1,...,5\}. \tag{1}$$

Each of 125 items within the Enterprise Knowledge Space possesses its own semantics and identifies the definite component of enterprise knowledge, which integrates 3 aspects of the enterprise: business (*B*), information technology (*T*) and knowledge (*K*) at the same level of elaboration. E. g., item *e*111 represents the integration of knowledge concerning 3 aspects of Enterprise management: the strategic business management activities, strategic knowledge management methods and particular IT types that are used at the strategic management level. There are 3 two-dimensional subspaces of the Enterprise Knowledge Space, namely, E1 = (*B*, *T*), E2 = (*B*, *K*), and E3 = (*T*, *K*).

The subspace E1 "Business - IT" (*B*, *T*) defines information technologies that are used to support business activities at a definite management level (strategic, knowledge, tactical knowledge etc.). The subspace E2 "Business - Knowledge" (*B*, *K*) describes business management methods and their interaction with the organizational knowledge.

The subspace E3 "IT - Knowledge" (*T*, *K*) characterizes the IT in the way it is used at each level of knowledge management. These subspaces of the Enterprise Knowledge Space support the analysis and integration of knowledge concerning different domains and aspects of Enterprise management activities.

For instance, the subspace "Business - Knowledge" (*B*, *K*) could be specified as follows:

E2= (*B* ={B1 - Strategic management level (this level embraces strategic management methods), B2 - Knowledge management level (this level embraces knowledge management methods), B3 - Tactical management level (this level includes tactical management methods), B4 - Operation management level (this level concerns operational management methods), B5 - Technological process control level (this level embraces process control and management methods));*K* = {K1 - Ontological modelling level; K2 - Meta-meta-modelling level, K3 - Meta-modelling level, K4 - Conceptual modelling level, K5 - Particular (instant) modelling level}).

For instance, the levels of decomposition of the aspect of Enterprise "information technology (*T*)" could be as follows: (T1 - Ontology modelling IT (methodologies and tools), T2 - meta-meta-modelling IT (methodologies and tools), T3 - meta-modelling IT (methodologies and tools), T4 - enterprise conceptual modelling IT (methods and tools), T5 - partial enterprise modelling IT (packages, patterns, plug-in, etc.)).

These two-dimensional models logically interrelate with such well-known models as Enterprise Information Architecture (ISA Framework) (Zachman, Sowa, 1992) and Multi-perspective Enterprise Modelling (MEMO) (Ulrich, 2002a).

Maes *et al.* (Maes et al., 2000) presents a three-dimensional Integrated Architecture Framework (IAF) for business-IT alignment. The IAF model is based on the ISA Framework (J. Zachman) and a well-known business-IT alignment model developed by Henderson and Venkatraman ((Henderson, Venkatraman, 1990).

The analysis of contemporary Enterprise knowledge modelling methods presented in (Gudas, Brundzaite, 2006, 2006a, 2006b) shows, that there are no methods which could directly suit for the integrated modelling the defined knowledge aspects at the defined levels of detail. Further we are going to discuss a business modelling method, which is intended to model 3 interrelated aspects (business, IT and knowledge) of an enterprise in the integrated way.

The identifiers of enterprise knowledge item. The formal description of the Modified Value Chain Model *M* with the knowledge management function *K* can be expressed as the Cartesian product in the following way:

$$M = (K) \times (F_1, ..., F_n) \times (P) \times (R) \times (R), \tag{2}$$

Where K - knowledge management function, F_1, ..., F_n - business management functions, P- business processes, R - business resources.

This means, that each enterprise knowledge model item $m \in M$ in the modified value chain model is related to the appropriate knowledge management function g ($k \in K$, business management function f ($f \in F$), business process p ($p \in P$), and resources r ($r \in R$). To put it in other terms, the enterprise knowledge model item is identified by a set of identifiers:

$$m(g; f; p; r) \in M. \tag{3}$$

The Enterprise Knowledge Model item m is located in the Enterprise Knowledge Space E (see Formula 1, Chapter 1.2), and is identified by additional identifiers. Enterprise knowledge model item m in the Enterprise Knowledge Space E (B, T, K) is defined as:

$$m_e \ (b; t; k; g; f; p; r; l) \in M_e; \tag{4}$$

Where l ($l \in L$) is the time period index, $m_e \in M_e$. Me is the enterprise knowledge model in consideration of the enterprise knowledge space.

The Enterprise Knowledge Model Me enables to shape the model of knowledge-based business, since it considers knowledge management function (the identifier g) as well as other process management functions (the identifier f), processes (the identifier p) and their interactions comprising all 3 aspects of Enterprise knowledge component (the identifiers b, t, k). Each aspect of Enterprise knowledge (b, t, k) is decomposed into 5 levels of details in the Enterprise Knowledge Space (Fig. 20).

10. Enterprise management layers and knowledge

An Enterprise Management System is a multilevel hierarchical structure. Enterprise management levels, knowledge hierarchy, semantics of the enterprise knowledge layers are investigated in (GERAM), (MOF, 2011), (Roboam et al., 1990) (Gudas, 2008), (Gudas, Brundzaite, 2006b), (Ulrich, 2002),(Laudon, Laudon, 2004), (Muller, Schappert, 1999). Semantics of Enterprise knowledge and management levels depends on the purpose of modeling, enterprise modeling point of view (Table 2).

Management layers of traditional Enterprise are as follows: strategic management, managerial, operational management. In case of Knowledge-Based Enterprise (KBE) semantics of Enterprise knowledge and management levels depends on the purpose of modeling and modeling point of view (see Table 1). Semantics of the enterprise Knowledge management layers in the different frameworks and models depends on the definite purpose (intention) of modeling as well as on the requirements of business control process and IT related requirements for enterprise management systems (Gudas, 2009).

For instance, the Enterprise model aimed for business and IT strategic alignment includes only two layer: strategy layer (business strategy and IT strategy) and infrastructure layer (business infrastructure and IT infrastructure) (Henderson, Venkatraman, 1990).

The management system of the IT-based enterprise includes layers as follows: strategic management, knowledge management, managerial, operational management layer (Laudon, Laudon, 2002).

According to J.M.Firestone (Firestone, 1999), organizational knowledge management activity "is aimed at integrating the various organizational agents, components, and activities of the organizational knowledge management system into a planned, directed process producing, maintaining and enhancing an organization's knowledge base".
The enterprise knowledge base along with its organizational and technological components constitutes enterprise knowledge management system (KMS). A key aspect in defining the KMS is that both its components and interactions must be fully designed. Knowledge management activity, as any other enterprise activity is arranged in a hierarchy, which can have infinite number of levels.
The first task is to identify finite number of design levels. According to MDA architecture, four modeling levels are recommended in Meta-Object Facility (MOF) **(Christian, 2005),** (MOF, 2011).
On the basis of these recommendations four hierarchically interrelated knowledge management levels (see Fig. 26) were identified. (Gudas, Brundzaite, 2006a).

Meta-modeling approach	**Modeling purpose, intention**	**Abstraction levels or views**
GERAM (GERAM, 1999)	Enterprise architecture model development	Generic; Partial;Particular
Meta-modeling approach to adaptive knowledge management (Süß, 2000)	Knowledge management	Abstract meta-model; Application specific model; Domain-specific models; Hypermedia information space; Real world
The Knowledge Factory (Müller, 1999)	Knowledge management	Knowledge; Information; Data
A. Liew (Liew, 2007)	Understanding Data, Information, Knowledge	Wisdom; Knowledge; Information; Data
A Multi-Layer Architecture for Knowledge Management Systems (Ulrich, 2002)	Architecture for Knowledge Management Systems	Views of a Knowledge Management System: Strategy view; Organizational view; Information System view. Abstraction levels:Generic knowledge; Specific knowledge.
Meta-Object Facility (MOF, 2011)	Object-oriented language description	Meta-meta model; Meta-model; Model; Information
Knowledge-Based Enterprise framework [5, 6, 8]	Architecture for Knowledge-Based Enterprise Management Systems	Enterprise strategic management ; Enterprise meta-knowledge management ; Enterprise knowledge management ; Enterprise management Business process management ;Manufacturing process management and control

Table 2. The overview of Enterprise management levels and knowledge

As it could be concluded from the overview of Enterprise modeling approaches (see the column "Abstraction levels or views" in Table 2), the enterprise management hierarchy levels and knowledge abstraction hierarchy are co-related. For instance, abstraction levels of knowledge could be *Generic knowledge; Specific knowledge, Partial knowledge, Domain-specific, Application specific, Meta-, Meta-Meta-* , and etc. (see Table 2).
Therefore the knowledge management modeling requires some complex hierarchical structures to be identified for adequate representation of the knowledge management activities and organizational units.

11. The knowledge-based enterprise framework

In the knowledge modelling field the process-oriented view is recognized as a success factor [18]. In the organizational management practice widely recognized the Porter's (VCM) represents a process-oriented view to business. The Porter's Value Chain Model (VCM) here is used as a basis for the enterprise knowledge modelling (Gudas, Brundzaite, 2006b).
The control view-based approach (Gudas et al., 2005) is focused on the informational interactions between two kinds of VCM activities -primary and support activities. The different nature of these two kinds of activities is revealed: support activities are information processing activities and are referred to as *Business Process Management Functions*; primary activities typically are material processing (technological) and are named *Processes*.
The interrelated elements *Function* and *Process* form the construct *Business Process* (B). The interaction of the elements *Process* and *Function* is formally assumed as a *Control Process* with the *Feedback Loop*, i.e. *Elementary Management Cycle* (*EMCp*). As the *Function* and *Process* interaction is already discussed in detail in (Gudas et al., 2005), let us concentrate on enterprise model constructs, which are related to the knowledge management.
The similar insights are represented in the organizational control systems modelling (OCSM) framework developed in (Kampfner, 1999).
According to the knowledge-based enterprise definition and structure (see Fig. 11, 12) there is a type of business activity – *knowledge management activity*, which is hidden within M.Porter's Value Chain Model. On the basis of these findings and other methods discussed above, the Value Chain Model is modified and Knowledge-Based Enterprise model is developed (see Fig. 21). Whereas the modified Value Chain Model is focused on the enterprise knowledge management activities and components, it is named *Knowledge-Based Enterprise Model.*
For the completeness of the model two important components of enterprise systems are included: *resources* (*R*) component and *information technology* (*IT*) component (Gudas, 2009).
The Knowledge-Based Enterprise model (KBEM) is a process-oriented model and it refines three different layers of enterprise management hierarchy (Fig. 21):

- knowledge management layer;
- business process management layer;
- infrastructure (management) layer.

The Knowledge-Based Enterprise (KBE) model is constructed from the following main components: *Business process* (*B*), *Knowledge management function* (*K*) component, *Information technology* (*T*) component and the *Resources* component (*R*).
The interaction of the components from different layers of the KBEM (management transaction) is considered as control loop (informational feedback) formally described in

(Gudas, Brundzaite, 2007) as *EMC* (*Elementary Management Cycle*). There are two different management transactions (*Elementary Management Cycles)* identified in the KBEM (Fig. 21): *Knowledge management cycle (EMCz*) and *Process management cycle(EMCp*) (Gudas, 2009).
The peculiarity of the developed model comparing with the M.Porter's Value Chain Model is that the developed model distinguishes between qualitatively different business management activities (*F, P* and *K* constructs in the Fig. 21) and allows formally represent interactions between these activities by using two types of the control activities (*EMCz* and *EMCp* with different semantics) (Gudas, 2009).

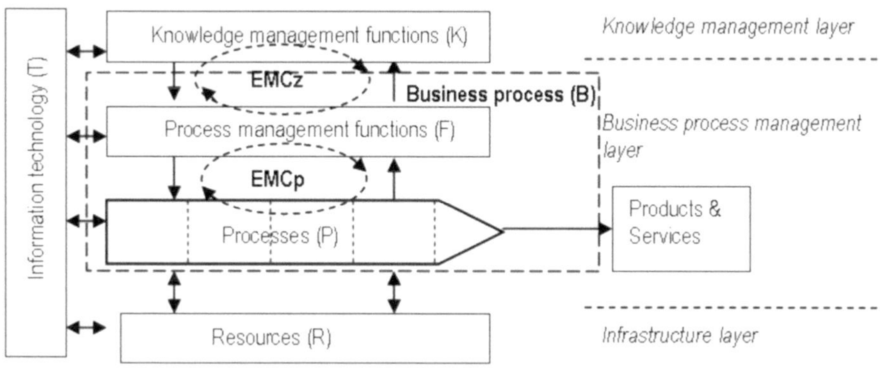

Fig. 21. Knowledge-Based Enterprise model

The semantics of identified management transactions *EMCp* and *EMCz* are different, and are defined as follows:

- *Process management cycle EMCp* – implements a set of *Process* management functions. *EMCp* is responsible for control of the component *Processes* (*P*) – primary activities of enterprise (development of products and services in the proper way (Quality, Time schedule, etc));
- *Knowledge management cycle EMCz* – is the higher level EMC, its component *Knowledge management functions* is responsible for the adequate activities of the *KBEM* component *Process management functions* (*F*). The *EMCz* is focused on the alignment of *Business process* (*B*) with the Enterprise strategic goals.

By definition (Gudas, Brundzaite, 2006b), an Elementary Management Cycle (*EMC)* consists of the predefined sequence of mandatory steps of information transformation (*Interpretation, Information Processing, Realization*); these steps compose a management cycle (a feedback loop). The content of information and semantics of transformation of these mandatory steps of *EMC* depends on the subject area (domain of the enterprise). For instance, the subject area of the *Knowledge management cycle EMCz* is a definite set of *Processes management functions*. It is evident that this subject area of *EMCz* (i.e. information and semantics of transformation of *EMCz*) is totally different from that of *Process management cycle EMCp*. The *EMCz* deals with the information about the characteristics of management functions (quality, effectiveness, etc.), meanwhile the Process management cycle *EMCp* controls characteristics of products, services and state of a *Process* (i.e. technological process).
Therefore, the content (semantics) of information (data, knowledge, goals) processed in these two management cycles (*EMCz* and *EMCp*) is unlike different. The mandatory steps (*Interpretation, Information Processing, Realization*) of the *Elementary Knowledge Management*

Cycle (*EMCz*) are defined as an information transferring processes focused on the control of the content of management functions *F*.
As it was concluded from the overview of Enterprise modeling approaches (see the column "Abstraction levels or views" in Table 2), representation of the enterprise knowledge management activities requires some hierarchical structure to be defined.
Therefore, the *Knowledge management component (K)* in the Fig. 25 is decomposed as hierarchical system and the Knowledge-Based Enterprise (KBE) framework (Fig. 26) developed (Gudas, Brundzaite, 2006, 2006a, 2006b).
The Knowledge management component (K) consist of the internal components as follows (Fig. 29): Business Process (BP), Resources (R), BP knowledge management (K4), Enterprise knowledge management (K3), Knowledge Base management (K2) and Business/IT strategic alignment (K1). These components shape a hierarchy of KBE management levels as follows:
Level 1 .Enterprise strategic management (Business and IT strategic alignment activities);
Level 2. Enterprise meta-knowledge management (Enterprise meta-modeling activities);
Level 3. Enterprise knowledge management (Enterprise knowledge for BP management);
Level 4. Enterprise management (BP knowledge management: knowledge acquisition for BP management, required by Enterprise strategy, defined at level 1);
Level 5. Business process management (managerial activities: Implementation of management functions, directing and controlling (manufacturing) Process);
Level 6. Process management and control (manufacturing control activities).
These enterprise management levels differ in the content of knowledge, required for KBE components for implementation of management activities.
The *KBE framework* is a process-oriented model and it refines two different layers (Fig. 26) of enterprise management hierarchy. The *Knowledge management domain* (*K*) is aimed to control activities of the component *Business domain* (B). The *Business domain* (B) includes management and control of manufacturing activities (the component *Processes* (*P*).
The Knowledge-Based Enterprise framework is based on the management (control) view (Gudas, et al., 2005), formally defined using the concept of Elementary Management Cycle (EMC). In brief, the concept EMC is a formalized description of the Enterprise management control as interaction of *Process* and *Function* - as two core components of enterprise from the control point of view (Gudas, 1991), (Gudas et al., 2005). The interaction of core elements *Management Function* and *Process* is formally assumed as a *Control Process* with the *Feedback Loop* between *Process P*(*j*) and *Management Function F*(*i*).
The interactions of the different management levels (including levels 1 - 6) of the *KBE framework* are management transactions, which are considered as control loops (informational feedback) between corresponding KBE components, that is formally described as *EMC* (the *Elementary Management Cycle*). The semantics of identified management transactions *EMCp* and *EMCz* are different, and are defined as follows:

- Process management cycle *EMCp* implements a set of *Process* management functions. The *EMCp* is responsible for control of the component *Processes* (*P*) - primary activities of enterprise (development of products and services in the proper way (Quality, Time schedule, etc));
- Knowledge management cycle *EMCz* is a higher level EMC, its component *Knowledge management functions* is responsible for the adequate activities of the *KBE framework* component *Process management functions* (*F*). The *EMCz* is focused on the alignment of *Business process (B)* with the Enterprise strategic goals.

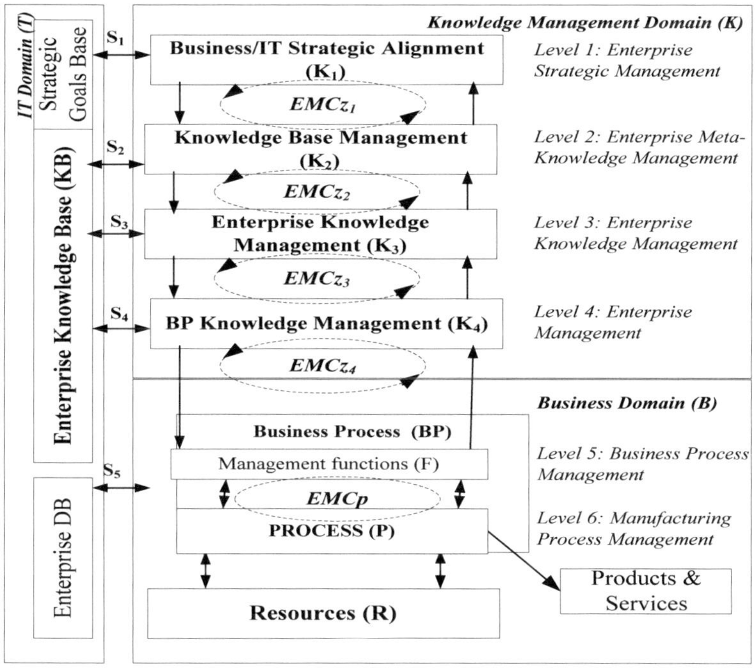

Fig. 22. Knowledge-Based Enterprise management framework

Every higher management level is related with the lower level by the Elementary Management Cycles (*EMCz1, EMCz2, EMCz3, and EMCZ4*) [8]. Each *EMCz* has different semantics.

Thus, from the management control point of view, *Knowledge Management Layer* of the Knowledge-Based Enterprise [Gudas, 2009), (Gudas, 2009a) is decomposed into four structural elements as follows:

- The component *K4* - *Business Process Knowledge Management Functions* (KM level 4 – *Enterprise Management Level*). K4 forms management control attributes for Business Process (*B*) level. *K4* uses interface *S4* with the *Enterprise Knowledge Base* (*KB*) for the exchange knowledge about business processes management.
- Third component *K3* - *Enterprise Knowledge Management (*KM level 3 - *Enterprise Knowledge Management Level*) is aimed to complement knowledge of structural element *K4* by using knowledge, stored in Enterprise Knowledge base (KB) through interface *S3*. *K3* is related with KM level K4 by feedback loop *EMCz3*.
- The component *K2* – *Knowledge Base Management* (KM level 2 - Enterprise-Meta Knowledge *Management Level*) is aimed to improve the structure and content of the *Enterprise Knowledge Base* (*KB*), i. e. to adjust KB content with the business goals through the interface *S2*; Level *K2* in turn is related with third KM *K3* level by feedback loop *EMCz2*.
- Knowledge management is driven by organizational goals and objectives. In the highest KM level – (KM level 1 - *Enterprise Strategic Management Level)* the component *Business/IT Strategic Alignment* (*K1*) defines strategic requirements for the Enterprise Knowledge Base meta-modeling. Components *K1* and *K2* are interrelated by the feedback loop *EMCz1*.

Summing up, four management transactions (formally described as *EMC*), which have different semantics, are identified (Fig. 26):

- *EMCz1* - Enterprise Meta-Knowledge Management Cycle;
- *EMCz2* - Enterprise Knowledge Management Cycle;
- *EMCz3* - Business Process Knowledge Management Cycle;
- *EMCz4* - Business Process Management Cycle.

The semantics of structural components of these Enterprise Management Cycles further are described in detail.

12. Management transactions of Knowledge-Based Enterprise

The semantics of structural components of the Knowledge-Based Enterprise management framework are further described in detail (Gudas, Brundzaite, 2007), (Gudas, 2008), (Gudas, 2009), (Gudas, 2009a), (Gudas, 2010).

Business process management cycle (*EMCz4*). The component *BP Knowledge Management (K4)* is aimed to complement knowledge of the component *Business process* (BP) required by the *Management functions* (F) for management and control of the *Process* (P) on the level 6. *„Manufacturing Process management"*(see Fig. 22). This knowledge management transaction in the KBE framework is named *EMCz4* - Business Process Management Cycle. Business process management cycle (*EMCz4*) is presented in Fig. 23.

The work flow and semantics of Business Process Management Cycle *EMCz4* is as follows. The purpose of Business process management cycle (EMCz4) is the development (generation) of a particular knowledge to control an enterprise component *Business process* (BP). The component BP is comprised of a set of *Management functions* (F) and *Process* (P). The component BP is at *Business domain* (B), it is outside of the *Knowledge management domain* (K).

The semantics of steps of the *Business process management cycle* (EMCz4) (Fig. 27) are as follows: IN4 - interpretation of some facts (characteristics) related with the controlled object - an activity BP; IP4 - processing of interpreted information (data, knowledge) and decision making (it is aimed to control an activity BP); RE4 - realization of decision (management control making, including transferring of manipulated variables (a particular decision) and influencing a controlled object - the component "Business process (BP)".

The constraints on the Business process management cycle (EMCz4) are output of the component K3 (Enterprise knowledge management) and input of the interface S4 from Knowledge base (KB).

The activity IN4 performs an interpretation of the actual knowledge about the features (state) of the Business process (BP). Characteristics (data and knowledge about a state) of Management Functions (F) and Process (P) are captured, transferred and conceptualized, using some criterions from the Enterprise Knowledge Base (EKB). This captured actual semantics of the Business process (BP) is an input of the component BP knowledge management functions (K4). The activity IN4 comprises of a set of rules and procedures for transformation of the actual data and knowledge about a state of Business process (BP).

The step IP4 is knowledge processing activity, aimed to define a set of manipulated variables - decision to control Business process (BP). The activity IP4 is a system of data and knowledge manipulation procedures focused for alignment of the content of component Business process (BP) (i.e. IP4 modify a list and logic of management functions F) in accordance with requirements of the higher level component K3 (these requirements are the output of the step RE3 of the higher level management EMCz3) and actual knowledge accessed by interface S4 from the Enterprise knowledge base.

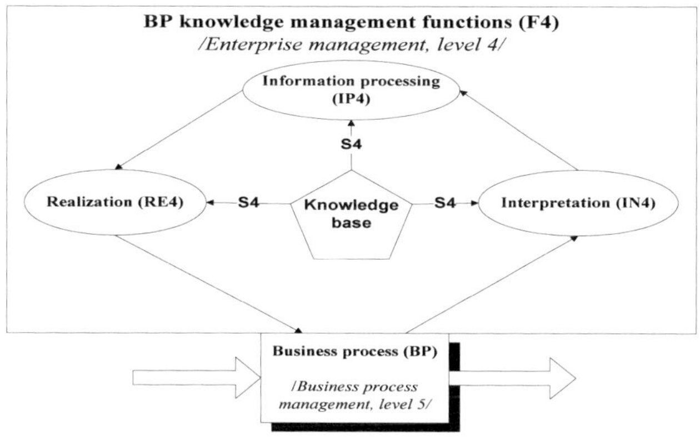

Fig. 23. Business process management cycle (EMCz4)

The step RE4 is the co-ordination activity, the feedback from higher level knowledge management component K4 to business process management level 5. The RE4 is aimed to transfer manipulated variables (decision) and to influence the component Business process (BP), namely to modify Management functions (F).

Business Process Knowledge Management Cycle (*EMCz3)*. The Business Process Knowledge Management Cycle (the management control EMCz3 in Fig. 22) is *knowledge adaptation cycle* (Fig. 28) aimed to integrate the component "BP knowledge management" (K4) with the actual content of the component "Enterprise Knowledge Base" (KB).

The Enterprise knowledge management cycle EMCz3 is aimed to development (generation) of particular new knowledge for business process management functions, which are depicted as the component K4 ("Business process management") in Fig. 26.

The semantics of steps of the Business process knowledge management cycle (EMCz3) are as follows (Fig. 24): IN3 - interpretation of facts (characteristics) related with the controlled object - an activity of the component K4, IP3 - processing of interpreted information (data, knowledge) and decision making (aimed to control the component K4), RE3 - realization of decision (making management control, including transferring of manipulated variables (a particular decision) and influencing a controlled object - the component K4. The constraints on the Business process knowledge management cycle (EMCz3) are output of the component K2 (Knowledge base management) and input of the interface S3 from Knowledge base (KB).

The activity IN3 performs an interpretation of the actual knowledge about the features (state) of BP knowledge management functions (F4). The step IN3 comprises of a set of interpretation rules and procedures for transformation of the actual data and knowledge about a state BP knowledge management functions (F4) for the integration with the step IP3. These transformations are aimed to fit the requirements of the IP3 - the next step of the enterprise knowledge management cycle EMCz3.

The step IP3 - knowledge processing activity, aimed to form a set of manipulated variables - decision to implement new features of the BP knowledge management functions. The IP3 is a system of data and knowledge manipulation procedures focused for modification of the content of component K4 with the requirements of the higher level component K2 (these requirements are the output the step RE2 of the higher level management EMCz2) and actual knowledge accessed by interface S3 from the Enterprise knowledge base.

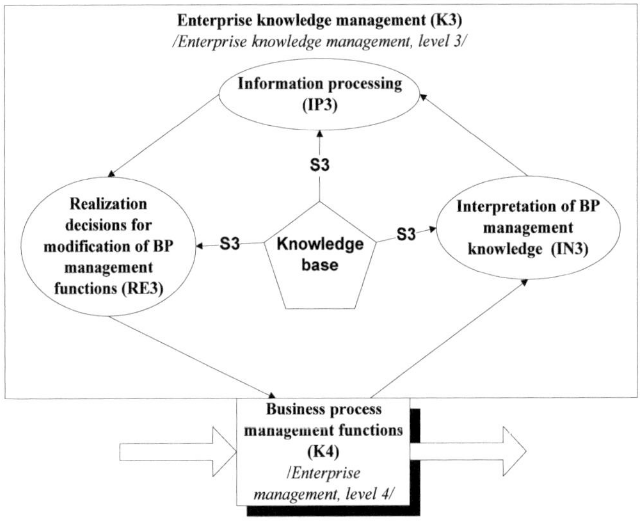

Fig. 24. The Business process knowledge management cycle (EMCz3)

The step RE3 - the co-ordination activity, the feedback from higher level Knowledge management component K3 to Business process knowledge management functions (K4). The step RE3 is aimed to transfer manipulated variables (decision) and to influence the component K4, namely to modify Business process knowledge management functions (F4).
Enterprise Knowledge Management Cycle (EMCz2.)
The component *K3 "Enterprise Knowledge Management"* (KM level 3 - *Enterprise Knowledge Management Level*) is aimed to complement knowledge of the component *K4 „BP Knowledge Management" by* required knowledge, stored in Enterprise Knowledge base (KB) using interface *S3*. The component *K3* is related with the next knowledge management level 4 by feedback loop *EMCz3* (related with component K4).
The component *Enterprise Knowledge Management (*K3) is interrelated with other knowledge management system components as follows:

- *EMCz2* - the Enterprise Knowledge (content) Management Cycle; based on the Enterprise meta-knowledge (Ontology) stored at the EKB (supported by the interface S2);
- The interface *S2* - service to component K2 for using meta-knowledge, stored in Enterprise Knowledge base (KB);
- *EMCz3* - the Business Process Knowledge (content) Management Cycle; based on the Enterprise knowledge stored at the Enterprise Knowledge Base EKB (supported by the interface S3);
- The interface *S3* - service to component K3 for using knowledge, stored at the Enterprise Knowledge Base (EKB).

The Enterprise Knowledge Management Cycle (the management control EMCz2 in Fig. 22) is a *higher level knowledge adaptation cycle* aimed to modify the component "Enterprise knowledge management" (K3) of Knowledge management (K) domain. The Enterprise knowledge management cycle EMCz2 is aimed to development (generation) of definite knowledge required to adapt a set of Enterprise knowledge Management functions to the new requirements of the Knowledge Base meta-model.

The semantics of steps of the Enterprise knowledge management cycle (EMCz2) are as follows (see Fig. 25): IN2 - interpretation of facts (characteristics) related with the controlled object - an activity of the component K3; IP2 - processing of interpreted information (data, knowledge) and decision making (aimed to control an activity of the component K3); RE2 - the step of realization (implementation) of decision aimed to influence a controlled object Enterprise management - the component K3.

The constraints on the Enterprise knowledge management cycle (EMCz2) are output of the component K1 ("Business and IT strategic alignment") and input of the interface S2 of Enterprise Knowledge base (KB).

The activity IN2 performs an interpretation of the actual knowledge about the features (state) of Enterprise knowledge management functions (F3). The step IN2 comprises of a set of interpretation rules and procedures for transformation the actual data and knowledge about a state of Enterprise knowledge management functions (F3) for the integration with the step IP2. These transformations are aimed to fit the requirements of the IP2 - the next step of the enterprise knowledge management cycle EMCz2.

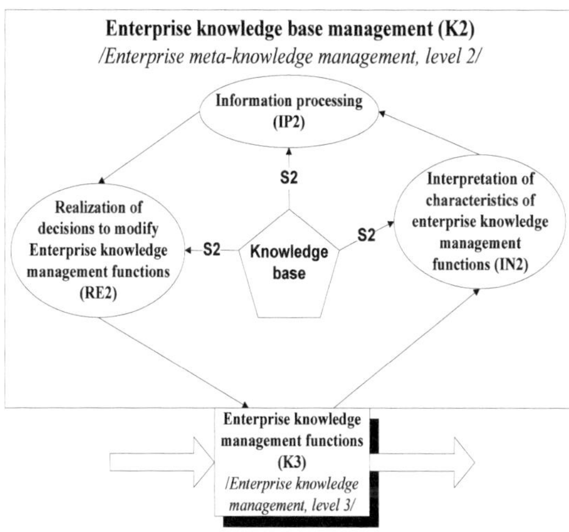

Fig. 25. The Enterprise knowledge management cycle (EMCz2)

The step IP2 - knowledge processing activity, aimed to form a set of manipulated variables - decision to modify the component Enterprise knowledge management (K3). The IP2 is a system of knowledge manipulation procedures focused for alignment of the content of component K3 with the requirements of the higher level component K1 (these requirements are the output the step RE1 of the higher level management EMCz1) and actual knowledge accessed by interface S2 from the Enterprise Knowledge Base.

The step RE2 is the co-ordination activity, the feedback from higher level component Knowledge base management (K2) to the component Enterprise knowledge management (K3). The step RE2 is aimed to transfer manipulated variables (decision) and to influence the component K3, namely to modify Enterprise knowledge management functions (F3) (Gudas, 2009).

Enterprise Meta-Knowledge Management Cycle (*EMCz1)*

Enterprise management as well as knowledge management is driven by organizational goals and objectives. At the highest level of knowledge management of the KBE framework *(Enterprise Strategic Management Level)* the component *Business/IT Strategic Alignment* (*K1*) defines strategic requirements for the Enterprise Knowledge Base management component (K2) and controls it by the feedback loop *EMCz1*.

The EMCz1 is *Enterprise meta-knowledge management cycle,* focused on the alignment of the enterprise knowledge base content (i.e. enterprise meta-knowledge model) and business/ IT strategic goals (Gudas, Brundzaite, 2007).

The management control EMCz1 is the t*op level knowledge management activity* focused on the requirements for the scope and content of Enterprise knowledge base (meta-knowledge). The component Knowledge base management (K2) is responsible for the meta-knowledge management (at level 2 of Knowledge management domain.).

The purpose of Enterprise meta-knowledge management cycle EMCz1 is development (generation) of a definite knowledge to modify the enterprise component Knowledge base management (K2) which is comprised of a set of Enterprise knowledge base management functions (F2).

The semantics of steps of the Enterprise meta-knowledge management cycle (EMCz1) are as follows (Fig. 26):

IN1 - interpretation of facts (characteristics) related with the controlled object - an activity of the component K2;

IP1 - processing of interpreted information (data, knowledge) and decision making (aimed to change the knowledge base meta-structure);

RE1 - realization of decision (a strategic decision) aimed to influence a controlled object - the component K2.

The constraints on the Enterprise meta-knowledge management cycle (EMCz1) are input of the interface S1 from the knowledge base *Strategic Goals.*

The activity IN1 performs an interpretation of the actual knowledge about the features (state) of enterprise knowledge base management functions (F2).

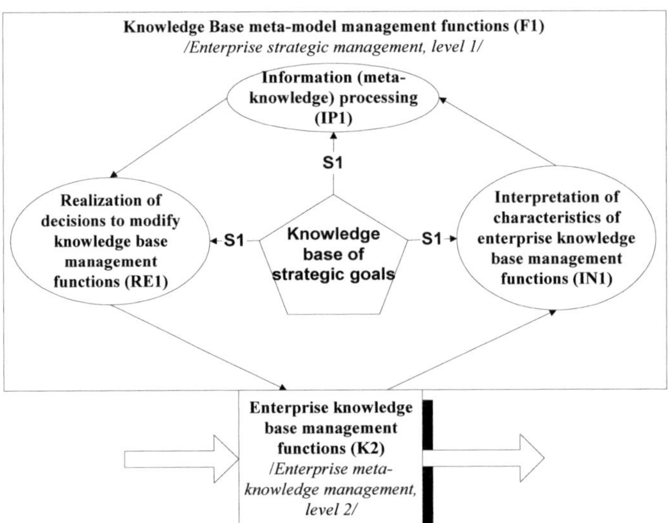

Fig. 26. Enterprise meta-knowledge management cycle (EMCz1)

The step IN1 comprises of a set of interpretation rules and procedures for transformation of the actual data and knowledge about a state enterprise knowledge base management functions (F2) for the integration with the step IP1. These transformations are aimed to fit the requirements of the IP1 - the next step of the enterprise knowledge management cycle EMCz1.

The step IP1 - a meta-knowledge processing activity, aimed to form a set of manipulated variables - decision to control the component Knowledge base management (K2). The IP1 is a system of knowledge manipulation procedures focused for alignment of the content of component K2 with the requirements of the actual knowledge accessed by interface S1 from the Enterprise Strategic Goals' Base.

The step RE1 - the co-ordination activity, it is the feedback from higher level component Business and IT alignment (K1) to the component Enterprise knowledge base management (K3). The step RE1 is aimed to transfer manipulated variables (a strategic decision) and to influence the component K2, namely to modify Enterprise knowledge base meta-model and knowledge base management functions (F2).

13. Components of knowledge management system

Knowledge management *Use Cases* and interfaces. The major knowledge management *Use Cases* and interfaces at the Enterprise knowledge management (K) domain are depicted at the *Use Case diagram* (UML) in Fig. 31. There are four types of *Actors* associated with particular level of the enterprise Knowledge management (K) domain: a top manager (a chief executive), a Knowledge base administrator, an enterprise management expert, and a business process manager (Gudas, Brundzaite, 2007).

The enterprise knowledge self-organization activity is a responsibility of a chief executive. It includes interfaces with use cases Strategic knowledge management functions (F1) and Knowledge base management functions (F2).

Responsibilities of a knowledge base administrator includes interfaces for administration of use cases Strategic knowledge management functions (F1), Knowledge base management functions (F2), "enterprise knowledge management functions (F3), and BP knowledge management functions (F4).

The responsibilities of an enterprise management expert are focused on the development of a definite new knowledge and requirements for improvement of BP management functions (using interfaces with use cases Enterprise knowledge management functions (F3), BP knowledge management functions (F4), and Knowledge base management functions (F2)).

The BP managers access definite knowledge aimed to perform BP management and BP management control (using interfaces with the use case BP management functions (F)), and use interface with BP knowledge management functions (F4) to access definite knowledge for modification of BP management functions.

The major Classes of Enterprise Knowledge base. Enterprise knowledge modelling method could be used for construction of the integrated enterprise knowledge base, which is considered as the basic component of the knowledge-based enterprise. Enterprise knowledge base will enable transformation of the enterprise into knowledge-based business as well as to solve business and IT alignment and enterprise IT management problems.

The major classes of the enterprise knowledge base are derived from formal description of Enterprise Knowledge Space and are defined as Enterprise Knowledge Model *M*.

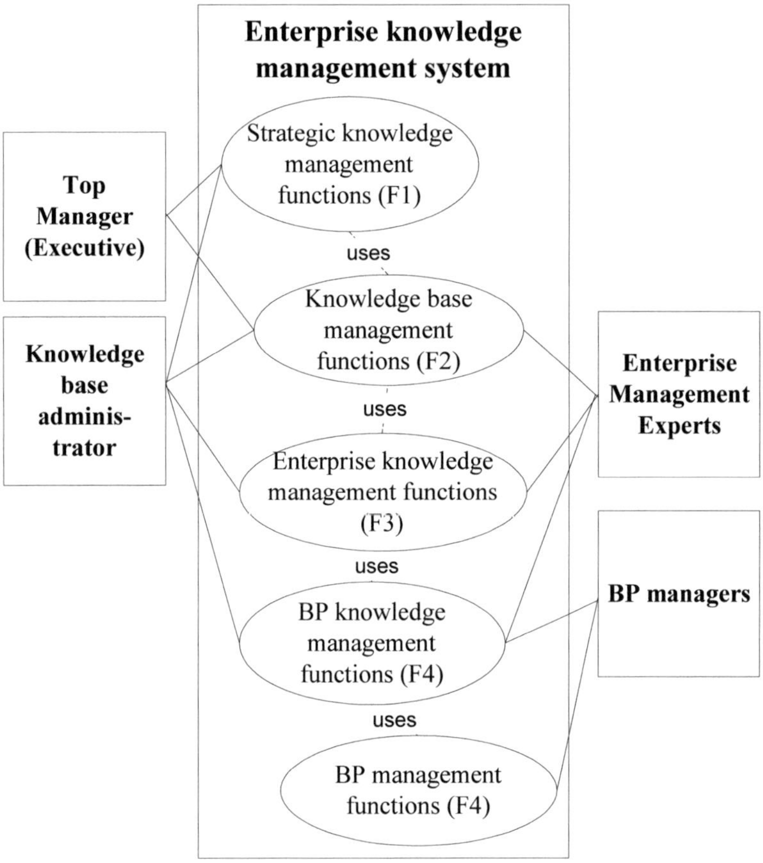

Fig. 27. The major interfaces of Enterprise knowledge management system

The formal description of the Enterprise Knowledge Model M can be expressed as the Cartesian product in the following way (Gudas, 2008):

$$M = (T) \times (K) \times (B) \times (R) \tag{5}$$

where T = information technology, K = knowledge, B = business process, R = business resources.

For the completeness of the model, *resources* (R) component was introduced into the model, as we consider knowledge as separate, but integrated enterprise aspect in contrary to the classical enterprise modelling methods which analyze knowledge alongside with other business resources.

This means, that each enterprise knowledge item m ($m \in M$) in Enterprise Knowledge Model M is related to the appropriate business process b ($b \in B$), knowledge k ($k \in K$), resources r ($r \in R$) and information technology t ($t \in T$). To put it in other terms, the enterprise knowledge model M item m is identified by a set of identifiers:

$$m(t;k;b;r;l) \in M \tag{6}$$

where l ($l \in L$) is time period index.

The Enterprise Knowledge Model *M* is composed of interrelated items *m* and enables modelling a knowledge-based business, as it considers enterprise modelling knowledge (identifier *k*), business processes (identifier *b*), IT (identifier *t*), and their interactions. Each aspect (*b, t, k*) is modelled into the 5 levels of detail in the Enterprise Knowledge Space (Fig. 20).
In Fig. 28, the Enterprise knowledge structure (subsets of knowledge) is presented by class diagram (UML).
Consequently, Enterprise Knowledge Base contains integrated knowledge about three enterprise domains: business (*B*), information technology (*T*) and knowledge (*K*), as well as various relationships of these domains.

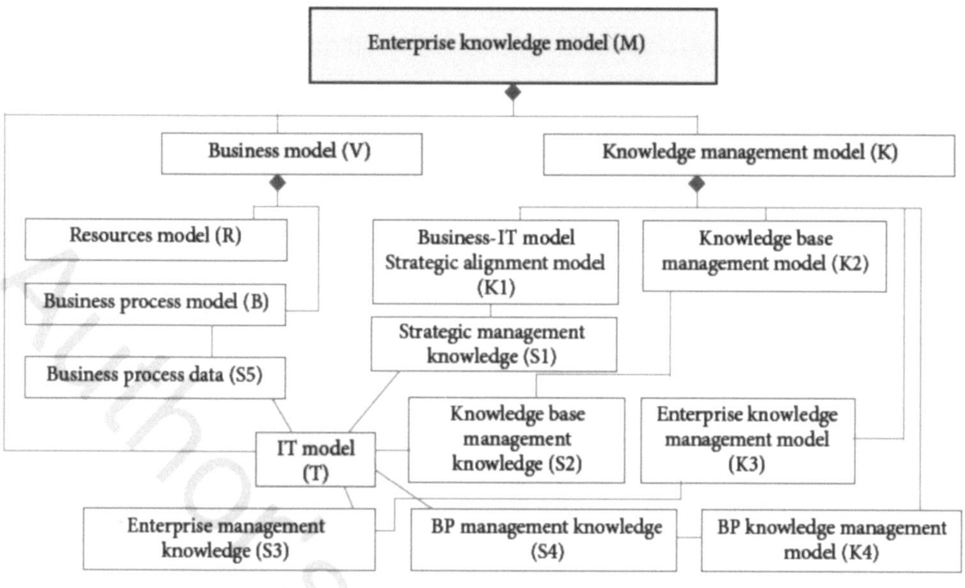

Fig. 28. The major knowledge subsets of the Enterprise Knowledge Base

14. Conclusions

The existing contemporary development methods of information systems that are based on enterprise modelling do not suit for the transformation of business into knowledge-based business, based on information technology.
From the knowledge management point of view, the conception of the Knowledge-Based Enterprise embodies the vision of the more mature and more advanced enterprise and is the step towards intelligent enterprise systems. Advancement is seen here as the high formalisation degree of the knowledge management activities which results in the more efficient management and automation of business process and knowledge processes in the enterprise (Gudas, 2009).

The Knowledge-Based Enterprise Model (KBEM) is presented by modifying Porter's Value Chain Model (VCM). The peculiarity of this KBEM is the identification of Knowledge management layer next to Business process management layer.

Interactions among layers of the KBEM are formally described as semantically different information feedback (control loops): the Process Management Cycle (*EMCp)* and the Knowledge Management Cycle (*EMCz*). The Knowledge-Based Enterprise model is represented as a modified value chain model featuring the knowledge management component.

The concepts of the *enterprise knowledge component* and *Enterprise Knowledge Space* delineates the boundaries and granularity of enterprise knowledge layers. The framework of the Enterprise Knowledge Space is based on the analysis of Enterprise domains and aspects of the various enterprise knowledge modelling approaches generalized by the following concept: the Enterprise Knowledge Component (*B*, *T*, *K*). The Enterprise Knowledge Space supports analysis and integration of knowledge about different domains and aspects of Enterprise management activities. The described Enterprise Knowledge Modelling framework is aimed to develop the method of enterprise knowledge modelling.

The developed Knowledge-Based Enterprise (KBE) framework more formally refines knowledge management activity in the enterprise and is the basis for the development of the Enterprise knowledge base, which is concerned as the main component of the KBE. Interactions among the levels of knowledge management are based on the concept of Elementary Management Cycle (EMC). The EMC concept is derived (Gudas et al., 2005) from the classical concept of control loop as the formal background for description of management information processing in the hierarchical organizational systems (Gudas, 1991).

The presented framework of the Knowledge-Based Enterprise Management System's architecture is aimed to the development of the practical methods for the Knowledge-Based Enterprise modelling and implementation.

The peculiarity of the KBE model is that it reveals another - knowledge management level - and defines interactions between those two management levels of the enterprise, using the same EMC concept. The knowledge management layer of the KBE model contains a hierarchy of the knowledge management activities, defined as the particular types of the EMC. All defined types of the EMC have their own semantics (Gudas, Brundzaite, 2007).

Another important feature of the developed model is that the interactions (defined as interfaces S) between knowledge management domain and information technology domain (Enterprise Knowledge base) are defined formally too.

The presented framework of the Knowledge-Based Enterprise is the basis for the development of the practical methods for the Knowledge-Based Enterprise Modelling and implementation.

15. References

Anthony, R., Govindarajan, V. (2003). *Management Control Systems* (11th Edition), McGraw Hill, ISBN 0-07-123227-3

Christian, S. (2005). Adaptive Knowledge Management: A Meta-Modeling Approach and its Binding to XML, In: *H.-J. Klein 12. GI-Workshop Grundlagen von Datenbanken, Pln, Christian-Albrechts- Universitt Kiel, Germany, 2000,* available from: http://citeseer.ist.psu.edu/christian00adaptive.html

ENV 40003 (1990) *Computer Integrated Manufacturing - Systems Architecture - Framework For Enterprise Modelling, CEN/CENELEC.*

Falkenberg, E.D. , Hesse, W. , Lindgreen, P. , Nilsson, B.E. , Oei, J.L.H. , Rolland, C. , Stamper, R.K. , Van Assche, F.J.M., Verrijn-Stuart, A.A. ,& Voss, K. (1998). *FRISCO – A Framework of Information System Concepts - The FRISCO Report.* IFIP WG 8.1 Task Group FRISCO, available from: ftp://ftp.leidenuniv.nl/pub/rul/fri-full.zip

Firestone, J. M. (1999). *Enterprise Knowledge Management Modeling and Distributed Knowledge Management Systems. Executive Information Systems, Inc.*,available from: http://www.dkms.com/papers/ekmdkms.pdf.

Gartner Group (1999). *White papers on knowledge management, Generalised Enterprise Reference Architecture and Methodology,* Version 1.6.3, IFIP–IFAC Task Force on Architectures for Enterprise Integration, Stamford, CT, GERAM: March 1999, available from: http://www.ict.griffith.edu.au/~bernus/taskforce/geram/versions/geram1-6-3/v1.6.3.html

(GERAM, 1999) GERAM: Generalised Enterprise Reference Architecture and Methodology, Version 1.6.3, IFIP–IFAC Task Force on Architectures for Enterprise Integration, March 1999, http://www.ict.griffith.edu.au/~bernus/taskforce/geram/versions/geram1-6-3/v1.6.3.html

Gudas, S. (1991). *A framework for research of information processing hierarchy in enterprise, Mathematics and Computers in Simulation,* No l. 33, pp. 281-285.

Gudas, S., Lopata, A. (2004). Žiniomis grindžiama informacijos sistemų inžinerija. In: *Informacijos mokslai, Mokslo darbai,* T.30, Vilnius, Vilniaus Universiteto leidykla, p.90-98 ISSN 1392-0561

Gudas, S., Lopata, A., & Skersys, T. (2005). *Approach to enterprise modelling for information systems engineering, Informatica,* Vol. 16, No.2, pp. 175-192, Feb. 2005. ISSN 0868-4952

Gudas, S., Brundzaitė, R. (2006a). *Knowledge-based enterprise modelling framework.* Lecture Notes in Computer Science : Advances in Information Systems, Berlin : Springer. ISSN 0302-9743. 2006, Vol.4243, p. 334-343.

Gudas, S., Brundzaite, R. (2006b). *Decomposition of the Enterprise Knowledge Management Layer.* Proceedings of the 2006 Seventh International Baltic Conference on Databases and Information Systems (Baltic DB&IS 2006), Vilnius: Technika; 2006, pp. 41 - 47

Gudas, S., Brundzaite, R. (2007a). *Approach to enterprise knowledge base development, Advances in Information Systems Development. New Methods and Practice for the Networked Societ,* Springer, p.61-72 ISBN-13 978-0-387-70760-0

Gudas, S., Brundzaite, R. (2007). *Interactions at the Enterprise knowledge management layer, Database and Information Systems IV.* Selected papers from the Seventh International

Baltic Conference DB&IS'2006, IOS Press, Amsterdam, pp.72-85 ISBN 978-1-58603-715-4

Gudas, S. (2008). *Enterprise Knowledge Management Aspects and Layers, Proceedings of the 12-th world multiconference on systemics, cybernetics and informatics* (WMSCI2008), June 29 – July 2th, 2008, Orlando, Florida, USA, Vol. V, p.160-165 ISBN -10: 1-9934272-35-3 (Volume V).

Gudas, S. (2009). *Architecture of Knowledge-Based Enterprise Management Systems: a Control View.* Proceedings of the 13th world multiconference on systemics, cybernetics and informatics (WMSCI2009),) July 10 – 13, Orlando, Florida, USA, Vol. III, p.161-266 ISBN -10: 1-9934272-61-2 (Volume III). ISBN -13: 978-1-9934272-61-9 (Volume III)

Gudas, S. (2009a). *Enterprise knowledge modelling domains and aspects, Technological and economical development of Economy,* v.15, No.2, p.p.281-293 ISSN 1392-8619 print/ISSN 1822-3613 online

Gudas, S. (2010). *Two-Dimensional Decomposition of Bussiness Enterprise Goals, Transformations in Business and Economics,* Vol. 9, No. 2(20) Supplement B, 2010, p.447 – 466 ISSN 1648-4460

Gupta, M.M., Sinha, N.K. (1996). *Intelligent Control Systems; Theory and Applications.* The Institute of Electrical and Electronic Engineers, Inc., New York, 856 p.

Henderson, J., Venkatraman. N.(1990). *Strategic alignment: A model for organization transformation via information technology,* Massachusetts Institute of Technology, Working Paper 3223-90

Hettinger, M.K. (2003). *Model-Driven Architecture, processes and methodology from the perspective of the "Modeling Discipline",* In: MDA™ Implementers' Workshop Succeeding with Model Driven Systems

Richard C. H., Dattero, R., & Stuart D. G. (2006). *The five-tier knowledge management hierarchy,* Vol. 10, No. 1 Journal of Knowledge Management, pp. 19-31

Holsapple, C. W., Joshi, K. D., (1999). *Description and Analysis of Existing Knowledge Management Frameworks,* Proceedings oh the 32nd Hawaii International Conference on System Sciences, 1999, available from: csdl.computer.org/comp/proceedings/hicss/1999/0001/01/00011072.PDF

Iyer, B. , Gottlieb, R. (2004). *The Four-Domain Architecture: An approach to support enterprise architecture design,* IBM Systems Journal, Volume 43, Number 3, available from: http://www.research.ibm.com/journal/sj/433/iyer.pdf

Merchant, K.A. (1998). *Modern Management Control Systems. Text and cases,* Prentice Hall, ISBN 0-13-554155-7 (MOF, 2011) Meta-Object Facility (MOF), available from: http://www.omg.org/mof/

Kampfner, R.R. (1999). *Modeling the Information-Processing Aspect of Organizational Functions.* IEEE

Laudon, J. P., Laudon, K. C (2004). *Laudon Management Information Systems. Managing the Digital Firm* (8th edition), Prentice Hall, ISBN 0-13-120681-8

Liew, A. (2007). *Understanding Data, Information, Knowledge And Their Inter- Relationships,* in: Journal of Knowledge Management Practice, Vol. 8, No. 2, available from: http://www.tlainc.com/articl134.htm

Maier,R. (2004). *Knowledge Management Systems: Information and Communication Technologies for Knowledge Management*, Springer

Malhotra, Y. (2005). *Integrating knowledge management technologies in organizational business processes: getting real time enterprises to deliver real business performance*, in: Journal of Knowledge Management, Vol. 9, No. 1, 2005, pp. 7-28

Maes, R., Rijsenbrij, D., Truijens, O., & Goedvolk, H. (2000). *Redefining business - IT alignment through a unified framework*, Universiteit van Amsterdam, available from: imwww.fee.uva.nl/~maestro/PDF/2000-19.pdf

(MOF, 2011) Meta-Object Facility (MOF), http://www.omg.org/mof/

Muller, H.J. , Schapert, A. (1999).*The Knowledge Factory – a Generic Knowledge Management Architecture*, Proceedings of International Joint Conference on Artificial Intelligence, (2011 08 29)p.1 -10, available from: http://citeseerx.ist.psu.edu/viewdoc/summary?doi=10.1.1.33.3708

Müller, H. J. (1999). *The Knowledge Factory – A Generic Knowledge Management Architecture*, Proceedings of International Joint Conference on Artificial Intelligence, available from: http://www-sop.inria.fr/acacia/WORKSHOPS/IJCAI99-OM/PAPERS/Mueller-IJCAI99-OM.pdf

Porter, M.E. (1985). *Competitive Strategy: Creating and Sustaining Superior Performance*, The Free Press, New York.

Roboam, M., Fox, M.S., & Sycara, K. (1990). *Enterprise ManagementNetwork Architecture The Organization Layer*, CMU-RL-TR-90-22 Center for Integrated Manufacturing Decision Systems The Robotics Institute Carnegie Mellon University Pittsburgh, Pennsylvania 1521 3, Carnegie Mellon University

Schekkerman, J. (2003). *How to survive in the jungle of Enterprise Architecture Frameworks*, Trafford, 2003, ISBN 1-4120-1607-x

Scheer,A.W. (1999). ARIS - Business Process Modeling (2nd ed.), Berlin et al. , Süß, C. (2005). *Adaptive Knowledge Management: A Meta-Modeling Approach and its Binding to XML*,GI-Workshop Grundlagen von Datenbanken, Plön, TR 2005, Christian-Albrechts-Universität, http://www.oasis-open.org/cover/suessS00-2000-.pdf

Frank, U. (2002). *A Multi-Layer Architecture for Knowledge Management Systems*, University of Koblenz-Landau

Frank, U. (2002a). *Multi-Perspective Enterprise Modeling (MEMO) – Conceptual Framework and Modeling Languages*, in: 35th Hawaii International Conference on System Sciences, available at: csdl.computer.org/comp/proceedings/hicss/2002/1435/03/14350072.pdf

Vernadat, F. (2002). *UEML: towards a unified enterprise modelling language*, International Journal of Production Research, Volume 40, Number 17, 20 November 2002 , pp. 4309-4321(13), available from: http://www.utt.fr/mosim01/pdf/invite/ARTICLE-invite-vernadat.pdf

Zachman, J. A., Sowa, J.F. (1992). *Extending and Formalizing the Framework for Information Systems Architecture*, in: IBM Systems Journal, vol. 31, no. 3, 1992. IBM Publication

Zack M.H. (2003). *Rethinking the knowledge-based organization*, in: Sloan management review, vol. 44, no. 4, summer 2003, pp 67-71, available from: http://web.cba.neu.edu/~mzack/articles/kbo/kbo.htm

Williams T.J., Hong Li, (1995). *A Specification and Statement of Requirements for GERAM (The Generalised Enterprise Reference Architecture and Methodology) with all Requirements illustrated by Examples from the Purdue Enterprise Reference Architecture and Methodology PERA*, Research Report 159, Purdue Laboratory for Applied Industrial Control, (November 1995), Version 1.1

10

Transcending Knowledge Management, Shaping Knowledge Governance

László Z. Karvalics
University of Szeged, Department of Library and Human Information Science
Hungary

1. Introduction

From knowledge management to knowledge governance

„*Knowledge management as an academic discipline is realizing phenomenal growth and international acceptance.*" However, reviewing three of the most popular models - Nonaka's SECI (Japan), March's Ex-Ex (USA) and Boisot's I-space (Europe) - Curado and Bontis have to confess, that „*there still exists no universally accepted framework or model of knowledge management*" (Curado & Bontis, 2011). But it seems to be a minor problem, if we recognize, that the major approaches of classical knowledge management, distilled to cook-book definitions and consultant practices, are increasingly viewed as inadequate in addressing the growing complexity of information and knowledge flows in modern organizations and societies facing with rapidly changing environments. It is enough to refer to the VUCA-paradigm (*volatility, uncertainty, complexity and ambiguity*) or the disruptive market and technology transformations.

Reflecting a new normative push towards conceptual innovation, knowledge governance has emerged as a new paradigm to describe, understand, and analyze the expanding "knowledge domain" in a holistic and comprehensive way. Knowledge governance involves the design of structures and mechanisms to support the processes of sharing and creating knowledge in the (almost) exclusive frame of strategic management. In this chapter we try to draw the portrait of this pretender theory and practice with deep case studies.

2. Forerunners of knowledge governance

During the "ruling decades" (1975-2005) of knowledge management, every innovative approach, dealing with the "knowledge domain" was introduced as a fruitful contribution to the mainstream knowledge management literature. Then again some of them had more complex scope and abstraction level, but their alternative classification became possible only in the last few years, identifying them as early attempts to find broader and more comprehensive framework. We have to start with the short review of these pioneer approaches and models[1].

---

[1] Part 2-3 is a slightly modified version of our papers with Nikunj Dalal. (Dalal & Z. Karvalics, 2009, 2011)

2.1 Management cybernetics

Stafford Beer was the first to apply cybernetics to management in the 1960s, calling it the "science of effective organization". Management cybernetics focuses on the study of organizational design, and the regulation and self-regulation of organizations from a systems theory perspective (Beer, 1985). Beer's viable system model (VSM) can be used to study different aspects of knowledge management in an individual, organization or network and to model knowledge processes dynamically over time with the goal of improving the organizational systems (Leonard, 2000). Management cybernetic approaches have led to the transformation of organizations particularly of public bodies such as governments and the advancement of new forms of governance.

2.2 Learning organizations and communities of practice

According to the influential vision of Peter Senge, learning organizations are: "*organizations where people continually expand their capacity to create the results they truly desire, where new and expansive patterns of thinking are nurtured, where collective aspiration is set free, and where people are continually learning to see the whole together.*" (Senge, 1990). From the perspective of learning organizations, the focus of knowledge creation should begin with individuals and in helping them to learn using tools such as: systems thinking, personal mastery, mental models, building a shared vision, and team learning (Senge, 1990). Arising from the field of organizational learning, the notion of communities of practice refers loosely to interest groups that get together at work and in social settings into which newcomers can enter and learn the sociocultural practices of the community. A community of practice is defined as "a unique combination of three elements: a *domain* of knowledge, which defines a set of issues; a *community* of people who care about this domain; and the shared *practice* that they are developing to be effective in their domain" (Wenger et al., 2002). From our perspective, a community of practice within an organization can be seen as a practical way to connect people, share existing tacit knowledge, and create new knowledge.

2.3 Knowledge communities and knowledge ecology

Closely allied to the notion of learning organizations, the concept and practices of knowledge communities and knowledge ecology recognize the systemic and holistic nature of knowledge and aspire to go beyond knowledge management to develop shared intelligence and collective wisdom. Members of several communities of practice will often interact with one another in wider knowledge communities. George Pór describes communities as those that connect islands of knowledge into self-organizing networks that share knowledge. Knowledge ecology, in contrast to command and control hierarchies, aims to unleash the full potential of its participants in order to design and support self-organizing knowledge ecosystems, whereby information, knowledge, intelligence, and wisdom can cross-fertilize and feed on one other (Pór, 2000). The practices of knowledge ecology seem to be more distributed, discipline-transcending, and customer-or problem focused than communities of practice.

2.4 Knowledge and policy networks

Knowledge networks can be seen as being larger, more diffuse and distributed, and less cohesive and practice-oriented than communities of practice or knowledge communities (Jordan & Schubert, 1992). Networks are neither solely organized like a market nor do they have official hierarchic regulatory structures. Rather, while they may share some characteristics with markets and hierarchies, they are more likely to have informal practices of coordination, common goals or interests, and transaction mechanisms based on attributes such as trust and recommendations rather than prices or administrative orders (Thompson, 2003). Knowledge networks provide an effective coordination mechanism for creating, sharing, and distributing knowledge within and across organizations as well as in specialized domains such as cancer and climate change. Policy networks may be seen as special types of knowledge networks in the political domain which attempt to relate private and public actors.

2.5 Knowledge asset management and knowledge markets

Knowledge asset management views knowledge as an organization's intellectual capital (Boisot, 1998) and as a strategic asset. This view attempts to combine process-centric approaches that views knowledge management as a set of communication processes and the product-centric approach that focuses on the documents, creation, and reuse. In the early knowledge management literature, the knowledge market was generally described as a mechanism for distributing knowledge resources between providers and users. It was Albert Simard, who developed a cyclic end-to-end knowledge-market model (Simard, 2006). The model is based on nine stages: generate, transform, manage, use internally, transfer, add value, use professionally, use personally, and evaluate. The latest (third generation) vision of knowledge markets is even more ambitious: It views knowledge markets as formal or informal community contexts, platforms, or environments (real or virtual) used to promote knowledge commerce, trade and exchange, demand and supply, between knowledge buyers and sellers. They are used to organize, coordinate, aggregate, facilitate, communicate, broker, and network flows and exchanges of knowledge between knowledge seekers and knowledge providers (Davis, 2007).

2.6. Wisdom management

Many recent approaches have begun to recognize that the focus on mere knowledge is not enough. Many organizational and societal crises are crises not because of a lack of information, knowledge or other resources but because of greed, lack of values, and a dearth of wisdom. While wisdom has been a focus of philosophical and religious traditions since antiquity, only in recent times are we seeing attempts to understand wisdom from an organizational science perspective. Combining the notions of wisdom, communities of practice, and networks, Nikunj Dalal has proposed the vision of wisdom networks as communities that aim to actualize and inculcate wisdom in specific domains (Dalal, 2008). Wisdom networks are involved in inquiry of key issues in a domain, the creation and dissemination of wisdom-based learning, counseling, participation in community initiatives, and in building linkages with other wisdom networks.

2.7 Chief knowledge officers

It was Thomas H. Davenport, one of the „founding fathers" of Knowledge Management who has successfully introduced the concept and described the „activity portfolio" of the Chief Knowledge Officer (CKO), fertilizing the discussion about the „knowledge leadership" of an organization (Davenport, 1994). Michael J. Earl and Ian I. Scott created a well-itemized tipology of the CKO's, as integrator and synchronizators of all the relevant aspects of the corporate knowledge flow, building and maintaining a network from knowledge champions, knowledge sponsors, knowledge partners and knowledge skeptics (Earl & Scott, 1999). The expression itself became very popular, but the appearance of CKO's in a corporate leadership hierarchy was very limited in the last decade. Conversely, the sweep of Knowledge Governance could bring the "big time" for the new generation CKO's.

3. The birth of a narrative: Coining and defining knowledge governance

In recent years, based on the work of Nicolai Foss and others, the concept of knowledge governance is expanding and gaining popularity. The primary underlying premise of knowledge governance is that knowledge creation, retention, and sharing processes can be influenced and directed through the deployment of organizational governance mechanisms and other coordination mechanisms.

In Foss's theoretical works, knowledge governance is a distinctive approach, having many cross-connections with knowledge management (Foss, 2005). In his early works, he refers to only the cross-points of general management, strategic issues and human resource management (Foss, 2007) and defines knowledge governance as follows: "*The 'knowledge governance approach' is characterized as a distinctive, emerging approach that cuts across the fields of knowledge management, organisation studies, strategy, and human resource management. Knowledge governance is taken up with how the deployment of governance mechanisms influences knowledge processes, such as sharing, retaining and creating knowledge. It insists on clear micro (behavioural) foundations, adopts an economizing perspective, and examines the links between knowledge-based units of analysis with diverse characteristics and governance mechanisms with diverse capabilities of handling these transactions.*" But over the next two years, Foss gradually broadened the scope of knowledge governance to connect with the management of intellectual capital, innovation theory, technology strategy, and the international business itself (Foss & Michailova, 2009). In the current vocabulary of Foss, knowledge governance "*refers to choosing structures and mechanisms that can influence the processes of sharing and creating knowledge* (Foss & Michailova, 2009)."

4. Knowledge governance in corporate environment

There is no doubt, that the most distinctive area of knowledge governance research is the corporate scene. In the lack of systematized, course book-like summaries, first of all I present a nine element table to highlight the differences between the „old" and the „new" paradigms, portraying the most substantive deviations and distinctions. After that I share the experiences of one of our knowledge governance fieldworks as case study, and finally I briefly present our innovative methodology to understand the Corporate Mind from a knowledge governance perspective.

4.1 Face to face with the knowledge management

Although more and more special aspects of knowledge governance are already discussed (see for example Antonelli, 2005, Sacchetti & Sugden, 2008), the main identity constitutor of this new approach is an ability to make strict distinction between the main characteristics of knowledge management and knowledge governance. Since we can find independent discourses behind every item with extended literature background, it seems to be enough to show the main arguments, the basic aspects – in a simple table format.

	Information and Knowledge Management	Knowledge Governance
Organizational focus, operative basis and nature	*Divisional* by the division of labour of corporate units, having additive character (1+1=2)	*Company as a whole* by information interfaces, having complementer character (1&1=3)
Leadership approach	Effectivity, return, value-proportionality, rationalisation, optimalisation of the business, production and decision processes	Coordinative effectivity, adaptation and reaction skills in changing environments, ability for regenerational capacity improvement
Main knowledge work	*Learning*	*Knowledge building* (Hong, Scardamalia and Zhang, 2010)
Control	Distributed CIO (*Chief Information Officer*), Education/Training director, Leader of Research and Development, Director of Human Resources, PR and communication	Integrated CKO (*Chief Knowledge Officer*)
Approaching problems	inductive, deductive reasoning	abductive reasoning
Way of thinking	*technical thinking*: analytic certainties	*design thinking*: interpretational probabilities
Technological macro-environment	„instant" software products, consultant-driven implementations, platform and solution development by the IT units, information center	revealing and interpreting the points of relevance, planning, building and operation of knowledge environments, coaching, facilitation of knowledge transfer
Tipical domains and forms of activity	Business and operations information systems, ERP (Enterprise Resource Planning), CRM (Customer Relationship Manageemnt), DSS (Decision Support Systems), DMS (Document Management Systems), data mining, market research, corporate Intranet, training, etc.	problem solving based on environmental scanning and the development of related skills, maintenance and development of constructive and creative technologies, detection and organic elimination of knowledge deficiencies
Consultant strategy	Work *for* the corporate partner Selling existing solutions	Work *with* the corporate partner Finding tailored solutions

Table 1. Knowledge Management versus Knowledge Governance - a comparison

4.2 Knowledge governance in action: A case study[2]

A prominent Hungarian service provider invited us to conduct a Knowledge Governance audit of his organisation. Through our initial discussions we learned that in an effort to make the incumbent company a more agile competitor of its industry they have already had a corporate risk profile audit completed and another one focusing on corporate culture. They wanted to concentrate on knowledge because there was a shared understanding

[2] The research was conducted by DEAK Zrt,, a joint research and development company of the University of Szeged and Hungarian Academy of Sciences, established in 2008 to enhance industrial cooperations, international innovation relations, and the development of knowledge based economy. The field work and desk research was supported by the New Hungary Development Plan GOP-1.1.2-07/1-2008-0007 „Multidisciplinary research and development by DEAK KKK". The main author of this summary is *Judit Benczik*.

within the organisation that the experience they cumulated under their belt, an experience base that earned them the third place as the most trusted profession (right after the fire department and the medical profession) is an untapped resource. A resource they wanted to make better use of since competitive dynamics created a setup in which it proved increasingly more and more difficult for the giant to meet both owners' and customers' expectations in equal measure.

In the first phase of the research we wanted to develop a bird's eye view on the most important organisational 'pain points' that top decision makers felt cut deeply into their overall performance. The interview series conducted revealed three problems and the situation was ripe for the company to make significant changes in how it made use of its existing knowledge and how it was handling the need to fill its knowledge gaps. The three problem areas were:

- despite of its outstanding reputation the organisation had an issue with how to turn this brand-related knowledge around and capitalise on it;
- decision making processes suffered from substantial inefficiencies as knowledge instead of flowing through the system got stuck in various parts of the organisational structure;
- and in terms of performance impact local knowledge had very little bearing on actual outcomes.

Once the initial findings were formulated we had a session with the General Manager confirming that the issues our analysis highlighted were indeed on the organisational agenda - though not phrased in knowledge terms - for a while and the need to address them initiated both the risk and the corporate culture studies. (We did not ask for such a brief prior to formulating our initial findings so that the value of a fresh perspective could be fully exploited.) This feedback struck a chord with us: if there was ample evidence and reasoning put forward in the available diagnoses (provided by both internal and external sources) how come the organisation was still not making decisive progress on its most pressing issues, not even when sizeable chunks of the market were taken over by competitors? So, we looked again into our research material but this time instead of looking for identifiable problem sets, we looked for signs that could provide a reasonable backdrop against which such a perceived reluctance could be explained.

Having completed this second phase of the research we came up with a framework. In this framework the explanatory power of our findings got an extra kick since we were able to demonstrate that the three elements were in crucial ways interlinked. The framework also provided clues to the broader question, as to why in an organisation where all the right calls seemed to have been made the elements on the activity field still did not come together to power up the performance engine and drag the system out of what seemed to be slowly becoming an inwardly spiralling cyclical trap. The link among the findings can be found once we depict the organisation as a self-sustaining entity that gains its identity through constructing its performance by managing a network of three models: its business model (how the organisation makes money), its operational model (how its interactions are designed across its domains), and its organisational model (how it allocates various rights and duties).

The issue of *how to turn the existing brand-related knowledge around to capitalise on it ties in with the business model*. The issue of knowledge getting stuck at various parts of the system ties in with the operational model. The issue of local knowledge playing a somewhat marginalised role ties in with the organisational model. In sum, we can state the entire architecture of the organisational identity was being challenged. This made the need to address the issues we highlighted apparent from a competitiveness point of view but did not provide a clue as to why such recommendations (plural is used to refer to earlier diagnoses as well that articulated points similar ours) are received reluctantly. It could be argued, of course, that to integrate modifications at such scale are complex hence the less than heartfelt reception. And it is also only fair to say that there were many attempts made (all of which were outlined in great detail in the interviews) during the last decade but none were powerful enough to stop the erosion of the company's market position.

Having accumulated from the interviews a fair understanding of what the three major re-organisation attempts of the past decade entailed and juxtaposing those goals to the organisation's current strategic goals we could see that although the characteristics of issues evolved over time, the underlying structures showed an eery resemblance throughout this time period. The company launched many initiatives to react to the changing needs of its customer base but most of those initiatives did not bring the expected results. A fair percentage of those actions were partially at odds with what the customers really wanted to accomplish by using this particular service provider. In other words, the solutions applied by the company did not or only to a degree matched customers' expectation about the realisable benefits of dealing with the company. This recurring pattern was confirmation enough for our hypothesis that the corporate identity crisis is not the cause but the symptom of the company's ailing health and we should dig deeper to find a possible cause.

We compiled a full list of the most important initiatives introduced that populated the company's activity field. A short extract of which:

- introduction of new products that utilise the existing distribution channel and also add to the company's modernised profile → targeted to lead to improved customer perception
- investment into technological solutions that help to streamline customer throughput → designed to monetize efficiency gains and to increase satisfaction generated by professional customer handling
- establishing quality insurance processes and qualifying for the relevant international title that acknowledges it → intended to ensure priority setting in the operation and remove inefficiencies that add to the company's cost base
- installing a reporting system that ties appropriate accountabilities into the planning process → designed to establish clear line of sight
- allocating funding to training & development → implemented not only to upgrade the knowledge base but also to motivate those who are eager learn
- adopting performance assessment techniques → intended to support the integration of appropriate behavioral pattern into daily work, behaviours that match customer expectation

Even this list shows clearly that customer and cost based issues were tackled together with individual and organisational development needs. The company's reaction repertoire to the challenges of toughening competition was broad enough to save them the criticism of inaction. It was not what they did, but how they did it. In order to be able to elaborate on this point further we have to introduce a distinction into the concept of organisational 'reaction'. According to the view to be presented here the capability to react involves at least two processes: that of 'reproduction' and that of 'regeneration'. The two processes are distinctively different in how they 'respond' to competitive pressure. In the first case the major concern is throughput, in the latter finding the right fit. As long as we regard reaction as a unified process during which an organisation adapts its practices to generate competitive advantage it is hard to see why so much effort might still not be 'good enough'. Irrespective of the disciplinary field's mindset applied as a filter to scan through management science for solutions to advance organisational competitiveness, there will be an abundant supply of ideas. For the sake of example, in a quite arbitrary fashion, let's take a strategic perspective now. We've been through the cycles of scale economies, market positioning algorithms, resource views and capability structures and they all added an understanding to what consitutes to 'success' - however that might be defined and measured by the given organisation. What appears to be unchanged are the fundamentals of 'competitive pressure'.

Even if the formulation of it slightly changes, at its core is the concept of a uniform process whereby the component parts that make up the conditions and circumstances within which the organisation operate set the framework for the organisational activity field. According to the view presented here however, competitive pressure has a double-decker nature. It operates as a mechanism that allows every organisational solution to thrive if it does not limit the organisation's capacity to stay in the game; and as another mechanism that sorts out how those solution sets rank compared to each other. This is not a simple theoretical whim. Quite the contrary. It has important implications for knowledge management. The differentiation we are to describe will allow us not only to give an answer to the question why our client's actions - that were mostly in line with that of its competitors - did not help it defend its highly profitable income streams, but it also helps us in our attempt to create an adequate foundation for how to incorporate knowledge management into organisational problem solving under incrising competitive pressure.

So let's reformulate our point proposed here. Do conditions and circumstances shape the directions an organisation can take? The answer is a resounding yes. Can we exclusively explain by looking at the same forces what determines the rank ordering of organisational performance of those participating in the same ball game? Well, not so sure about it. And if there is doubt, there is room for further investigation. We developed a special model for the company to plan the interventions[3].

4.3 A knowledge governance model of a corporate mind

We regard organisations as self-sustaining entities that gain their identity by managing their performance construct. We also put forward the argument that in order to better understand the contribution potential of knowledge governance to this performance construct the 'sanctity' of competitive pressure has to be dismantled. Since both of these premises are fairly complex especially when put into the context of high stake management dilemmas, not to mention the fact that their relationship to each other was expected to appear as counter-intiutive to our client, we decided to work out a model that captures the most important dynamics of how these components interact. Our model, dubbed the 'Corporate Mind', is based on the analogies that the connections of brain-mind-intelligence offer.

The Corporate Mind as a metaphor was very popular in the late 80's and early 90' (see Zaleznik, 1985, Hampden & Turner, 1990, Cornwell, 1992) and reflected to Stafford Beer's early classics, The Brain of the Firm (Beer, 1972). We use the expression as a pure help to visualize the main relationships.

---

[3] The model, the figures and the methodology is a property of the developer partner, *Zebnick & Associates.* The main author of this chapter is Judit Benczik.

The underlying message of placing informed decision making into a model that reflects the double-decker nature of competitive pressure under which organisational decisions are made is to point out that the key to the appropriateness of those decisions is not 'out there' but is 'in here'. The replies and reactions that a given Corporate Mind produces will reflect how it handles the inherent difficulties that come with accomodating the double-deckedness of competitive pressure. Results of which will show up in the overall competitiveness of the firm. It also follows from the above, that the appropriateness of an action and the utilisation of relevant knowledge cannot be simply derived from the relationships between the attributes of desired change and that of competitive conditions and how the two sets correlate with each other in a complex situation. Obviously, such connections do exist, no question about that. But if we are interested in understanding what makes one solution work better for one organisation and not the other, we need to look elsewhere.
Our Corporate Mind model simplifies the behaviour of the more complex organisational decision making system but it can still sufficiently represent the connections that help describe the observed phenomena - that of under-achievement in the presence of appropriate actions. Just like in the individual case, the way the Corporate Mind works is by running a mental model in which one or more concepts interact - the communication between those concepts are expressed by arrows.

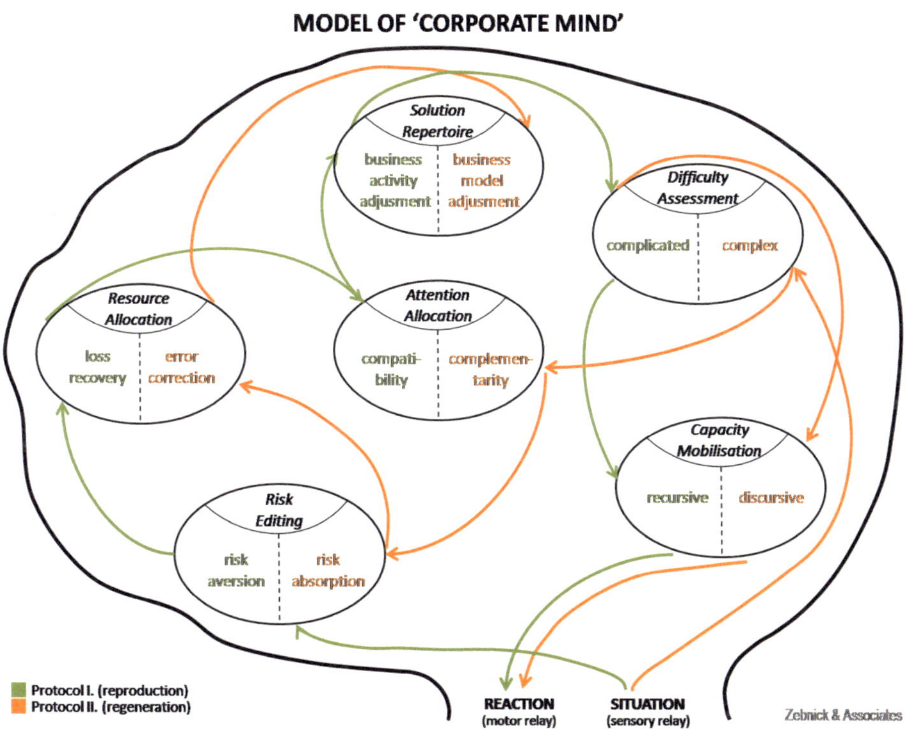

Fig. 1. Model of the Corporate Mind

In the given organisational situation information is extracted and flows from feature extraction through percept to concept formation. It is important to emphasise here that according to this view the representations that this process creates are in a constant flux as transformations are conducted with the information obtained. In this regard, the Corporate Mind's task is maintaining both the mechanism and the construct that creates the representation of reality, so that the organisation can trace changes in it as closely as possible. *Any flaw in this activity will hinder the organisation's ability to reply appropriately.* Interaction among the concepts, as far as our current knowledge goes, appear to go on throughout the entire cerebral cortex. But the functions of different regions put this capacity to different uses. The six major regions in the brain are: the limbic system, the executive functions, the integrative functions, the motor program selection, the sensory processing and feature extraction, and the motor program execution. We mapped out the regions of the Corporate Mind accordingly.

Coming back to the point about the double-decker nature of competitive pressure, we proposed that it operates both as a mechanism that allows alternative solutions to thrive and as a mechanism that rank orders those solutions. One is there to navigate the maze and to find what's applicable, the other to opt for the 'best'. The former is more of a complex task, whereas the latter is more of a complicated task. And because of the intrinsic differences of complexity and complicatedness, they are best handled by deploying alternative protocols. In our model the seven green lines represent the loop that is more geared towards tackling complicatedness, whereas the other seven orange lines represent the loop that is better tailored to handle complexity.

The problem however for organisational decision makers is that situations do not emerge nicely labeled 'complicated' or 'complex' for the sake of managerial convenience. As if this was not enough, due to the pressures of globalisation, regulatory changes, technological advances and an increasing demand for new services, the issue becomes further exacerbated. In most industries where these four forces exert pressure on the reaction capabilities of organisations - and it is hard to point to one where they wouldn't - they made it ever more prevalent that the flow and charactersitics of knowledge and the context in which it is applied is changing quicker than we are mostly ready to admit it.

The Corporate Mind model in itself does not answer the question of how to address specific situational constellations. It is there to highlight the fact that in order to process the double demands of competitive pressure (that of finding and that of choosing) the Competitive Mind has to run the double protocol depicted by the model. Why? Because one loop is governed by the principle of compatibility to give the best result, the other by complementarity to do the same (see the middle region of 'Attention Allocation' in Figure 1.) The situation itself will not determine which one to deploy because the risks the organisation will take by opting for one action rather than the other will depend on what it deems learnable about the situation. By running the green loop, the Corporate Mind makes the organisation ready to learn from mustering complicatedness that will most benefit performance through efficiencies of reproductive success. This learning greatly enhances the organisation's ability to come up with consistent performance time period upon time period. By running the orange loop, the Corporate Mind allows the organisation to learn from holding up to complexity that will most benefit performance through efficiencies of regenerative success. This learning supports the organisation's ability to self-correct or recover, as the case might be. Hence the name of the two loops in our model.

How the balance between the two loops will be managed over time is unique to any organisation. The shifts will be reflective of when and how the Corporate Mind adjusts the representation of its reality by activating either one of the loops. The more generalisable message of the model, however, is that loop dominance – i.e. frequenting the approbriable benefits of either the Reproductive cycle or that of the Regenerative cycle - will sooner or later strain the ability of the organisation to meet its own targets. Why? Because no lopsided Corporate Mind can fully engage with the dialogue that is going on in its marketplace and the organisation will either come to false conclusions about what aspects of its activity field need to be aligned, or about the relevance of its business model. In case a Corporate Mind allows for an over-drive to happen (that is one loop over-powering the other), it will sooner or later find itself in a self-inflicted trap. The longer it keeps postponing the need to address both requirements that competitive pressure presents, the tighter the grasp of self-inflicted trap will become.

In sum, as the Corporate Mind switches from a double protocol to a single protocol - which often happens in an effort to recover losses from unexpected performance decrease - it tries to release resources (time, money, energy) from alternative uses that may divert efforts from recovery. Which is just as well. But the solution begins to backfire when reallocation restrains the permeability of the system. In every region of the Corporate Mind the two protocols are to inform each other, otherwise one of the aspects of competitive pressure is not being addressed. If reallocation severes the knowledge transfer ties between the two protocols, the organisation is a strong candidate for implementing actions that do not bring the expected results. But the explanation is not in the action itself, but how it was achieved. If due to the lack of permeability there was minimal or no referencing of the knowledge base that can appropriately handle either the complicatedness or the complexity aspects of the situation, there will be no fit between what the situation calls for and the reaction provided.

Often times, managers of stressed organisations propose arguments, solutions that go into intricate analytical details that are designed to prove a particular point. The analyis is mostly valid but by their very nature of being recursive most analyis is ill equipped to handle ambiguities, incongruities and parallel definitions of the same phenomema that are characterisitc features of juggling to find most of the viable solutions that allow the organisation to stay part of the gameand ranking them at the same time. Analyes typically open only a small window to the discursive space where the juggling is going on and by doing so they can limit access to the relevant knowledge base. Juggling is the task of the Corporate Mind. Analysis is only a part of it.

This brief interpretation of how the model works, hopefully illustrated the proposition that ignoring the double-decker nature of competitive pressure - which most Corporate Minds in a single protocol over-drive do - is a self-inflicted wound that limits the organisation's capacity to decipher meaning from what's going on in and around its competitive landscape.

4.3.1 The dynamic model

As it was emphasised in the previous chapter, the concept network in the Corporate Mind is created by the transformational activites that happen when loop-specific knowledge is exchanged through the permeable boundaries of the regions. This malleable characteristic enables the Corporate Mind to update its cognitive map. Learning takes place as new concepts join and leave. New links can be made at all levels and old links can fade if not reinforced. What's even better from a performance improvement potential point of view is that old links can be inhibited when new links have a contradictory or dampening effect on earlier associations. The performance intelligence of an organisation can be assessed by looking at the activities that go in the Corporate Mind.

It is much like doing brain diagnosis with a fMRI (functional magnetic resonance imaging). This non-invasive specialised scanning technology picks up change of blood flow related to neural activity. Stimuli will activate different areas of the brain and will show up as dense colour patches over the areas involved. Adopting this method of investigation we have created a diagnostic toolkit that helps us detect the activity of Corporate Mind. Dynamic choice sets and visual aids help us identify the signs the Corporate Mind pays attention to in a given situation. By asking organisation members to place a dot representing their selected items into a stylised schemata we call the Meta-filter, we can demonstrate what the information that the Corporate Mind picked up is used for. Figure 2. shows the basic skeleton of the Meta-filter.

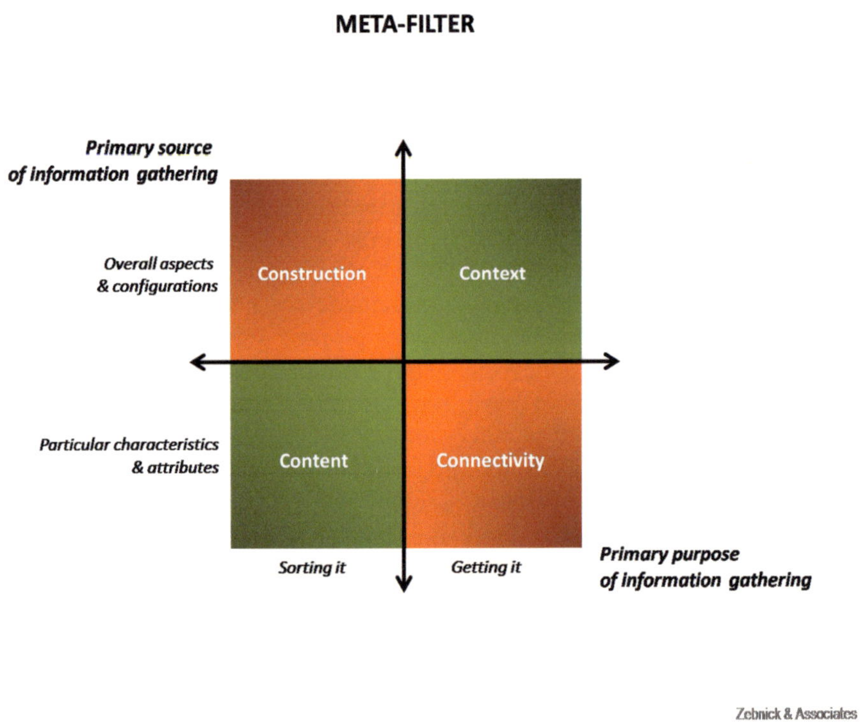

Fig. 2. Meta-filter

When information is used to perfect every operational flaw and wrinkle the Corporate Mind is focused on realising efficiency gains of its reproductive potential. To do this it has to dig deep, so to speak, and the dots will mostly populate the areas of 'content' and 'context' . When information is used to look into every nook and cranny of the operation the Corporate Mind is focused on realising efficiency gains of its regenerative potential. To do this it has to go broad, so to speak, and the dots will mostly populate the areas of 'connectivity' and 'construction'.

The diagnostic results of a Corporate Mind that tries to tackle the double-decked nature of competitive pressure will show activity over a wide spread. Not necessarily covering all areas proportionately. Actual distribution will depend on the situation. But a wider spread is indicative of the Corporate Mind embracing the challenges that the double-decker nature of competitive pressure presents. The more asymmetry is present, that is one area being over-populated (see illustration in Figure 3.), the more characteristic it will be that to boost its performance, the organisation will concentrate on what its tools can accomplish rather than realising reproductive and regenerative efficiency gains. This kind of self-referencing is often enough to set the vicious circle of an inwardly spiralling cyclical trap into motion. Therefore, whenever this over-population is present it is high time to update the cognitive map. In other words, in all such cases the Corporate Mind is not supporting enough the reality tracing ability of the organisation.

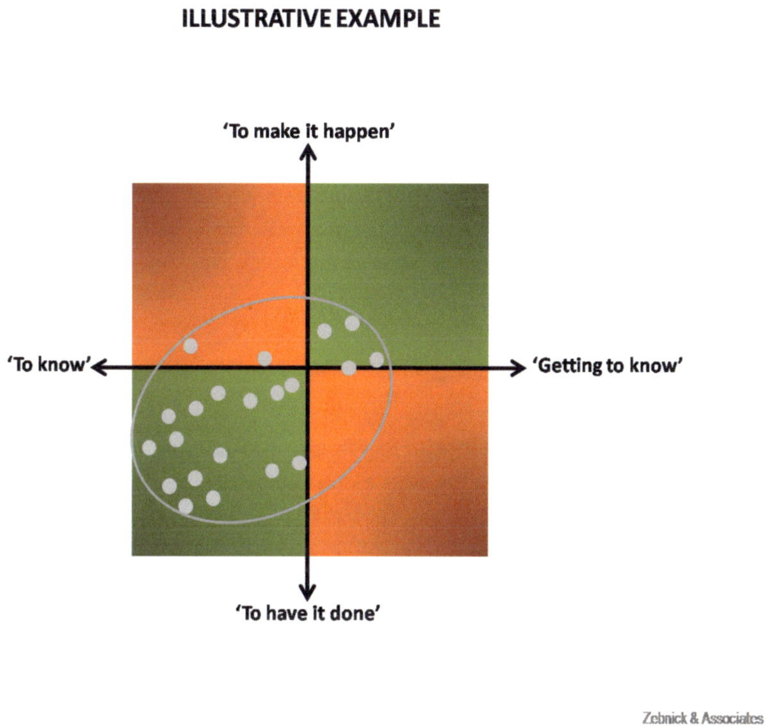

Fig. 3. Operationalization of the model design

4.3.2 Results

By outlining the specificities of reproduction and regeneration we hopefully demonstrated that in order for an organisation to improve its competitiveness it must not ignore the double-decked nature of competitive pressure. It has to run a parallel mental process that ensures continuity as well as recovery. By taking the analogy offered by the scientific dialogue that is going on about the interlinkages of the brain-mind-intelligence construct we outlined in a model the basic characteristics of a Corporate Mind that is tailored to address this challenge. In this model, the Corporate Mind is both a control system that activates coordinated responses and an 'organ' of perception.

A brief overview was also given as to how the model can be operationalised in a real life situation. The model and its related diagnostic tools powerfully demonstrated to our client that the key to understand the systematic nature of under-achievement in the presence of

appropriate actions is neither in the actions themselves, nor in the what's 'out there'. We could also show that our knowledge governance audit can not only tie together the findings of all other available diagnoses (this we showed by describing the contributing factors to the corporate identity crises and how it related to risk management and corporate culture issues) but can answer the seeming reluctance of the organisation to make progress on its most presssing issues (this we demonstrated by preparing the Meta-filter diagnosis that showed on overwhelming presence of loop-dominance in the content area).
The relevance of our model to knowledge governance is in emphasising that by taking into account the characteristics of both protocols that interact to create a representation of the organisation's reality, it is easier to see that appropriateness of action and utilisation of relevant knowledge will harbor on how the Corporate Mind orchestrates the interactive linkages among its own functions. Successfully mobilised and coordinated knowledge bases will promote a degree of organisational cohesion that supports performance progress. In case of the less successful ones, their very own actions will be putting strain on the permeability of the system that in turn prevents relevant knowledge to bear on decisions. In sum, the approach taken here proposes that knowledge as it pertains to the development of an appropriate reaction to competitive pressure, one that takes both the complicatedness and complexity of the business issue into account, is the key the driving factor behind organisational success.

5. The extension of knowledge governance framework

Knowledge governance has two main interpretation levels in the early literature: the company- (micro-) and the national (macro-) level. For example, knowledge governance has been discussed as a profitability issue at the company level and as an effectiveness issue at the government level in the research project series of the University of Bonn. Whitley (2000) conceptually classified knowledge governance as: 1) *enterpreneurial knowledge governance* based upon knowledge codification and privatization, and the organizational methods of generation and usage of new corporate knowledge, and 2) *associative knowledge governance,* which addresses the macro-level distribution of the complex forms of knowledge.

<table>
<tr><th>Original model</th><th>Advanced model</th><th>The Dalal-Z.Karvalics model 2009</th><th>Z. Karvalics four layer model 2011</th></tr>
<tr><td rowspan="4">Company/
Corporate/
Enterpreneurial</td><td rowspan="2">Company
Micro-level</td><td rowspan="2">Company
Micro-level</td><td>Individual
Nano-level</td></tr>
<tr><td>Company
Micro-level</td></tr>
<tr><td rowspan="2">Nation(al)
Macro-level</td><td>Nation(al)
Meso-level</td><td>Nation(al)
Meso-level</td></tr>
<tr><td>Global
Macro-level</td><td>Global
Macro-level</td></tr>
</table>

Table 2. Development of Knowledge Governance Models

Entrepreneurial and associative knowledge governance are simultaneously evolving narratives sharing many similarities such as the inclusion of holistic approaches and high-level planning and control functions. Smits and Moor composed an indicator system to measure the effectivity of corporate knowledge management, dubbing it the "Knowledge

Governance Framework" (Smits & Moor, 2004), while Mariussen used it to address the integration of the knowledge system and managing on a nation-state level (Mariussen, 2003).

However, we could successfully define and describe 3 levels with their main characteristic features with Nikunj Dalal, adding the *Global Knowledge Governance* (Dalal & Z. Karvalics, 2009) to the basic model. And, finally, the model has currently upgraded with the *Personal Knowledge Governance* layer.

5.1 Personal Knowledge Governance (PKG)

Once upon a time the discourse has started with the Personal Information Management (PIM), the practice and training of skills professionals need *„to process the information, save time, and work more effectively"*(Etzel & Thomas, 1999) in organizational (business) environment. With other words: how to manage the constantly and rapidly changing Personal Information Technologies (PIT's - hardware and software components, methods, services, etc.) in work. Later (Jones, 2007) and recently (Jones & Marchionini, 2011) William Jones has started to broaden the definition: Personal information management (PIM) is *„the practice and study of the activities people perform to acquire, organize, maintain, and retrieve information for everyday use"*, more generally: *PIM is about taking charge of the information in our lives.*

David Pauleen was the first to go one step beyond, introducing the „Personal Knowledge Management" (PKM) (Pauleen, 2011), *„coping with complex environmental changes and developments...* as a *„form of sophisticated career and life management.* "Personal Knowledge Management" is an emerginging concept *„that focuses on the importance of individual growth and learning as much as on the technology and management processes traditionally associated with organizational knowledge management".*

The „physical" infrastructure of its individual „nano-level" constituted by the concept of Personal Area Network (PAN). Integrating the existing Personal Information Technologies (PIT's), Personal Information Management (PIM) and Personal Knowledge Management (PKM) approaches and combining it with the emerging Personal Learning Environments (PLE), it seems to be very topical to define a new, synthetic Personal Knowledge Governance frame. It contains all the mentioned parts, bundling up into a (personal) set of planning and performance activities, based on values, goals, personal and family considerations.

5.2 National Knowledge Governance (NKG)

Although the term itself is rarely used, the national (and local, regional) knowledge governance discourse is very old starting with the thousand years old brain drain practices (Dedijer, 1968). National Knowledge Governance sometimes a simple reformulation of traditional policy discourses (see for example the bright analysis about the monopoly of knowledge production and diffusion in China since 1949 (Zhenglai (2000), sometimes it generates innovative approaches - as Johann Peter Murmann discovered the role of applied scientific knowledge and the national institutions in the dawn of industrial era in his classics (Murmann, 2003).

5.2.1 Fields and topics: A first look

Since the number of relevant fields are too high and the narratives are well-known, there is no time and reason for systematic mapping of National Knowledge Governance issues. But it can be very useful to illustrate the changing face of traditional discourses listing recent, "hot" topics, and reviewing nation state employment strategies as knowledge governance responses for the economic crisis.

„Traditional" policy fields	New type of narratives and interventions
Innovation policy	Capacity building, data and knowledge asset policy, „national crowdsourcing" models
Science policy	Planning the structure and resource map of Natural-, Life-, Technical Sciences and Humanities
Education policy and literacy	Information literacy, talent management, lifelong learning schemes
Media and dissemination of scientific information	Nation-state reactions on current brain drain, brain gain, and brain sharing issues
Knowledge Industry Development (Fostering attractivity and visibility)	Competition in creative industries, talent hunting
Copyright, patent issues	Indigenous knowledge management, copyleft

Table 4. National Knowledge Governance discourses - examples (Dalal-Z. Karvalics, 2009)

5.2.2 How to increase knowledge-based employment? A case study[4]

As a special response for the worldwide economic crisis, lot of nations turned to a radical increase of employment in research and development, accepting, that it is critical for business, innovation, higher education and the political, economic and media elite, would be timely and could serve as a strategic point of departure in and of itself.

In the United States, one key element of the *American Reinvestment and Recovery Act* package (ARRA), launched in response to the economic crisis, was the supplemental support to be given to the sciences (Lane, 2009) in the form of billions of dollars provided to various scientific agencies. This support was granted based on the conviction that the new value produced as a result of scientific activities serves as the basis of economic growth and results in the creation of new workplaces. Decision-makers were convinced that investing in science leads to more competitive firms, as well as more and better workplaces. Naturally, they were able to rely on forecasts from organizations such as the *Information Technology and Innovation Foundation*; ITIF's report suggested that an extra investment of 20 billion USD in the sciences leads to the creation of over 400 thousand new jobs within one year. Julia Lane quotes a study showing that 50 thousand new jobs in the biotechnology and electronic sectors – in the high-tech zone outside San Diego – may be traced back to the work of four (!) scientific researchers at the University of California in San Diego.

It is stunningly insightful that the real questions for Lane are how money can be well spent and how its use may best be measured. Given, however, that sufficient information was not yet available to answer these questions, or to explore the subtle correlations between scientific development and economic growth, an NSF program was immediately established to provide scientific policies with appropriate input in the matter.

4 Excerpt from my brochure on *„dual flue effect"* of knowledge-based employment (Z.Karvalics, 2011).

According to the Obama administration, the major question is how employees are able to benefit from the kinds of skills and abilities which will ensure their competitiveness in the labor market of the future. The number of jobs requiring higher education degrees will increase twice as fast as the number of jobs not necessitating such qualifications; therefore, says Obama, it has never been more important to ensure that learning continues past the secondary school stage. The goal, then, is for the United States to be the world's leader in advanced professional training by 2020. Thanks to an impressive development program providing schools with funding for infrastructure development, asset purchases and online courses, the number of students graduating from the community colleges of specific states will increase by five million. The schools themselves will become 21st century job training centers.

Great Britain also found a similar point of departure, reaching eerily similar conclusions[5]. They simply placed their basic structural data from the past forty years next to each other. The figures indicate that the percentage of the population employed in knowledge-based sectors increased from 25% in 1970 to 50% today. This sector was also the creadle of new job creation, increasing the share of value-added activities and exports (specifically: business, finances, high-tech services, creative and cultural industries, advanced technology manufacture, education and healthcare). In 1970, the share of investments in intangibles was only 40% of the amount put toward buildings, vehicles and machinery. In 2004, investments in design, software, databases, research and development, as well as human and organizational capital have reversed the previous figures, and - at 120% - have taken the lead. In 1970, 60% of the labor force did not possess appropriate qualifications; their numbers dropped to 10% by 2005. For Great Britain, the findings led to the following results: the launching of business and employment development programs centered on the pivotal role of the knowledge sector, together with the increase of the numbers and quality of higher education programs and graduates.

Ireland's latest action plan, *Technology Actions to Support the Smart Economy*, aims to create 30 thousand new jobs in the next decade. These would all be created in the field of smart economy - digital industry and network technologies. The International Content Services Center, to support over one thousand Irish companies, is expected to create ten thousand new jobs by 2020, primarily in the world of creative digital arts (film, games, music and animation) and in communications, legal and other services.

It is hardly surprising that the same focal points are seen in China's latest initiatives in the field of scientific policy: new and improved innovations capacities are expected to support economic restructuring and transform development practices. China's State Council augmented its fifteen-year medium-term science development plan, adopted in 2006 for the period 2006-2020, with a fifty-year long-term plan adopted in July 2009 (and compiled by the Chinese Academy of Science). The long-term plan was designed in the understanding that the next 10-20 years will see yet another "technological and industrial revolution" in many areas of science, and that these must be identified in due course. The plan recognized the fostering of innovation as the strongest possible answer to the global economic crisis. The plan points to 18 focus areas, demonstrating a strong "green" commitment: agriculture,

---

[5] Based on the latest report (*The Knowledge Economy Programme*) of the strategic U.K. think tank Work Foundation; the report outlines plans to restore and develop the knowledge economy of the United Kingdom by 2020. http://www.theworkfoundation.com/research/keconomy.aspx

ecology, environment, health, oceanography and "clean" and renewable energy resources are in the center. Certainly, the areas selected are not limited to the specific supporting sciences: multidisciplinary teams stand the greatest chance of arriving at solutions to particular problems (in the case of healthcare, for instance: biology, environmental sciences, psychology and social sciences). The two most important motives are talent programs and institutional reform. The central question as far as China's scientific and technological future is concerned is how talented young people can be drawn toward the sciences and how their talents may best be used. The answer is fairly general, but certainly points in the right direction: the kind of fertile environment must be created for them which will bring forth their "best creative thoughts."

In Japan, the state has shown extraordinary planning and care in its expansive central developments of the past decade (science towns, intellectually creative society, "ubiquitous Japan"); the efforts of Japanese companies also point in much the same direction. A survey of 253 large Japanese companies (Rowley, 2009) showed that despite difficulties in sales, companies keep their contributions to research and development activities high. Much of these funds go toward alternative energy and environmentally friendly technologies; and while unemployment has increased in virtually every sector, research and development has continued to see high rates of employment.

5.3 Global knowledge governance (GKG)

The very popular Global Knowledge Managament (GKM) discourse is not else than a knowledge management practice of *global companies* (Gu, 2004). In contrary, the Global Knowledge Governance is not else than managing *global issues, raised in and connected to the knowledge domain.*

On the economic scene the discourse is an organic continuation of the worldwide economic development planning efforts, that's why the University of Oxford's Global Economic Governance Programme has recently (in November, 2009) launched it's independent *Expert Taskforce on Global Knowledge Governance*[6] to propose a *„set of principles and options for the future of global knowledge governance"*. However, the „scope" is much more broader, than the „economy" itself: there are lot of knowledge-related relevant cultural, scientific, media and technology challenges at the global level, including the need for new generation *international knowledge institutions* (Miller, 2007).

5.3.1 Towards a knowlege governance-based new vocabulary of global issues

Knowledge Governance issues are mainly reinterpretations and re-integrations of old problems (see Deere Birkbeck's forthcoming book on intellectual property management from global knowledge governance aspects (Birkbeck, 2012), combining this „texture" with fresh reflections and reactions to the emergent, new fields, like the globalization of the scientific community and it's knowledge infrastructure, the global library building efforts from Project Gutenberg to Google Books. The results of this hybridization are new terms and tools: we will be able to talk about a set of the main civilization problems in a new language.

---

[6] http://www.globaleconomicgovernance.org/wp-content/uploads/KnowledgeTaskforceoverview-8-Dec. pdf

„Phenomena" to reflect	Scientific domain	Development/ Policy/ Planning issues
International cooperation in the fields of education, science and communication	Cultural politics, Communication politics	Reengineering of UNESCO-type global coordination
Collaborative Research Megaprojects	Sociology of Science	New generation workflow tools, Regulation challenges
Knowledge readiness (knowledge development indicators)	General politics	Narrowing the gap between the developed and underdeveloped nations and regions
Global Conference and Publication Industry	Knowledge Management	Re-thinking of the channels of distribution of knowledge
Circulation of Brains	(Im)migration, Demography, Sociology	Equation mechanisms, regulation, monitoring
Globalized higher education, virtual universities	Pedagogy, Economy	Quality management, equivalence and interoperability issues
„Global" libraries, common scientific repositories (data silos)	Library and Information Science	Regulation, standardization

Table 5. Mapping the Global Knowledge Governance scene (Dalal-Z. Karvalics, 2009)

5.3.2 Case study: Approaching the future of UNESCO

UNESCO, a specialized organization of the UN has been the symbol of cultural progress and dialogue since its foundation in 1945, as "antithesis" to the war. In the past decades it has contributed significantly to the dissemination of basic civilizational values, it has helped raise awareness regarding the universality of the cultural heritage, has launched several successful projects aiming at the preservation, popularization of this heritage, as well as at ensuring the accessibility of the same. It has established (more than fifty) institutions of long-lasting impact, has helped achieving significant scientific results, has tried, with steadfast policy and dedicated action, to balance differences in the development of groups of countries. All these have probably contributed to the fact that, in a world burdened with fear, insecurity and mutual distrust, it managed to become a highly supported trans-national institution, and could maintain its crucial role in the long run[7].

However, in case we wish to scrutinize UNESCO regarding the importance of its role in key areas (natural sciences, social sciences and humanities, public education, and the world of culture and information and communication networks) and compare it to the goals set in its Mission Statement, we see that apart from its success at emblematically successful areas, its position has been increasingly weakening, the organization has been losing its reputation and significance in almost every respect. We witnesses a process

[7] On the latest goals, programs, organizational structure see UNESCO's exemplarily well maintained website at http://www.unesco.org/new/en/unesco/

during which the unsustainability of the organizational model is clearly revealed, pointing towards the need for redesigning the future, the essence and the whole organizational structure of the institution, replacing the present practice of debating scrupulously minor amendments to the budget. The time has come that we state clearly and firmly, beyond the context of standing receptions with their background noise, that everything has to be rebuilt from the base, since the success of minor reforms only delays the unavoidable fundamental reform.

Only little can be felt from all the above - both from the inside and the outside. An increasing number of people acknowledge that the compulsions of the diplomatic context that are officially and legally governing UNESCO are too tight. In the labyrinths of the offices career diplomats, as representatives of national interest, delegated by member states pass the time trading with memberships and positions. Instead of acting as sites for exchanging ideas, the biennial General Assemblies and their sections are generally about communicating presence; while ceremonial greetings and the formal approval of minor opinions takes more time than anything else. Such contributions are combined with lengthy and completely ineffective debates about the meaning of prepositions included in the documents. The single *pro forma* goal of these strenuous meetings is the legitimization of the budget and of the related circle of planned activities. The process is seemingly democratic and seemingly launched from the grassroots level, since member states have the opportunity to make remarks and give recommendations regarding the quotas and priorities. However, unchanged conceptual frames, the significant divisional separation of large fields of activities and the documents that are prepared by officials - who are biased towards the program structures of previous terms - predetermine the discussions, and member states have very little scope to contribute significantly to the forming the future. For a considerable time now UNESCO has been merely *capable of following talks, but cannot create, launch or initiate discussions*. The organization is increasingly lagging behind "state-of-art" situations, and *cannot reflect adequately on the latest problems of global scope*. Such a structure has both an illusion and a rhetoric: from the point of view of the sociology of organization it would be possible to understand the preference of the staff towards minor changes, however, officers in the position of making decisions are interested in the exact opposite of what can be interpreted as progressive, brave and pioneering initiatives. The more long-term these ideas are, the more they hurt various national and business interests, and thus any undertaking can be aborted very quickly by referring to "diplomatic correctness" in its bad sense and interpreting the principle of *paritas* mechanically.

The reason for this, on the one hand, is that the main directions, the basic activities and the possible interventions are not formed by "cases" or the nature of represented areas, nor by recommendations of experts or communities, but by the compromises of cultural diplomacy set by the 193 member states. The scope of activities, the norms and compliance to these norms are defined by the interstate and international legal context. Professional initiatives can be realized only vis-à-vis this pact system of *Realpolitik*. On the other hand, the reason is that the amount of funds at disposal restricts all activities in the first place. UNESCO is not able to solve, nor to moderate contradictions deriving from unequal development. Even challenges that can be interpreted as cultural are too big to be affected by the choice of the organization between several programs. This is why UNESCO has never been, and cannot ever be a development agency, at the same time its activities would seem incomplete if it had not offered "traditionally" direct resources for the realization of local projects. These, however, amount next to nothing, no matter how important they seem for "poorer" countries that always make sure to apply for the help of "donor" countries. In the meantime, in the past ten-fifteen years a certain takeover has occurred, since dynamic and effective civil organizations, NGOs and foundations are supporting hundreds of progressive projects independently of UNESCO, with funds way beyond the ones at UNESCO's disposal.

The real obstacles, the ones which have to be overcome independently of the management and apparatus of the organization, are to be found elsewhere. If we wish to understand the root of the increasing anachronism of UNESCO, we have to start analyzing the problem from a different perspective. In the last third of the 19th century capitalist "center-countries" found themselves in a curious position. In the well-developed territories the overall success and transformation power of big industry lead to a crisis of management in economy, society, and politics (or control crisis in James Beniger's widely spread words), which could be overcome by the massive and creative use of modern information and knowledge technology (Beniger, 1986). The nature of the solution was similar in all sub-systems. The management and competitiveness of companies and of the administrative "industry" of states were based upon systems using almost identical solutions, and the same applied to modern systems of public education as well as institutions of academic management and academic organization. Relying on James Beniger's model we can say that the revolution of bureaucratic control took place in the scope of just a few decades, and it proved highly successful. This control revolution contributed most significantly to the realization of the civilizational change which was launched before the First World War, continued during the interwar period, and was completed in the decades succeeding the Second World War - while the industrial period was flourishing.

The success of the industrial civilization, however, was much shorter than what may be deducted based on history coursebooks or the statistics of "developed industrial countries". As opposed to the agrarian sector and parallel to the rise of industry already at the end of the 19th century, the service and the information-knowledge sector started increasing its share regarding both production and consumption. The success of the bureaucratic control revolution not only revived the industrial civilization, but it also gave birth to informational society as well, which soon put an end to the world dominated by traditional industries. In other, slightly simplified words, the next civilizational change, the birth of information society took place in the sixties in the United States, at the beginning of the seventies in Japan, and at the beginning of the nineties in Western-Europe, while for developing countries somewhere around the turn of the millennium. Still, the bureaucratic control revolution was so successful that the structures of the industrial era could be well maintained within the context of the information society. In the schools of the information society the order that has to be followed by teachers and students alike has been formed to match the objective functions of the bureaucratic control revolution of the industrial era. The science of information society is financially bound by national and ideological interests, as well as business and commercial commitments that - regarding the logic of management and distribution - have been inherited from the industrial era. The industrial era, optimized for nation states, created the organizational and institutional structure of transnational coordination, and this system tries to cope with coordination of information society at a global level with the old, tried and tested algorithms of bureaucratic control.

It is increasingly clear, however, that the technologies used fruitfully by bureaucratic control have started successfully to restructure society, economics, and even culture. As it has been noticed by many, we are heading towards a next control crisis, and the way out of it is a next control revolution: networks instead of hierarchies, human technology next to machine technology, cooperative and "multistakeholder" management instead of single-center organization, sustainability and humanization instead of profit-oriented growth function, as well as local and global coordination based on reciprocity, voluntarity and solidarity.

This perspective shows clearly the nature of the multiple trap in which UNESCO is caught. The organization (with its goals, mission, networks of interest and its organizational structure) is a (top) product of the industrial era. The organization has moved forward from its past rooting in the industrial era with the fact that not so long ago the area of "information and communication" has been integrated into its main scopes of activities as the fifth pillar, and thus the rhetoric of information society have also been included into its documents. In order to reach a civilizational change, the organization should go beyond its restrictions in information-age science, in information-age education, and should think along a radically innovative logic regarding the production, consumption and the geography of culture. It has to perform this task in a way that it also takes into consideration that countries of crucial importance - let us just think of the BRIC group (Brazil, Russia, China and India) - are still fighting for the industrialization and modernization of their own country, and are very far from patterns of employment, consumption, stratification of society and culture typical of information society, but enjoy all the advantages of up-to-date information technology. And we have not mentioned yet agrarian countries that are in a pre-industrial stage… All this does not contradict the idea that norms and relationships typical of information society should be taken as guidelines for action: in a concrete information society an urgent task in development is bridging the gap between areas and social groups at different levels of development, and similarly, it is important to keep on the agenda that nations that are seemingly the furthest from the global information society are included into its network.

As long as UNESCO functions as the rear-guard of the industrial era, it cannot act as vanguard of information society in order to replace bureaucratic control via creating social control structures and alternative value chains. If it cannot and does not wish to be a "laboratory of future", which supports the future control revolution relying on systems of producing, distributing and consuming knowledge, and which is based upon a model of culture and society or world-view that is typical of the information age, if it does not face conflicts with the monstrous interest relations of the industrial age, then it will deteriorate rather quickly into an empty display of a declining era.

Luckily, there is still potential to fulfill. Despite all its problems, UNESCO is an authentic "brand". It managed to address and keep working with several dedicated, well-prepared experts who have a mission, as well as to build a network of cooperation with NGOs, and its activity has always been formed along the lines of preserving and fostering values. Thus, it has a significant amount of opportunity points and trust capital that it can still turn towards a change of philosophy and organization required for solving global problems that are included into its mission statement, instead of maintaining the organization as an end in itself. If this effort is successful, the moulds and paths will be formed almost automatically, through which UNESCO can become a decisive and accepted actor of a new control revolution in the governance of global knowledge and literacy.

6. Conclusion and further research directions

Research on Knowledge Governance has a two-way future. The theoretical clarification and the development of everyday practice are interactively and mutually influencing each other. Similarly, the national and global actors can learn a lot from the consolisated experiences and best practices of the corporate arena. In the same way, scientists, consultants, policy experts and CKO's can start a fruitful conversation about the Knowledge Governance basics and specialities.

From a „disciplinary and theoretical perspective" (Foss & Michailova, 2009), *region, culture and business sector-specific research programmes* are very important to aggregate field experiences, supporting the formation of general statements, methods and next generation research questions. The Knowledge Governance Program of the Center for Development Research at University of Bonn, led by Hans-Dieter Evers is currently in its fourth project phase. This comparative research is simultaneously studies the practice of large corporations and small and medium enterprises in South-East Asia and Africa. Their results successfully demonstrated, that *„Asian nations differ greatly in their success in closing the gap between local and global knowledge"*[8]. The fresh, sustainability-oriented Knowledge Governance program of the transdisciplinary Canadian POLIS Project on Ecological Governance explores *„complex philosophical, ethical, legal and political issues"* in the context of academic and indigenous knowledge, concentrating to the *„collaborative knowledge creation and sharing of associated rights and responsibilities beyond the corporate partnership model"*[9]. The Knowledge Governance Fora of KEI (Knowledge Ecology International)[10] joins with the main global representatives of the legal field.

From a „methodology perspective", knowledge governance experts have to find convincing and standardizable solutions for the most painful organizational challenges: how to develop new methods to reengineer the channels of knowledge aquisition? How to insert the culture of knowledge building into the center of strategic thinking? How to design new, effective knowledge environments for decision makers, and how to make them *abductive*? It would be easy to produce far longer question lists and more dense keyword maps, but detecting the dynamics is currently more important than providing full analytic descriptions.

7. References

Beniger, J. (1986): The Control Revolution. Technological and Economic Origins of the Information Society, Harvard University Press

Beer, S. (1972): Brain of the Firm: Managerial Cybernetics of Organization, Allen Lane

Beer, S. (1985): Diagnosing the System for Organizations, John Wiley & Sons, Chichester

Birkbeck, D. (2012): Global Knowledge Governance and the World Intellectual Property Organisation, Edward Elgar Publishing (forthcoming)

[8] http://www.zef.de/606.html

[9] http://polisproject.org/researchareas/knowledgegovernance

[10] http://keionline.org/fora

Boisot, M.H. (1988): Knowledge Assets. Securing Competitive Advantage in the Information Economy Oxford University Press

Cornwell, A.W. (1992): Freeing the Corporate Mind: How to Spur Innovation in Business Execu-Press

Curado, C., Bontis, N. (2011) Parallels in knowledge cycles *Computers in Human Behavior* Vol. 27, No.4 July pp. 1438-1444.

Dalal, N. (2006): Toward Reflective Dialogue based Inquiring Systems. In: The 12th Americas Conference on Information Systems, Acapulco, Mexico, August 4-6.

Dalal, N., Z. Karvalics, L. (2009): An Extended Model of Knowledge Governance In: Best Practices for the Knowledge Society - Knowledge, Learning, Development and Technology for All. Second World Summit on the Knowledge Society, WSKS 2009, Chania, Crete, Greece, September 16-18, 2009. Proceedings. Series: Communications in Computer and Information Science , Vol. 49 Lytras, M.D.; Ordóñez de Pablos, P.; Damiani, E.; Avison, D.; Naeve, A.; Horner, D.G. (Eds.), XXVIII, 586 p.

Dalal, N., Z. Karvalics, L. (2011): Beyond Knowledge Management. An extended model of Knowledge Governance *International Journal of Knowledge Society Research* Vol.2, No.4.

Davenport, T. H. (1994): Coming soon: The CKO, *Information Week*, (491). September, pp. 95.

Davis, B. (2007): Harnessing Knowledge Markets Research Program Kaieteur Institute for Knowledge Management Toronto, 2007

Dedijer, S. (1968): Early migration In: Adams, W. (Ed.): The Brain Drain New York, The Macmillan Company pp. 9-28.

Earl, M.J., Scott, I.A. (1999): What is a Chief Knowledge Officer? Opinion. *Sloan Management Review* Vol. 40. No. 2; p. 29

Etzel, B., Thomas, P. (1999) Personal Information Management: Tools and Techniques for Achieving Professional Effectiveness, NYU Press

Foss, N. J.: The Knowledge Governance Approach In: Copenhagen Business School Center for Strategic Management and Globalization *Working Paper Series* (2005). Available from: http://ssrn.com/abstract=981353

Foss, N. J.: The Emerging Knowledge Governance Approach: Challenges and Characteristics Knowledge Governance Primer *Organization;* 14: 29-52.o. (2007) Available from: http://organizationsandmarkets.com/2007/02/05/knowledge-governance-primer/

Foss, N.J., Michailova, S. (Ed.): *Knowledge Governance. Processes and Perspectives* Oxford University Press (2009)

Gu, Y. (2004): Global knowledge management research: A bibliometric analysis *Scientiometrics* Vol.61. No.2. pp. 171-190.

Hampden-Turner, C. (1990): Charting the Corporate Mind, Free Press

Hong, H., Scardamalia, M., Zhang, J (2010): Knowledge Society Network: Toward a Dynamic, Sustained Network for Building Knowledge *Canadian Journal of Learning and Technology*, Vol. 36.No.1. Available from: http://www.cjlt.ca/index.php/cjlt/article/view/579/282

Jones, W. (2007): Keeping Found Things Found: The Study and Practice of Personal Information Management (Interactive Technologies) Morgan Kaufmann

Jones, W. , Marchionini, G. (2011): Personal Information Management (Synthesis Lectures on Information Concepts, Retrieval, and Services) Morgan Claypool

Jordan, G. and Schubert, K. (eds.). (1992). Policy Networks. *European Journal of Political Research*, Special Issue, 21, 1-2.

Lane, J. (2009) : Science Innovation: Assessing the Impact of Science Funding *Science*, Vol. 324. No. 5932, pp. 1273 - 1275

Leonard, A. (2000): The viable system model and knowledge management, *Kybernetes*, Vol. 29, No. 5/6; p. 710

Mariussen, A. (2003): New forms of knowledge governance. Basic outline of a social system approach to innovation policy DRUID Summer Conference: Creating, Sharing and Transferring Knowledge Copenhagen, June 12-14. Available from: http://www.druid.dk/uploads/tx_picturedb/ds2003-832.pdf.

Miller, C. A. (2007): Democratization, International Knowledge Institutions, and Global Governance *Governance: An International Journal of Policy, Administration, and Institutions*, Vol. 20, No. 2, pp. 325–357.

Murmann, J.P. (2003): Knowledge and competitive advantage: the coevolution of firms, technology and national institutions, Cambridge University Press

Pauleen, D. (2011): Personal Knowledge Management: Individual, Organizational and Social Perspectives, Gower Pub Co.

Por, G. (2000): Nurturing systemic wisdom through knowledge ecology. *The Systems Thinker*, Vol. 11 No.8. pp. 1–5.

Rowley, I. (2009): Japan Inc. Continues to Spend Big on R&D Despite the Recession. *Business Week*, August 5. Available from: http://www.businessweek.com/globalbiz/blog/eyeonasia/archives/2009/08/japan_maintains.html

Senge, P. (1990): The Fifth Discipline: the Art and Practice of the Learning Organization. New York: Doubleday. p.3.

Simard, A. (2006).: Knowledge markets: More than Providers and Users. *IPSI BgD Internet Research Society Transactions* Vol.2 No.2 pp.4-9.

Smits, M., Moor, A.D (2004): Measuring Knowledge Management Effectiveness in Communities of Practice. *Proceedings of the 37th Hawaii International Conference on System Sciences* pp.236-244.

Thomson, G. (2003): Between Hierarchies & Markets: the logic and limits of network forms of organization, Oxford University Press

Wenger, E., McDermott, R., & Snyder, W. M. (2002): Cultivating communities of practice: A guide to managing knowledge.Boston: Harvard Business School Press p.27.

Whitley, R. D. (2000): The Institutional Structuring of Innovation Strategies: Business Systems, Firm Types and Patterns of Technical Change is Different Market Economies *Organizational Studies* 21, 855-886.

Zaleznik, A. (1985): Power and the Corporate Mind: How to Use Rather Than Misuse Leadership Bonus Books; 2nd edition

Zhenglai, D. (2000): Civil society and reconstruction of national knowledge governance system: growth and role of unofficial knowledge diffusion mechanism. China's state control of books and accesss to knowledge and information. *Civil Society and Governance Programme*, IDS Available from: http://www.eldis.org/assets/Docs/11467.html

Z.Karvalics, L. (2011): The Dual Flue Effect. A Model and an Action Plan to Increase Knowledge-based Employment. Endorsement to the IBM White Book 1. JATE Press, Szeged, pp. 1-31. Available from: http://www-05.ibm.com/hu/feherkonyv/pdf/Tanulmanyok_az_IBM_Feher_Konyvhoz_angolul.pdf

11

Creating a Culture of Learning and Knowledge Sharing in Libraries and Information Services

Octavia-Luciana Porumbeanu Madge
University of Bucharest
Romania

1. Introduction

Organizations have focused over the last two decades on finding a solution which could help them achieve success in a society dominated by changes that maintain and enhance competition permanently. The solution identified by organizations is represented by a new managerial process that concentrates on the most valuable resource currently available to them, namely the knowledge held both at the level of the employees individually and of the processes and practices specific to each organization. Implementation of knowledge management process is largely seen as a critical element in contemporary organizations which will enable and facilitate their survival and success, preservation of their position on the market, and growth of their performance.

Awareness of the importance which knowledge resources have concerning the performance of organizations has led to structural changes and massive investment for implementing knowledge management in organizations. Any discussion and any initiative in this regard involves the recognition of the need to make significant changes at organizational level that refer to the transformation of the way organizations relate to competition, to change and how they act in order to meet the challenges of society. Any knowledge management approach should consider hence that key element enabling organizations to adapt continuously to the changing environment, namely learning. This plays a leading role in transforming organizations and therefore in the implementation of knowledge management, and from there to the discussion on the need for their transformation into learning organizations is only one step.

Competitive advantage, which is often mentioned in literature, is based on the knowledge resources and the learning capacity of organizations (Argyris & Schon as cited in Tschaitschian et al., 2000; Prusak, 1996). It depends according to analysts on the organization's ability to acquire knowledge assets by planning and facilitating organizational learning (Pucik, 1996) which leads to the development, consolidation and growth of these resources, both through internal actions and collaborations, alliances, and partnerships with other organizations. Knowledge sharing too contributes to increasing competitive advantage (Teece, 2002) because value creation is based not only on the possession of knowledge and other assets, but also on the ability to transfer, assimilate, and combine knowledge and other assets.

Knowledge resources as such, their collecting, storage, processing and organization, but also learning as a simple process do not guarantee organizations they will obtain performance in their work environment, just as simple application of knowledge management models that proved successful in some organizations do not ensure success in a different context. It is necessary to share knowledge and generate new knowledge, and in order to talk about learning, not only at individual, but also at organizational level, and transforming an organization into a learning organization, it requires a clear strategy to help organizations be able to anticipate, react and respond to the changing environment (Senge, 1990). Similarly, any attempt of implementing knowledge management in an organization must start from the need to adapt this process to the conditions in that organization, from studying the context and characteristics of its field of activity and from designing an appropriate model adapted for that organization.

Learning, knowledge sharing and knowledge generation are in a relationship of interdependence. All these processes depend on people, and this refers to the importance of human resources and organizational culture. Even if there is no consensus at this point, after so many years since the breaking out of interest in knowledge management, on its definition, its components, most experts agree on the importance of organizational culture in any knowledge management initiative. The role of organizational culture in the process of knowledge management implementation and in the action of transforming organizations into learning organizations is constantly highlighted in literature. It becomes clear therefore that an organizational culture that fosters learning and knowledge sharing is essential for contemporary organizations seeking increase of their performance and a leading position in their field. Forwards we address this issue.

2. Knowledge management and organizational culture

Among the major themes investigated in recent literature on knowledge management, that referring to the change of organizational culture so as to create a culture that promotes learning and the transformation of organizations in learning organizations has a special place. The concept of the learning organization is essential for any knowledge management project because the improvement of knowledge sharing and learning in organizations is at the basis of knowledge management (Skyrme & Amidon, 2002). Researchers and managers have realized that organizations good at learning will range ahead of the competition (Abell & Oxbrow, 2002), and the strong links between learning and knowledge management are often pointed out in literature (Addleson, 2000; Ali et al., 2006; Skyrme & Amidon, 2002). Learning is intrinsic for knowledge management, contributing to the ability of individuals to share knowledge (Ali et al., 2006) and some analysts understand knowledge management as facilitating interaction among people and groups, this interaction being the real source of knowledge creation and sharing (Addleson, 2000). We can say that an organizational culture oriented towards learning, innovation and performance, supporting communication, collaboration, participation, creativity and sharing of knowledge is essential and facilitate any knowledge management initiative or approach.

2.1 Learning and knowledge sharing in organizations

Experts agree on the need to maximize the responsiveness of organizations to the complexity of the challenges, both in the external environment and within the organization. And learning with the aim of regeneration and development of organizational knowledge is seen as the appropriate response of organizations to what some researchers call the endemic change in society (Quintas, 2002). Turoff at his turn believes that organizations will succeed based on their ability to learn and adapt (Turoff, 1998, as cited in Gregory, 2000).

No matter how we choose to call the successful organization, competent organization (Sanchez, 2001), intelligent organization (Sydänmaanlakka, 2002), open organization (Addleson, 2000) etc., this is based on learning, it is an organization with a culture where people can interact and share knowledge. The learning organization is indicated as the ideal model to which all structures should turn, although building a learning organization is considered a risky activity (Gregory, 2000) in that it involves creating a new organizational culture. But what is a learning organization? In short, we remember the five main activities which Garvin considers as defining for learning organizations "systematic problem solving, experimentation with new approaches, learning from past experiences, learning from the best practices of others, and transferring knowledge quickly and efficiently throughout the organization" (Garvin, 1993, as cited in Gregory, 2000).

Many researchers make references to the individual as a decisive successful factor for knowledge management, despite the importance which is given to teams and groups (Stacey, 2001). And indeed when it comes to learning and knowledge creation and sharing, one must start from the individual and then reach organizational culture which must support these processes massively (Jacobson, 2006), the individual being the one who can interpret and communicate knowledge with other individuals, groups and organizations (King, 2006). But even if individual talent and creativity are at the basis of learning and innovation, ultimately it is the organizational culture that supports these processes (Kanter, 1996).

Learning is seen as a very complex creative process (Sydänmaanlakka, 2002), it is a social activity (Stamps, 2000) and "the natural connection between working and innovating" (Brown & Duguid, 2000). Some experts even speak of generative learning, ie learning that "increases the organization's ability to adapt to dynamic and unexpected situations and to respond creatively to them" (Ali et al., 2006).

Learning takes place at three different levels: individual, group/team and organizational level and specialists refer to the circular interaction between the individual level and the group/organizational level (Stacey, 2001; Sydänmaanlakka, 2002). There have been created many models in this sense. For example, Sanchez proposed the model of the five learning cycles according to which "individuals in organizations create knowledge, individuals and the groups they work in interact to create shared knowledge and to generate new knowledge and groups use their knowledge to undertake coordinated action and to jointly develop new organizational competences" (Sanchez, 2001). For some specialists it seems more appropriate to talk about organizational learning, ie "the ability of the organization to renew itself by changing its values, practices and processes" (Sydänmaanlakka, 2002) than about the learning organization. Analysts of the learning process forewarn not only about the importance and difficulty of learning how to learn, but also about the need to unlearn, to leave behind old knowledge and practices that would not be useful in the future but could represent obstacles to new activities and new forms of management at organizational level (Cope, 2000; Quintas, 2002).

2.2 Organizational culture

The greatest influence on the organization's performance is thus exerted by the organizational culture with all its components, and its transformation, meaning a greater emphasis on knowledge sharing, must be the key point in the organization's strategy (Webb, 1998). The elements of organizational culture exert their influence on the way organization "thinks, feels and acts" (Hofstede, 1996). This influence is exercised not only on the organization long-term activity, it also refers to its daily work and thus reflects on the organization's overall performance. A thoroughly investigation and understanding of organizational culture must cover all its components and also all levels on which they manifest, from physical features of the organization, to perception, relationships between employees, practices, habits and values promoted within the organization.

The existence of a shared vision guides the organization in one direction, creates an environment that allows and encourages learning. The same workculture as well as common language and ground lead to better communication and better sharing of knowledge (Davenport & Prusak, 1998) and actually create competitive advantage. Because the essential difference between organizations and which leads eventually to market advantage and success is given by the state in which these resources are found, namely, whether knowledge is found only in the minds of employees, if shared among employees or recognized and used throughout the organization (Sanchez, 2001).

Generating new knowledge is dependent on the organizational culture and in order to improve knowledge sharing and generation an interactive context must be developed and maintained. Because only when organizational culture allows and encourages change, expression of ideas, participation, communication, and dialogue, then learning and knowledge sharing are possible.

When discussing about knowledge resources and their flow in organizations, cultural, physical and organizational barriers should not be overlooked (Barrett, 2000). In terms of knowledge sharing, studying and understanding how this takes place can provide ways to identify and overcome these barriers (Lindsey, 2006). However there are researchers (Firestone & McElroy, 2003) who do not consider that failure of knowledge sharing in organizations is due to cultural barriers and do not give so much importance to the process of changing the organizational culture for implementing knowledge management in that it has only a small role and there are many other factors that influence knowledge management processes.

In the context of all these issues discussed in recent literature that analyzes the knowledge economy with its global competition and continuous changes, the process of knowledge management and the importance of organizational culture, we turned our attention to a particular type of organizations that play a key role in the knowledge-based society, namely libraries and information services, and we proposed to investigate how they could implement knowledge management in order to meet the challenges of the current environment. Thus, we conducted a research that spanned a period of five years to develop a general model for implementing knowledge management in libraries and information services and to identify and outline the directions for creating in these organizations a culture of a learning and knowledge sharing. Developing organizational practices and a culture centered on the ability to create and assimilate new knowledge and to share knowledge will assist libraries and information services with protecting themselves in front of changes and redesigning their management systems.

3. Libraries and information services in the knowledge-based society

Libraries and information services, like other organizations in current society are faced with an acceleration of changes and a growing competition. The environment in which libraries operate, the way people search and access information have changed in recent decades, mainly due to the developments in the information and communication technology area. Libraries are no longer the only providers of information and globalization and networking bring serious challenges to these institutions. But libraries should make use now, as so often in the past of the changes in society and exploit them for their advantage and become more competitive. Libraries and information services need an analysis and a change of their functioning models so that they can adapt to the conditions in the market of information transfer and deal with the more specific requirements of users.

Libraries are organizations with a very long history. They have always adapted to the needs and requirements of society, but kept their core mission and objectives, that is conservation of written cultural and scientific heritage and information dissemination. Libraries have survived many changes because they knew how to adapt. They have transformed their structure and reorganized their services to meet changes and maintain their position in society. Transformations that libraries have gone through over the years have followed the changes in society and come to meet society demands. Libraries and information services have demonstrated a great openness to change, entering into new paradigms many times along their history.

At present, for surviving in a globalized economy and for maintaining their position as important players in the knowledge market, libraries and information services must continue to redesign their management systems. They need for this to promote flexibility, transparency, organizational learning, improve efficiency and effectiveness, and they also need permanent training of staff, reassessment and adaptation of working methods to contemporary requirements. At the same time, libraries should give major importance to the policy of competence and co-operation and should have a modern approach to project management, that is results-orientated and centered on the capitalization of the major strategic resources of the current society - information and knowledge - that define and shape actions, interactions, human activities and institutions. Higher levels of performance and continuous innovation can be achieved by libraries and information services through the identification and development of better ways to manage and exploit knowledge assets.

It appears that knowledge management is nowadays the foundation of organizational development in all fields of activity. And the relationship between knowledge management and libraries and information services is "an organic one, based on the movement forms of information as a joint constituent element" (Stoica, 2006). For being successful in this globalized world, libraries and information services should become knowledge driven organizations. Knowledge management practices will allow them to function effectively and efficiently in this environment. Some libraries have already turned into learning and knowledge centres, others invest now in implementing solutions for managing better their knowledge resources, but these initiatives should consider how librarians create, acquire, share and use knowledge effectively. Development of practices that allow collective experience and learning is important in libraries and information services too because the benefits will be for the individual, the group and the organization as a whole. Roberts and Rowley emphasize in the context of libraries the need to understand the complexity and significance of the individual, groups and teams (Roberts & Rowley, 2004).

Libraries and information services should act as "living organizations", should build and develop a culture that fosters thinking, learning, creating and sharing knowledge. For sharing knowledge is necessary to have within libraries open communication, interpersonal context, trust, transparency of decision making, appropriate rewards, teamwork, cooperation, etc. All these aspects enable, support and facilitate learning. In libraries and information services it must be understood the way in which new knowledge is generated at the group level, what motivates librarians to share what they know, how knowledge is shared and managed among the employees.

In this study we address some of the issues to be considered when they want to transform the organizational culture and orientate it towards learning and knowledge sharing and to implement knowledge management in libraries and information services.

Libraries and information services should encourage and support at organizational level training and development of well-knit communities that collaborate and learn. They should encourage employees to develop and express new ideas, to participate in all activities and decisions within the library. Participation and knowledge sharing contribute to the development and transformation of libraries and information services into learning and also long-term successful organizations.

4. Conducting the research

This study is based on research conducted between October 2004 and December 2009. For the data collection we used a multi-method approach which included questionnaire surveys in large Romanian libraries, semi-structured interviews with the library staff and participant observation of staff meetings in one of the library on which we focused our research beginning with March 2007. The combination of these three methods gave us the possibility to use data obtained through these different techniques and offered a large and complete perspective of the aspects investigated. This approach helped us with a better understanding of the collected data and ensured an increased validity of the results. We proposed in 2004 to carry out a study on knowledge management in Romanian libraries and information services and starting from the first results we focused on the organizational culture in Romanian libraries and on the aspects that could lead to the transformation of the organizational culture in one that encourages learning and knowledge sharing and on the elements of a model for implementing knowledge management in libraries and information services.

An initial study, the first ever in Romania regarding knowledge management in the field of library and information services, took place between October-November 2004 in four Romanian libraries and information services and it investigated on the basis of a questionnaire consisting of 14 questions whether a favourable climate for effective knowledge management could be identified. Eighty questionnaires were randomly distributed to the library staff in the participant institutions. There was a response rate of 85%. We identified enough elements that could support the creation of such a culture over the next few years. Most of the librarians who participated in this study were familiar with this new process, having a fairly good perception of what knowledge management represents, were open to the idea of knowledge sharing and considered the implementation of a knowledge management strategy by their organizations as necessary and beneficial (Porumbeanu, 2006; Madge, 2010).

Starting from the results of this first study that showed that a culture of knowledge sharing amongst the participant librarians did not exist, we undertook a second questionnaire survey between December 2006 and January 2007 which analyzed the particular characteristics of the organizational culture in five large Romanian academic libraries, namely the values promoted by this culture, their policies concerning staff, and organizational development, their managerial style, knowledge sharing, their embracing of creativity, innovation, performance, communication, change, collaboration and continuous professional development amongst other elements. The questionnaire consisted of 10 questions and eighty questionnaires were distributed at random to the library staff in the five participant institutions. There was a satisfactory reply rate of 82.5%. The results showed that regarding the values promoted by the organizational culture in their library, the participants indicated performance, professionalism, efficiency, teamwork, communication, competition, and innovation. Most of the librarians in the survey were open to the idea of knowledge sharing and many of them characterized the managerial style in their organizations as being one that creates a stimulating climate (Porumbeanu, 2010).

The methodology of the study evolved over time and because we considered that for studying the organizational culture we needed more direct contact with the library staff and the organization environment, and a greater closeness to the specific values and the activity of that organization, we included other two methods, interviews and observation. Starting with March 2007 we focused our reserach just on one library, the Central Library of the "Carol Davila" University of Medicine and Pharmacy - Bucharest. We decided to focus our research only on one of the libraries surveyed in the previous study, having in view that the results were similar in the participant libraries and also considering that in the case of a smaller scale study we would be able to come with some concrete solutions, suitable for that library. We chose this library also because it proved a great availability over the years for research, this library being involved in other studies too, for example user studies (Porumbeanu, 2008, 2009a, 2009b). 28 semi-structured interviews of approximately 30 minutes in length with staff from all levels were conducted to ensure an adequate representation. There were also six informal follow-up interviews. They all took place between March-June 2007. The third method, observation of meetings refers to observations of eight staff meetings at the same library between September 2007 and December 2009. The interviews and observations offered us data from "inside", staff points of view and clarified specific aspects of the organizational culture in the library studied.

By analyzing the data collected and the results achieved we could design in 2006 a strategic model for implementing knowledge management (Madge, 2011) and after that, in 2010 we also outlined courses of action to create a culture of learning and knowledge sharing in libraries and information services. However, detailed presentation of the results of this research is not subject to material. We propose in this paper to present briefly the model for implementing knowledge management in libraries and information services and the outline of the framework for creating an organizational culture oriented towards learning and knowledge sharing in this type of organizations.

5. Strategic model for implementing knowledge management in libraries and information services

Despite some common elements and depending on their particular field of activity, organizations present a number of features including the nature of the products and services they produce, their clientele or the public. They therefore require appropriate ways of implementing the new functions of management corresponding to specific conditions found in each organization. Starting with these issues, based on our research results but also reports of applications of knowledge management in organizations from different countries and industries identified in a review of the literature, and bearing in mind the characteristics

of the institutions involved in the information transfer, we believe that in order to obtain optimal results in the implementation of this new function in libraries and information services, managers must focus on creating a specific model, adapted to the needs and conditions of their structures. The model should be based on an in-depth analysis of the organization and the relationships within it, and those with the external environment. We designed in 2006 a strategic model (Figure 1) and formulated a few basic ideas which could be the starting point in implementing knowledge management in libraries and information services (Porumbeanu, 2006, 2009c).
The value of products and services provided by libraries and other information services has always relied not only on tangible resources, but also on the intangible ones, their knowledge assets. And today, these organizations may have a higher performance compared to other structures that appear in the market of information transfer, because they have a better knowledge of the ways in which they can create and provide quality information products and services to meet user needs. And this is thanks to their long institutional experience and also to their staff and their specialist training. The organizational knowledge, both in its practices and procedures and which the specialists possess, is difficult to imitate, it is unique and can be transformed into strategic benefits in the long term.

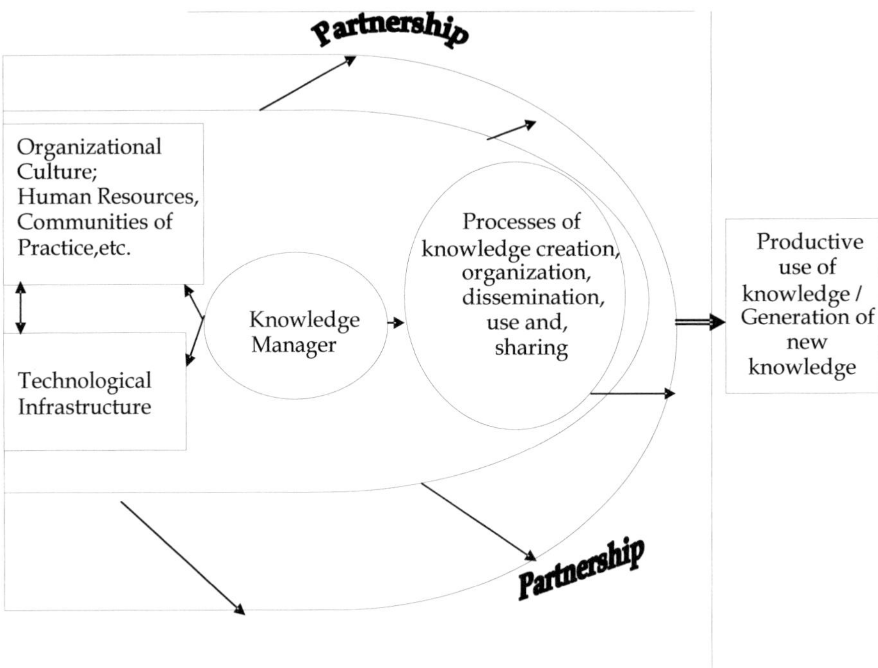

Fig. 1. Strategic model for knowledge management in libraries and information services

Therefore, the fundamental idea from which our model starts is that in contemporary society, the essential skills, based on knowledge, underlying the few activities which libraries and information services do best, are their key organizational assets. Developing unique products and services or developing them at a lower cost than competitors is based on superior knowledge of these processes. In the case of libraries and information services these activities are knowledge organization and preservation, information search and retrieval, information dissemination and development of added value information products. To know how to carry out these activities effectively and efficiently, in ways that other organizations cannot copy is a primary source of value that cannot be purchased from external markets. Therefore, firstly libraries and information services should identify and focus on those few processes which they do best, developing and improving them all the time. Through a variety of mechanisms of organizational learning, libraries and information services can create, collect, and use the knowledge necessary in these processes. Based on this knowledge, they can develop new operating procedures and improve the existing ones. Organizational learning is essential and it must be fostered and enhanced continuously.

The second fundamental element of our model is represented by the people, the human resources and the organizational culture. The chances of success in the implementation of knowledge management is almost non-existent in any kind of organization, including libraries and information services, without development of a collective culture open to change. Here learning, creativity and quality are valued and sought, where the acquisition of new skills and knowledge is an ongoing process, where investment in human capital, in the further training of employees, is essential. Developing a better strategy for communication, creating a coherent context for the systems and the people in the organization are steps that necessarily must be taken. The existence of a unified culture will reduce the barriers of communication and will lead to closer co-operation within the organization. There must be, therefore, a framework created whose components (vision, strategy, values, etc.) recognize the benefits that derive from supporting organizational learning and knowledge sharing. Communities of practice (an important source of expertise for the organization) should be encouraged, as should communication and a team culture where exchange of ideas and information leads to the creation of added value. For an increased efficiency in knowledge management an online discussion forum may be created, which certainly will improve the processes of organizational learning, sharing of knowledge and expertise. Managers must take appropriate measures so that knowledge sharing takes place, perhaps leading to the establishment of organizational changes to encourage greater use of this forum. Changes could include, for example, recording weekly statistics indicating the system users by employee. Frequent users could be rewarded. Internal procedures could also be changed to ensure the immediate capture and use of information during the various projects undertaken by the organization. A system must be set up for periodic evaluations and rewards to encourage people to contribute with their knowledge and to use the knowledge of others.

This brings us to the third fundamental element of our model, namely the technology that can underpin the process of knowledge management by improving the methods of organizational learning and knowledge sharing. Technology plays a fundamental role in creating a culture and an infrastructure to stimulate and enable access to knowledge and expertise existing in the organization. Knowledge management systems based on the new technologies may collect the relevant knowledge and experience in an organization and may make it available anywhere and anytime, thus supporting the processes taking place and decisions that are taken within the library or the information service. They can also connect these institutions to external sources of knowledge. Knowledge management systems support the processes of identification and codification, sharing and distribution of knowledge, and also the processes of generation of new knowledge and integration of this into the organization. Applications of knowledge management support libraries and information services in creating knowledge maps, registers of the collective knowledge of employees, indicating specific areas of their expertise. It also provides support in identifying and sharing best practices, in encoding experts' knowledge so that it can be registered on the information system and used by other members of the organization. Information systems can promote organizational learning. With these systems, knowledge can be preserved in the organizational memory for the training of future employees and for helping them in making decisions. People can be directed to specific areas of expertise, can get in touch with those who possess knowledge, can easily identify experts and tacit knowledge can be shared. The role of information technology underpins the ability to raise and improve collaboration and communication among employees, and between them and practitioners and experts from outside the institution. This helps enormously in the innovation process. Technology makes available the organizational knowledge. But precisely the type of system that can facilitate information flow and knowledge management in libraries and information services must be identified. Specifically systems that help these organizations understand and respond better to the requirements of their environment. External and internal networks, databases, techniques for extracting data, and other applications based on the new technologies of information and communications can also help libraries and information services in capturing, organizing and using the knowledge base they possess.

We introduce here the fourth fundamental element of the model, networks, the partnerships with other structures of the same type or with structures with similar activities. Libraries and information services should be organized in networks, which through all the human, information, knowledge and technology resources they possess, will have more ways to use human knowledge productively and thereby will be more efficient and more competitive. By applying information and knowledge they will be able to generate new knowledge, will be able to process information and develop advanced communication tools. Also, as part of a network they will be able to focus on creating and improving the facilities and infrastructure that encourage and support learning. Designing, implementing and managing partnership programmes with other public or private organizations are necessary actions to stimulate research, innovation and new knowledge generation. Libraries and information services have to be constantly in search of new opportunities for collaboration. They must identify, develop and use the best practices in scientific co-operation, exploit the potential of information and communication technologies to help develop strategies and activities in co-operation with other organizations. Expanding partnerships, involvement in international research programmes, development of modern applications for their actions, the interconnection of all their departments, will enhance the quality of activities of libraries and information services and of the products and services they provide to users. Through partnerships and networks, libraries and information services will have more knowledge assets, and although many difficulties can appear in sharing these assets, information and communications technologies can provide solutions to overcome these difficulties.

A fifth key element for the success of the knowledge management project is the creation of the position of knowledge manager. Its holder will deal with all that makes up the knowledge strategy for that organization. They will co-ordinate the technological infrastructure, human resources, the processes of creation, use and sharing of knowledge, the co-operative relationships of the organization (Figure 2). They will be responsible for the smooth running of the process of knowledge management within the library or the information service, will co-ordinate the design and implementation of knowledge management programmes and systems, will find new sources of knowledge and will identify new ways of effective use of knowledge in the organization.

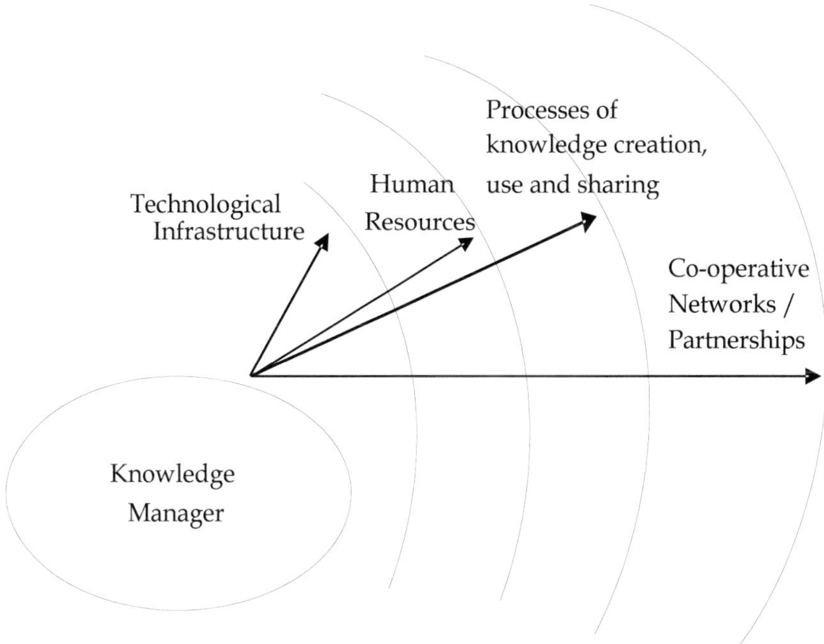

Fig. 2. The role of knowledge manager

Our model centrally places the knowledge assets of the organization (which are in the minds of people, in the organization processes, practices and activities) and those from the external environment, at organizational level where there are co-operative relationships, and is designed to support the expansion and improvement of those main activities deployed by libraries and information services: the acquisition, organization, processing, and preservation of documents; information search and retrieval; information dissemination; development of information products; provision of information services for users, etc.

The phases of the model (Figure 3) are not necessarily dependent on each other, so that we need not complete a stage and only then move to the next. They can also be addressed in a different order, not only in that set out below. These steps should rather be seen as some steps to be taken, regardless of the path chosen, each library or information service setting out on an individual basis, depending on the specific functions and resources (human, financial, time, etc.) available, the importance of these stages in order to achieve the goals and the order in which these steps must be completed. For example, developing an organizational culture open to sharing knowledge can be the first action that a library initiates, as is perhaps the most important step, but the most difficult in any project for implementation of knowledge management. Also, creating a post of knowledge manager may well be a decision that is put into practice as soon as a library has decided to implement knowledge management.

The model includes a series of relationships which should be established at library or information service level, but also at the level of the partnerships established with other organizations. The relationships within the partners should be at the knowledge managers' level for effective coordination and functioning of co-operation or directly between specialists in the libraries and information services who can co-operate in various activities in which they are engaged. These relationships are represented schematically in Figure 4.

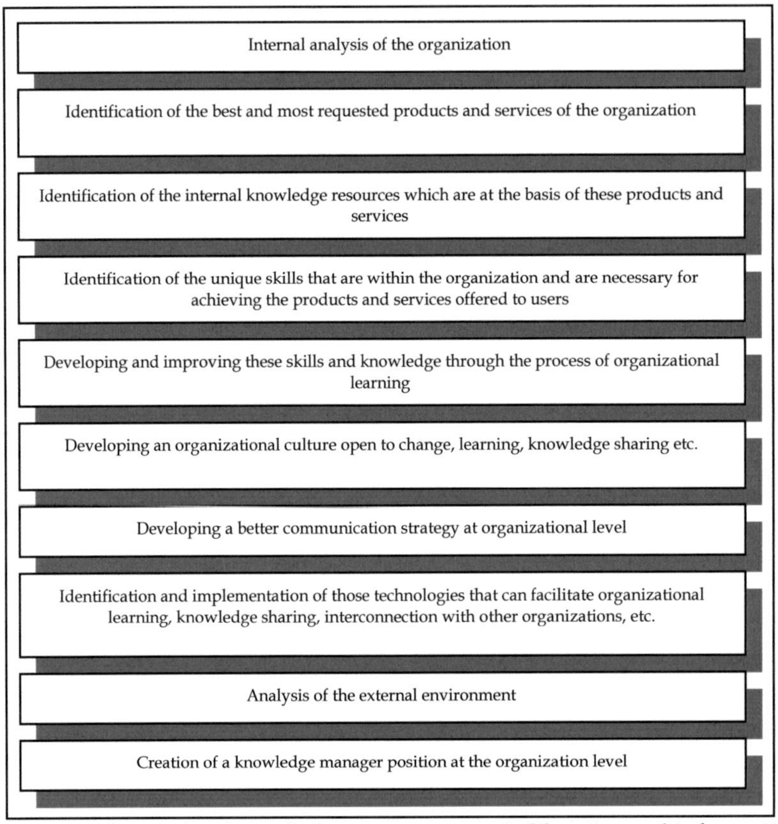

Fig. 3. Phases in implementing knowledge management in libraries and information services

Modes of action must be decided at organizational level by each manager because each institution has a specific environment, the characteristics of organizational culture being different in all structures. As a whole each organization will react in a specific way differently from other structures, even if they are the same type. For example, for operational changes to the organizational culture, each structure must identify the best ways to motivate people to share and use knowledge.

The consequences of the implementation of a knowledge management project can be manifested in different ways. Results of actions may occur faster or slower depending on the circumstances in each library or information service. Acting in the same way in two different organizations, we will not achieve the same results.

In the case of libraries, partnerships for knowledge management can be established through existing networks at public, school and university level by the interconnection of all these institutions, then a partnership at national level could be constructed through the participation of these structural networks, but also of others (Figure 5). In the case of academic libraries, for example, co-operation at the level of the field / discipline can lead to expansion both in breadth and depth.

The model of implementation of knowledge management in libraries and information services allows:

- identification of the most important processes, products and services of libraries and information services and their evaluation;

- identification of knowledge resources and skills in the organization in order to exploit these resources;
- identification of the potential external partners for collaboration.

Implementing knowledge management in libraries and information services will lead to the improved ability of these organizations to learn, identify and use knowledge from internal and external resources in their processes and activities. It will also lead to the generation of new knowledge, to the development of new procedures and practices to optimize integration and sharing of knowledge within organizations. A knowledge management programme tailored to the specific conditions in libraries and information services, once put into practice, can reduce costs, increase revenue, increase staff efficiency, improve the activities, products and services offered to users, in short improve the performance of libraries and information services and secure a good position for them in the knowledge market.

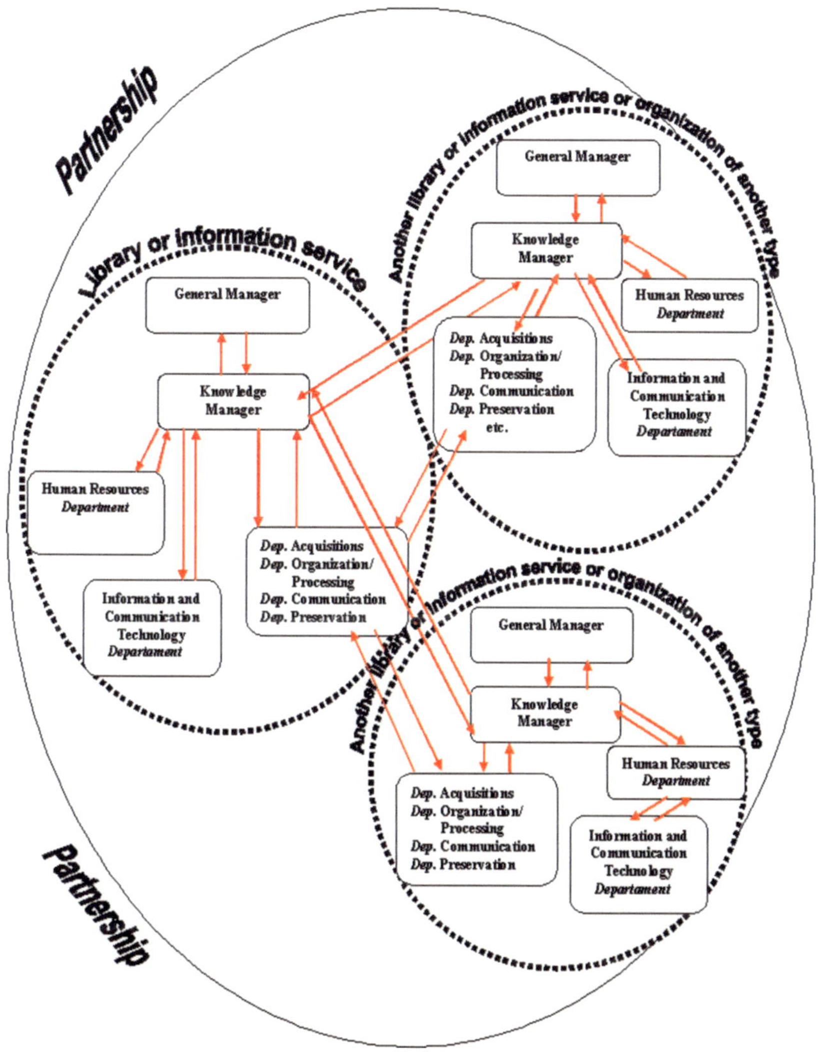

Fig. 4. Relationships at the library or information service and at partnership level

6. Framework for creating a learning and knowledge sharing culture in libraries and information services

Orientation of organizational culture towards learning and knowledge sharing will help ensure success and long-term development of organizations, including libraries and information services. If the knowledge manager or the chief knowledge officer is generally considered to have three major responsibilities which involve creating a knowledge management infrastructure, creating a knowledge culture and making these structures pay off economically (Lester & Kohler, 2003), we believe that in libraries and information services and in the context of the strategic model that we proposed, the knowledge manager should firstly focus his efforts and start his approach of managing the knowledge resources strategy from issues related to building an adequate organizational culture. Such an organizational culture should support libraries and information services in the future in order to adapt to the globalized environment by reinventing themselves continuously. This could allow them to respond creatively to change and maintain an important position on the market of information transfer.

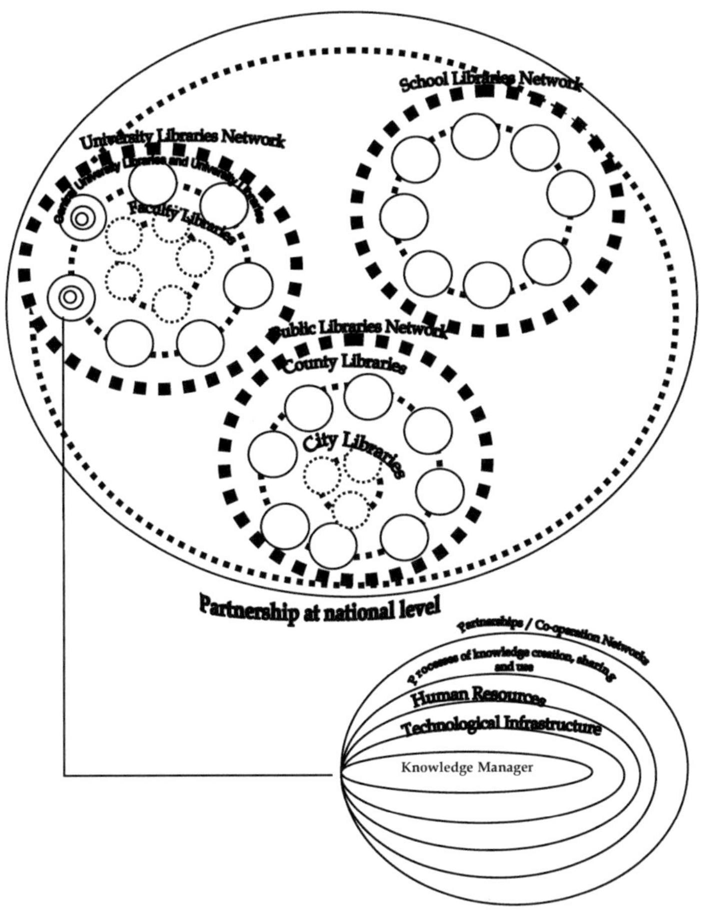

Fig. 5. Partnership for knowledge management at national level in libraries and information services

In the specific context of libraries and information services as key players in this market, everything must be designed taking into account the challenges which the information and knowledge society has brought in their domain, the impact it has had on the role of librarians and on the information needs of users, the fast development of information and communication technologies and the explosion of digital information resources to which libraries have increasingly turned and which have led to significant changes of the way in which information services are provided to users (Hornby & Clarke, 2003; Limb, 2004). Libraries must use to their advantage all these changes regarding digital resources and networks.

The importance of organizational culture comes also from the fact that it has influence on so many organizational levels: mission and objectives, policies and procedures, decision making, communication process, continuing professional development of employees, employee attitudes and behavior, values promoted by the organization, management style, the position libraries and information services occupy in their domain, relationships with the external environment, employee motivation, performance etc.

According to our model, the knowledge manager tasks and responsibilities are (Figure 6):

- to identify necessary changes at the organizational culture level and to find ways to implement these changes;
- to support and promote organizational learning;
- to work for building a culture that fosters open communication, experts networking, etc., in short a culture oriented towards learning and knowledge sharing;
- to work for developing forms of co-operation;
- to design the knowledge strategy at the level of the whole organization;
- to work for building a knowledge management infrastructure (design, implementation, monitoring, evaluation of human, library, and technological resources, etc.);
- to handle the identification, acquirement, organization, protection, distribution, and sharing of knowledge resources;
- to coordinate knowledge management programs and systems;
- to coordinate the process of creating and using knowledge (development of new products and services, market research etc.);
- to coordinate the relationships with external partners and providers of information and knowledge.

Vision and leadership are essential for this whole approach because they will support achievement of these tasks and responsibilities.

For creating a culture of learning and knowledge sharing in libraries and information services we believe that action must be taken in four major directions (Figure 7) aimed at:

- the communication process at organizational level;
- the motivation and reward system for employees;
- the policy on training and continuing professional development of employees;
- the system of the values promoted at organizational level.

Communication plays a vital role in the efficient functioning of any organization. The existence of a shared vision depends on how communication occurs in the organization. It is not possible to know and understand very good the library mission, its objectives, and policies etc. without effective communication. Participation, involvement, dialogue, expressing new ideas, empowering employees should be encouraged, but this is not possible without creating conditions for effective communication and facilitating multidirectional communication

channels. Development of a strategy that reflects the shared vision of the employees in that library must be based on a process of open and effective communication.
The communication process is also crucial in terms of employee perception of their organization, the values promoted within that organization and how this is perceived by the external environment. Benefits that new information and communication technologies currently offer can be exploited to create fast, open and multidirectional communication channels. A communication strategy that takes into account support for learning, knowledge sharing, and in fact knowledge management systems, should consider creating the necessary conditions for developing communities of practice and an interactive environment within the library. In promoting and facilitating learning opportunities, the knowledge manager can play a key role by encouraging communities of practice and developing teams to learn and generate knowledge (Abell & Oxbrow, 2002; Lester & Kohler, 2003).

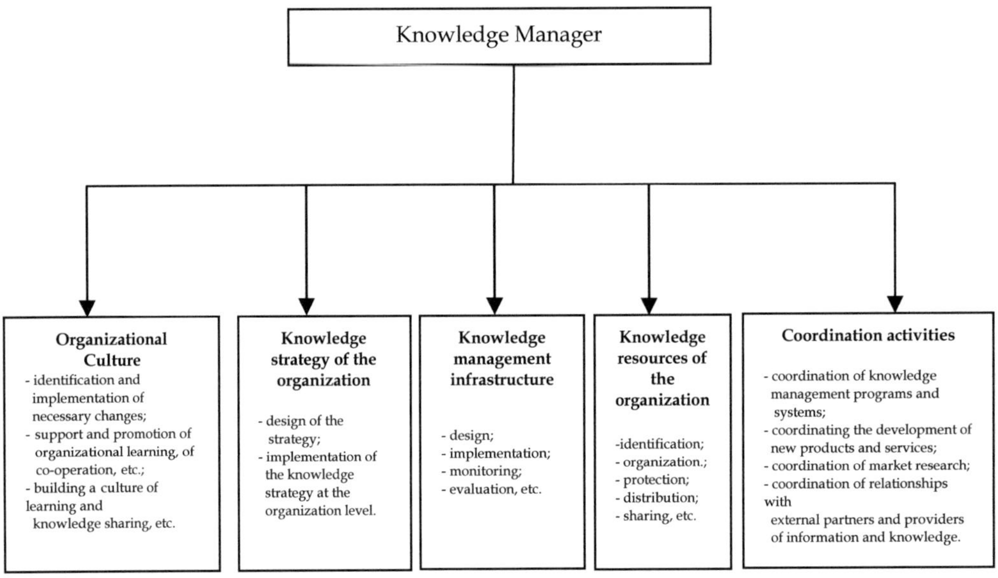

Fig. 6. Tasks and responsibilities of the knowledge manager

In the action of improving communication process in libraries and information services, both formal and informal communication together with their related channels should be considered. Informal communication, face to face, group and team meetings must be encouraged because people communicate and learn better in an informal context. Informal communication also contributes to the confidence that library staff develops in each other. Managers should also not neglect the barriers of various types that may occur in communication and also the complexity of this process that can take place in so many ways and forms (Condon & Yousef, 2002).
The values and attitudes promoted in libraries and information services, their encouragement and development at the employee level have a major influence in supporting processes such as learning and knowledge sharing. Among the values with a key role in the success of organizations on the globalized knowledge market which should be promoted (Figure 8), libraries and information services should give great importance to

the following: open communication, knowledge sharing, learning, collaboration, dialogue, performance, creativity, flexibility, change, responsiveness to new ideas, teamwork, professional co-operation, exchange of experience, transparency, empowerment, participation, etc.

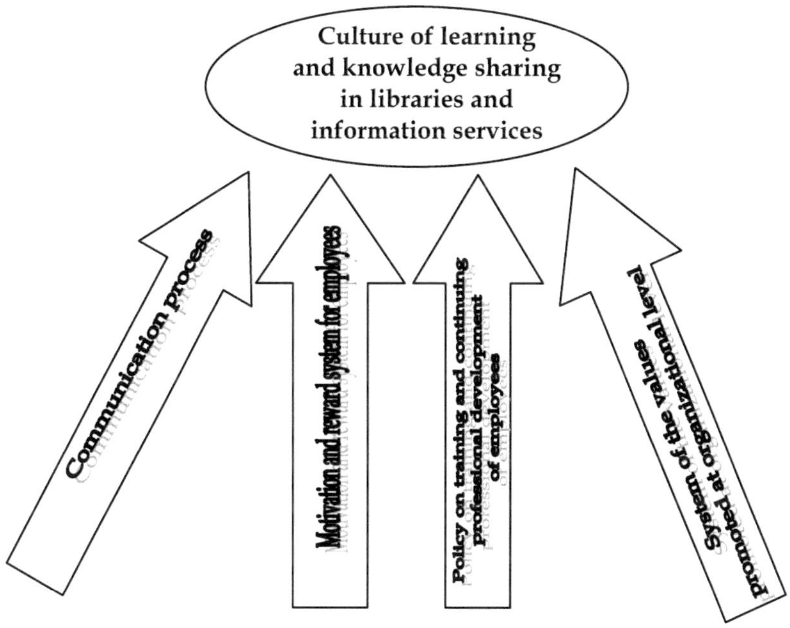

Fig. 7. Major directions of action for creating a culture of learning and knowledge sharing in libraries and information services

But in the field of libraries and information services, we can also talk about professional values specific to these organizations (Roberts & Rowley, 2004) which should not be overlooked by managers: the value of information, accessibility to information and services, user orientation, social inclusion, providing selective information, that is evaluated, validated, directly exploitable, current and quickly obtained information, etc. Promoting these values which facilitate and stimulate learning and knowledge sharing among employees is very important in libraries.

The policy of training and professional development of employees in libraries and information services strongly influences the learning process. Libraries have the advantage of various tools for continuing professional development: reading and updating, coaching or mentoring, job exchanges or job shadowing, conferences, distance education, training others, meetings, networking, learning from others, etc. (Roberts & Rowley, 2004). How employees will pertain and respond to growth and improvement of their speciality knowledge, their involvement in various forms of training and professional development, their active/passive attitude towards these aspects of professional development are influenced by the organization policy and the importance libraries and information services give to these issues. Building programmes of training and professional development at internal level, encouraging employee participation in external training and professional development programmes, offering them material support to participate in such programmes, encouragement of their participation in conferences, and preparation of communications and articles, their involvement in research concerning the library's activity should be taken into consideration because learning and increasing employee knowledge are supported by such actions.

In libraries, learning at individual, group/team and organizational level and also knowledge sharing need to take into account the existing types of groups and teams in these organizations, namely: operational team, strategic team, multi-skill teams, virtual teams, networks and communities of practice, etc. (Roberts & Rowley, 2004).

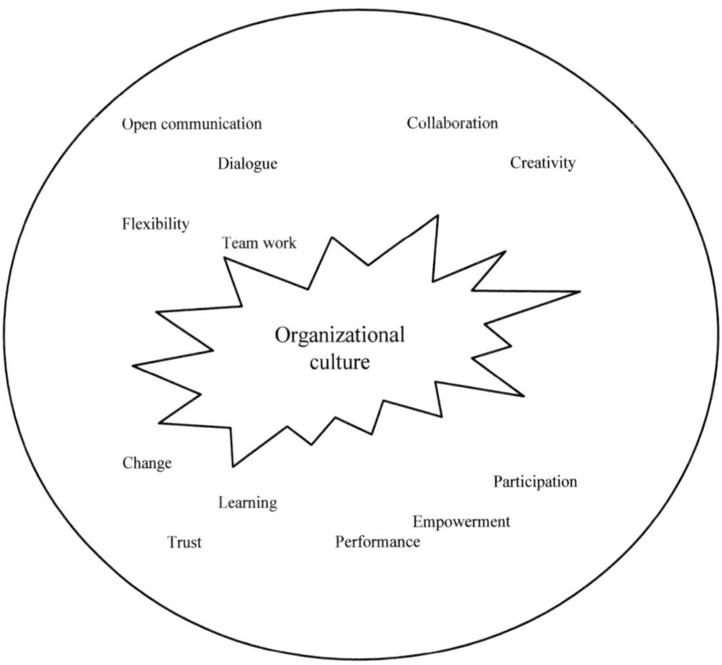

Fig. 8. Values which should be promoted by the organizational culture in libraries and information services

The motivation and reward system for employees is very important in the process of sharing knowledge. Staff should be motivated to learn, develop professionally, enhance their expertise, be active professionally. Rewarding employee performance may be at material level or by promoting their career, by supporting their participation in various professional events, etc. In libraries and information services, for increasing employee satisfaction we have at hand specific approaches, namely creation of new roles, of new teams, introduction of various new practices and patterns of work like flexible working, job sharing, etc. (Roberts & Rowley, 2004). The factors that motivate the staff and which impact on their activities, and the management practices and methods that support performance among employees have been investigated (Tampoe, 1996). But the motivation and reward system for employees must be well developed and be based on the analysis and the specific situation of each organization and its employees.

The data collected between 2004-2009 in our research and the results from these data analysis sent us to the conclusion that for creating a culture of learning and knowledge sharing in libraries, all these issues should be considered and action is needed in these four directions.

The model and framework which we propose offer a possible solution to implement knowledge management and create a culture of learning and knowledge sharing in libraries and information services (Figure 9). Their novelty, importance and usefulness stay in that they are general, allowing adjustments depending on the peculiarity and scale of each library. They are flexible and can be used in any library with the necessary adaptations, they will certainly lead to obtaining high performance and are a starting point for developing other specific models.

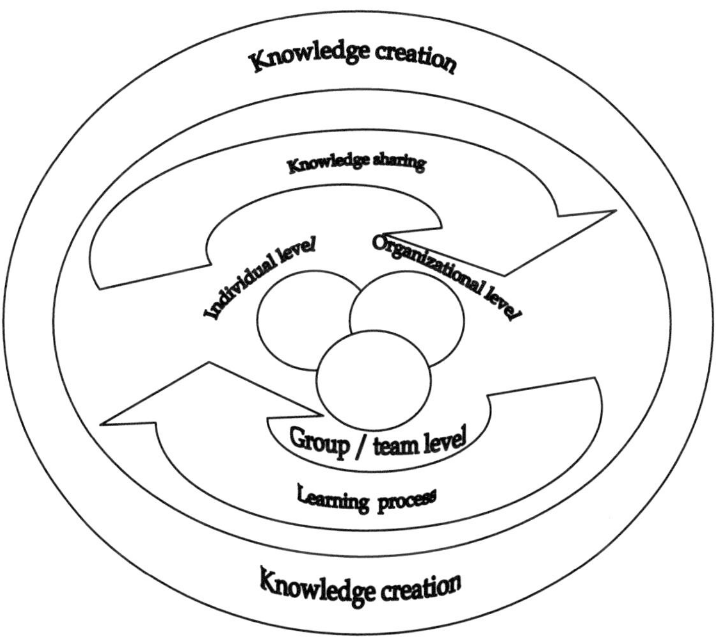

Fig. 9. Learning and knowledge sharing in libraries and information services

Even if the design of the model has in view large libraries which develop well defined workflows and have employees with higher skills and training, its elements can keep up their validity till the smallest libraries. The model can lead to a successful implementation of knowledge management in libraries and information services through a strategic vision of a knowledge manager and the systemic relationship which include the organizational assets, the new technologies and the human resources in the context of networks (Stoica, 2006).

Though, in very distinct contexts things may be different from the situation in the libraries examined by us and our model may appear incomplete or unsatisfactory. Also, some may see a weakness in that it does not go into details, in depth and offers only general guidelines, outlining the general directions of action to follow.

We believe, however, that this openness provides general application and it is an advantage. The model and framework designed by us can be adapted and completed, just from the fact that each library applying knowledge management process should develop a suitable way to implement it according to its own activities, practices and circumstances.

7. Future research

Together with other studies in literature, our research contributes to a deeper understanding of a category of organizations that occupies a special place in the knowledge-based society, namely libraries and information services, which are involved the most in knowledge management. Implementing knowledge management in any organization should start from understanding the context in which it operates, its mission and objectives, its activities and its characteristic elements and the external factors that influence it.

In literature, approaches to knowledge management application in libraries and information services are fragmentary. Our study provides a starting point for future research to explore in greater depth and go in more details about the elements of the model and framework and answer questions such as How should be developed a system to motivate staff in libraries? How communication can be improved at the library level? etc. The model and the framework we designed starting from our research offer the basis for understanding the context of libraries and for creating a culture of learning and knowledge sharing in these structures. Future research should develop more systematic and detailed approaches and ways to manage and improve knowledge sharing in libraries. This could bring great advantages by increasing the efficiency of these organizations in the globalized knowledge-based society.

8. Conclusion

Knowledge management is a way of thinking and action, it is not based solely on the use of knowledge, but becomes at the same time, an instrument of its development. "By implementing knowledge management organizations gain intelligence, learn, adapt, change themselves and change the environment, produce not only specific performance, but a special kind of tacit performance that penetrates gradually deep into the organizational fiber and gene. And all these through general awareness and participation" (Stoica, 2006). Recent literature is rich in researches that analyze, present and underline the benefits of applying the knowledge management process in organizations, the need to change the organizational culture and improve the organizational learning. The importance of these issues is evident for the future of organizations in the knowledge-based society.

Various studies have dealt with the libraries and information services domain too. But things are far from clear. Researchers agree that it is necessary to create a culture of learning and knowledge sharing and it is the best way for libraries and information services to follow, but how to do this as well is not completely understood. Aspects of organizational culture, organizational learning and knowledge sharing should be considered when approaching implementation of knowledge management in libraries. However, research has focused so far on the importance of culture and less on creating a framework for building such a culture.

This study is just one of the researches that focus on knowledge management in libraries and information services, it provides a model for implementing knowledge management in these organizations and highlights the directions on which library managers should concentrate when they operate changes at the organizational culture level. Future research on organizational culture in libraries and information services and on the learning and knowledge sharing processes can help deepen this field and provide a stronger basis to be useful to libraries and information services and their managers.

9. References

Abell, A. & Oxbrow, N. (2002). *Competing with Knowledge. The Information Professional in the Knowledge Management Age,* Library Association Publishing, ISBN 1-85604-339-8, London, UK

Addleson, M. (2000). Organizing to Know and to Learn: Reflections on Organization and Knowledge Management, In: *Knowledge Management for the Information Professional,* T. K. Srikantaiah & M. E. D. Koenig, (Eds.), pp. 137-160, Information Today, Inc., ISBN 1-57387-079-X, Medford, USA

Ali, I., Warne, L. & Pascoe, C. (2006). Learning in Organizations, In: *Encyclopedia of Knowledge Management,* D. G. Schwartz, (Ed.), pp. 561-568, Idea Group Reference, ISBN 1-59140-573-4, Hershey, USA

Barrett, W., Lau, L. M. S. & Dew, P. M. (2000). Facilitating Knowledge Transfer in an R & D Environment: A Case Study, In: *Internet-Based Organizational Memory and Knowledge Management,* D. G. Schwartz, M. Diviniti & T. Brasethvik, (Eds.), pp. 147-169, Idea Group Publishing, ISBN 1-878289-82-9, London, UK

Brown, J. S. & Duguid, P. (2000). Organizational Learning and Communities of Practice: Towards a Unified View of Working, Learning, and Innovation, In: *Knowledge and Communities,* E. L. Lesser, M. A. Fontaine & J. A. Slusher, (Eds.), pp. 99-121, Butterworth-Heinemann, ISBN 0-7506-7293-5, Boston, USA

Condon, J. C. & Yousef, F. S. (2002). Communication Perspectives, In: *Managing Knowledge. An Essential Reader,* S. Little, P. Quintas & T. Ray, (Eds.), pp. 214-237, The Open University and Sage Publications, ISBN 0-7619-7212-9, London, UK

Cope, M. (2000). *Know Your Value? Manage Your Knowledge and Make it Pay,* Prentice Hall, ISBN 0-273-65032-7, London, UK

Davenport, T. D. & Prusak, L. (1998). *Working Knowledge. How Organizations Manage What They Know,* Harvard Business School Press, ISBN 0-87584-655-6, Boston, USA

Firestone, J. M. & McElroy, M. W. (2003). *Key Issues in the New Knowledge Management,* Butterworth Heinemann, ISBN 0-7506-7655-8, Boston, USA

Gregory, V. L. (2000). Knowledge Management and Building the Learning Organization, In: *Knowledge Management for the Information Professional,* T. K. Srikantaiah & M. E. D. Koenig, (Eds.), pp. 161-179, Information Today, Inc., ISBN 1-57387-079-X, Medford, USA

Hofstede, G. H. (1996). *Managementul Structurilor Multiculturale: Software-ul Gândirii,* Editura Economică, ISBN 973-919-801-5, Bucureşti, Romania

Hornby, S. & Clarke, Z. (Eds.). (2003). *Challenge and Change in the Information Society,* Facet Publishing, ISBN 1-85604-453-X, London, UK

Kanter, R. M. (1996). When a Thousand Flowers Bloom: Structural, Collective, and Social Conditions for Innovation in Organizations, In: *Knowledge Management and*

Organizational Design, P. S. Myers, (Ed.), pp. 93-131, Butterworth-Heinemann, ISBN 0-7506-9749-0, Boston, USA

King, W. R. (2006). Knowledge Sharing, In: *Encyclopedia of Knowledge Management,* D. G. Schwartz, (Ed.), pp. 493-498, Idea Group Reference, ISBN 1-59140-573-4, Hershey, USA

Jacobson, C. M. (2006). Knowledge Sharing between Individuals, In: *Encyclopedia of Knowledge Management,* D. G. Schwartz, (Ed.), pp. 507-514, Idea Group Reference, ISBN 1-59140-573-4, Hershey, USA

Lester, J. & Koehler, W. C. (2003). *Fundamentals of Information Studies. Understanding Information and its Environment,* Neal-Schuman Publishers, Inc., ISBN 1-55570-474-3, New York, USA

Limb, P. (2004). *Digital Dilemmas and Solutions,* Chandos Publishing, ISBN 1-84334-039-9, Oxford, UK

Lindsey, K. L. (2006). Knowledge Sharing Barriers, In: *Encyclopedia of Knowledge Management,* D. G. Schwartz, (Ed.), pp. 499-506, Idea Group Reference, ISBN 1-59140-573-4, Hershey, USA

Lorino, P. (2001). A Pragmatic Analysis of the Role of Management Systems in Organizational Learning, In: *Knowledge Management and Organizational Competence,* R. Sanchez, (Ed.), pp. 177-209, Oxford Univeristy Press, ISBN 0-19-924028-0, Oxford, UK

Madge, O. L. (2010). Managementul Cunoaşterii în Biblioteci / Knowledge Management in Libraries. *Studii de Biblioteconomie şi Ştiinţa Informării / Library and Information Science Research,* No. 14/2010, Editura Universităţii din Bucureşti, pp. 85-98, ISSN 1453-5386

Madge, O. L. (2011). Knowledge Management in Medical Libraries in the Web 2.0 Age, *Proceedings of the International Symposium The Book. Romania. Europe 3rd Edition,* pp. 151-160, ISSN 2068-9756, Bucharest, Romania, September 20-24, 2010.

Porumbeanu, O. L. (2006). *Managementul Cunoaşterii şi Structurile Infodocumentare,* Editura Universităţii din Bucureşti, ISBN (10) 973-737-203-4, Bucureşti, Romania

Porumbeanu, O. L. (2008). Identifying the Implications of the Use of Electronic Resources and New Technologies in Academic Medical Libraries, *Proceedings of MLA 08 Connections: Bridging the Gaps,* p. 32, Chicago, USA, May 16-21, 2008, 30. 08. 2011, Available from: <http://www.mlanet.org/am/am2008/pdf/08_abstracts.pdf>

Porumbeanu, O. L. (2009a). The Impact of Electronic Resources and New Technology in Academic Medical Libraries in Romania. *Health Information and Libraries Journal,* 26, pp. 152-155, ISSN 1471-1834

Porumbeanu, O. L. (2009b). Is Electronic Always the Right Choice?, *Proceedings of Positioning the Profession: the Tenth International Congress on Medical Librarianship,* Brisbane, Australia, August 31-September 4, 2009, 30.08.2011, Available from: <http://espace.library.uq.edu.au/eserv/UQ:179724/n2_5_Wed_Porumbeanu_160.pdf>

Porumbeanu, O. L. (2009c). Model Strategic pentru Implementarea Managementului Cunoaşterii în Structurile Infodocumentare / Strategic Model for Implementing

Knowledge Management in Libraries and Information Services. *Studii de Biblioteconomie şi Ştiinţa Informării / Library and Information Science Research,* No. 13/2009, Editura Universităţii din Bucureşti, pp. 71-105, ISSN 1453-5386

Porumbeanu, O. L. (2010). Implementing Knowledge Management in Romanian Academic Libraries: Identifying the Elements that Characterize their Organizational Culture. *Journal of Academic Librarianship,* Vol. 36, No. 6, (November 2010), pp. 549-552, ISSN 0099-1333

Prusak, L. (1996). Introduction to Series - Why Knowledge, Why Now?, In: *Knowledge Management and Organizational Design,* P. S. Myers, (Ed.), pp. IX-X, Butterworth-Heinemann, ISBN 0-7506-9749-0, Boston, USA

Pucik, V. (1996). Strategic Alliances, Organizational Learning, and Competitive Advantage: The HRM Agenda, In: *Knowledge Management and Organizational Design,* P. S. Myers, (Ed.), pp. 151-165, Butterworth-Heinemann, ISBN 0-7506-9749-0, Boston, USA

Quintas, P. (2002). Managing Knowledge in a New Century, In: *Managing Knowledge. An Essential Reader,* S. Little, P. Quintas & T. Ray, (Eds.), pp. 1-14, The Open University and Sage Publications, ISBN 0-7619-7212-9, London, UK

Roberts, S. & Rowley, J. (2004). *Managing Information Services,* Facet Publishing, ISBN 1-85604-515-3, London, UK

Sanchez, R. (2001). Managing Knowledge into Competence: The Five Learning Cycles of the Competent Organization, In: *Knowledge Management and Organizational Competence,* R. Sanchez, (Ed.), pp. 3-37, Oxford Univeristy Press, ISBN 0-19-924028-0, Oxford, UK

Senge, P. M. (1990). *The Fifth Discipline: The Art and Practice of the Learning Organization,* Doubleday, ISBN 0-385-26094-6 New York, USA

Skyrme, D. J. & Amidon, D. M. (2002). The Learning Organization, In: *Managing Knowledge. An Essential Reader,* S. Little, P. Quintas & T. Ray, (Eds.), pp. 264-271, The Open University and Sage Publications, ISBN 0-7619-7212-9, London, UK

Stacey, R. D. (2001). *Complex Responsive Processes in Organizations. Learning and Knowledge Creation,* Routledge, ISBN 0-415-24918-8, London, UK

Stamps, D. (2000). Communities of Practice: Learning is Social. Training is Irrelevant?, In: *Knowledge and Communities,* E. L. Lesser, M. A. Fontaine & J. A. Slusher, (Eds.), pp. 53-64, Butterworth-Heinemann, ISBN 0-7506-7293-5, Boston, USA

Stoica, I. (2006). Cuvânt înainte, In: Porumbeanu, O. L. (2006). *Managementul Cunoaşterii şi Structurile Infodocumentare,* pp. 7-12, Editura Universităţii din Bucureşti, ISBN (10) 973-737-203-4, Bucureşti, Romania

Sydänmaanlakka, P. (2002). *An Intelligent Organization. Integrating Performance, Competence and Knowledge Management,* Capstone, ISBN 1-84112-048-0, Oxford, UK

Tampoe, M. (1996). Motivating Knowledge Workers - The Challenge for the 1990s, In: *Knowledge Management and Organizational Design,* P. S. Myers, (Ed.), pp. 179-189, Butterworth-Heinemann, ISBN 0-7506-9749-0, Boston, USA

Teece, D. J. (2002). *Managing Intellectual Capital. Organizational, Strategic and Policy Dimensions,* University Press, ISBN 0-19-829541-3, Oxford, UK

Tschaitschian, B., Abecker, A., Hackstein, J. & Zakaoui, J. (2000). Internet Enabled Corporate Knowledge Sharing and Utilization, In: *Internet-Based Organizational Memory and Knowledge Management,* D. G. Schwartz, M. Diviniti & T. Brasethvik, (Eds.), pp. 25-41, Idea Group Publishing, ISBN 1-878289-82-9, London, UK

Webb, S. P. (1998). *Knowledge Management: Linchpin of Change. Some Practical Guidelines,* Aslib, ISBN 0-85142-414-7, London, UK

12

Exploring the Risks of Knowledge Leakage: An Information Systems Case Study Approach

Fenio Annansingh
Plymouth University
United Kingdom

1. Introduction

Companies in high-tech industries are increasingly investing in 3D and virtual reality (VR) packages to support customers in understanding and using their products. These packages are now taking the form of 3D virtual reality environments (VREs) where employees can navigate, browse and learn in an authentic, close to reality context. These products supported by combinations of photographic techniques and virtual reality programming platforms are becoming increasingly popular and indeed very effective training tools. They provide for realistic contexts and easily navigable environments, which are ideal media for training in complex and specialised settings.

These VREs promote specialised knowledge and technical skills within authentic environments and reinforce acquired knowledge by increased interactions with both the environment and the objects that compose it. These user-friendly and intuitive interactions encourage creativity and innovative thinking (Nunes & Annansingh, 2003). Furthermore, because these environments are usually web-based applications, hyperlinks enable access to vast amounts of both company specific and general information. This combination of use with precise descriptions of operational details have been identified by companies using them as posing possible risk of knowledge leakage (KL) exposure, thus, representing a threat to organisational knowledge management (KM). This chapter will discuss the findings of a study which explore this exact issue.

Therefore, the motivation behind this chapter is based on the identification and characterisation of KL risks associated with information systems (IS), namely VREs. The concept of KL has now evolved and increasingly literature searches indicate that KL is now emerging as a major consideration for businesses and academia alike. The definition for KL used in this chapter is:

> *"knowledge leakage is the deliberate or accidental loss of knowledge to unauthorised personnel within or outside of an organisational boundary". (Annansingh, 2004)*

In the past, IS projects have adopted a positivist approach, which focuses primarily on the development process associated with the technology rather than the perception and perspectives of the people involved in the developmental process (Bharadwaj, 2004). From an IS point of view interpretivist is an epistemological stance, concerned with the users' understanding of reality. It embraces a wide range of philosophical and sociological stances, which share the common characteristics of attempting to understand and explain the social world from the perspective of the actors directly involved in the social process (Burrell &

Morgan, 1985). It assumes that knowledge, within the domain of human action, is a necessary social construction and therefore inevitably subjective (Walsham, 1993). Hence an interpretivist paradigm was used with the research design comprising of two stages: an exploratory case-study and a cross-sectional sector wide survey used in order to validate the findings emerging from the first phase. Thus a mixed method approach using interviews and survey was employed.

The results show that knowledge embodiment and use in projects occurred during systems development and dissemination owing to the actual utilisation of the 3D models during business transactions and training activities. Since one of the primary goals of KM is to share, transfer and disseminate explicit knowledge, the sharing of this knowledge if done in an ad hoc manner can result in KL. Even the best laid KM policy or framework can be a source of KL due to the absence of an integrated risk management approach. In addition, the general nature of the KM models allows for KL, this weakness or discrepancy occurs where policies and practices do not merge. Another reason for KL is the fact that KM models have failed to consider the protection of knowledge within the organisation and across it boundaries.

In addition, current risk identification process in organisations tends to occur via two pathways. This is clearly based on the relationship between an interacting company and their direct customers and the resulting risks from this relationship. Risk identification and assessment have been characterised as fundamental for business continuity and to maintain a competitive advantage over ones competitor. It is essential for the successful business relationship between developing companies and its direct customers, and may ultimately be crucial for the acceptance and success of the 3D modelling solutions proposed. Each party should have an interest in determining the risk associated with acquiring and interacting with the 3D environments in their own organisation.

2. Organisational knowledge management (KM)

Knowledge is recognised as a valuable asset by organisations and has gained a great deal of attention in academic and business world alike. Interest in KM stems from the realisation that organisational knowledge is a strategic corporate asset that needs to be generated, represented, stored, transferred, transformed and applied to future organisational problems (Shultze & Stabell, 2004). Thus enhancing companies' competitive advantage as it improves efficiency and performance and enhances innovation (Nonaka & Takeuchi, 1995; Nonaka, 1991). Consequently, KM practices are now considered as established practice in large organisations (Srikantaiah & Koenig, 2000).

KM is concerned with how this knowledge is created, used, transferred and applied (Nonaka & Takeuchi, 1995; Nonaka & Konno, 1998). KM therefore should focus on information in relevant context and having an understanding of interrelationships and behaviour (Nonaka & Teece, 2001; Wenger et al., 2002; Nonaka, 1994). Furthermore, authors such as Davenport & Prusak (1998) and Coleman (1999) have promoted KM as a practice with implications beyond that of simply developing information and communication technology (ICT) infrastructures, with information sharing and retrieval potential. For example, according to Pollard (2003) the expectations are mostly of organisational gains in terms of:

- Growth and innovation
- Productivity and efficiency

- Customer relationships
- Employee learning, satisfaction and retention, and
- Management decision-making.

In general, KM in organisations should be seen as the process of critically managing knowledge to meet existing needs, to identify and exploit existing and acquired knowledge and to develop new knowledge in order to take advantage of new opportunities and challenges (Quintas et al., 1997). Strategically, KM must be seen as an approach to: manage organisational knowledge assets, support management decision making; enhance competitiveness, and increase capacity for creativity and innovation (Zyngier et al., 2004). Operationally, KM should be viewed as a cycle that starts with knowledge creation, which is followed by knowledge interpretation, knowledge dissemination and use, and knowledge retention and refinement (De Jarnett, 1996).

2.1 Knowledge management characterisation

There are several classifications of knowledge with the most common being explicit, implicit and tacit knowledge (Nonaka & Takeuchi, 1995; McInerney & Koenig, 2011; Polanyi, 1974). Explicit knowledge can be transmitted using logical language and hence can easily be shared and stored (Srikantaiah & Koenig, 2000). Tacit knowledge on the other hand is intangible; it is not easily codified and articulated in formal languages. Nonetheless according to Nonaka & Takeuchi (1995) both types of knowledge do not compete with each other, but rather be supplemented by each other. Implicit knowledge can be transferred, but without a conscious process, during learning (Jones & Miller, 2008).

However, regardless of the philosophical stance adopted about knowledge and KM this research focuses on the leakage of knowledge rather than its classification and management meanings ascribed to this concept. KM activities and in particular the forgone are prone to KL due to its very nature because KM processes are coupled with the use of VRE.

3. KM and risk management thinking

IS development activities consume a significant amount of time, energy and resources in most organisations, yet there are many instances when the potential benefits from these activities do not materialised. Much of the difficultly lies with the uncertainty faced during these projects - which is inherent in their development. It is well recognised that effective development and implementation of IS projects requires considerable planning. Quite often project management techniques are used to ensure the efficient and timely execution of a project. However, the deployment of human resources and scheduling of the project activities are not without uncertainty which leads to risks (Alter & Ginzberg, 1978).

Risks are an inevitable reality, however, attempting to recognise and manage them does not constitutes a futile exercise (McCarthy, 2001). According to Williams et al., (1999), the more one understands risk the better-equipped one is to manage it. According to Boehm, (1989) risks is: *"the probability of loss"*. Ensuing discussion, therefore, is primarily based on this simplistic definition of risks. There are two factors inextricably associated with risk, namely:

- the probability of failing to achieve a goal or a particular outcome; and
- the consequences of failing to achieve said outcome (Parry, 1999).

Many IS projects fail not because of technological or project management reasons but because of organisational pressures (McCarthy, 2001). Hence the importance of exploring and maintaining such strategic risk management framework and the relevance of incorporating this framework with the strategic management policy of the organisation is paramount for success. Besides the strategic focus particular attention needs to be paid to operational risks with continuous risk management thinking.

The application of risk management allows for continuous improvement in decision-making processes. The objective therefore is to provide new insights, thus empowering managers to make informed decisions. One of the key issues arising from the risk management process is risk assessment. This constitutes a number of phases, which are primarily the identification, analysis and prioritisation of such risks (Yeates & Cadle, 2007; Pate-Cornell, 2001; Kliem & Ludin, 2000).

Since risk investigation in KL in VREs is lacking, the focus of the chapter is on the identification and analysis of such risk factors. Thus from the stages in the risk management process only the risk identification and analysis phases is considered relevant in this discussion. Consequently, special consideration is given to risk identification techniques in IS so as to provide the underlining framework for classification. The risk identification process will focus on software risks since VREs falls under this generic heading with specific attention given KL risks.

4. The company

This research was initially triggered by a company which specialises in large-scale metrology, quality engineering, and aerospace. Company 3D specialise in alignment services and CAD drawings for its customers. Since then it has grown and now provides a wide range of services in all engineering disciplines including:

- Measurement Services
- Training
- Equipment Sales
- Systems integration.

One of the important areas of expertise is the creation of 3D models and 3D photographic databases of numerous artefacts which can be navigated in a PC environment using a variety of 3D viewing packages. These environments create authentic and detailed virtual models that are easily navigable and contain comprehensive and detailed information that can be easily queried by users or employees.

Central to the authoring tool is the photographic database created by using special surveying and photographic equipment. The environments produced are implemented using VRML, which the company use to produce realistic, accurate and visually matter-of-fact environments which are easily navigable by simple walk-through. Individual entities within the environment can also be linked to external sources using a number of interfaces such as Hypertext Mark-up Language (HTML). These environments are also easily and efficiently upgraded and revised to reflect innovations, changes, new data, explore other technologies, and archive reference information. One major reason for the popularity of these 3D model databases is based on the fact that traditionally database information is composed of text and figures. This makes such databases very complex and time consuming to use, as traditional searching facilities are less intuitive than browsing through natural representations of reality. Thus, these 3D models provide a more intuitive interface for a non-expert user to explore more readily (Annansingh & Nunes, 2005). The intuitive user interface allows a broad cross-section of company personnel, from low-level maintenance, to senior engineers to have access to whatever information is needed to populate the database. These environments are also easily accessible and can be navigated by even those with very limited training (Annansingh & Nunes, 2005). This is a dynamic environment which encourages creativity and risks taking.

5. Research methodology

IS research traditionally adopted a positivist approach. However, since the objective of this chapter is to:

- characterise and identify risks from the case study.
- use a questionnaire survey to validate and assess risks identified in the literature review and case study.

It was believed the perception and perspectives of participants would provide deeper understanding into issues surrounding the development of this software and associated risks, rather than a positivists' approach which prohibits such rich descriptions (Bharadwaj, 2004). Consequently, a constructivist rather than a positivist paradigm is adopted. The constructivist paradigm according to Denzin & Lincoln (1998: 27) "assumes a relativist ontology (there are multiple realities), a subjectivist epistemology, (knower and subject create understandings), and a naturalistic (in the natural world) set of methodological procedures". The interpretivist paradigm which falls under the general umbrella of social constructivism focuses on the understanding of the world as it is, as well as an understanding of the social world from the level of subjective experience. Burrell and Morgan (1985:28) claims that an interpretivist paradigm "seeks explanation within the realm of individual consciousness and subjectivity, within the frame of reference of the participant as opposed to the observer of the action". Based on these arguments and the need to extract the perceptions and perspectives of participants, an interpretivist stance seems appropriate.

From an ontological perspective, interpretivist researchers view the social world as extremely complex and problematic, where everyday life is an incredible achievement. The interpretivist researcher therefore seeks to interpret, understand, experience or produce the very basis and source of social reality (Burrell & Morgan, 1985; Mason 2002). Additionally this study is an exploratory case study research. The adoption of an interpretivist approach rather than positivist is selected on the basis that the validity of an extrapolation does not depend on the statistical representation of such case/s in a statistical sense but rather on the plausibility and clarity of the logical reasoning used in describing the results and drawing conclusions from the cases (Walsham, 1993).

5.1 Research design

The main function of the research design is to:

- conceptualise the operational plan to undertake the different procedures and tasks necessary for the execution of the research;
- ensure that the procedures are sufficient to obtain valid, objective and accurate answers to the research question (Kumar, 2011).

There are three main approaches to research. According to Creswell (2003), these are qualitative, quantitative and mixed method approach.

A mixed method approach is adopted with a dominant qualitative method and supporting quantitative method (QUAL - quan) (Creswell, 2003). One of the reasons for conducting a qualitative study is the research is exploratory and involves the use of a case study. In order to validate the results from this case study a cross sectional questionnaire survey is used. Thus, the study is theoretically driven by a qualitative case study research method with a complementary quantitative cross sectional survey (Tashakkori & Teddlie, 1998; Creswell 1994). Additionally, since not much has been written about the risk of KL resulting from VREs, obtaining both the perceptions and perspectives of various individuals as well as reaching a consensus within a population will assist with the generalisation of the findings. The mixed method procedure used to accomplish this is sequential as described by Creswell (2003). The underlying principle driving this research is the qualitative method as interviews provide the bulk of the information, in addition to the use of both open and closed ended questions in the questionnaires.

Having established the research paradigm, design and chosen methodology, the next logical step is to define the strategy necessary to achieve this goal. A number of IS taxonomy were examined, however none of these models were viewed as being singularly appropriate for this study. As such, an adaptation was done to Galliers (1992) IS taxonomy. Therefore, the rationale for the study consists of identifying the base-events that may trigger the risks, defining and characterising the risks, and finally proposing recommendations on how to minimise and remediate their occurrence.

This research develops and uses the practice-based IS research (PB-ISR) framework presented in Figure 1. This PB-ISR framework is particularly useful for projects where research questions emerge from real-life organisational processes and problems encountered in practice. Thus the formulation of the research question is inherently linked with practice rather than theory (Annansingh & Nunes, 2005).

5.1.1 Research question

Foreshadowed problems are the starting point of any research (Hammersley & Atkinson, 1994). In this study, the foreshadowed problem emerges from the unexpected fact, that using VREs may result in risks of KL.

In fact, despite the many advantages offered by VREs, their very nature poses risks exposure owing to the fact that the environments produced are intuitive, realistic, browsable and link to comprehensive specialised and technical databases. For Company 3D, the problem is particularly complex, since they produce these virtual environments on behalf of very specialised and high-tech companies, which in turn make these 3D models available both internally and externally to their customers. Thus the research question driving this project emerged from the increasing awareness by Company 3D, that these risks could become crucial in the success of their products and services.

5.1.2 Case study research

The use of case studies as a research tool has become increasingly important, as they are excellent at simplifying complex issues or objects and can draw on experience and/or add to the strength of information from other researchers (Soy, 1998). A case study strategy, can be used for either one of three purposes - exploratory, descriptive or exploratory (Yin, 2003; Walsham, 1993). A single exploratory case study was employed using Company 3D since it was considered typical of other SMEs involved with 3D models. Owing to this, a case-study research design was implemented based on the triangulation of methods presented.

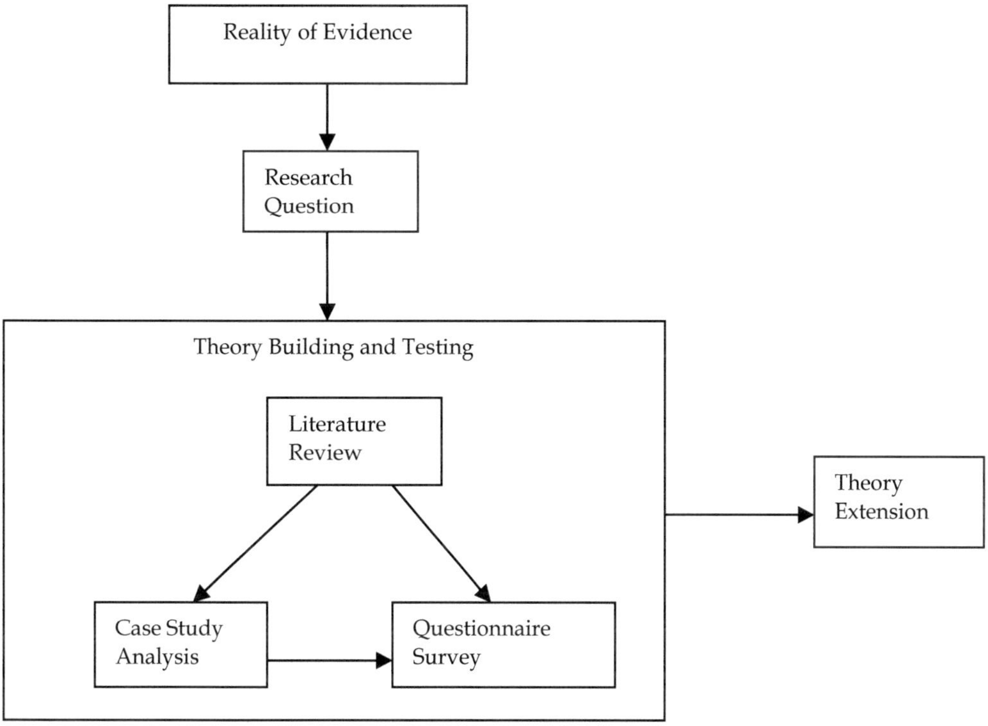

Fig. 1. The PB-ISR framework: a research framework to support Practice-based IS research questions (Annansingh & Nunes, 2005).

Nonetheless, risk analysis is inherently a causal and explanatory analysis which requires special attention to internal validity (Yin, 2003). This is essential whenever a study aims at establishing explanations and causal relations. Internal validity establishes that certain conditions lead to others and requires the use of multiple pieces of evidence from multiple sources to uncover convergent lines of inquiry. Therefore, throughout the study there was an on-going interaction between theory and the data collected. Concept maps were used to represent the data collected as they allow for the establishment of chains of evidence forward and backward. These concept maps allowed a comparative analysis between the results collected from the case study with the theoretical stance, as well as a constant re-interpretation of new findings and already accepted causal chains. Thus the data gained through exploratory interviews were based on the knowledge, experience and perspectives of the respondents. Consequently, a cross sectional survey of similar companies in the UK interacting with 3D models was considered appropriate in order to gain a more holistic understanding of the leakage risks (Annansingh & Nunes, 2005).

5.1.2.1 Interviews

Supported by risk typologies and conceptual understandings drawn from the literature review, initial exploratory interviews were undertaken with the Technical Director (TD), the Development Director (DD), Security and Database Administrator (SDA), Sales and Marketing Director (SMD), Lead Software Developer (LSD) and members of his team. These interviews allowed for an early identification and assessment of risks and were used to provide greater insight into KL risks with such systems.

5.1.2.1.1 Data analysis interviews

Data analysis of qualitative data begins with the identification of key themes and patterns (Coffey & Atkinson, 1996). Base on the interviews, initial data analysis was conducted via a question by question summary. Following this, open coding was used to identify, name, categorise and describe significant themes and issues found in the interview scripts. The codes emerged from actual terms used by the participants as well as those in existing theory and the literature (Saunders et al., 2009). Consequently, for open coding each sentence in the interview scripts were scrutinised in relation to risks identification and KL risks in VREs, this enabled the broadening of the research focus while keeping within the exploratory confines.

Further to the use of open coding, axial coding was used. Axial coding was used to identify the relationships between the categories of data that emerged from the open coding process. As the relationship between categories were identified they were rearranged based on a hierarchal system with sub-categories emerging (Saunders et al., 2009). Axial coding was used to determine the risks arising from each vulnerability as well as the consequences associated with the risks identified (Coffey & Atkinson, 1996). Here based on the key concepts and the associated risks, the properties or consequences of each were examined via a combination of inductive and deductive thinking.

From these categories, selective coding was used to group the different types of risks into key concepts around KL. Since selective coding was used to identify the main concepts from the sub-categories, a number of key concepts emerged (Saunders et al., 2009). Concepts were used as they provide useful mental images or perceptions. Since concepts are subjective impressions—their understandings may differ from person to person—which if measured would cause problems in comparing responses (Kumar, 2011). The decision to assign concepts to the data was done to facilitate data condensation, thus making it more manageable. A number of key concepts were identified from this set of data, namely: organisational KL risks, KL from the KM process and technological KL.

From these concepts, relevant phenomena and examples were identified and selected to support such occurrences. Here similarities and differences were identified with a number of emerging patterns and structures, thus facilitating a more diverse analytical scrutiny (Coffey & Atkinson, 1996). Based on the risks and key concepts identified from employing open, axial and selective coding, testing of these phenomena was done via the use of a questionnaire survey.

5.1.2.2 Questionnaires

Having completed the analysis and representation of the data from the interviews a cross sectional survey was sent to companies in the UK. This questionnaire survey was used as a validation tool, that is, it was conducted to validate the findings of the case-study by querying the industry sectors that are involved in the design, development and use of 3D virtual models. This approach was adopted as recommended in De Vaus (1996). The aim was to determine whether risks identified from the case study were a true representation of perceptions in the sector. Postal questionnaires were sent to SMEs and targeted a wide group within the organisation with different job functions. 300 companies were selected as matching the criteria of designing and developing 3D models, 40 however had ceased trading and 50 useable questionnaires were returned.

5.1.2.2.1 Data analysis questionnaire

The use of descriptive data analysis facilitates the exploration of key issues. Like the questionnaire in the case study, descriptive data analysis is used to analysed the data from the cross sectional survey. Descriptive data analysis provides simple summaries about the sample and the measures adopted. Together with simple graphic analysis, it forms the basis of quantitative data analysis. Both descriptive univariate and bivariate analysis were conducted and made use of percentages, frequencies, diagrams, cross tabulation and correlations (De Vaus, 2002).

6. Presentation and discussion of the findings

KL occurs via three main pathways: organisational KL, technological KL and from the KM Process. Based on each of these pathways a discussion now ensue which focuses on the different types of KL.

6.1 Organisational knowledge leakage

A firm's competitive advantage lies in its ability to prevent the loss of knowledge across the organisation's boundaries (Brown & Duguid 2000). KL occurs when the ideas develop in the originating company - where it is being used -- are leaked to the production line of its competitors. The combination of a virtual reality world with a precise description of construction and operational details has been identified as a possible knowledge exposure risk and a threat to internal KM. The use of VREs therefore is a fantastic tool for competitors and other unauthorised personnel to detect, understand and monitor events in the organisation. This is based on the fact that even though organisations have established formal and bounded structures of practice, informal and fluid networks are constantly evolving. Once instituted, these networks adopt an entirely different role from those formally established in the organisation. Thus as individuals in the organisation *"work collaboratively and vital interstitial communities are continually being formed and reformed"* (Brown & Duguid, 2000), knowledge is being disseminated and shared. The dissemination and sharing of this knowledge can result in KL. Quite often networks are formed and established outside the confines of the regular organisational structure and even outside its boundaries. Therefore, due to these processes and activities KL is not only occurring internally but also externally.

In addition, from the results several risks were identified as being particular to 3D models as well as those generic to IS projects. The fact that the creation of these environments is fairly new, highlights additional problems for developers, outside the regular software development problems, as development of this sort, can result in longer project cycles and a number of generic vulnerabilities which can lead to project and software risks that affected the quality and performance of the system. Thus it was expressed by developer's that customers would experience problems with the expected performance of the system especially with regards to the information retrieval and storage, real time responses, and database response, contentions or access. The probability of these problems occurring was seen as 'high'. This phenomenon was however, not surprising owing to the fact that the use of 3D models to produce VREs is constantly emerging. These applications are then navigated in a PC environment using a variety of 3D viewing packages. These environments create authentic and detailed virtual models of artefacts that are easily navigable and contain comprehensive information which are queried by users or employees at the click of the mouse (Nunes & Annansingh, 2003). Consequently, evidence indicates the following are most likely risks to occur thus leading to KL, theft; data readily interpreted, easy analysis of information; easy accessibility. In addition, due to the verisimilitude nature these environments make it difficult to monitor environmental changes which could lead to incorrect decision making. Owing to the fact that there is need for constant update users need to be aware that environments are based on supposition and that information easily is out-dated.

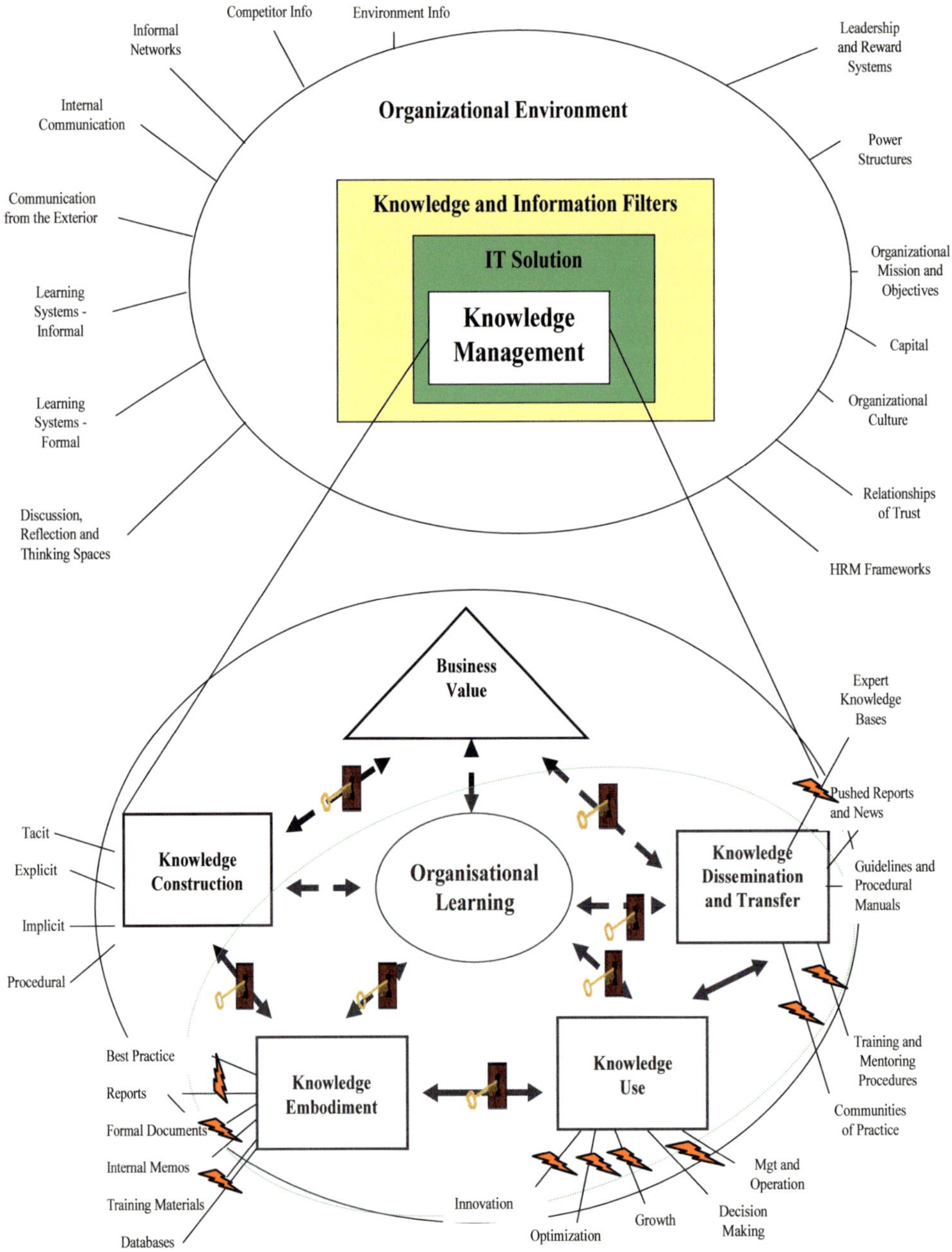

Fig. 2. The Knowledge Intensive KM (KIKoM) Model indicating areas of KL (Nunes et al., 2005)

6.2 Leakage from knowledge management process

The ease in which knowledge is transferred - that is leaky knowledge - will depend on whether it is tacit or explicit knowledge. Tacit knowledge is difficult to transfer while explicit knowledge leaves the organisation quite readily (Alavi, 2002). From the models of KM and as seen in Figure 2 (Nunes et al., 2005), one of the primary goals of KM is to share, transfer and disseminate explicit knowledge. The sharing of this knowledge however is sometimes done in an ad hoc manner and can result in KL. Like larger corporation, SMEs need appropriate and current knowledge in order to compete. However, SMEs tend to be more susceptible to problems of high staff turnover and knowledge retention than their larger counterpart. Thus, knowledge within these companies should be appropriately managed, disseminated and retained. Even though KM processes are onerous in terms of both direct and indirect costs, the consequences for a SME of not maintaining those processes can create vulnerabilities to KL and consequently losses in efficiency, productivity and competitiveness.

From the case study it was noted that while Company 3D encourage employees to obtain knowledge from external sources, the company lacked an explicit KM strategy to collate, share and disseminate this information once captured. Therefore, a lack of formal mechanisms existed for the identification and protection of strategic knowledge within the organisation. In addition, making this information available to the different employee's increased the probability of KL risks, as security mechanisms were quite often inadequate within the databases to prevent unauthorised access or systematic downloading of information.

Subsequently, whether these practices were typical of the industry was sought in the questionnaire. From which, it was seen that 41.2% indicated not having an explicit KM strategy, while 32.4% believed such a strategy did not exist. Nonetheless, a low indication of explicit KM strategy in these organisations was not surprising as the majority of participants were from SMEs. For which, studies have shown that SMEs in general, tend not to adopt or implement KM strategy or its principles (Nunes et al., 2005). Even though a number of these companies reported not having an explicit KM strategy, 81.2% had knowledge storage mechanisms in place. While these practices are recommended for the business continuity, integration and dissemination, the protection of this knowledge from KL - both internally and externally— should be considered strategically. The need for the risk and KL assessment cannot be over emphasised, since within any organisation not all knowledge can be or should be shared with all employees, thus it is necessary that employees be given information on a need to know basis. This knowledge should be protected by the organisation from external sources as in fact it is part of its intellectual property. Figure 2 highlights the areas of possible KL risks in organisations. The lightly shaded blue areas of the model indicate where in the KM process KL during activities such as: collaborations, narrations, group discussions and communities of practices. A key is used to symbolise where KL risks is most likely to occur between the different processes.

In addition, the red arrows highlight the areas where knowledge is being shared or transferred from one form to another, and represent the areas in the KM process where KL will most likely occur. Consequently, risk management and security measures should be adapted to prevent such loss. For those areas without a red arrow, this is not an indication for an absence of KL risks but rather that within these areas the probability of

KL occurring was seen as unlikely. From a KM perspective, Figure 2 provides a breakdown of the areas where holistic risk management should occur in the organisation. In addition, it supplies the reader with a simplistic view of the areas where KL risks will occur.

6.3 Technological knowledge leakage

With the various developments in the previous decade which has seen the reduction in the cost of computer technology and its easy availability, organisations are increasingly reliant upon the use of electronic media, more specifically electronic mail (email) for inter-organisational communication. In addition to email messaging, most organisations typically use a variety of communication technologies to send and receive information. This information is then processed and stored in a number of ways, one of which is through electronic database. The Internet and electronic databases in general, provide users with easy access to vast amounts of information which may not always be intended for general dissemination. This knowledge sometimes gets into the public domain, whether deliberately or unintentionally. Based on the rationale behind the development of this software system, which was for the representation of organisational information via the use of 3D models in a database, and since information in these databases is often interlinked, the system therefore becomes susceptible to attacks of theft, hacking and unauthorised access. Nonetheless, where the models were used for training and maintenance purposes, it was especially prone to attacks from unauthorised personnel, as some employees during training may have been given access to areas of the system which was previously prohibited. During maintenance and training the probability of KL risks occurring were identified as 'high' by the interviewees owing to the nature of the software. Therefore, it is possible for employees or any unauthorised personnel to steal or walk out with any of the organisation's assets including valuable information without being detected as this information has been internalised into tacit knowledge.

> *[]… VR model is a fantastic tool for competitors to see how the system is designed, or why a competitor is so efficient []" (LSD).*

As organisations grow more sophisticated systems have to be installed, thus increasing the challenges of managing communication and change. A number of organisations do not have formal approach to documentation thus it is difficult to pinpoint exactly where there are potential problems or how these problems may arise. However, without proper documentation the risk of failure and reduced efficiency increases when the organisations attempt to upgrade or implement a new system to meet new requirements. The simplistic answer to these problems is provided very bluntly by Frank (2002): "The easiest way to reduce knowledge loss is to avoid losing it in the first place". This is not a possibility in the majority of scenarios, as the acceptance, usefulness and even success of the product designs and solutions offered by an organisation depends to a large extent on the good and efficient training of the employees in the third party companies. Several risks which are indirectly related to the use of the models were also identified especially during maintenance. One of the main contributors of these risks was due to staffs' inexperience in carrying out these maintenance services.

The case study shows KL could be intentional or accidental. Thus, the concept of KL covers a number of risks management issues such as organisational and security risks. It was perceived by the interviewees that while internally it is possible to regulate KL, to some extent, through the use of employment contracts and confidentiality clause, there were unequivocal concern from alliances formed with suppliers and third party companies interacting with the system. In addition, KL resulting from employees was basically prevented by having:

"critical information held on read only files but in reality there is little to stop systematic downloading over a period of time"(LSD).

Even though, there are obvious technical awareness of the dangers of KL, from the case study there is no risk management strategy existing within the organisation to mitigate, control or prevent these risks. Therefore, it was generally perceived that little would be done to prevent KL, especially over time, and was consequently viewed as a secondary factor. Nonetheless, attempts to protect against intra-organisational leakage were made via the use of firewalls and password protected screensavers. This however, was seen as inadequate since the probability and impact of intra-organisational KL risk occurring was rated as 'medium'. This can result in an unprecedented number of unauthorised copies being made and distributed quite rapidly to unauthorised or unidentified recipients. It is also not uncommon that a lapse in procedures often results in an original document being carelessly left in some unprotected location where literally any unauthorised person can access it. Hence education and training of employees is necessary to prevent KL owing to carelessness, naïf acts and during informal discussions.

The cross sectional survey shows the 87.6% of respondents being also aware of KL, with 51.3% rating the probability of KL occurring as ranging from "medium" to "very high". 49.7% of these companies had precautionary measures to protect against internal and external KL. Consequently, the mechanisms in place to prevent internal KL shows most organisations opted for:

- rules for appropriate level of physical access; and
- the implementation of host based firewalls between segregated networks.

Since these companies had obviously implemented measures to prevent intra - organisational risks, the probability of KL risks occurring was rated by 54.5% as ranging from "medium" to "very high" with 45.4% rating the impact as "medium" and 20.6% as "high". Therefore the impact of KL on the organisation was rated higher than the probability of the risks occurring.

In addition to the measures used to protect it against KL risks - internally or externally - there were other factors which contributed to KL. One such factor is the loss of employees, thus it was important to obtain the perception of people within the industry. The results show a cumulative total of 74.7% either "agreeing" or "strongly agreeing" that loss of employees is one of the main causes of KL. However, not all companies took precautionary measures to retain knowledge in the organisation before employees leave, the justification provided were:

- Employees work in teams— no one person has all the knowledge it is share among the group;
- No formal measures have been established;
- Low staff turnover.

Regardless of the size of the organisation and the staff turnover rate, KL risks should be addressed and the relevant actions taken to prevent or mitigate its occurrence. A comparison of the size of the organisations with the security or risk management measures adopted to prevent KL, shows the size of the organisation had no influenced on either the risk management or security measure used. Although, a significant number (87.6%) of respondents claimed to be aware of the dangers of KL within the organisations there were no evidence of an explicit consideration for KL prevention. This again highlights a flaw within the risk management thinking of these organisations.

From the case study, concerns were raised about KL resulting from suppliers and third party companies, rather than employees, as it was believed that it is possible to regulate KL through the use of employment contracts and confidential statements. Thus, Company 3D took no action to formalise policies on KL or knowledge capture and acquisition even though the TD claimed.

"....this is a new development and we always run a risk when introducing new facilities".

Therefore, this and any new technology was seen as being associated with some degree of uncertainty.

The risk identified by respondents from the use of VREs as having the highest impact on the organisation was the loss of competitive advantage. This was regardless of the purpose for which the software was employed. Theft of proprietary information was not regarded as factor of major concern as the expected impact on the organisation was rated as 'medium'. In addition to the aforementioned risks, others were identified in the literature and case study which are also associated with the practice of delivering software across the Internet. Hence risks negotiations need to occur between all parties involved in the design, development and use of the VREs.

From a client's perspective one of the key questions emerging from this study is whether presenting the information in a VRE would result in greater risks implications for the organisations concerned. In addition, to being a valuable resource for competitors the use of VREs raises concerns regarding system updates. These concerns are based on the verisimilitude nature of such software. Since models for the system were done using photographs, in a dynamic environment changes will not be evident. This is particularly important, for example, for maintenance work and health and safety issues, where every detail is significant and will determine the difference between life and death.

7. Conclusions

In this study, particular attention was given to the embodiment, use, and dissemination of knowledge as a result of the employment of VREs. Knowledge embodiment and use in projects occurred during systems development and dissemination owing to the actual utilisation of the 3D models during business transactions and training activities. Since one of the primary goals of KM is to share, transfer and disseminate explicit knowledge the sharing of this knowledge if done in an ad hoc manner can result in KL. The results shows that even the best laid KM policy or framework can be source of KL due to the absence of an integrated risk management approach. In addition, the general nature of the KM models allows for KL, this weakness or discrepancy occurs where policies and practices do not merge.

Another reason for KL is the fact that KM models have failed to consider the protection of knowledge within the organisation and across it boundaries. Consequently the risk assessment process in any organisation cannot be reduced to the simple negotiation of risk between two f companies. As a result third party companies should be explicitly involved in the risk assessment process since the greater risks of exposure and leakage are related to such interactions.

It is recommended that once the risk assessment process is completed, risk thinking on knowledge exposure and leakage should not be abandoned. Knowledge exposure concerns should be part of the continuous risk management approach from the beginning of a project until the outcomes are realised. Knowledge leakage risks should be continually assessed and monitored and whenever needed contingency measures considered. This attitude towards this type of risk should influence technical and design decisions as well as provide insights on technical options, thus empowering managers to make informed decisions.

8. References

Alavi, M. (2002). Managing Organizational Knowledge, 31.03.03, Available from: http://www.pinnaflex.com/pdf/framing/CH02.pdf

Alter, S. & Ginzberg, M. (1978). Managing uncertainty in MIS Implementation. *Sloan Management Review*, Vol.20, No.1, (Fall 1978), pp.23-31, ISSN 1532-9194

Annansingh, F. & Nunes, JM. (2003). The Risks of Virtual Reality. *The Institute for the Management of Information Systems Journal*, Vol. 13, No.5, pp.17-20

Annansingh, F. & Baptista Nunes, JM. (2005). Validating Interpretivist Research: Using a Cross-Sectional Survey to Validate Case-Study Elicitation of Knowledge Leakage Risks Associated with the Use of Virtual Reality Models, *Proceedings of the 4th European Conference on Research Methodology for Business and Management Studies*, Université Paris Dauphine Paris, France, April 2005

Bharadwaj, SA. (2004). Integrating Positivist and Interpretive Approaches Ro Information Systems Research: A Lakatosian Model, In: *Emory University*, 04.02.05, Available from:
http://hsb.baylor.edu/ramsower/ais.ac.96/papers/bharadwa.htm

Boehm, BW. (1989). *Software Risk Management.* IEEE Computer Society Press, Washington

Brown, J.S. & Duguid, P. (2000). Knowledge and the Organization A Social- Practice Perspective, *Organization Science* Vol. 12, No. 2, (March/April 2000), pp. 198-213, ISSN 1047-7039

Burrell, G. & Morgan, G. (1985). *Sociological Paradigms and Organizational Analysis*, Gower ISBN 978-056-6051-49-4, Aldershot

Coffey, A., and Atkinson, P. (1996). *Making Sense of Qualitative Data: Complementary Research Strategies*, Sage, ISBN 978-080-3970-53-3, Thousand Oaks, CA

Coleman, D. (1999). Groupware: Collaboration and Knowledge Sharing, In: *Knowledge Management Handbook*, Liebowitz, J. pp. 12-1 12-15, CRC Press, ISBN 978-084-9302-38-1, London

Creswell, JW. (1994). *Research Design: Qualitative and Quantitative Approaches*, Sage, ISBN 978-080-3952-54-6, Thousand Oaks, CA

Creswell, JW. (2003). *Research Design: Qualitative, Quantitative, and Mixed Methods Approaches*, Sage, ISBN 978-076-1924-41-8, London

Davenport, TH. & Prusak, L. (1998). *Working Knowledge: How Organizations Manage What They Know*, Harvard Business School Press, ISBN 978-087-5846-55-2, Boston, MA

De Jarnett, L. (1996). Knowledge the latest thing. *Information Strategy The Executive Journal*, Vol.12, No. 2, (Winter 1996), pp. 3 –5, ISSN 0743-8613

Denzin, NK. & Lincoln, YS (Eds.). (1998). *The Landscape of Qualitative Research: Theories and Issues*, Sage, ISBN 978-076-1914-33-4, Thousand Oaks, CA

De Vaus, DA. (1996). *Surveys in Social Research,* UCL Press Limited, ISBN 978-185-7285-42-0, London

De Vaus, DA (2002). *Analyzing Social Science Data: 50 Key Problems in Data Analysis,* Sage, ISBN 978-076-1959-38-0, London

Frank, B. (2002). Five Tips to Reduce Knowledge Loss. *The Journal of the Knowledge and Innovation Management Professional Society (KMPro*), (December 2002), pp. 1-3

Galliers, R. (1992). *Information Systems Research: Issues, Methods and Practical Guidelines,* Blackwell Scientific, ISBN 978-063-2028-64-1, Oxford

Hammersley, M. & Atkinson, P. (1994). *Ethnography. Principles and Practice,* Routledge, ISBN 978-041-5086-64-6, London

Jones, B. & Miller, B. (2008). *Innovation Diffusion in the New Economy: The Tacit Component,* Routledge, Retrieved from: http://www.gbv.de/dms/zbw/585834733.pdf

Kliem, RL. & Ludin, IS. (2000). *Reducing Project Risk,* Gower, ISBN 978-056-6077-99-9, Hampshire

Kumar, R. (2011). *Research Methodology: A Step by Step Guide for Beginners* (3rd edition), Sage, ISBN 978-184-9203-00-5, London

Mason, J. (2002). *Qualitative Researching* (2nd edition), Sage, ISBN 978-076-1974-28-4, London

McCarthy, J. (2001). MS Solutions Framework: Risk Management Overview, In: *Microsoft Corporation*, 12.02.2002, Available from: http://www.microsoft.com/TechNet/

McInerney, CR & Koenig, MED. (2011). *Knowledge Management (KM) Processes in Organizations. Theoretical Foundations and Practice,* Morgan & Claypool, ISBN 159-829-9565

Nonaka, I. (1991). The Knowledge - Creating Company. *Harvard Business Review,* Vol. 69, (Nov-Dec 1991), pp. 96-104, ISSN 0017-8012

Nonaka, I. (1994). A Dynamic Theory of Organizational Knowledge Creation. *Organization Science,* Vol. 5, No. 1, (Feb 1994), pp. 14- 37, ISSN 1047-7039

Nonaka, I. & Konno, N. (1998). The Concept of Ba: Building a Foundation for Knowledge Creation. *California Management Review*, Vol. 40, No. 3, (Spring 1998), pp. 41- 53, ISSN 0008-1256

Nonaka, I & Takeuchi, H. (1995). *The Knowledge-creating Company: How Japanese Companies Create the Dynamics of Innovation*, Oxford University Press, ISBN 978-019-5092-69-1, New York

Nonaka, I. and Teece, D. (2001). *Managing Industrial Knowledge - Creation, Transfer and Utilization*, Sage, ISBN 978-076-1954-98-9, London

Nunes, MB.; Annansingh, F.; Eaglestone, B. &Wakefield, R. (2006). Knowledge Management Issues in Knowledge-intensive SMEs. *Journal of Documentation*, Vol. 62, No. 1, pp. 101-119, ISSN 0022-0418

Nunes, MB. & Annansingh, F. (2003). Knowledge Exposure due to Internet -Based Virtual Reality Training, *Proceedings of the IADIS International e-Society Conference*, Lisbon, Portugal, June 2003.

Parry, T. (1999). Generic Risk Management Plan, In: Defense Acquisition University, 04.11.2006, Available from: http://www.acq.osd.mil/io/se/risk_management/papers

Pate-Cornell, E. (2001). Risk Uncertainty Analysis in Government Safety Decisions, In: Stanford University, 23.11.2001, Available from: http://www.ce.nesu.edu/risk/

Polanyi, M. (1974). *Personal Knowledge: Towards a Post-critical Philosophy*, University of Chicago, ISBN 978-022-6672-88-5, Chicago

Pollard, D. (2003). The Future of Knowledge Management: Discussion Paper, 20.08.2006, Available from: http://blogs.salon.com/0002007/images/TheFutureofKnowledgeManagement.doc

Quintas, P.; Lefrere, P. & Jones, G. (1997). Knowledge Management: A Strategic Agenda. *Journal of Long Range Planning*, Vol. 30, No. 3, (June 1997), pp. 385-91, ISSN 0024-6301

Saunders, M.; Lewis, P. & Thornhill, A. (2009). *Research Methods for Business Students* (5th edition), Prentice Hall, ISBN 978-0273716860, London

Schultze, U. & Stabell, C. (2004). Knowing What You Don't Know: Discourses and Contradictions in Knowledge Management. *Journal of Management Studies*, Vol. 41, No. 4, (June 2004), pp. 549-573, ISSN 1467-6486

Soy, S. (1998). The Case Study as a Research Method, In: *University of Texas*, 12.03.2002, Available from: http://www.gslis.utexas.edu/%7Essoy/usesusers/l391d1b.htm

Srikantaiah, TK & Koenig, MED (eds.) (2000). *Knowledge Management for the Information Professional*. American Society for Information Science Medford, ISBN 978-157-3870-79-5, New Jersey

Tashakkori, A. & Teddlie, C. (1998). *Mixed Methodology: Combining Qualitative and Quantitative Approaches*. Sage, ISBN 978-076-1900-71-9, Thousand Oaks London

Walsham, G. (1993). *Interpreting Information Systems in Organizations*. John Wiley & Sons, ISBN 978-047-1938-14-9, Chichester

Wenger, E.; McDermott, R. & Snyder, WM. (2002). *Cultivating Communities of Practice: A Guide to Managing Knowledge -Seven Principles for Cultivating Communities of Practice*. Harvard Business Press, ISBN 978-157-8513-30-7, Cambridge

Williams, RC.; Pandelions, GJ. & Behrens, SG. (1999). Software Risk Evaluation (SRE) Method Description - Overview of Risk Management, In: *Carnegie Mellon University*, 04.11.2008, Available from: http://www.sei.cmu.edu/pub

Yeates, D. & Cadle, J. (eds.) (2007). *Project Management for Information Systems*, Pitman Publishing, ISBN 978-013-2068-58-1, London

Yin, RK. (2003). *Case Study Research: Design and Methods*, Sage, ISBN 978-076-1925-52-1, California

Zyngier, S.; Burstein, FV. & McKay, J. (2004). Knowledge Management Governance: A Multifaceted Approach to Organizational Decision and Innovation Support, *Proceedings of the 2004 IFIP International Conference on Decision Support Systems (DSS2004)*, Prato, Italy, July 2004,.

13

Knowledge Management Maturity Model in the Interpretativist Perspective

Edgar Serna M.
University of San Buenaventura Medellín
Medellín
Colombia

1. Introduction

Since the last years of the 20th century a strong social revolution has begun; it is a revolution based on information and knowledge, which is driven by the developments in informatics and communications technologies ICT. "*We are entering –or we have already entered– in the knowledge society, in which the basic economic resource … is the knowledge itself... and where the worker of knowledge will perform a central role*" (Drucker, 1993).
Emerging global economy progressively becomes more distinguished by intensive knowledge enterprises that need specialized workers, exhibiting knowledge that diversify and develop unique competences, and that get involved with the collaboration to create new knowledge for the improvement of the company performance. The ICT´s progresses perform an integrating role within these companies as a way for the achievement of the shared learning. These changes have resulted in the need for the improvement of knowledge management, which in turn leads to more changes in the same companies. Different authors (Hedlund, 1994; Nonaka & Takeuchi, 1995; Tenkasi & Boland, 1996; Schultze, 1998; Brown & Duguid, 1998) have proposed categorizations for the knowledge management –KM– approaches, being the most outstanding the *functionalist* and *interpretativist* approaches. In the functionalist approach, the knowledge is considered like an "*static object*" that exists in a number of ways and localizations; in the interpretativist approach, it is considered that knowledge does not exist being independent of human experience, social practice, the knowledge itself and its use, where it is shaped by the social practices of the communities, because it is "*active and dynamic*".
This work focuses in reviewing, analyzing and presenting a study about the interpretativist perspective, and describing a maturity model to turn operative the knowledge management based on it. The work begins with a discussion of the concept of knowledge management. Later, the current knowledge management perspectives are described; the functionalist and interpretativist. Finally we propose a maturity model to turn operative the knowledge management in the interpretativist perspective.

2. The knowledge

Knowledge definition. In the context of knowledge management this term can be defined in different ways in such a way that it reflects the different research perspectives. Most of the definitions belong to one of the following categories: 1) it can be defined by means of comparison or relation with data and information (Marshall, 1997; Burton-Jones, 1999; Kanter, 1999); and 2) it can be defined as knowledge *per se,* that is, without any direct relation with data and information (Nonaka & Takeuchi, 1995; OECD, 1996; Rennie, 1999; Davenport & Prusak, 2000).

In the first category it is considered as an entity which is located in an authority level higher than data and information (Stewart, 1997). Data is a set of discrete facts about events (Davenport & Prusak, 2000), while information is *"data provided of relevance and with a purpose"* (Drucker, 1988) that can be created by adding value to data through contextualization, categorization, calculation, correction and condensation (Davenport & Prusak, 2000). Therefore knowledge is described like *"information suitable to be processed"* (O'Dell et al., 1998; Tiwana, 2000), which provides *"the power to act and to take decisions that produces value"* (Kanter, 1999). On the one hand, however, in the real world, it is not always possible to distinguish among knowledge, information and data, because the differences between these terms are simply a matter of degree (Davenport & Prusak, 2000). On the other hand, in accordance with the importance of the knowledge and the knowledge base of individuals, that which is considered as information for some people is interpreted as knowledge by others and vice versa (Bhatt, 2001).

The second category presents the features of knowledge, quality and components, instead of contrasting it with information and data. Therefore, avoid the particular distinction between knowledge and information. An example within this category is Davenport & Prusak (2000), who define knowledge like *"a smoothly mixture with a backdrop which consists of experiences, values, context information and expert's visions, who provide a framework to evaluate and to incorporate new experiences and information"*. Apart from this, knowledge also is defined like a series of *know-what, know-how and know-who* (OECD, 1996; Rennie, 1999), a *"dynamic human process to justify the personal beliefs about truth"* (Nonaka & Takeuchi, 1995) and the result of learning process (Orange *et al.*, 2000).

Knowledge economy. To understand knowledge management is necessary to see the subject within the whole context of the big changes which occur in the global economic framework (Neef, 1999). It is argued that western society entered since the last part of the 20th century in a deep revolution, a second industrial revolution based on the information and does not on the energy, related with the development of the computational sciences (UNESCO, 2005). The economist Fritz Machlup (Checkland & Holwell, 1998) declares that already in 1960 there was an increasing proportion of knowledge workers, and coined in his discussions the sentences *"knowledge industries"*.

Marshall (2008), an ancestor of the neo-classic economy, was one of the first authors that recognized explicitly the importance of the knowledge in the economic issues: *"Capital is formed mostly by knowledge and organization … and knowledge is our more powerful production tool"*. However, like point out Nonaka & Takeuchi (1995), the neo-classic economists were concerned only about the usage of existent knowledge, not for the creation of new knowledge.

In 1993 Peter Drucker, talking about manufacture, services and information said: *"We are entering –or we have already entered- in the society of knowledge, in which the basic economic resource…is knowledge… and where the knowledge worker will perform a central role"*. The changes in the computing technology of middle 80's were the key for this change and, because of the exponential growing of computer science in speed, cost reduction and availability of applications, for the first time the companies were able to capture, to code and to spread in a fast way big amounts of information all over the world (Tapscott, 1997).

Because of that growth it was possible to redesign company processes, which modified the way in which worked the companies. Such "reengineering" of business processes provide a valuable profitability on investment, but in Europe and USA it had bad press because the changes, often, were too much for the company culture to manage it (Neef, 1999); this lead to Snowden (2000) to describe it like the *"last breath of the Tailorism"*. The fast increase of technology in the workplace requires new skills from employees, therefore the companies became aware that it was necessary the management of information and knowledge in different ways. This implies to help the employees to react before changes, to promote creativity and innovation, and to learn and to boost productivity (Neef, 1999). Companies need to turn into *"knowledge companies"*.

Davenport & Prusak (1998) suggest that companies having more than two hundred or three hundred employees are too big for people can have a comprehension of company collective knowledge, for this reason this becomes a need *"to know what is known"* (Sieloff, 1999). If knowledge turns into a valuable company asset, therefore it must be accessed, developed and used (Davenport & Prusak, 1998). Knowledge management started because of the wish to improve company knowledge; however, it occurred without a definition of this widely accepted. Nonaka & Takeuchi (1995) define the company-knowledge through its ability to adapt itself to the environmental changes by creating new knowledge, effective spreading and put into practice; the only task of a *"knowledge creating"* company is continuous innovation (Nonaka *et al.*, 2000; Nonaka, 2008).

Knowledge Managemente. Describing this term is usually difficult because there is little agreement about its definition (Neef, 1999; Bhatt, 2001). Raub & Ruling (2001) point out in their study that there is not a unique area accepted for the discourse in the academic or management-related literature. Many authors simply avoid the term, and prefer to focus on specific issues of the subject like knowledge, innovation or learning (Costello, 1996). Others argue that knowledge management is deeply related with concepts like company learning, company memory, information exchange and collaborative work (Schultze, 1998).

As we have seen, there is no consensus about a definition of knowledge management, and many authors avoid the epistemological discussion about its definition by comparing knowledge with information and data (Alavi & Leidner, 2001). A generalized opinion is that data consists of facts and raw numbers, that information are processed data and that knowledge is the authenticated information (Alavi & Leidner 2001). Through a review of the literature on knowledge management, Scarbrough *et al.* (1999) define knowledge management like *"any process or practice of creating, acquiring, capturing, sharing and using knowledge, wherever it lies, to improve the performance and learning of the companies"*. Hedlund (1994) suggests that knowledge management refers itself to the generation, representation, storage, transfer, transformation, application, insertion and protection of company's knowledge. Such definitions, apart from incorporate many aspects of the "process" around the knowledge management, implies an essentially objectivist vision of the subject. Even the vendors of technology emphasize more on the influence of technology in the knowledge management, for instance, the following definition of knowledge management was quoted in the web page of Microsoft (Brown & Duguid, 1998):

Knowledge management is the use of technology to make that information become important and accessible wherever is located. To perform this efficiently it is required the appropriated application of the proper technology for the specific situation. The knowledge management incorporates systematic processes to find, select, organize and present the information in such a way that it improves both the employee comprehension and the use of company's assets.

Others argue their own points of view about knowledge and point out that it also occupies itself of creating an environment and a culture in which knowledge can evolve (Davenport & Prusak 1998; Wenger, 1998; Wenger & Snyder, 2000). For example, already in 1996 Davenport et al. criticize the technologies approaches for KM:
The emphasis of encoding in the KM literature probably reflects the predominance of the vision of information systems: many articles have been focused on the development and implementation of the KM databases, of tools -for example, decision supporting tools- and techniques despite the recognition, now very wide, that most spectacular improvements in the KM capacity in the next ten year will be in the human and managing issues.
The lack of a rigorous definition and the aggressive promotion of technologists, has lead many people to point out that knowledge management is a fashion-like subject. Although the subject clearly exhibits the features of a fashion issue (Davenport & Grover, 2001), and even can be analyzed from the fashion perspective (Raub & Ruling, 2001), the consultancy firm TFPL (1999) considers that is probable that concepts and values of the knowledge management practice are deeply-rooted in the basic managing processes of the companies.
Knowledge management models. Because of the divergence of points of view, opinions and ideas having the general motto of the knowledge management, it is necessary to identify a set of structures that allow that subjects make sense, a challenge that have been assumed by different researchers. An example, frequently cited, is that of Earl (2001), who proposes seven strategic schools for knowledge management, as can be seen in Table 1.

TECHNOCRATICS			ECONOMICS	BEHAVIOURAL		
Systems	**Cartographic**	**Engineering-based**	**Commercial**	**Company-Related**	**Spatial**	**Strategical**
Technology	Maps	Processes	Incomes	Networks	Space	Mentality
Bases	Directories	Flows	Goods	Agreements	Interchang	Abilities
Coding	Conectivity	Capacity	Marketing	Collaboration	Interconexión	Inventiveness

Table 1. Schools of Knowledge Management by Earl (2001)

These schools identify the types of strategies that use the companies for knowledge management, and Earl categorizes them in three large types: Technocratic, Economical and Behavioral. The approach of Technocratic ones is to manage the knowledge through the information or management of the technologies that support and condition the employees in their daily tasks; the Economical ones explicitly have the goal of produce incomes by exploiting knowledge like an asset; the approach of the Behavioral ones is to manage the knowledge from a behavior-based perspective, in which they manage and encourage to directors and managers for creating, sharing and proactively using the knowledge resources (Earl, 2001).
While these schools provide a useful classification of specific approaches, mainly in the issues related to how is used technology within a knowledge management initiative, it is considered that they do not achieve the emphasis of the epistemological base of the strategies of knowledge management, particularly because they do not efficiently classify the social aspects. Earl's social interaction model only is fully applied in the spatial school, which is centered in using the space the exchange of knowledge, like a chat in which is discussed about how to cool the water, o when builds are designed for knowledge exchange (Schultze & Boland, 2000; Ward & Holtham, 2000). However, many authors think that

knowledge social interaction is more complex than this (McAdam & McCreedy, 1999-a; Nonaka*et al.*, 2000; Von-Krogh*et al.*, 2000).
McAdam & McCreedy (1999; 1999-a) provide an alternative structure for the comprehension of knowledge management and they propose three model categories for it: 1) the intellectual capital, in which the knowledge is like a material good; 2) the knowledge category models, in which the knowledge is identified by categories; and 3) the social constructivism models, in which knowledge is intrinsically tied to the learning and social processes.
Knowledge management usually treats on systematize, organize and use the knowledge inside a company for transforming it and storing it with the objective of improving the performance (KPMG, 1998); additionally, exists, as we have already pointed out, a big number of available definition for KM, all of these trying to encapsulate what it is and how it must be done (Quintas *et al.*, 1997; O'Leary, 2001; Diakoulakis*et al.*, 2004; Nicolas, 2004), but until now, there is no consensus.

2.1 Tacit and explicit knowledge

The following is an "official" definition of its differentiation:
On the one hand tacit knowledge is personal, context-specific and for this reason it is difficult to formalize and to communicate. The explicit knowledge is "codified", on the other hand, has to do with knowledge that can be transmitted in a formal and systematic language...Therefore, scientific objectivity is not the only source of knowledge. Much of our knowledge is the result of our determined effort to relate ourselves with the world... (Nonaka & Takeuchi, 1995, pp. 59-60).
The explicit knowledge requires being not subjective and can lie on databases, written reports, among others. In addition to this tacit knowledge subdivides itself in two categories not fully different:
Tacit knowledge includes cognitive and technical elements... mental models, cognitive elements, like schemes, paradigms, perspectives, beliefs and points of view, which help individuals to perceive and define its world. Opposite to that, knowledge technical elements include concrete know-how, jobs and abilities. This is important because cognitive elements of tacit knowledge are referred to single pictures of reality and to visions for the future; this is "what it is" and "what should be" (Nonaka & Takeuchi, 1995, p. 60).
It is important take notice that technical skills are mainly body-related skills.

3. Perspectives of knowledge management

Applying the Burrel & Morgan framework (1979) in a social and company-related research, Schultze (1998) identified four research paradigms in KM: radical humanism, radical structuralism, interpretativism and functionalism, as it is showed in the Table 2.
Among these paradigms exist a continuity between the subjective and objective perspectives: from the objective's point of view, knowledge is considered as an object awaiting to be discovered, that can exist in a number of forms –tacit or explicit–, and in a number of places -individual, group or organization (Schultze, 1998)-; from subjective point of view it is pointed out that knowledge emerge through a continuous elaboration, it is determined by social practices of communities, and cannot be located in an specific place because it cannot exist independently of human experience and social practices of knowing (Schultze, 1998).

According to these paradigms, functionalism prevails on KM current research, that frequently contrast with the interpretativism, because exist a lack *"of structuralist perspectives or humanists in the research on knowledge management"* (Jashapara, 2004). Probably the weight of both perspectives can be affected by its incapability to accept post-structural theories (Schultze, 1998), for this reason they must be mixed in a *"critical perspective"* to accept them (Schultze, 1998; Venters, 2002).

	The sociology of change		
Subjectivism	**Radical Humanism** ▪ Knowledge as social practice of knowing ▪ The value of knowledge and work is refuted, and it becomes a source of conflict	**Radical Structuralism** ▪ Knowledge as an object that can exist independently of human actions and perceptions ▪ The value of knowledge and work is refuted, and it becomes a source of conflict	**Objectivism**
	Interpretativism ▪ Knowledge as social practice of knowing ▪ There is a consensus about the value of knowledge and work	**Functionalism** ▪ Knowledge as an object that can exist independently of human actions and perceptions ▪ There is a consensus about the value of knowledge and work	
	Sociology of regulation		

Table 2. The four paradigms in the KM research (Schultze, 1998)

Schultze applies a framework developed by Burrell & Morgan (1979), with the objective of locating the theories of knowledge management. In the application of this framework the following perspectives are identified.

3.1 The functionalist perspective

Knowledge exists as an objective representation of the world that is waiting for being discovered by a human agent. Schultze (1998) argues that this approach, that can be found in Hedlund (1994) and in Nonaka & Takeuchi (1995), represents an objectivist perspective of knowledge because it considers that it exist in different ways and places. Besides inheriting the features of the objectivist perspective, the functionalist approach is highly scientific, it uses quantification methods, coding and of structure to make the most of knowledge, and depends the most of technology and of the *"activities managed by the databases"* to achieve their objectives (Venters, 2002).

In the last decade, relatively, there has been an explosion of literature on the knowledge management field. Almost all of this literature is managerialist and is supported on the belief that competitive advantages can be derived from knowledge exploitation –both for companies and countries– in the developed countries. A typical argument is:

The widely forecasted "information society" and "knowledge economy" are emerging like concrete "facts. The main theoretical researchers on management point out that is much more profitable for a company to invest a certain amount on its knowledge assets instead of investing the same amount of money on material goods (Probst *et al.*, 2000, p. 3).

The challenge is for both; creating new knowledge and exploiting the previous one –inside a company– in a more aggressive way being different to the way it has been until now. The work of Nonaka & Takeuchi (1995) have one of the seminal accounts of these processes, and offer prescriptions –for the managers of foreign companies–, related to how creating and exploiting knowledge. They argue that, with the goal of persist; the companies must continuously offer new products and competitive services.

Many years of research in Japanese companies -and other western companies- convince us that knowledge creation has been the most important source of their international competitiveness (Nonaka & Takeuchi, 1995, p. viii).

In view of the fact that market is conceived like dynamic, it is inferred that constantly it is needed new knowledge to support the existence of a company.

We called knowledge creation as the ability of a company, as a whole, for creating new knowledge, spread it out, and incorporate it in products, services and systems… The objective of this study is formalizing a general model of the creation of company knowledge (Nonaka & Takeuchi, 1995, pp. vii-ix).

This approach –and many others in the field of knowledge management– hypothesize and, undoubtedly encourage, a desire without precedents for the knowledge in the company. As Orlikowski (2002) points out, this has little to do with a –picturesque- desire based in the curiosity for knowledge. The knowledge management literature is focused in the needs of the competitive companies - or maybe in their stockholders–:

The comprehension that knowledge is the new competitiveness resource, has affected like a thunder to the West world. But all this talks about the importance of knowledge-for companies and countries-make little contribution to understand how is created the knowledge (Nonaka & Takeuchi, 1995, p. 7).

Philosophically this is significant. The current epistemology is in a big extent a regulatory activity; most of philosophers have occupied themselves of the issue of how to assess the demand of knowledge, and they have abandoned at a great extent the generative issues. The knowledge management literature emphasizes on the generative aspects and let uncovered a big part of regulatory aspects -in fact, the consequence is that these problems have been solved. Sometimes, one has the secure impression that while useful things are produced, the debates about its trustiness are limited to the scholasticism.

There are deep implications of this point of view, but the complimentary discussions are out of the scope of this work. At a certain extent, it can be pointed out, from a critic perspective; Lyotard (1984) established these arguments in the 70's. A key argument of Nonaka & Takeuchi (1995) is that knowledge is divided in different categories; the main difference is that the authors indicate is that of tacit and explicit knowledge.

3.1.1 Lyotard's performativity principle

Lyotard (1984) was one of the first persons in associate, in a systemic way; the production of knowledge to the economic wellness and, at a certain extent, the knowledge management literature is a kind of "non-rigorous" extension of this thesis:

Cannot be denied the current predominant existence of techno-science, which is the massive subordination of cognitive declarations to the finality of the best possible performance, which is the technologic criterion. But mechanics and industrial, especially when entering fields traditionally reserved for the artists, carry with them much more power effects. The objects and thoughts originated in scientific knowledge and capitalist economy transmit one of the rules that support their possibility: the rule that there is no reality if it is not verified by a consensus among the partners between a concrete knowledge and concrete compromises. This rule is not of little consequence it is the footprint made over the policies of the scientists and the capital manager through a kind of scape from reality based on the metaphysic facts, religious and politics that the mind thinks that supported it. This escape is absolutely necessary for the arousal of science and capitalism (Lyotard, 1984, pp. 76-77).

However, like has been already mentioned, Nonaka & Takeuchi establish a difference between the tacit and explicit knowledge; from which, […] the most important type of knowledge is the tacit knowledge (Nonaka & Takeuchi, 1995, p. viii).

Curiously, if Nonaka & Takeuchi seriously considered - and the management literature seems to make it- therefore, for critic purposes, the tacit knowledge is where must be focused the attention. However, a big part of the Lyotard's argument it is referred to, more or less completely, explicit knowledge; the tacit knowledge do not consider it predominantly textual. Consequently, in this context, the critic solution for the problems of the performativity principles proposed by Lyotard, would not be sustainable anymore:

Finally we are in position of understand how the computerization of the society affects this problems. Could be become in the "dreamed" instrument for controlling and regulating the market system, extended to include own knowledge and ruled exclusively for the performativity principle…But also might help to the groups…, to provide them with information of what generally lack for taking decisions. The line to follow for the computerization when taking the second of these roads is, at the beginning, quite simple: to allow the public free access to the memory and to the data banks. The language games could be information games perfect at any specific moment (Lyotard, 1984, p.67).

A critic theory on the diffusion of tacit knowledge must take an approach very different. Apart from this, Lyotard has little to say about active management of knowledge process creation in a place like a competitive company.

3.1.2 The process of creation of dynamic knowledge

Which specific interventions are involved in the creation of knowledge in the literature of knowledge management? An answer could be arrogant because exist so many answers to this short question, ¡as books on knowledge management! Nonaka & Takeuchi (1995) reach some conclusions to explain their theoretical and pragmatic suppositions, and help to provide guidance about the questions with which must be managed. To start, we could ask ourselves, ¿how can totally be created the knowledge? Of course, is of enough common sense to point out that the creation of knowledge it is not "by casualty", but also seems of enough common sense to point out that knowledge generally is discovered instead of be generated. The key point here is to point out that the use of the term "created" involves an active process; in fact, different dynamic processes are adopted:

In our theory of company knowledge creation we adopt the traditional definition of knowledge like "true belief justified". It is important to notice, however, that if it is true that western epistemology has been centered like the essential attribute of knowledge, we remark the nature of knowledge as "justified belief"… While traditional epistemology emphasize on the absolute feature, static, and non-human of knowledge, typically expressed in propositions and formal logic, we consider knowledge as a dynamic human process for justifying the personal belief towards "truth" (Nonaka & Takeuchi, 1995, p. 58).

Truth is, very probably with quotation marks, because the justification for the generated "thing" must be based in the future: in the acceptance of the consumer of the products or services, produced like the result of "knowledge" generated in the competitive market- instead of be generated in a direct evidence of truthfulness. In a sense, this is perhaps the final conclusion of the justification argument for perfomativity presented by Lyotard (1984).

The different issue is that the exploitation –or liberation– of explicit knowledge, do not is enough, or even important. Apart from that, the involved processes in the active management of the process of dynamic knowledge creation –for example, knowledge management– have escaped themselves in a big extent of the critic attention until now. To critically analyze the tacit dimension, other approaches can give important trails, like the analysis of the pastoral power of Foucault as far it provide the beginning of a genealogic approach for the analysis of the relationships power/knowledge, intrinsic in the typical contemporary descriptions –and the prescriptions– of knowledge management –tacit– in the competitive companies.

3.1.3 The pastoral power and the knowledge management in Foucault

Foucault characterize this way of power in this way:

This way of power it is applied itself to the daily life that categorize the individual, it mark him by his own individuality, gives himself his own identity, it imposes him a truth law which must be recognized and that other people must recognize in him. It is a way of power that make individual subjects … The modern western State has integrated, in a new politic way, an old technique of power that was originated in the Christian institutions. We can call this technique of power that was originated in the Christian institutions. We can call this technique pastoral power… This way of power does not can be exerted without knowing the inside of people's mind, without exploring their soul, without making them reveal their most deep secrets. This implies knowledge of the conscience, and the ability for detecting it (Foucault, 1982, pp. 212-214).

One of the main techniques of the pastoral power was the religious confession, vital to obtain a deep knowledge of the subjects: their intentions, aspirations, secrets … The original objective of the pastoral power –and its confessional technologies associated– was the religious salvation. Of course, in the lay western societies, mainly, the religious salvation can had lost their traditional meaning, however Foucault points out that the pastoral power, like a way of power, still prevails, but in other ways:

We can see a change in its objective. This is not anymore a matter of people led to their salvation in the other world, but instead of that it has to do with guarantee it in this that world. And, in this context, the world salvation has different meanings: health, wellness-that is enough wealth, life status- security, protection against accidents. A set of "worldly" objectives pretends to occupy the place of the religious aims of the traditional pastoral… (Foucault, 1982, p. 215).

The origin of the legitimization of the active management of knowledge creation processes is in the calling to the secular salvation. Additionally, it is about processes that transcend the normal limits of the management, conceived as an aspect of the traditional relationships capital-work. Foucault traces the genealogy of this conception back to the old Hebrew, Greek and Roman civilizations. A key concept in the indicated topics is that the pastor:

I only want to show some typical topics of the pastoral power…The pastor call together, guides and lead his flock…that pastor call together are dispersed individuals. They come together when heard his voice: "I whistle and they congregate themselves"…In other words, the immediate presence of the pastor and the direct action make that the flock exist… the act of watching them is important. Become evident two aspects of the pastor devotion: in first place, he acts, works, exercises, for those who he fed and that are asleep; in the second place, that takes care of them, he pay attention to all and watch for everyone. He has to know their flock as a whole and in detailed way. Apart from knowing where are the good pastures, the current laws and the order of the things, but he must know the particular needs of each of them...The power of the pastor implies to pay attention to each member of the herd (Foucault, 1982a, pp. 61-63).

The CEO's of the knowledge creation companies - in theory - express many of these features, because their role is to take advantage from both tacit and explicit knowledge, generated in the lower levels of the company, to obtain competitive advantages:

The basic function of knowledge agents, who are the company's CEOs, is the management of the whole creation process at company level...The officials of knowledge must be aware that their aspirations and ideals determine the quality of the knowledge that the company creates. It is a fact that the senior manager's ideals are important, they by themselves are not enough; they must promote a high degree of personal commitment for other members of the knowledge creation team. For that, is preferable an open and erroneous view, that is sensitive to a number of interpretations. A more erroneous view allows team members of the same company the freedom and autonomy to establish their own goals, creating on them more compromise to ascertain which really means the management ideals (Nonaka & Takeuchi, 1995, pp. 156-157).

The management of knowledge creation cannot be achieved by using the old technique of disciplinary/hierarchical management. Managing the "herd" of potential creators of knowledge involves a considerable number of classic foucaultian power/knowledge topics, particularly "subjectivation" –ways in which persons become themselves in subjects–, that was explained by Rabinow:

The third mode of Foucault's objectivation represents his more original contribution. We are going to call it "subjectivation". The process is systematically different from the other two modes...The dividing practices, roughly speaking, are domination techniques...The interaction between these domination modes and the diverse social scientific ways of classification, despite of the new clarity and the power given by Foucault in his analysis and historic studies, has been recognized by other thinkers...On the contrary, in the third mode, the "subjectivation", Foucault analyzes processes of self-education in which the person is immerse (Rabinov, 1984, pp. 10-11).

The creation process of tacit knowledge requires than the actors be dynamic self-educated to produce their own tacit knowledge, which can be transmitted, by different methods, to other company members for their commercial exploitation.

Let's begin with the ontological dimension. Strictly speaking, the knowledge is created only by individuals. A company cannot create knowledge without individuals. The company support individuals' creativity or provides the contexts for them can create knowledge (Nonaka & Takeuchi, 1995, p. 59).

However, to exploit such knowledge it will be necessary put it available for others in the company.

The explanation of how Japanese companies create new knowledge is limited to the conversion of tacit knowledge into explicit knowledge. To have an idea or personal premonition is a low-value issue for the company, unless that which is isolated can be converted into explicit knowledge (Nonaka & Takeuchi, 1995, p. 11).

The employee must accept to perform the self-education activities in different ways, both physical and cognitive, because tacit knowledge can be created in the two ways. This is essentially the subjectivation process identified by Foucault,

This self-education…it is carried out through different operation on the self-body of the persons, in their own souls, in their own behavior (Rabinov, 1984, p.11).

A part of the behavioral management requirements will be the "pastoral" function of turning isolated tacit knowledge into socialized explicit knowledge.

3.1.4 Knowledge creation processes

Nonaka & Takeuchi (1995) provide four models of knowledge "conversion":

- *From tacit to tacit.* The described process for this conversion is the "socialization", because tacit knowledge is acquired through experience and is possible to transmit it to other people; personal education is as important as anything in this cognitive process. This education occurs at a big extent by own initiative, and requires proper arrangements and pastoral incentives. It is important to point out that, in theory, the disciplinary procedures have no role, or very little, in this process.
- *From tacit to explicit.* The described process for this conversion is called "externalization", and essentially consists in textually describing, at a big extent, the personal knowledge; although not always it will be possible to express directly this knowledge in prose or charts,

When we cannot find an expression for an image by deductive or inducement analytic methods, we have to use a non-analytic method. Therefore the externalization is, often led by metaphors and/or analogies (Nonaka & Takeuchi, 1995, p.65).

However, for this to be useful, this knowledge must be codified in a very precise language. It can be a considerable margin to encourage the critic research referred to this mode of speech.

- *From explicit to explicit.* This process describe like "combination", in which any cognitive learning, mainly coming text sources -for example, databases-, falls under the paraph of "combination". It is interesting the -politics- pretext from Lyotard (1984) of "giving to the audience free access to the memory and databanks", because, it has been considered within the borders of the knowledge creating company. Discussing about the Kao company –in Japan–, Nonaka & Takeuchi point out the following:

For granting "the free access to the information", computer systems has been introduced in all Kao company, with all the information filed in a database. Through this system, any person in Kao can access the databases included in the sales information systems, marketing, production, distribution, and the complete information network that includes all its offices in Japan. The unique feature of this system is that any member, without being of importance their job or the section that it belongs to within the company system, has full access to the database -except a limited amount of personal information. In other words, any person can access the rich explicit knowledge base that exists within the company system by this "free access to the information system" (Nonaka & Takeuchi, 1995, p. 172).

In certain way, surprisingly, the risk is perceived like a result of this politic, which indicates a considerable difference between this approach, where security and the "need of knowing" problems is essential, and the old "disciplinary" approaches for managing.

- *From explicit to tacit.* The described process for this conversion is the "internalization", something that is difficult to describe. Nonaka & Takeuchi (1995) suggest "learning-by-doing" (p. 69-70). Once again the person is the center, because he learns to express formally in writings. The explicit operations in the person are the essential thing here, as is showed in:

An internalization example trough "learning-by-doing" can be seen in Matsushita, when he implemented a policy in all the company to reduce the working day to 1800 hours in 1993...The objective of the policy was not to reduce costs, but innovating the way of thinking and managing by reducing working day, and to increase person's creativity. Many departments were confused about how to implement that policy, that was clearly communicated like explicit knowledge...It was indicated to all the departments that it must experiment with the policy of 150 work hours during a month. Through an own experience the employees have to learn how it would be to work 1800 hours a year. An explicit concept, to reduce the work time to 1800 hours, was internalized through one-month experience (Nonaka & Takeuchi, 1995, p. 70).

In this way, the written prescriptions were internalized like person's processes and activities. These four knowledge conversion modes explicitly involve operations on all the body and the mind. The adjustments in which they must occur hardly seem to be "disciplinary" companies of the past; however, there are strong traits that should be occurring subjectivation processes.

3.2 The interpretativist perspective

The knowledge cannot be located in a specific place because it has not independent existence of human experience and social practices (Schultze, 1998). Schultze argues that this approach, that can be observed in authors like Tenkasi & Boland (1996) and Brown & Duguid (1998), represent a perspective more subjective or intersubjective, because it considers that knowledge is generated continuously through social practice of communities. This approach inherits the features of the subjectivist perspective and is centered in supporting the social processes and structures in which is shared knowledge, and does not consider technology as a solution by itself, instead of that it considers it a support to the social activity of knowledge exchange (Venters, 2002). The features of the problem of the research problem in KM suggest adopting the interpretativist perspective. As Walsham (1995) points out, the interpretativist methods suppose that knowledge of reality is a social construction of human agents. To understand the KM problems inside a company and try to solve them, are processes strongly based on the opinions of the participants in the company.

For this perspective the functionalism, based on the empiricist and rationalist approach, can be pertinent to know about the rational world, but they do not consider the role of the individuals as part of knowledge in social world. This is based on Immanuel Kant's studies, in which is accepted that the mind it is not a passive *tabula rasa* or a blank leaf, but that actively participates in the organization of the sensorial experiences; the argument is that the direct knowledge of things by themselves –which Kant call "*noumena*"– is impossible. The *noumena* are not knowledge by themselves, but the understanding of that is achieved through the application of our a priori knowledge for creating cognitive phenomena to ourselves (Johnson & Duberley, 2000). The point of view here is that human knowledge is achieved through experience and that is "*intrinsically undetermined*" (Tsoukas, 1996; Davenport & Prusak, 1998).

This point of view also considers the work of Karl Marx –accepting that it is centered on the action instead of being centered on knowledge-, who observe the perception as an interaction between the cognoscente subject -subject- and that known -object-; and, particularly in which the truth is demonstrated in practice, which provides a tie between knowledge creation and action (Russel, 1967). Do not considers that knowledge exist *a priori* awaiting to be acquired, through experimentation or by thought; instead of that, these approaches point out that it is required an interaction between the ego and the external world; which is evident in the Edmunf Husserl work about phenomenology and, particularly, that of Martin Heidegger (Inwood, 2002). These perspectives point out that even the simplest learning consists of a complex social process; the individuals interpret the world and learn from it through these forms of social interaction (Daft & Weick, 1984).

The interpretativist perspective emphasize on the action inside practice. "*Work practice ... seems to be essential to understand the identity and knowledge acquisition when working*" (Brown & Duguid, 2001), and the meaning is created through action within a specific social context (Cook & Brown, 1999). A particular interpretativist KM model emphasize on the construction of knowledge, inside company, through an exchange social process in which knowledge is consecrated within their own company structures (Demarest, 1997). Once it has been incorpored to the organization, the knowledge it is disseminated through social processes (Demarest, 1997; McAdams & Mc Creedy, 1999, 1999a). This fact of emerging is a similar practice to the interpretativist work about KM of Orlikowski (2002), who presents knowledge as "*emergent from actions located and occurring that company members commit themselves to perform*". Orlikowski suggest that knowledge is promulgated every day and each practice of persons, which suggest that the debate about knowledge must be intrinsically related to practice. In his work, the emphasis on practice indicates that knowledge must be seen like "*in a particular moment, that which have been made by practice*" with knowledge, and the practice must be considered like mutually constitutive.

This entire works suggest that an interpretativist approach for the management of knowledge must consider knowledge like an active object, because is like embedded in recurrent human practices (Venters et al, 2002). Transference of knowledge from one place to other does not mean that knowledge be an object that become mobile when is transmitted, codified or is offered like a basic service. On the contrary, knowledge becomes mobile like a product embedded permanently in all human activity within a social context (Venters *et al.*, 2002).

When using an interpretativist approach is emphasized in the social nature of the creation of knowledge, which leads to approaches for its management that are centered on human interaction instead of being centered on information. Knowledge is considered like a continuous achievement (Kogut & Zander, 1996), and a process rather than an object (Spender, 1996). These approaches consider, within the KM interpretativist approaches, concepts like "sense construction" and "practice community", because they are centered in social practices of creation and application of knowledge. Also is introduced the concept of "*thought on the action*", aimed to conceptualize the creation of knowledge by thought on practice. Apart from that, they consider the communication role in KM through the concept of a company's dialogue.

3.2.1 KM Maturity model in the interpretativist perspective

The maturity models proposed from this perspective are of evolutionary nature, this is, consist of a number of stages in which the complexity level is increased from one to another searching for perfection; additionally, are considered like strengthen models that have operational conditions to satisfactorily maximize the changes in the companies. The maturity models, particularly these of evolutionary nature, are characterized by the presence of multiple optimal stages that normally refer to the development stages in the maturity model.

A proposal of this kind of models (Desouza, 2006) consists of five levels or stages to evaluate the efforts of the company in KM, whose maturity can be described in a progressive scale: predisposed, reactive, appreciative, organized and optimized. The four components of knowledge management that are assigned to the maturity scale are: sources, analytics, significant and action, This model is similar to that proposed in other disciplines, and the control of its cognitive dimension of learning is based on Bloom's taxonomy (1956), whose points of view provide a valuable way of consider the semiotic for the study of KM.

This taxonomy uses value systems to control the personal behavior: penetrating, consistent and foreseeable; for which the proposed model basis starts from the affective and psychomotor dimensions of such taxonomy. The first is the way how humans share their feelings, values, opinions, enthusiasm, motivations and attitudes, as can be seen in Table 3; while the second one provide a point of view in which are not seen diverse objectives of learning but hierarchical levels, as described in Table 4.

These spheres provide a good point of view to study the maturity practice of the knowledge management in companies. The work of knowledge management, specially the maturity analysis of KM, can be beneficiated of the perspective proposed by Bloom in the affective and psychomotor spheres.

Reception	The individuals pay attention in passive way; they have the skill for listening and receiving emotional phenomena; without this level cannot be learning
Answer	The individuals participate actively in the learning process; not only react to stimulus, but they also react in some way, and assign value judgments to the phenomena
Valoration	The individuals can assign a value judgment to the objects, phenomena or to information
Organization	They are able to create and organize a value system; they develop the skill of assign priorities to contrast different values, solving conflicts between them and creating an unique value system
Characterization	They have a particular value or belief that now exert influence on their behavior, therefore it becomes a feature; they build character or personality

Table 3. Levels of the affective sphere by Bloom (1956)

Perception	It is the skill to use sensorial signals to guide the motor activity
Disposition	Is a disposition to act, where he is able not only of perceive environment signals, but also to plan action sequences to follow
Guided Answer	The individuals have the skill to follow a guided answer
Automatic Answer	They can present complex public answers
Conscious execution	They create new movement patterns to perform task in new environments

Table 4. Levels of the psychomotor sphere by Bloom (1956)

4. Operationalization of a maturity KM model exhibiting interpretativist traits

To summarize, argue and dispose of a KM operationalization model having interpretativist features it is proposed the following proposal:

1. In the *predetermined* level the company does not have a proper capacity to answer or to attend the information coming from external and internal environments. Some entities

inside him could be specialized to and for listening and answering to the environment's information, but they will be limited to the local level. The company lacks of proper competences in all the activities of the psychomotor sphere, because exist a poor perception and ignorance on the information sources. It can be possible that individuals or units have a proper management of these sources, but in the same way it can be within a very local environment. Because of the low perception capacity, the company will have difficulties to properly answer to the learning process. This is natural because the company, at this level, do not has the skill to develop mechanisms, complex public answers, adaptations or to participate in creations, and can exist entities, inside the company that know how to lead these activities, but this not meant that the company know how to do it.

2. In the *reactive* level the company answers to the external pressure to improve the knowledge management; for example, implement strategies to attend and answer the signals in a selected sphere. The company learns to manage in a better way the information coming from the selected sources. At this point, is possible to find the analogy with the perception that has a baby about the information coming from his parents: the baby starts to tune with their voices and gestures, but still is difficult to him to recognize the persons that does not belong to their surrounding family. At this level is expected that the company improve the perception, the disposition to act, and that show answers to the learning between the centers and the selected areas.
3. In the *appreciative* level the company start to give value to the need of establish interdisciplinary agreements and comprehensive analysis to achieve a better appreciation for the information sources, the used analysis for processing it and the meaning acts and of action management. The company starts to increase their range of perception, improves the disposition to act, and starts to maturate in its capacity to learn guided answers. This because now is connected by knowledge management activities through the entities, and start to develop mechanisms and instances limited to complex open answers. To develop these answers a company needs to have coordination of its knowledge management activities through entities.
4. In the *organized* level the company presents an organized architecture around knowledge: resource management, analytic management, significant management and active management; and it will be able of carry out all the activities: perception, disposition to act, guided answer, mechanisms, complex answers, adaptation and creation, which can be attributed to the presence of a holistic structure of knowledge management.
5. Finally, in the *optimized* level, are observed similarities between the personality and character construction concepts in the knowledge management. With the aim of operating this level, the company will benefit itself from the opening to continuous improvement, and will support on the practices and current skills of the different KM components. The company optimizes its ability for adaptation and creation. The objective is to decrease the time necessary to adapt to the environment changes, and increase the fluency and abilities coming from new actions, with the objective of being more proactive instead of being reactive.

In the Table 5 are described the levels and features of the operationalization of the proposed maturity model.

Levels	Features Resources Management	Analytic Management	Significant Management	Active Management
Disposed	The individuals, as agents, will have their own resources and the responsibility of managing the information they consider necessary to perform their tasks	There is no standard definition for the information objects; each agent will define the necessary objects. As a result the analytic opinions have low quality and will lack of portability. The generated analysis for each agent will be not harmonic or compatible.	Individual agents interpret the meaning, but is incomplete and usually do not is shared in an effective way with the other people. As a result of bad calibrated will be the necessity of company's knowledge generation and application.	Any action will be based on personal intuitive feelings, and there is no disposition for feedback aimed to the monitoring on the effectiveness of the action.
Reactive	With the objective of managing the convergence or the conflicts in the information, are created centers for managing the information and to start to standardize a management process of sources, by creating definitions and the mapping of their origins. As a consequence of local map creation the sources become integrated within the center. The member belonging to the center will have tools to retrieve the pertinent information for each center.	The centers will be standardized regarding to the procedures for the analytic regulation, the deployments, and the repository management. This contributes to the effective transformation of the information in the center.	The meanings are shared within the center, and a common language arises that is related to information. It is interchanged, compared, and actively debated -it is feed backed- with the aim of improving the planned indicators for the actions.	The regulated actions within the centers will be based on the meaning, which leads to a higher efficiency of the operations and allows flexibility at this level. At this moment, the feedback actions related to actions will be restricted to inside the center.
Appreciative	Alliances are formed between the center with the objective of promoting the integration and a source management more effective. The	The centers shares their analysis processes with other centers. The analysis is redefined, and its	The meanings are shared through functions. This process requires translators in order to agree	The alliances of the centers will generate wider ways of action-share experiences-and also will be able

	definition of information, maps, and management efforts will widen the scope of the processes.	development is best understood. The analyzed information increases their scope. The analysis repositories grow and become more sophisticated as studied information volume increases.	about the syntax and the terminology. The members of different centers start to take into account external points of view in its work practices.	to see the reaction of the actions throughout a wider context-outside the same centers. This will result in an efficiency increase, in addition to changes in the effectiveness.
Organized	The company has developed a repertory that gradually increases talking about their interest sources. These sources will be mapped to examine its convergence and the conflicts in the emitted information. It is developed one standardized architecture to easy the information retrieval. The company will have an almost complete map of their interest sources, having the possibility of receiving information coming from these sources.	The company will be able of generate sophisticated analysis, based on a proper definition of the information and in the element classes themselves. It is conformed a company repository feasible to promote the reuse of all the analysis for the permanent feedback cycles.	The meanings generated in the analysis are deep and are shared with the company members. The company will be able of managing the company's language diversity and to promote the dialogue based on meanings.	The company will be able of designing unique actions supported on the new meanings. A repository will be created of the existent actions, which will ease the reuse of the existent knowledge. The actions' feedback process is effective, and will contribute to the evaluation of the actions.
Optimized	The company will commit itself to critically respect the new sources of information, to review the source inventories, and to periodically upgrading the information and the recovery mechanisms. The map of the sources is upgraded and it refines constantly to	The company is committed to search in a more effective way better methods to evaluate the analysis. The purpose is to rationalize the processes of generation and application of the analysis.	It will be put into operation mechanisms to ease the permanent review of the generated meanings. Furthermore, it will be a compromise to train agents with the objective of keeping their	The actions will be reviewed based on a schedule with the objective of keeping the company's operations updated and at the proper time. The metrics for evaluating the actions permanently will be upgraded,

	represent the changes in the company's internal and external environments.		skills upgraded, in the same manner the compromise to keep, as much as possible, the efficiency of the compatible mechanisms.	always thinking in executing them as soon as possible. The company will have a diverse repository of actions to take advantage, and it will be updated on a regular basis.

Table 5. Operationalization of the maturity model of KM having an interpretative trait

5. Discussion and conclusions

There is no doubt that the selection of a KM management perspective depends on considering the knowledge as true facts about the world or considering it as a social construction. Although both perspectives can be epistemologically mutually exclusive, as is implicit in the analyzed literature, in practice the elements of one of them is used indistinctly by the other. Because of this, that really should matter is the way in which each perspective is introduced and is used to manage knowledge in the company. What is the practical meaning of this? In first place, you can adopt an approach through the appreciation and understanding of the "environment" in which knowledge management is planned; however, the construction of that knowledge is not trivial. Subsequently, you must select a set of methods and management techniques to implement any approach; this requires drawing a matrix that establishes relationships between the environment, the approach and the application method selected. Finally, the selection must be implemented for KM.

It is evident, in the functionalist perspective, that the knowledge creating company is, at least in theory, a "beast" very different to the disciplinary company. Much of the later Foucault subjects, about power and subjectivity, undoubtedly seem to be more adequate to analyze the effects of the power that use the knowledge creating companies, but it is necessary to doubt about whether these analysis can go beyond thematic conclusions. The most important examples given by Nonaka & Takeuchi (1995) are inside Japanese companies - most of the genealogic studies have been European.

Considering that the USA-based companies follow many social patterns seen in European companies, there is big similarities between North America's history and Western Europe history at the genealogic/ideological level –very few genealogic materials is available in Japan. Until recent times there was not much cross fertilization exchange –of ideologies, social structures, etc.– among Europe, North America and Japan, despite that is worthy a review on the influence of United States of America –in Japan–, immediately after 1945.

However, that referred to the genealogy itself, which is with are formed the management styles and other things, is easily accepted by people. In this sense, is worthy to revisit many Foucault's subjects, particularly those relative to subjectivation, when the management styles defended by Nonaka & Takeuchi are so ephemeral. But, is it that way? The knowledge management already shows many aspects of the current mode, which is a result of the established modern literature related to bad management. The analysis of the knowledge functionalist perspective is centered on the work by Nonaka & Takeuchi, precisely because if this become wider to consider the multiple approaches in the knowledge management subject, available in the literature, probably must result impossible to make a serious analysis of all. Apart from that, much of the literature on knowledge management is centered on technology, particularly on IT, instead of management. At this point it is worthy to say that Nonaka & Takeuchi just include a wide debate on the Information Systems but there is nothing about IT in their whole 1995 book. Supposing that their work will be last –in this moment–, a technology-based approach seems to lose all homilies about the importance of tacit knowledge, especially its personal condition.

Additionally, on this respect it can be argued that the changes in the management, apparently defended by Nonaka & Takeuchi, can appear proposals for changes in the production relationships in the European and American companies, instead of being changes in the production (Adorno, 1968). Apart from that, is an illusion that these changes and ideas, proposed in the production relationships, be critically so substantive as to originate academic enthusiastic acceptances in North America and Europe, while really they are that because they are simple extensions/formalizations of the management techniques that have become stronger, at least since 1960's decade, and that can explain the enthusiasm demonstrated by the proposer of these ideas.

The interpretativist perspective seems to be more complex to implement and to model by using ICTs. However, the interest for taking it in this document is to share the object named knowledge based on the support, mapping, storage, understanding and dissemination, to support and to create the many possible activities performed by people through the application of their knowledge. The technological action based on this proposal ranges from the idea that technology can help to "manage knowledge" to the idea that the technologies and approaches for knowledge management can improve the different and complex activities of persons dedicated to create knowledge. These philosophies not necessarily can use different technologies or approaches, but, is different the way in which such technologies are designed and deployed. Curiously, as an interpretativist epistemic commitment it is suggested that any technology developed should be extensible and adaptable to the different actions taken by knowledge creators.

This approach is based on interpretative interactionism to recognize the natural perspective of knowledge. Evidently, seems to be that always have been ignored the complexity of the environment in which it is developed and the recurrent interaction between technology, organization and persons, therefore any knowledge management process originates itself in an organizational context through human, social and political interactions. However, because of the complexity and unpredictability of human behavior, strong questions arise about the effectiveness of the search for general laws capable of predicting that behavior. The evolution in the field of KM research and the development of interactionism reasoning emphasize more on the human issue, thus requiring more resources of the interpretativist perspective, in such a way that it offer to the different actors the means to understand and act in the reality.

The interpretivist perspective, suggest many of the authors referred and, in a number of industrial applications, is becoming the dominant paradigm. In the different practices, reality is observed as a subjective phenomenon, knowledge is considered as context-dependent, learning as a social practice that takes place between people, and has been established that knowledge cannot be stored indistinctly because it is determined by each specific situation. But, as mentioned above, from this perspective is difficult to manage, to measure and to understand the meaning of company learning. The interpretivist perspective puts these tasks on the shifting sands of relativism and contextualization. Relativism turns measurement almost impossible because their constantly changing rules. If the situation or context is the key factor for knowledge, the learning should not be based on the foundation of truth but on the environment. The implications of this perspective include comprehensive concepts like business ethics and cultural morality; therefore, selecting this perspective is a task that must be taken seriously.

As a final comment, and, because the subject of knowledge management generates a huge amount of material coming from researchers and practice, it is suggested to continuously review the material in order to achieve the construction of a broader vision. Additionally, to have a minimum understanding on KM, it is suggested the review of some closely-related issues like person and company learning, communication processes, computer support to collaborative work, company changes and information systems.

6. References

Adorno, T. W. (1968). Late Capitalism or Industrial Society? Is Marx Obsolete? *Diogenes*, No. 64, pp. 1-16, ISSN: 0392-1921.

Alavi, M. & Leidner, D. (2001). Review: Knowledge Management and Knowledge Management Systems: Conceptual Foundations and Research Issues. *MIS Quarterly*, Vol. 25, No. 1, pp. 107-136, ISSN: 02767783.

Bhatt, G. D. (2001). Knowledge management in organizations. *Journal of Knowledge Management*, Vol. 5, No. 1, pp. 68-75. ISSN: 1367-3270.

Bloom, B. S. (1956). *Taxonomy of Educational Objectives: The classification of educational goals, Handbook 1: Cognitive Domain*. Addison Wesley Publishing Company, ISBN-13: 978-0582280106, USA.

Brown, J. & Duguid, P. (1998). Organizing knowledge. *California Management Review*, Vol. 40, No. 3, pp. 90-112, ISSN: 0008-1256.

Brown, J. S. & Duguid, P. (2001). Knowledge and Organization: A Social-Practice Perspective. *Organization Science*, Vol. 12, No. 2, pp. 198-213, ISSN: 1047-7039.

Burrell, G. & Morgan, G. (1979). *Sociological Paradigms and Organizational Analysis*. Ashgate Publishing, ISBN-13: 978-1857421149, London.

Burton-Jones, A. (1999). *Knowledge Capitalism: Business, Work and Learning in the New Economy*. Oxford University Press, ISBN-13: 978-0198296225, Oxford.

Checkland, P. & Holwell, S. (1998). *Information, Systems and Information Systems*. John Wiley & Sons, ISBN-13: 978-0471958208, USA.

Cook, S. D. N. & Brown, J. S. (1999). Bridging Epistemologies: The Generative Dance between Organizational Knowledge and Organizational Knowing. *Organization Science*, Vol. 10, No. 4, pp. 381-400, ISSN: 1047-7039.

Costello, G. (1996). *Knowledge Management in Strategic alliances: The Role of Information Technology*. University of Oxford, Oxford.

Daft, R. & Weick, K. (1984). Towards a model of organizations as interpretation systems. *Academy of Management Review*, Vol. 9, No. 2, pp. 284-295, ISSN: 0363-7425.

Davenport, T. & Grover, V. (2001). Special Issue: Knowledge Management (editorial). *Journal of Management Information Systems*, Vol. 18, No. 1, pp. 3-4, ISSN: 0742-1222.

Davenport, T. H. & Prusak, L. (1998). *Working Knowledge: How organizations manage what they know*. Harvard Business School Press, ISBN-13: 978-1578513017, Boston.

Davenport, T. H. & Prusak, L. (2000). *Working Knowledge: How organizations manage what they know*. Harvard Business School Press, ISBN-13: 978-0875846552, Boston.

Davenport, T. H.; Jarvenpaa, S. & Beers, M. (1996). Improving knowledge work processes. *Sloan Management Review*, Vol. 37, No. 4, pp. 53-65, ISSN: 0019-848X.

Demarest, M. (1997). Understanding Knowledge Management. *Long Range Planning*, Vol. 30, No. 3, pp. 374-384, ISSN: 0024-6301.

Desouza, K. C. (2006). *Knowledge Management Maturity Model: Theoretical development and preliminary empirical testing*. PhD dissertation: University of Illinois at Chicago.

Diakoulakis, I. E.; Georgopoulos, N. B.; Koulouriotis, D. E. & Emiris, D. M. (2004). Towards a holistic knowledge management model. *Knowledge Management*, Vol. 8, No. 1, pp. 32-46, ISSN: 1367-3270.

Drucker, P. F. (1988). The coming of the new organization. *Harvard Business Review*. Jan-Feb, pp. 1-11. ISSN: 0017-8012.

Drucker, P. F. (1993). *Post-Capitalist Society*. Harper Paperbacks, ISBN-13: 978-0887306617, Oxford.

Earl, M. (2001). Knowledge management strategies: Toward a taxonomy. *Journal of Management Information Systems*, Vol. 18, No. 1, pp. 215-233, ISSN: 0742-1222.

Foucault, M. (1982). *The subject and power*. In H. L. Dreyfus and P. Rabinov (Eds.): Michel Foucault: Beyond Structuralism and Hermeneutics. Chicago University Press, pp. 208-226, ISBN: 0226163121, Chicago.

Foucault, M. (1982a). *The Archaeology of Knowledge & The Discourse on Language*. Vintage, ISBN: 9780394711065, UK.

Hedlund, G. (1994). A Model of Knowledge Management and the N-form Corporation. *Strategic Management Journal*, Vol. 15, No. S2, pp. 73-90, ISSN: 00246301.

Inwood, M. (2002). *Heidegger: A Very Short Introduction*. Oxford University Press, ISBN-13: 978-0192854100, Oxford.

Jashapara, A. (2004) *Knowledge Management: An Integrated Approach*. Pearson Education Limited, ISBN-13: 978-0273682981, UK,

Johnson, P. & Duberley, J. (2000). *Understanding Management Research: An Introduction to Epistemology*. Sage, ISBN-13: 978-0761969181, London.

Kanter, J. (1999). Knowledge management practically speaking. *Information Systems Management*, Vol. 16, No. 4, pp. 7-15, ISSN: 1934-8703.

Kogut, B. & Zander, U. (1996). What Firms do? Coordination, Identity and Learning. *Organization Science*, Vol. 7, No. 5, pp. 502-518, ISSN: 1047-7039.

KPMG (1998). *Knowledge Management. Research Report 1998*. KPMG Management Consulting. On line: http://www.brint.com/papers/submit/knowmgmt.pdf, [Apr. 2011].

Lyotard, J. F. (1984). *The Postmodern Condition*. Manchester University Press, ISBN: ISBN: 0-8166-1173-4, Manchester.

Marshall, A. (2008). *Principles of Economics*. Evergreen Review, ISBN: 9781573921404, London.

Marshall, L. (1997). Facilitating knowledge management and knowledge sharing: New opportunities for information professionals. *Online*, Vol. 21, No. 5, pp. 92-102, ISSN: 0146-5422.

McAdam, R. & McCreedy, S. (1999). A critical review of knowledge management models. *The Learning Organization*, Vol. 6, No. 3, pp. 91-101, ISSN: 0969-6474.

McAdam, R. & McCreedy, S. (1999a). The process of Knowledge Management within Organizations: a Critical Assessment of both Theory and Practice. *Knowledge and Process Management*, Vol. 6, No. 2, pp. 101-113, ISSN 1092 4604.

Neef, D. (1999). Making the case for knowledge management: the bigger picture. *Management Decision*, Vol. 37, No. 1, pp. 72-78, ISSN: 0025-1747.

Nicolas, R. (2004). Knowledge management impacts on decision making process. *Knowledge Management*, Vol. 8, No. 1, pp. 20-31, ISSN: 1367-3270.

Nonaka, I. & Takeuchi, H. (1995). *The Knowledge-Creating Company: How Japanese companies create the dynamics of innovation*. Oxford University Press, ISBN-13: 978-0195092691, Oxford.

Nonaka, I. (2008). *The Knowledge Creating Company*. Harvard Business Review, ISBN-13: 978-1422179741, Boston.

Nonaka, I.; Toyama, R. & Konno, N. (2000). SECI, Ba and Leadership: a Unified Model of Dynamic Knowledge Creation. *Long Range Planning*, Vol. 33, No. 1, pp. 5-34, ISSN: 0024-6301.

O'Dell, C. S.; Essaides, N.; Ostro, N. & Grayson, C. (1998). *If Only We Knew What We Know: The Transfer of Internal Knowledge and Best Practice*. Free Press, ISBN-13: 978-0684844749, New York.

O'Leary, D. E. (2001). How knowledge reuse informs effective system design and implementation. *IEEE Intelligent Systems*, Vol. 16, No. 1, pp. 44-49, ISSN: 1541-1672.

OECD, Organisation for Economic Co-Operation and Development (1996). *The Knowledge-Based Economy*. OECD, OCDE/GD(96)102, Paris.

Orange, G.; Dugat, J. & Acker, P. (2000). Ductal®: New ultra high performance concretes – Damageres istance and micromechanical analysis. *Proceedings of BEFIB-V*, ISBN: 2-912143-18-7, pp. 781-790, Lyon, France, Sep. 12-15.

Orlikowski, W. J. (2002). Knowing in Practice: Enacting a Collective Capability in Distributed Organizing. *Organization Science*, Vol. 13, No. 3, pp. 249-273, ISSN: 1047-7039.

Probst, G., Raub, S. & Romhardt, K. (2000). *Managing Knowledge*. Wiley, ISBN-10: 0471997684, Chichester.

Quintas, P.; Lefrere, P. & Jones, G. (1997) Knowledge management: A strategic agenda. *Long Range Planning*, Vol. 30, No. 3, pp. 385–991, ISSN: 0024-630.

Rabinov, P. (1984). *Introduction*. In P. Rabinov (Ed), *The Foucault Reader*, Penguin, ISBN: 0394713400, Harmonds worth.

Raub, S. & Ruling, C. C. (2001). The knowledge management tussle – speech communities and rhetorical strategies in the development of knowledge management. *Journal of Information Technology*, Vol. 16, No. 2, pp. 113-130, ISSN: 0268-3962.

Rennie, M. (1999). Accounting for knowledge assets: Do we need a new financial statement? *International Journal of Technology Management*, Vol. 18, No. 5-8, pp. 648-659. ISSN: 0267-5730.

Russell, B. (1967). *A History of Western Philosophy*. Simon & Schuster, ISBN-13: 978-0671201586, London.

Scarbrough, H.; Swan, J. A. & Preston, J. C. (1999). *Knowledge Management: A literature review*. Chartered Institute of Personnel & Development, ISBN-13: 978-0852927991, London.

Schultze, U. & Boland, R. (2000). Place, Space and knowledge work: a study of outsourced computer systems administrators. *Accounting, Management and Information Technology*, Vol. 10, No. 3, pp. 187-219, ISSN: 0959-8022.

Schultze, U. (1998). Investigating the contradictions in knowledge management. *Proceedings of IFIP Working Groups 8.2 and 8.6 Joint working conference on information systems: current issues and future changes*, Helsinki, Finland, Dec. 10 - 13.

Sieloff, C. G. (1999). If only HP knew what HP knows: the roots of knowledge management at Hewlett-Packard. *Journal of Knowledge Management*, Vol. 3, No. 1, pp. 47-53, ISSN: 1367-3270.

Snowden, D. (2000). Private Presentation. Senior Consultant on Knowledge Management at IBM. *In T. B. Council (Ed.)*. Oxford.

Spender, J. (1996). Organizational knowledge, learning and memory: Three concepts in search of a theory. *Journal of Organizational Change Management*, Vol. 9, No. 1, pp. 63-78, ISSN: 0953-4814.

Stewart, T. A. (1997). *Intellectual Capital: The New Wealth of Organizations*. Doubleday, ISBN-13: 978-0385483810, New York.

Tapscott, D. (1997). *Digital Economy*. McGraw-Hill, ISBN-13: 978-0071353199, New York.

Tenkasi, R. V. & Boland, R. J. (1996). Exploring Knowledge diversity in knowledge intensive firms: a new role for information systems. *Journal of Organizational Change Management*, Vol. 9, No. 1, pp. 79-91, ISSN: 0953-4814.

TFPL (1999). *Skills for knowledge management: building a knowledge economy*. White Paper. London: TFPL Ltd., 17-18 Britton Street London EC1M 5TL.

Tiwana, A. (2000). *The Knowledge Management Toolkit*. Prentice Hall, ISBN-13: 978-0130128539, New Jersey.

Tsoukas, H. (1996). The firm as a distributed knowledge system: A constructionist approach. *Strategic Management Journal*, 17, Winter Special, pp. 11-25, ISSN: 0143-2095.

UNESCO (2005). Hacia las sociedades del conocimiento. Ediciones UNESCO, ISBN 92-3-304000-3, Paris.

Venters, W. (2002). Literature for C-Sand: Knowledge management. *C-SandD/WP/1002/2*. On line: http://www.c-sand.org.uk/Documents/WP1001-02-KMLitRev.pdf. [Apr. 2011].

Venters, W.; Cushman, M. & Cornford, T. (2002). Creating Knowledge for Sustainability: Using SSM for Describing Knowledge Environments and Conceptualizing Technological Interventions. *Proceedings of Third European Conference on Organizational Knowledge, Learning and Capabilities*, Athens, Greece, Apr. 5-6.

Von-Krogh, G.; Ichijo, K. & Nonaka, I. (2000). *Enabling Knowledge Creation: How to Unlock the Mystery of Tacit Knowledge and Release the Power of Innovation*. Oxford University Press, ISBN-13: 978-0195126167, Oxford.

Walsham, G. 1995. The emergence of interpretivism in IS research. *Information Systems Research*, Vol. 6, No. 4, pp. 376-394, ISSN: 1526-5536.

Ward, V. &Holtham, C. (2000). The role of private and public space in knowledge management. *Proceedings of Knowledge Management: Concepts and Controversies*, Coventry, UK, Freb. 10-11.

Wenger, E. & Snyder, W. (2000). Communities of Practice: The Organizational Frontier. *Harvard Business Review*, pp. 139-145, ISSN: 0017-8012.

Wenger, E. (1998). *Communities of practice: Learning, meaning and identity.* Cambridge University Press, ISBN-13: 978-0521663632, Cambridge.

14

Implementation Process of a Knowledge Management Initiative: Yellow Pages

Stéphanie Gretsch, Heinz Mandl and Raphaela Schätz
Ludwig-Maximilian-University
Germany

1. Introduction

Knowledge management has often been identified as an important challenge for sustained organizational success and as a prerequisite for the productivity and flexibility of corporate and non-corporate organizations. Due to the global interconnectedness of markets today, the scope and quality of individual employees' knowledge have taken their place alongside more traditional organizational resources such as work and capital. Knowledge of employees is considered as the most important knowledge source within organizations. Therefore, it is necessary to explicitly plan and manage the development, consolidation, representation and application of the knowledge of organizations and individuals to support a learning organization. Above all, knowledge communication between employees is essential for growth of learning. When employees share knowledge with other colleagues within their organization, that knowledge can become a source of competitive advantage (Solano, 2010). The issue is finding the colleagues within an organization who can provide the knowledge and skills needed in a given situation. This is particularly true in large organizations, such as an international corporation with geographically distributed departments. Within the domain of knowledge management, the problem of finding a suitable expert is usually solved with the help of expert finding systems such as company yellow pages or similar tools. This article presents a case study in a biotechnological company concerning the implementation of yellow pages. The implementation process included four phases. Phase 1 comprehends a knowledge management diagnosis, including a differentiated needs analysis concerning knowledge management domains. Phase 2 is concerned about the design and phase 3 is comprehends the realization of this intervention; and in phase 4 the rollout of the intervention takes place (Tarlatt, 2001; Winkler & Mandl, 2007).

2. Knowledge management in organizations

Especially in the global situation of competitive pressure, organizations acknowledge the importance of developing innovative concepts for using their own resources and existing synergies to have an optimum effect while simultaneously minimizing costs. Innovative knowledge generation and utilization in for-profit and non-profit organizations are essential for the future and therefore require an intelligent, responsible and human knowledge management.

Among the precursors of knowledge management is the engineering approach, in which technology is of great importance. Even today, technologies are an integral part of modern knowledge management. Until now, most knowledge management strategies could be categorized under the approach of business administration. In this approach, especially organizational aspects are important, such as knowledge for business goals and strategies as well as the role of staff development for knowledge management.
Another approach, the recent line of development, is concerned with the psychological approach to knowledge management. Here a central role is given to human and its individual handling of knowledge through tools and strategies (Reinmann & Mandl 2010). Finally knowledge management has a social logical sense, covering topics such as knowledge society, organization development and system theories.
In connection to these approaches, knowledge management is referred to as the systematic and reasoned dealing of knowledge concerning economic, employment or human resources. Dealing means both the supply and design of frameworks, methods and technical tools as well as the optimization of technical, organizational and mental processes (Reinmann & Mandl 2010, p. 1050). In this sense, human, organization and technology together form the three key components of knowledge management, considering also the relation to society (Mandl, 2010; Reinmann-Rothmeier & Mandl, 2000).

- The first component *human* is about the promotion and creation of knowledge, skills and competencies of the organization members, which form the carrier of relevant knowledge and the core of all knowledge management as the actual "driving forces" of continuous learning.
- The second component *organization* implies the development of a knowledge- and learning-friendly environment and culture in the organization and creating a framework that will facilitate the management of knowledge resources.
- The third component *technology* deals with the implementation and design of information and communication infrastructures and tools, supporting the knowledge-based processes in an efficient and user-friendly manner.

2.1 Knowledge management models

Knowledge management models are intended to support knowledge and decision-making processes by depicting "actions that are intended to result in anticipated business outcomes; and actions that emerge as a result of the many complex activities that are undertaken within an organization" (Callaghan, 2000). Knowledge management models can represent goals, measures, structures, and processes to provide roadmaps for how to document, communicate, generate and utilize knowledge. They have useful functions such as providing a framework amongst the multitude of possible knowledge management methods and tools and helping to prevent unreflective practice. Models also act as a potential anchor for knowledge to analyze issues in organizations and act as a starting point for organization-specific knowledge management concepts and their implementation or help to highlight the ultimate integrative role of knowledge management to better coordinate different tasks (Reinmann, 2009).
Several diverse models have been developed to conceptually describe the processes involved with knowledge management. One of the most well known models is the model of the Geneva School. This model is based on setting goals relative to the individual processes of knowledge identification, knowledge acquisition, knowledge development, knowledge

dissemination, knowledge utilization, knowledge retention and knowledge evaluation and concludes with an evaluation of these processes. The evaluation serves as a basis for reformulating the knowledge goals (Probst et al., 2010). Nonaka and Takeuchi's (1997) knowledge spiral has also achieved widespread recognition. In this model, the processes of socialization, combination, externalization and internalization are described. These processes involve the transformation of implicit and explicit knowledge within organizations.

When examining each of these approaches more closely, it becomes clear that they are often quite complex to apply in practice or as Callaghan (2000) states "knowledge strategies are often inflexible and unable to cope with the emergent properties that characterize the complex and dynamic environments of the 'knowledge age'". In addition, most models do not allow for conclusions to be drawn about individual knowledge management processes. However, some aspects can be identified that are relevant both for individuals and organizations and which also integrate the process models that have been formulated to date. These relate to aspects of goal setting and evaluation, knowledge documentation, knowledge communication, knowledge generation and finally knowledge utilization, for example, as described in the Munich reference model of knowledge management (Reinmann-Rothmeier et al., 2001; Mandl & Schnurer, 2007).

- **Knowledge Documentation**

The aspect of knowledge documentation includes all methods and processes that can be implemented to make knowledge transparent. From an organizational perspective, databases, knowledge cards and strategies for the dissemination of information within an organization play a key role. From an individual perspective, it is possible to externally represent knowledge by using elaboration strategies that relate to internal representation and mapping techniques or other visualization techniques. The presentation of knowledge, both internal and external, forms the basis for the communication of knowledge.

- **Knowledge Communication**

This aspect includes all processes and methods for sharing and disseminating knowledge. On an organizational level, these involve incentives and career structures that may be designed to promote or hinder the dissemination of knowledge. These processes may also involve the use of technical support tools such as, for example, the Intranet, E-mail or Business TV. On an individual level, it is important to consider the competence, motivation and volition of the knowledge communication. In this context, the organization also needs to train its employees in these key competence areas and must also offer structures that are likely to facilitate the communication of knowledge (e.g. through suggestion schemes or the relevant career paths). This illustrates that the communication of knowledge is a key element for linking the individual to the organization. Knowledge communication not only facilitates the circulation of information, but also leads to the generation of new knowledge.

- **Knowledge Generation**

In modern society, each organization must create competitive advantage through innovations, new ideas and products. Therefore, an organization that does not continue to develop and does not generate new knowledge will not be capable of surviving. Individual departments, such as pre-manufacturing, research and development, may often promote the generation of knowledge within the organization. Idea competitions or creativity workshops could also help to keep the organization flexible and innovative. For a "learning organization" it is important not to overlook the learning individual. From an individual perspective, it is the goal of optimal knowledge generation to create knowledge structures that allow knowledge to be transferred to other contexts and used in a flexible manner. In the sense of knowledge management, this means that the organization must create structures that allow for the most practice-based learning possible within the organization.

- **Knowledge Utilization**

Only knowledge that has been previously represented, communicated and generated can be applied in practice, either at an organizational level through concrete products or services or on an individual level when applying acquired knowledge. Alone the fact that knowledge has been represented, communicated or acquired does not guarantee its application. In knowledge management models to date, knowledge utilization has been of rather undifferentiated significance. Some practice reports and empirical studies to date (Bullinger et al., 1998) have concluded that problems in implementing knowledge management are mainly due to problems with knowledge utilization. Despite this fact, there are rarely concrete instruments or strategies provided for the effective and targeted utilization of knowledge.

In a manner similar to the model of Probst et al. (2010), partial processes are initiated through setting a goal and are completed with an evaluation.

Unfortunately, the above-mentioned knowledge management models do not provide a framework of how knowledge management can be implemented in concrete business and production processes. Above all, we must emphasize that knowledge management is not one unitary vacuum that can be implemented adhoc, but that projects must emerge concerning specific knowledge management interventions and strategies which foster the idea of knowledge management by being sub-processes. Introducing knowledge management interventions, strategies or even innovations in organizations is seldom unproblematic. In many cases, the purpose of introducing a new concept, such as a knowledge management initiative, is unclear, too abstract or too generally formulated. Consequently, newly developed tools are often doomed to failure from the outset. This is either due to the fact that there is no adequate target group for utilization or it fails to win the intended users' acceptance. One reason is that many innovations do not meet the actual needs of employees (Akhavan et al., 2005 & Chua & Lam, 2005).

To overcome these shortcomings, there is a need for a systematic implementation process to ensure the sustainable acceptance and utilization of knowledge management initiatives.

3. The Implementation process of knowledge management

The term implementation can be derived from Latin and means "fulfillment" or "filling up". Implementation is understood as the accomplished conversion of solutions, which are present in the design and through conversion leading to specific action (Tarlatt, 2001). An implementation plan can be considered as transforming an actual condition into a target state, as an idea spread into new areas of application or as the replacement of an old concept by a new one (Reiss, 1995). One characteristic of an implementation process is that a part of a new concept is embedded in an existing system or environment. The aim is to compatibly integrate plans, models or concepts while taking into account different conditions in an existing system. The implementation is considered successful if, after completing all the necessary implementation measures, the desired application level takes place (Bauermann, 1988). Since implementations usually do not run smoothly, but are confronted with various obstacles, a standardized implementation process should be

developed considering various situations, influences and conditions of different organizations to ensure a successful implementation process.
In the following section, an implementation process is presented which relies primarily on the model of Tarlatt (2001) and Kremer (2003). The implementation process comprises four main phases that complement each other. Phase 1 involves a knowledge management diagnosis, including a differentiated needs analysis concerning knowledge management domains. Phase 2 is concerned about the design and phase 3 is concerned about the realization of the intervention. In phase 4, the rollout of the intervention takes place (Tarlatt, 2001; Winkler & Mandl, 2007) (see figure 1).

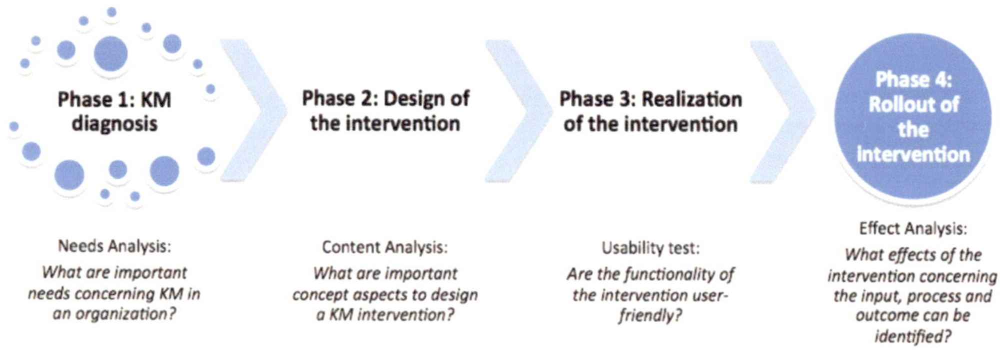

Fig. 1. Implementation process of knowledge management intervention

3.1 Phase 1: Knowledge management diagnosis

Before implementing a knowledge management intervention, it is fundamental to analyze the specific needs for such a system and to make sure that there are appropriate context conditions with regards to content, organizational and technical aspects. Based on a vision (e.g. optimization of business processes), a diagnosis of knowledge management problems should be realized. The diagnosis should take the Munich knowledge management model into consideration with its four dimensions of knowledge documentation, communication, generation and utilization. There are different methodological approaches (interviews, questionnaire) to analyze needs. The target group of respondents should include managers and employees as well as the general organizational conditions to make the actual situation visible and to clarify the desired goals for formulating goal settings for potential interventions (see figure 2).
In this context, it is evident that a comprehensive procedure for a purposeful and acceptance-oriented implementation must precede the introduction of the intervention. This procedure should concentrate on the needs of the end user in order to actually contribute to the optimization of their business processes. Based on the diagnosis, management makes decisions taking into account the order of priority concerning the analyzed needs as well as the financial, technical and personal resources. In addition, management should retain the business case providing the implementation project with its first written framework. The business case describes the vision of the organization concerning knowledge management, the results of the needs analysis and its goal settings as well as the detailed decision-making concerning one concrete knowledge management intervention. Concerning the knowledge

management intervention, there should be a detailed budget plan should be estimated as well as an initial draft of the cost-benefit relationship. This information is essential for getting funds from corporate financial administration (Winkler & Mandl, 2007). Furthermore, it is necessary to define a task force to distribute responsibilities concerning the implementation of the knowledge management intervention, including the design (phase 1), the realization (phase 2) and the rollout (phase 3, formed with employees from different areas, e.g. business related, IT, human resources, worker council, and management.

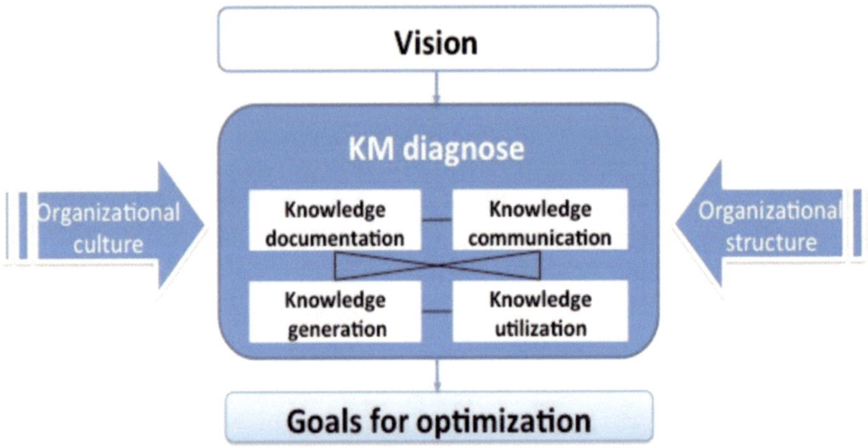

Fig. 2. Knowledge management needs analysis model

3.2 Phase 2: Design of the intervention

To design an acceptance-oriented knowledge management intervention, a specific content analysis should be conducted making visible the actual situation and the desired goals of the planned knowledge management intervention. The content analysis should take into account individual, organizational and technical aspects.

- Individual aspects include the participation of employees and specific qualifications. It is important to include employees in the process from the outset in order to ensure that their actual needs are met. Even during the planning and conception phase, feedback of employees should be gathered continuously (Hinkofer & Mandl, 2004). To ease the employee's introduction to the innovation, it is necessary to implement qualifications that facilitate the utilization of the intervention (VBM, 2000; Tartlet, 2001). Moreover the content of the intervention should be practice-oriented and demand-oriented to foster the use of the intervention.
- Concerning organizational aspects, management support is a basic requirement for facilitating acceptance (VBM, 2000). The importance of the project is communicated to employees when it becomes integrated into the overall mission of the organization.
- Technical aspects are considered when using technical instruments to support knowledge management measures. It is crucial to select a suitable technology that focuses on the concrete needs of employees. The technology selection must also meet the requirements for user-friendliness.

Using the results of the content analysis, a differentiated concept concerning individual, organizational and technical aspects can be developed.

3.3 Phase 3: Realization of the intervention

Based on the conceptualization, considering individual, organizational and technical aspects, the realization of the intervention should take place. The realization of the intervention often is implemented on a technical system. Defining working groups responsible for different aspects e.g. technology are helpful and promote acceptance by employee participation. A usability test should be carried out to control the new intervention. Usability is a quality attribute that assesses the simplicity in dealing with user interfaces. Usability is defined by several quality components: learn ability, efficiency, memorability, errors, satisfaction or utility (Nielsen, 1994). It is advantageous to use multiple methods to identify as many constraints as possible. This could be done by a think-aloud method with task scenarios followed by a usability test through a questionnaire (based e.g. on QUIS and IsoMetrics). The QUIS (Questionnaire for User Interaction Satisfaction) was designed to assess users' subjective satisfaction with specific aspects of the human-computer interface. It includes specific *interface factors* such as screen factors, terminology and system feedback and *learning factors* such as system capabilities, technical manuals, on-line tutorials, multimedia, teleconferencing, and software installation (Chin et al., 1988). IsoMetrics is a user-oriented approach in software evaluation based on ISO 9241 Part 10 that includes seven dialogue principles: suitability for the task, self-descriptiveness, controllability, conformity with user expectations, error tolerance, suitability for individualization, and suitability for learning (Gediga et al., 1999). After revision, the intervention will be ready for a pilot phase. Interviews and observations could identify some more obstacles that need to be solved before rollout.

3.4 Phase 4: Rollout of the intervention

The rollout of the intervention should follow a well-elaborated communication strategy, which takes into account the communication before, in-between and after the rollout. After the rollout, the intervention should be evaluated according to the goal setting with regard to the effects, including input factors on the individual, organizational and technical level, process factors concerning the implementation of the intervention and the outcome factors including the acceptance and utilization, individual and organizational effects. Moreover, a cost-benefit analysis can be taken into consideration. A summative evaluation of the project is crucial for ensuring continuous process improvements and the project's adaptation to the needs of the users.

4. Case study: Part 1

The next section presents the first part of a case study. Part 1 of the study comprises the phase 1 concerning the knowledge management diagnosis according to our implementation process model (chapter 3.1). The aim of the knowledge management diagnosis is to identify possible needs concerning knowledge management to gather potential interventions to consciously introduce and improve knowledge management processes within the company. The case study took place in the Research and Development (R&D) department of an international biotechnological company. The R&D department was widely distributed geographically with two R&D sites in Germany, one in Switzerland, two in the United States and one in Australia.

4.1 Phase 1: Knowledge management diagnosis

Concerning the knowledge management diagnosis, 163 employees from different sites of the R&D department took part in an online questionnaire study to analyze specific knowledge management needs. The study showed highly differentiated results concerning knowledge documentation, knowledge communication, knowledge generation and knowledge utilization.

With regard to **knowledge documentation**, 50.3% of the respondents indicated a need for general improvements in this area. Specifically, the biggest need was identified for improving documentation on the specific expertise of individual employees (47.3%) and on product-specific regulatory strategies (41.8%). Moreover, respondents identified a number of needs for improving the documentation of experiences with projects (45.9%), or with external cooperation partners (42.5%). Referring to **knowledge communication**, 54.1% of respondents identified that there is an overall need for improvements in this domain. Respondents indicated that knowledge relevant for the whole site is not always made available to all colleagues (34.2%) and that there are no appropriate opportunities for knowledge communication (38.2%). Moreover there were no appropriate opportunities for networking with relevant colleagues (38.1%) and no sufficient knowledge exchange (36.7%). Concerning **knowledge generation** respondent mentioned that there are no sufficient opportunities to acquire new knowledge by job rotation. In regard to **knowledge utilization** there could be identified an overall need for improvements (47.3%). Especially respondent indicated that there are no standard operating procedures for using existing experiences (50.4%) and no standard operating procedures for using existing knowledge (45.9%).

Due to the highly differentiated needs assessment very specific needs of employees to improve knowledge management could be determined. In particular, the specific analysis of needs with regard to different knowledge management dimensions revealed that there is an explicit need for improving documentation of specific expertise and of experiences with projects. Moreover there is a need for improving the communication and availability of knowledge as well as standard operating procedures for using existing knowledge and experiences within the company and its different R&D sites. To meet these needs, the company decided to develop and implement a "corporate yellow pages" expert finding system as an initial improvement project. Corporate yellow pages are an optimal knowledge management intervention to encourage aspects of knowledge documentation and, above all, *knowledge about the specific expertise of individual employees* and *experiences with projects and external cooperation partners* by creating profiles of employees and documenting their expert knowledge, experiences or networks. In terms of knowledge communication, especially regarding *opportunities for exchanging and networking with employees from other R&D sites,* corporate yellow pages provide the opportunity to search for experts and for employees to interact by exchanging knowledge and experiences. Knowledge utilization, such as the *use of knowledge and experiences in new projects* is supported by corporate yellow pages, while exchanging knowledge between experts, expert knowledge and experiences can be transferred into new projects. The next chapter outlines the topic of yellow pages in detail.

5. Yellow pages: General issues

The following chapter will introduce general theoretical and practical approaches of yellow pages, which should serve as a basis for the further implementation phases (chapter 6). The chapter includes a definition of yellow pages, their appearance, functionalities and creation, their differences to other tools, their conceptualization and finally their potential influence on knowledge communication.

5.1 Definition of yellow pages

Expert finding systems (a.k.a. corporate "corporate yellow pages") are considered to be an effective and less time-consuming instrument, mainly used to support knowledge communication in organizations (Probst et al., 2010).

Corporate yellow pages aim to assist users in finding experts with specific knowledge, competencies, or experiences within the company. They cover the specific knowledge of all relevant organizational members, independent of their position. The goal of yellow pages is to foster knowledge communication between employees through the strategic finding of experts (Conway, 2004). The communication between the person searching for knowledge and the knowledge owner is made easier by making it transparent who knows what (Kukat, 1999). The system does not maintain the knowledge itself, but only the meta-knowledge pertaining to the available knowledge of employees (Lehner, 2008). Information about employees is saved in directories, indicating expertise such as competencies, experiences and further information about the person (Ehrlich, 2003). They are expected to help members of large, often widely geographically dispersed organizations in finding out who has specific expertise in a problem area. This is essential for finding support in complex problem-solving situations, or for obtaining critical knowledge for making decisions. Expert finding systems can stimulate learning and exchange processes in the organization (Lehner, 2009). Other potential advantages mentioned in the literature are that expert knowledge is made visible to all employees, that communities of experts can emerge, and that novice employees can find support from relevant experts more quickly. Accordingly, expert finding systems are expected to improve information searches for work processes and knowledge development.

5.2 Appearance, functionalities and creation of yellow pages

In general, yellow pages are based on a digital, Intranet-based database (Heinrich & Stelzer, 2009). The further technical components are a user interface and a search engine (Idinopulos & Kempler, 2006). The user interface can be provided through a browser and allow the employee to access the underlying yellow page database. Entries can be made and search requests can be entered with the help of the search engine (Gray & Tehrani, 2004). The results of the search are then presented through the browser. The contents of the database are the employee profiles. The main components are information about their expertise (Debitz, 2007) and options on how to contact them (Kilian et al., 2007). A profile can also be expanded in a number of ways, for example through photos, videos or other personal information (Davenport & Prusak, 1998).

There are three different approaches for filling the yellow pages with content: manual entry, automatic generation (Conway, 2004) and importing data from existing sources (Becks et al. 2004). Manual entry requires that employees create their own profile into which they enter their own relevant data through the user interface (Becks, et al., 2004). The second approach follows the basic principle that data already exists that provides information about the expertise of the individual employees, such as sent emails, presentations they have created, or project reports. Specifically designed algorithms then filter out the expert areas of the author of the data, which then become the contents of the yellow pages (Idinopulos & Kempler, 2006). Becks et al. (2004) describe the third way as importing existing data. For example, this could be from entries in the human resource databases such as contact information and other master file data.

5.3 Differences to other tools

In order to more clearly differentiate yellow pages from other tools and to identify the terms more clearly, the following section briefly describes the tools that are similar to yellow pages, but which have a different focus.

A tool that is very similar to the yellow pages is the so-called **blue pages**. Blue pages function according to the same principle as yellow pages with the difference that they do not list company-internal experts, but rather experts that are external to the organization, such as customers, consultants, suppliers or other service providers (Lehner, 2008).

Another very similar tool that is sometimes referred to as the basis for yellow pages is **knowledge cards** (Pircher, 2010). A major differentiating factor to yellow pages is, however, that knowledge cards visualize the carrier, structure, level or application of knowledge (Kilian et al., 2007). Through graphic representation in the form of nets, MindMaps or other schematic visualization, specific knowledge gaps can be identified (Schuhbauer & Schwinghammer, 2005). In addition to their use for knowledge communication in everyday business, knowledge cards also function increasingly as a tool for the human resources department. Knowledge cards are similar to yellow pages in that they do not contain the knowledge itself, but rather describe the path to that knowledge.

Additional tools which provide answers to specific questions as yellow pages do, but which use a different approach, are the so-called **question and answer systems** (Iske & Boersma, 2005) and also forums in which questions are posed and answered (Metze et al., 2007). In these tools, employees do not present a profile with their areas of expertise and do not react to specific and personal requests on the part of a person seeking information. This instrument only uses a pull strategy for knowledge communication. This means that a question is posed in a forum and then experts can provide an answer to the topics relevant to them. The communication takes place in Intranet-based forums, which has the advantage that answers are provided in written format and are therefore automatically saved for future information seekers. In that way, there are additional benefits because a type of database is created alongside the communication (Iske & Boersma, 2005).

5.4 Conceptualization of yellow pages

The following chapter describes which aspects must be considered in the concept phase of yellow pages. These can be differentiated into individual aspects, organizational aspects and technical aspects. The result is a written document, which describes and establishes the characteristics of the product that is to be developed (Döring & Ingerl, 2008).

5.4.1 Individual aspects

Individual aspects comprise the kinds of information which may be contained in a single corporate yellow pages profile and describe the conceptual points that directly affect the employee. These aspects include the knowledge itself including domain of knowledge, the quality of knowledge and level of detail of the entries, a common ground, as well as contact information that reflects the availability and accessibility of relevant employees.

- **Knowledge**: Each employee's knowledge is an essential aspect, as without knowing what someone else knows, it is not possible to find a person with specific expertise (Cross et al., 2006). Knowledge domains that can be relevant include technical knowledge, experiential knowledge from previous projects, as well as knowledge on research, products, or customers. To facilitate searching for experts in specific knowledge domains, it may be important to predefine a closed set or taxonomy of knowledge domains relevant for the organization (Helm et al., 2007). However, it is important to limit the number of predefined domains (Lehner, 2008) and keep them flexible for future additions. In addition to knowledge domains, information on the validity, credibility, or soundness of the expert's knowledge may be an important aspect of a person's entry (Woudstra & Van den Hooff, 2008). The general principle is that the size of the entry should be as detailed as necessary, but also be kept as brief as possible. The person seeking information should have the amount of information available to differentiate between entries and to make a selection. In order to prescribe the entries, which are especially relevant for manually created profiles, it is necessary to use structuring aids and to limit the input options (Twietmeyer et al., 2008).

- **Common ground:** An important factor for ensuring the successful communication of knowledge is mutual trust. When supplementary information about the expert provides some common ground between the person searching for information and the expert, this promotes trust and thereby also promotes the communication of knowledge (Davenport & Prusak, 1998). Davenport and Prusak (1998) also suggest including a photo or even a short video of the expert in their profile. This can increase a sense of closeness and trust and gives a first impression of the person (Bettoni et al., 2007). Especially in large companies, it is often the case that people recognize a face, but don't necessarily know a person's name. A photo can help jog their memory.
- **Contact information:** How to contact an expert is trivial, yet essential content for Yellow Page entries (Woudstra & Van den Hooff, 2008). Instructions about how to reach the colleague and their availability are important. The instructions tell the person searching for information if and how the expert can be contacted. Employees prefer to make contact with a colleague when that person is in close physical or organizational proximity, even if communication media such as email or telephone are used (Ehrlich, 2003).

5.4.2 Organizational aspects

Organizational aspects refer to the structures, processes, and rules associated with the expert finding system in the organization. These concern mainly the organizational climate including participation, motivation, qualification, and voluntary participation of employees, the support of management, as well as the common language; and the regulations concerning the utilization of yellow pages.

- **Organizational climate**: Trust and responsible handling of entries are important aspects for dealing with corporate yellow pages (Lehner, 2008; Soliman & Spooner, 2000). These aspects can be strengthened by participation, motivation and qualification of employees and their voluntariness to use yellow pages, which are fundamental for the successful implementation of corporate yellow pages.

Support from top management: Support from management is crucial for the success of knowledge management as they are providing time for employees to exchange knowledge. They are allocating sufficient budget for implementing knowledge management, they are introducing a "new mindset" and are acting as example by completing their own profile in the system. This demonstrates by example that they are giving priority to knowledge management (Helm et al., 2007).

Participation: Firstly, it means that the needs and the requirements of the users can be directly considered (Moser & Schaffner, 2004). Secondly, playing a part in the development process

increases their ability to identify with the new instrument (see Frey & Schnabel, 1999; Kraus, et al., 2004). It is also important to integrate other stakeholder groups within the organization. According to Böhm (1999), this includes those responsible for data security, members of the workers' council and personnel board as well as all members of the management team.
Motivation: Motivational measures could include a transparent and comprehensive communication strategy, measures of qualification, management support, as well as participation of employees (Finke & Will, 2003). Stimuli can be used (Ehrlich, 2003) to keep employers motivated to continuously make updates. These could include monetary rewards (see Chap. 2.5.1) or be as simple as reminder systems.
Voluntary participation: Entering one' own profile should be voluntary. Participation in the system should reflect a sincere readiness to exchange knowledge and to support one's colleagues (Hofmann et al., 2010). Even if the creation of profiles for the yellow pages is obligatory, this does not mean that motivation is generated by the mere requirement to create them. This could lead to profiles of poorer quality. All employees should also be aware of the personal benefits they can gain by utilizing yellow pages (Below, 1999).
Qualification: When introducing new instruments, it is important to make sure that employees are sufficiently trained to use them (Winkler & Mandl, 2007). If the technical and methods-related skills or the willingness to use the tools are lacking, trainings may be helpful (Helm et al., 2007). To ensure acceptance, the specific purpose of the training and the needs of the individual target group determine which training is suitable for meeting individual needs (Tarlatt, 2001).

- **Common language:** In general, developing an appropriate taxonomy is a task that is not to be underestimated. Ample time should be planned for this activity during the conception phase of the yellow pages (Ehrlich, 2003). In each case, it is recommended that a function-based and a cross-hierarchy work group be created to work on the development and specification of a company-specific taxonomy. This approach has the positive secondary effect that a common language can be developed through this teamwork. The team has to agree to certain formulations and develop a common understanding of the chosen terms. A common language amongst the employees is ultimately essential for the successful utilization of yellow pages (Ehrlich, 2003).
- **Regulation for using yellow pages:** There are basically three different methods for creating profiles in yellow pages. First of all, there is the approach of using specific software from existing data sources to generate the profiles automatically. Secondly, there is an option for a person to manually create and complete the profile. The third method utilizes existing data sources and exports them to the yellow pages profile. Entries and updates of personnel profiles within the corporate yellow pages system should be entered by employees themselves, as they are the ones who are most competent to do so (Lehner, 2008). Including information on how recently an entry has been checked for being up to date helps in rating the entry (Woudstra & Van den Hooff, 2008). Keeping the yellow pages profile current is seen as one of the most critical success factors (Ehrlich, 2003). This is because older or even incorrect data would taint the results of the search. This then defeats the purpose of the yellow pages which is to find a competent contact to help with a specific problem.

5.4.3 Technical aspects

Technology facilitates the necessary processes, but is not the driving force behind the project. Davenport and Prusak (1998) refer to the one-third rule. If more than a third of the numbers of resources are used for technology and design, the project runs the risk of no longer serving knowledge management, but rather technology. Despite this fact, it is necessary to consciously and purposely include information and communication technologies. These form the infrastructure for knowledge communication and enable important information to be accessed quickly (Gray & Tehrani, 2004). Technical aspects refer to design features of the hard- and software of the platform used to realize the expert finding system including user interface, design and user friendliness.

- **User interface:** Knowing what someone else knows is only useful if there is prompt access to this information (Woudstra & Van den Hooff, 2008). The user interface refers to what the user perceives from the system or the software and what he/she can do with the software (Chlebek, 2006). In the case of yellow pages, this includes the profile entry, search entry, list of results and presentation of the profile. These four basic elements can be complemented by an introduction and detailed help tips. The interaction with the system can take place in several forms. One of these forms includes graphical entry tools, such as the mouse, which control the position of the cursor. Actions such as clicking, dragging and double-clicking make the entries which facilitate the interaction with the system (Raskin, 2001). Another option is using the keyboard, in which each key performs different functions (Dahm, 2006). Navigation is also an important aspect that should be considered in the concept for the user interface. It is the goal of the navigation to provide an overview of the current location, the target and the path to reach the target. Ultimately all aspects of the user interface, the forms of interaction, the actions, the input masks and the navigation should be documented in the interface description. This serves to provide the structure and is helpful for the realization of the concept during the implementation process (Chlebeck, 2006). The technical challenge is developing a search engine that meets the needs of the employees. Since it cannot be assumed that there is a significant technical difference between searching for people and searching for documents (Shami et al., 2008), there are basically three different methods available: index search, search in a constructed catalog, and a combination of these two variants. The last one provides a hybrid method that combines both of the variations we have presented. This can refine the search in such a way that the results are often more satisfactory (Twietmeyer et al., 2008). When presenting the search results, it is recommended that they are ordered logically, because in practice it is often the case that only the first search results are utilized (Strzolka, 2006). Therefore, the best results should be in the top position.
- **Design and user friendliness**: Fundamental design aspects to be considered are perception, color, typography, orientation, navigation, layout, style guide, and screen and information design (Stapelkamp, 2007; Döring & Ingerl, 2008). It is important that the design is tailored to the contents as well as to the function of the instrument and that it also supports both of these aspects (Idinopulos & Kempler, 2006). In terms of user friendliness, there are also other important concepts such as simplicity, structure, brevity and conciseness and mixing things up through motivating add-ons (Schnotz& Heiss, 2004). Requirements which are important for optimizing the usability of the system include perceptibility, operability, intelligibility, and sustainability (Stapelkamp, 2007). In order to develop user-friendly software, it is necessary to adapt the application to the skills of the users. The other and less successful way would be to use training and instruction to help the users gain the skills needed to utilize the product. However, this method is often less successful and significantly more costly (Groner et al., 2008). There

are several guidelines and design tips to provide information about the ways in which software and, in this case, yellow pages, can be designed in a user-friendly manner. Nielsen and Tahir (2001) provide a total of 112 suggestions for creating user-friendly websites. The quality management norm DIN EN ISO 9241 talks about the ergonomics of the interaction between people and systems (Stapelkamp, 2007). The large number of rules relating to user-friendliness can all be simplified into four principles: usability, learnability, efficiency and satisfaction.

Yellow pages are considered as a tool to promote knowledge management in organizations. Especially as in our case yellow pages can facilitate knowledge communication between employees which will be demonstrated in the next paragraph.

5.5 Knowledge communication through yellow pages

Within organizations, the goal of knowledge communication is first and foremost „taking existing isolated knowledge and making it useful to the organization as a whole" (Hespe, 2007, p. 27). In order to achieve this goal, Gray and Tehrani (2004) suggest the following three strategies. The first variation is based on the notion that information can be distributed to all employees through **the „watering can" principle**. This means that a central decision is made about what will be communicated and what will not (Probst et al., 2010). This so-called push strategy is attractive because all employees are provided with all of the information. However, this can also be seen as a disadvantage because a flood of information must then be processed by each individual employee (Bodendorf, 2010). A common tool that is used for communicating using the push principle is a newsletter which is sent via email. The **pull strategy** is the opposite approach. In this strategy, each employee is specifically responsible for getting the information they require (Gray & Tehrani, 2004). This is a way to prevent the flood of information. The challenge is whether each employee will receive the information they require despite a shortage of time, interest and knowledge (Hespe, 2007). For example, one tool that can be used is a database that stores all the information that can be retrieved on the initiative of the employee. The use of the pull strategy is additionally supported by information and communication technology, which makes it easier to search for specific knowledge in a cost-effective manner (North, 2011). If a person is only given the location where the information can be found and is not provided with the information directly, it is referred to as a **point strategy** (Gray & Tehrani, 2004). This approach is especially positive when dealing with complicated knowledge topics depending on the type of knowledge. For example, yellow pages support the point strategy, in which the expert does not have to make their personal knowledge explicit and log it in a database. This is because the interested party can be in direct contact with the expert, thereby facilitating knowledge communication.

In order to be able to analyze the benefits and challenges of knowledge communication using yellow pages, the following section provides a more detailed description of the process of knowledge communication with the support of yellow pages. The entire communication process that is initiated by yellow pages can be broken down into three components (see figure 3).

First, expert profiles must be created. The core and main component of corporate yellow pages are employee profiles (Idinopulos & Kempler, 2006). Employees externalize descriptions of their implicit knowledge domains by articulation of this knowledge into words, numbers and pictures (Polanyi, 1966). In general, employees are the main agents who communicate knowledge about their expertise to the tool (Conway, 2004). The employee therefore takes on a classical sender roll. The difference is that the receiver is not clearly identified and or that potentially all colleagues will receive the information. The goal of these profiles is to give the intended searcher a basis for deciding whether someone is an adequate expert for a specific problem or not. Moreover, profiles are the basis for knowledge communication, which should be initiated through the use of corporate yellow pages (Lin et al., 2008).

Fig. 3. Communication process with yellow pages

The second step involves searching for an expert. In this step, an employee sends his request to the system that contains the information that was input in the first step (Gray & Tehrani, 2004). The employee then receives an answer in the form of the profile that another employee had entered previously. The person who reads the results of the search is the receiver of the message sent in the first step. By using information and communication technologies, it is possible that a message only needs to be sent one time, but that can be received as often as desired.

The third step involves the interaction between the identified experts and the person searching for the information. The employee that placed the search request (second step) makes contact with one of the colleagues identified as an expert. The process thereby ends as a classic communication situation that can take place face-to-face or through another medium.

Yellow pages can encourage the exchange of knowledge and experiences, thus giving employees the opportunity to translate implicit knowledge into explicit knowledge (Eppler, 2003). Sharing tacit knowledge is only possible if the knowledge is externalized by articulation of this knowledge into words, numbers and pictures, above all during discussion and knowledge exchange (Polanyi, 1966). The exchange between experts by means of an expert finding system can provide an opportunity to exchange tacit knowledge in a highly situated context between employees and consequently help employees acquire new knowledge in a work-integrated learning environment.

6. Case study: Part 2

Based on the theoretical and practical approaches of yellow pages, this chapter will present the development and implementation of yellow pages within the R&D department of the international biotechnological company. It will refer to the implementation process concerning phase 2: design of the intervention, phase 3: realization of the intervention and phase 4: rollout of the intervention (see chapter 3).

6.1 Phase 2: Design of the intervention

According to our case study concerning the acceptance concept, a specific content analysis was conducted, including individual, organizational and technical aspects (see chapter 5.4). Thirty-five employees from different parts of R&D were interviewed concerning their needs for yellow pages. The findings of interviews gave important information about individual aspects, organizational aspects and technical aspects. Respondents confirmed the urgent need for an expert finding system. Concerning **individual questions,** respondents spoke in favor of the following aspects to be considered in corporate yellow pages: contact details (N=24), experiences with projects (N=20), knowledge domains of R&D expertise (N=19), qualifications (N=17), work experience (N=17), and experiences with products (N=11). With regard to **organizational aspects,** eight of 35 respondents mentioned that the entry should be voluntary, seven respondents were in favor of obligatory entry and five for a combination of both. 16 respondents were in favor of each employee updating his or her own profile. To ensure the acceptance of corporate yellow pages, suggestions were also collected concerning *conditions, measures* and *obstacles*. Regarding *conditions,* respondents mentioned: support by manager (N=14), communication measures (N=13), usability (N=10), and company-wide introduction of corporate yellow pages (N=9). As adequate *measures* for the success of corporate yellow pages, respondents named trainings (N=9) and the function of a knowledge manager (N=6). Six respondents were against incentives. Besides this, respondents also mentioned some *obstacles* that could influence the success if corporate yellow pages: time factors (N=8), complicated handling (N=7) or not enough communication measures from management (N=4). Finally, with regard to **technical questions**, specifications for the technical implementation and user interface design were clarified. For example, nine respondents mentioned that SharePoint could be suitable. Concerning the search form, respondents (N=15) preferred a combination of search functions, keyword search and searching by categories.

Results of the content analysis give essential information about the individual, organizational and technical aspects concerning corporate yellow pages and serve as a central basis for the conceptualization. The selection of individual, organizational and technical aspects was chosen according to the amount of entries from respondents and discussions between the task force members.

Concerning the **individual concept,** the following main content fields will be integrated in corporate yellow pages: Contact details; expert knowledge domains related to R&D, developed products, current product development projects, networks and qualifications. Above all contact details (see chapter 5.4.1) are essential for yellow pages. Concerning the individual knowledge of each employee different aspects could be determined which are important for the every day working in the R&D department. To facilitate the search for the category expert knowledge domain, it was decided to develop a closed taxonomy. This task was taken over by a working group composed of staff from different areas and regions.

With regard to the **organizational concept,** it was decided that all entries should be voluntary except for contact details to gather sincere readiness to exchange knowledge and to support colleagues (see chapter 5.4.2) This decision point was also strongly related to the claims of the workers' council. Moreover, to ensure the acceptance of corporate yellow pages, managers are obligated to support their employees concerning the utilization of corporate yellow pages (e.g. giving more time for utilization) and to carry out communication measures (e.g. company wide introduction). There is a plan to provide employees with opportunities for gaining practical knowledge about the handling of corporate yellow pages through trainings and tutorials. According to Lehner (2008) employees will enter their profile by themselves, as they are the ones who are most competent to do so. In order to keep yellow pages up to date, there will be a contact person for support and for sending up-dating reminders regularly to employees. A detailed communication strategy will be worked out supporting the motivation of employees. Moreover employees are involved in development steps, e.g. task force, technical workgroup, knowledge workgroup or several evaluations with employees, and get the opportunity to participate in the development of yellow pages.

Relating to the **technical concept**, a technical workgroup of R&D members and external consultants were working in collaboration to design and develop corporate yellow pages according to user interface, design and user-friendly principles. As system basis, a customized SharePoint was used that included combination of search functions, keyword search and searching by categories. Furthermore, to test if the developed technical system is user-friendly and enable the practical use usability tests was conducted. Results will be presented in phase 3.

6.2 Phase 3: Realization of the intervention

According to the conceptualization yellow pages was technical realized by a technical workgroup including internal and external IT specialists. After the technical realization of yellow pages, four task force members individually analyzed the functionality according to specific individual, organizational and technical aspects. To do this, they used a checklist and summarized the results in a discussion round. Based on their feedback, the technical workgroup updated the expert finding system.

In a second step after the technical revision of the expert finding system, an analysis was conducted regarding the usability in a multi-evaluation model. The study involved a performance and diagnostic evaluation with intended users. Ten organizational members from the R&D department tested the usability of corporate yellow pages through the think-aloud method (performance evaluation) with task scenarios followed by a usability test (diagnostic evaluation) through a questionnaire (based on QUIS and IsoMetrics). The think-aloud analysis revealed about 43 hints that may influence the usability of yellow pages in the company. In detail, 24 hints were mentioned concerning the edit of profiles, e.g. *explanations should be placed directly under the field name* or *field size should be the same everywhere;* eight hints were mentioned concerning the search functions, e.g. *link to the advanced search should be more visible;* six hints were mentioned concerning the selection of results, e.g. *hyperlinks in the text should be removed as they are confusing;* and finally five hints were mentioned concerning the refinement of results, e.g. *the title should be renamed, for example "Filter Results".* Beside the comments of open answers in the questionnaire, which were similar to those in the previous method, the results of closed answers (1=not agree to

5=completely agree) showed only few hints that should be revised, e.g. *error messages are helpful* (M=2,80); *correcting my mistakes is easy* (M=3,14) or *it is easy for me to move back and forth between different screens* (M=3,25).
Results of the usability test showed important hints concerning the user-friendliness of the system. About all the method of thinking aloud was crucial. It was very interesting that our sample of ten intended users from different positions and pre-knowledge could make 43 valid recommendations for improvement. The usability test plays a central role, as the test users are evaluating an unknown system. Taskforce members and managers involved in the development agreed about the importance of the test, and even declared they had become blinkered in their work, as they did not realize the relevant recommendations for improvement mentioned from the test user.
After the test the technical workgroup revises the expert finding system, which is currently under process, and then it will be launched according to a step-by-step communication strategy in the whole R&D department.

6.3 Phase 4: Rollout of the intervention

A summative evaluation of the project is crucial for ensuring continuous process improvements and the project's adaptation to the needs of the users. After the rollout of corporate yellow pages, a comprehensive and systematic evaluation should take into consideration the entire chain of effects from the initialization of the implementation process to the final impact of the intervention.
In doing so, different evaluation activities may refer to three main components:

1. **Input factors** comprising *individual factors* such as motivation, willingness and job relevance; *organizational factors* such as the infrastructure of knowledge management which results from the implementation process including attitude of management, support measures or organizational culture and *technical factors* as design and usability.
2. **Process factors** including any knowledge management *process* due to the intervention for example interaction among employees.
3. **Outcome factors** referring to the *utilization* as quality of support or frequency; *acceptance* of attitude and behavior; *individual effects* as time saving, problem solving or increase of employee and customer satisfaction; and *organizational effects* like improvement of decision-making processes, improvement of product developments and project realizations, reduction of mistakes or cost savings (Hanley & Malafsky, 2003; Tiwana, 2000).

In focus of interest are also potential relationships between these effects, and what the single factors and processes contribute to the intended outcomes. An important goal will be the formative improvement of the infrastructure and the implementation of knowledge management for optimizing effects.

7. Conclusion

As demonstrated, the implementation of knowledge management measures in organizations is a complex undertaking. Especially the importance of the human factor should not be underestimated. A successful implementation can be achieved through well thought-out, employee-oriented implementation processes. By using a process model, it is possible to strategically support employee-oriented implementation processes that prevent reactance and increase employee's acceptance of the innovation (Winkler & Mandl, 2007). It is very important to integrate employees in different phases of the implementation.

At the beginning of our case study, a needs analysis was carried out, questioning all R&D members. On the basis of the results of the needs analysis, a decision was made to develop and to implement an expert finding system. A task force responsible for the project was formed and included employees from different positions and regions. To conceptualize the expert finding system, a content analysis was conducted by interviewing employees. Two workgroups with different employees were formed on the one hand for building a taxonomy for knowledge domains and on the other hand for the technical realization of the system. Moreover, a usability test with employees concerning the technical realization was executed. Finally after revision sessions, the rollout of the expert finding system is ongoing respecting a step-by-step communication and introduction strategy. We expect that the final evaluation show positive results and confirm our highly differentiated implementation approach.

8. Acknowledgements

This research is supported by the National Research Fund Luxembourg.

aides à la formation recherche

Fonds National de la Recherche Luxembourg

9. References

Akhavan, P., Jafari, M. & Fathian, F. (2005). Exploring Failure-Factors Of Implementing Knowledge Management Systems in Organizations, *Journal of Knowledge Management Practice,* Vol. 10, No. 1.

Bauermann, R. (1988). Die Implementierung organisatorischer und softwaretechnologischer Methoden und Techniken: Probleme und Lösungsansätze. Frankfurt: Lang.

Becks, A., Reichling, T. & Wulf, V. (2004). Expertise Finding: Approaches to Foster Social Capital. In M. Huysman & V. Wulf (Hrsg.), *Social Capital and Information Technology* (S. 333-354). Cambridge: MIT Press.

Below, C. von. (1999). Wissen preisgeben: Die Angst der Experten vor dem Machtverlust. In C. H. Antoni & T. Sommerlatte (Hrsg.), *Report Wissensmanagement. Wie deutsche Firmen ihr Wissen profitabel machen* (S. 67-72). Düsseldorf: Symposion.

Bettoni, M., Bernhard, W., Borter, F. & Doennges, G. (2007). The Yellow Tool - Making Yellow Pages More Social and Visible. In D. Remenyi (Hrsg.), *Proceedings of the 8th European Conference on Knowledge Management* (S. 118-124). Kidmore End: Academic Conferences.

Bodendorf, F. (2006). *Daten- und Wissensmanagement.* Berlin: Springer.

Böhm, I. (1999). Mitarbeiterprofile. In C. H. Antoni & T. Sommerlatte (Hrsg.), *Report Wissensmanagement. Wie deutsche Firmen ihr Wissen profitabel machen* (S. 119-127). Düsseldorf: Symposion.

Bullinger, H., Warschat, J., Prieto, J. & Wörner, K. (1998). Wissensmanagement - Anspruch und Wirklichkeit: Ergebnisse einer Unternehmensstudie in Deutschland, *Information Management,* Ausgabe 1/98, S. 7-23.

Callahan, S. (2000). *Crafting a knowledge strategy.* Anecdote Pty Ltd, Melbourne.

Chin, J. P., Diehl, V. A. and Norman, K. L., 1988. Development of an instrument measuring user satisfaction of the human-computer interface. *Proceedings of SIGCHI '88*, (pp. 213-218), New York: ACM/SIGCHI.

Chlebek, P. (2006). *User Interface-orientierte Softwarearchitektur*. Wiesbaden: Vieweg.

Chua, A. & Lam, W. (2005). Why KM Projects Fail: a Multi-case Analysis, Journal of Knowledge Management Vol. 9, No. 3, pp. 6-17.

Conway, S. (2004). Knowledge Searching and Services. In C. W Holsapple (Hrsg.), *Handbook on Knowledge Management 2. Knowledge Directions*. (S. 69-83). Berlin: Springer.

Cross, R. & Borgatti, S. P. (2004). The Ties That Share: Relational Characteristics That Facilitate Information Seeking. In M. Huysman & V. Wulf (Hrsg.), *Social Capital and Information Technology* (S. 137-161). Cambridge: MIT Press.

Dahm, M. (2006). *Grundlagen der Mensch-Computer-Interaktion*. München: Pearson Studium.

Davenport, T. H. & Prusak, L. (1998). *Wenn Ihr Unternehmen wüßte, was es alles weiß... Das Praxishandbuch zum Wissensmanagement*. Landsberg/Lech: Moderne Industrie.

Debitz, U. (2007). *Findefreundliche Wissensdokumentation. Hilfsmittel für die Dokumentation, das Suchen und Finden von Informationen und Wissensbeständen im Unternehmenskontext. Eine aktuelle Übersicht* (Projektberichte Heft 57). Dresden: Technische Universität Dresden, Institut für Psychologie I, Arbeitsgruppe Wissen - Denken - Handeln.

Döring, N. & Ingerl, A. (2008). Medienkonzeption. In B. Batinic & M. Appel (Hrsg.), *Medienpsychologie* (S. 403-424). Heidelberg: Springer.

Ehrlich, K. (2003). Locating Expertise. Design Issues for an Expertise Locator System. In M. S. Ackerman, V. Pipek & V. Wulf (Hrsg.), *Sharing Expertise. Beyond Knowledge Management* (S. 137-158). Cambridge: MIT Press.

Eppler, M. J., 2003. Making Knowledge Visible through Knowledge Maps: Concepts, Elements, Cases. In C. Holsapple, *Handbook on Knowledge Management, 1. Knowledge Matters*, Berlin: Springer, 2003.

Finke, I., Will, M. & Schnalzer, K. (2005). Humanbezogenes Wissensmanagement. In Fraunhofer-Wissensmanagement Community (Hrsg.), *Wissen und Information 2005* (S. 33-50). Stuttgart: Fraunhofer IRB-Verlag.

Frey, D. & Schnabel, A. (1999). Change Management – der Mensch im Mittelpunkt. *Die Bank. Zeitschrift für Bankpolitik und Bankpraxis* (1), 44-49.

Gediga, G., Hamborg, K-C., & Düntsch, I., 1999. The IsoMetrics Usability Inventory: An operationalisation of ISO 9241-10, *Behaviour and Information Technology*, 18, 151 - 164.

Gray, P. & Tehrani, S. (2004). Technologies for Disseminating Knowledge. In C. W Holsapple (Hrsg.), *Handbook on Knowledge Management 2. Knowledge Directions.* (S. 109-127). Berlin: Springer.

Groner, R., Raess, S. & Sury, P. (2008). Usability: Systematische Gestaltung und Optimierung von Benutzerschnittstellen. In B. Batinic & M. Appel (Hrsg.), *Medienpsychologie* (S. 425-446). Heidelberg: Springer.

Hanley, S. & Malafsky, G., 2003. A Guide for Measuring the Value of KM Investments. In C. Holsapple, *Handbook on Knowledge Management, 2. Knowledge Directions*, Berlin: Springer.

Heinrich, L. J & Stelzer, D. (2009). *Informationsmanagement: Grundlagen, Aufgaben, Methoden*. München: Oldenbourg.

Helm, R., Meckl, R. & Sodeik, N. (2007). Systematisierung der Erfolgsfaktoren von Wissensmanagement auf Basis der bisherigen empirischen Forschung. *Zeitschrift für Betriebswirtschaft, 77* (2), 211-241.

Hense, J. & Mandl, H., 2010. *Knowledge Management and Evaluation (Wissensmanagement und Evaluation)* (Studientext Seminar Bern). Ludwig-Maximilians-Universität München Empirische Pädagogik und Pädagogische Psychologie.

Hespe, C. (2007). *Motivation zur Wissenskommunikation als Führungsaufgabe*. Hamburg: Kovač.

Hinkofer, L., & Mandl, H. (2004). Implementation von E-Learning in einem Pharmaunternehmen. In G. Zinke, & M. Härtel (Eds.), *E-Learning: Qualität und Nutzerakzeptanz sichern* (pp. 126-139). Bielefeld: Bertelsmann.

Hofmann, K., Balog, K., Bogers, T. & de Rijke, M. (2010). Contextual Factors for Finding Similar Experts. *Journal of the American Society for Information Science and Technology, 61* (5), 994-1014.

Idinopulos, M. & Kempler, L. (2006). Do You Know Who Your Experts Are? In L. Prusak & E. Matson (Hrsg.), *Knowledge Management and Organizational Learning: A Reader* (S. 334-340). Oxford: Oxford University Press.

Iske, P. (2002). *Building a Corporate KM Community*. In IK Magazine. Verfügbar unter: http://www.ikmagazine.com/xq/asp/sid.0/articleid.3FD08B70-6013-465C-A84C-CB04C6F2776D/eTitle.Building_a_corporate_KM_community/qx/display.htm (29.03.2011).

Kilian, D., Krismer, R., Loreck, S., Sagmeister, A. & Sigl, K. (2007). *Wissensmanagement. Werkzeuge für Praktiker*. Wien: Linde.

Kraus, G., Becker-Kolle, C. & Fischer, T. (2004). *Handbuch Change-Management: Steuerung von Veränderungsprozessen in Organisationen, Einflussfaktoren und Beteiligte, Konzepte, Instrumente und Methoden*. Berlin: Cornelsen.

Kremer, H.-H. (2003). *Implementation didaktischer Theorie – Innovationen gestalten. Annäherungen an eine theoretische Grundlegung im Kontext der Einführung lernfeldstrukturierter Curricula*. Paderborn: Eusl.

Kukat, F. (1999). Wissen teilen und bewahren. Die Wissensnetzwerke der Siemens AG. In C. H. Antoni & T. Sommerlatte (Hrsg.), *Report Wissensmanagement. Wie deutsche Firmen ihr Wissen profitabel machen* (S. 77-81). Düsseldorf: Symposion.

Lehner, F. (2008). *Wissensmanagement: Grundlagen, Methoden und technische Unterstützung*. München: Hanser.

Lin, C.-Y., Ehrlich, K., Griffiths-Fisher, V. & Desforges, C., 2008. SmallBlue: People Mining for Expertise Search. *IEEE Multimedia, 15* (1), 78-84.

Mandl, H. (2010). Wissensmanagement: Kompetenter Umgang mit Wissen - die Grundlage für Innovation. In R. Oerter, D. Frey, H. Mandl, L. v. Rosenstiel, & K. Schneewind („Münchener Innovationsgruppe")(Hrsg.), *Neue Wege wagen: Innovation in Bildung, Wirtschaft und Gesellschaft* (S. 197-203). Stuttgart: Lucius & Lucius.

Mandl, H., & Schnurer, K. (2007). Wissensmanagement. In H.-E. Tenorth, & R. Tippelt (Hrsg.), *Beltz-Lexikon Pädagogik* (S. 772-773). Weinheim: Beltz.

Metze, F., Bauckhage, C. & Alpcan, T. (2007, September). *The "Spree" Expert Finding System*. Paper presented at the International Conference on Semantic Computing, Irvine.

Moser, K. S. & Schaffner, D. (2004). Die Bedeutung der Wissenskooperation für ein nachhaltiges Wissensmanagement. In B. Wyssusek (Hrsg.), *Wissensmanagement komplex. Perspektiven und soziale Praxis* (S. 227-242). Berlin: Schmidt.

Nielsen, J., 1994. *Usability engineering* [Updated ed.]. San Francisco, Calif: Morgan Kaufmann Publishers.

Nielsen, J. & Tahir, M. (2001). *Homepage Usability 50 Websites Deconstructed*. In Lucas Training. Verfügbar unter: http://www.lucastraining.es /herramientas /e_marketing/Website%20Usability%20Guidelines,%20Nielsen,%20Tahir.pdf (19.2.2011).

Nonaka, I. & Takeuchi, H. (1997). *Die Organisation des Wissens. Wie japanische Unternehmen eine brachliegende Ressource nutzbar machen*. Frankfurt: Campus.

North, K. (2011). *Wissensorientierte Unternehmensführung. Wertschöpfung durch Wissen.* Wiesbaden: Gabler.

Pircher, R. (2010). Organisatorisches Wissensmanagement. In R. Pircher (Hrsg.), *Wissensmanagement, Wissenstransfer, Wissensnetzwerke* (S. 17–59). Erlangen: Publicis.

Polanyi, M., 1966. *The Tacit Dimension.* Routledge and Kegan Paul: London.

Probst, G., Raub, S. & Romhardt, K. (2010). *Wissen managen: Wie Unternehmen ihre wertvollste Ressource optimal nutzen.* Wiesbaden: Gabler.

Raskin, J. (2001). *Das intelligente Interface: Neue Ansätze für die Entwicklung interaktiver Benutzerschnittstellen.* München: Addison-Wesley.

Reinmann, G. (2009). *Studientext Wissensmanagement.* Verfügbar unter: http://gabi-reinmann.de/wp-content/uploads/2009/07/WM_Studientext09.pdf (12.09.2011)

Reinmann-Rothmeier, G. & Mandl, H. (2000). Wissensmanagement in Unternehmen - Eine Herausforderung für die Repräsentation, Kommunikation und Nutzung von Wissen. In C. Maar, H. U. Obrist & E. Pöppel (Hrsg.), *Weltwissen - Wissenswelt* (S. 271-282). Köln: DuMont.

Reinmann, G. & Mandl, H. (2010). Wissensmanagement in Weiterbildung. In R. Tippelt & A. von Hippel (Hrsg.), *Handbuch Erwachsenenbildung/Weiterbildung* (S. 1049–1066). VS Verlag.

Reinmann-Rothmeier, G., Mandl, H., Erlach, C. & Neubauer, A. (2001). *Wissensmanagement lernen. Ein Leitfaden zur Gestaltung von Workshops und zum Selbstlernen.* Weinheim: Beltz.

Reiss, M. (1995). Implementierung. In H. v. Corsten & M. Reiss (Hrsg.), *Handbuch Unternehmensführung* (S.291-315). Wiesbaden: Gabler.

Schnotz, W. & Heiss, S. F. (2004). Die Bedeutung der Sprache im Wissensmanagement. In G. Reinmann & H. Mandl (Hrsg.), *Psychologie des Wissensmanagements. Perspektiven, Theorien und Methoden* (S. 41-52). Göttingen: Hogrefe.

Schuhbauer, H. & Schwinghammer, J. (2005). Anwendung von Wissenslandkarten im Wissensmanagementprozess. *HMD Praxis der Wirtschaftsinformatik, 42* (246), 67-75.

Shami, N. S., Ehrlich, K. & Millen, D. R. (2008, April). Pick Me! Link Selection in Expertise Search Results. Paper presented at the 26th Annual SIGCHI Conference on Human Factors in Computing Systems, Florence.

Soliman, F. & Spooner, K., 2000. Strategies for Implementing Knowledge Management: Role of Human Resources Management, *Journal of Knowledge Management,* Vol. 4, No. 4, pp. 337-345.

Solano, B. R. (2010). *Organizational politics, personality and willingness to share knowledge: The meditational role of employee engagement.* ProQuest Dissertations & Theses

Stapelkamp, T. (2007). *Screen- und Interfacedesign. Gestaltung und Usability für Hard- und Software.* Berlin: Springer.

Strzolka, R. (2006). *Suchmaschinenkunde. Arbeiten zur Bibliotheks- und Dokumentationspraxis.* Hannover: Koechert.

Tarlatt, A. (2001). Implementierung von Strategien im Unternehmen. Wiesbaden: Gabler.

Tiwana, A., 2000. *The Knowledge Management Toolkit. Practical Techniques for Building a Knowledge Management System.* NJ: Prentice Hall, 2000.

Twietmeyer, G. A., Lyth, D. M., Mallak, L. A. & Aller, B. M. (2008). Evaluating a New Knowledge Management Tool. *Engineering Management Journal, 20* (1), 10-18.

Verband der Bayerischen Metall- und Elektroindustrie e.V. (VBM) (Hrsg.). (2000). *Wissensmanagement für die Praxis.* München: VBM.

Winkler, K. & Mandl, H. (2007). Implementation of Knowledge Management in Organizations, *Learning Inquiry,* Vol. 1, No. 1, pp. 71-81.

Woudstra, L. & van den Hooff, B. (2008). Inside the Source Selection Process: Selection Criteria for Human Information Sources. *Information Processing & Management, 44* (3), 1267-1278.

15

Agents and Processes in Knowledge Creation and Management in Educational Organisations

Joaquín Gairín, David Rodríguez-Gómez and Carme Armengol
Department of Applied Pedagogy, Universitat Autonòma de Barcelona
Spain

1. Introduction

Today's society has enshrined knowledge and worker training as strategic elements in organisations, viewing individual and collective intellectual capital as one of the main resources available to them in achieving their mission. In this context, organisations are seeking new strategies that enable their employees to share experiences, impressions and knowledge, aware that what makes an organisation competitive is its ability to develop the human capital it has at its disposal.

Isolated professionals that interact solely with themselves or with their materials no longer make sense; rather what truly matters is the configuration of human groups that are in constant interaction through networks or communities. Therefore, it should come as no surprise that organisations are determinedly seeking how to foster collaborative processes and the development of the environments that facilitate them (Gairín, 2011).

Education professionals and school networks are an excellent tool to instigate improvements in the educational systems. These networks can be established between professionals at the same schools, between schools and education and social services from a same town, between educational and professional centres from different towns and communities or even between professionals from different countries.

The information and communication technologies can be an opportunity and a powerful weapon when setting up a new collaborative professional culture, which is so necessary in our day. First, they open up and improve the possibilities for collaboration, which is further enhanced with the implementation and gradual development of tools related to the concept of Web 2.0; secondly, when used properly, ICTs help to systematise the processes of knowledge exchange, creation and management that take place. The desirable knowledge-based organisation which not only stimulates the creation and management of knowledge but also fosters its transfer and support in diverse media is becoming more of a reality to us.

The new forms of work based on the virtual network, such as virtual communities, remote networks and collaborative work environments thus fulfil their objective with the aid of technology, which becomes a fundamental tool for the exchange of information, knowledge, learning and experiences and for the creation of new knowledge.

Several studies and publications confirm that the establishment of networks and communities encourages knowledge creation and professional development processes (Aubusson et al., 2007; Dering, Cunningham & Whitby, 2006; Kimmble & Hildreth, 2005;

Klein, Connel & Meyer, 2005; Leinonen & Järvelä, 2006; Jeon, Kim & Koh, 2011; Ragachari, 2011, Schenkel & Teigland, 2008; Usora et al, 2007; Wenger, 1999, Zang & Watts, 2007).
"Among the chief reasons why communities of practice are efficient tools for knowledge generation and sharing is the fact that the most of a firm's competitive advantage is embedded in the intangible, tacit knowledge of its people and that competencies do not exist apart from the people who develop them" (Ardichvili, Page & Wentling, 2003, p. 65).
From a relational approach, knowledge is understood as socially constructed resource and, therefore, Knowledge Creation and Management (henceforth KCM) processes should be concentrated on social relations and/or professionals who connect the different agents involved. In this sense, it is obvious that organisational solutions that foster those relations, such as communities of practice (CoPs), are an interesting way of promoting KCM.
Over and above the use of CoPs, the development of KCM strategies entails the theoretical and practical command of processes for measuring, creating and disseminating individual and collective knowledge, and the participation of different agents with a clear definition of responsibilities and functions which ensure the proper development of these processes and, therefore, the success of the KCM strategy.
The handful of KCM studies and experiences in the field of education (Petrides & Nguyen, 2006; Sallis & Jones, 2002) which provide theoretical and practical knowledge on the processes and agents of KCM are the motivation behind this article,[1] which aims to provide practical answers for the development of KCM processes in educational organisations.
In this chapter, we shall note the requirements and benefits of collaborative work among professionals, develop a theoretical survey of the leading processes and agents traditionally linked to KCM processes based on Communities of Practice (henceforth CoPs) and, based on the research, outline a proposal on the essential roles, functions and processes for the design, development and evaluation of any KCM strategy in educational organisations.

2. Collaboration among professionals

Desirable professional development cannot isolate itself from a consideration of the workplace contexts in which it takes place. The goal is to extend beyond the individual action that has traditionally characterised professional interventions and consider the organisation where these individuals act and their context of action. Taking on institutional commitments to professionalisation, fostering structures for cooperative work and generating processes of internal dynamisation is a personal and institutional challenge, but they are impossible without a change in today's macro- and micro-structural conditions which always exist and in which professionals operate.
Cooperation among professionals *is considered necessary* in today's educational settings, since many of the existing problems cannot be resolved based on limited specialisation and instead require group thinking and teamwork. Likewise, professional action is not individual but group and coordinated if we think about broad intervention processes over time and in the variety of people affected. Collaborative work enables our knowledge to be enriched, expanded and compared in the quest for solutions to the problems posed by the

[1] This article is also based on the broader ACCELERA study (Rodríguez-Gómez, 2009; Gairín-Sallán & Rodríguez-Gómez, 2010; Gairín-Sallán, Rodríguez-Gómez & Armengol, 2010; Gairín, 2011), launched in 2003 by the EDO team (http://edo.uab.cat) and financed by the National RDI plan of the Spanish Ministry of Science and Technology (projects SEC2003-08366 and SEJ2007-67093/EDUC).

reality around us. Likewise, we must act from or with institutional frameworks where the goal is to generate synergies and leave an embedded capacity related to strategies, procedures and positive attitudes towards change.

Collaboration among professionals *is considered useful* in that it helps to overcome the individualism to which professional activities often lead. In fact, collective work can help us to shift from one activity with others, to one activity in conjunction with others, a collaborative activity, and ultimately it can facilitate a community of interests and a shared culture. Collaboration boosts the creative potential of the resulting team, and the technology of the solutions that they adopt is more proven. We can also mention higher performance in human resources and how they make more profitable use of the material and functional resources available to them. Collaboration enables and challenges reflection on one's own activity, with connotations of personal, collective and institutional improvement. In fact, professional exchanges can broaden perspectives and improve ways of doing things, such as by augmenting the participants' professionalism. Duly channelled in the organisation's processes and results, collaboration provides the members of the organisation with the skill and experience already existing in the organisation and enables new members to integrate quickly and fully. Finally, collaboration strengthens collective activity and a view of organisations as communities of training and professional development.

Collaboration among professionals *is considered possible,* as denoted by the numerous examples and existing evidence. As proof we can cite the collaborative processes which are taking place in the world of education and internally encompass both the coordination of certain students' problems and the organisation and operation of teams of teachers, while externally they encompass associations of schools under the same organisational parameters, groups of schools in rural areas, associations of adult schools, networks of schools, associations between secondary schools and companies or between schools and universities, and collaborative actions promoted within broader contexts such as environmental plans, the City Educational Project and the Innova portal (www.portalinnova.org).

Our current models of social, cultural and economic functioning increasingly support collective undertakings and participatory processes. This is the result of not only living in democratic contexts but also the conviction that in complex settings like ours today innovation and change depend more on the outcome of a collective activity than on the existence of extraordinary individuals capable of motivating desires and overcoming difficulties by themselves.

As has been suggested, the creation of networks and communities fosters collaboration among professions and processes of knowledge creation and professional development, thus justifying many organisations' interest in fostering social and professional ties among their members. We can find references in this vein in professional **Communities of Practice** (henceforth CoPs).

Many authors (Bolam et al., 2005, Collison & Parcell, 2003, Dalkir, 2005, Hardon, 2005, Hargreaves & Giles, 2003, Milton, 2005) use the terms 'network' and 'community' synonymously. However, it is important to point out that some experts distinguish clearly between the two (Cummings & Van Zee, 2005, Despres & Chauvel, 2000, Müller-Prothmann, 2006, Wenger & Snyder, 2000), basing this distinction on the boundaries, from the standpoint of social interaction and belonging, which characterise Communities of Practice (henceforth CoP) yet do not exist in networks. Table 1 outlines some of the characteristics which can help us to differentiate between terms similar to 'community of practice'.

Kind of Organisation	Purpose	Membership	Cohesion	Duration
Community of Practice	Developing their members' capacities, constructing and exchanging knowledge	Self-selection	Passion, commitment, identification with the group's expert knowledge	Until the interest in maintaining the community disappears
Interest group	Sharing knowledge, learning, creating knowledge	Voluntary, open involvement	Commitment and identification with the target of interest	Until the interest disappears
Formal working group	Providing a product or service	Formal membership	Workplace requirements and shared goals	Until the next reorganisation
Project team or target community	Carrying out specific tasks	Formal assignment (by a senior manager)	Milestones and goals of the project	Until the project is finished
Formal network	Carrying out specific tasks within a given domain of knowledge	Formal assignment (by a senior manager)	Workplace requirements and shared goals	Until the next reorganisation or until the task is finished
Informal network	Exchange of knowledge in a given domain	Voluntary involvement (colleagues, friends, acquaintances, etc.)	Mutual needs and individual interest	Until the members lose interest in being connected

Table 1. Kinds of structures similar to CoPs (based on Al-Hawamdeh, 2003; Collison & Parcell, 2003; Hislop, 2005; Müller-Prothmann, 2006 and Wenger & Snyder, 2000)

One of the core aspects of the concept of CoP as set forth by Lave and Wenger (1991) is the role played by "legitimate peripheral participation", which describes how knowledge and competences are transferred in groups through different kinds of guidance, implicit learning and active participation in communities. The members of the community fradually shift from "peripheral participation" to "full participation".

The second fundamental concept in the theories of Lave & Wenger (1991) is that of "situational learning", which states that learning should take place in the same context in which it will be applied. This "situational learning" is characterised by two basic principles (Smith, 2009):

- It makes no sense to talk about decontextualised, abstract or general knowledge.
- The new knowledge and learning are only conceived properly when they are located inside communities of practice.

The smooth running of CoPs depends on the existence of the following facilitators (Cummings & van Zee, 2005; Gannon-Leary & Fontainha, 2007; Kimble y Hildreth, 2005; Milton, 2005): institutional changes that facilitate their development; the quest for effective models for their operation; progress in the technical innovations needed and the provision of tools that foster modern, flexible environments; open participation and horizontal operating structures; collaborative group work; the right coordinator; participation by recognised experts; a launch meeting; the right degree of autonomy given their functions and characteristics; structures for the communication, interaction and storage of shared knowledge; regular, frequent interaction; task-orientation and deadlines; shared interests, desires and motivations; sound use of technology; and finally, alignment with the organisational strategy.

If these conditions are in place, the benefits can be manifold because: by using dialogue as the cornerstone of the process, there is better interaction and participation; shared responsibility encourages all the members of the community to participate in the learning process; knowledge is viewed as dynamic and the process of building knowledge as an active, collaborative process; and the active stimulus to share knowledge contributes to the development, capture and transfer of good practices.

Ever since they first appeared, CoPs were quickly integrated into organisational management and design, since they offer a new approach for dealing with knowledge in organisations which is focused on people and social structures, and this in turn allows the members of the organisation to learn from each other. Wenger (2007) mentions some of the characteristics that explain *organisations' interest in CoPs* as a means of developing strategic capacities:

- They enable practitioners to shoulder collective responsibility for managing the knowledge they need, thus recognising that if they have the right structure, they are better poised to do so.
- They create the perfect link between learning and performance since the people who belong to CoPs are also members of other organisational units.
- The participants can address both the dynamic and tacit aspects of sharing and creating as well as the most explicit aspects.
- CoPs are not limited by formal structures; the connections among their members extend beyond geographic and organisational limits.

The kind of relationships that are established between CoPs and the organisation are quite varied and can range from a total lack of recognition of the CoP by the organisation to total institutionalisation (Despres & Chauvel, 2000). In any case, the integration of CoPs into organisations implies consideration of the four challenges to cultivating CoPs proposed by McDermott (2001):

- Management: This must focus on important aspects for the organisation and its members by finding a member respected by the organisation to coordinate the community, ensuring that people have the time and willingness to participate and basing the community on the organisation's core values.
- Community: Getting the key leaders involved, developing personal relationships among the members and developing a passionate / heavily involved core group, and creating forums for thinking together and systems for sharing information.
- Technology: Facilitating access to technology and contributions to the community.
- Personal: Generating a real dialogue on important, timely issues.

The importance of CoPs for KCM processes within organisations is based on their ability to totally integrate the knowledge and lessons into their social practices without treating them as isolated processes with no connection to day-to-day operations (Lave & Wenger, 1991).

The usefulness of CoPs in KCM processes, either online or offline (Table 2), depends not only on the knowledge they can share but also on other basic factors such as a shared identity and values. If these elements are present, the knowledge processes are facilitated and communication of the tacit knowledge becomes simplified, since their existence prompts the social conditions and trust needed to create and manage knowledge (Hislop, 2005).

	Online communities	Offline communities
Ease of participation	Depends on the group dynamics, but it is relatively easy (users should only type in their comments).	Depends on the design of the community, the group dynamics and the degree of comfort at speaking in public.
Usefulness for geographically disperse organisations	Extremely useful. In fact, this is often the only solution for effective, affordable networking.	Complicated and expensive. However, occasional gatherings (e.g., yearly) can be highly productive and generate synergies and trust.
Reusability of the discussions and archives	Very high.	Low; special steps are need for documentation and archives (such as transcriptions of recordings).
Generation of trust and ties	Complicated.	Easy.
Tools to analyse knowledge-related behaviours	Data mining, creation of clusters, analyses of social networks (interviews + digital real time analyses).	Analyses of social networks (interviews).

Table 2. Online vs. offline communities of practice (Rao, 2005, p. 42)

3. Agents and processes in knowledge creation and management

The development of KCM strategies implies theoretical and practical mastery of processes of mediating, creating and disseminating individual and collective knowledge and the participation of different agents with a clear delimitation of responsibilities which ensures the proper functioning of these processes and thus the success of the KCM strategy.

3.1 Processes for knowledge creation and management

The delimitation and understanding of the **processes involved** in KCM within organisations necessitates a previous outline of the purpose of this knowledge creation and management. Based on epistemological and ontological dimensions and on the interaction between tacit and explicit knowledge, Nonaka & Takeuchi (1999) have outlined four processes, now classics in the field (see Figure 1):

- **Socialisation:** A process in which knowledge is created by sharing one's experience and culture with other people (organisational culture).

- **Externalisation:** This entails the formalisation and structuring of tacit knowledge into explicit knowledge through dialogue, schemas, formulas, metaphors, analogies, models, etc. This is perhaps the most important form of knowledge conversion, since it enables explicit new concepts to be created based on tacit knowledge (production - innovation).
- **Combination**: This is a process of systematisation (analysis, comparison, categorisation, etc.) of the explicit knowledge existing to create new explicit knowledge (information processing).
- **Internalisation**: Through this process, individuals absorb the explicit knowledge, include it in their cognitive structures and transform it into tacit knowledge (organisational learning).

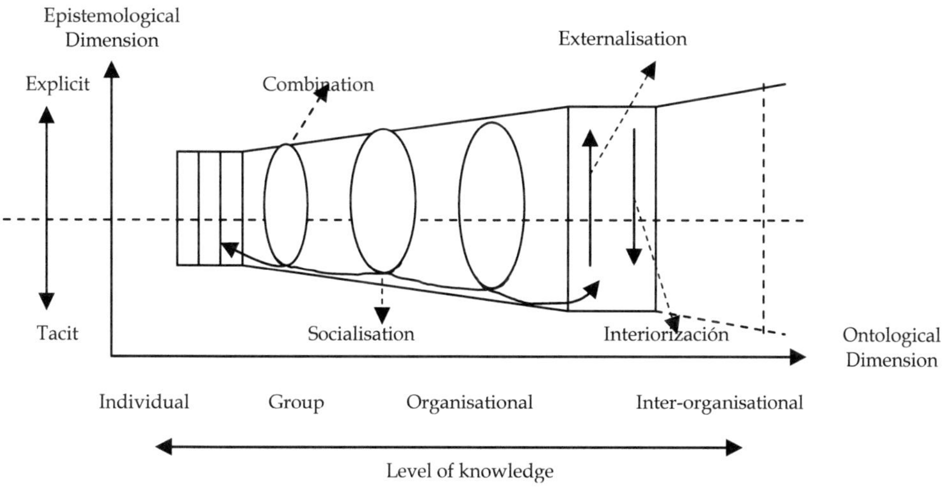

Fig. 1. Spiral of the creation of organisational knowledge (Nonaka & Takeuchi, 1999, p. 81)

Compared to what we could call the "first generation of knowledge management" spearheaded by Nonaka & Takeuchi's "knowledge specialist" (1999), which assumes that valuable knowledge already exists within the organisation, through the Knowledge Management Consortium International (www.kmci.org) Firestone & McElroy (2003) are advocating the second generation of KCM, which is much more inclusive in terms of people, processes and social initiatives. It believes that knowledge does not exist a priori; rather it is something we produce as part of social systems and that we make through individual and shared processes.
As we can see, the main processes involved in KCM can be grouped as follows (Rodríguez-Gómez, 2009):

1. **Initial**: Concentrating, storing, controlling, capturing, getting, accessing, planning, coordinating, formulating, identifying and locating.
2. **Processual**: Understanding, valuing, measuring, evaluating, developing, creating and transforming.
3. **Final**: Applying, exploiting, using, renewing, transforming, sharing and distributing.

In addition to the basic and typical processes of KCM, developing an intervention of this kind in any organisation must necessarily take into account the generic aspects of project management, such as the project's appropriateness and pertinence to the characteristics, demands and needs of the organisation and its environment; the involvement of personnel in the design and development of the process; and the communication to and awareness-raising of the members of the organisation, including many other factors.

3.2 The roles and functions of the agents involved

People are at the heart of KCM processes (Collison & Parcell, 2003; Firestone, 2008; Gorelick, Milton & April, 2004; Milton, 2005; Petrides & Nguyen, 2006; Wiig, 2004), just as they are in any intervention that takes place within the organisational setting.

Usually all the functions related to information, contents, documentation, publications databases and organisational relations, among others, are associated with KCM. The functions, jobs and responsibilities that are usually associated with the people linked to KCM are as follows (Dalkir, 2005):

- Designing information systems (design, evaluation and selection of contents, indexing and representation of knowledge, structure of databases, etc.).
- Managing information systems (maintenance of integrity, quality and value of the data, updating and improvements of the system, etc.).
- Managing information resources to support organisational actions.
- Training.
- Acting as information agencies (information management consultants).
- Providing intelligence on the competition.
- Maintaining client relations with information systems and technologies.
- Designing and producing information services and products.
- Acting as knowledge journalists.
- Acting as KCM policy analysts.

In any event, there is little consensus on who should be in charge of KCM in an organisation or the profile these individuals should have (Al-Hawamdeh, 2003). Rodríguez-Gómez (2009) identify several key personnel categories more or less intensely involved in KCM processes (Dalkir, 2005; Davenport & Prusak, 2001; Frappaolo, 2006; Gorelick, Milton & April, 2004; Liebowitz, 1999; Milton, 2005):

- **Knowledge-oriented personnel**: This includes all individuals who are part of the organisation and create, share, investigate and use knowledge fundamental in the functioning of the organisation in their day-to-day jobs.
- **Knowledge management workers - experts - or knowledge engineers**: This includes the members of the organisation who are capable of identifying and extracting knowledge from the people who possess it and of organising, storing and updating it.
- **Administrators of knowledge projects**: This includes people who are in charge of specific projects and must therefore have knowledge of the sphere of the project and understand how the people working on it are, think and act. They perform jobs like: "developing the project objectives, setting up and administering work teams, determining and administering the client expectations, supervising budgets and project programmes, and identifying and resolving problems in the projects" (Davenport & Prusak, 2001, p. 129)
- **Knowledge analyst**: This is the person in charge of gathering, organising and disseminating the knowledge, usually on demand. He or she is in charge of analysing and storing good practices.
- **Knowledge manager**: This is usually a coordinator of the knowledge processes and is thus appropriate in organisations with the need for several groups of people to participate in the knowledge management processes.

- **Chief Knowledge Officer (CKO)**: This is a well-known figure in KCM, similar to the "learning director", "director of intellectual capital", "director of human resources" and similar positions. Thurow (2004) asserts that in light of the characteristics of our society, all organisations should have a CKO on their managerial teams. Some of the responsibilities and/or functions of the CKO include (Dalkir, 2005; Davenport & Prusak, 2001): defending knowledge and its learning; formulating the knowledge management strategy; designing, implementing and supervising the knowledge infrastructure; administering relations with outside suppliers of information and knowledge; providing critical information in the process of creating and using knowledge in the entire company; designing and implementing a company's knowledge codification methods; measuring and administering the value of knowledge; managing the knowledge management operations; managing the knowledge management professionals in the organisation; spearheading the development of a knowledge strategy; positively influencing organisational change; developing a knowledge culture; maximising the return on KCM investment; improving the innovation and commercialisation of ideas; and preventing the loss of knowledge.
- **Chief Learning Officer** (CLO): The CLO is in charge of spearheading the professional development in the organisation, focusing on the organisational culture, the kind of knowledge and lessons and the technology used. Ultimately, this person must foster organisational learning.

Some of these categories of KCM professionals are part of what De Tena (2004) calls the "core team" (see Table 3).

"While the knowledge worker is any member of the organisation involved in a knowledge-intensive job, the knowledge professional is one who serves as a bridge between the knowledge workers and the decision-makers. These people have the competences needed to deal with the organisational knowledge and promote KM within the organisation" (Al-Hawamdeh, 2003, p. 181).

According to the majority of authors (CEN, 2004; Dalkir, 2005; Gallego & Ongallo, 2004; Gorelick, Milton & April, 2004; Milton, 2005), the basic KCM team would include four people who would focus on KCM more or less exclusively and intensely according to the resources available.

Technical Coordinator	He or she suggests the conceptual approach to the system by analysing the processes, the context and individuals' capacities. This position is the most similar to a CKO.
Encourager	This person remains close to the workers, getting the most from each of them.
Technology Coordinator	This person's place is near the technology, creating the "motorways of interaction".
Moderator	His or her job is the content: linking it, directing it, validating it.
Network Knowledge Manager	His or her job is to extract outside knowledge to feed the system.

Table 3. Functions of the "core team" (De Tena, 2004, p. 169)

4. Method

During the second stage in the ACCELERA project, which was carried out between 2006 and 2009, the activities centred on analysing the roles of the agents and processes that are involved and take part in KCM in virtual environments. The objective was twofold:

- To describe and analyse the characteristics of the different agents that take part in KCM networks (participants, moderators and knowledge managers) as well as the strategies they use during the processes they carry out.
- To analyse some of the fundamental processes and factors in the proper development of online KCM, including participation, motivation, group dynamics (cohesion, productivity, etc.), ethics, communication processes and content analysis.

The final sample in the study was made up of 343 people (14 CoP moderators, 28 institutional managers and 301 CoP participants) in fourteen CoPs chosen intentionally according to three criteria: a) they develop KCM processes in socio-educational/training environments; b) their KCM is based on online and/or in-person communities of practice; and c) the participants had easy access to the CoP.

The CoPs ultimately chosen came from the Centre for Legal Studies and Specialised Training of the Generalitat de Catalunya (4 CoPs), the Health Protection Agency of the Generalitat de Catalunya (4 CoPs), the Educational Management Support Network in Latin America (2 CoPs), the Coyahique Commune in Chile (2 CoPs) and the Autonomous University of Barcelona (2 CoPs).

The methods used to gather information included an exploratory interview with the institutional managers, knowledge managers and moderators of the fourteen communities, content analysis of the forums based on the Community of Inquiry model (Garrison, Anderson & Archer, 2001), analysis of the general operation of the communities, and questionnaires for the participants and two discussion groups with the participation of some members of the communities, institutional managers and experts in various fields of KCM.

All the instruments were devised based on the following measures, which were in turn drawn from the basic dimensions of any KCM process (Collison & Parcell, 2003; Gorelick, Milton a& April, 2004; Milton, 2005; Petrides & Nguyen, 2006, Rodríguez-Gomez, 2009):

1. Information and communication technologies for KCM: Today it is difficult to imagine a KCM system that does not entail the use of ICTs, especially in the processes of transferring, storing, processing, accessing and organising data, information and knowledge. However, a disproportionate use of ICTs can pervert KCM systems and make them resemble data and information management systems.
2. KCM processes: It is crucial to plan all the KCM-related processes. The novelty and complexity of KCM processes means that organisations focus on and invest many resources into planning pilot tests and later forget to disseminate this project to the rest of the organisation. For example, the absence or lack of clarity in the KCM goals can serve as an impediment to the success of a project, as can the clarity of the language and goals or fitting the breadth of interpretations attributable to the concepts used in this field (such as knowledge, information, learning, etc.). Likewise, it is important to stress that KCM initiatives can end up in failure without a prior diagnostic evaluation that helps us to contextualise their development and indicates how and why to proceed, if the personal responsibilities are not clarified and established or if the existence of a KCM team devoted especially to designing, developing and evaluating the process is not promoted.

3. People in KCM, particularly their competences, motivations, attitudes, beliefs and values: If knowledge is personal and sticky, it is crucial to motivate and encourage the members of the organisation to share, use and create it on a regular basis. KCM is impossible if people do not value the importance of knowledge, are unwilling to share and create knowledge or do not have the competences needed to so do.

5. Results

The analysis and validation of the data obtained from the participants and institutional managers of the fourteen CoPs analysed, as well as the contributions from the numerous experts invited to participate in the discussion groups on the study, enable us to present a proposal for KCM processes and agents based on CoPs and on the ACCELERA model for KCM.

The smooth functioning of online KCM requires the involvement of at least five agents with specified functions, profiles, spaces for participation and roles. What is more, we should consider the fact that online KCM entails different stages of planning, development and dissemination, and in this sense, the participation of any given agent can be related to each of the processes involved (see Figure 2).

In the case of the ACCELERA KCM model, the agents involved in the design and development of any process are the following (Rodríguez-Gómez, Armengol, Fuentes & Muñoz, 2011, p.169-170):

- **Institutional Manager (IM).** This is the person who takes the decision to offer, provide, suggest and even impose a way of working focused on KCM. They prescribe what the goals and objectives to be achieved are, and they assign the Network Director to design and supervise the KCM network in the institution that they run.
- **Network Director (D).** They suggest to institutions that they participate in the online KCM for organisational and institutional improvement. They must provide answers to these organisations' specific requests based on initial diagnostics that end up in specific proposals for personalised, well-coordinated interventions based on the leadership position they hold. This person is in charge of planning and supervising the development of the intervention and the functioning of the network. Sometimes they may also hold the intellectual rights to the platform which is used to support the development of the network.
- **ICT Facilitator (IT).** This person takes all the steps needed to ensure that the support tool used is ready to go for the participants. They take part in the design of simple interaction tools that are user-friendly, functional and practical, according to the standards of usability, accessibility and security, always focusing on the user. Once the design has been made, they must ensure its execution and the administration of the network by ensuring its functioning, supporting the participants, following up and providing technical maintenance of the network, working in close cooperation with the network moderators and creating, if needed, technical guides, while also participating in establishing quality criteria (relevance, focus, precision, exhaustiveness, reliability, punctuality, detail, format and comprehensibility) for more effective, efficient communication.
- **Network Moderator (NM).** This person starts forums of debate or other activities which can be conducted online, guides the process, intervenes if the debate becomes complicated or does not happen, orders the information and synthesises the knowledge that is generated and proposes outside content to feed the debate if needed. They also play a key role in motivating the participants and promoting the socialisation and

generation of a culture that fosters autonomy and self-regulation in order to improve the quality and continuity of the KCM.

- **Participants (P).** The participants are the users of the network, and they are truly at its core since the network has no raison d'être without them. They must shoulder the responsibility of joining the network and participating in it periodically. There are numerous kinds of users, although practice distinguishes three roles: the core active group, the peripheral group with more sporadic participation and the lurkers or passive participants.

The participants must converse with each other and establish an enriching dialogue that promotes the exchange of information based on criteria established by the director and moderator of the network. Their participation should produce new and relevant information for the joint construction of knowledge. The interaction they engage in should be sustained on the outline of ideas, the formulation of questions, discussions on different alternative approaches, contributions of relevant materials and documentation, reflections on the topics proposed and their practice, the sharing of their own or familiar experiences, briefings and criticisms of works, doubts, successes, difficulties and more.

KCM professionals require a multidisciplinary set of competences which enable them to successful deal with any of the processes inherent in KCM (Rodríguez-Gómez, 2009), such as searching for information, using knowledge, evaluating information and knowledge, reformulating questions, filtering information and knowledge, generating contents, synthesising, and organising and classifying data and information. Al-Hawamdeh (2003) groups the set of competences that KCM professionals should have into six categories: technology, information, communication, leadership and management, analysis and personal qualities.

As well as these considerations, it should be borne in mind that in addition to the objective of the network and the desirable active participation of its users, the size of the groups, the number of participants, the forms of participation and the distribution of roles and responsibilities of all the agents affect the KCM. In particular, the entire set of aptitudes and attitudes of each agent involved; the planning, categorisation and distribution of jobs; control over the interactions as the foundation of the communication systems; ethics and the governance of the network or the type of structures that govern the organisation; and the management of the content flow are just a few of the issues which should be taken into consideration.

An integration of phases, agents and processes validated in ACCELERA is shown in Table 4. The PRIOR phase includes the presentation of the KCM through an organisational and cultural diagnostic, which enables the needs to be detected and prioritised. Thus, the map of existing knowledge in the organisation can be completed with the contributions by the participants in the development phase.

After the organisational structure has been evaluated and the strengths and weaknesses identified comes the PLANNING stage. The first step is to assemble a team that will design and develop the KCM process. The members of this team must complement each other and have diverse knowledge (intellectual capital, technology systems, organisational learning, training, management of cultural change, group dynamics, etc.). The members of the group must obviously include the Institutional Manager and the Network Director. At the same time, direct contacts should be forged with the Network Moderator and the ICT Facilitator.

The processes in the IMPLEMENTATION phase refer to the nature of the communication (characteristics, contents, processes, etc.), the participatory processes (natural or induced), the cohesion among the members of the network and their motivation. The start of this phase enables the participants to access the network so that they can shift from tacit (personal) knowledge to explicit (shared) knowledge. This is when a socialisation process gets underway in which the participants share their individual knowledge (theoretical and practical, aptitudes, attitudes, etc.), with the goal of contributing to the KCM.

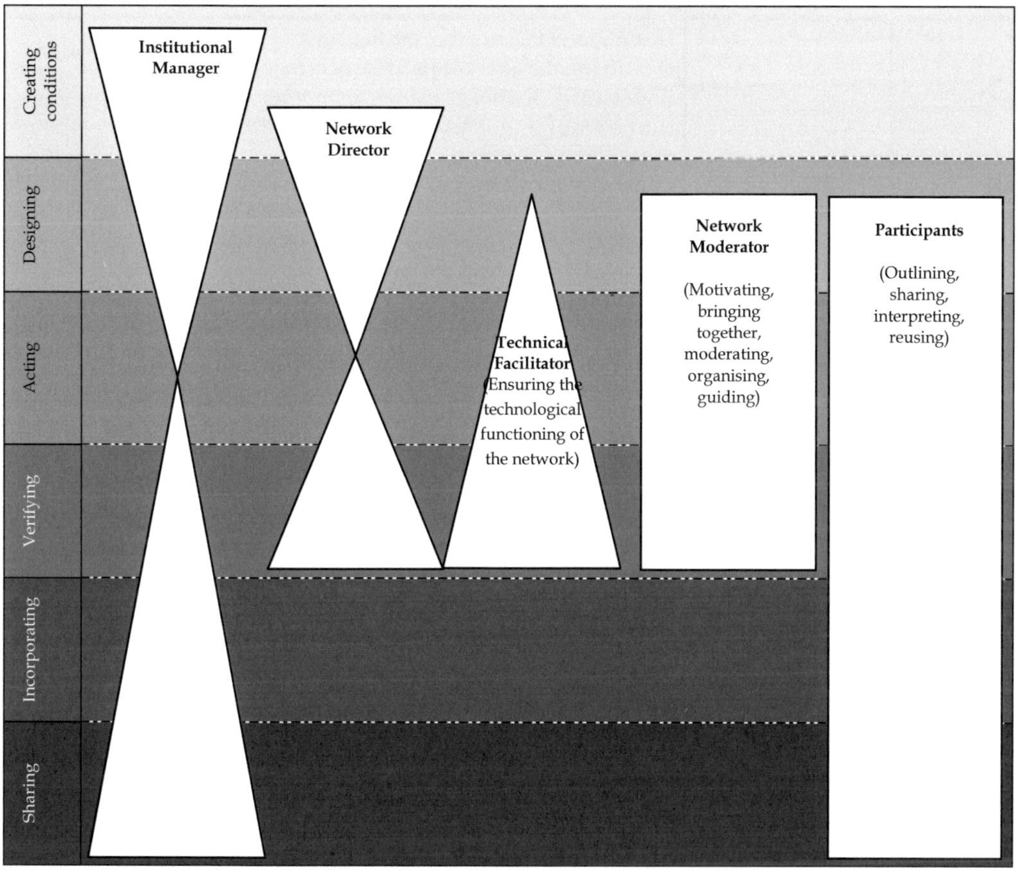

Fig. 2. Roles and processes in KCM

The Network Moderator appointed must guide and stimulate the debate, help with group cohesion through regular monitoring of the network, and organise the information and knowledge that are generated through precise moderation. The participants' interventions entail sharing their experience and culture, making their personal knowledge explicit, interpreting and reusing their colleagues' contributions, reflecting on their own beliefs and culture, socially elaborating information and formalising shared knowledge, among others.

One important way to improve the efficacy of a KCM network is to encourage the participants to start a dialogue that grows as they share schema, formulas, metaphors, analogies, documents, bibliographic references, thoughts, feelings, beliefs, models, etc. and to encourage the contributions to be analysed, compared, categorised, interpreted, processes, criticised, reused, systematised, etc.

This dialogue takes on meaning by combining externalisation and individual explanation with the reflection on a social network, giving rise to the creation and internalisation of new knowledge, knowledge that can be organisational and which, if it is, should directly contribute to institutional improvement.

PHASES	ACTIONS	DESCRIPTION	AGENT RESPONSIBLE
PRIOR PHASE "Creating conditions"	KNOWLEDGE OF THE CONTEXT OF ACTION	Determining the origin of the demand. Identifying the ultimate purpose of creating the KM network: to change values, to improve the curriculum, for professional development, for organisational reasons... Contextual conditions: a) analysis of external factors: administrative, academic and economic autonomy, and b) analysis of internal factors: culture and climate of the institution, educational purposes, structures, interactive system, role of the managerial team, tradition of teamwork, tradition of reflexive processes of analysis and problem-solving.	Institutional Manager
	DETECTION OF NEEDS	Categorisation and prioritisation.	Institutional Manager Network Director
	DETECTION OF OBSTACLES TO LAUNCHING THE NETWORK	Degree of motivation. Degree of integration in relations. Group working dynamic. Capacity to adjust to new situations. Level of harmony to create shared visions. Existence of leaders with the ability to motivate. Involvement and support of initiatives.	
	IDENTIFICATION OF ISSUES THAT MIGHT BE ADDRESSED	Degree of efficiency of processes. New challenges and demands. Nature of the contents to be improved: structural, academic, management, etc.	
PLANNING "Designing"	SETTING THE OBJECTIVES OF THE NETWORK	Clarification and precise formulation of the problems and dysfunctions which can be improved or issues to be addressed.	Institutional Manager Participants
	GENERAL AND SPECIFIC ACTION PLANS	Organisation of general avenues of action, definition of the working methodology and outline of the action plan: step-by-step actions (specific, identifiable, observable, matching the objectives), logistical planning to carry them out, definition of a timeline. Defining the roles and functions of the people involved and agreeing on the process and mechanisms of participation and control. Mobilisation of the resources needed. Assessment of the costs, risks and opportunities of embarking upon a KCM	Institutional Manager Network Director ICT Facilitator Participants Moderator

		process. Deciding on the most appropriate kinds of strategies and instruments to inform the stakeholders. Defining the training needs to participate in a virtual KCM network. Defining the mechanisms to motivate the participants.	
	PLAN FOR THE EVALUATION PROCESS	Defining evaluation criteria and designing the revision process and instruments: data gathering, drawing up reports, timeline... Design of feedback mechanisms. Dissemination of the results of the evaluation regarding the process and the agreements reached. Timeline of the evaluation plan.	Institutional Manager Network Director
IMPLEMENTATION - SPECIFIC REVISION "Acting"	DEVELOPMENT OF ACTION PLAN	Presenting the guide to using the platform. Fostering access to the network and resolving technical problems, if there are any. Guiding the project towards the objectives established. Motivating and creating a pleasant climate. Establishing moderation criteria and ensuring that they are followed. Organising and suggesting work. Offering feedback and redirecting the topics, if necessary. Reinforcing relationships among people; organising and coordination interaction among the participants. Facilitating the KCM: Discovering the hot points in discussions, guaranteeing the relevancy and quality of the contributions, introducing external information when necessary. Ascertaining the problems as they arise in order to affect them. Proposing syntheses and/or conclusions.	ICT Facilitator Moderator
	PARTICIPATION IN THE NETWORK DESIGNED	Active and constructive participation in the KCM network launched.	Participants
	DEVELOPMENT OF FOLLOW-UP AND REVISION MECHANISMS	Writing efficacy reports or suggestions during the course of the network, detecting difficulties and progress, launching self-observation and revision mechanisms, launching feedback mechanisms.	ICT Facilitator Moderator

EVALUATION OVERALL REVISION "Verifying"	DETECTION OF DYSFUNCTIONS	The interaction or inter-dependence of the factors that trigger the dysfunctions noticed.	All the stakeholders
	SEARCH FOR ALTERNATIVES	Searching for solutions to the problems that arise. Introducing modifications to the initial plan to rectify the dysfunctions noticed.	All the stakeholders
	OVERALL ASSESSMENT REPORT	Drawing up an overall evaluative report based on the observation and monitoring plan and on the reports from the revision process. Criticism and reflection on the process and practice.	Network Director, ICT Facilitator and Moderator
INSTITUTIO NALISATION "Incorporating"	MAKING THE MECHANISMS ESTABLISHED ROUTINE	Including KCM into the organisational structure.	Institutional Manager Participants
	ADDRESSING NEW ISSUES	Creating dynamics that encourage the adoption of new KCM networks.	
	SURVIVAL OVER TIME	Establishing support mechanisms. Improvements above and beyond the people who launched it.	
DISSEMINATION "Sharing"	EXTERNALISATI ON	Drawing up strategies to disseminate the experience. Motivating the participants to share the experience.	

Table 4. Phases and actions in the ACCELERA network (based on Gairín, 2002)

The end of cycles must signal EVALUATION processes. Drawing up evaluation reports from the vantage point of each of the stakeholders involved should allow the planning (objectives, tasks proposed, timing, etc.), construction and selection of instruments and technological resources, information outlining and gathering and the agility and effectiveness of the knowledge generated to be assessed.

Likewise, it is important to evaluate to what extent the benefits of online KCM may last over time and become a valuable asset, that is, to assess the impact of the network on the institution.

Finally, the experience must be INSTITUTIONALISED. Communication of the experience online can give rise to organisational knowledge which must be internally disseminated in order to promote institutional improvement and lead, if possible, to generating inter-organisational knowledge. The external DISSEMINATION is extremely important for organising the knowledge generated and exploiting it in a way that enables the participating organisations to keep and/or generate a competitive advantage.

6. Conclusions

The concern with innovation and improvement in educational centres has always been present in the individuals involved in their management and operation, although the focal points have changed according to the successes achieved and expected. The initial importance of extraordinary teaching staff is no longer as important compared as have the necessary collective, coordinated efforts when the period of schooling is on the rise. Here we are discussing schools as spaces of innovation, and the stress is on collaborative work.

Making the concern with endowing educational institutions with a shared, common culture promotes consensus and the clarification of objectives (reformulating the educational project, the curricular project, the normative regulations, etc.) and the transformation of structures (spaces and times for meetings, development of catalysts, etc.); that is, the goal is to reinforce the organisation as a global reality by developing a support structure and collaborative work.

This structural concern has not been sufficient to achieve the effects sought, and thus in recent years the importance of people and organisational processes has been reconsidered. First, the personal characteristics and contextual conditions related to professional collaboration have been analysed, while secondly there has been an attempt to identify effective processes associated with professional and organisational development.

The concepts of learning community and community of practice developed in this vein include the feeling of belonging, as well as a clearly determined orientation: the interaction among the members of the community should enable each and every member to progress while also strengthening a shared culture and the possibility that learning and organisational improvement can come to fruition. This is the individual and collective learning that justifies calling these communities formative, even if they adopt different guises, such as professional communities of practice.

Professional communities of practice (CoPs) can be set up and developed either in person or through the web. Virtual communities of practice offer several advantages over the more traditional method of working teams: (a) they make it possible to forge asynchronic relationships that facilitate collaborative activities without threatening individual autonomy, thus leading to the acquisition of knowledge constructively and with high social interaction; (b) they facilitate processes of collaboration in which the participants produce knowledge actively by formulating ideas in writing which are shared and constructed based on others' reactions and responses; (c) in the opinion of Silva (2004), they allow more time to consider opinions after reflection and to discuss complex ideas; (d) our knowledge can be extended because of the diversity of the other participants; and (e) they take advantage of the emancipating capacity of certain uses of technology, its capacity to impact users and their environment, improvements in coordinating actions and a reduction in costs (Smith & Kollock, 2003).

However, we should bear in mind several limitations: (a) a restriction due to the written language, which is linked to finding the right tone, the fluidity of the conversation and the loss of richness from gestural language, especially for those with lower writing skills; (b) excess information: over-saturation of information, high time demands and complications in managing all this information; (c) the lack of training in the use of the platform by both the moderators and the other participants is yet another stumbling block that must be overcome for the online training actions to be effective; and (d) the most appropriate materials and/or knowledge are not always available, leading to technical problem related to the set-up of the system and the access to and use of the network.

However, the working models used and the tools that accompany them are as important as the people. Their facilitating or limiting role is closely tied to the choices made and implemented. Given the novelty of this field of education, the effective creation and management of the collective knowledge generated by professionals requires specific models, strategies and instruments.

The ACCELERA model, which is specific to KCM in the field of education, has enabled us to analyse, experiment with and validate the working processes among education professionals based on a collective reflection grounded on questions. Likewise, it has also helped to clarify the roles and functions of the stakeholders involved in KCM.

Even though KCM should involve all the members of the organisation, the team in charge of it should plan the process to be used by aligning its objectives with the organisational strategy by defining the resources needed, designing KCM-specific strategies and dynamics, giving instructions for individual and/or group tasks, either guided or independent, choosing models of good practices, proposing case studies and readings, assessing and choosing the technologies needed (groupware, e-learning platforms, databases, blogs, wikis, repositories, messengers, social bookmarkers, etc.) and determining the evaluation system in an integrated, continuous fashion throughout the entire process.

However, improving the efforts of the KCM agents requires them to keep further pursuing several directions. Our studies have experimented with KCM models by delimiting the role of the managers and moderators, using varied motivation and participation strategies and further examining the usefulness of synchronous or asynchronous tools, while always using voluntary professional groups on an occasional basis. The crux of the matter is that if we want to promote significant developments, we have to consider the involvement of the entire organisation or most of it in KCM processes and thus overcome the dilemma of volunteers "versus" everyone in the organisation.

Likewise, despite the considerable surge in studies on KCM, it is worth continuing to work based on specific approaches in and from the field of education which enable us to evaluate, propose and validate procedures to create and manage knowledge in both in-person and online communities of practice according to the stage of education and the target groups. The goal is to analyse the personal, organisational and social effects entailed by the intensive use of CoPs by an organisation, while also providing instruments for self-evaluation to improve their functioning and tools to identify and validate the informal learning they generate.

However, the effective, widespread development of KCM approaches would not be possible without the implementation and development of strategies to support them. In this respect, headway is needed in identifying strategies for personal knowledge linked to the resistances to collective work and the development of the individuals in the organisation, such as peer guidance, mentoring or coaching.

Therefore, the problem is not so much one of conception as primarily one of development. The goal is to more deeply define the models and strategies that enable professionals to work together collaboratively, and then for their collaboration to generate positive results and effects for both individuals and the organisation.

7. Acknowledgment

Contributions from the study "Agentes y procesos en la gestión del conocimiento en red"(Agents and process in networked knowledge management). Ministry of Education and Culture, National R&D Plan (ref. SEJ2007-67093/EDUC), supervised by Joaquín Gairín.

8. References

Al-Hawamdeh, S. (2003). *Knowledge Management. Cultivating knowledge professionals,* Chandos, ISBN 978-1843340379, Publishing, Oxford.

Anderson, T. & Kanuka, H. (1997). *On-Line Forums: new platforms for professional development and Group Collaboration.* Retrieved from <http://www.ascuscs.org.jcmc/vol3/issue3/anderson.html>

Ardichvili, A., Page, V, & Wentling, T. (2003). Motivation and barriers to participation in virtual knowledge sharing teams. *Journal of Knowledge Management, 7*(1), pp. 64-77, ISSN 1367-3270

Armengol, C. & Rodríguez, D. (2006). La moderación de redes: algunos aspectos a considerar. *Educar,* 37, pp.85-100, ISSN 0211-819X

Aubusson, P. Steele, F., Dinham, S. & Brady, L. (2007). Action learning in teacher learning community formation: informative or transformative? *Teacher Development,* 11, 2, pp. 133-148, ISSN 1366-4530

Ballester, L., Orte, C., Oliver, J.L. & MARCH, M.X. (2006). Metodología para el trabajo socioeducativo en red. Comunicación presentada en el IV Congreso Estatal del Educador Social, Retrieved from <http://www.eduso.net/archivos/IVcongreso/comunicaciones/c65.pdf>

Bolam, R., McMahon, A. Stoll, L., Thomas, S., Wallace, M., Greenwood, A., Hawkey, K., Ingram, M., Atkinson, A. & Smith, M. (2005). *Creating and Sustaining Effective Professional Learning Communities.* University of Bristol, Bristol, Retrieved from <www.dcsf.gov.uk/research/data/uploadfiles/RR637.pdf >

Cabero, J. & Llorente, M.C. (2007). Propuesta de colaboración en educación a distancia y tecnología para el aprendizaje. *Edutec. Revista Electrónica de Tecnología Educativa,* 23, ISSN 1135-9250, Retrieved from <http://edutec.rediris.es/Revelec2/revelec23/jcabero/jcabero.html>

CEN (2004). *European Guide to good Practice in Knowledge Management - Part 3. SME Implementation.* CEN, Brussels, Retrieved from <http://www.cen.eu/cenorm/sectors/sectors/isss/cen+workshop+agreements/knowledge+management.asp>

Collison, C. & Parcell, G. (2003). *La Gestión del Conocimiento. Lecciones prácticas de una empresa líder.* Paidós, ISBN 9788449313677, Barcelona.

Cummings, S. & van Zee, A. (2005). Communities of practice and Networks: reviewing two perspectives on social learning. *Knowledge Management for Development Journal,* 1, 1, pp. 8-22, ISSN 1947-4199

Dalkir, K. (2005). *Knowledge Management in Theory and Practice.* Elsevier, ISBN 978-0750678643, Oxford

Davenport, T. & Prusak, L. (2001). *Conocimiento en Acción. Cómo las organizaciones manejan lo que saben.* Pearson Education, ISBN 9789879460290, Buenos Aries

De Benito, B. (1999). Taller: Redes y trabajo colaborativo entre profesores. *Proceedings of* EDUTEC 99. Retrieved from <http://gte.uib.es/articulo/EDUTEC99.pdf>

De Tena Rubio, R. (2004). La implantación de sistemas de gestión del conocimiento. In: *Conocimiento y Gestión,* D. Gallego & C. Ongallo (Eds.), (pp. 145-180). Pearson Educación, ISBN 9788420541129, Madrid

Dering, A., Cunninghan, S. & Withby, K. (2006). Developing leadership teams within an EAZ network: what makes for success? *School leadership and Management*, 26, 2, pp.107-123, ISSN 1363-2434

Despres, CH. & Chauvel, D. (Eds.) (2000). *Knowledge Horizons. The present and the promise of Knowledge Management*, Butterworth-Heinemann, ISBN 978-0750672474, Boston

Fernández-Enguita, M. (2008). ¿Qué hay de nuevo bajo el sol? De las organizaciones y los grupos a las redes. *Cuadernos de Pedagogía*, 385, pp.12-19, ISSN 0210-0630

Firestone, J. M. (2008). On Doing Knowledge Management. *Knowledge Management Research & Practice*, 6, pp. 13-22, ISSN 1477-8238

Firestone, J. M. & McElroy, M. W. (2003). *Key issues in the New Knowledge Management*, Elsevier, ISBN 978-0750676557, Burlington

Frappaolo, C. (2006). *Knowledge Management.* Capstone Publishing, ISBN 978-1841127057, West Susex

Gairín, J. (2006). Las comunidades virtuales de aprendizaje. *Educar* ,37, pp. 41-64, ISSN 0211-819X

Gairín, J. (2008). Las comunidades formativas de aprendizaje en el contexto institucional. *Gestión de centros.com.* Wolters Kluver Educación, Madrid

Gairín, J., Rodríguez-Gómez, D. & Armengol, C. (2010). Who exactly is the moderator? A consideration of online knowledge management network moderation in educational organisations. *Computers & Education,* 55, 1, pp. 304-312, ISSN 0360-1315

Garín, J. (2011) (Ed.). *El trabajo colaborativo en red. Actores y procesos en la creación y gestión del conocimiento colectivo*, DaVinci, ISBN 9788492651481, Barcelona

Gallego, D. & Ongallo, C. (Eds). (2004). *Conocimiento y gestión. La gestión del conocimiento para la mejora de las personas y las organizaciones,* Pearson Prentice Hall, ISBN 9788420541129, Madrid

Gannon-Leary,P. & Fontainha, E. (2007). Communities of practice and virtual learning communities: benefits, barriers and success factors. *E-learning Papers*, 5, Retrieved from <http://www.elearningeuropa.info/files/media/media13563.pdf>

Gea, M., Gutierrez, F. L., Garrido, J. L. & Cañas, J. (2002). *AMENITIES: Metodología de Modelado de Sistemas Cooperativos. Proceedings of III Congreso Internacional de Interacción Persona-Ordenador*, Madrid. Retrieved from <http://lsi.ugr.es/~mgea/workshops/coline02/Articulos/mgea.pdf>

González, A. P. (2005). *La Organización del trabajo y la formación en los nuevos escenarios: el papel de las TIC. Proceedings of Congreso: IV CIFO. IV Congreso de Formación para el trabajo: Nuevos escenarios de trabajo y nuevos retos en la Formación,* Retrieved from <http://tecnologiaedu.us.es/formaytrabajo/Documentos/pon3.pdf>

Gorelick, C., Milton, N. & April, K. (2004). *Performance Through Learning. Knowledge Management in Practice.* Elsevier, ISBN 978-0750675826, Burlington

Hardon, A. (2005). Virtual knowledge communities: lessons learned in making them work. *Knowledge Management for Development Journal*, 1, 1, pp. 71-78, ISSN 1947-4199

Hargreaves, A. & Giles, C. (2003). The Knowledge Society School: An Endangered Entity. In: *Teaching in the Knowledge Society: Education in the Age of Insecurity,* A. Hargreaves (Ed.), pp. 127-159, Open University Press, ISBN 978-0807743591, Philadelphia

Hislop, D. (2005). *Knowledge Management in Organizations. A critical introduction.* Oxford University Press, ISBN-13: 978-0199262069, Oxford

Huang, K-T., Lee, Y.W. & Wang, R. (1999). *Calidad de la información y gestión del conocimiento*. Aenor, ISBN 9788481431902, Madrid

Jeon, S., Kim, Y.G. & Koh, J. (2011). An integrative model for knowledge sharing in communities-of-practice. *Journal of Knowledge Management*, 15, 2, pp. 251-269, ISSN 1367-3270

Kimmble, C. & Hildreth, P. (2005). Dualities, distributed communities of practice and knowledge management. *Journal of Knowledge Management*, 9, 4, pp. 102-113, ISSN 1367-3270

Klein, J. H., Connell, N. & Meyer, E. (2005). Knowledge characteristics of communities of practice. *Knowledge Management Research & Practice*, 3, pp. 106-114, ISSN 1477-8238

Lave, J. & Wenger, E. (1991). *Situated Learning: Legitimate Peripheral Participation*. Cambridge University Press, ISBN 978-0521423748, New York

Leinonen, P. & Järvelä, S. (2006). Facilitating interpersonal evaluation of knowledge in a context of distributed team collaboration. *British Journal of Educational Technology*, 37, 6, pp. 897-916, ISSN 1467-8535

Liebowitz, J. (1999). *Knowledge Management Handbook*. CRC Press, ISBN 978-1439878033, Danvers, MA.

López, A. (2009). Dossier de treball: Treball col·laboratiu, visions disciplinàries. *Papers. Revista sobre la societat del coneixement*, 8, pp. 1-2, ISSN 1885-1541, Retrieved from <http://www.uoc.edu/uocpapers/8/dt/cat/presentacio.pdf>

McDermott, R. & O'Dell, C. (2001). Overcoming Cultural Barriers to Knowledge Sharing. *Journal of Knowledge Management*, 5, 1, pp. 76-85, ISSN 1367-3270

Milton, N. (2005). *Knowledge Management for teams and projects*. Chandos cop, ISBN-13: 978-1843341147, Oxford

Müller-Prothmann, T. (2006). *Leveraging Knowledge Communication for Innovation. Framework, Methods and Applications of Social Network Analysis in Research and Development*. Tesis doctoral. Retrieved from <http://www.diss.fu-berlin.de/diss/receive/FUDISS_thesis_000000002367 >

Nonaka, I. & Takeuchi, H. (1999). *La organización creadora de conocimiento*. Oxford University Press, ISBN 978-970613454, México

Petrides, L.A. & Nguyen, L. (2006). Knowledge Management Trends: Challegenes and Opportunities for Educational Institutions. In: *Knowledge Management and Higher Education. A critical analysis*, A. Scott (Ed.), (pp. 21-33). Idea Group Inc, ISBN 978-1591405108, Hershey

Polanyi, M. (1967). *The tacit dimension*. Routledge and Kegan Paul, ISBN 978-0844659992, London

Polanyi, M. (1983). *Personal knowledge: towards a post-critical philosophy*. Routledge and Kegan Paul, ISBN 978-0226672885, London

Ragachari, P. (2011). Knowledge sharing networks in professional complex systems. *Journal of Knowledge Management*, 13, 3, pp. 132-145, ISSN 1367-3270

Rao, M. (Ed.) (2005). *Knowledge Management Tools and Techniques. Practitioners and Experts Evaluate KM Solutions*. Elsevier, ISBN 978-0750678186, Burlington

Resnick, M. (2002). Rethinking Learning in the Digital Age. In: *The global Information Technology Report: Readiness for the Networked World*, G. Kirkman (Ed.) (pp.32-37). University Press, ISBN 978-0195152586, Oxford

Rodríguez-Gómez, D. (2009). *La creación y gestión del conocimiento en las organizaciones educativas: barreras y facilitadores.* Tesis doctoral. Universitat Autònoma de Barcelona.

Rodríguez-Gómez, D., Armengol, C., Fuentes, M. & Muñoz, J.L (2011). Roles y funciones en la creación y gestión del conocimiento. In: *El trabajo colaborativo en red. Actores y procesos en la creación y gestión del conocimiento colectivo,* J. GAIRÍN (Ed.), (pp. 161-180). DaVinci, ISBN 9788492651481, Barcelona

Saez, F., Garcia, O., Palao, J. & Rojo, P. (2009). Capital Humano (y II): Gestión del Conocimiento e-Learning y Modelos sociotécnicos. In: *Temas Básicos de Innovación tecnológica en las empresas.* Retrieved from <http://www.gsi.dit.upm.es/~fsaez/intl/indicecontenidos.html>

Sallis, E. & Jones, G. (2002). *Knowledge Management in Education: enchancing leaning and education.* Kogan Page Limited, ISBN 978-0749434953, London

Schenkel, A. & Teigland, R. (2008). Improved organizational performance through communities of practice. *Journal of Knowledge Management,* 12, 1, pp. 106-118, ISSN 1367-3270

Silva, J. (2004). El rol moderador del tutor en la conferencia mediada por computador. Edutec. *Revista Electrónica de Tecnología Educativa,* ISSN 1135-9250, Retrieved from <http://edutec.rediris.es/Revelec2/revelec17/silva_16a.htm>

Smith, M. K. (2009). *Communities of Practice. The encyclopedia of informal education.* Retrieved from <http://www.infed.org/biblio/communities_of_practice.htm>

Smith, M.A. & Kollock, P. (Eds.) (2003). *Comunidades en el ciberespacio.* Ediuoc, *Comunidades en el ciberespacio,* Barcelona

Sveiby, K.E. (2000). *Capital intelectual. La nueva riqueza de las empresas. Cómo medir y gestionar los activos intangibles para crear valor.* Gestión 2000, Máxima Laurent du Mesnil Éditeur, ISBN 9788480885454, Barcelona

Towsen, A., De Marie, S. & Hendrickson, A.R. (1998). Virtual teams: technology and the workplace of the future. *Academic of Management Executive,* 12, 3, pp. 17-29, ISSN 0896-3789

Usoro, A., Sharratt, M.W., Tsui, E. & Shekhar, S. (2007). Trust as an antecedent to knowledge sharing in virtual communities of practice. *Knowledge Management Research & Practice,* 5, pp. 199-212, ISSN 1477-8238

Ward, J. & Peppard, J. (2002). *Strategic Planning for Information Systems.* Weley, ISBN 978-0470841471, Chichester

Wenger, E. (2007). *Communities of Practice. A brief Introduction.* April 18th, 2009, Available from: <http://www.ewenger.com/theory/communities_of_practice_intro_WRD.doc>

Wenger,E. & Snyder, W. M. (2000). Communities of Practice: The Organizational Frontier. *Harvard Business Review,* 78, pp. 139-145, ISSN 0017- 8012

Wiig, K.M. (2004). *People-focused Knowledge Management. How effective Decision Making leads to corporate success.* Elsevier Butterworth-Heinemann, ISBN 978-0750677776, Oxford

Zang, W. & Watts, S. (2008). Online communities as communities of practice: a case study. *Journal of Knowledge Management,* 12, 4, pp. 55-71, ISSN 1367-3270

16

Talent Management in Knowledge-Intensive Organizations

Melissa Schroevers and Paul Hendriks
Radboud University Nijmegen, Nijmegen School of Management
The Netherlands

1. Introduction

In many organizations knowledge becomes increasingly important for sustaining competitive advantage. Knowledge-intensive firms (KIFs; Alvesson, 2004) gain competitive advantage by continuous adaptation to their environment. This constant adaptation to the competitive environment is realized by the unremitting generation and use of new knowledge (Harrison & Kessels, 2004, p. 3). Thus, for KIFs the strategic capacity to compete flows from knowledge; this knowledge is mainly derived from people (Kessels, 2004). Therefore it is assumed that managing their workforce's knowledge has become ever more critical to organizations. The relevance of HRM to knowledge management debates has long been noticed (e.g. Haesli & Boxall, 2005; Scarbrough, 2003; Storey & Quintas, 2002). Knowledge presumes knowing subjects, and therefore management focusing on knowledge and learning needs to pay attention to these subjects. Because of the emphasis on the knowledge people in knowledge-intensive firms possess and may create, organizations constantly need to find ways to make better use of this knowledge. Here, improved knowledge usage does not just concern better exploitation of existing knowledge sources but also leveraging the knowledge creation capability hidden in available knowledge. Even the most intelligent knowledge-based systems remain void of knowledge without intelligent users of these systems. As Kaulingfreks (2002) argues, knowledge management in an ICT-oriented approach easily runs the risk of producing erudite folly because of its preoccupation with information. What gets lost in even the most user-friendly and fully updated storage of best practices, Kaulingfreks argues, is the contextual, individual, non-transferrable, purposeless activity that knowledge is. Introductions into KM nowadays are considered incomplete if they do not pay sufficient attention to HRM and HRM handbooks typically include a chapter or section on knowledge and learning (e.g. Harrison & Kessels, 2004; Redman & Wilkinson, 2006; Adams, 2006).

A possibly interesting yet mostly unexplored domain of managing knowledge via HRM is by means of talent management. Since the late 1990s the interest in the topic of talent management has grown considerably. In 1997 a group of McKinsey consultants formulated the importance of talent for the performance of organizations by coining the 'War for Talent'. Since then the topic of talent management has received a remarkable degree of practitioner and academic interest (Gollings & Mellahi, 2009, p. 2). Changes in the environments of organizations such as globalization, growing operational complexity, an aging workforce, scarcity of talent, and greater international workforce mobility made the competition for talented knowledge workers a business case. 'Talent is the oil of the future and is the key to strategic success. Talent means all people in an organisation that contribute to its goals and competitive advantage' (Van der Sluis, 2009). Nowadays, most companies are experiencing a shortage of top talent as well as tough competition for talent (Heinen & O'Neill, 2004, p. 67). In 1998 Fishman already predicted a growing interest in the field of talent management in the near future: 'The most important corporate resource over the next 20 years will be talent: smart, sophisticated business people who are technologically literate, globally astute, and operationally agile. And as the demand for talent goes up, the supply of it will be going down' (Fishman, 1998, p. 1).

Connections between talent and its management on the one hand and subjects of knowledge and learning in organizations on the other seem logical and possibly fruitful. Yet subjects of knowledge management hardly receive any systematic attention in the talent management literature. Also the knowledge management and organizational learning literatures do not seem to have embraced notions of talent management. This paper aims to explore the potential of linking the fields of talent management and knowledge management, The method taken in this research is that of a literature review of the emerging stream of talent management studies via a knowledge and learning perspective that is derived from a literature review of the knowledge management literature. To meet these objectives, the chapter addresses three questions:

1. What is the definition of talent management; what do different literature views say about the definitions on talent management and their scopes?
2. Why should we aim at linking talent management to debates on knowledge management and organizational learning? What debates regarding the latter two fields can be supported by adding insights from the talent management domain?
3. How would talent management when linked to KM/OL help envision practical implementation of management programmes around knowledge and learning? This question refers to the objectives as well as the means of talent management in light of knowledge-related challenges and problems. For example, a relevant debate concerns which HR practices can be applied to achieve the objectives of talent management to support knowledge and learning processes. Which approaches does talent management offer that may help organizations meet their knowledge-related objectives?

2. Towards a definition of talent management

It is no easy task to find a unanimously accepted definition of talent management. A key limitation in the field of talent management is its lack of a consistent definition (Collings & Mellahi, 2009, p. 1; Lewis & Heckman, 2006, p. 139; Cappelli, 2008, p. 74). 'There isn't a single consistent or concise definition of talent management' (Ashton & Morton, 2005, p. 30). Lewis & Heckman (2006, p. 139) speak of a 'disturbing lack of clarity regarding the definition, scope and overall goals of talent management'. As Lewis & Heckman (2006, p. 143) mention: 'Talent management, as defined currently, is not well grounded in research, not distinct from traditional HR practices or disciplines, and is supported mainly by anecdote'. Also, the terms 'talent management', 'talent strategy', 'succession management' and 'human resource planning' are often used interchangeably (Lewis & Heckman, 2006, p. 140). Thus, despite a growing popularity in the field of talent management and despite hopeful debates between authors, the concept of talent management remains unclear (Collings & Mellahi, 2009, p. 3).

A useful starting point for finding a navigation path through the definitional maze that surrounds the talent management concept is provided by Lewis & Heckman (2006) who identify three distinct streams of thought regarding talent management. First, some studies merely substitute the label of human resource management with talent management by focusing on human resource practices, functions, activities such as recruiting, selection, development and career succession management (Lewis & Heckman, 2006, p. 140). A second perspective on talent management primarily highlights the concept of 'talent pools' by focusing on 'projecting employee/staffing needs and managing the progression of employee through positions' (Lewis & Heckman, 2006, p. 140). These approaches typically build on earlier research in the manpower planning/human resource planning or succession planning literature. A third perspective on talent management emphasizes the management of talented people; this perspective involves is a clear focus on talent generically (Collings & Mellahi, 2009; Lewis & Heckman, 2006, p. 141). With this approach, all roles within the organization should be filled with employees who are considered 'A performers' or 'top grading' (Smart, 1999).

Two assertions can be made. First, of these three streams only the third type of definition seems to offer a serious attempt to provide a foothold for asking who is to be considered a 'talent' and what is the 'talent' that this person has or should have. The first two classes (talents as substitute for HR or talent as element of a pool to be developed) seem to use the concept of talent just for labelling reasons - and perhaps even for rhetoric or advertisement reasons. They would need further elaboration of the concept of talent. And second, the three types of definition do not represent approaches that are conceptually at odds with one another, but provide perspectives that may be combined (e.g. one can easily combine stream 3 typified by its focus on A-performers with the attention for talent pools in stream 2). To explore these linkages we can inspect some of the definitions of talent management given in the literature.

Cappelli (2008, p. 74-76) defines talent management as 'a matter of anticipating the need for human capital and then setting out a plan to meet it'. He mentions the need for a fundamentally new approach to talent management that takes into account the great uncertainty businesses face today. By borrowing lessons from operations and supply chain research, firms can forge a new model to make talent management better suited to today's realities (Cappelli, 2008, p. 76). Cappelli's definition fits with the third perspective on talent management because of the focus on (the management of) talented human capital.

Another example that fits the third stream is provided by Frank and Taylor (2008). These authors acknowledge the evolutionary changes that will permanently affect how we approach talent management. 'Workplaces everywhere are facing an increasingly complex and ever-changing landscape in their efforts to acquire, retain, motivate and develop the talent needed to keep their organizations operating efficiently and competitively' (Frank and Taylor, 2008, p. 34). This definition also acknowledges the need for talent and therefore their definition of talent management also fits in the third stream of thought regarding the concept of talent management as identified by Lewis & Heckman (2006). However, because of their focus on human resource practices such as recruitment and development of employees and because of the emphasis on strategic goals ('operate efficiently and competitively'), this definition adds elements of the first perspective on talent management: 'talent management as a substitute for strategic human resource practices'.

A third example, also within the third stream, can be found in Fishman (1998). According to this author, talent management refers to the skills of attracting highly skilled workers, of integrating new workers, and developing and retaining current workers to meet current and future business objectives. This process of attracting and retaining profitable employees in order to strive for competitive and strategic advantage has come to be known as 'the war for talent'. Because it acknowledges the need for talent in order to achieve business objectives, the definition of Fishman (1998) is consistent with the third perspective on talent management which emphasizes the management of talented people. But here too this is combined with the first perspective on talent management, given the focus on human resource practices.

Several other authors emphasize the interests and strategic objectives of the organization in implementing talent management practices when defining talent management. For example, Van Aken (1991) defines talent management as 'the way in which managers manage their employees in order to deploy their talents as much as possible for the benefit of the success of the organization'. The success and competitive advantage of the organization is also emphasized in the following definition of Mensink (1991). According to Mensink (1991), 'talent management is the stimulation of people/employees to perform as well as possible to shed light upon the success of the organization'. Also Van der Sluis (2009) recognizes the importance of talent in achieving organizational objectives: 'Talent means all people in an organisation that contribute to its goals and competitive advantage' (Van der Sluis, 2009). Because of the focus on strategic objectives, these definitions too fit the third, general perspective on talent management in which there is a clear focus on the management of talent in general in order to strive for competitive advantages.

Next to the two remarks regarding Lewis and Heckman's (2006) triplet of talent management approaches made above, a third remark has to be that the three streams identified by these authors do not cover the full breadth of the talent management debates. Collings & Mellahi (2009) add an emerging fourth stream of thought regarding talent management to these three key streams. These authors define *strategic talent management* as: 'activities and processes that involve the systematic identification of key positions which differentially contribute to the organization's sustainable competitive advantage, the development of a talent pool of high potential and high performing incumbents to fill these roles, and the development of a differentiated human resource architecture to facilitate filling these positions with competent incumbents and to ensure their continued commitment to the organization' (Collings & Mellahi, 2009, p. 9). They recognize an emphasis on the identification of key positions rather than talented individuals per se (Collings & Mellahi, 2009, p. 6). This emphasis is not present in any of the other three streams, which justifies assigning definitions of talent management in terms of key positions to a fourth stream.

In summary, it can be concluded that a clear, broadly accepted definition of talent management is lacking in the literature. Because of this, an integrated definition of talent management cannot simply be derived from the extant literature but needs to be constructed. What the assorted definitions show is that a key element involves a focus on the talent of employees in order to enhance the organizational performance. The concept of talent should be read as a combination of (1) people ('A-performers'), (2) the specific skills and competencies of these individuals (the talents of the A-performers) and (3) key positions within the firm to address the linkage between these talented individuals and their organizational role (in the talent management domain, someone is not to be considered a talent because of her individual traits in isolation but always in connection to organizational processes and objectives). Human resource practices and talent pool programmes can then be perceived and designed as means to stimulate organizational success via these talents. This allows us to conceive of the conceptual unity that binds the four streams on talent management that have been distinguished. These four streams are: 'talent management as HR practices', 'talent pools', 'the management of talented people' and the 'identification of key positions'. The latter two appear as the home base for coming to grips with the concept of talent as a domain for management, with the first two as extensions to allow the specification of management programmes and approaches.

3. Why look for linkages between talent management and knowledge management?

The second question identified in the introduction concerns the reasons for linking talent management to knowledge management and organizational learning. To answer this question, an inspection of the knowledge management field is called for. Two main streams can be discerned in the development of the knowledge management field (e.g. Hislop, 2009; Chiva & Alegre, 2005; Schultze & Stabell, 2004). One stream approaches knowledge as a functional resource, and provides a perspective for how that resource can be approached to identify its unique strategic potential (Zack, 1999) as a starting point for drafting management programmes for achieving that potential by knowledge management programmes and tools. Historically, especially the class of ICT tools has attracted much attention but within this functionalist approach to KM also several authors discuss the possibilities of HR programmes. A second stream has emerged, which can now be seen as an integral element of the knowledge management perspective, adopting a critical stance with regard to the functionalist perspective (e.g. Alvesson, 2004; Tsoukas, 2005; Brown & Duguid, 1998; Cook & Brown, 1999). This stream challenges the potential of knowledge as a functionalist resource, because thinking of knowledge as a resource would involve a conceptual impoverishment in our understanding of the very nature of knowledge (e.g. the way functionalist KM thinkers treat the fundamental category of tacit knowledge leads Tsoukas, 2003, to ask the question of 'Do we really understanding tacit knowledge?' - needless to say that his answer is 'no', not the way it was intended by Michael Polanyi, the intellectual father of the concept). These authors stress the importance of social processes and social context in which knowledge is created, and recreated. When divorced from social context, as happens when only the content side to knowledge is recognized as the basis for 'knowledge' storage in ICT systems or when knowledge domains are specified in HR development programmes, knowledge is considered to be void of meaning. Within that second stream, knowledge management is considered by many authors as a vague and ambiguous field of study. Knowledge management is a term which is difficult to understand because knowledge is something which cannot really be managed.

Several authors, including Alvesson (1993, 2001), Becker (2001), Sewell (2005) and Tsoukas (1996), identify a focus on 'ambiguity' when describing the dominance and understanding of the nature and significance of 'knowledge' in contemporary companies and in particular in knowledge-intensive firms. These authors emphasize the ambiguity of knowledge work and the struggle knowledge-intensive organizations have with it. Not only the concept of knowledge is ambiguous, but also the role of knowledge in a knowledge-intensive company is ambiguous. "Ambiguity, (involving uncertainty, contradictions that cannot be resolved or reconciled, absence on agreement on boundaries, clear principles or solutions), then is seen as a crucial element in work and organization" (Alvesson, 1993, p. 1002). Ambiguity is different from uncertainty, because more information does remove the uncertainty, but does not delete ambiguity. Ambiguity refers to the reduction of the ability to make a qualified judgement on a certain situation (Alvesson, 1993; Becker, 2001; Tsoukas, 1996).

Institutionalized myths are a way of claiming to be knowledge-intensive. Beliefs that are taken for granted bridge the gap between claims of rationality and the ambiguity within the organization. Hence, the focus changes from the formal knowledge to the strategies that persuade all stakeholders involved to convince them of the expertise and knowledge that is employed by the organization (Alvesson, 1993). KIFs are typically more concerned with being socially recognized as being an expert than ultimately being one. Consequently, various rhetorical strategies are employed to create a rhetoric that stresses the personal qualities, besides the knowledge base that knowledge workers are claimed upon, that knowledge workers must possess to appear qualified. In this myth perspective, knowledge has other roles such as:

"a) a means for creating community and social identity through offering organizational members a shared language and promoting their self-esteem, b) a resource for persuasion in, for example, PR work and interactions with customers, c) providing the company with a profile (an intended image targeted at the market), d) creating legitimacy and good faith regarding actions and outcomes, and e) obscuring uncertainty and counteraction reflection" (Alvesson, 1993, p. 1011).

The expertise of the knowledge worker is not only expressed by an objective result, but also symbolizes rationality, intelligence, quality etc. Knowledge can hence not be isolated and be seen as a particular that is in itself important and the success of knowledge-intensive work is contingent upon beliefs about knowledge workers offering something specific (Alvesson, 2000). Knowledge does not exist separate from the social processes of interpretation and meaning creation (Alvesson, 2000). Ambiguity involved in meaning creation processes is the foundation for the 'quality' of knowledge.

Alvesson (1993; 2000; 2001) proposes a new theoretical framework for the concepts of knowledge and knowledge work, involving three kinds of ambiguity: 1) ambiguity of knowledge, 2) ambiguity of the significance of knowledge, and 3) ambiguity of results claimed to be contingent upon knowledge work. The ambiguity of knowledge refers to the claimed core product and the varying definitions on what knowledge is claimed to be in knowledge-intensive firms. Second, knowledge is not necessarily significant in work, because it is connected to flexibility, motivation, social skills, ways of operating, and other elements that are involved in doing knowledge-intensive work. Finally, the work results of knowledge work are very hard to evaluate, while knowledge work is a very intangible and complex 'product'. The work results are often subject to uncertainty, because criteria for evaluating the quality are lacking. They are more based on the perception of the client about the degree to which their problem is solved or the outcomes meet the expectations. "Institutionalized assumptions, expectations, recognitions, reputation, images etcetera are important to how the products of KIFOWs [KIFs] are perceived" (Alvesson, 1993, p. 1007). As a result, KIFs can be defined as being very 'ambiguity-intensive', as Alvesson (1993) calls it.

As Alvesson & Karreman (2001) argue, the term knowledge management has the threat of falling into pieces when both knowledge and management are taken seriously. The functionalist stream with its focus on knowledge as strategic resource and the deployment of knowledge management tools takes management very seriously, which results in an impoverished understanding of knowledge which is hardly different from information. The critical, social-constructivist stream of social-practice approaches to knowledge management and organizational learning aims at building a more fully-fledged conceptual image of knowledge, yet at the expense of sidestepping a systematic analysis of the management side. Building a meaningful combination of the two - knowledge ánd management - appears hard, simply because the realm of management stops when ambiguity enters. Or, as Ten Bos (2002) puts it: "The urge to manage knowledge stems from the need to offer management professionals what we know in a neat and well-structured fashion. I believe, however, that knowledge that has been structured and arranged this way, in a certain sense no longer qualifies as knowledge. To put it differently, whoever manages, gives up every claim of knowledge. [...] Management necessarily involves the exclusion of many contents and the attempt to capture, document and clarify what cannot be excluded. The price you pay is that knowledge is no longer subversive, revealing, creative or even exciting." Ambiguity and critical thinking are crucial in the complex situations knowledge-intensive firms face nowadays (Alvesson, 2004). In addition to this focus on ambiguity when describing knowledge and learning in organizations, Alvesson (2004) also claims the label of knowledge management is sometimes overstretched and that it should be used with a greater sense of its drawbacks.

The same applies to the concepts of 'organizational learning' and the 'learning organization', critics also have suggested that the learning organization can be construed as an ideology which is far from reality in organizations as we know them today (e.g. Driver, 2002). Therefore, concepts like knowledge management and learning organizations are frequently seen as 'management trends' for which the effectiveness is difficult to demonstrate.

What is argued here is that one way of bridging this ambiguity and vagueness of knowledge and associated learning processes and the legitimate desire to intentionally regulate organizational matters is to insert a focus on talent management to establish a relation between knowledge management and performance. Talent and knowledge are closely related subjects (e.g. Arab & Plucker, 2002). What makes talent management an attractive candidate for managing in knowledge-intensive situations relates to the triplet identified above of talent as a specific class of individuals ('A-performers'; these would become knowledge workers or knowledge subjects when approached from a knowledge perspective), a specific content (talent as high-level skills involves a key element of potential, and is meaningless without some domain that the talent applies to) and organizational positions (key positions refer to the organizational perspective, and thus may be used to step beyond the individual focus on people with their personal knowledge). Talent management can thus be used to avoid a limited functionalist approach to knowledge. By focusing on the talents of the workforce and by specifying these talents in knowledge related terminology (e.g. the content side to talent specified in relation to specific knowledge domains, the dynamic aspects of talents explored with respect to such processes as knowledge sharing and knowledge creation), knowledge enters the management domain in a way that avoids the risks of conceptual erosion of the knowledge concept. Knowledge functions as a gauge to select and specify talents considered crucial for meaningful persistence of the organization; it does not become the direct object of management. Also the concepts of talent management can function as a suited selection and specification vehicle within the broader HRM domain. Obviously, the social-practice sides to knowledge and learning processes call for a management focus on individuals and groups of individuals in connection to their organizational tasks and roles. Yet simply thinking of knowledge management as incomplete without human resource management would provide a not well-informed guide into the HRM field. Talent management is proposed here as a highly suited candidate for providing the missing link between the people side to management and knowledge-related challenges and problems within organizations.

Knowledge and learning are of fundamental importance in understanding organizations as adaptive systems. Regarding the strategic domain (viz. the discussion couched in terms of knowledge as a strategic resource or strategic capability) the use of talent management offers an attractive option to establish a positive relation between knowledge and learning on the one hand and the performance of organizations on the other. A reformulation and elaboration of knowledge-related talent management in strategic knowledge management terminology involves honouring the distinctive position that specific knowledge and learning capabilities may entail in a way that enables us to avoid a functionalist, objectivist perspective on knowledge without losing sight of the potential strategic boons of a knowledgeable workforce. Thus, a combined talent-knowledge focus on strategic positioning involves a potentially rich elaboration of *strategic* human resource management.

At the infrastructural level, talent management with a focus on the knowledge-related talents of employees also provides a powerful perspective on potentials and limitations of management in knowledge-intensive environments. Alvesson (2004) defines 'knowledge-intensive firms' as follows: 'organizations that offer to the market the use of fairly sophisticated knowledge or knowledge-based products. The core activities in these companies are based on the intellectual skills of a very large proportion of the labour force deployed in development, and often also in the sale of products and in service work' (Alvesson, 2004, p. 17). In these kinds of organizations, there is a strong focus on knowledge and on attracting and retaining knowledge workers who possess this knowledge. Therefore, within knowledge-intensive organizations, talent management can be significant in recruiting, developing and retaining talent. Within knowledge-intensive organizations, talented employees and their knowledge are considered important in producing those goods and services that yield and maintain competitive advantage. Connecting talent management to knowledge processes allows envisioning knowledge-related objectives as manageable entities. As examples of these knowledge processes and the way these would perceived via their relation to talent management, consider the processes of knowledge retention, knowledge sharing and knowledge creation. The first of these, knowledge retention, translates into identifying the key domains of knowledge that should not get lost into specific talents attached to these domains without modelling these domains (cf. the risks involved in knowledge modelling as identified by Ten Bos), and opens the door to specifying which A-performers, which talents and which key positions are pivotal in maintaining appropriate levels of organizational knowledge. Knowledge sharing as a talent-related theme allows focusing on the tacit and explicit sides to knowledge without unduly treating these as separate categories. Perceiving of knowledge creation as a talent-related process allows focusing management attention not so much on the current knowledge per se, but on the potential current insight and associated reflection have for future insights that develop because of current knowledge yet deviate from it. The ambiguity and intransparancy of exactly this knowledge creation process thus remains centre stage in management efforts aimed at enhancing the creativity of the organization. Also broader conditions for these knowledge processes, such as the culture of the organization or shared worldviews among groups of personnel, may earn their appropriate place on the management agenda. The infrastructure of organizations needs to be regulated in a way that talent management can be established. When organizations launch talent management activities, a proper learning and working climate needs to be at hand (Christaensen et al., 2009). Therefore, without an existing learning climate, talent management activities cannot be launched in knowledge-intensive organizations.

4. On how to manage talent as knowledge management

To further elaborate on how a perspective on knowledge-related talent management provides an insight into possible management programmes and tools, attention needs to be paid to how objectives of talent management are to be specified. This concerns a necessary preparation for answering the third question posed in the introduction regarding the management practices of what can be labelled as 'knowledge-intensive talent management'. According to Van Beers (2005), the objectives of talent management are 'the optimal obtaining, mobilizing, developing and retaining of the talents which are needed for organizations to distinguish themselves on the market and in their provision of services'. This definition identifies two classes of objectives. Firstly, external objectives are included that concern distinguishing the organization from competitors or establishing its external identity (talents as vehicles for strategic positioning). These objectives link to the strong relation that exists between talent management and the strategic organizational objectives of the organization (Mensink, 1991; Van der Sluis, 2009). Thus the objectives of talent management can be described in terms of achieving competitive advantages and increased organizational performance. As signalled above, what talents are from a knowledge perspective is exactly those organizational knowing and learning capabilities that can be used to gain a competitive edge. To identify what strategic talents are, the knowledge management literature offers suited support in the processes of defining a knowledge strategy (e.g. the approach developed by Zack, 1999) that could be used in connection with a focus on talent to around knowledge domains, A-performers on these domains and key positions associated with the processing of these knowledge domains.

Next to these strategic objectives in Van Beers' definition, it also refers to the 'optimal obtaining, mobilizing, developing and retaining of the talents'. These objectives refer to organization-internal prerequisites for effective external positioning via talents. We will label this second class of objectives as infrastructural objectives: the objective of the organizational infrastructure will be to make sure that talents are and remain indoor that are indispensible for meeting the strategic objectives. A further specification of these infrastructural objectives is provided by Van der Sluis (2009) who states that 'talent management is about the finding, binding, captivating and flourishing of people in organizations with the goal of optimizing the labour productivity of their workforce'. Van der Sluis (2009) distinguishes the following three steps:

- Appoint and attract talent;
- Deploy and guide talent;
- Develop and bind talent.

When combining goals of talent management as presented by Van der Sluis (2009) and Van Beers (2005) the following list of infrastructural goals of talent management emerges:

- *Finding:* recruitment and selection.
- *Binding:* contracts, engagements/arrangements and inspiring confidence
- *Captivating*: providing perspective, professionalism and collegiality.
- *Flourishing:* performance, learning, innovation and excel, focus on talent development.
- *Development:* stimulate learning and development (career development).

- *Retain talent:* by providing enough challenge in the work of professionals.

In addition to these objectives, Horowitz (2003: in Redman and Wilkinson, 2006), list the following objectives of talent management which are effective in motivating ('captivating'), developing and retaining talented knowledge workers:

- *Having fundamentally interesting work:* the work needs to be intrinsically, and continuously satisfying and stimulating;
- *High levels of autonomy:* workers need to be free to choose their own work activities and projects;
- *Significant opportunities for self-development*: there is a high need for continuous development under knowledge workers, which is a distinctive characteristic of this group of workers (Horowitz, 2003: in Redman & Wilkinson, 2006, pp. 415-416).

Again, a clear connection can be observed when linking the concepts of knowledge and learning in organizations to the objectives of talent management. When pursuing the objectives of finding, binding, captivating, flourishing, developing and retaining talented employees (Van der Sluis, 2009; Van Beers, 2005) and by providing fundamentally interesting work, high levels of autonomy and significant opportunities for self-development (Horowitz, 2003 in Redman & Wilkinson, 2006), talent management will be most effective. By using talent management as a means to fill in the performance side to knowledge management, a positive relationship between knowledge management and performance in organizations can be established. Pursuing the objectives of talent management as presented in this paragraph therefore can be used to strive for a higher knowledge-related performance of organizations.

The means for achieving these classes of talent management objectives provided in the literature and practice of talent management (e.g. Bhatnagar, 2007; Cseres & Kelly, 2006; Farley, 2005; Frank et al., 2004; Romans et al., 2006; Romans & Lardner, 2005), specifically concern a series of human resource practices. Talent management can be employed by making use of several practices; by implementing these practices it is assumed that the strategic objectives of talent management will be reached. Authors argue that organizations need to come up with 'bundles of HR practices' which are effective for motivating, developing and retaining talented knowledge workers (Redman and Wilkinson, 2006). Talent management practices are referred to in 'bundles', given the recognition that these processes need to be well integrated. Without a cohesive system of talent management practices, the required high performance will not be achieved (Heinen and O'Neill, 2004). The objectives of talent management as distinguished by Van der Sluis (2009) and Van Beers (2005) will again be used here to discuss the most suitable human resource practices. The bundles of human resource practices consist of:

- *Recruitment and selection:* find the talented employees organizations search for by means of applying accurate recruitment and selection practices. With recruitment and selection practices there has to be a proper 'fit' between new talent and the organization's current strategy and culture (Van der Sluis, 2009). Recruitment practices are vital in getting the right talent at the right place (Blass, 2009). When attracting talent, knowledge-intensive companies have to depict themselves as organizations having a clear focus on the personal development of these talented workers in a diverse environment.
- *Contracts, arrangements and pay:* to attach your talented employees to an organization, the organization has to provide knowledge workers with attractive levels of pay and reward packages (Horowitz, 2003: in Redman & Wilkinson, 2006, p. 416). Talent-oriented companies should provide talented employees with performance-based

compensation packages, quality of life considerations and career development in an environment that promotes diversity and communicate these conditions of employment to the people they want to attract (Blass, 2009, p. 13).

- *Providing perspective, professionalism and collegiality:* in addition to the contractual arrangements, a confidential environment is important in binding talented employees to the organization (Van der Sluis, 2009). To captivate as well as motivate talent, the organization has to provide perspective in the form of opportunities to develop and by offering enough learning opportunities (Van der Sluis, 2009) which is in line with the next HR practice of talent development.
- *Talent development:* focus on innovation, performance and learning in order to develop the talents of employees. Talent development supports employees through their life cycle with the organization (Schiemann, 2009, p. 45). With talent development an existing learning climate has to be at hand (Christiaensen et al., 2009) to enable knowledge workers to constantly adapt their knowledge to new situations. Besides, every talented employee needs performance feedback on previous stated objectives of personal growth/development (Schiemann, 2009).
- *Career development:* to retain talented knowledge workers, enough career prospects have to be provided. A common problem in many knowledge-intensive organizations is for talented employees to leave their jobs because they are not being allowed to do as much as they would like to do for their organizations (Blass, 2009). Talented workers should be stimulated to constantly develop their talents in working towards higher job levels. Retaining talented workers also flows from constantly providing enough challenge in the work of professionals and again from contractual arrangements such as specific levels of pay (Van der Sluis, 2009; Van Beers, 2005).

In the description of these different human resource practices of talent management, a clear connection between these practices and knowledge and learning in organization becomes visible. In recruiting and selecting talented employees a strong focus can be put on the knowledge of these talented employees. Besides, in certain knowledge-intensive firms (Alvesson, 2004), potential employees will only be selected from a certain level of education (for instance an academic degree). The knowledge these talented employees possess is assumed to be strategic and decisive in achieving competitive advantage. The 'War for Talent' (Fishman, 1998) consists of attracting highly skilled, knowledgeable workers. Learning in organizations is also significant in, for example, the practices of 'career development', 'talent development' and providing 'perspective'. Without a learning climate, talented knowledge workers will not get the opportunity to develop themselves (Christiaensen et al., 2009); this learning climate is therefore very important when considering these practices. A learning climate means having enough possibilities to constantly adapt knowledge workers' knowledge to new situations. Because of this learning climate, the knowledge worker is constantly learning and will be provided enough challenges to remain within the organization.

5. Conclusion

By means of a literature review of talent management, the main objective of this paper was to explore the connections between knowledge and learning in organizations and talent management. More specifically, talent management has been used as a potentially interesting specification vehicle for establishing the relationship between knowledge management and organizational performance. In this paper four different streams of talent management have been identified, and sorted into the two main streams of approaching talent as 'A-performers' and key positions along with two auxiliary streams addressing associated HR practices and talent pool management activities. It has been argued that because of the vagueness, broadness and ambiguity of knowledge, a direct link between knowledge and organizational performance remains evasive. Given the assertion that knowledge is first and foremost organizationally relevant if and when it forms the basis for generating new knowledge - and thus when present knowledge is not enough for securing a viable and meaningful strategic position for organizations - using knowledge as the guiding light when drafting strategic courses would appear futile. What would such strategic choice look like when based on vagueness, ambiguity, and dispute centred on what organizations do not know (which is strategically highly relevant) as opposed to the certainties of what they do know (which in themselves are strategically hardly interesting)? Talent management, when aimed at combining insights on 'A-performers' with insights on key positions, has been proposed as a means to fill in the performance side of knowledge management in organizations as talent concerns exactly the type of conditions not just to apply current knowledge but also to generate new insights and foster deep learning.

What the talent management literature shows is that setting the goals of finding, binding, captivating, flourishing, developing and retaining talented employees (Van der Sluis, 2009; Van Beers, 2005) and providing fundamentally interesting work, high levels of autonomy and significant opportunities for self-development (Horowitz, 2003, in Redman and Wilkinson, 2006), will result in making talent management most effective. Furthermore, the human resource practices 'recruitment and selection', 'contracts, arrangements and pay', 'providing perspective, professionalism and collegiality', talent development' and 'career development' should be integrated and aligned with the firm's business strategy in order to pursue these stated goals. In this paper it has been argued that by focusing on talented employees and by using their capabilities in order to strive for performance, the 'black box' between HRM practices and performance can be opened up.

The importance of HRM practices for effective knowledge management has been acknowledged by many authors in the knowledge management field (Hislop, 2009, p. 239). By developing the commitment and loyalty of workers to share, codify and create knowledge, HRM policies can play a crucial role in supporting organizational knowledge management (Hislop, 2009). In this debate talent management has not yet been recognized as a means to specify the HRM practices of knowledge management. When considering knowledge and learning in organizations it appears natural to focus on talented employees because they possess the specific creative abilities needed to survive in a knowledge-intensive environment. Several authors emphasize the importance of talent management when striving for organizational performance (Fishman, 1998). According to Heinen and O'Neill (2004), talent management practices can create the most enduring competitive advantages. Sustained competitive advantage comes from talent management practices, how the organization attracts, develops, motivates, manages and rewards its talent (Heinen and O'Neill, 2004, p. 67). Talent management can become effective only when talent management processes are integrated into a firm's business strategy. As a consequence, to be successful, the talent strategy must be aligned with an organization's business strategy and human capital context (Heinen and O'Neill, 2004). Talent management practices are supposed to create the most enduring competitive advantages (Heinen and O'Neill, 2004). But because of a lack of research-based evidence, the productive link between talent

management and performance has not been empirically confirmed (Lewis & Heckman, 2006). Establishing a concrete link between talent management programs and performance metrics proves to remain difficult (Farley, 2005). 'The topic talent management has been enthusiastically pursued in the trade and popular press without being systematically linked to peer-reviewed, research-based findings' (Lewis & Heckman, 2006, p. 142).
Despite the lack of research-based evidence regarding the relationship between talent management and performance of organizations, this paper has argued that managing around talent in light of knowledge-related challenges and problems may serve as a useful beacon in attempts to increase performance. A condition that has to be met, however, is that talent management practices are well integrated and aligned with the firm's business strategy. More research is needed to determine whether, how and when implementing talent management activities will actually lead to business success when knowledge and learning are defined as key beacons for setting a strategic course and providing the organizational conditions when needed to adjust the course while following to it. The effectiveness of talent management as a potentially powerful specification of a knowledge management approach therefore needs to be further examined by future empirical research.
To conclude this paper we offer some discussion elements regarding possible future studies and KM practices in the combined domain of knowledge management and talent management. Talent management has been interpreted here as a means to increase organizational performance. It should be seen as a potential HR system (bundle of practices) for managing knowledge in knowledge-intensive settings. Implementing the bundles of human resource practices in talent management programmes (e.g. Blass, 2009; Schiemann, 2009; Van Beers, 2005; Van der Sluis, 2009), as has been distinguished in paragraph 4, will help knowledge-intensive organizations in establishing a concrete link between managing knowledge and learning on the one hand and striving for organizational performance on the other. By implementing the proper recruitment and selection practices, personnel with a specific knowledge level will enter the organization. Their knowledge will be managed by means of providing them with adequate arrangements and development possibilities. When these talented employees develop their skills and knowledge within the organization, the organization is assumed to benefit as well. Furthermore, by means of these talent management-geared HR practices, knowledge workers (also defined as 'talent' or 'A performers'), are assumed to constantly learn within this organizational environment. Talent management has therefore been interpreted as an attempt to increase the organizational performance. Future studies regarding the effectiveness of talent management are required to broaden our understandings regarding the connections between knowledge management and increased performance rates of organizations. Recommendations for subjects to be addressed in future studies elaborating the talent management-knowledge management connection include:

- How to enable talented workers to share their knowledge;
- How to create a learning climate in which talented workers will gain enough possibilities for developing themselves (personally as well as technically);

6. References

Adams, J. (2006). *Managing People in Organizations: contemporary theory and practice*, Palgrave, Houndmills

Alvesson, M. (1993). Organizations as Rhetoric - Knowledge-Intensive Firms and the Struggle with Ambiguity. *Journal of Management Studies*, Vol. 30, No. 6, pp. 997-1015

Alvesson, M. (2001). Knowledge work: Ambiguity, image and identity. *Human Relations*, Vol. 54, No. 7, pp. 863-886

Alvesson, M. (2004). *Knowledge work and knowledge-intensive firms*, Oxford University Press, Oxford

Alvesson, M., & Karreman, D. (2001). Odd couple: Making sense of the curious concept of knowledge management. *Journal of Management Studies*, Vol. 38, No. 7, pp. 995-1018

Ashton, C. & Morton, L. (2005). Managing Talent for Competitive Advantage, *Strategic HR Review*, Vol. 4, No. 5, pp. 28-31

Barab, S.A., & Plucker, J.A. (2002). Smart People or Smart Contexts? Cognition, ability and talent development in an age of situated approaches to knowing and learning. *Educational Psychologist*, Vol. 37, No. 3, pp. 165-182

Becker, M. C. (2001). Managing dispersed knowledge: Organizational problems, managerial strategies, and their effectiveness. *Journal of Management Studies*, Vol. 38, No. 7, pp. 1037-1051

Bhatnagar, J. (2007). Talent management strategy of employee engagement in Indian ITES employees: key to retention. *Employee Relations*, Vol. 29, No. 6, pp. 640-663

Blass, E. (2009). *Talent management: cases and commentary*, Palgrave Macmillan (Palgrave connect online services), New York

Boselie, P. , Dietz, G. & Boon, C. (2005). Commonalities and contradictions in HRM and performance research, *Human Resource Management Journal*, Vol. 15, pp. 67-94

Boxall, P. & Purcell, J. (2008). *Strategy and Human Resource Management* (second edition), Palgrave Macmillan, Basingstoke

Brown, J.S. & Duguid, P. (1998). Organizing knowledge. *California Management Review*, Vol. 40, No. 3, pp. 90-111

Cappelli, P. (2008). Talent management for the 21st century, *Harvard Business Review*, March 2008, pp. 74-81

Chiva, R. & Alegre, J. (2005). Organizational learning and organizational knowledge - Towards the integration of two approaches. *Management Learning*, Vol. 36, No. 1, pp. 49-68

Christiaensen, R., Dochy, F., Kinschots, C., Kyndt, E., Marcelis, V., Philips, K., Van Cauwenberghe, H., Van den Bogaert, T. & Vervaeke, A. (2009). *Talent and Talent development: a literature review [Talent en Talentontwikkeling: een literatuurstudie]*, University of Leuven, Leuven

Collings, D.G. & Mellahi, K. (2009). Strategic Talent Management: A review and research agenda, *Human Resource Management Review*, Vol. 19, No. 4, pp. 304-313

Cook, S.D.N. & Brown, J.S. (1999). Bridging epistemologies: The generative dance between organizational knowledge and organizational knowing. *Organization Science*, Vol. 10, No. 4, pp. 381-400

Cseres, P. , & Kelly, N. (2006). Restructuring talent sourcing at DuPont. *Strategic Human Resource Review*, Vol. 6, No. 1, pp. 28-31

Driver, M. (2002). The learning organization: Foucauldian gloom or Utopian sunshine? *Human Relations. Vol.* 55, No. 1, pp. 33-53

Farley, C. (2005). HR's role in talent management and driving business results. *Employment Relations Today*, Vol. 32, No. 1, pp. 55-61

Fishman, C. (1998). *The war for talent.* http://www.accordsyst.com/papers/talent_war.doc

Frank F. D., Finnegan, R. P. & Taylor C. R. (2004). The race for talent: Retaining and engaging workers in de 21st century. *Human Resource Planning*, Vol. 27, No 3, pp. 12-25

Frank, F.D. & Taylor, R.C. (2008). Talent management: Trends that will shape the future, *Human Resource planning*, Vol. 27, No. 1, pp. 33-42

Haesli, A. & Boxall, P. (2005). When knowledge management meets HR strategy: an exploration of personalization-retention and codification-recruitment configurations. *International Journal of Human Resource Management*, Vol. 16, No. 11, pp. 1955-1975

Harrison, R. & Kessels, J. (2004). *Human Resource Development in a Knowledge Economy – An organisational view*, Palgrave Macmillan, New York

Heinen, J.S. & O'Neill, C. (2009). Managing Talent to Maximize Performance, *Employment Relations Today*, Vol. 31, No. 2, pp. 67-82

Hislop, D. (2009). *Knowledge Management in Organizations* (second edition), Oxford University Press, Oxford

Kaulingfreks, R. (2002). Reflections on Knowledge, Management and Thinking [Bedenkingen over Kennis, Management en Denken], In: *Kennis en Management*, P. v. Baalen, M. Weggeman & A. Witteveen (Eds.), pp. 208-232, Scriptum, Schiedam

Kessels, J.W.M. (2004). The knowledge revolution and the knowledge economy: the challenge for HRD, In: *New Frontiers in HRD*, Woodall, J., Lee, M. & Stewart, J. (Eds.), pp. 165-179. Routledge, London

Lewis, R.E. & Heckman, R.J. (2006). Talent management: A critical review, *Human Resource Management Review*, Vol. 16, pp. 139-154

Mensink, J.C.M. (1991). *Dynamics in human resource management: using talents as policy [Dynamiek in human resource management: talenten benutten als beleid]*, Lemma, Utrecht

Nonaka, I. (1994). A dynamic theory of organizational knowledge creation, *Organization Science*, Vol. 5, No. 1, pp. 14-37.

Redman, T. & Wilkinson, A. (2006). *Contemporary Human Resource Management – Text and Cases*. Second edition, Pearson Education Limited, Harlow

Romans, J., & Lardner, L. (2005). Integrated talent management at BD Japan. Strategic Human Resource Review, Vol. 4. No. 5, pp. 16-19

Romans, J., Frost, A., & Ford, S. (2006). Developing high – potential talent at Hughes Supply, Strategic Human Resource Review, Vol. 5, No. 3, pp. 32-35

Scarbrough, H. (2003). Knowledge management, HRM and the innovation process. *International Journal of Manpower*, Vol. 24, No. 5, pp. 501-516

Schiemann, W.A. (2009). *Reinventing Talent Management, How to Maximize Performance in the New Marketplace*, Wiley, Hoboken (New Jersey)

Schultze, U. & Stabell, C. (2004). Knowing what you don't know? Discourses and contradictions in knowledge management research. *Journal of Management Studies*, Vol. 41, No. 4. pp. 549-573

Sewell, G. (2005). Nice work? Rethinking managerial control in an era of knowledge work. *Organization*, Vol. 12, No. 5, pp. 685-704

Smart, B.D. (1999). *Top grading: How leading companies win by hiring, coaching, and keeping the best people*, Prentice Hall Press, Paramus, NJ

Storey, J. & Quintas, P. (2002). Knowledge Management and HRM. In J. Storey (Ed.), *Human Resource Management: A Critical Text* (2nd Ed.), pp. 339-363, Thomson Learning, London

Ten Bos, R. (2002). Paradigms and the organization of knowledge [Paradigma's en de organisatie van kennis]. In: *Kennis en management*, P. v. Baalen, M. Weggeman & A. Witteveen (Eds.), pp. 33-52, Scriptum, Schiedam

Tsoukas, H. (1996). The firm as a distributed knowledge system: a constructionist approach. *Strategic Management Journal*, Vol. 17, Special Issue Winter 1996, pp. 11-26.

Tsoukas, H. (2003). Do we really understand tacit knowledge? In: *The Blackwell Handbook of Organizational Learning and Knowledge Management*, M. Easterby-Smith & M.A. Lyles (Eds), pp. 410-427, Blackwell, Malden

Tsoukas, H. (2005). *Complex knowledge: studies in organizational epistemology*, Oxford University Press, Oxford

Van Aken, T. (1991). Talent management: deploying talent of vital importance to organizational success [Talent management: inzet van talent van levensbelang voor succes van organisaties]. *Personeelbeleid*, Vol. 27, No. 9, pp. 458-478

Van Beers, W. (2005). Performance management, competency management and talent management: three sides of a coin? [Performance management, competentie management en talentmanagement: drie kanten van één medaille?]. *Opleiding & Ontwikkeling*, Vol. 18, No. 5, pp. 26-28

Van der Sluis, L. (2009). *Competing for talent*, Van Gorcum, Assen

Zack, M.H. (1999). Developing a knowledge strategy. *California Management Review*, Vol. 41, No. 3, pp. 125-145

17

Academic Landscape Based on Network Analysis Considering Analysis of Variation in the Years of Lucubration Publishing

Akira Otsuki and Ayumi Kawakami
Ochanomizu University, Tokyo
Japan

1. Introduction

Recent development in the field of Academic Landscape consists mainly in quotation network analysis. It is possible to sort tens of thousands of academic papers into clusters automatically by making full use of the various techniques that we describe in Section 2. However, it is not yet possible to automatically define the characteristics of each field identified by clustering as well as to automatically extract major papers in each field. Thus, We research the method to automatically identify major papers in each field recognized by clustering. Specifically, We examine the variance of years when a paper was quoted; then we apply the variance to the page rank algorithm to calculate the importance of a paper. We also aim to build up a hiangle map with a temporal axis based on the importance.
Finally, We describe the constitution of this paper. Section 2 surveys the preceding studies of network analysis, clustering and bibliometrics that are element technologies to realize Academic Landscape. Section 3 describes the purpose of this study and proposed method. Furthermore, Section 4 refers to the result of experimental evaluation of the proposed method before the conclusion in Section 5.

2. Related studies

Academic Landscape is kind of network analyses. Network analyses have long history. Network analysis is based on graph theory [1] by Leonhard Euler in the 18th century. There are a various analysis types to Network analysis. For example, "Complex Networks", "Network Optimization", "Small World Phenomenon", „Analysis of the degree distribution", "Clustering". Currently, the most important technology is "Clustering" in the Academic Landscape.
Clustering is the method to divide data into clusters. Clustering can be a simplify the structure of the vast amounts of data by having a common feature of the each clusters. The initial clustering algorithm was focused on the central link, and the common method was disconnect the center link to the first, then disconnect the around links to the second. On the other hand, Girvan and Newman [2-4] proposed a new algorithm that uses the modularity as an Evaluation function. Modularity is focused on links that mediate between the best cluster and disconnect the link from the link-mediated higher.

Then, Bibliometrics is a method developed by Garfield and Price. Bibliometrics is a method to support the resarch activity. It does analysis of academic papers or patents, Then, It can be understand that: "What is hot research topics?", "Which a large number of cited papers?", "Which are important papers?", "Which is related to that area?", "Who is important researcher?", "Which is the important research institute?"
There are three methods of Bibliometrics analysis (Fig. 1.).
The first is the "Direct Citation". It is regarded there is a link between paper A and paper B, If paper A is cited in the Paper C. In this case, there are 2 nodes and 1 link in the network. Papers are regarded as having any link between the papers themselves has been cited, when using a"Direct Citation".
The second is the " Co-Citation". It is the method proposed by Small [5]. Then it is regarded there is a link between paper A and paper B, If paper A and paper B is cited by paper C. In this case, there are 2 nodes and 1 link in the network. Be considered that there are a links between a pairs of those papers that all papers are listed in the bibliographies.
The third is the " Bibliographic Coupling". It is the method proposed by Kessler [6]. Then it i regarded there is a link between paper D and paper E, If paper C is cited in the Paper D and paper E. In this case, there are 2 nodes and 1 link in the network. Be considered that there are links for all pairs of papers that cite.

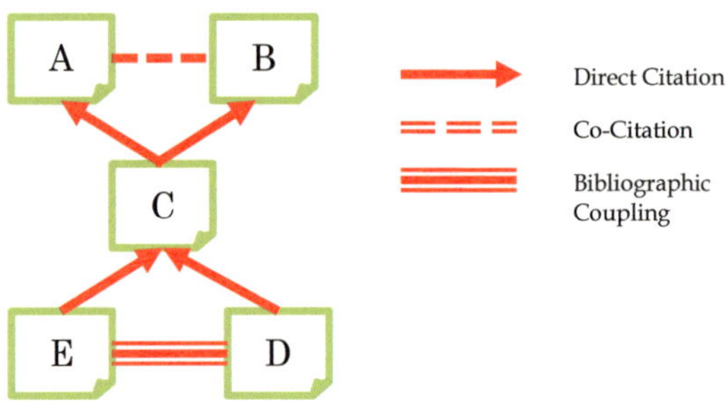

Fig. 1. The kinds of citation analysis

It became possible to analyse the academic landscape by combining these studies. Specifically, Each phase of the "Build of citation networks", "Getting the largest connected components", "Clustering" and "Visualization" will be processed automatically. But each area cannot automatically interpret. It is currently being analysed by the experts (Fig. 2).

3. Methods

In this study, to consider about automatic extraction of major paper in the each area to solve the issue of previous section. To calculate the severity by the traditional citation analysis is difficult, because shall be interpreted differently even if the same number of citations. For example, the cases that have been cited in many papers during the same period, and, the cases that cited in the long-term.
Therefore, in this study we consider a digraph assuming a paper is a node and a quotation is an edge for each "case" mentioned above. Then, We try to calculate the importance of each node by examining the variance of release years of source nodes whose edges enter into a node after allocating release years to each node. And we aim to establish a hiangle map with

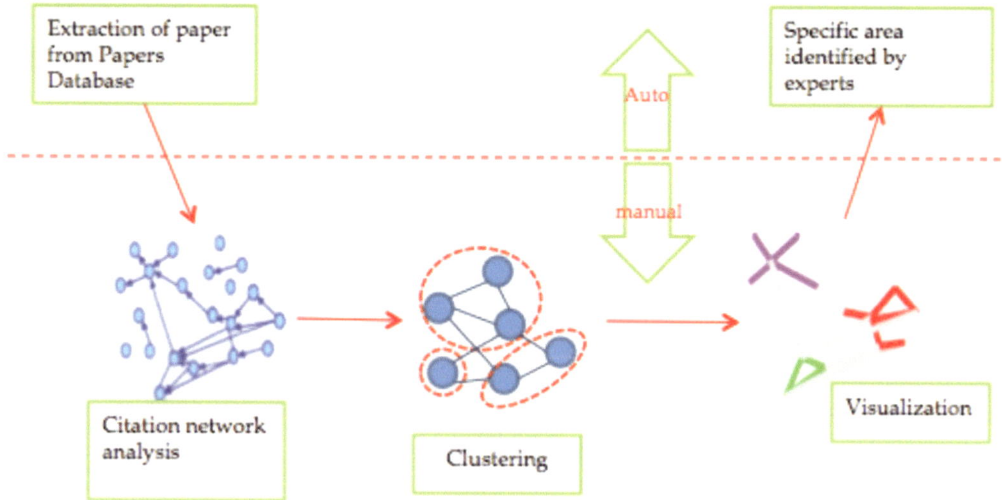

Fig. 2. Procedure of Academic Landscape based on network analysis

1. To narrow down the number of papers by keyword (query) search in the publication databases.
2. To make a list of quotations (papers) for a target papers.
3. To analyze the variance of release years of the papers in the list above to weight each target papers.
4. To calculate the importance of each target papers by applying the page rank algorithm with the weight above.
5. To visualize the result based on the importance (node & edge)

3.1 Publication databases and search query

This study used SCOPUS for publication databases. As a result of narrowing down the number of papers by "clustering" as query, the number of papers for this study became 87,399.

3.2 Publication year analysis of variance and weight of each cited papers

Follow the steps 1) to 3) below to weight paper:

Step 1. To extract the maximum value in the histogram, the year with the maximum number of quotations is extracted by using the function below and save it in MaxYear.

$$MaxYear = max\{y(x) \mid y(x) := \text{Number of times the references in year } Y\} \quad (1)$$

Step 2. To identify the quotation period, find out the maximum year by examining the release years chronologically; the year with the number of quotations exceeding 10% of the maximum year's quotations for the first time should be the start year and it is saved in StartYear. Then, the year with the number of quotations getting below 10% should be the end year and it is saved in LastYear. The period of quotation is achieved by the formula below:

$$Period := (LastYear + 1) - StartYear \quad (2)$$

In addition, if there are two or more peaks in the histogram as shown in Fig. 3., the steps above should be repeated and the periods are saved in Period0,1,2,,,,n.

Step 3. To calculate the variance (standard deviation) of a histogram, it can be defined how long paper has been quoted by examining the variance (standard deviation) of the release years of the papers that referred to the target paper. The following shows a common way to obtain standard deviation; the obtained standard deviation is saved in Variance.

$$Variance = \frac{\sum (x - \bar{x})^2}{n} \quad (3)$$

Again, if the histogram is not normally-distributed (it has two or more peaks) as shown in Fig. 3., the variances (standard deviations) of different periods (Period0,1,,,n) is calculated and the average of them is to be saved in Variance. Then, the value in Variance is used for weighing of the target paper.

3.3 Calculation of the severity of each cited papers

The PageRank algorithm [7] is a technique to calculate quantitatively which page is most important if there are cross reference relations among pages such as the hyperlink structure. In this study, We calculate the importance of papers by utilizing this algorithm. The calculation follows the steps below:

(1)Each Paper have a unique scores. and each cited have a unique score,too.

(2) Assuming there is paper (X);

- The score of X is P,
- When X is quoted by other papers, X obtains scores, $Variance_1,,,,Variance_n$,
- When X quoted other papers, X provides scores to others,$O_1,,,,O_m$.

Where, the statement below is assumed to be true:

$$\boldsymbol{Variance_1 + \ldots + Variance_n = P}$$

$$O_1 = \cdots = O_m = \frac{p}{m}\left(= \frac{\sum_{i=1}^{n} Variance_i}{m}\right)$$

In other words, assuming that the total score of "out going" quotation for paper should be equal to the total score of "in coming", the total score should be considered to be the base of the paper. Then, paper should be considered to be more important as the score becomes higher. Thus, We intend to identify major papers in each field by applying the value in Variance to calculation of the "in coming" score for paper. In the conventional algorithm, if there are more than one "in coming" quotations, the score of each quotation was thought to be equal. On the contrary, in this research a quotation with a larger value in Variance should be thought to have a larger score. In this algorithm, the importance of paper can be calculated with the factor of quoted years reflected.

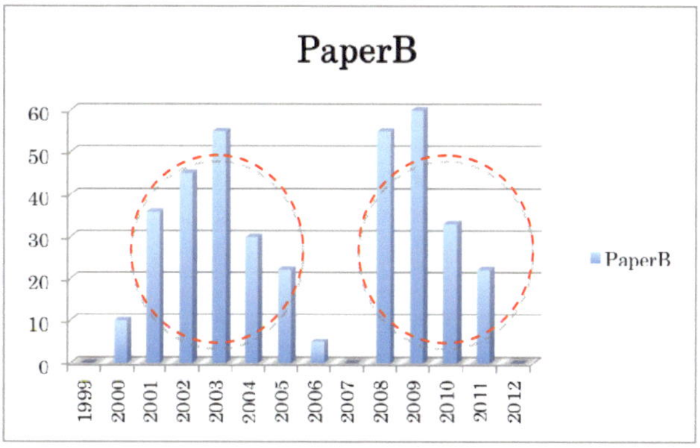

Fig. 3. Outside the normal distribution case that the shape of the histogram

3.4 Visualization based on the severity

Fig. 4. shows a visualization of the quotation network based on the importance obtained in the previous section. Each nodes has the title of paper displayed. As described in the previous section, a node with a larger importance is displayed as a larger node. In addition, this tool is called SciHi (**Sci**ence **Hi**ghangle).

Fig. 4. Example of Academic Landscape based on weight of each cited papers

4. Evaluation experiment

In the survey report on study trend published in 2004, Tatsubori et al. used the publication databases of IBM to survey the research trend of software architecture after 1999. They manually extracted 51 major papers [8]. In this study, we examine how well the automated method can extract the major papers that were manually extracted by experts.

Tatsubori et al. used GoogleScholar to obtain the number of quotations for each year and extracted top 40 papers in a year. In addition to them, they extracted 11 more papers about software architecture by identifying international conferences that they thought particularly important, resulting in 51 major papers. Furthermore, they adopted a unique classification method in order to evaluate study trend quantitatively. Specifically, they classified 51 papers by defining each paper focused on which one of the following five roles that software architecture played in software development process. Fig.5. shows the classification result.

R: Requirements for the system of various stakeholders are reflected in the architecture.
M: Architect designs the architecture based on the meta-model.
A: The architecture is actually build up/modified.
C: If all the requirements cannot be met, the architecture is changed to meet the requirements.
S: If the architecture is abstract, it must be modified so that it can be implemented in a working system. Contrary, if the system has some changes, the changes should be reflected to the architecture.

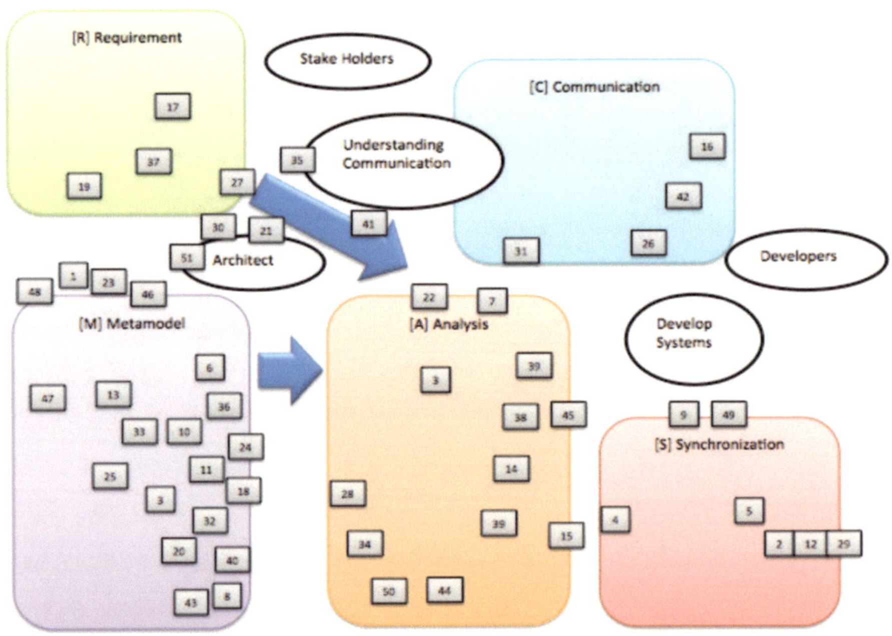

Fig. 5. An image of classification of papers by five roles of software architecture

Fig.6. shows the major papers extracted by SciHi in a similar manner to that of Tachibori et al. Fig.5. and Fig.6. both indicate the paper numbers.
The following describes the way of extraction by SciHi: We used SCOPUS as publication databases. Then, we selected “Software Architecture” for query and “1999 to 2004” for the period for extraction of papers. Among 51 papers, 28 papers were not included because they did not exist in SCOPUS (see the papers numbers in Fig.5. : 1, 5, 12~14, 16~19, 21, 24, 27, 29,

30, 32~39, 41~43 and 49~51). Regarding five roles in Fig.5., we manually made minute adjustment for SciHi (see Fig.6.) because they were an original classification set by Tatsubori et al. for quantitative evaluation of research trend.

As shown in Fig.6., visualization result by the page rank algorithm (hereafter, it is referred as this algorithm) with the variance value of a target paper taken into consideration as weight showed all the 23 papers were extracted as major papers. Especially, the papers (44~58 in Fig.6.) were extracted manually by Tatsubori et al. and all of them were extracted as major papers.

Thus, this algorithm can automatically extract major papers that are the same papers manually extracted by experts. However, SciHi extracted major papers that were not extracted by Tatsubori et al. such as a large (green) node in the cluster of [R]. As a future task we will examine these papers to see what meaning they have.

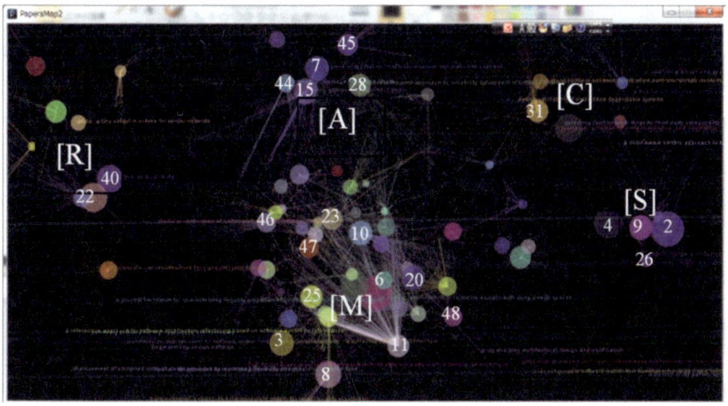

Fig. 6. An image of extraction of papers by SciHi

5. Conclusion

In this study on the network analysis of quoted academic papers, we tried automated extraction of major papers in each one of the fields identified by clustering. Specifically, we analyzed the variance of the release years of papers quoting the target paper; applied the result to the page rank algorithm to calculate the importance of the target paper. Then, we examined how well the automated method can extract the major papers that were extracted by experts by comparing the result with the report on research trend in the software architecture field that was published by Tatsubori et al. in 2004. As a result, this algorithm could extract all the target papers as major papers. In other words, this algorithm could automatically extract major papers with the same result as what experts manually obtained. Last of all, in our experiment for evaluation, SciHi also extracted major papers that experts did not manually. As a future task we will examine what these papers mean.

6. References

[1] R•J•Wilson .(2001). *Introduction to Graph Theory*, Kindai Kagaku Sha Co.,Ltd.

[2] M. E. J. Newman and M. Girvan.(2004). *Finding and evaluating community structure in networks*, Physical Review E, Vol. 69.

[3] M. E. J. Newman. (2004).*Fast algorithm for detecting community structure in networks,* PHYSICAL REVIEW E 69, 066133, pp1-5, 2004 ·

[4] M. E. J. Newman. (2005). *A measure of betweenness centrality based on random walks, Social Networks*, Vol. 27, No.1, pp. 39-54.

[5] H. Small. (1973). *Co-citation in the scientific literature: a new measure on the relationship between two documents,* Journal of the American Society for Information Science, Vol. 24, pp. 28-31.

[6] M. Kessler. (1963). *Bibliographic coupling between scientific papers,* American Documentation Volume 14, Issue 1, pages 10–25.

[7] Lawrence Page, Sergey Brin, Rajeev Motwani, Terry Winograd. (1998). *The PageRank Citation Ranking*. Bringing Order to the Web'.

[8] M.Tachibori,H.Maruyama,M.Kobayashi,D.Yellin,N.Yoshida,N.Kawai .(2005). *A Survey Report Digest on Research Trends in Software Architecture* , IPSJ SIG Technical Report, pp45-52.

18

Some Collaborative Systems Approaches in Knowledge-Based Environments

Mihaela I. Muntean
West University of Timisoara, Faculty of Economics and Business Administration
Romania

1. Introduction

Collaboration represents a strategic alternative to the monolithic approach to business development and competition. It involves a different approach to business - focused on managing business relationships between people, within or without groups, and within and between organizations.

Fig. 1. Collaboration – A Business Strategy (http://literacy.kent.edu/CommonGood)

In the present global economy, strongly influenced by IT (information technology) and information systems evolution, the modern organizations try to face the challanges by adjusting their strategies and restructuring their activities, for aligning them to the new economy requirements. It is certain, that the enterprise's performance will depend on the capacity to sustain collaborative work. The evolution of information systems in these collaborative environments led to a sudden necessity to adopt, for maintaining all kind of virtual activities/processes, the latest technologies/systems that are capable to support integrated collaboration in business services.

It is obvious that, all collaborative environments (workgroups, practice communities, collaborative enterprises) are based on knowledge, and between collaboration and knowledge management (KM) there is a strong interdependence. Therefore, we focused on how collaborative systems are capable to sustain knowledge management and their impact on optimizing the KM life cycle. Some issues regarding collaborative systems are explored and a portal-based IT solution that sustains the KM life cycle is highlighted. In addition, an agile development framework for portals will be proposed

2. Collaborative environments

To collaborate effectively, people work in various virtual teams, created quickly, spread around the world, and comprising colleagues, customers and partners. Working in these global team-based environments, people establish relationships that may be short-term project-focused or long-term and are evolving over time. With each new relationship, companies invest in selecting the right people, learning how to work together, and determining how to extract the most value in terms of revenues and profits (Pflaging, 2001). Integrating collaborative services with business functions allows companies to gain a significant competitive advantage. Information is shared more effectively, communication is more efficient, and companies can make quicker, more informed decisions. More specifically, companies can shorten sales cycles, accelerate product development, generate more transactions, increase partner/customer retention, and expedite problem resolution.

Effective collaboration requires actions on multiple fronts: early involvement and the availability of resources to effectively collaborate; a culture that encourages teamwork, cooperation and collaboration; effective teamwork and team member cooperation; defined team member responsibilities based on collaboration; a defined product development process based on early sharing of information and knowledge; collocation or virtual collocation; collaboration technology.

Collaborative enterprises differ from other businesses in a number of ways and collaborative working needs to be simultaneously a business philosophy, strategy and operational working. Resuming, collaborative enterprises are (Pflaging, 2001): (1) - networked and collaborative; (2) - core-competence focused and virtual; (3) - transparent to customer and partners; (4) -customer and partners centric; (5) - multi-disciplinary, (6) - community and team-based; (7) - strategically agile; (8) - change resilient and risk taking; (9) - knowledge creating and sharing; (10) - web-enabled; (11) - empowered and responsive.

The more collaborative the environment is, the more knowledge will be available to make right decisions the first time (Collins, 2004). In non-collaborative environment, a large knowledge/decision gap exists early on. Using enterprise collaborative techniques, it is possible to make better use of a group's core understanding, thereby raising the starting level of knowledge available on an initiative and closing the gap.

Establishing business processes and strategies for collaborative environments supposes : (1) - defining virtual collaboration and what it means for an organization; (2) - assessing the activities, tasks and initiatives that would benefit from virtual collaboration or virtual team work; (3) - examining work practices and the cultural implications of working within collaborative environments; understanding the role of trust among virtual team members for better awareness of group dynamics and social interactions; (4) - exploring with senior management the benefits of collaborative environments and teamwork, and their impacts on business models; (5) - developing a set of guidelines and a framework for a clearer definition of the changing nature of current work practices; and (6) - incorporating the performance metrics and the success of virtual collaborative environments.

3. Some collaborative systems

Collaborative technologies fundament a large range of tools, systems and IT platforms that sustain collaboration in the modern global economy, contributing decisively on the consolidation of different types of virtual collaborative communities, virtual world constituting a reality superstructure.

The orientation toward a collaborative business represents a necessity for developing a competitive business in the actual global economy (Muntean 2006; Ghilic-Micu, Stoica, Mircea, 2008). At the end of 2008, Forrester Research Inc. surveyed business environment inquiring about companies' opening towards adopting new IT collaborative platforms; a trend was obvious, more than 50% heading to collaborative technologies. Based on our research, we propose the adoption of portal platforms at the level of collaborative communities/environments, and followed by integration of a series of systems, collaborative instruments, and enterprise applications which help to consolidate portal's SOA architecture (Service Oriented Architecture) meant to sustain collaboration as a business strategy. It is obvious that collaborative systems maintain knowledge management (KM) at the level of collaborative environments, interfering into all stages of KM life cycle (subject will be developed in paragraph 4).

Without iterating different consecrated approaches in the field of collaborative systems (Mooney, 1974; Giboin, 2000; Marakas, 2003; Crabtree, 2003; Pels, Wortmann, 2003; Cil, Altrup, Yazgan, 2005; Kurdel, Sebestyenova, 2007; Nițchi, 2006, 2007, 2008), we will develop our scientific intercession around some consideration towards:

- collaborative systems based on software agents;
- collaborative tools (in fact, conversational tools);
- portal-based IT platforms; initiative sustained by the following considerations:

1. in the actual global economy, in which collaboration is imposed as a business strategy, collaborative environments based on any kind of knowledge presume the existence of informatics systems, tools and technologies being able to maintain collaborative work, collaborative solving of different tasks, collaborative decisions and consolidating value;
2. multi-agent systems imposed themselves as facilitating collaboration, maintaining economic processes/activities, as well as collaborative solving of specific complex problems;
3. on the other hand, collaborative tools are indispensable in every collaborative organization/community, concurring on sustaining the knowledge dissemination between its members;
4. but, the IT infrastructure of collaborative communities presumes the existence of complex platforms, with various capabilities in order to virtualize a big part of the communities' reality.

This can be achieved only with the help of portal technologies, at their level being integrated multi-agent systems with specific functions as well as a diverse range of conversational tools.

3.1 Considerations regarding multi-agent systems

Multi-agent systems (MAS) are computer based environments that contain multiple software agents to perform certain tasks (Turban, 2007). Multi-agent systems offer an innovative perspective on the capacity of configuration virtual communities. But some of their capabilities must be perfected, as follows (Muntean, 2009):

- incrementing the intelligence level of the agents through perfecting their capabilities, aiming autonomy, cooperation and learning;
- introducing new valences as for agents collaboration within MAS (Multi-Agent Systems) and, maybe even new approaches at protocol level and communication languages (KQML, KIF, COOL, etc.);

- upgrading the MAS's security level (processes, systems, respectively network security – securing communication between agents).

Agents in a multi-agent system are characterized by autonomy, adaptability, interoperability and dynamism. A multi-agent model includes a number of informative agents who share their results with a just-in-time middle agent (Maracine, 2007). The middle agent does not only suggest its own documents of relevance, but information found by other agents as well. Agents deposit information for later use by themselves or by other agents. In this way, knowledge sharing between agents is possible, but it is controlled in such a manner as to allow modular inclusion of agents within the framework.

From the knowledge management point of view different ways of sustaining this process must be developed, an important part being held by manipulation agents' knowledge in different ways.

It is obvious that developing MAS is a complex process which can raise real problems virtualizing some collaborative communities. In the last years it is ascertained the emergence of some specialized platforms for developing multi-agent systems, which contributes substantially to reducing the effort of developing those kinds of systems.

3.2 Considerations on collaborative tools

Collaboration tools or groupware, were the first tools to be used to enhance tacit knowledge transfer within an organization. Social or conversational technologies imposed themselves in the last years as tools that sustain knowledge management in collaborative environment (Wagner, Bolloju, 2004; Roll, 2004; Anghel, 2009).

Bypassing the stage of simple conversational support, these instruments maintain tacit knowledge dissemination at the community level, consolidating collaboration through offering various facilities of collaboration based on the considered environments' demands/necessities, in literature contouring the concept of „on demand collaboration anytime/ anywhere" (Marcus, Coleman, 2006). Therefore, it is recommended the integration of this kind of tools in IT virtualizing collaborative environments platforms.

We consider that:

- collaboration within different work groups, communities, virtual environments, can't be achieved without the help of social/conversational tools. These are the first to be adopted, adding, based on the community's demands and necessities, advanced collaborative systems and technologies;
- from the knowledge management point of view, tools such as forum, blog, wiki, etc. bypassed a long time ago the level of a simple conversational instrument, sustaining it's life cycle stages;
- developing of some collaborative tools, in the last years, implies using technologies and web programming, because of the boom of open-source solutions, in order to reduce their development effort.

3.3 Considerations regarding portal technologies

With each portal generation, portal producers promise amending of work quality through supplying extra services for the members of collaborative communities. These services are the result of integration and unification of different applications, information system and collaborative tools, necessary to maintain current activities, business processes held at the level of virtualized environment.

Integration represents the key concept, around which portal technologies developed, with the help of some integration mechanisms/schemes like portlet, gadget, iView, skin or dashboard (Guruge, 2003). Portlets became the most popular ones, being the most efficient integrator in portal type architecture (Sullivan, 2003), the majority of portal server developers adopting this concept.

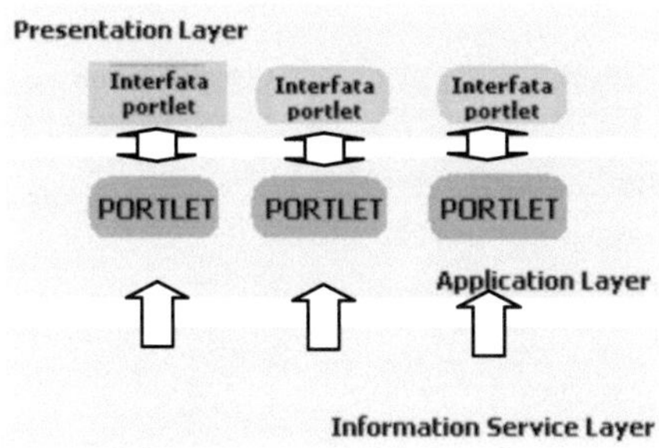

Fig. 2. Integration & Portlets

In essence, the role of portlets at Application Layer is to be in charge of the correct functioning of information systems integrated into the portal's platform management, to make the necessary links with the Presentation Layer, and with the different sources of information/knowledge at Information Service Layer (Figure 2). Portlets permit the maintaining of attached applications independent of the rest of the portal. They cover the presentation level and business logic, but are connected to information/knowledge sources from back-end.

Collaborative and integration portal platform:

- offers to all extended community members un unique, personalized, based on user roles access, to the multitude of integrated systems and applications (including enterprise applications ERP, SCM, CRM, HR); these enterprise applications can be constituted in sub-portals, being integrated into the collaborative environment, based on knowledge, unitary platform portal;
- in the last years we can ascertain the developing of some facilities of remote accessing of the portal with the help of some mobile devices and vocal systems;
- promotes dynamic and efficient communication, including virtual collaboration spaces maintained by a series of collaboration tools;
- permits business process modeling and deploying in dynamic environments, the applications that sustain them covering the whole chain value;
- offers the managers the information/knowledge and the necessary tools for making a decision in the shortest time; with the help of some dedicated portlets the integration of Business Intelligent modules that sustain decisional processes at any level is possible;
- a collaboration management is promoted at the collaborative organization level, decision making processes being marked by this desideratum.

Being an important factor from the KM triad, information technology, through collaborative systems exponents, contributes essentially to maximize knowledge value (Bair, 1998; Cain, 1999; Firestone, 2000, 2001, 2002; White, 2000; Bock, 2001; Barette, 2003; Guruge, 2003; Sullivan, 2003; Torsten, 2004; Collins, 2004; Hoolahen, 2005; Herrmann, 2006).

All these systems produce changes into the organizational structure, exercising managerial functions into business models throughout the world.

4. Developing portals

Starting from the metodologies, methods and techniques used generally in the development of information systems, an approach regarding quick development of portals will been introduced. The agile development framework, which proposes the use of prototype technique enriched with MDA (Model Driven Architecture) speciffic valences, includes the following phases (Figure 3):

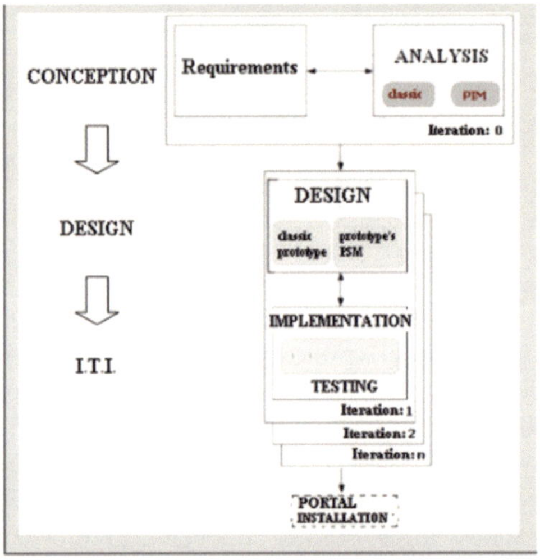

Fig. 3. Agile development of portals

- Conception: at the level of this phase the PIM (Plarform Independend Model) model elaboration is targeted, according to the requirements of the knowledge based collaborative community; Prior, a feasibility study is made for justifying the efficiency and efficacy of the project, being also made a business plan for demonstrating that the project does or does not bring a measurable benefit; the modelling of the requirements will lead to the outlining of the functionalities of the portal, of the user communities, all this being represented at a level of PIM model;
- Design: targets the elaboration of the PSM (Platform Specific Model) model specific for the portal prototype, i.e. the finalisation of the architecture of this model, taking into account all details regarding the IT infrastructure, which must sustain the unitary, integrating vision of the PIM model. The building of the PSM model will take into account the future implementaion solution of the prototype by relating the model to a certain IT platform and to certain maintenance technologies;
- I.T.I (Implementing-Testing-Installation): has the goal to implement the portal prototype according to the PSM model, followed by the testing of the prototype. Often, the prototype invalidation as a result of testing its functionality, leads to the revision of the PSM model and aims at correcting some aspects related to technology and the considered IT platform. Practically, the final version of the portal prototype is obtained by an iterative process, which regards the adjustment of the PSM, its implementation and the testing of the prototype solutions for verifying the imposed requirements. After the validation of the prototype follows the portal installation and its transfer to the users, who posess knowledge of the collaborative community.

We propose the following basic functional architecture (Figure 4) for a collaborative knowledge portal, having as an objective to facilitate the access to the knowledge base (as part of the organizational knowledge, which has been transposed to the portal) of the collaborative community members, the knowledge exchange between them and generally to provide a knowledge flow in the whole virtual community.

Among the functional components of the knowledge portal we have highlighted the following four major categories: process support, collaboration, content management and personalization (Note. The four major functionalities (content/document management, collaboration, process support and personalization), guide to the outlining of the service oriented architecture, unlike other functionalities, which only provide the operation of the portal in the imposed parameters or, indirectly, sustain these four.)

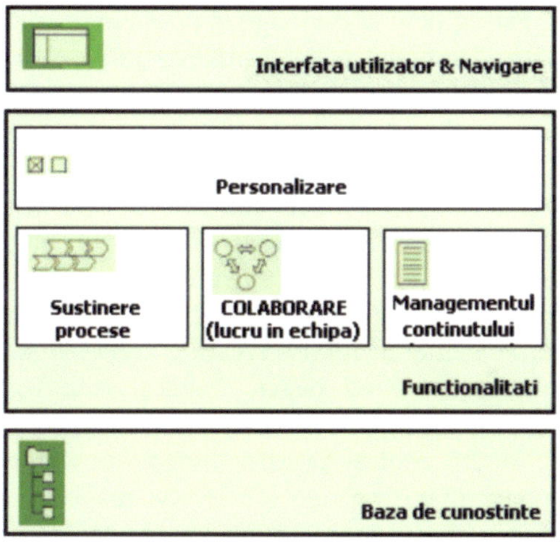

Fig. 4. The functional architecture of a knowledge portal (Jansen, Bach, Osterle, 2000)

5. Knowledge management approaches

According to the defined collaboration, knowledge management comes to consolidate the collaborative community and through the client orientation it opens the environment to the necessities and requirements of the clients. The level of interest in knowledge management has grown rapidly during recent years as enterprises recognize that they operate in a knowledge economy and that knowledge is their most valuable asset. At the same time knowledge management theories and technologies have reached the maturity level required for business confidence and endorsement.

5.1 A model for the knowledge management life cycle

Considering the knowledge management life cycle consisting of phases like (Muntean, 2009):

1. knowledge generation,
2. knowledge management/storage,
3. knowledge dissemination,
4. knowledge auditing,

we present a possible maintenance based on a knowledge portal infrastructure (Figure 6).

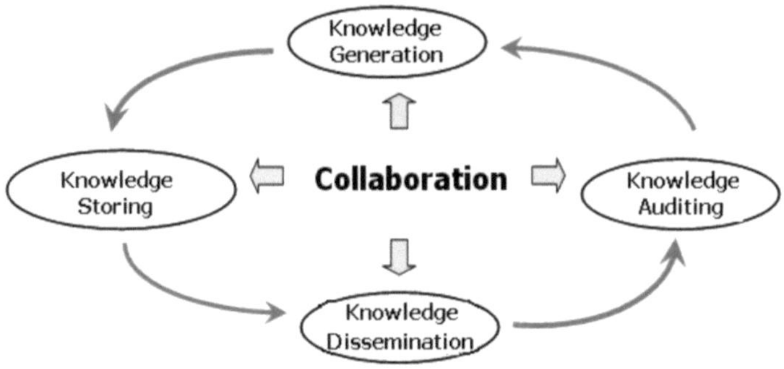

Fig. 5. A Model for KM Life cycle

1. At the portal level, creating new knowledge is possible through acquiring/attaining of some knowledge pieces from the collaborative organizational environment (or even external from the organization), or is a following of some intelligent reasoning made by modules of artificial intelligence incorporated in the portal's architecture. The knowledge created that way is collected and refined to eliminate unjustified redundancies and filtering the ones most "valuable" for the organization.
   Creating documents represents a significant percentage of the current activities, so the less time is allocated to this activity, more time will remain for the members of the organization to achieve the other tasks. Therefore, at the portal level, we will have to integrate some instruments that facilitates creating knowledge of a document type, such as: text editors, multimedia, Web pages, images, sounds, video editing systems, spreadsheet editors, graphic programming's.
   At the portal level, in the central or distributed knowledge database (meta-base), different kinds of knowledge are coded efficiently, assuring quality, accessibility, and their representativeness with the help of some specific tools/technologies.
2. Knowledge can be stored in data warehouses, knowledge databases specific to artificial intelligence, content specific structures or in a documents management system; all these will form the portal knowledge meta-base. One of the forms in which knowledge can be stored is knowledge repository, which stores knowledge that is often text-based and has very different characteristics. It is also referred to as organizational knowledge base. A knowledge repository is not a knowledge base of an expert system, the repository containing all the organizational knowledge, not only the one needed in solving a specific problem. Concordant with the different knowledge storing technologies, we will use specific methods/techniques to access/locate them.
3. Collaborative tools sustain and facilitate the transfer of knowledge. Some tools and technologies facilitates the use of knowledge: Business Intelligence tools, expert systems, simulations of dynamic complex processes, decision support systems, ERP applications (Enterprise Resource Planning), CRM (Customer Relation Management) and other enterprise applications, visualizing tools that permit understanding of some complex knowledge structures, etc.
4. Practice proved that if we don't take into account aspects of economic efficiency, the costs of maintaining the informatics systems are much more that the profit and most of the time the life cycle reduces drastically.

Auditing represents a complex activity of verifying the conformity degree of the knowledge database with the standards in that domain, and its capacity to sustain the achievement of the strategic objectives of the organization. The main subjects tested are regarding the reliability and performance of the product, the efficiency of the operations and, not last, the security facilities (Lungu, 2003). Auditing the organizational knowledge implies analyzing its impact on decisional processes, the contribution of each piece of knowledge in optimizing business processes, therefore in raising the quality of the products and services offered. At the end of this process, it is possible to have to regenerate some knowledge pieces.

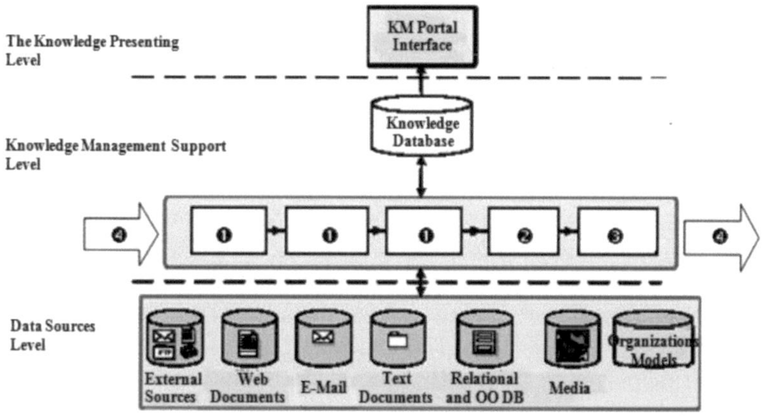

Fig. 6. KM lifecycle phases' implementation at the portal level (Kerschberg, 2003)

A collaborative enterprise represents an adequate environment for developing a strategy for a better performance of knowledge management, taking into consideration the social and cultural specific aspects and having an adequate IT infrastructure.

The portal provides a new work environment for enterprise knowledge workers, one that is aligned with, and supports and partially automates, their individual and collaborative workflow in creating, distributing and using data, information and knowledge, and in making and implementing decisions and actions (Firestone, 1999). The enterprise knowledge portal (EKP) combines enterprise information portal (EIP) aspects while also capturing tacit knowledge, integrating access to expertise and management application (Firestone, 2002). Giving users one-stop interaction with appropriate intellectual capital, applications and expertise, the EKP speeds innovation and reduces the amount of rework in an organization. EKPs also integrate and support a number of e-business processes that transcend the enterprise. EKPs are themselves eBusiness applications that web-enable knowledge processing and knowledge management within the enterprise.

5.2 Distributed knowledge management

In the global economy, interconnected organizations that forms a collaborative network can be considered, based on their cumulative know-how, to be inter-connected knowledge nodes (KN) (Bonifacio, Bouquet, Cuel, 2000, 2002). In this approach, the collaborative community becomes an environment that must sustain two different kinds of processes:

1. knowledge management specific to each node (organization);
2. coordination of different knowledge nodes.

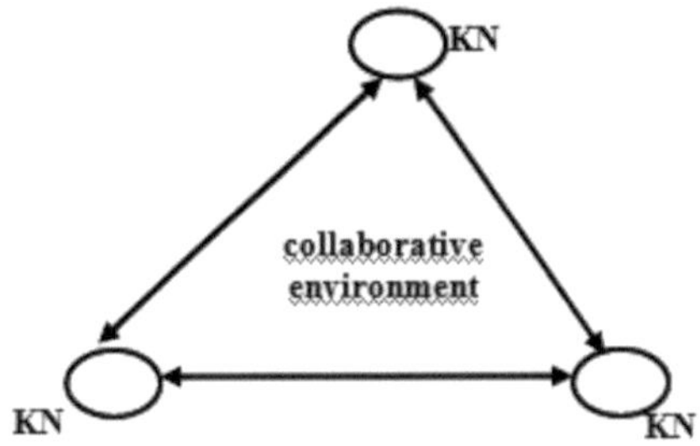

Fig. 7. Inter-connected knowledge nodes

Each organization is an absolute manager (from conceptual and technical point of view) of its organizational knowledge. Coordinating different KN arises some problems that can be overcome from the technological point of view by adopting some knowledge-based portals with intelligent capabilities of communication at the level of the nodes. Starting from the technical architecture proposed by Firestone in 2001, 2002, 2003 for a knowledge-based portal, collaboration between KNs can be accomplished with some collaborative intelligent software agents that are integrated into the organizational portals (Muntean, 2005). These agents assist the members of a KN to formulate queries (requests of knowledge) to other nodes and they respond to queries that came from the other KNs.

We support the strategy of a distributed KM approach based on two general principles:

1. Autonomy Principle - each node/organization manages its own knowledge; the enterprise portal will represent a unique access point to the knowledge meta-base, that stores a part of the organizational knowledge;
2. Coordination Principle - each node must permit exchange of knowledge with other nodes, without having to adopt a unique interpretative scheme at the level of collaborative network, but through a mapping mechanism of the context of the node queried to its own context, taking into consideration their own perspective on knowledge.

As any distributed system, this one will also have to fulfill some requirements such as connecting users and resources, failure safety, scalability and standardization.

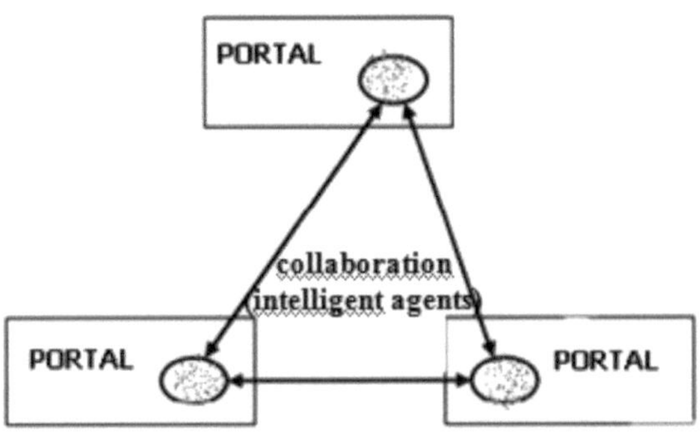

Fig. 8. Infrastructure based on portals sustaining a distributed KM

This will be achieved with the help of some collaborative intelligent agents specially integrated, with this purpose, in the nodes' portals. In these last years, software agents

evolved spectacularly, gaining unexpected intelligent capabilities being able to sustain virtual collaborative environments. (Weiss, 2000; Kimatura, Yamada, Kokubu, 2001; AgentLink, 2004; Dang, 2004; Silaghi, 2005; Sycara, Sukthankar, 2006).
Knowledge management demands cultural flexibility, strong management of knowledge management project CSFs and an adequate technical collaborative foundation. If done right, knowledge management is supposed to create a collaborative environment.

6. Collaboration & knowledge management

Collaboration facilities improve decisions, increase knowledge. They facilitate better distribution of knowledge, improve planning and development cycles and create more functional and productive relationships within teams. This in turn increases productivity and company understanding of internal and external environments. Overall, employees will begin to have a better view of corporate information and the power to make informed decisions more effectively.
A collaborative enterprise organization is a more agile organization. The ability of employees to quickly share their insights contributes to an organization's collective knowledge, and has a direct impact on its success. Successful companies continually seek and refine ways to make effective use of their employees' collective knowledge and experience. Information technologies that contribute to knowledge management solutions, such as enterprise portals, improve the enterprise's business intelligence and its collaboration capabilities. Collaboration is becoming an enterprise's business strategy sustained by IT technology. Integrating collaborative services with business functions allows companies to gain a significant competitive advantage. The benefits of collaboration within a portal are clear. It will continually facilitate and enrich the knowledge management process.
An interesting aspect of the increased globalization of the business world is the cultural diversity of the workforce involved in collaborative virtual work. As a result, the performance of a global virtual team may be contingent not only upon technology and task factors, but also upon a virtual group's cultural homogeneity or heterogeneity. A culturally heterogeneous group is expected to display types of behavior and interactions that are different from those displayed by a culturally homogeneous group. In a virtual setting, the impact of cultural heterogeneity on group performance might ultimately result in performance outcomes that are different from those generated by a culturally homogeneous group. Managers may reduce the influence of national cultures and cultural differences in collaborative enterprises by developing a strong organizational culture. Internalization of a strong organizational culture is done through training, suitable knowledge management approaches, developing appropriate information systems, using integrating practices such as enforcing quality, super ordinate goals, promoting linking between different cultural groups.
There are many different approaches toward knowledge management. Many concepts focus on social and cultural aspects only and ignore the role of technology. There are other approaches that are very technology-minded but provide no solutions to cultural challenges of knowledge management. Therefore, many companies have sophisticated concepts on how to manage knowledge, but have little understanding of how to implement and deploy them. The implementation of efficient knowledge management solution often proves to be very challenging.

7. The place of our debate within the european research programs

Organizations that promote collaboration within them and in their extended environment, that contains different actors from economic/business environment, are identified by the name of collaborative organizations, presenting the following specific features (Skyrme, 2003):

- collaborative - from the business philosophy, the strategy adopted and all the operational activities;
- team-work oriented;
- centered on collaborative formation of organizational competences & knowledge;
- client and partner centered;
- adaptable to changes;
- agile from the strategic point of view.

IT represents an indispensable sustainer of collaborative organizations, of collaborative environments in general [Harmon, Rosen, Guttman, 2001]. These represent (virtual) communities which, even if they are not subordinated to a business objective, adopt the collaboration and elaborate knowledge management principles.

Strategic demarches are scheduled in order to achieve this objective, at the level of different research networks specialized in setting up visionary studies - business models evolution collaborative enterprises related (Figure 9). The focus on collaborative business processes orientation dictates identification and configuration of the collaborative technologies capable of sustaining these processes.

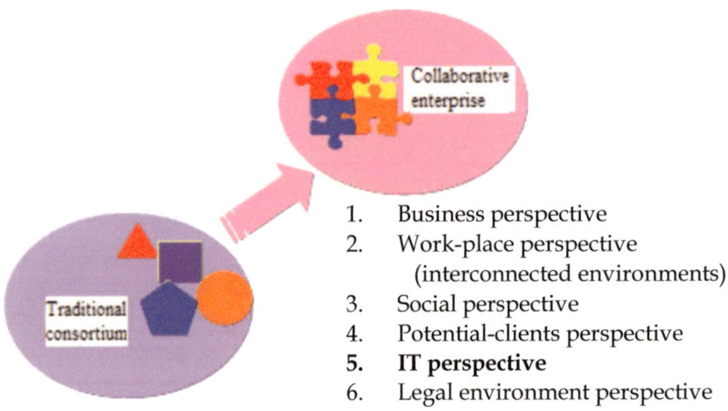

Fig. 9. Strategy to evolve to the collaborative enterprise model (CE-NET Consortium, 2004)

Portal technology that permit building a fundament for a collaborative virtual environment based on knowledge was imposed, the presented approaches being an innovative scientific demarche of the IT perspective indicated in figure 9.

We consider that:

1. it is important for the organizations to have the capacity of underlying and putting forward tacit knowledge pieces (individual or collective ones, belonging to an informal group, being the result of some accumulated practical experience; they can be categorized as being „contextualized", non-fundamented, less accessible, difficult to describe and maybe unconscious) through their integration within organization functions. We refer to an organizational learning process sustained by KM and

collaboration, developed at the collaborative environment level and which contributes decisively to the process of competitive knowledge pieces generating (Kim, 1993; Nonaka, Takeuchi, 1995; Malhotra, 1998; Flood, 1999; Bontis, 2002). At the collaborative organization level, creation of a knowledge capital is the main desideratum, organized under the form of organizational knowledge (best practices, expertise, learned lessons, competences), in the same time focusing on the best IT solutions, capable of incorporating as much as possible from the organization know-how, under the form of a knowledge base (meta-base).

2. knowing the clients represents an important asset in all business. To remain competitive, organizations must collaborate with clients (or suppliers and even competitors) in order to remix their capacities with the ones of possible partners.
3. At the level of network organizations, KM applies within each organizational entity, considered a knowledge node, as well as to sustain collaboration between these KNs. A portal based IT infrastructure, like the one presented in figure 7, is vital to sustaining management strategy of distributed knowledge.
4. For developing portals an agile framework is recommended; the desired functionalities, like content/document management, collaboration, personalization and business process modeling are obtained. By means of the facilities offered by the UML language the specifc models of these functionalities are built; the PIM and PSM model are consolidated. The developed portal will satisfy the requirements of the collaborative environment, being able to store the knowledge from certain area of expertise, concern and activity.

8. Conclusions

It is obvious that inside every collaborative environment, starting with small work-groups or practice communities (of interests, scope, action, etc.) and ending with the collaborative environment, there is a strong fundament based on knowledge and a powerful interdependence between collaboration and knowledge management. Collaborative communities represent organizational manifestation forms that wish to remain competitive in the competitive environment. Being entirely or partially transposed into the virtual environment, they have to adopt a malleable business strategy, to take fundamental decisions based on knowledge regarding consumers, suppliers, stockholders, investors or even competitors.

Collaborative systems, tools and technologies sustain work teams, communities and collaborative enterprises, portal type IT platforms proving their efficiency as infrastructures of those environments:

- depending on particularities of each organization/community (organization dimension, working needs, etc) it can be chose from an unique portal solution or one based on a distributed model;
- in a distributed approach, collaborative community can be assimilated with a network of knowledge nodes at which level it is recommended a policy of distributed knowledge nodes;
- portal based IT infrastructure must sustain KM distributed strategy, therefore knowledge management at the level of each node and the communication between them;
- integration of necessary collaborative tools, MAS and enterprise applications at each portal's level in order to satisfy its needs.

Collaborative enterprises represent the solution for companies, which wish to remain competitive in the business environment. Being entirely or partly transposed in the virtual environment, they have to adopt a malleable strategy, to make decisions based on knowledge, which regards the consumers, suppliers, shareholders, investors or even competitors. Many innovative companies have long appreciated the value of knowledge management to improve their processes, products and customer service and to create competitive advantage. Research studies show that by managing the knowledge of their customers, corporations are more likely to sense emerging market opportunities before their competitors, to constructively challenge the established wisdom of "doing things around here", and to create economic value for the corporation, its shareholders and its customers.
In our future work our attention will be focused on optimizing the technical architecture of the referred portals, studies that will be made by the research interdisciplinary team of the on-roll grant[1]. But, paradoxally, the success of any portal-based collaborative environment (any new technology-enabled business model) relies, more than ever, on people's ability to build relationships based on mutual trust. Further research will also refer how to manage business relationships between people, within or without groups, and within and between organizations according to a knowledge management approach. Future research streams will include work in intercultural communication and collaboration, temporal coordination, and trust in virtual teams.
For Romania, as well as for the countries were these approaches are not familiar, the relevance of the collaborative enterprise concept results from the engagement of the states in the evolution of the informational society - knowledge society. It would be risky to assume, that given the differences with highly developed countries, the collaborative (knowledge based) enterprise would represent, on national scale, only a future problem or an exaggerated sophistry.

9. References

Bair, J. (1998), The Knowledge portal: Adding Knowledge to Intranets, *Gartner*, T-06-2507

Barette, J. (2003), Deploying the Next Generation of Enterprise Portals, *DM Review*, Vol.13, No.2

Bock, G. E. (2001), *Enterprise Portal Promise to Put an End to Corporate Intranet Haos, Enterprise Applications Webtop*, vol. 440

Bonifacio, M. & Bouquet, P. & Cuel, R. (2002), Knowledge Nodes: The Building Blocks of a Distributed Approach to Knowledge Management, Journal of Universal Computer Sciences, 8(6), Springer Pub & Co

Bonifacio, M. & Cuel, R. & Mameli & G., Nori, M. (2000). A Peer-to-Peer Architecture for Distributed Knowledge Management, http://eprints.biblio.unitn.it/archive

Cain, M. (1999), Enterprise portals: A Publishing Mode, Meta Group, Workgroup Computing Strategies, Delta File no. 837

Cil, I., Altrup, O., Yazgan, H.R. (2005), *A New Collaborative System Framework Based on Multiple Perspective Approach*, Digital Press

Collins, H. (2004), *Corporate Portals: Revolutionizing Information Access to Increase Productivity and Drive the Bottom Line*, AMACOM, New York

[1] ANCS-CNMP project PN II - 92-100/2008-2011

Crabtree, A. (2003), *Designing Collaborative Systems: A Practical Guide to Etnography (Computer Supported Cooperative Work)*, Springer Verlag

Dang, V.D.(2004), *Coalition Formation and Operation in Virtual Organizations*, University of Southhampton

Firestone, J. (2001), Estimating Benefits of Knowledge Management Initiatives: Concepts, Methodology and Tools, *Journal of the KMCI*

Firestone, J. (2000), *The Metaprise, The AKMS and The Enterprise Knowledge Portal*, http://www.dkms. com/White_Papers.htm

Firestone, J. (2002), *The New Knowledge Management: A Paradigm and its Problems*, http://www.kmci.org/media/Firestone-tnkmparadigm.pdf;

Ghilic-Micu, B., Stoica, M., Mircea, M. (2008), *How to Succed in Business Intelligence Initiative: A Case Study for Acquisitions in Romanian Public Institutions*, WSEAS Transactons on Business and Economics, ISSN 1109-9526, Issue 6, Volume 5, June 2008

Giboin, A., Dien, R., Karsenty, L., De Michelis, G. (2000), Designing Cooperative Systems, The Use of Theories and Models, *Proceedings of the 5-th International Conference on the Design of Cooperative Systems* (COOP'2000),

Guran, M. (2008), Knowledge Management using Intranets and Enterprise Portals, *Int. J. of Computers, Communications & Control*, ISSN 1841-9836, E-ISSN 1841-9844, 2000, Vol. III, Proceedings of ICCCC 2008, pp. 75-81, http://www.journal.univagora.ro/download/pdf/259.pdf

Guruge, A. (2003), *Corporate Portals Empowered with XML and Web Services*, Digital Press

Hoolahen, G. (2005), Applying Adaptive Enterprise Principles to Collaborative Business Infrastructure. Bases Solution Design, *HP White Paper*, http://www.sveiby.com.au/KnowledgeManagement.html;

Kimatura, Y., Yamada, T., Kokubu, T. (2001), *Interactive Integration of Information Agents on the Web, in Cooperative Information Agents*, LNAI, Springer Verlag;

Kerschberg, L. (2003), *Knowledge Management in Heterogeneous Data Warehouse Environment*, http://eceb.gmu.edu/pubs/KerschbergDaWak 2001. pdf;

Lungu I., Sabau Gh., Velicanu M., Muntean M., Ionescu S., Posdarie E., Sandu D. (2003), *Informatics systems. The analysis, projecting and implementing*, Ed. Economica, Bucharest

Malhotra, Y. (1998), Knowledge management for the new world of business, www.brint.com/ km/whatis.htm;

Maracine, V. (2007), Agent-based Modeling in the Sharing Knowledge Processes, *Informatics in Knowledge Society*, The proceedings of the Eigth International Conference on Informatics in Economy, Editura Economica, Bucharest

Marakas, M. (2003), Decision Support Systems In the 21st Century, Prentice Hall

Marcus, A., Coleman, D. (2006), The Future of Collaboration, Collaborative Strategies LLC

Mooney, J. D. (1974), The Coordination Principle - retipărit în Koontz & O'Donnell, Readings in Management, McGraw

Muntean, M. (2005), Knowledge Management in Collaborative Environments, *Proceedings of the 2th International Conference on Economics and Management of Networks*, Budapest;

Muntean, M., Muntean, C. (2006), *Collaborative Environments – A Framework for Business Intelligence*, WSEAS Transactions on Business and Economics, ISSN 1109-9526, Issue 8, Volume 3, August 2006

Muntean, M. (2009), Portal-Based Collaborative Environmen, *Megatrend Review*, Belgrad

Niculescu C. (2009), Knowledge Product Management in Knowledge based Organizations, *"The Proceedings of the Ninth International Conference on Informatics in economy"*, Bucharest

Nonaka, I., Takeuchi, H. (1995), The Knowledge-Creating Company: How Japanese Companies Create the Dynamics of Innovation, Oxford Universuty Press

Pflaging, J. (2001), Enterprise Collaboration: The Big Payoff,KMWorld, available at: http://www.kmworld.com/publications/whitepapers

Pels, H.J., Wortmann, J.C. (2003), Collaborative Systems for Production Management, Kluver Academic Publishing

Rablou C. (2009), Considerations about Distributed Systems, *"The Proceedings of the Ninth International Conference on Informatics in economy"*, Bucharest;

Silaghi, C. (2005), *Collaborative Multi-Agent Systems. Conception,* Design and Development, Ed. RisoPrint, Cluj-Napoca;

Sullivan, D. (2003), *Proven Portals. Best Practices for Planning, Designing and Developing Enterprise Portals,* Addison-Wesley Press

Sycara, K., Sukthankar, G. (2006), *Robust Recognition of Physical Team Behaviors Using Spatio-Temporal Methods,* http://citeseer. comp.nus.edu.sg/751889.html

Torsten, P.(2004), INWISS - *Integrative enterprise knowledge portal,* Department of Information Systems, University of Regensburg, D-93040 Regensburg

Turban, E., Aronson, J., Liang T.-P., Sharda, R. (2007), *Decision Support and Intelligence Systems,* Prentice Hall, New Jersey

Wagner, C., Bolloju, N. (2004), Supporting Knowledge Management in Organizations with Conversational Technologies: Discussion Forums, Webblog and Wikis

Weiss, G. (2000), Multiagent Systems, A Modern Approach to Distributed Artificial Artificial Intelligence, *The MIT Press*

White, M. (2000), Enterprise Information Portal, *The Electronic Library,* vol. 18, no. 5, 2000, MCB University Press

Wickramasinghe, N. (2005), *Knowledge-Based Enterprise. Theories and Fundamentals,* Idea Group Publishing, Hershey, SUA

Wiig, K.. (2000), The Intelligent Enterprise and Knowledge Management, *Life Support Encyclopedia – UNESCO*

19

The Liberation of Intellectual Capital Through the Natural Evolution of Knowledge Management Systems

Harold M. Campbell*
Vaal University of Technology
South Africa

1. Introduction

The research literature on knowledge management (KM) suggests that the valuation and measurement of intellectual capital (IC) is important to business intelligence (BI) and organisational performance. Harnessing the power of KM requires an effective communication interface which will allow the successful process integration of IC with organisational performance. The seminal research of Nonaka & Takeuchi (1995), and Brown & Duguid (1998) among others, established that effective communication of knowledge obtained from an organisational milieu is essential to organisational performance.

For this to happen, the organisation needs to craft an innovative and viable design of its business systems. A business system design (BSD) comprises of a dynamic architecture which is isomorphic across firms in space and time. It is a dense dynamic nexus of social capital, human capital and KM. A firm's IC, is seen as the resultant of its knowledge management network, as posited by von Krogh et al. (2000). Intellectual capital (IC) represents a firm's meta-capability aimed at exploiting opportunities in its continual pursuit of value creation. This process has been one of the most important sources of international competitiveness for some time.

This chapter takes the view that knowledge is shared among organisational members, because, it is connected to the firm's history and experiences, and will soon become the ultimate replacement of other resources. This notion underpins a more general idea that economies of the future will be education-led (Eftekharzadeh (2008)). It means that the capacity to manage knowledge-based intellect will be the critical skill of this era.

If there is one distinguishing feature of the new economy that has developed as a result of powerful forces such as global competition, it is the ascendancy of IC. Competitive, technological, and market pressures have made continuous organisational learning a critical imperative in global strategy effectiveness (Day & Tate (2006), Hislop (2005), and Campbell (2009)).

Allied to this is the seminal work of Nonaka & Takeuchi (1995), on knowledge creation, where their theory of knowledge creation identified four categories of knowledge assets. These being:

1. experiential knowledge assets (tacit knowledge, shared through experience);

---

*H. M. Campbell is the HoD: Department of Industrial Engineering, Vaal University of Technology.

2. conceptual knowledge assets (tacit knowledge, in the form of symbols and language);
3. routine knowledge assets (tacit knowledge, embedded in organisational routines and practices), and
4. systemic knowledge assets (systematized explicit knowledge).

These categories of knowledge are linked to Nonaka & Takeuchi (1995) modes of knowledge creation and the type of *ba*[1] involved. These platforms aid in giving form to the impact of knowledge on innovation processes, in terms of the characteristics of knowledge. There are three such characteristics which influence the innovation dynamics. These are:

- the degree of tacitness;
- the level of complexity, and
- the degree of relatedness between bodies of knowledge being linked together.

These characteristics of knowledge inform the central role of tacit knowledge to innovation processes is well recognised (Gous & Schutte (2009); Campbell (2005); von Krogh et al. (2000); Campbell (2009); Eftekharzadeh (2008)).
The rest of the chapter is divided into five sections:

1. KM Research concepts - a review of the recent literature which includes definitions of terms as well as a conceptual model for business intelligence, asynchronous groupware, organisational learning, structural capital, and human capital;
2. Research goal - insights from the literature surveyed, a discussion of the innovation processes and network dynamics in terms of the need for intra-organisational collaboration, and the possible types of strategies organisations must devise through external networks, so as to access the requisite knowledge for competitive advantage and BI;
3. *Drupal*[2] - highlights of the analysis, limitations of the research and the contribution of the current technologies of content management aimed at managing the integrated knowledge network of organisations,
4. Directorate - a summary of a case study, which describes an iteration of the AR cycle conducted at Directorate, one of the human resources departments of the public service in Botswana, and
5. Concluding remarks - the chapter then points to the way forward for practitioners, and organisations alike.

We now discuss these concepts in greater detail in the next five sections.

2. KM research

The most common classification of knowledge in the KM literature may be considered to be that of von Krogh et al. (2000), to date, where an ambiguous distinction between *'explicit knowledge'* and *'tacit knowledge'* is proffered. Explicit knowledge is codified or articulatable in a formal manner (Nonaka & Takeuchi (1995)). Explicit knowledge can be easily passed on from one medium to another; that is, it's transferable. 'Tacit knowledge', on the other hand, may be seen as implicit knowledge or hidden knowledge, as opposed to explicit knowledge. Tacit knowledge is personal knowledge, which is bound to the individual.

[1] *Ba* - platforms for knowledge creation.
[2] Drupal - *www.Drupal.org* is the official website of Drupal, an open source content management platform.

This is not embedded in some process nor easily transmitted and shared without some systematic effort. The characteristics of tacit knowledge are a subjective view or understanding of a topic, an artefact, an intuition or an internal feeling in the sense of a cultural prejudice, experience, tradition or belief. Tacit knowledge is based on informal metrics, non-standard experience, personal conceptions or convictions. The literature supports this view of tacit knowledge (Nonaka & Takeuchi (1995), von Krogh et al. (2000), and Campbell (2005)).

Current principle \ Future principle	Tacit knowledge	Explicit knowledge
Tacit knowledge	Share experience, discuss ideas, opinions, etc.	Articulate experience in formal models, embed experience into equipment, software, etc.
Explicit knowledge	Convert models and formulas into tacit skills; learn/teach how to use equipment, etc.	Reformulate formal models and data, convert codes, etc.

Fig. 1. Modes of knowledge common in the knowledge spiral (Campbell (2005))

The classification of the foregoing is represented as the modes of knowledge, common in the knowledge spiral, as are illustrated in Fig.1. This figure seeks to explain how active knowledge sharing may be conceived in an organisational milieu. Active knowledge sharing, according to Campbell (2005), subsumes that most organisations will be focusing on one or more of the following four areas: (a) innovation, (b) responsiveness, (c) productivity, and (d) competency, as discussed in Campbell (2005). Consequently, this research takes cognisance of the processes of gathering, searching, filtering, conceptualizing, and transferring of knowledge, at the firm level (Campbell (2005), Hislop (2005), Day & Tate (2006), and Eftekharzadeh (2008)). As such, aligned to the four areas of active KM, are the following five processes, of KM:

1. business intelligence;
2. asynchronous groupware;
3. organisational learning;
4. structural capital, and
5. human knowledge,

in which Campbell (2005), discusses how technologies can be used in the context of KM projects. These five KM processes are discussed next.

2.1 Business intelligence

In his study, Campbell (2005) argues that KM effectiveness depends on how one organizes the generation of new knowledge, and the transfer of existing knowledge within the organisation. The views expressed in that study, are supported by recent studies, as they relate to the growing interest in knowledge sharing practices (Davenport & Prusak (2000), Hislop (2005), and Richard C. Hicks (2007)). It is now commonplace, to find that both scholars and practitioners alike (Sveiby & Simons (2002)), are robustly discussing the benefits of knowledge transfer and knowledge sharing. Allied also with this is a debate on how organisations can effectively demonstrate their internal knowledge value that is their intellectual capital (Richard C. Hicks (2007)), and of particular relevance is the work of Majchrzak et al. (2004), as it resonates with the idea of knowledge reuse, sharing and conceptualization of meta-knowledge into business intelligence.

Fig. 2. A framework for knowledge enablement (Nonaka & Nishiguchi (2001))

In perusing both the literature, and in the study, the researcher found that, one of the most important objectives of KM is to have organisations consolidate their intellectual resources and make them available across organisational boundaries (Martin (2004), and Campbell (2005)). The fact that many of these organisations fail to harness the latent resources of their IC into BI, begs the case for an integrated knowledge network.

2.2 Asynchronous groupware

Apart from the development of new knowledge in the enterprise and the acquisition of knowledge from external sources, the knowledge that employees already have should not be ignored. In practice, it is found that most employees find it rather difficult to share their knowledge with each other. The problem is due in part to the nature of the organisational culture, or sometimes, to the modes of operation, in terms of how they synchronize with, or co-ordinate with their KM efforts. If employees espouse the *"knowledge is power"* mentality, then, there will be a conflict between their personal interests, and the interests of the enterprise in knowledge sharing. An organisational structure, which is favourable for sharing knowledge, must develop a perspective, which does not let this conflict grow out of control.

Knowledge sharing must be understood as a natural part of the organisation's business, and strategic landscape, in the development of a KM strategy. This is the theme of Fig. 2.
On the part of management, there should be executive commitment to the KM strategy. It cannot be expected that employees will share their knowledge, if structures and mechanisms for this cultural change is not provided, in the organisational basic conditions of operations. The approach will be one that begins with the basic conditions, which provides for the individual employee to have the requisite time for sharing his/her knowledge, and also where necessary, the introduction of non-financial incentive systems as motivation for knowledge sharing.
It is to be understood that knowledge sharing is not only achieved through direct communication. It may take place over a cup of coffee or in a formal session. The concern here, is when it does takes place, where employees enter the codified knowledge in an information system. A substantial aspect for the motivation of employees to use the system depends on the efficiency and the user friendliness of this system. The systems where all participants interact in real-time are called synchronous groupware systems, and performance considerations (such as fast response time) are especially important here. On the other hand, e-mail and messaging systems are examples of asynchronous groupware (van der Aalst & Kumar (2001)). The metrics governing asynchronous groupware systems will be discussed next.
Campbell (2005), defines groupware as follows:

> ... *Groupware is a generic term for computer-based systems which are particularly used to support groups of people engaged in common tasks in organisations. Typically, these groups are small; businesses oriented, and have relevant tasks with definite deadlines [cf. Fig. 1]. There are several taxonomies for groupware. The two most commonly accepted are the application-level taxonomy, based on the main functions the system provides to its users; and the time-space taxonomy, based on the users' temporal and physical distribution while interacting through the system.*

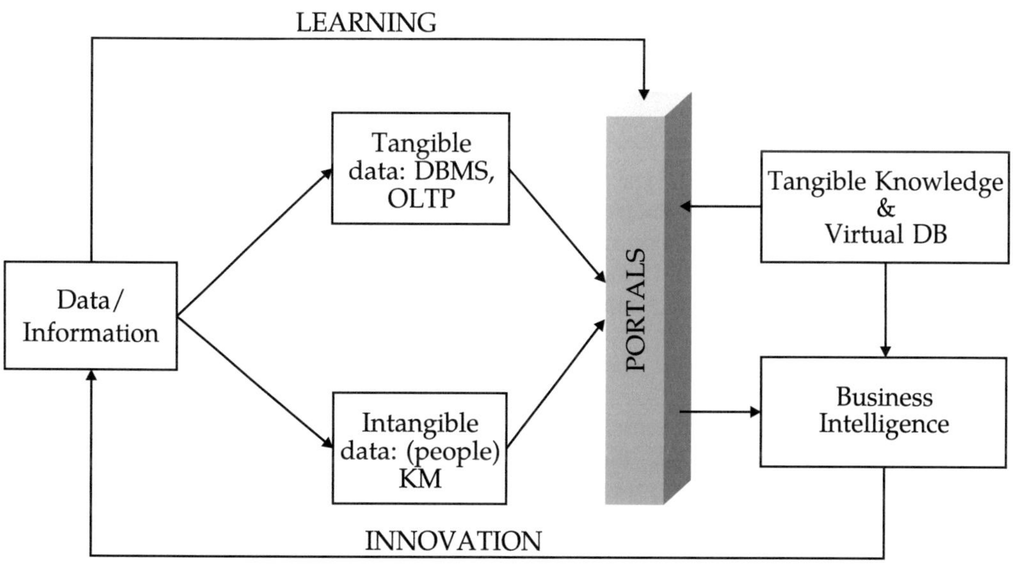

Fig. 3. KM - BI Model (Campbell (2005))

Knowledge is information in action. It includes what people know about any process or approach. The conceptual KM-BI model of Fig. 3 suggests that with good information, people can make better decisions and take intelligent action, which leads to business intelligence at the organisational level. This model relates well with the framework for knowledge enablement in Fig. 2. KM is seen as a systematic process - as conceptualised from the KM-BI model, in this chapter, to:

1. *Identify important knowledge:* The KM-BI model acts as a framework for facilitating knowledge creation and transfer. The model assumes that the organisation's internal structural and cultural dimensions in which knowledge work processes must take place are already enabled.
2. *Create a space and system for people to share what they know and create new knowledge:* The environment in which knowledge work processes are realized "*comprise social interaction and communication processes on an individual or group level. These processes may be categorized according to the transformation that knowledge undergoes as a result of the activity*" (Schutte & Preez (2008)). These being :
   (a) *Socialization* - comprises the exchange of tacit knowledge between individuals in order to convey personal knowledge and experience.;
   (b) *Externalization* - involves the conversion of implicit into explicit knowledge, and the exchange of knowledge between individuals and a group;
   (c) *Systematization* - transforms explicit knowledge into more complex and more systematized explicit knowledge, and
   (d) *Internalization* - is the conversion of organisation-wide, explicit knowledge into the implicit knowledge of the individual. These four knowledge work processes combine to form a spiral representing all the knowledge creation and transfer activities within the network.
3. *Capture, collect and manage best practices and useful information in a form that other people can use in the future:* This component of the model is the business intelligence which results from the resulting organisational learning, and the empowerment thereof. The KM-BI model (Campbell (2005)), and the knowledge network architecture (Seufert et al. (1999)) consist of tools that are used to facilitate social relationships, and include organisational, as well as information and communication protocols aimed at enabling or improving knowledge work processes. Gous & Schutte (2009) suggest that a tool classification framework may be employed to divide the combination of organisational information system tools into four main categories: communication and coordination tools, organisation and management tools, intelligent tools and integration and database tools. This is with a view to ensure maximum impact on the knowledge network, these tools are used in combination to form "*solution frameworks*" (Seufert et al. (1999)) instead of operating as modular tools.
4. *Transfer information, knowledge and best practices to others who can use it (von Krogh et al. (2000)).:* Fig.1. sets out the modes of knowledge common in the knowledge spiral (Campbell (2009)), which, with the use of an Asynchronous Groupware (AG) infrastructure will facilitate this systematic process. The work of (Gous & Schutte (2009)), concurs with the previous views of Campbell (2005), that "*the creation of a knowledge portal to provide access to the knowledge network may be realized with modern web-based technologies. This provides a single point of access to the knowledge objects and all underlying systems. Such a knowledge portal should be configurable and adaptable to the needs of knowledge networks as well as the needs of their members*" (Campbell (2009)).

2.3 Organisational learning

Knowledge transfer is not a one directional movement of knowledge. Effective knowledge transfer is more than the movement of knowledge from one location to another. It is proposed that organisations can gain significant learning benefits through transferring knowledge between units and people. Competence tends to improve with those who transfer and share knowledge, because knowledge does not leave the owner when it has been transferred. As a result, the value of knowledge grows each time a transfer takes place. And, the key to knowledge transfer strategies should be based on the internal and the external structure of the organisation. As such, there are three main approaches to knowledge transfer, in terms of technology and organisational culture. The first approach, emphasizes the importance of the technological means and tools for effective knowledge transfer. The second, focuses more on the social interactions and underlying importance of cultural aspects. The third approach, is a comprehensive one, that aims to combine the technological perimeter with the socio-cultural perimeter of KM.

The challenge here is that managers either need to ensure the creation of unique knowledge that can be unleash in value-creating activity, or establish better use of public knowledge that is generally available to the organisation and its competitors (von Krogh et al. (2000)). The chapter reports this as organisational learning, in the KM-BI model (Campbell (2009) as illustrated in Fig. 3.

2.4 Structural capital

Knowledge is meaningful when it is codified, classified, given a shape, put in a useful format and stored. Only then can it be used by the right person, at the right time, in the right way. Storage and codification of knowledge is not only important for the effective use of knowledge, but also for re-using knowledge when it is needed; so the knowledge in question belongs to the organisation rather than the knower (Campbell (2005)). In this chapter, KM is viewed as a process. It is the process through which organisations create and use their institutional or collective knowledge. It has three sub-processes:

1. *Organisational learning* - the process through which the organisation acquires information and/or knowledge;
2. *Knowledge production* - the process that transforms and integrates raw information into knowledge which in turn creates BI, and is useful to solve business problems, and
3. *Knowledge distribution* - the process that allows members of the organisation to access and use the collective knowledge - corporate memory of the organisation.

The question one may ask is, how does this inform the concept of a knowledge system? In the context of the present chapter, a *'knowledge system'*, means the web of processes, behaviour and tools which enables the organisation to develop and apply knowledge to its business processes. It includes the infrastructure for implementing the KM process. There are usually two components here (Campbell (2005)):

Firstly, there is a robust IT infrastructure, including the organisation's database, computer networks, and software applicationns. This chapter is not advocating the need for just a good or popular relational database, or a sophisticated groupware, or email system - the Asynchronous Groupware component of the knowledge system [cf. Figure 3], it subsumes that there must be an organisational infrastructure, which supports innovation. This prescript resonates with the views of du Plessis (2007), who defines innovation,

> ... *as the creation of new knowledge and ideas to facilitate new business outcomes, aimed at improving internal business processes and structures and to create market driven products and services. Innovation encompasses both radical and incremental innovation.*

This includes the soft characteristics of the system. There are incentives schemes, organisational culture, critical people and teams which are involved in the KM sub-processes. This also accounts for, most importantly, the internal rules that govern these sub-processes. This is the structural (knowledge) capital component of the knowledge system [cf. Figure 4]. In the structural capital framework, one should think of data as information devoid of context. Information is data in context, while knowledge is information with causal links. So within the logic of the knowledge system, the more structure that is added to a pool of information, the easier it will be for one to achieve the benefits of a knowledge system [cf. KM-BI model]. In this regard, the definition of a meaningful KM initiative should be aligned to the enterprise strategy. This would, therefore, mean the development of formal KM strategies, from which realistic and concrete goals can be derived. These strategies should be closely aligned with the three drivers of the application of knowledge in innovation advocated by Marina du Plessis (du Plessis (2007)):

> *The first basic driver for knowledge management's role in innovation in today's business environment is to create, build and maintain competitive advantage through utilization of knowledge and through collaboration practices. Cavusgil et al. (2003) indicate that building and sustaining an innovation program has, however, become increasingly complex due to changing customer needs, extensive competitive pressure and rapid technological change. organisations find it increasingly difficult to internalize innovations. Some large organisations such as Xerox and Hitachi have therefore started working collaboratively across organisational boundaries to ensure sustained innovation and competitive advantage (Cavusgil et al. (2003)). Knowledge management can facilitate such collaboration. Close collaborative relationships can provide access to the processes other organisations use that could be applied in different contexts. Acquiring knowledge and skills through collaboration is considered to be an effective and efficient way of successful innovation.*

The second driver of the role of knowledge management in innovation is that knowledge is a resource used to reduce complexity in the innovation process, and managing knowledge as resource will consequently be of significant importance. Innovation is extremely dependent on the availability of knowledge and therefore the complexity created by the explosion of richness and reach of knowledge has to be recognized and managed [Adams & Lamont (2003); Cardinal et al. (2003); Darroch & McNaughton (2002); Pyka (2002); **?**]. According to **?** the upsurge in the amount of knowledge that is readily available to organisations seems to add increased complexity to the design and management of new product development, but this complexity can be addressed by knowledge management and knowledge-intensive units in the organisation that are strategic in nature. Cavusgil et al. (2003) agree that knowledge management is a mechanism through which innovation complexity can be addressed. It assists in managing new knowledge created through the innovation process, but also in managing existing knowledge as a resource used as input to the innovation process. Cavusgil et al. (2003) are of the opinion that firms that create and use knowledge rapidly and effectively are able to innovate faster and more successfully than those that do not. According to Pyka (2002), creation of innovation networks are driven by synergistic creation and management of knowledge.

The third driver of applying knowledge management to the benefit of the innovation process is the integration of knowledge both internal and external to the organisation, thus making it more available and accessible. Knowledge integration implies that timely insights can be made available to be drawn at the appropriate juncture for sense making, i.e. knowledge can be exchanged, shared, evolved, refined and made available at the point of need. Knowledge integration via knowledge management platforms, tools and processes must therefore facilitate reflection and dialogue to allow personal and organisational learning and innovation. This requires linkability, adaptability and dynamic representation of business information and knowledge. Without effective information and knowledge management that drives knowledge integration, which in turn underpins innovation, organisations could be underutilizing knowledge as an innovation resource [Baddi & Sharif (2003); Chen et al. (2004)]. The above three drivers resonate with the prescript for organisational learning, knowledge production, and knowledge distribution, which define the concept of a knowledge system, and a basic requirement for the enablement of structural capital. Given the foregoing, we can now explore the component of human capital.

2.5 Human knowledge

The focus of this component, human knowledge, of the knowledge system is on knowledge creation and knowledge dissemination. This is not to suggest, in any way, that knowledge utilisation is not just as important. Rather, the elements comprising knowledge utilisation are subsumed here. The component of human knowledge involves the process of knowledge acquisition, which looks at the integration of external knowledge in the enterprise. This integration is by means of recruiting knowledge workers, specialists with particular value adding expertise, who usually bring relevant experience to the enterprise to assist it to meet its strategic objectives. The period over which this method of knowledge acquisition is used can be for different life cycles, ranging from permanent to project specific duration.

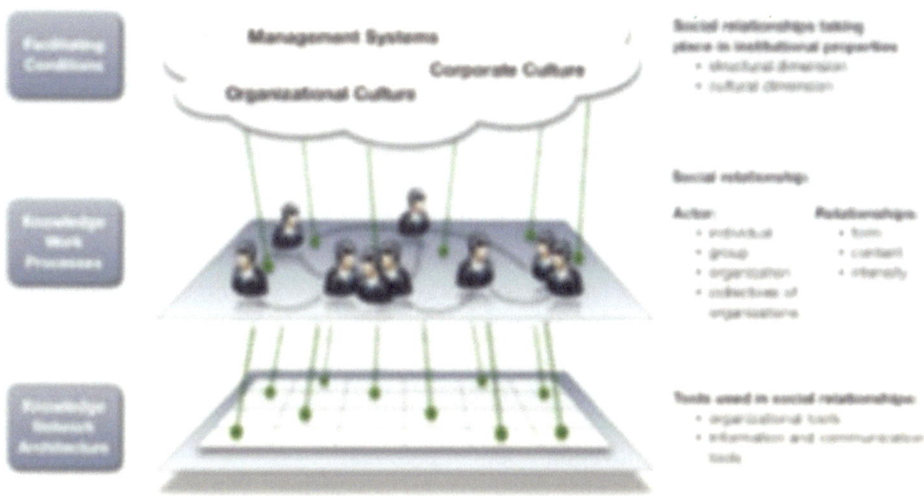

Fig. 4. A framework for knowledge networks (Gous & Schutte (2009))

Allied to this, though, is the active process of knowledge development, which involves not only the functions of knowledge production in the formal sense of the concept of the development of a process, or a product, or service for consumption in terms of the commercial milieu, but it also includes the performance metrics of an organisation. This is not to say that, that the development of knowledge and knowledge creation initiatives, in the physical sense, in the organisation's R and D department is not important. One is arguing that the processes used in the investigation and communication of that knowledge is more important than in the context of product creation and production. The generation of new ideas, abilities and products (of course) must be considered in addition to the other innovative processes of the enterprise. A central role of knowledge development is the promotion of creativity and communication among employees through the integration of enabling knowledge sharing strategies and an appropriate collaboration framework.

The presence of an appropriate organisational culture is a prerequisite for successful knowledge development. The analogy is like the role played by technological devices and tools within the spectra from telephones and whiteboards, to videoconferences and groupware, but more specifically asynchronous groupware (AG). Nonaka & Takeuchi (1995) argue that knowledge development is based on the interaction of implicit and explicit knowledge as the basis for the generation of new knowledge. Also, from the literature, Nonaka & Nishiguchi (2001) specifies a model for organisational knowledge development, which he calls the spiral of knowledge. This model is replicated in Fig. 1.

3. Research goal

The research goal of this chapter is to provide some insights from the literature surveyed and suggest how the innovation processes and network dynamics in terms of the need for intra-organisational collaboration, and the possible types of strategies organisations must devise through external networks. So they would be able to access the requisite knowledge for competitive advantage and business intelligence. This is with a view to lead to a robust discussion on how innovation may be supported by an integrated knowledge network, and whether the current ICT architecture available to organisations can offer the necessary functionality.

The research problem is conceptualized on the premise that: *"innovation within a globalized economy requires that a wide range of role-players along a knowledge management network of collaboration by transferring and creating knowledge."* A mechanism that offers this functionality is required.

This chapter, therefore, hypothesized that "innovation may be supported by an integrated knowledge network, that is an ICT architecture that offers the following functionality, such as:

- support for all the necessary knowledge work processes needed for knowledge creation and transfer within an Integrated Knowledge Network, and
- support for the full innovation life cycle of projects that develop within the integrated knowledge network." Gous & Schutte (2009)

3.1 Value proposition in the innovation-oriented process

Such a system would be circumscribed by an articulated value proposition. The value proposition of the role of knowledge management in an innovation-oriented intellectual capital milieu plays an invaluable role in fostering business intelligence, and intellectual capital, organisational knowledge, and structural knowledge, towards enabling an organisation's competitive advantage. Marina du Plessis [du Plessis (2007)] defines this value proposition as follows:

1. Knowledge management assists in creating tools, platforms and processes for tacit knowledge creation, sharing and leverage in the organisation, which plays an important role in the innovation process. Knowledge management provides a focus in the organisation on the value of tacit knowledge and assists in creating the environment for tacit knowledge creation, sharing and leverage to take place. An example would be through creation of communities of practice around areas of innovation that requires attention in the organisation. Knowledge could also provide other platforms and processes for tacit knowledge sharing, such as breakfast briefings. Knowledge management can also facilitate tacit knowledge transfer across organisational and inter-organisational boundaries through ensuring that experts with relevant expert knowledge have opportunities to share their tacit knowledge through collaboration. Knowledge management can also assist in identifying stocks of available tacit knowledge.
2. Knowledge management assists in converting tacit knowledge to explicit knowledge. It can provide both the platforms as well as the processes to ensure that tacit knowledge becomes explicit. Examples of codification platforms include discussion databases or online collaborative communities of practice. An example of a process to codify tacit knowledge to explicit knowledge is the capturing of tacit knowledge at tacit knowledge sharing events such as breakfast briefings into an electronic form where the knowledge can be organized and retrieved for later use. This adds a lot of value to the organisation as it is known what knowledge is available, and it is retrievable for future re-use.
3. Knowledge management facilitates collaboration in the innovation process. Knowledge management allows collaboration across functional boundaries within organisations, but also across organisational boundaries through online collaboration forums as well as organisational tools and platforms such as intranets and extranets. These collaboration forums are extremely valuable as they ensure the codification of knowledge utilized as input to the innovation process, but also generated as output of the innovation process. It provides accessibility to the knowledge and provides identification of collaborators in the knowledge sharing and innovation process, thus building up a reference of expertise and where it resides in the organisation. It also ensures that knowledge external to the organisation relevant to the organisation's innovation processes is available and accessible.
4. Knowledge management ensures the availability and accessibility of both tacit and explicit knowledge used in the innovation process using knowledge organisation and retrieval skills and tools, such as taxonomies. It allows the organisation and retrieval knowledge in a structured way according to the unique structures and value chain of the organisation. It also provides search facilities and tools (e.g. Autonomy, Convera, and others) to enable staff to search for knowledge required in the innovation process. It provides a unique corporate structure to the corporate knowledge base. It can also make tacit knowledge more accessible through directories that identify individuals' areas of expertise in the organisation.
5. Knowledge management ensures the flow of knowledge used in the innovation process. Through the provision of collaboration forums and knowledge management processes, knowledge required for the innovation process can flow easily across functional boundaries as well as across organisational boundaries to facilitate internal and external collaboration. Creation of a knowledge sharing culture, which is an essential part of any knowledge management program, also stimulates knowledge flow, which is beneficial for innovation.

6. Knowledge management provides platforms, tools and processes to ensure integration of an organisation's knowledge base. Through knowledge management structures such as taxonomies, knowledge management can ensure the integration of the corporate knowledge base. This enables staff members to have an integrated view of what knowledge is available, where it can be accessed, and also what the gaps in the knowledge base are. This is extremely important in the innovation process to ensure that knowledge as resource is utilized to its maximum benefit and to ensure that knowledge is not recreated in the innovation process.
7. Knowledge management assists in identifying gaps in the knowledge base and provides processes to fill the gaps in order to aid innovation. Through the structured provision of access to knowledge, knowledge management provides an overview of what is available in the organisation. This allows the organisation to understand in which areas knowledge is lacking and to systematically build the knowledge base in these areas. The organisation may do this through the innovation program itself if the gaps are in strategic areas, but it may also do it through knowledge management processes or operational business processes.
8. Knowledge management assists in building competencies required in the innovation process. Through knowledge accessibility and knowledge flow, staff members are able to increase their skills levels and knowledge both formally and informally. An increase in skills can improve the quality of innovation. The flow of knowledge across functional boundaries ensures that a wider base of knowledge is available to employees than only the knowledge they use in their day-to-day activities. Employees therefore have a wider frame of reference of the context in which they work and will therefore be able to innovate more efficiently. Knowledge management also provides a culture of knowledge sharing and accessibility of knowledge, creating an environment conducive to skills and competency building, which aids innovation.
9. Knowledge management provides organisational context to the body of knowledge in the organisation. Every organisation's corporate memory is unique. The structures provided to organize and retrieve knowledge from the corporate knowledge base will therefore be providing a unique context to each particular organisational knowledge base. Provision of organisational context is critical in the innovation process, as innovation in the organisation also takes place within a very specific business context. Knowledge management assists in identifying and understanding this organisational context.
10. Knowledge management assists in steady growth of the knowledge base through gathering and capturing of explicit and tacit knowledge. It also assists specifically in addressing gaps in the knowledge base through specific acquisition of knowledge in those areas where gaps exist, or through knowledge creation and innovation itself. This in turn feeds the innovation process through creation of a much broader knowledge base that is available as resource for the innovation process. The tacit knowledge base also grows through building of skills due to the availability of knowledge.
11. Knowledge management provides a knowledge-driven culture within which innovations can be incubated. Knowledge sharing is enhanced by a culture where the role of knowledge, knowledge management, innovation and creative thinking is encouraged. Most knowledge management programs have a strong knowledge culture element through which an organisational culture of knowledge generation and sharing is emphasized. This benefits innovation programs as it provides knowledge as resource,

but it also provides a culture within which innovation, creativity and learning through mistakes are encouraged and valued.

The goal of this chapter is therefore to suggest the design of an information system that facilitates an integrated knowledge network, or a knowledge management - business intelligence (KM-BI) portal [cf. Fig. 3.], while providing support for the full life cycle of innovation projects that develop within this network, following from the work of Gous & Schutte (2009).

4. Drupal

During the implementation phase of the computerised personnel management system (CPMS) project at Directorate, we found that the available innovation management software did not provide much ICT solutions with regard to an integrated knowledge network. The literature also had only few successful projects which had integrated knowledge networks as a part of their web technologies. The few available web technologies, we found, offer remote connectivity, content management, media-rich environments, community building and social networking.

All these technologies had relevance to the nature and scope of the requirements of the Information Systems project definition of Directorate in terms of its integrated knowledge management work processes and value chain. The literature supports the view that an organisation's integrated knowledge network is *"...a cradle for Innovation in a modern environment, and the exact features many of these technologies boast"* [Gous & Schutte (2009)]. We found that the latest web technologies which were noteworthy, are mainly open-source content management system, among these are WordPress, Joomla, and Drupal [Buytaert (n.d.)], which support content management. We also found that the standard release of Drupal, known as "Drupal core", contains basic features common to most Content Management Systems (CMS). These include the ability to register and maintain individual user accounts, administration menus, RSS-feeds, customizable layout, flexible account privileges, logging, a blogging system, an Internet forum, and options to create an interactive community website [Gous & Schutte (2009)] We concur with Gous & Schutte (2009) that "*Drupal was also designed to allow new features and custom behaviour to be added by third parties. For this reason, Drupal is sometimes described as a* "Content Management Framework." *Although Drupal offers a sophisticated programming interface for developers, no programming skills are required for basic web site installation and administration."*

At Directorate, the system was designed to support the integrated work carried out by the personnel administration, recruitment, and placement divisions. Internal users of the system were intended to be able to store up-to-date information about public officers in their ministries, and keep track of policy development provided by Directorate through the online Policy Database. In order to meet this requirement, some of the positive and negative considerations of Drupal are set out next

1. Positive aspects of Drupal:
   - Flexible framework for the development of web-based applications
   - Vibrant developer community on the Drupal site
   - New content types are easily created and may be extended with the Content Construction Kit module
   - Fully customizable user permissions
   - The Organic Groups module provides unrivalled community building functions

- Dynamic approach to content handling
- The Taxonomy module is unparalleled in the CMS landscape and allows for predefined content classification, as well as free tagging
- The Views module allows for custom views of any content within the content pool

2. Negative aspects of Drupal:
    - Limited availability of themes
    - Steeper learning curve than many other CMS packages

Despite Drupal's steep learning curve, it creates a framework that offers extendibility far beyond most other CMS packages and is supported by a vibrant and helpful community of knowledgeable developers and users. Drupal includes a number of features and extensions (Taxonomy, Organic Groups, Content Construction Kit, Views) that allow developers to create highly customized web-based community platforms. Drupal was therefore chosen as the basis of the proposed Information System.

5. Directorate

This section describes an iteration of the action research (AR) cycle conducted at Directorate[3], one of the human resources department of the public service in Botswana. Directorate had a staff complement of 435, and 8 functional divisions at the start of the iteration. These divisions are spread over four offices throughout the country. Communication between these offices is via traditional means: post, telephone, facsimile and also the application of groupware technology, namely email (Lotus Notes[4], and a corporate intranet. The Government Data Network (GDN) supports the groupware application. All four offices were connected via the GDN. All senior officers had computers in their individual offices, which were networked in a campus network, and connected to the GDN. They all had access to the Lotus Notes mail server, and Domino Docs[5] database.
Each officer had an email address assigned to him/her, and was able to communicate with each other without any difficulty.

5.1 System requirements and design

A multi-layer approach was used to ensure that all the requirements of the aforementioned solution are considered. The information system architecture requirements of an integrated knowledge network (i.e. the knowledge network architecture and the knowledge work processes) of CPMS at Directorate were considered first, after which a similar set of requirements was derived for the innovation life cycle [cf. Fig. 5].
Combining these requirement sets provided an information system architecture specification that was used to develop the Information System that serves as a proposed solution for the problem at Directorate. After about two years of development, the system finally achieved an acceptable level of efficiency. It was decided by management to introduce new technologies which would provide greater understanding and knowledge on the core processes. An external consultant was engaged to define these processes. Interviews were conducted to this end. The approach followed is discussed next.
Before decentralisation, Directorate was nearly 100% responsible for keeping the CPMS system up-to-date. Since decentralisation the following is true:

[3] The Directorate is the short name for the Directorate of Public Service Management.(DPSM)
[4] Lotus Notes Corporation
[5] Data Base Management System of Lotus Corporation

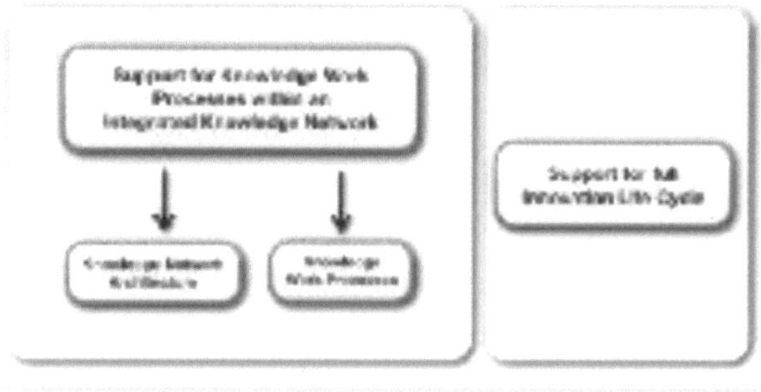

Fig. 5. A multilayer approach for the systems requirement (Gous & Schutte (2009))

1. The Recruitment, Personnel Administration, and Training Divisions, which were the major players using the system, have now become occasional users;
2. The Manpower Planning Division owns the responsibility to create and change positions in the Establishment Register; and
3. The Industrial Class Division, which was already decentralized only, needs the system for enquiries. For the ministries, however, there was a big increase in usage and responsibility to keep the computer system up-to-date. The ministries now have complete ownership of the system except for the creation and changing of positions which still belongs to the Manpower Planning Division. The effect that decentralisation has had on the CPMS is three-fold:
   - where the system had one owner, responsible for the usage and ensuring that the information in the system was being kept up-to-date, there were now 18 ministries and independent departments that were responsible;
   - no roles and responsibilities were formally clarified, which created confusion. This confusion forced the project to stop its planned work on the HRM Workflow Management System (WMS), as a WMS needs a very disciplined and focused environment, with every-one concerned knowing exactly what were their roles and areas of responsibility; and
   - system training was not only required at the Directorate level anymore, but at also at ministries' as well. This necessitated the change in scope and focus of the implementation of the CPMS project. For the project team to successfully implement the system at the ministries' level, it was imperative to ensure that the HR processes used by them were integrated with the CPMS. In the process of identifying this requirement, two other issues came to light, namely:
     - whether the ministries had any formalised processes to build on, and
     - ownership of the HR processes (personnel actions). The need that was jointly identified for the project, Directorate and the ministries, was a requirement for a process manual with each HR process defined where the following is clarified:
       * what must be done, and
       * who is responsible.

This process manual could then be used to compile the operational manual by adding 'how' each step must be done. The key benefit from this manual is that it would enable Directorate, and the identified trainers to teach and train all the ministries in what must be done and how it should be done, using the computer system, in order to ensure that the system is kept up-to-date. For the CPMS to succeed in the Public Service, it requires that each ministry must keep their information in the system up-to-date. If the ministries fail to comply, the money already spent on the implementation phase of the project would go to waste, and the data would become outdated and useless. The only way, it was felt, to ensure that the system is updated, and is available, is by ensuring that no personnel action can be executed without the use of the computer system in the process. For example, public officer should not be able to:

- hire without using the CPMS;
- promote someone without using the CPMS, and
- send someone for training without using the CPMS.

Several unstructured interviews conducted at this stage revealed symptoms of an organisation in which the process of learning involved in adapting to a fast changing business environment was the sole responsibility of its top management. Permanent Secretaries of ministries were unhappy with the current system. Government expressed dissatisfaction with the lack of service delivery of the system. A major reengineering of the system was required. Employees were unmotivated, reporting as the most important reason for their lack of motivation was the excessive centralisation of decisions by the divisional managers. Employees showed no interest in either improving business processes, or learning new methods and techniques. It was noted by one manager that: *"What keeps [the employees] working are their monthly pay cheques and the prospects of overseas per diems, travel, seminars and training at international colleges and universities."*

The inability to motivate officers at the Directorate called for changes in the management approach. Some techniques for enhancing the level of employee participation in decisions were tested; among these techniques were brainstorming sessions, suggestion boxes, and campaigns for new ideas to solve specific problems.

None of these techniques generated the expected gains, due to two reasons. Firstly, they were strictly based on the assumption that front-line workers should have an active role in management and solution of problems, which is one of the several facets of process improvement. For example, employees were called to participate in routine strategic decisions [Campbell (2005)]. However, this proved to be a counter-productive strategy, supporting the assumption that group decisions may not be better than individual decisions. Strategic decisions to form new partnerships or sign a large government contract, for example, were found to be better made only by managers as usual.

Directorate experience suggested that sharing the responsibility of taking some types of decisions with large groups of employees not directly involved with decision making on a daily basis simply delayed what could not be delayed, undermining both the employee' and management's confidence in participatory management principles. There were a number of problems experienced during this phase. These were exacerbated due to a lack of ownership on the part of management. They include such issues as budgeting and funding concerns, the rigid structure of the ministry management, massive staff turnover, poor project ownership, and the absence of a proper system protocol, and data availability regime. Secondly, the analysis and redesign of the human resource processes received a low priority status in the public sector's reform initiatives, and national development plans.

For example, by the time this research iteration had begun, the whole set of interrelated activities involved in reviewing the pay structures and performance incentives, from consultants engaged to study the relationships between private sector and public sector remuneration, and the Presidential Commission on salary structures coupled with the

implementation difficulties of the performance management system (PMS), had not been addressed by government in at least three years. The emphasis was on having employees participate in management decisions, rather than in the analysis of how activities were executed and improvements could be attained. Moreover, new ideas for improvement coming from employees covered an overly broad range of subjects, from new designs for promotional material to better wages, leading to a vast amount of contributions coming from staff that had little knowledge about the work of the areas likely to be affected by the ideas. This, and the repetition of ideas, progressively undermined the interest of managers, and consequently employees' motivation to generate new improvement ideas.
The researcher will now discuss the experiences observed in implementing a KM system.

5.2 Diagnosing

Directorate decentralised its portfolio responsibilities to the human resources (HR) divisions of client ministries in 1998. The new role of Directorate was now one of policy formulation, etc. Directorate is one of the leaders in facilitating the nation's Vision 2016, and it has a number of reform initiatives currently being implemented. However as the public sector has grown, problems have arisen in the effective managementof the human resources management (HRM). Directorate gets its authority from the Public Service Act, (1998). Several unstructured interviews conducted at this stage revealed symptoms of the computerised personnel management system (CPMS), and a number of suggestions were provided as to how Directorate may alleviate them. The system had a number of problems at the onset. This was because the model of Directorate and the clients it serves were not properly specified. The Management of Directorate relied on the services of the commercial brokers to advise them on the choice of the HRM solution to purchase. All this was done before a proper system operations and user requirements documents was completed and proved by the senior management of Directorate. Additionally, systems personnel and developers for both the administrative and technical areas required for staffing the new infrastructure were not implemented. There was a major concern about the budgeting requirements for the different phases of the project.
The system was designed to support the integrated work carried out by the personnel administration and recruitment and placement divisions. Internal users of the system were intended to be able to store up-to-date information about public officers in ministries and keep track of policy development provided by Directorate through the online Policy Database. These processes are listed in paragraph 5.3 [cf. List of core processes].

5.3 List of core processes

After about two years of development, the system finally achieved an acceptable level of efficiency. It was decided by management to introduce new technologies which would provide greater understanding and knowledge on the core processes. An external consultant, was engaged to define these processes. Interviews were conducted to this end. The approach followed is discussed next. Before decentralisation, Directorate was nearly 100% responsible for keeping the CPMS system up-to-date. Since decentralisation the following is true:

- The Recruitment, Personnel Administration, and Training Divisions, which were the major players using the system, have now become occasional users;
- The Manpower Planning Division owns the responsibility to create and change positions in the Establishment Register; and

- The Industrial Class Division, which is already decentralized only needs the system for enquiries.

For the ministries, however, there was a big increase in usage and responsibility to keep the computer system up-to-date. The ministries now have complete ownership of the system except for the creation and changing of positions which still belongs to the Manpower Planning Division. The effect that decentralisation has had on the CPMS is three-fold:

- where the system had one owner responsible for the usage and ensuring that the information in the system was being kept up-to-date, there are now 18 ministries and independent departments that are responsible;
- no roles and responsibilities were formally clarified, which created confusion. This confusion forced the project to stop its planned work on the HRM Workflow Management System (WMS), as a WMS needs a very disciplined and focused environment, with everyone concerned knowing exactly what are their roles and areas of responsibility; and
- system training was not only required at the Directorate level anymore, but at ministries as well. This necessitated the change in scope and focus of the implementation of the CPMS project.

To enable the project to successfully implement the system at the ministries, it was imperative to ensure that the HR processes used by the ministries are integrated with the CPMS. In identifying this requirement, two other issues came to light, namely:

- whether the ministries had any formalised processes to build on, and
- ownership of the HR processes (personnel actions). The need that was jointly identified for the project, Directorate and the ministries, was a requirement for a process manual with each HR process defined where the following is clarified:
  - what must be done, and
  - who is responsible.

This manual could then be used to compile the operational manual by adding 'how' each step must be done. The key benefit from this manual is that it would enable Directorate, and the identified trainers to teach and train all the ministries in what must be done and how it should be done, using the computer system, in order to ensure that the system is kept up-to-date. For the CPMS to succeed in the Government, it requires that each ministry must keep their information in the system up-to-date. If the ministries fail to comply, the amount already spent on the implementation phase of the project would go to waste, and the data would become outdated and useless. The only way, it was felt, to ensure that the system is updated, and is available, is by ensuring that no personnel action can be executed without the use of the computer system in the process. For example, and officer should not be able to:

- hire without using the CPMS;
- promote someone without using the CPMS, and
- send someone for training without using the CPMS.

The following is the models used in developing the processes in the process manual. The core processes included in the manual, which show officers the process to follow, in terms of the identified personnel actions are also set out. The process manual when completed is expected to be used in conjunction with the system's Procedure Manual, where the process shows an activity to be done by the CPMS.

5.4 The high-level enterprise model

HRM in the Botswana Government can be illustrated as set out in the policy-making framework, on people management, of Figure ??. Furthermore, in theory, any successful organisation and department needs four different types of groups of processes to function effectively. These groups types are presented in Figure ?? [cf. Figure ?? Different groups of process in organisational management].

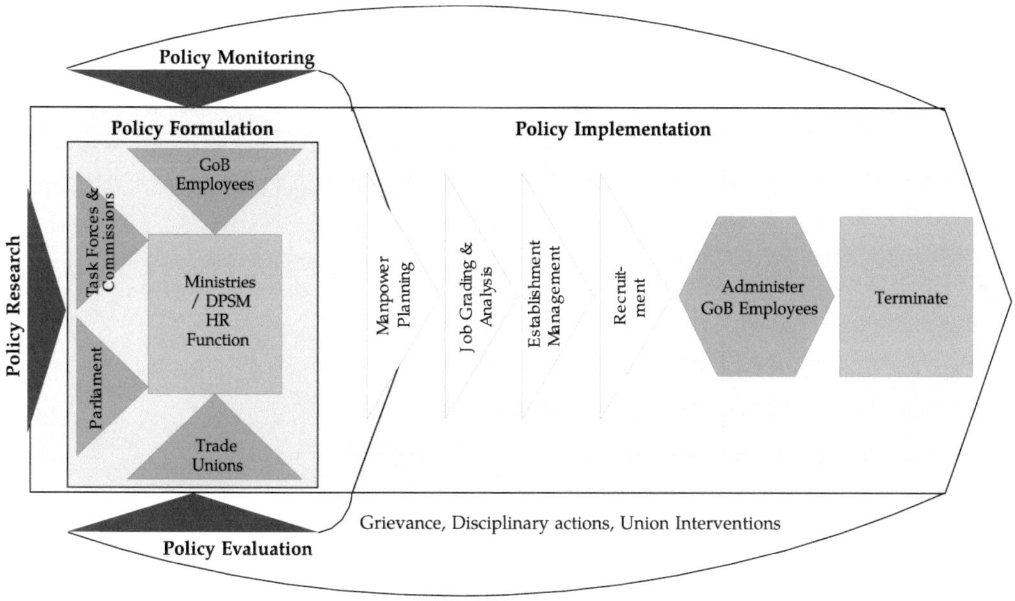

Fig. 6. HRM policy-making framework

Based on the researcher's knowledge of HRM, as well as the theory regarding processes and process groupings, the HR processes can now be broken down into these four groups. This is set out in Table 1 [cf. Table 1 List of processes]. Each process performed by the HRM function should be able to fit into one of these four groupings. If there are, for example, no processes in the Governing Processes group, it means that there is currently no control function and policymaking in terms of HRM. The study uses this information, to compile an enterprise model for the HRM function in the Botswana Government. An enterprise model is a holistic picture of the HRM function within the Botswana Government, which shows all the high level processes and the links between them.

The enterprise model has the same form as the physical building in which the ministries are situated:

- Roof: The customer interfacing processes (the part of one organisation that the customer can see);
- Walls: The enabling and governing processes (the barriers in between, in which one has to function);
- Floor: The processes, which assist one in delivering a first-class service,. For example, research and development, etc; and
- Living area: The main reason for having the house, that is, the value-adding processes of the HRM function.

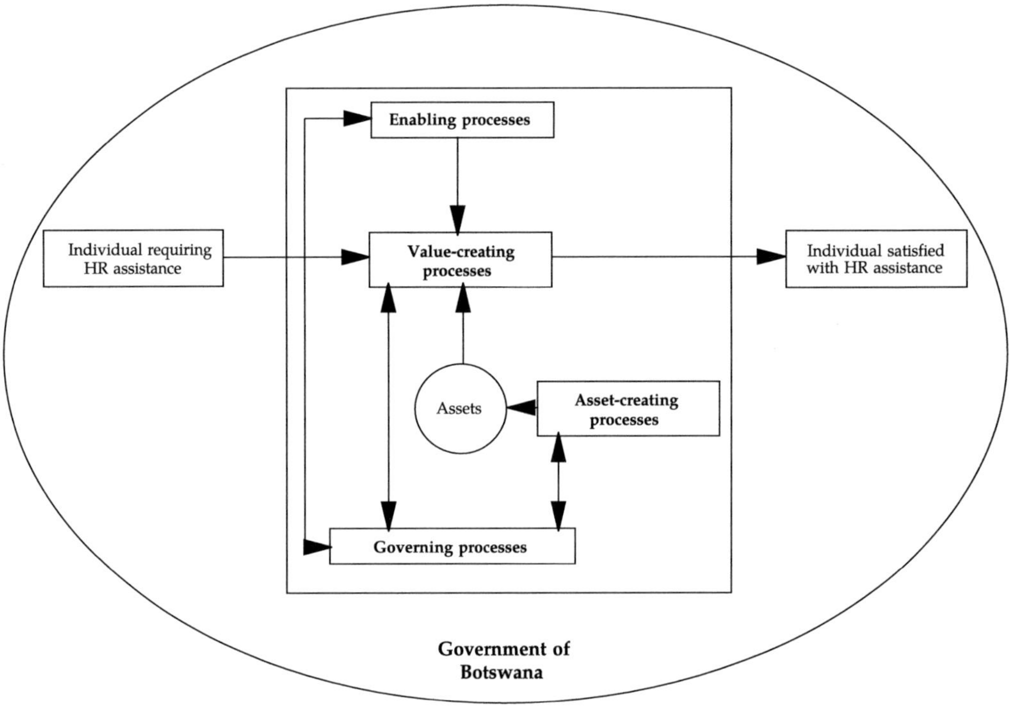

Fig. 7. Different groups of process in organisational management

Governing processes	Value-creating processes	Asset-creating processes	Enabling processes
• Align with Vision 2016 • Align with National Development Plan • Determine Budgets • Formulate Policy • Monitor Policy • Evaluate Policy	• Analyse jobs • Plan manpower • Recruit • Administer • Terminate	• HR Research • HR System • Knowledge System	• Financial management • Records keeping • Advertising • Public Relations • Employee Relations (Law) • Operations (Ministries & Parastatals) • IT Operations

Table 1. List of processes

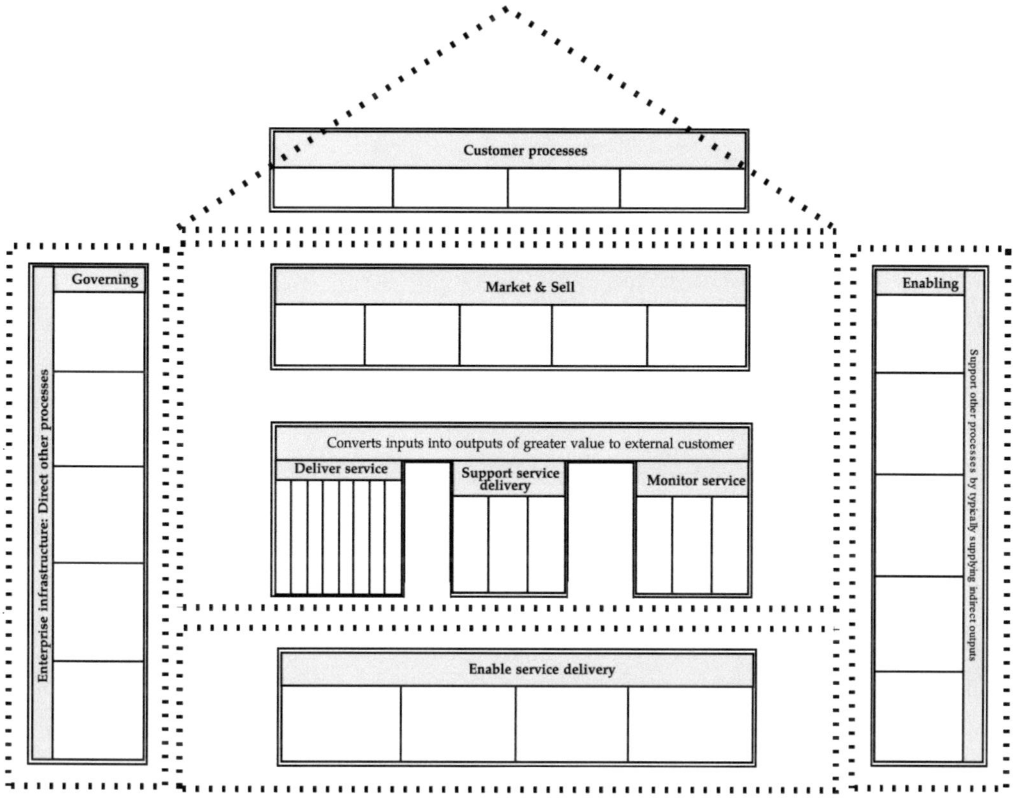

Fig. 8. Conceptual model of the HR function Source: Government of Botswana, 2000

There are a number of reasons, for having an enterprise model, in an organisation. The following reasons were used in Botswana, for building the enterprise model for this project:

- It's an articulation of the personnel action's strategic intent;
- It tells the story of how HR faces its "customers";
- It provides a non-traditional perspective that stimulates other non-traditional ideas;
- It provides a context for integration;
- It's irrelevant whether it is the "As is" or the "To be"
- It tells us what we do, not how we do it;
- It's a description of what the business is all about, and
- It's how we pick our targets for re-engineering.

Characteristics of a good enterprise model:

- Shows the interfaces with the customer processes;
- Contains a logical flow;
- Has only a few clear processes;
- Has clearly definable and measurable results;
- Is action oriented;

- Not generic;
- Centres on value-adding processes;
- Describes everything that occurs in the organisation;
- Uses pictures, not words.

The High-level Enterprise Model, for the HRM function of the Government of Botswana, may then be modelled in the following process:

(i) Recruitment process;

(ii) Promotion process;

(iii) Upgrading process;

(iv) Transfer process v. Personnel Updates – Where the Employee requests an update (e.g. Personal Information);

(v) Personnel Updates – Where the Line Manager requests an update (e.g. Confirmation);

(vi) Termination – Retirement;

(vii) Termination – Resignation;

(viii) Termination – Dismissal;

(ix) Termination – Death;

(x) Termination – Probation;

(xi) Training – Planning;

(xii) Training – Budgeting;

(xiii) Training – Administration;

(xiv) Manpower Planning; and

(xv) Industrial Class.

Several unstructured interviews conducted at this stage revealed symptoms of an organisation in which the process of learning involved in adapting to a fast changing business environment was the sole responsibility of its top management. Permanent Secretaries of ministries were unhappy with the current system. Government expressed dissatisfaction with the lack of service delivery of the system. A major reengineering of the system was required. Employees were unmotivated, reporting as the most important reason for their lack of motivation was the excessive centralisation of decisions by the divisional managers. Employees showed no interest in either improving business processes, or learning new methods and techniques. It was noted by one manager that: "What keeps [the employees] working are their monthly pay cheques and the prospects of overseas per diems, travel, seminars and training at international colleges and universities". The inability to motivate officers at the Directorate called for changes in the management approach. Some techniques for enhancing the level of employee participation in decisions were tested; among these techniques were brainstorming sessions, suggestion boxes, and campaigns for new ideas to solve specific problems.

None of these techniques generated the expected gains, due to two reasons. Firstly, they were strictly based on the assumption that front-line workers should have an active role in management and solution of problems, which is one of the several facets of process improvement. For example, employees were called to participate in routine strategic decisions. However, this proved to be a counterproductive strategy, supporting the

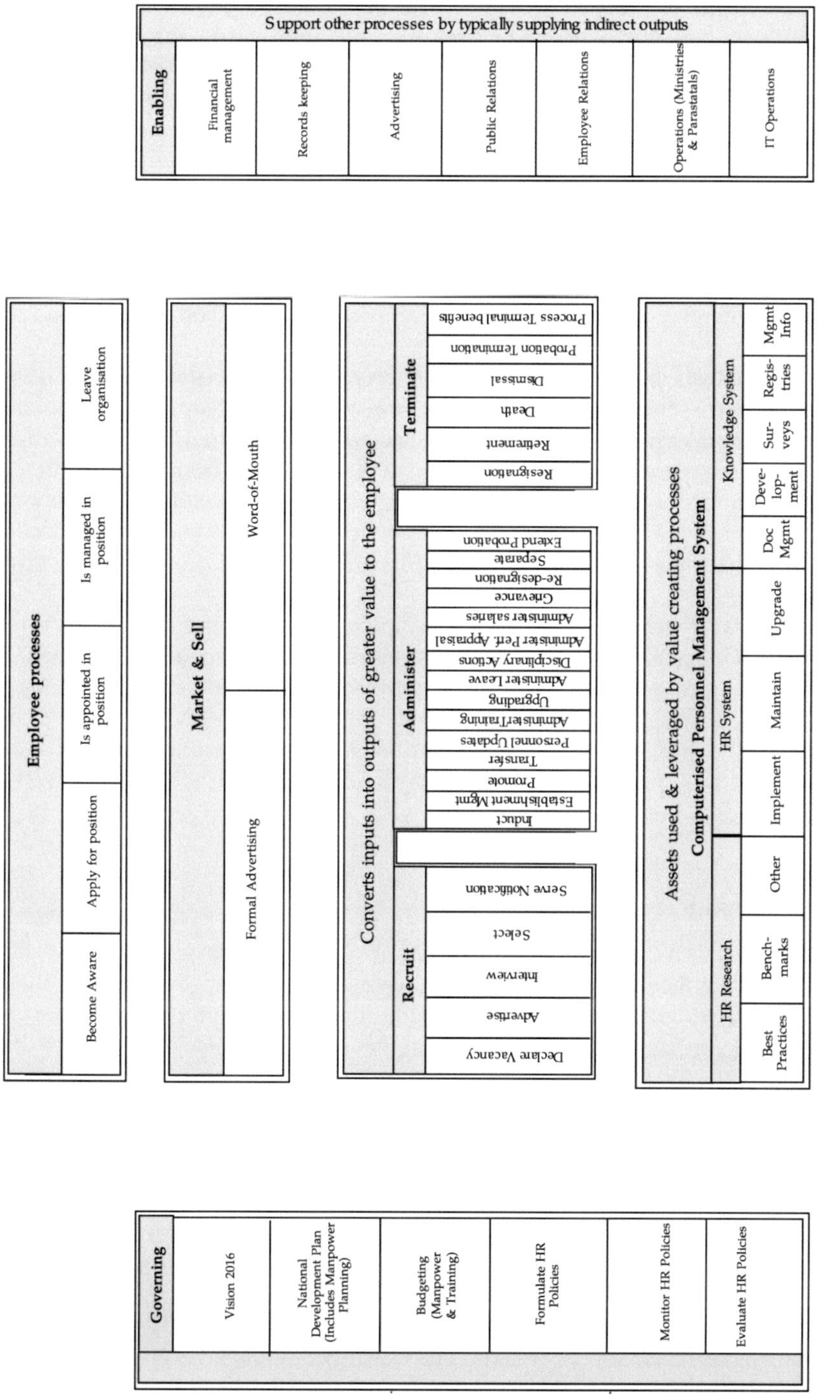

Fig. 9. The high-level Enterprise Model for the HR function (Source: Government of Botswana, 2000)

assumption that group decisions may not be better than individual decisions. Strategic decisions to form new partnerships or sign a large government contract, for example, were found to be better made only by managers as usual. Directorate experience suggested that sharing the responsibility of taking some types of decisions with large groups of employees not directly involved with decision making on a daily basis simply delayed what could not be delayed, undermining both the employees and management's confidence in participatory management.

There were a number of problems experienced during this phase. These were exacerbated due to a lack of ownership on the part of management. They include such issues as budgeting and funding concerns, the rigid structure of the ministry management, massive staff turnover, poor project ownership, and the absence of a proper system protocol and data availability regime.

Secondly, the analysis and redesign of the human resource processes received a low priority status in the public sector's reform initiatives, and national development plans. For example, by the time this research iteration had begun, the whole set of interrelated activities involved in reviewing the pay structures and performance incentives, from consultants engaged to study the relationships between private sector and public sector remuneration, and the Presidential Commission on salary structures coupled with the implementation difficulties of the performance management system (PMS), had not been addressed by government in at least three years.

The emphasis was on having employees participate in management decisions, rather than in the analysis of how activities were executed and improvements could be attained. Moreover, new ideas for improvement coming from employees covered an overly broad range of subjects, from new designs for promotional material to better wages, leading to a vast amount of contributions coming from staff that had little knowledge about the work of the areas likely to be affected by the ideas. This, and the repetition of ideas, progressively undermined the interest of managers, and consequently employees' motivation to generate new improvement ideas.

6. Action planning

The researcher was a consultant with the Management Services' Division (MSD), of the Directorate. MSD is the internal management consultancy arm of government. The researcher was assigned the responsibility of re-engineering the remaining 6 processes, which were not done by the IBM consultants. The project team was expected to tackle a number of problems, both at the local level in the Directorate, and at the level of the human resource departments of client ministries. The researcher was also expected to help coordinate the use of information technology (IT) as an enabler in the implementation of the workflow proposals which came as a result of the human resource process re-engineering. The research iteration was expected to last approximately one year, for the duration of the Directorate's annual performance plan (APP). The researcher and the process owners (Heads of Divisions – Senior Assistant Directors of Directorate, participated in this training exercises and became project champions for the role-out of the CPMS to ministries.

Directorate is a super Department of the ministry of State President. The Directorate is headed by a permanent secretary level Director. The executive management team of the Directorate comprised the Director, two Deputy Directors, and eight Senior Assistant Directors, who are the functional heads of the Divisions of the Department.) They decided that the iteration would begin with a number of training sessions, involving line managers of client ministries,

in which officers would receive formal hands-on training on HRM techniques based on a methodology developed by the researcher and the IBM Consulting team.
The training sessions were planned so as to include practical HRM exercises, to be done in groups, comprising ten members each. Participating officers from ministries and independent departments were expected to replicate these exercises with real organisational processes after the sessions, using the infinium's (the Human Resources Management Information Systems (HRMIS), personnel actions along with the user manual, of the HRMIS.

6.1 Recommended workflow points

The group noted and recommended the following workflow points:

- When a vacancy is declared by the Line Manager, a template in Lotus Notes should be e-mailed, to the Directorate and the Ministry; advising them about the vacancy.
- The Ministry and the Directorate are required to acknowledge the existence of the vacancy to the Line Manager, which should ideally be a response template of Recommendation;
- Directorate and the Line Manager should be notified via Lotus Notes when the vacancy has been actually created in the CPMS;
- If there are recommendations from within the system - all the applicable officers should be notified via Lotus Notes of the vacancy;
- All the job descriptions and advertisements should be kept in a Lotus Notes database and taken from there for electronic approval by the HR ministries;
- The Appointing Board should be notified via Lotus Notes from the system of interview times and dates;
- A database should be set up with rejection letters that are automatically generated from the system;
- The Appointment Board should notify and verify interview times via Lotus Notes;
- The same database in Lotus Notes, should generate the letters of invitation inviting an applicant to come to an interview;
- Notify the Appointment Board that an offer letter has been sent out to the applicant;
- Once the start date is confirmed a form is generated (Casualty Return) and send to the relevant Departments (Accountant General, Directorate, Auditor General, HRM ministries);
- Casualty Return should be triggered by the CPMS, and filled in, in a softcopy format. This should then trigger an e-mail (asynchronously), to be sent to the appropriate parties; and
- Once the employee has actually started his/her duties, the Ministry should be formally notified via e-mail (Lotus Notes).

The researcher and the project team, in diagnosing the problem and the service delivery requirements of the decentralised personnel system, decided to develop an interactive WMS using Lotus Workflow release 3.0. This application was selected because the Directorate was using 'Lotus Notes' and 'Domino Doc', already. Lotus Workflow 3 is one of the product group from the Lotus Corporation groupware solution suite. This KM group was expected to complete the analysis and redesign of each HRM business processes within four to six weeks. After that, a proposal should be generated and implemented, under the coordination of the group leader, who would then prepare a report for approval by Government.

7. Action taking

Seven training sessions were held over a two-week period. These sessions involved all HR managers and officers, lasted one day each, and were conducted by the researcher.

7.1 Core KM groups

The core KM groups were tasked to review the following processes:

1. Recruitment, and
2. Personnel Administration.

The evaluation had earlier on, set out how these processes fit within the overall structure of the Directorate. This analysis is set out in section **??**: List of core processes, and present the six process maps for the Recruitment process, in section **??** [cf. **??**]. These processes are also relevant to how these processes translate into the Directorate Policy Databases. The remaining processes were completed within the specified time, and successfully implemented.
Three high-level KM groups were formed involving the Director and the two Deputy Directors. All three groups had 10 to 14 members, were led by the Deputy Director, or the Senior Assistant Director, and facilitated by the researcher (The members were of similar seniority in the three groups). These groups targeted three main core processes at Directorate: (a) Recruitment process; (b) Personnel Administration, and (c) Policy Database.
The KM group working on the recruitment process made a number of recommendations which were implemented by management within six months of those recommendations being made. The main recommendations are indicted in paragraph 6.1 for the recruitment process. The group also felt that the unit responsible for managing the technical infrastructure of the CPMS should be elevated to the status of a Division with the Directorate structure. This was done within the same time period, as is evidenced by the Functional Structure in Figure **??**.
The Directorate and HRM ministries were encouraged to use the process maps as templates for carrying out any personnel action. They were also asked to use the CPMS network, and the LotusNotes groupware system whenever they must carry out any personnel action.
Although a number of technical problems were reported by Line managers, during the implementation phase of the CPMS, in general, the system, (the computerised Policy database, and the Infinium HRM applications) were running on the Directorate – Ministry intranet seamlessly, and users of the system, in general, reported significant efficiency gains in their respective local processes (Line ministries) due to the resulting decentralisation of access to data relevant to their activities/personnel actions.
In line with this development, the Directorate implemented version 5, of the Lotus Notes, groupware system, in order to provide greater functionality to users. This email system was linked seamlessly in an integrated suite of tools with the Domino Docs, a database application, which is a sister product of Lotus Notes. This was the kernel on which the Policy Database was built.
The email system (ES) was used as a vehicle to conduct personnel actions. The ES was widely accepted by all the process owners. There were much concerns about issues of confidentially and security in the use of officers personal information, and the protection of the personnel record and data of the Directorate. There were no observed or reported resistance or reluctance, in using the ES for the processing of personnel actions. The researcher surmised this to be due in part to the prior experience officers have in the usage of ES for interaction on a personal basis with family, friends and colleagues. The use of the ES for facilitating KM group work and BPI for the purposes of improving the workflow interactions were implemented for all the 14 processes which were proposed by the consultant.

7.2 Local KM groups

The researcher recommended the use of ministry specific KM groups, using the principles of WITS to target processes cutting across only a few departments within the Ministry. This was the reason for calling them "local" KM groups. One of the rationales for these groups was to improve the ownership of the changes, which were introduced in the processes. These groups had very short-term projects. Some of them lasted only for a few weeks to a month; while others only for a few days. The researcher found that this short-term group duration were particularly linked to a narrow target process scope. Also, that the shortest groups being those targeting very localised processes at the departmental and divisional level. Local WITS groups were led by management as well as line staff.

In the case of Directorate, which was the agency responsible for implementing the PMS in the Public Service, local KM groups abound. There was a long tradition of WITS projects and usage within this agency. So, there was no resistance to the setting up of local KM groups – teams. About seven months after the research iteration had begun four KM groups had completed their work. These groups met exclusively face-to-face, as the ES was unavailable at that stage. As the Directorate had 50 management level staff working in a campus environment, and considering that, a group would last on average of 4 weeks, the Directorate's maximum WITS group capacity was approximately of 4 five-member groups at a time. Some of the groups recommend very impressive alternatives to some of the Directorate processes, while others concentrate on short-term problems. This apparent tendency of some groups to focus on problems rather than on underlying processes has also been pointed out by previous research on both gradual and radical KM groups/community of practice interaction, and occurred in spite of the one-day training sessions previously mentioned.

Some of the Directorate's employees who did not take part in any of the KM groups, reported as one of the reasons for non-participation as being the inability to attend KM group meetings because they were engaged in external activities (e.g. meeting with a client) during scheduled group meetings. Since all the Directorate staff had access to the intranet – the GDN, this problem called for the introduction of the ES prototype developed by the researcher as a tool to allow KM group members to interact from their own computers at different times. This prototype was built on the Lotus Notes infrastructure. Each KM group was assigned a group mailbox upon its creation. KM group mailbox topics were suggestive of the business process under consideration, and held postings from group members' related to different stages of the KM methodology (i.e. process definition, analysis, and redesign). Some KM group mailboxes allowed public access within the organisation to group postings so other public officers could participate in the ongoing discussions. However, some of the KM group mailboxes had restricted access to group members, whenever the discussion was perceived as addressing confidential issues (e.g. possible dismissals as a result of process changes, terminal benefits, termination, etc.).

In addition, a number of public mailboxes were created and gradually populated with information regarding the core business processes of the HRM policies and regulations. This information was previously held in the conventional paper-based "General Orders," and other policy document, such as "savingram"[6]. These mailboxes also contained some regularly updated postings with information about efficiency, PMS outcomes, and service delivery, and ministries and clients complaints for each business process. Employees were instructed

[6] SAVINGRAM – A circular/memorandum document, which provides information on policy/regulation issues that subsequently, becomes part of the "General Order".

about how to use the Lotus Notes system (ES) to support KM group communication and retrieval of previously posted information, and were encouraged to use the ES as much as possible. None of the local WITS was directly facilitated by the researcher, as was the case of the core KM groups. The reason for this was that the researcher's support was restricted to troubleshooting and orientation meetings with other group facilitators. This means that the researcher's facilitation of local KM groups was indirect.

8. Evaluating

In this stage of the AR iteration, one observed a number of patterns evolving into practical learning opportunities. This was against the basic action research routine advocated by Stringer (1999:19). This 'road map', is set out below, in Figure **??**, and Table **??**. These were related to both face-to face and the ES supported KM groups. The patterns observe in face-to-face discussions related only to the core KM groups, and are summarised in the next three sub-sections [cf. 8].

The pattern observed in the ES-supported KM groups relate to apparent ES-support challenges, and effects on the groups' effectiveness and relevance of the process emerging as a result of these collaborative efforts.

9. Conclusion

In this chapter, the first iteration of the AR cycle, was described, which were carried out over a period of approximately one year at Directorate, a Public Administration department, in the Republic of Botswana. At most thirty six public officers were directly involved in this AR iteration. They were all trained based on a methodology developed by the researcher on how to conduct, and participate in KM groups.

With our field research study of KM systems and a literature study of KM research as a basis, we draw four main conclusions:

1. Evolution, which refers to the process in which organisations and their information systems change over time, is an important dimension of KM system implementation and use.
2. Managing the evolution of KM systems on an ad hoc basis and treating them as standalone systems can lead to unnecessary complexity and KM systems failures. The evolution of KM systems needs to be managed by deliberately managing both the systems within the organisation and the organisational change process from a long-term perspective.
3. The KM research has paid little attention to the evolution of KM systems. Limited support and guidelines for managing KM systems' evolution are available in the mainstream KM research literature. Consequently, this is an important issue to add to the KM research discourse. The predominantly design oriented KM research needs to be extended by more implementation and management oriented studies.
4. The implementation of a portal, such as that of the proposed KM-BI model [Fig. 3], will facilitate this process, with the ultimate development of more robust content management systems for integrated knowledge networks for the evolution of innovation and business intelligence through the harnessing of intellectual capital.

Based on this research, it is clear that knowledge management plays a significant role in the liberation of intellectual capital.

9.1 Future research direction

This section summarizes ideas for potential future work, as it relates to the design of a KM system, for the deployment of BI. This list does not include minor improvements or cosmetic changes that are in the implications of implementation of the KM-BI framework.

Therefore, further research may proved valuable, in investigating the potential role of the evolution of knowledge management in knowledge systems, and how the value of intellectual capital can be leveraged to maximized the use of knowledge systems in organisational processes, and to ensure a more efficient and effective liberation of intellectual capital processes and flows.

Allied to the foregoing, impact studies in this area maybe extremely valuable, especially in organisations that have distinct knowledge management systems oriented programs. It is important for knowledge management professionals to understand the systemic relationship between the concepts and the value that can be generated in respect of creating and maintaining sustainable competitive advantage for organisations and naturing, and liberating the natural evolution of intellectual capital.

Ideas for potential future work, as it relates to the design of a KM system, for the deployment of BI are summarized. This list does not include minor improvements or cosmetic changes that are implicit in an organization's implementation of their KM-BI framework.

9.2 Future work on a learning-oriented KM system

The literature called for the information systems (IS) field to begin to develop theory based on endogenous paradigms rather than based on other disciplines. The learning-oriented component (OL) of one's model for KM strategy, deals with IS, and as such impacts on the use of the IT infrastructure, as it relates to groupware technologies to aid OL.

There is a need, however, to use a systematic approach to the implementation of this IT infrastructure, which would enable the conceptualize of a robust IS based on expert systems theory. This research has suggested how a KM system may be specified by proposing a high-level casual model of latent factors which impact the implementation of KM practices in an organisational milieu. The portal in the KM-BI model requires the development of the conceptual heuristics so as to operationalise the model. This therefore, requires the testing of individual components [BI, AG, SC, Ol, and HK] validation, where appropriate when applying management theories at the implementation process level.

This work involves the use of systems theory, at a design level, to conceptualize both a learning-oriented, and strategy-oriented KM system.

The literature addressed both the design product and the design process. This research presents the design product in our KM-BI model (the conceptualized learning-oriented and the portal components, of the KM-BI system) and portions of the design process (the components). The method of design for the other potential components identified as a result of this research is the conceptualization of methods to achieve other meta-requirements, such as the use of the IT instrastructure. Such work would be analogous to the normalization procedure of a design method that achieves the goal of reducing certain anomalies in a database. Each of the components identified in this research has the ability to achieve the meta-design for our hypothesized KM-BI system.

The findings in this research offer a number of approaches firms may use to implement their KM projects. The underlying dialogue is that managers need a corporate-wide strategy to implement their KM practices. The researcher discussed throughout this work, and intimated that any successful BI oriented strategy should have the following components:

1. Definition of the system to be assessed;

2. Identification of relevant stakeholders and their expectations;
3. Definition of the knowledge vision;
4. Deduction of factors of influence and use-and-effect patterns;
5. Identification of the most important drivers;
6. Prioritisation of the impact of the drivers on the expectations of the stakeholders, and
7. Development of an action plan.

These components are distilled from the results of the research. However, the approaches firms may use in implementing KM strategies, by the supported of AG systems have been fully explored. Some of these are summarised next.

- Use information flow and knowledge transfer to improve the competitive advantage and enhanced BI, of the firm through the use of innovative applications of tangible and intangible resources.
- Use new and emerging technologies to improve CA and enhanced BI, of the firm through the use of innovative applications of tangible and intangible technological resources.
- The technological effects of the organizational and environmental evolution needs to be validated with further research on contextualising effects on KM effectiveness. This would include such dimensions as trust and management (leadership) support. The related metrics need to be developed so as to validate the groupware-supported social facilitation factors, which were found in the group domain of the study.
- Understand the impact of organizational learning on information flow, knowledge transfer and new and emerging technologies, through the development of a systematic design model, which our KM-BI framework sought to initiate.

They are therefore constraining their firms from leveraging the BI which could be achieved through the proper use of the technological infrastructure which is a requisite of KM deployment. The observed failure to harness the full potential of the technological infrastructure goes to the heart of the difficulty firms have in selling KM as a management technique to their employees. Technology has changed the way many firms do business globally. In most cases, it has improved their business, though there remain some areas where much improvements may arguably be made. The study found, and ascribe to the belief that the management of technology, has not added value to many organisations' BI.

Our proposed KM-BI model, one believes should afford firms the opportunity to have immediate access to vast stores of processed, timely and relevant knowledge with which they can make decisions. In fact the study found that much of the technology, although new and has been implemented as organizations have begun to experiment with new ways of using it. If a sound business strategy is crafted, then all organisations need to do, when they implement the necessary technology, is to populate it with data so as to make it worth using and to add real benefit to their *bottom-line*. This in turn means that organisations must focus on keeping the information up-to-date on an on-going basis, and develop a programme of removing out-of-date information and committing resources to this task. The researcher recommend that, in order to obtain the full benefits, organisations need to take a fresh look at the available technology from a KM perspective to realize the potential, in aiding in the liberation of intellectual capital.

Given that the constructs and findings of this study lend support to the validity of our KM-BI framework, a logical next step would be to develop and test more complex theoretical models.

10. References

Adams, G. & Lamont, B. (2003). Knowledge management systems and developing sustainable competitive advantage, *Journal of Knowledge Management* 7(2): pp. 142–54.

Baddi, A. & Sharif, A. (2003). Information management and knowledge integration for enterprise innovation, *Logistics Information Management* 16(2): pp. 145–55.

Brown, J. S. & Duguid, P. (1998). Organizing knowledge., *California Management Review* 40(3): 90 – 111.
URL: *http://0-search.ebscohost.com.library.vut.ac.za/login.aspx?direct=true&db=buh&AN=738859&site=bsi-live*

Buytaert, D. (n.d.). Core drupal.

Campbell, H. (2005). *A study of knowledge management strategies as enabled by the support of asynchronous groupware systems*, PhD thesis, University of South Africa, Pretoria, South Africa. Also available at University of South Africa, Main Library.
URL: *http://uir.unisa.ac.za/handle/10500/2406?show=full*

Campbell, H. M. (2009). Linking knowledge management to business intelligence and organisational performance, SAIIE, p. 18.

Cardinal, L., Allessandri, T. & Turner, S. (2003). Knowledge codifiability, resources, and science based innovation, *Journal of Knowledge Management* 5(2): pp. 195 – 204.

Cavusgil, S., Calantone, R. & Zhao, Y. (2003). Tacit knowledge transfer and firm innovation capability, *Journal of Business & Industrial Marketing* 18(1): pp. 6 – 21.

Chen, J., Zhaohui, Z. & Xie, H. (2004). Measuring intellectual capital, *Journal of Intellectual Capital* 5(1): pp. 195 – 212.

Darroch, J. & McNaughton, R. (2002). Examining the link between knowledge management practices and types of innovation, *Journal of Intellectual Capital* 3(3): pp. 210 – 22.

Davenport, T. H. & Prusak, L. (2000). *Working Knowledge - How Organizations Manage What they Know*, Harvard Business School Press, Boston.

Day, D. & Tate, B. (2006). Continuous learning: Why is it still an issue, *in* F. D. e. in Francis J. Yammarino (ed.), *Multi-Level Issues in Social Systems (Research in Multi Level Issues*, Emerald Group Research Limited, pp. 173 – 188.

du Plessis, M. (2007). The role of organizational knowledge management in innovation, *Journal of Knowledge Management* 11(4): pp. 20–29.

Eftekharzadeh, R. (2008). Knowledge management implementation in developing countries: An experimental study., *Review of Business* 28(3): 44 – 58.
URL: *http://0-search.ebscohost.com.library.vut.ac.za/login.aspx?direct=true&db=buh&AN=34757419&site=bsi-live*

Gous, J. & Schutte, C. (2009). Using knowledge networks to support innovation, SAIIE, p. 18.

Hislop, D. (2005). *Knowledge Management in organizations – a critical introduction*, Oxford University Press, New York.

Majchrzak, A., Cooper, L. P. & Neece, O. E. (2004). Knowledge reuse for innovation, *Management Science* 50(2): pp. 174–188.
URL: *http://www.jstor.org/stable/30046057*

Martin, W. J. (2004). Demonstrating knowledge value: a broader perspective on metrics, *Journal of Intellectual Capital* 5(1): 77–79.

Nonaka, I. & Nishiguchi, T. (2001). *Knowledge Emergence*, Oxford University Press, New York.

Nonaka, I. & Takeuchi, H. (1995). *The Knowledge Creating Company*, Oxford University Press, New York.

Pyka, A. (2002). Innovation networks in economics: from the incentive-based to the knowledge based approaches, *European Journal of Innovation Managementt* 5(3): pp. 142–54.

Richard C. Hicks, Ronald Daltero, S. D. G. (2007). A metaphor for knowledge management: explicit islands in a tacit sea, *Journal of Knowledge Management* 11: 5 – 16.

Schutte, C. S. L. & Preez, N. D. D. (2008). Knowledge networks for managing innovation projects, PICMET.

Seufert, . A., von Krogh, G. & Bach, A. (1999). Towards knowledge networking, *Journal of Knowledge Management* 3: 10.

Sveiby, K. E. & Simons, R. (2002). Collaborative Climate and Effectiveness of Knowledge Work- An Empirical Study,, *Journal of Knowledge Management* 6(5): 420–433.

van der Aalst, . W. M. & Kumar, A. K. (2001). A reference model for team-enabled workflow management systems, *Data & Knowledge Engineering* 38: 28.

von Krogh, G., Ichijo, K. & Nonaka, I. (2000). *Knowledge Creation – How to unlock the mystery of tacit knowledge and release the power of innovation.*, Oxford University Press, New York.